Skyros
Evia
(Euboea)
Eretria
Thebes
Attica
Skala Oropou
Gulf of Euboea
Thiva
Amphiareion
Hag. Apostoli
Kalamos
Parnitha
Malakassa
Rhamnous
Aliki
Plataea
Kapandriti
Grammatiko
Phyle
Ino
Marathonas
Aigosthena
Marathon
Acharnes
Mandra
Aspropyrgos
Kifissia
Limenas
Pentelikon
Eleusis
Megara
Elevsina
Athens
(Athina)
Rafina
Loutraki
Moni Dafni
Moni Kaisariani
Salamina
Kalamaki
Loutsa
Ambelakia
Brauron
Hymettus
Vravrona
Aiantio
Piraeus
Glyfada
(Imittos)
Loutro Elenis
Salamis
(Pireas)
Porto Rafti
Tilos
Saronic Gulf
Voula
Vouliagmeni
Kato Almiri
Varkiza
Palaiokhora
Kaki Thalassa
Korfos
Aegina
Aphaia
Palea Fokea
Makronisos
Hag. Marina
Lavrio
(Laurion)
Perdhika
Aegina
Sounion
Kea
Epidaurus
Methana
Driopi
Poros
Poros
Iria
Troizen
Galatas
Iliokastro
Kythnos
Hydra (Idra)
Spetses
Serifos
Sifnos
Kimolos
Aegean Sea
Monemvasia
Milos
Neapoli
Kythera

Sailing ships at the port of Piraeus in 1921.

Athens at the turn of the century: the Parthenon and the rock of the Acropolis.

Bassae in 1930:
tourists visiting
the Temple of Apollo.

Numerous specialists and academics have contributed to this guide.
We would especially like to thank Monsieur Pierre Brulé.

Authors and editors: Gérard G. Aymonin, Achille Démétropoulos, Mme Bouras, W. D. Nesteroff, Catherine Koumarianou, Maria Couroucli, Nikos Platanos, Mme Papamanoli-Guest, Dina Couroucli, Thomas Morvan, Pierre Brulé, Stéphane Marcie, Alkis Pierrakos, Georges Tolias, Maryline Desbiolles, Maria Couroucli, Sandrine Duvillier, Amanda Michalopoulou, Maria Couroucli, Georges Tolias, Catherine Bray, John Freely, Charalambos Bouras, Yannis Saitas, Mme Triantafyllidou-Baladié, Georges Tolias, Marie-Dominique Nenna, Raoul Baladié, Gilles Touchais, Nicolas Yalouris, Manolis Korrès

Illustrators and iconographers: Sophie Lavaux, Jean Chevalier, Jean Bodin, Jean-François Péneau, Jean-François Binet, Pierre-Xavier Grézaud, Stéphane Marcie, Pierre-Xavier Grézaud, Jean-François Binet, Jean-François Péneau, Jean-François Binet, Jean-François Péneau, Pierre-Xavier Grézaud, Pierre-Xavier Grézaud

Photographers: I. Ioannides, L. Bartzioti, Constantin Pittas, Dimitris Tsoublekas, Bernard Hermann, Benoît Juge, Jean-Michel Belmer, Jean-François Binet, François Brosse, Édouard de Pazzis, Guido Alberto Rossi

We would also like to thank:
Charalambos Bouras, Cornelia Hatziaslani-Bouras, Evi Touloupas, Yannis Saitas, Mrs Goulandris, Yannis Mazarakis, Lila Marangou, François Lefèvre, Anna Lambrakis, E. J. Finopoulos, Manos Charitatos, Dimitri Daskalopoulos, Gérard G. Aymonin, Françoise Botkine, Pierre Mari, Vassia Karabélias, Montembault, B.G.K. Architects, M. Gregoris.

Translated by Anthony Roberts;
Edited and typeset by Book Creation Services, London.
Printed in Italy by Editoriale Libraria.

Everyman Guides
Published by David Campbell Publishers Ltd, London

ISBN 1-85715-801-6

Everyman Guides, 79 Berwick Street, London W1V 3PF

ATHENS
AND THE
PELOPONNESE

Contents

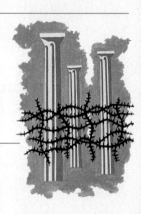

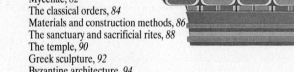

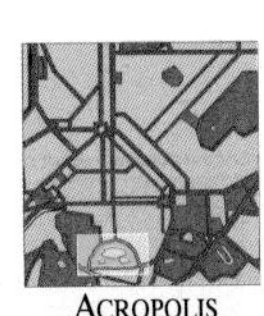

ACROPOLIS

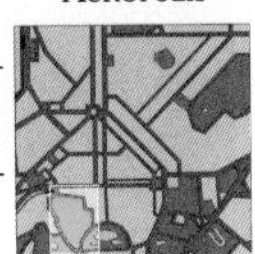

AGORA

KERAMEIKOS

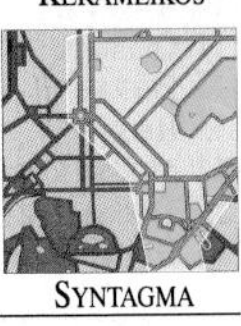

SYNTAGMA

ITINERARIES IN ATTICA, BOEOTIA AND THE PELOPONNESE

AROUND ATHENS

ATHENS AND CORINTH

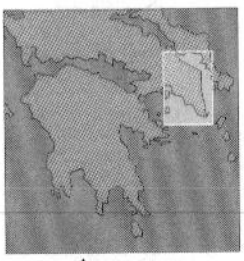

CORINTH AND NAUPLION

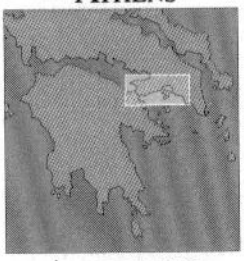

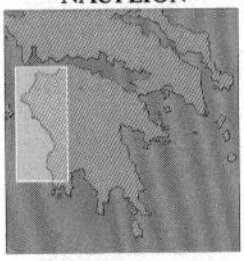

OLYMPIA AND PATRAS

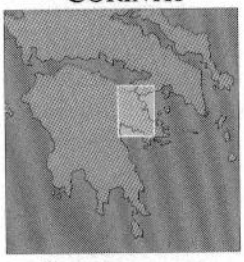

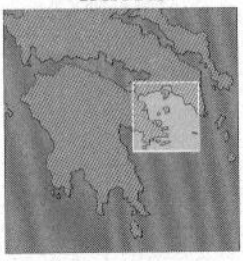

ISLANDS OF THE SARONIC GULF

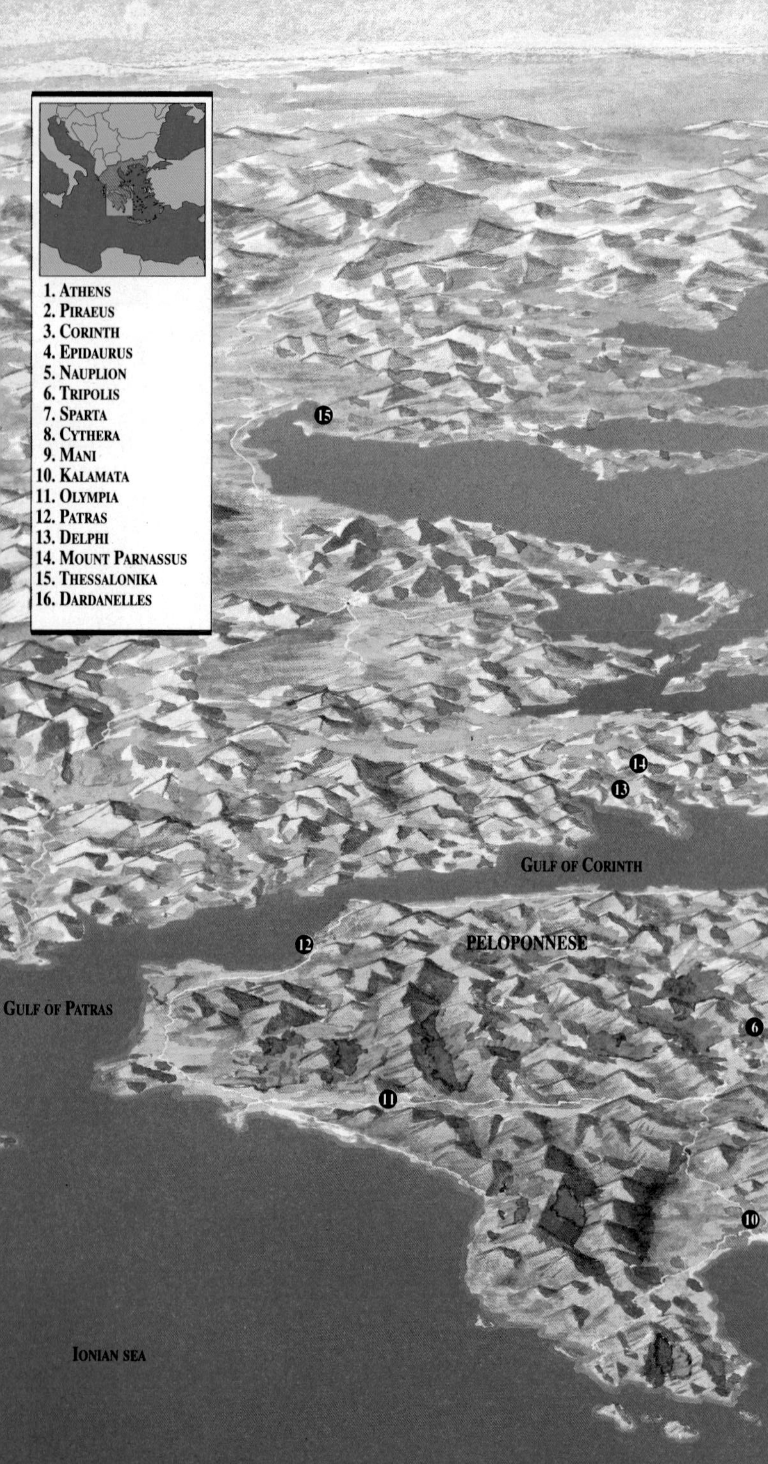
1. Athens
2. Piraeus
3. Corinth
4. Epidaurus
5. Nauplion
6. Tripolis
7. Sparta
8. Cythera
9. Mani
10. Kalamata
11. Olympia
12. Patras
13. Delphi
14. Mount Parnassus
15. Thessalonika
16. Dardanelles
Gulf of Corinth
Peloponnese
Gulf of Patras
Ionian sea

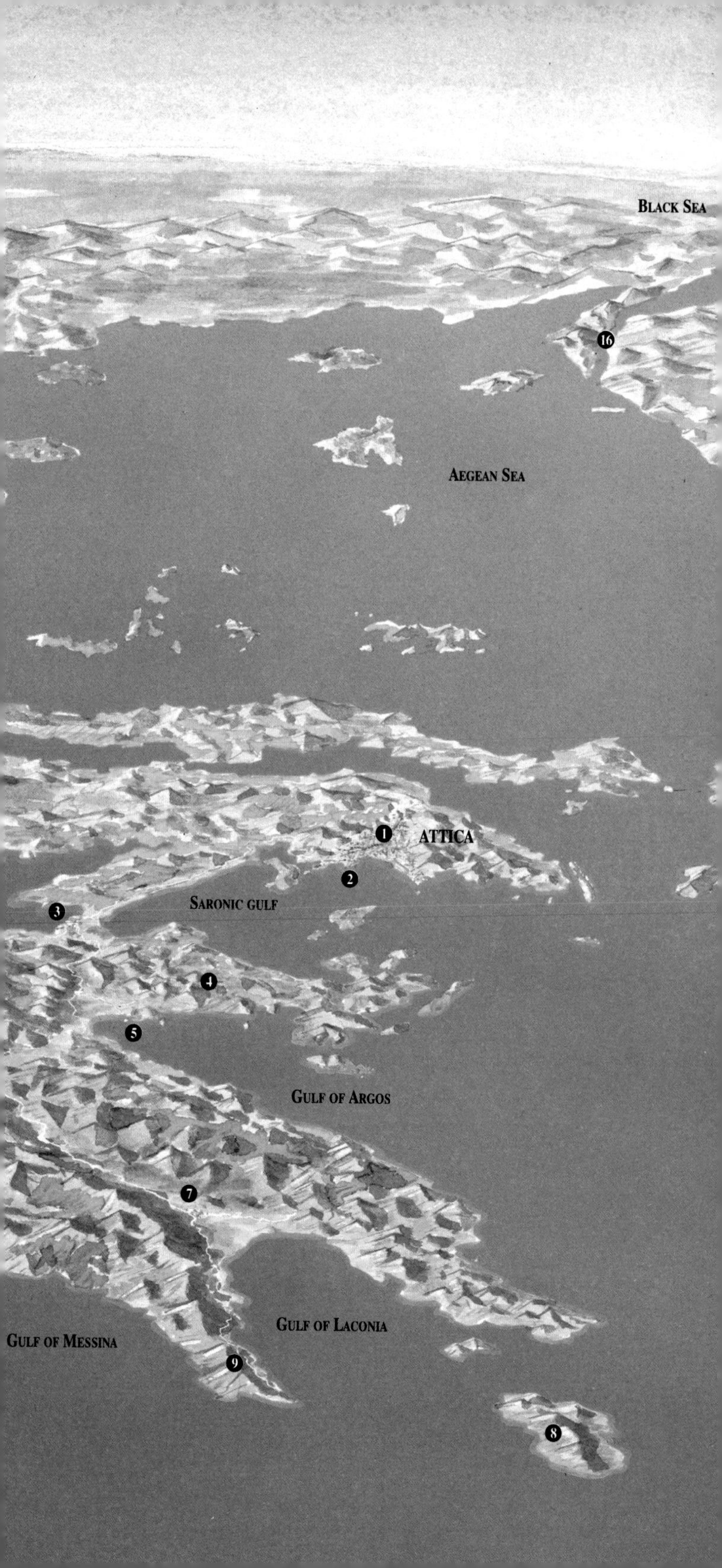

Black Sea

16

Aegean Sea

1 Attica

2

Saronic gulf

3

4

5

Gulf of Argos

7

Gulf of Laconia

Gulf of Messina

9

8

How to Use this Guide

(Sample page shown from the guide to Venice)

The symbols at the top of each page refer to the different parts of the guide.

■ Natural Environment

● Keys to Understanding

▲ Itineraries

◆ Practical Information

The itinerary map shows the main points of interest along the way and is intended to help you find your bearings.

The mini-map locates the particul itinerary within the wider area covered by the guide.

★ The star symbol signifies that a particular site has been singled out by the publishers for its special beauty, atmosphere or cultural interest.

At the beginning of each itinerary, the suggested means of transport to be used and the time it will take to cover the area ar indicated:

- By boat
- On foot
- By bicycle
- Duration

●▲■◆

The symbols alongside a title or within the text itself provide cross-references to a theme or place dealt with elsewhere in the guide.

The Gateway to Venice ★

Ponte della Liberta. Built by the Austrians 50 years after the Treaty of Campo Formio in 1797 ● *34,* to link Venice with Milan. The bridge ended the thousand-year separation from the mainland and shook the city's economy to its roots as Venice, already in the throes of the industrial revolution, saw

Half a day

Bridges to Venice

Nature

Marble

The ancient Greeks used the name "marble" for any stone that could produce a fine polish. For the construction and decoration of the great monuments of Athens they used marble from the quarries of Mount Pentelikon in Attica. This white, fine-grained stone takes on a golden patina with time and was the preferred material for building. For sculpture, Parian marble was more popular. Limestone without impurities makes white marble; when minerals other than calcite are present richly colored marbles of all kinds can be produced.

Marble cutting
The surface is planed flat with a mallet and chisel, and the dimensions marked off by a groove made with a saw. The blocks are then split with wooden wedges rammed into notches along the groove and soaked with water to make them expand. Blocks of marble are usually hewn roughly at the quarry, then given their finish on site.

Surface dressing
First the rough, uncut face (**A**) is hewn with a mason's axe (**1**) to produce an initial flat surface (**B**). It is then smoothed with "points" or "punches" (**2** and **3**), followed by broad-toothed chisels (**4**) and toothed hammers (**5**).
The result is dressed smooth with flat-edged chisels (**6**) to produce the final surface (**C**).

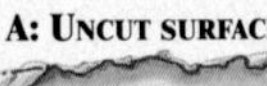

The quarries of Mount Pentelikon supplied marble for the temples of Athens.

Byzantine chapel
This small chapel was built against a rockface of Mount Pentelikon.

Mosaics
Mosaic paving adorned the shrines, monuments and private houses of ancient Greece. The one shown here is an *opus tessellatum,* made up of *tesserae* (tiny squares of marble) set into a design in fresh cement laid out with stencils. The idea was to imitate a carpet pattern in stone.

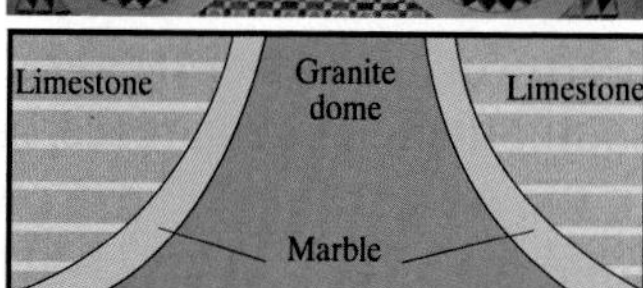

How marble is formed
Limestone is transformed into marble by natural recrystallization, under the influence of pressure and heat.

Rough limestone

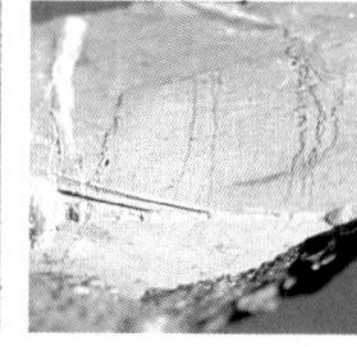

Compact limestone

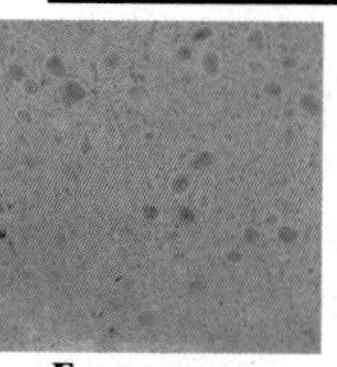

Fine-grained limestone

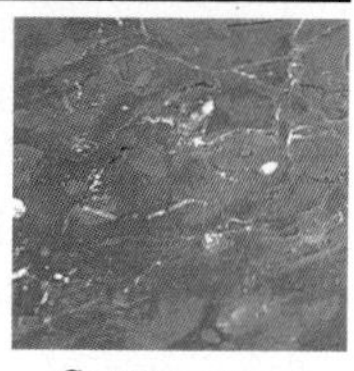

Cherry marble

Antique-red marble

Coarse-grained white marble

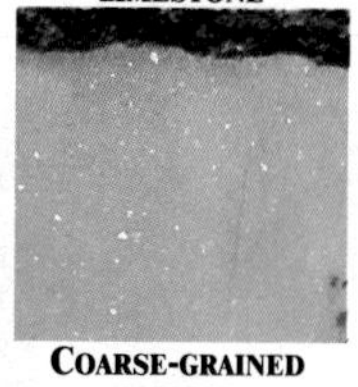

Coarse-grained marble

Large-crystal white marble

Fine-grained marble

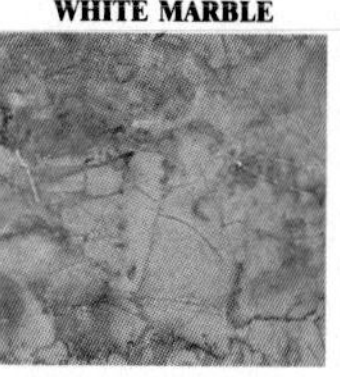

Yellow breche

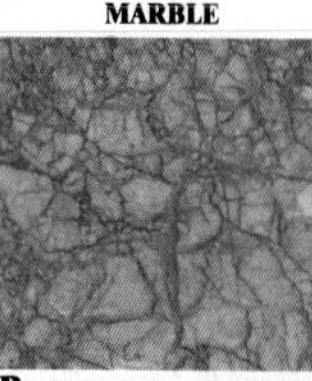

Brown breche with red veins

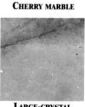

Veined yellow breche

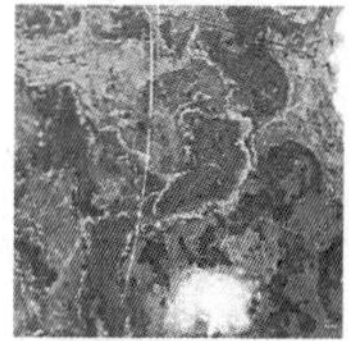

Brown marble

Yellow-ocher marble

Pink-and-grey marble

Yellow-ocher-and-grey marble

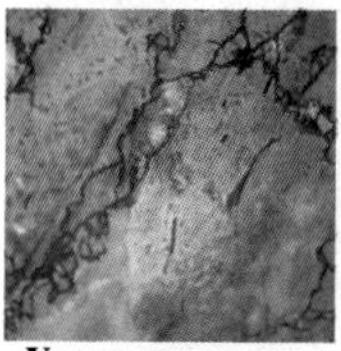

Veined pink-ochre marble

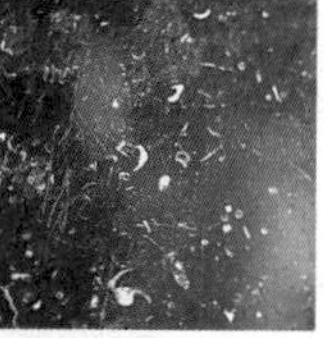

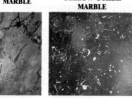

Black-and-white marble

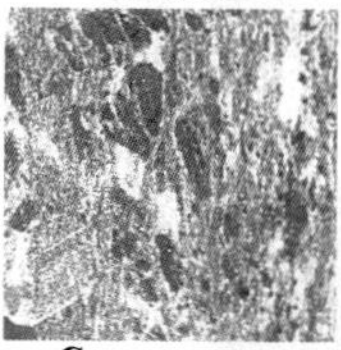

Grey-and-blue conglomerate

Grey-blue breche

Regions with Mediterranean climates are characterized by vegetation with thick, shiny evergreen foliage. This can be found in Mediterranean *maquis*, Californian *chaparral*, South African *fynbos* or the *mallee scrub* of southwestern Australia. Such vegetation often replaces forest destroyed by fires or overgrazing. In southern mainland Greece, as in the islands of the Aegean, *maquis* can cover the terrain from sea level to up to 2,000 feet. Evergreen trees such as holm oaks and kermes oaks may sprout above the undergrowth of white briars, cistus and other scented plants, which seldom exceeds ten feet in height.

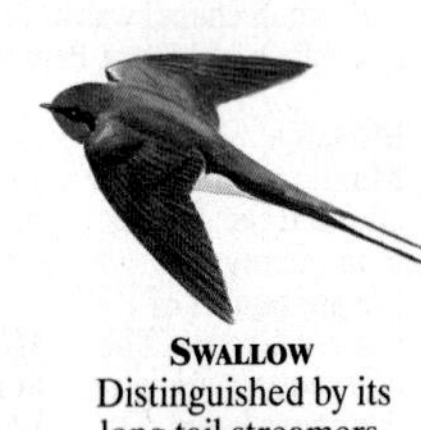

SWALLOW
Distinguished by its long tail streamers, buff underparts and russet throat.

Male

SARDINIAN WARBLER
Nests in low bushes.

SHINY EVERGREEN LEAF OF THE HOLM OAK

FOLIAGE AND FRUIT OF THE HOLM OAK

HOLM OAK
Grows in the *maquis*, up to 2,000 feet above sea level.

In Attica the plants that make up the *maquis* tend to have a bushy form due to grazing and frequent fires.

PISTACIA LENTISCUS (MASTIC TREE)
One year after being ravaged by fire, the *maquis* has recovered with foliage beginning to sprout again from the blackened trunks of the mastic trees.

Anemone blanda. This plant has starlike flowers with narrow petals.

The colors of the *maquis* in the spring are often magnificent, especially the blazing yellow of the gorse.

Laurustinus
Winter-flowering shrub.

Montpellier cistus
A small aromatic rock rose of low-lying *maquis*.

White briar
A many-leaved shrub, characteristic of Mediterranean *maquis*.

Arbutus
A small, elegant tough-barked tree whose wood is used in Greece for making flutes.

Myrtle
Known since ancient times as a symbol of peace and love.

Myrtle flowers
Myrtle has a heavy perfume. In ancient Greece it was called Daphne, for the nymph who changed into a myrtle tree to escape Apollo.

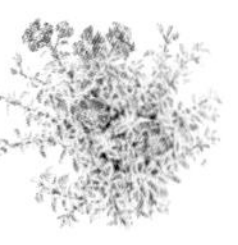

Cretan rock rose
From May to June the blossoms of this rock rose attract many insects.

Sage-leaf cistus
This bushy shrub grows in the thickest parts of the *maquis*.

Cyclamen
Grows in cool, shady parts of the *maquis*.

Mastic tree
This aromatic plant is covered with white blossom in spring.

Wild olive
This thorny, heavily-branched shrub – the wild original of the domestic olive – is the most common tree on the plains of Greece.

At the beginning of the 20th century the Greek rural economy was based on a combination of woodland, pasture and arable farming. After World War One, the *maquis* spread, and the quality of pasture diminished as a result. Brush fires were lit by shepherds to open up impenetrable areas of *maquis* for grazing; this began a cycle of burning and regrowth, with fires often reoccurring too frequently to allow woody vegetation to recover. The only way to prevent brush fires in Greece, as elsewhere, is to bring the old cultivated terraces back into use and to create open grazing areas as firebreaks.

BRUSH-FIRE VICTIMS
Birds are asphyxiated by the smoke, and snakes and other reptiles are unable to elude the flames.

Hermann's tortoise moves too slowly to escape the fire. The only creatures that have a good chance of surviving brush fires are scorpions, which hide from the flames in rock falls and scree.

KESTREL
The kestrel, as a predator of rodents and small birds, profits from the period of regrowth after a fire.

EUROPEAN BEE-EATER
An insect-eating species that benefits from the abundance of insects after a brush fire.

HOBBY
This insect-eating falcon, which nests in pine woods, loses its habitat to fires but gains by the increased insect population that follows them.

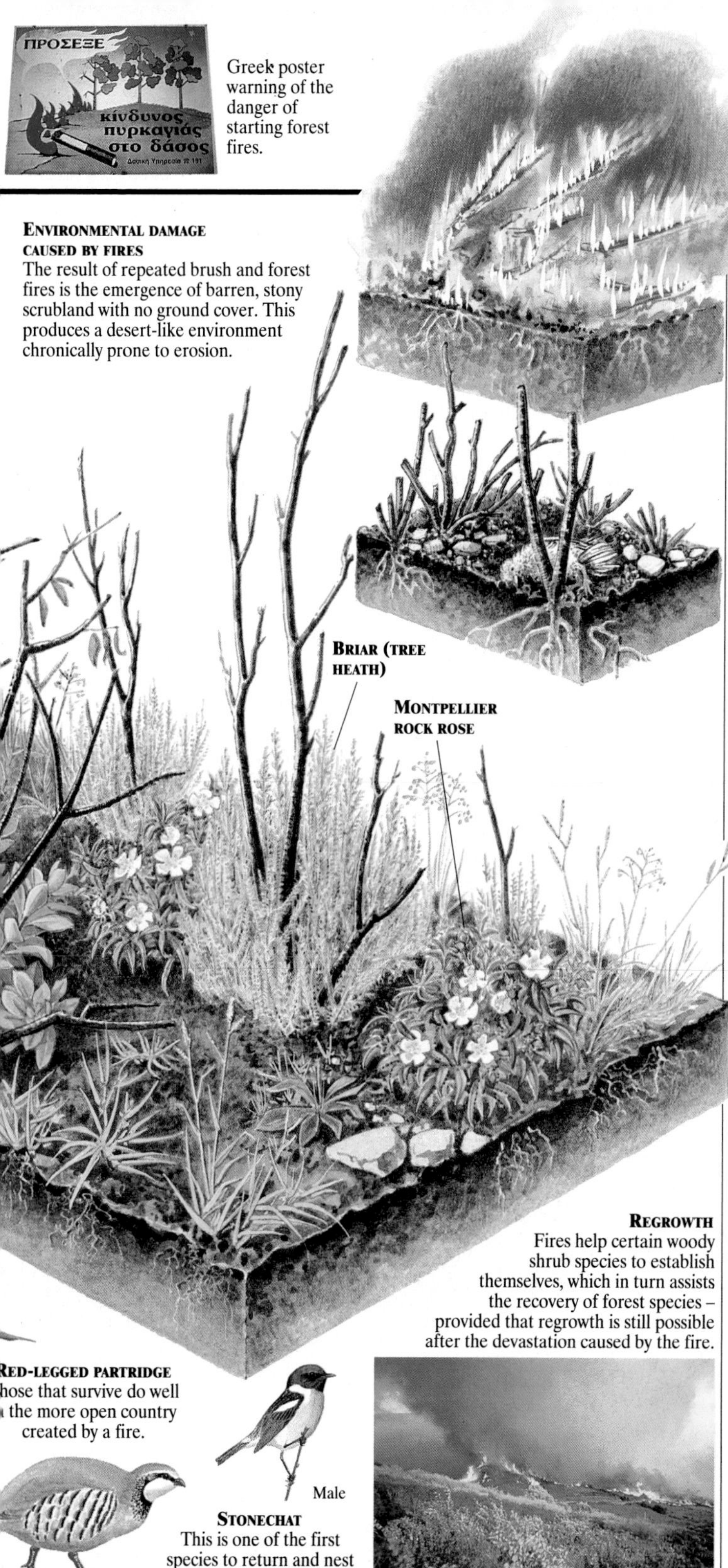

Greek poster warning of the danger of starting forest fires.

Environmental damage caused by fires
The result of repeated brush and forest fires is the emergence of barren, stony scrubland with no ground cover. This produces a desert-like environment chronically prone to erosion.

Regrowth
Fires help certain woody shrub species to establish themselves, which in turn assists the recovery of forest species – provided that regrowth is still possible after the devastation caused by the fire.

Red-legged partridge
hose that survive do well
the more open country
created by a fire.

Stonechat
This is one of the first species to return and nest in the scorched *maquis*.

Phrygana

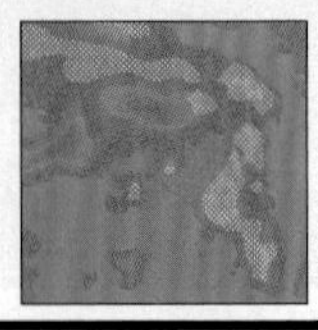

The term *phrygana*, from classical Greek, describes a type of vegetation approximating the French *garrigue* and the Spanish *tomillares.* It consists of low woody species, often thorny, which supply intermittent cover for dry, rocky and chalky soil. The type of herbaceous flora which occupies these zones emerges in spring and/or autumn. This type of terrain extends from the coasts to the high plateaux through areas that seem completely bare in the summer months. Nevertheless, the plants' deep root systems allow them to find enough moisture to survive far below the surface. *Phrygana* can evolve in areas that have been ravaged by overgrazing or fires. The animal population usually consists of birds, small mammals and reptiles.

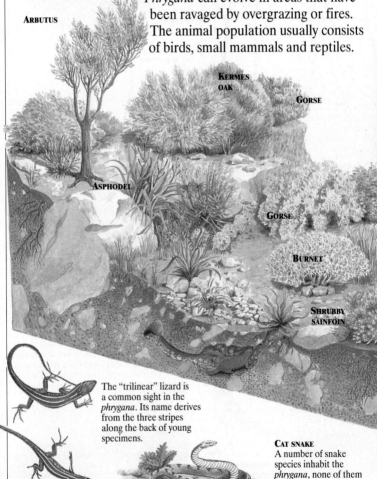

Chukar partridges live among thorny bushes. They are much sought after by hunters.

Arbutus

Kermes oak

Gorse

Asphodel

Gorse

Burnet

Shrubby sainfoin

The "trilinear" lizard is a common sight in the *phrygana*. Its name derives from the three stripes along the back of young specimens.

Cat snake
A number of snake species inhabit the *phrygana*, none of them venomous.

A typical stretch of *phrygana*, covered by spiky gorse bushes. The great explosion of blossom takes place in spring, but some of the aromatic plants – among them the native varieties of wild rosemary, sage, oregano and thyme – retain a powerful scent throughout the summer when the vegetation is very dry.

Blue rock thrush
The male's plumage is blue all over, with darker wings and tail.

Sardinian warbler
A charming songbird, which frequents wooded areas and clearings.

Ortolan
With its brown back, reddish belly and olive-brown breast, this bird nests at ground level in the *phrygana*.

Asphodel
With its deep root system, asphodel can stand dry conditions and thrives in Greece.

Hives and honey
Honey was greatly prized in antiquity. Bees feed on the nectar of aromatic blossoms of the *phrygana*; painted hives are placed in sites sheltered from the wind.

Uromenas elegans
A large species of cricket found in the *phrygana*.

Yellow orchid
One of many orchid species found in Greece.

In spring the flowers of the *phrygana* are particularly colorful.

The herbaceous plants of the *phrygana* are either short-lived annuals or perennials with an underground root system for storing reserves of nutrients. The seeds of both the annuals and the bulbs remain dormant during the dry season.

HOUSE SPARROW
A familiar inhabitant of the olive grove.

The cultivation of the olive, which was imported from Asia or Africa by the Minoans, reached the Mediterranean about 3,000 years ago. Since then the olive has spread throughout the Mediterranean basin, to such an extent that it has become its symbol. The ideal altitude for olives is below 1,000 feet, though they can grow at up to 2,000 feet above sea level. Green olives for eating are harvested in September and October, black ones between November and January. Olives for pressing are gathered from December to February.

HARVESTING OLIVES
Like their ancestors, present-day Greeks harvest olives by beating the branches with poles of different lengths. Since ancient times olive oil has had the same flavor.

The olive belongs to the family Oleaceae. The species grown in Greece is called *Olea europaea*.

Olive groves, usually quite small, need regular maintenance. An olive tree begins to bear fruit at three to four years old, and gives its highest yields between fifteen and thirty years of age. The trees are often cut short to facilitate picking; the spaces between them may be planted with other crops.

The olive grove is often worked side by side with vineyards, or used for pasture in spring, after the last black olives have been harvested. The ripe fruit falls on tarpaulins spread under the trees.

Only one flower in twenty produces an olive.

ROBIN
In the wooded hills of Greece robins are shy and skulking.

Male

BLACKCAP
This warbler can be either migratory or sedentary.

A PLAIN OF OLIVES
This magnificent olive grove is over 30 miles long. It contains many acres of young, geometrically planted trees, but also a number of venerable ones, with giant roots and scarred bark, that date from the 13th century – some of them still yielding as much as half a ton of olives each.

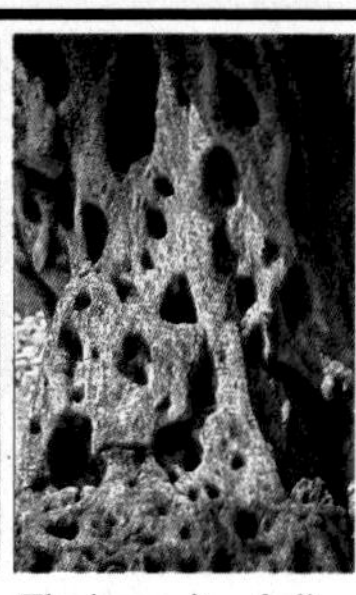

The longevity of olive trees is legendary: many still bear fruit at 150 years old.

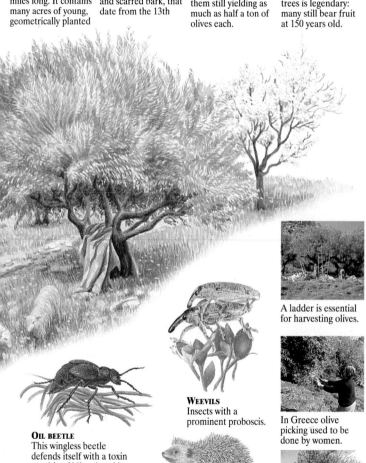

A ladder is essential for harvesting olives.

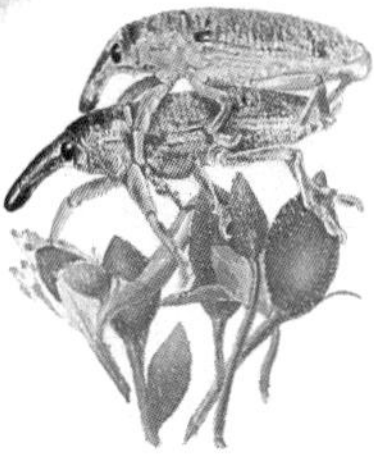

WEEVILS
Insects with a prominent proboscis.

In Greece olive picking used to be done by women.

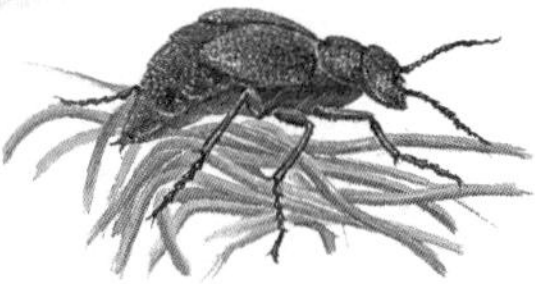

OIL BEETLE
This wingless beetle defends itself with a toxin capable of blistering skin.

EASTERN HEDGEHOG

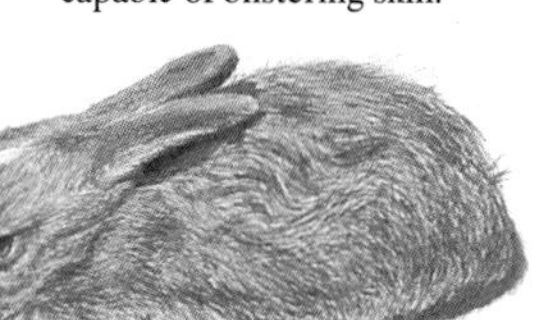

BROWN HARE
Found all over Greece.

Electric harvesting poles were introduced in the late 1980's.

Greek ports are full of small boats, mostly *trehadiri* (caïques with rounded bows and sterns). The fishermen use different techniques – depending on the season, the weather, the particular fishing ground and how they happen to feel – from hand lines to trawl lines and nets. They go out both by day and by night, seldom straying far from the shore, and bring back a great variety of fish.

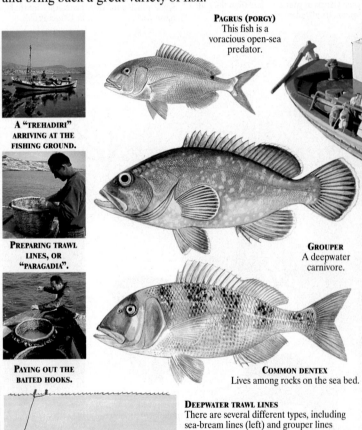

PAGRUS (PORGY)
This fish is a voracious open-sea predator.

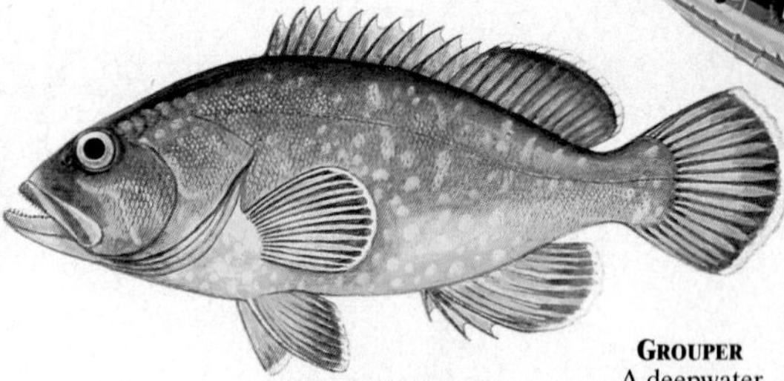

A "TREHADIRI" ARRIVING AT THE FISHING GROUND.

PREPARING TRAWL LINES, OR "PARAGADIA".

GROUPER
A deepwater carnivore.

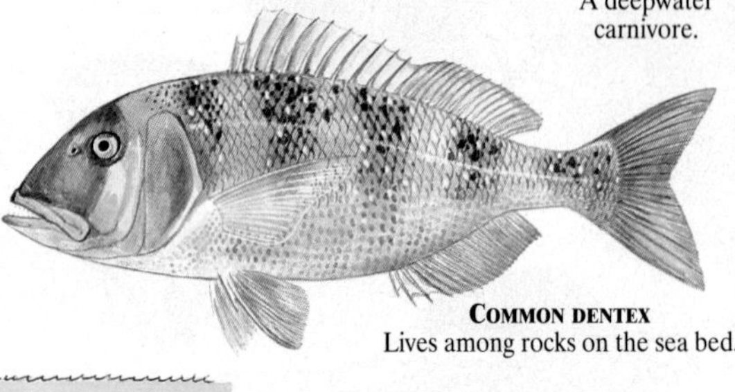

PAYING OUT THE BAITED HOOKS.

COMMON DENTEX
Lives among rocks on the sea bed.

DEEPWATER TRAWL LINES
There are several different types, including sea-bream lines (left) and grouper lines (below). They are pitched more or less close to the bottom, depending on which species the fisherman is after.

Trawl lines consist of leaders to which the hooks are attached, linked by a master line. Each trawl line may carry as many as five hundred hooks. This technique is used for catching top-grade fish.

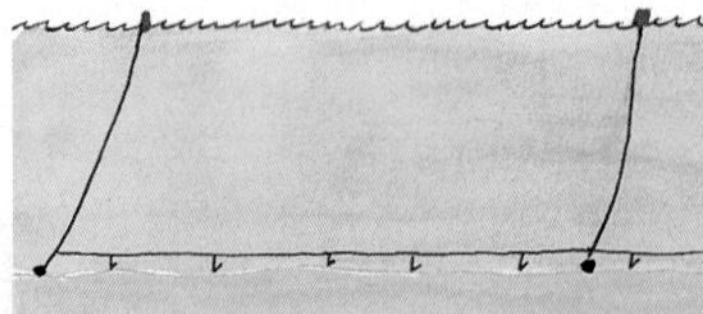

"THE SEA AWAKENS TO THE CRY OF GULLS, WHILE THE STARS STILL SLEEP IN HER DEPTHS."

M. DIMAKIS, *A SEASON AT SEA*

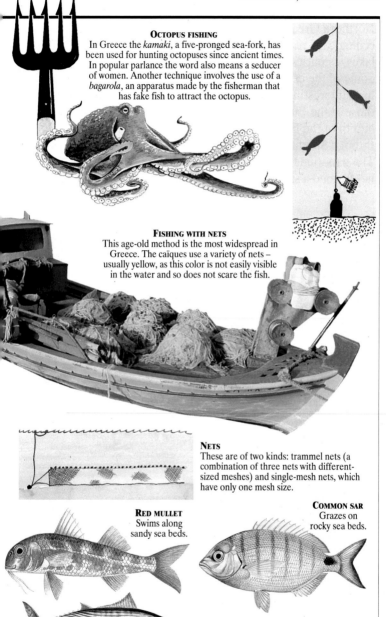

OCTOPUS FISHING

In Greece the *kamaki*, a five-pronged sea-fork, has been used for hunting octopuses since ancient times. In popular parlance the word also means a seducer of women. Another technique involves the use of a *bagarola*, an apparatus made by the fisherman that has fake fish to attract the octopus.

FISHING WITH NETS

This age-old method is the most widespread in Greece. The caïques use a variety of nets – usually yellow, as this color is not easily visible in the water and so does not scare the fish.

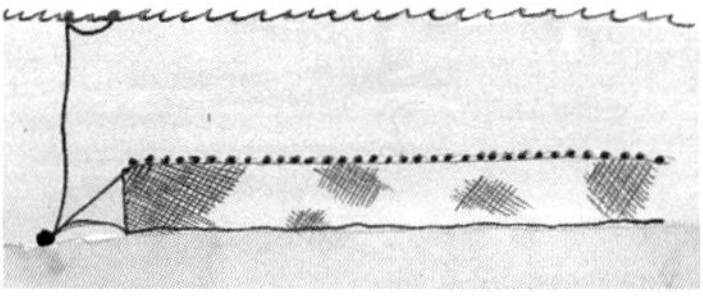

NETS

These are of two kinds: trammel nets (a combination of three nets with different-sized meshes) and single-mesh nets, which have only one mesh size.

RED MULLET

Swims along sandy sea beds.

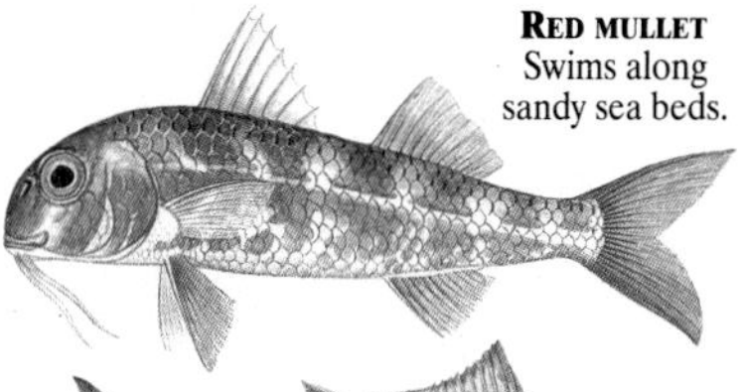

COMMON SAR

Grazes on rocky sea beds.

STRIPED BONITO

A denizen of the open sea.

"KARTERI" NET

Used for catching bonito and small tuna, the *karteri* consists of a line of wide-meshed nets.

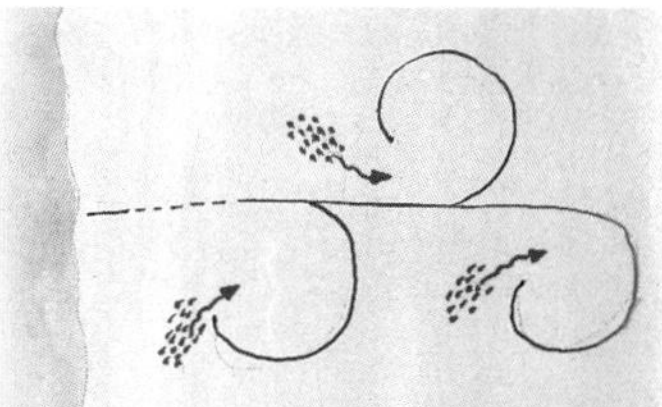

The Eurotas Estuary

Northern Greece boasts many ecologically rich wetlands around rivers, lakes, estuaries, ponds and marshland. Some of the estuaries of the Peloponnese have interesting inshore marshes, such as those at the Eurotas Estuary formed by the mouth of the Eurotas River, which flows through Sparta into the Gulf of Laconia. The panorama below shows how sediment has formed a sandy bar at the entrance to the bay, creating a brackish alluvial lagoon through which the river meanders.

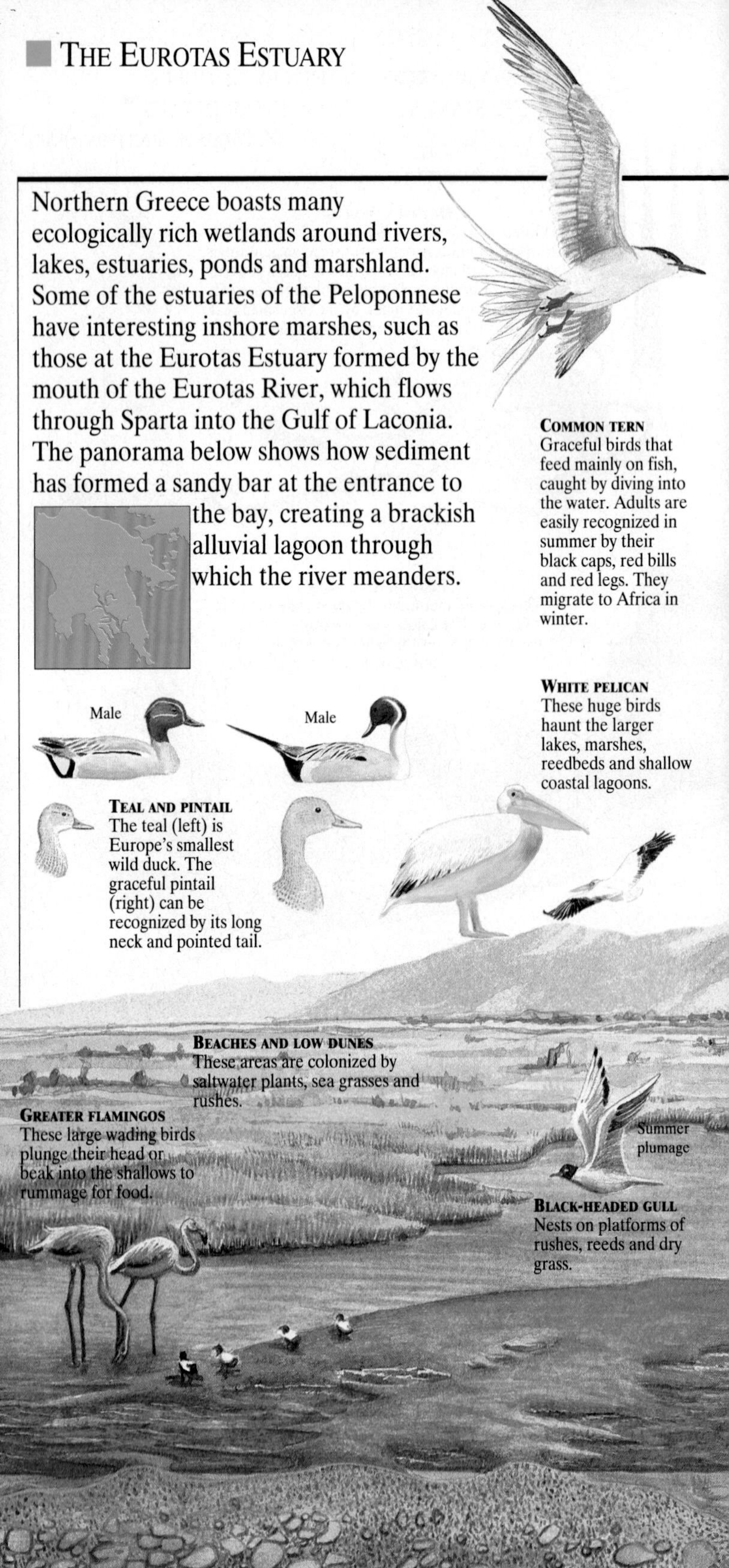

Common tern
Graceful birds that feed mainly on fish, caught by diving into the water. Adults are easily recognized in summer by their black caps, red bills and red legs. They migrate to Africa in winter.

White pelican
These huge birds haunt the larger lakes, marshes, reedbeds and shallow coastal lagoons.

Teal and pintail
The teal (left) is Europe's smallest wild duck. The graceful pintail (right) can be recognized by its long neck and pointed tail.

Beaches and low dunes
These areas are colonized by saltwater plants, sea grasses and rushes.

Greater flamingos
These large wading birds plunge their head or beak into the shallows to rummage for food.

Black-headed gull
Nests on platforms of rushes, reeds and dry grass.

FLORA. On the dunes and beaches of the delta sand plants such as sea reeds, couch grass, sea holly (*Eryngium maritimum*) and sand lilies are very plentiful. The saltmarshes support several different kinds of rushes and where the tamarisks end a variety of other plants that tolerate sea water flourish.

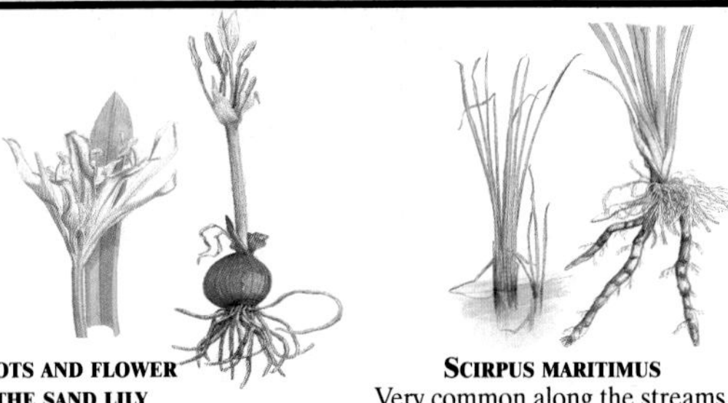

ROOTS AND FLOWER OF THE SAND LILY

SCIRPUS MARITIMUS
Very common along the streams.

POSIDONIA
This sea plant has leaves like dark green ribbons and a thick stem that looks like the tail of an animal. The dried stems can often be found strewn about on the dunes.

FAUNA
Loggerhead turtles lay their eggs in the sand. The estuary is also a habitat of the threatened golden jackal, as well as of kestrels, Bonelli's eagle and various species of owl.

CORMORANT
Cormorants winter in large numbers on deltas and coastal marshes.

CHASER DRAGONFLY
The most spectacular marshland insect.

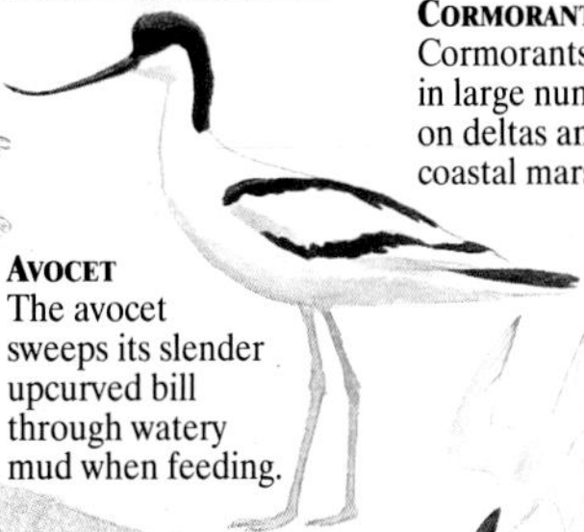

AVOCET
The avocet sweeps its slender upcurved bill through watery mud when feeding.

COMMON TERN
These terns nest in colonies along river banks and on beaches, sand dunes and islands.

GOLDEN JACKAL

EEL

BULRUSHES

The golden jackal is found all over Greece with the largest remaining populations in the Peloponnese and Sparta. Long considered to be a creature of the forests and mountains, the golden jackal is in fact an inhabitant of the Mediterranean *maquis* and similar low-lying areas. It belongs to the same family as the fox, wolf, dog and coyote, and lives on a diet of small mammals such as field mice and squirrels, as well as reptiles, fruit and carrion. It may occasionally kill poultry, rabbits and newborn lambs. The golden jackal lives in small groups; the males and females share their food and the duties of looking after cubs.

HABITAT
In Greece the golden jackal tends to inhabit damp areas – mainly estuaries and marshes.

The golden jackal often plays with its prey, as here with a dead field mouse.

A PROTECTED SPECIES
The jackal was long considered a pest; shepherds hunted it remorselessly with the sanction of the government forestry authorities. In the 1980's it was placed on the engangered list and designated a protected species. Nevertheless its survival in Greece is even more threatened than that of its cousin the wolf.

THE DEN
The jackal's den shown here (right) has just been dug. The cubs, which are born in the spring, remain underground for about three weeks.

THE JACKAL'S COAT
The color changes according to the season. Golden in summer, it becomes a yellowy brown with the onset of winter.

MILLER'S SHREW
A small rodent that feeds on insects and earthworms.

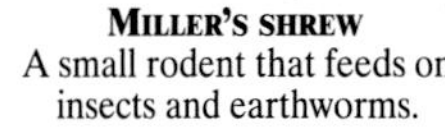

GREAT GREEN GRASSHOPPER

WOOD MOUSE
Like the shrew, this creature is part of the jackal's staple diet.

The Greek climate is Mediterranean in character, with a long dry summer and a cooler, wetter winter. A wide variety of plants have adapted to these conditions, including many with thick, hard, fleshy leaves. There are also thorny shrubs; short-lived annuals that flower and die in the spring; plants with deep, complex root systems or bulbs (such as lilies, irises and cyclamens); and plants with thick, clustering root systems (such as asphodel). All these plants accumulate reserves which allow them to flower every year. At certain times, particularly in spring, the ground is carpeted with the blossoms of anemones, tulips, orchids, crucifers and leguminous plants.

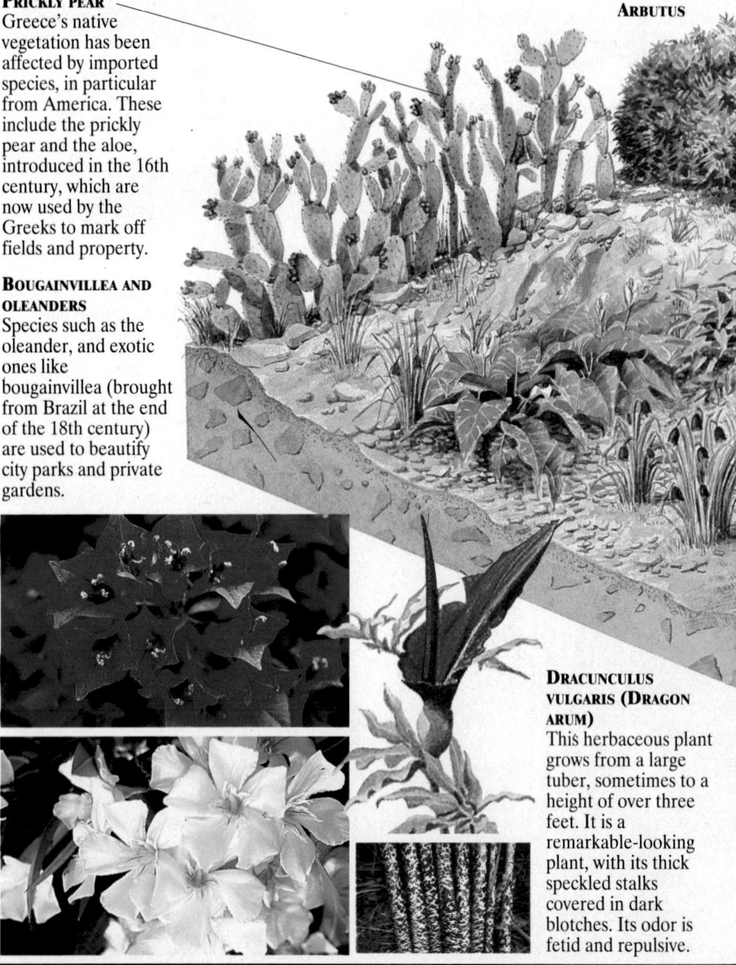

PRICKLY PEAR
Greece's native vegetation has been affected by imported species, in particular from America. These include the prickly pear and the aloe, introduced in the 16th century, which are now used by the Greeks to mark off fields and property.

ARBUTUS

BOUGAINVILLEA AND OLEANDERS
Species such as the oleander, and exotic ones like bougainvillea (brought from Brazil at the end of the 18th century) are used to beautify city parks and private gardens.

DRACUNCULUS VULGARIS (DRAGON ARUM)
This herbaceous plant grows from a large tuber, sometimes to a height of over three feet. It is a remarkable-looking plant, with its thick speckled stalks covered in dark blotches. Its odor is fetid and repulsive.

GARLIC FLOWERS AND BULB
Wild garlic produces tightly bunched clusters of flowers from May to July. It is very common on beaches and dry banks in Greece.

PISTACIA LENTISCUS (MASTIC TREE)
The perennial "mastic tree" grows in the *maquis* and in places in the *phrygana*, where it forms bushes or even small trees. It provides a resin that the Greeks eat.

WHITE BRIARS
There are two varieties, both with pinkish flowers, found all over the *maquis* and in dry woodlands.

ARBUTUS (STRAWBERRY TREE)
The arbutus produces globular orange-red berries that can be eaten from December onward.

ECBALLIUM ELATERIUM
This species of wild squash – known locally as *Agriangouria* or *Pikrangouria* – is very common in Greece, where it can be found growing in rocky crannies everywhere. From May to September the plant is covered with small yellow flowers. When the oval fruits are ripe, they burst open at the merest touch, spraying seeds everywhere. The leaves are thick and fleshy; the stalks, which lack tendrils, creep along the ground.

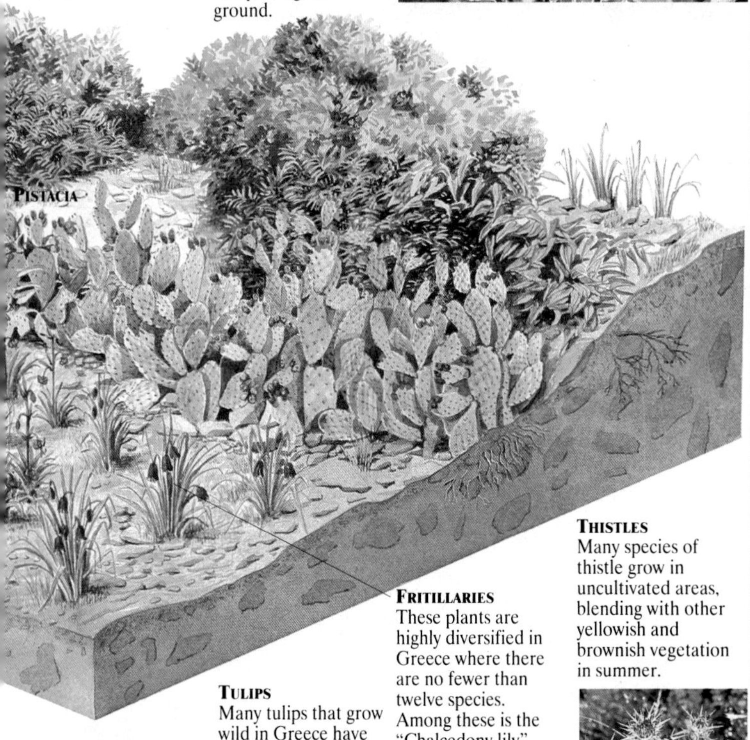

PISTACIA

TULIPS
Many tulips that grow wild in Greece have been domesticated by gardeners, notably deep-red species like the Boeotian tulip. Tulip leaves replenish reserves not only in their original bulb but also in the bulb that will replace it.

FRITILLARIES
These plants are highly diversified in Greece where there are no fewer than twelve species. Among these is the "Chalcedony lily", which has pendulous red flowers with outward-curving petals; the leaves grow in tufts and the flower stems sprout from the same level. It is found on rocky, wooded hillsides.

THISTLES
Many species of thistle grow in uncultivated areas, blending with other yellowish and brownish vegetation in summer.

THE NATIONAL GARDENS

When King Otto came to the throne of Greece in 1833 • *52*, there were almost no trees in Athens. It was therefore decided that public gardens should be laid out and trees planted along the capital's streets. The first of three parks created in the 19th century was the Royal Park, which opened its gates to the public in 1923 and was renamed the National Gardens. The excavation of Hadrian's aqueduct resolved the problem of irrigation, and the park was endowed with several canals and ponds, along with more than five hundred species of shrubs and trees.

The planting of rare exotic plants proved a disaster: the only ones to survive more than a few years were a pair of gingkos. As a result the gardeners decided to focus on native Greek plants, and at the end of the 19th century cypresses, olives and orange trees were planted along with other local species.

Queen Eugenia, who took a special interest in the park, wanted a garden of rarities. The latest soil enrichment, irrigation and fertilization techniques were used to acclimatize no fewer than 1,500 species imported from Italy, many of them exotic. Unfortunately, the persistent dryness and winds destroyed most of these plants.

LAYOUT OF THE GARDENS
The National Gardens are made up of a network of broad, curving avenues in the 18th-century English style which was still fashionable in Europe in the 19th century. There are several monuments, both ancient and modern, consisting mainly of statues, small pavilions and mosaics.

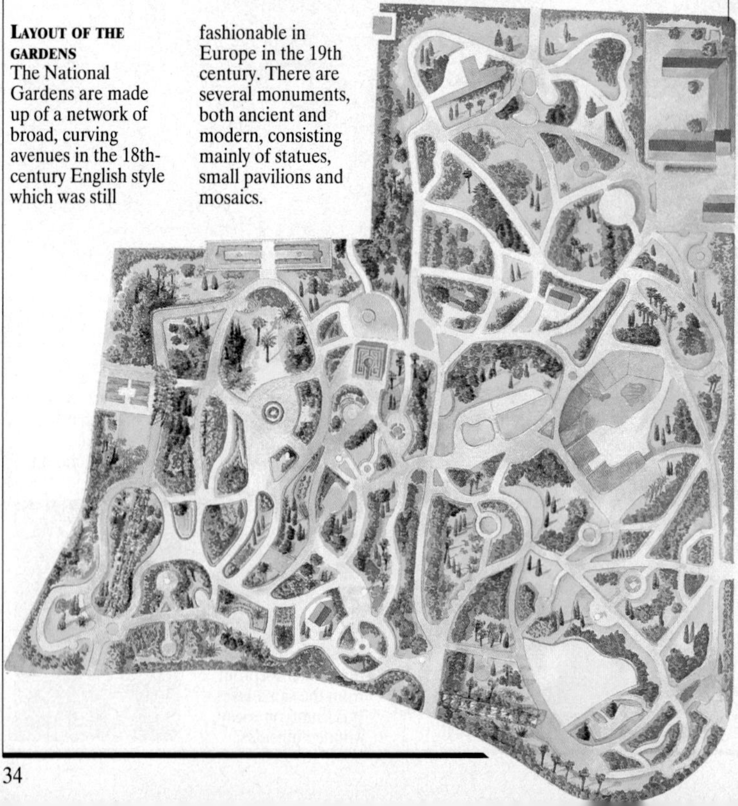

History

The various gods that made up the Greek pantheon in classical times were already firmly established in mythology by the Mycenean era. As the spiritual and religious foundation of ancient Greece, mythology stimulated a ferment of artistic creativity; represented over and over again in art, its stories illustrated man's dual relationship with the divine. The gods were included both in the rituals of ordinary piety and in an awareness of the limitations of human life, as delineated by the gods themselves. The mythical scenes and situations that the ancient Greeks reproduced in art reminded them of the divinely determined boundaries beyond which they could not venture, and this in turn enabled them to understand themselves and their place in the cosmic order.

IO TURNED INTO A COW AS PUNISHMENT FOR SEDUCING ZEUS
Humans are often metamorphosized after intimacy with a god or goddess.

OEDIPUS AND THE SPHINX
The riddle of the sphinx was: "What animal goes on all fours in the morning, two feet at noon and three feet in the evening?" Oedipus, holding a cane, replied: "Man." Here he is man in the evening of his days; age and experience have led him to surpass himself, to become different while remaining the same.

MEDEA KILLING HER SON
Medea the sorceress epitomizes extreme behavior: she is as skillful at manipulating the passions of others as she is incapable of controlling her own. Her career exemplifies absolute injustice and extravagance.

HERAKLES FIGHTING THE SERPENTS OF HERA
So great is the power of the gods that they need not await adulthood before performing great exploits: the demi-god Herakles is already his heroic self even as a newborn.

Poseidon in combat with a giant
Giant-killing symbolized the cosmic opposition between the ages of the world.

Meleager and the boar of Calydon
Meleager's destiny is decided by his encounter with the boar. His death does not result from the act of slaying the animal, but from his refusal to share the spoils of the hunt – thus ignoring his peers and destroying the bonds of kinship that keep the tribe together.

Piety and long tradition created a sense of intimacy between the Greeks and their gods, lending harmony and stability to their daily existence. The images of ordinary life depicted on Greek vases have been a rich and important source of information for understanding life in ancient times. Such vases mirrored daily existence, though transformed by art.

COUPLE POURING A LIBATION
Libations were performed before meals, banquets and other important events in daily life, such as departures or assemblies. The ritual consisted of pouring out the first few drops of a beverage, either on the ground or on an altar. This sanctified the moment by placing it under the protection of one of the gods (usually one of the earth divinities). The beverage might be pure wine, wine mixed with water, wine mixed with honey and water, or pure milk.

MOURNERS AROUND A DEAD MAN
Funerary rites had five stages: the washing and dressing of the corpse; displaying it on a ceremonial couch; the procession to the necropolis; cremation or burial; and the purification of the deceased's home. For the ancient Greeks, to die was to complete one's destiny as a human being – but this could not be accomplished fully without the rites that gave meaning to death. The tears shed by the mourners were seen as drops of human essence offered as a libation.

WEDDING SCENE
Marriage was preceded by vows in the presence of the suitor's witnesses and the father or guardian of the prospective bride. Wedding celebrations lasted three days. On the first night the bride purified herself with a ritual bath and made offerings to Artemis, the protectress of virginity. On the day of the wedding the groom led his bride by the hand to her new home, and on the third day the couple received gifts from their guests. According to Aristotle, the ideal age to marry was about 37 for men and about 18 for women.

BANQUET SCENE
The banquet is typical of Greek culture, in which people never ate without indulging in speeches too. In general, Greeks took the view that the food which went into their mouths counted for less than the words that came out of them.

A HOPLITE
The hoplite was the model Greek warrior. He was well-armed with helmet, shield and lance, greaves and usually a corslet. The representation of the hoplite looking back as he runs forward is designed to represent the craftiness and intelligence as necessary to the soldier as his armor.

THE BARBARIAN
The way the clothes of this figure are rendered shows how well the Greeks understood cultural differences. To them "barbarians" were not savages, merely men belonging to different civilizations speaking different languages.

DEPARTURE OF A WARRIOR
This scene illustrates one of the main differences between Greeks and barbarians, notably Persians. A Greek only took up arms to defend his family and his country: he saw himself as a bulwark against aggression, rather than as a member of a clan.

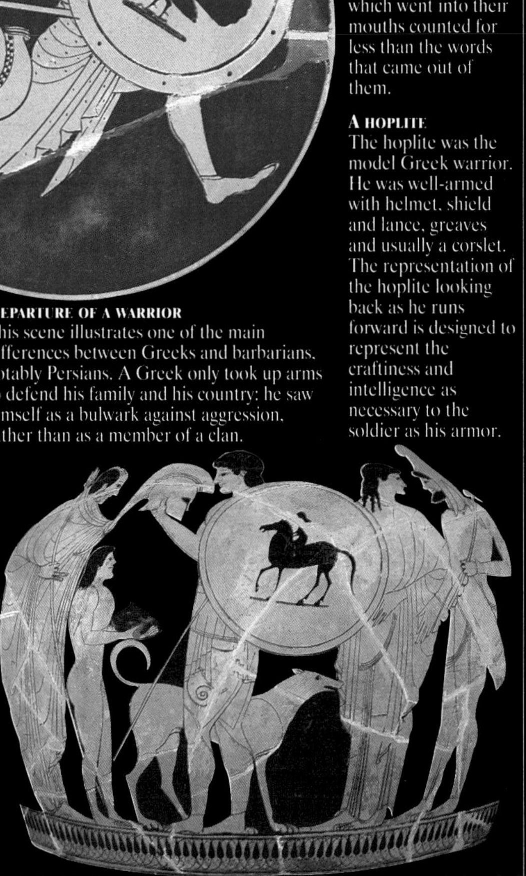

The origins of tragedy lie in the cult of Dionysos, and particularly in the great Festival of Dionysos, a feast of special magnificence celebrated in Athens from the 6th century BC onward. At the beginning of spring people came to Athens from the four corners of Attica to participate in several days of processions and orgies in celebration of the god of wine and nature. The high point of the festivities came with the poetry and singing contests, when bards and singers matched their skills before a rapt audience. Their performances eventually developed into the art of tragedy.

MELPOMENE
The muse Melpomene received the gift of song from Apollo, and the gift of tragedy from Dionysos. Here she is shown holding an actor's mask.

Of the various events that took place during the festival of Dionysos, the most lavish was the procession in honor of the god. Magistrates, priests and maidens bearing baskets of gifts to be distributed among the crowd lead a statue of Dionysos on a procession around the city. Musicians and dancers, dressed up as Silenuses and Satyrs, traditionally broke up the solemnity of this occasion: the dithyramb evolved from their comic antics.

SATYRS ET SILENUSES
Half men, half animals, these minor deities were included in the retinue of Dionysos by virtue of their skills as musicians and dancers. Greek tragedy later adopted their more fanciful characteristics: the actors' masks and costumes imitated the features of the animals with which they were associated.

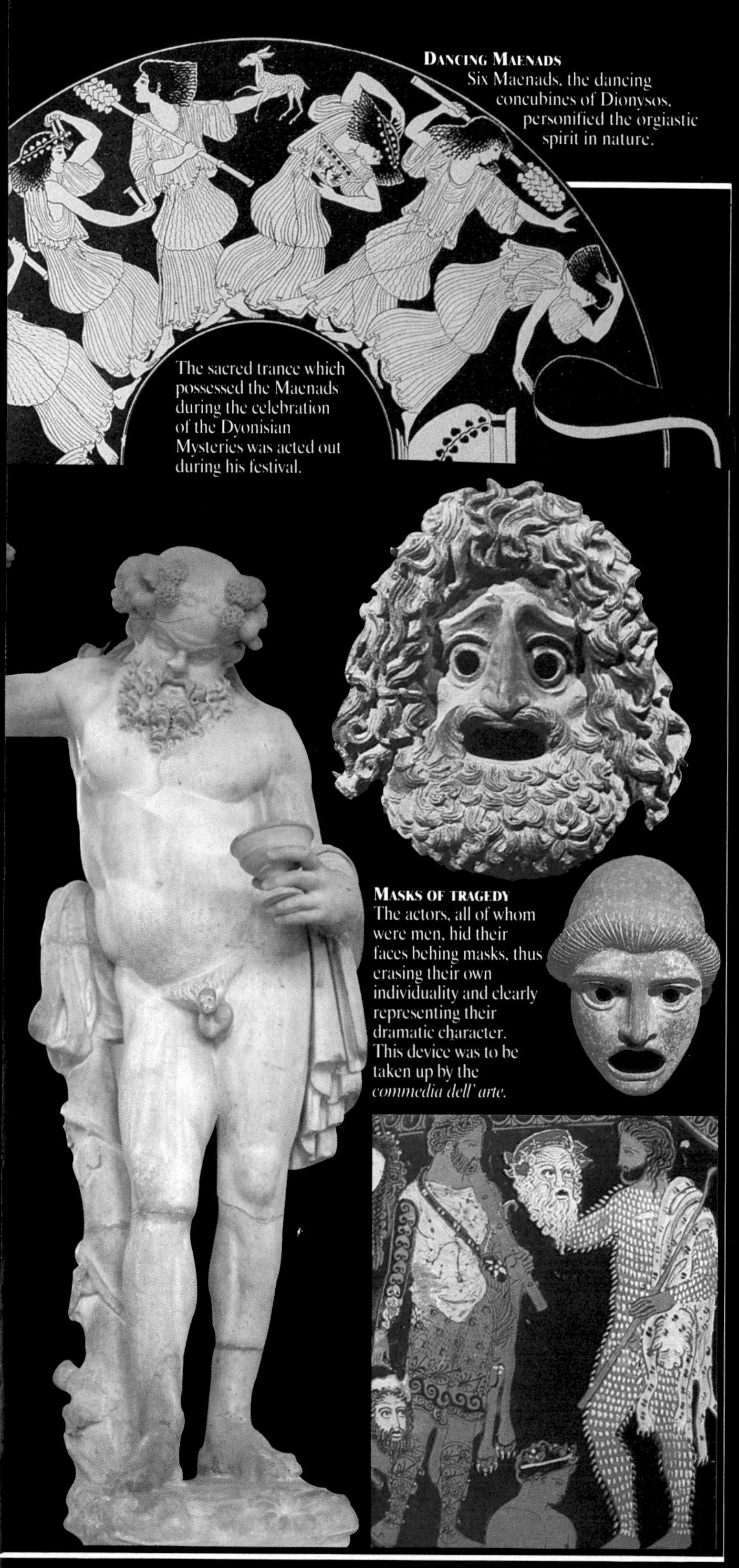

Dancing Maenads Six Maenads, the dancing concubines of Dionysos, personified the orgiastic spirit in nature.

The sacred trance which possessed the Maenads during the celebration of the Dyonisian Mysteries was acted out during his festival.

Masks of tragedy The actors, all of whom were men, hid their faces behing masks, thus erasing their own individuality and clearly representing their dramatic character. This device was to be taken up by the *commedia dell' arte.*

CYCLADIC CIVILIZATION

Small Minoan vase, 3000–2200 BC.

The temperate climate of the Cyclades favored human settlement from the Bronze Age onward. Moreover the relative calm of the Aegean facilitated communications between these islands and the coasts of Greece and Asia Minor. Vestiges of settlements scattered along the shores of the Cyclades. These were not fortified – a sign that the inhabitants, whose lives were dominated by the sea, lived in peace. Between 2800 and 2200 BC the settlements appear in groups with defensive walls on hillsides, suggesting a threat from invaders.

3650–1300 BC
Minoan civilization.

3200–2200 BC
Cycladic civilization.

THE ART OF THE CYCLADES. Numerous objects, either ceramic or sculpted in marble, show the originality of Cycladic art, in painted vases, tools, weapons and statuettes.

MINOAN CIVILIZATION

Cycladic art: Head of a marble figurine, c. 3200–2800 BC. The 3rd millennium BC (the Ancient Cycladic era) furnishes the most original creations – including idols and female figurines, usually in marble. The statuettes known as the Plastiras group are handled in a natural style, with anatomical details such as ears, eyes and full-lipped mouths.

Aegean civilization was born in Crete, the largest island in the eastern Mediterranean and the richest in arable land. While the first traces of human occupation of Crete date from the Neolithic era, it was not until 2000 BC that Cretan civilization reached its first high point, with the construction of the palaces of Knossos, Phaistos and Malia. All of these were destroyed around 1700 BC, in all probability by an earthquake. A second important period began with their reconstruction, after which Minoan civilization dominated the eastern Mediterranean from 1700 to 1300 BC. Crete's political, social and religious life, along with its economic and cultural exchanges with other Mediterranean countries, attest to the great wealth and dynamism of its society. In particular Crete influenced Mycenean civilization.

MINOAN ART. Sir Arthur Evans' excavations at the close of the 19th century, continued by Greek archeologists, revealed the full achievement of this brilliant civilization. Evans found evidence of sophisticated architecture, sculptures, frescos, jewelry, finely wrought precious metals, inscriptions (the Gortys disk) and writing (Linear A).

2000–1570 BC
Unfortified Minoan palaces.

1850–1600 BC
The first invasions of the "Greeks."

1600–1150 BC
Monumental Minoan palaces.

1570–1425 BC
Minoan maritime hegemony.

Naval expedition, fresco of 1600–1500 BC.

“THE LAND OF CRETE RISES, BEAUTIFUL AND FERTILE, OUT OF THE WINE-DARK SEA; THEREIN LIVE MEN BEYOND COUNT… OVER THEM ALL IS SET THE GREAT CITY OF KNOSSOS, WHERE MINOS REIGNED.” *THE ODYSSEY*

MYCENEAN CIVILIZATION

The city of Mycenae, in the center of the Argolid Plain, was for many centuries the principal power in the Greek world. As the base of influential kings, its political influence extended to Attica, Boeotia and Thessaly. The city's geographical situation and easy access to the sea allowed it to develop its commercial activities throughout the Mediterranean.

MYCENEAN ART. Without reaching the heights attained by Minoan art, the Myceneans did produce some major works – discovered by Heinrich Schliemann, in 1874, and his successors: the Treasury of Atreus, gold funerary offerings, royal palaces, domed tombs, Cyclopean walls and the Lion Gate. Another important element in this culture was mythology. The cycle of the royal line of Atreus, the Trojan War and the voyage of the Argonauts inspired the great tragic poets of Greece and later artists of all eras and all nations.

Painted stucco head, 13th century BC.

1500–1150 BC
Mycenean civilization.

CIRCA 1425 BC
Destruction of the Palace of Knossos.

MIGRATION OF THE GREEKS, 1200–1000 BC

A new era began around 1125 BC with the arrival of a second wave of “Greeks” in the Peloponnese. They brought with them a new civilization, in which the Hellenic element was much stronger. It was unified by the worship of certain divinities, a tradition of athletic games, mythology and the language and alphabet called “Phoenician”, which became the basis of the Greek alphabet. The Achaeans, who had created Mycenae, were driven from the Peloponnese by the invading Dorians, a warrior race whose discipline and iron weapons gave them distinct military superiority.

Minoan Palace of Knossos: the great staircase.

GEOMETRIC ART. The dawn of recorded history (c. 1100 BC) coincided with the birth of geometric art, and the ceramic designs of that era are considered to be the precursors of fully fledged Hellenic art. The freedom of the artists who produced this work is evident in their inventions of new forms and in the variety of the scenes they represented. Mythology, however, remained the principal source of inspiration. Also at this time the first bronze figurines appeared; and craftsmen of the period created jewelry and small decorative objects in bronze and gold, which attest to the abundant wealth accumulated from the 8th century BC onward.

CIRCA 1400 BC
Construction of domed tombs.

CIRCA 1250 BC
Destruction of Troy.

CIRCA 900 BC
Foundation of Sparta.

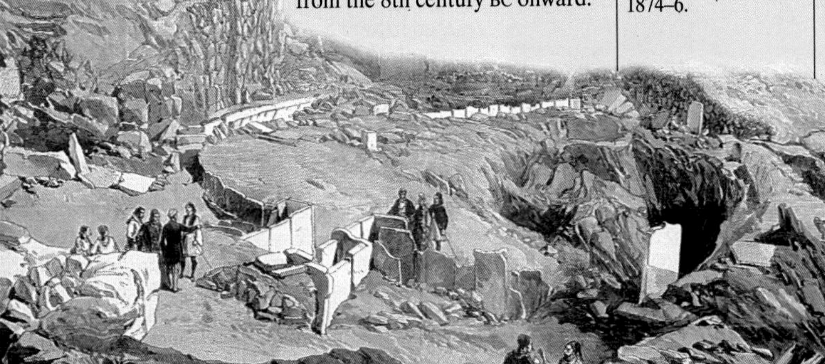
Schliemann's excavation of the acropolis at Mycenae, 1874–6.

THE ARCHAIC PERIOD, 8TH–6TH CENTURIES BC

Statue of a woman, Acropolis, Athens.

Around 800 BC, during the era known to us as the Archaic period, appeared the Greek world's most original political invention, the city-state. From about 770 BC, the smaller Greek metropolises founded colonies throughout the Mediterranean basin and around the Black Sea. The city-states were a unique phenomenon: economically independent and politically autonomous, they were the crucible for a whole array of different political systems that are still in operation today. Progressing from authority personified by a strategist-king to aristocratic or tyrannical regimes, they eventually gave birth to a purely democratic system. This was based on a city, its territories and its citizens, which formed an entity called a *polis*. The *polis* was under the protection of a divinity which sometimes gave it its name, as Athena did for Athens.

750–700 BC
Homeric poetry.

7TH CENTURY BC
Advent of tyranny.

683 BC
The archonate takes the place of the monarchy in Athens.

Kouros of Anavyssos, 530 BC.

660–640 BC
Spartan oligarchy.

594 BC
Solon elected archon.

GREEK COLONIZATION, 770–550 BC. For social, agricultural and demographic reasons, colonization proceeded at a great rate between 770 and 550 BC. Hellenic civilization expanded into Ionia and along the coast of Asia Minor, eventually penetrating southern Italy; the city-states also founded colonies in Gaul, Spain and Africa, where Greek culture quickly took root. Philosophy, poetry, science and architecture thus became established everywhere on the Mediterranean seaboard.

MILETUS. The most brilliant Greek colonies were those of Italy and Asia Minor. The Ionian colony of Miletus in turn founded trading outposts on the Black Sea coast, while itself remaining pre-eminent and producing a galaxy of great thinkers and artists. Among these were Hecataeus, one of the first writers on history and geography; the philosophers Thales and Anaximenes; the poet Phocylides; and later the urban architect Hippodamos and the poets Timotheus and Aspasia, the *hetaira* (mistress) of Pericles. In the domain of the visual arts, the oriental influence predominated at Miletus, with numerous naturalistic plant and animal motifs.

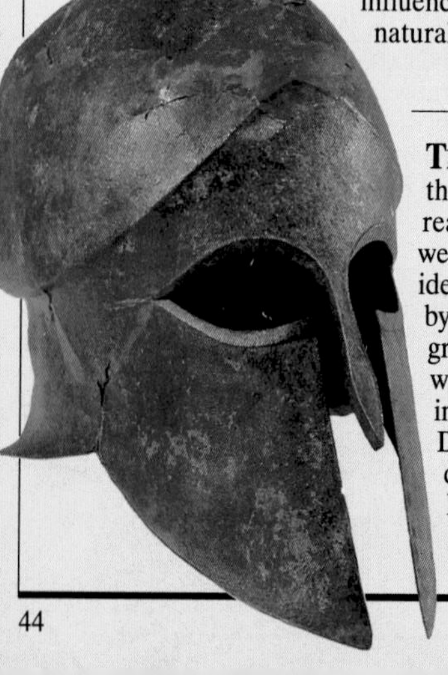

Corinthian helmet, late 6th century BC.

THE PERSIAN WARS

THE FIRST PERSIAN WAR. At the close of the 6th century BC the Persian Empire had reached its zenith and began to look to its western flank, desiring a universal empire – an idea conceived as early as the 3rd millennium BC by the Assyrians and Babylonians. In 499 BC the great Persian king Darius' dreams of conquest were set back by a revolt fomented by Athens in the Ionian city-states of Asia Minor. By 494 Darius had crushed the Ionians and decided to do the same to Athens. But in 490 the great Persian army was defeated at Marathon. Athens gained huge credit from this historic victory, and a reputation for invincibility.

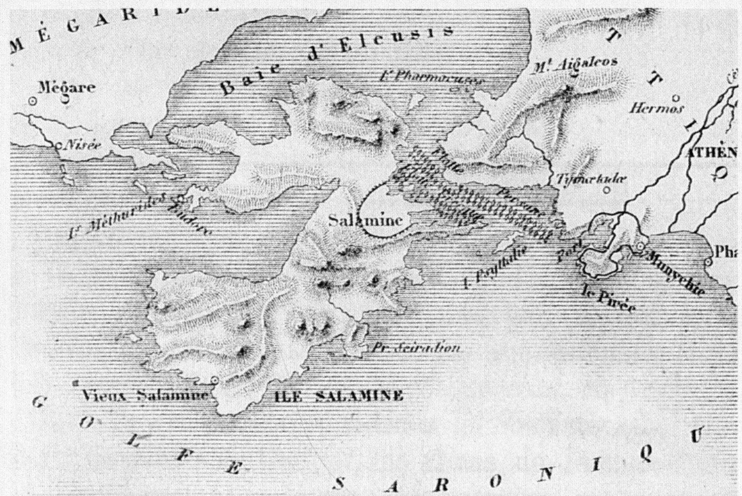

Battle of Salamis: the positions of the Greek and Persian fleets.

THE SECOND PERSIAN WAR. Xerxes was the next king of the Persians to attack Greece, at the head of an army of 100,000 men. In 481 BC Leonidas and his 300 Spartans met Xerxes at Thermopylae, in a legendary battle that gave Athens time to organize its defenses. The Athenians fell back on the island of Salamis while the Persians swept through Boeotia, destroying every city they overwhelmed, including Athens itself. But the tables were turned in 480 BC when the Persian fleet was decimated by the Athenians at Salamis. In the following year Xerxes' army was broken at Plataea, and the remnant of his fleet destroyed near Mycale in Asia Minor.

560–510 BC
Pisistratus' tyranny.

493 BC
Archonate of Themistocles.

490 BC
Battle of Marathon.

THE APOGEE OF ATHENS

With the elimination of the Persian menace, the old rivalries between Athens, Sparta and Thebes were revived. In the 5th century BC, under Pericles (444–429 BC), Athens possessed the greatest political power, the greatest wealth and the most brilliant civilization in the West, with the city at the head of a powerful maritime confederation. At the suggestion of Themistocles, Piraeus was turned into Athens' principal port; and in 460–457 BC Greece's largest fortifications, the Long Walls, were built, linking the city to Piraeus.

ATHENIAN DEMOCRACY. The model of democracy devised at Athens was adopted both in the metropolises and in the city-states of the Aegean, Asia Minor, Sicily and Magna Graecia in Italy. In 477 BC Aristides created the Delian League; this federation became a kind of empire with Athens at its head, creating new military colonies, notably in Thrace.

CLASSICAL ART. The democratic epoch brought about a new flowering of art and culture. First of all, the marriage of the Doric and Ionic styles found its most perfect expression in the masterpieces of the Acropolis. Phidias' sculptures for the friezes and pediments of the Parthenon allied extraordinary originality with technical perfection. The tragedians Aeschylus, Sophocles and Euripides and the comic playwright Aristophanes laid the foundations of modern theater. Meanwhile the Attic dialect, polished by philosophers, writers and orators, became an incomparable tool for expression. In Asia Minor, the cities of Miletus, Ephesus, Priene and Didyma were embellished with major architectural works.

480 BC
Battle of Salamis.

479 BC
Battle of Plataea.

470–460 BC
Construction of the Temple of Zeus at Olympia.

Amphora by Exekias, 6th century BC.

456 BC
Euripides' first tragedy.

477–406 BC
Rebuilding of the Acropolis.

THE PELOPONNESIAN WAR

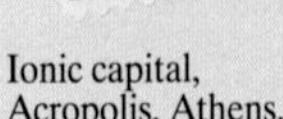

Ionic capital, Acropolis, Athens.

In the years following the Persian Wars the alliances between the city-states gradually disintegrated. The conflict that broke out in 431 BC between Sparta (which was Dorian and aristocratic) and Athens (which was Ionian and democratic) threatened the city-states' independence by drawing them into a web of outside alliances. In less than thirty years Athens was brought to its knees, its maritime empire ruined. In 404 BC the Athenians capitulated. The oligarchic regime of the Thirty Tyrants replaced democracy for one year, a sign of irrevocable decline. Thebes then gained ascendancy for a while, thanks to Epaminondas, who crushed the Spartan army in 371 BC; but this period ended with the great Theban general's death in 362 BC.

445 BC
30-year peace between Athens and Sparta.

427 BC
Aristophanes' first comedy (now lost).

399 BC
Trial and death of Socrates.

367 BC
Plato's Republic.

Effigy of Philip II on a Macedonian coin.

352–342 BC
The Macedonians seize control of Thessaly and Thrace.

MACEDONIAN HEGEMONY. Philip II of Macedon (359–336 BC), having built up his state and his army, annexed the territories of Peonia, Thrace and Thessaly. Then, by a series of brilliant diplomatic and military moves, he managed to gain a foothold in southern Greece, imposing his authority over the entire Hellenic world and reducing the last of the Greek city-states to obedience with a stunning victory at Chaeronea in 338 BC. A year after this decisive event the states were all represented at the federal council of Corinth, which brought the Corinthian League into being. The League gave Philip the titles of "Hegemon" (leader) and general, placing him at the head of a Hellenic army for an expedition against the Persians. However, he was assassinated in 336 BC, by Pausanias, and was unable to complete his life's ambition of uniting all the Greeks. His son, Alexander, was to accomplish this in his stead.

ALEXANDER THE GREAT

334 BC
Aristotle founds the Lyceum in Athens.

Recent excavations at major archeological sites in Macedonia have revealed that Alexander grew up in surroundings of extraordinary esthetic refinement. In addition to his high-level military and political training, the young prince was tutored personally by the great philosopher Aristotle. After his father's assassination Alexander repressed the revolt of the Greek city-states, annihilating Thebes but sparing Athens. Having re-established Greek unity, he set out to subjugate Asia, conquering the Persian Empire and pushing on to the borders of India. By this time Alexander bore the titles of King of the Persians, Hegemon of the Corinthian League and King of Macedonia. He encouraged the development of scientific and geographical knowledge, notably by the exploration of the Indus delta. Greek became the common language of his immense empire, and Greek institutions spread throughout the oriental world. No fewer than seventy cities bearing the name of Alexandria were constructed, which became centers for the expansion of Greek civilization.

Portrait of Alexander, 4th century BC.

“THE SUN NEVER SETS ON MY EMPIRE.”

ALEXANDER THE GREAT

Alexander died age 32, on June 13, 323 BC, while preparing an expedition to conquer the western Mediterranean. His personality, brilliant strategy, many military victories, heroic style and vast achievements gave him a legendary dimension. Deified in his own lifetime as the son of Zeus, Alexander was the subject of countless historical, literary and artistic works and remains to this day one of the great Greek heroes.

330 BC
Alexander burns Persepolis, to avenge the destruction of the Acropolis in 480. End of the Panhellenic League.

Alexander the Great, mural painting by Theophilos (1868–1934).

323–280 BC
Wars of the successors.

3RD CENTURY BC
Foundation of the museum in Alexandria and the library in Pergamum.

267 BC
Sack of Athens by the Heruli.

196 BC
Autonomy of the Greek cities proclaimed by Flaminius.

167 BC
Destruction of the Macedonian monarchy by the Romans.

HELLENISTIC KINGDOMS AND GREECE UNDER THE ROMANS

After the death of Alexander his generals fell to fighting over his legacy, and after thirty years of war three monarchies emerged: the Antigonids in Macedonia, the Seleucids in Asia Minor and the Ptolemies in Egypt. While the organization of the Greek cities remained much the same, in foreign affairs the kings appropriated the old prerogatives for their own advantage. One of the most brilliant cities of the day was Alexandria, which attracted droves of artists and scholars, while in Pergamum architects revised the old concepts of urban design. This was the era of the mathematicians Euclid (c. 300 BC) and Archimedes of Syracuse (c. 280–212 BC). Numerous artistic masterpieces were created, such as the *Winged Victory of Samothrace*. Apollonius of Rhodes wrote his *Argonautica*, and the philosophers Epicurus of Samos and Zeno of Citium, founder of Stoicism, taught in Athens.

GREECE UNDER THE ROMANS. The defeat of Perseus, king of Macedonia, at Pydna in 168 BC marked the beginning of the Roman Republic’s annexation of Greece. The old Greek kingdoms were conquered one by one. Under the empire, Athens attracted the special attention of Hadrian (AD 117–38), becoming the emblem of the Hellenization of the Roman world and of the renaissance of Greek art and letters.

146 BC
Greece becomes a Roman province.

Demosthenes, sculpted 288 BC.

64 BC
The Seleucid Kingdom becomes a Roman province.

30 BC
The Ptolemaic Kingdom becomes a Roman province.

THE BYZANTINE EMPIRE

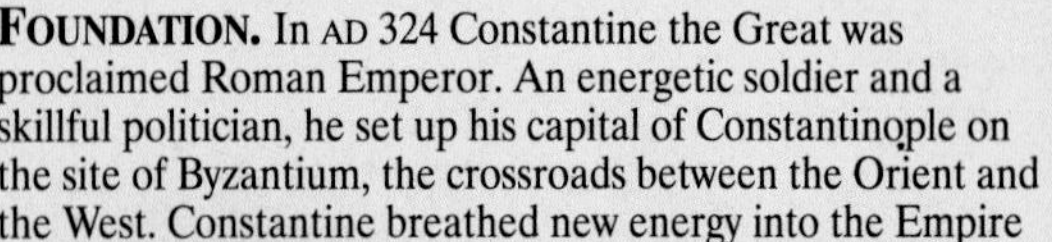

Emperor Constantine and his wife, early-16th-century icon.

FOUNDATION. In AD 324 Constantine the Great was proclaimed Roman Emperor. An energetic soldier and a skillful politician, he set up his capital of Constantinople on the site of Byzantium, the crossroads between the Orient and the West. Constantine breathed new energy into the Empire by combining the military, administrative, legislative and political structures of the West with the intellectual and artistic potential of the East, supplementing Greek thought with Christian fervor.

JUSTINIAN. On the death of Theodosius I in 395, the Roman Empire split in two, the Orient falling to his elder son, Arcadius, and the Occident to his younger son, Honorius. Repeated barbarian invasions brought about the collapse of the Western Empire in 476; the Eastern Empire had also to face invasions, in addition to internal crises. Emperor Justinian (527–60) succeeded in restoring order to a state riven by social and religious strife (notably the Nika riots in 532). His military campaigns restored the empire to its former borders, but at a crippling cost. Justinian oversaw sweeping reforms in the law, the renovation and construction of cities, immense public works and above all the creation of an architectural masterpiece, the Basilica of St Sophia, with its phenomenal mosaics. Religion, particularly monasticism, assumed a primary role in the life of the empire.

330
Foundation of Constantinople.

476
Collapse of the Western Empire.

Saint Gregory, mosaic in Hosios Loukas.

529
Justinian closes the schools of philosophy in Athens.

537
Inauguration of the Basilica of St Sophia.

EMPEROR HERACLIUS 610–41. The founder of the Heraclid dynasty reorganized the defenses of the empire and forced the Persians to retreat from Egypt, which they had conquered. He created the *themai* (regions) of Asia Minor, and imposed Greek as an official language, promoting the Hellenization of the empire.

THE ICONOCLASTIC CONTROVERSY. Religious dissensions culminated in the Iconoclastic Controversy in the 8th century. The Isaurian Emperor Leo III (717–41) prohibited the veneration of religious pictures. For nearly 120 years the empire was divided between worshippers of icons (*iconoduli*) and those who rejected them (*iconoclasts*). Finally a compromise was reached when in 843 Empress Theodora legalized religious imagery. Nevertheless, the gulf between the Eastern and Western churches continued to widen during the 9th century.

Saint Luke, mosaic in Hosios Loukas.

CONSTANTINE VII PORPHYROGENITUS 905–59. The last great emperor of the Macedonian dynasty, in addition to his legislative, educational and administrative reforms, was an active supporter of arts and letters. A century later Michael Psellos (1018–78), also a man of letters and a learned scientist, wrote the lives of the Byzantine emperors.

Iznik pottery, circa 1600.

DECLINE. Under the Macedonian dynasty Constantinople achieved economic and political power at the expense of the provinces. This led to conflict between the central and provincial authorities and a loss of cohesion which proved disastrous for the empire during the first invasion of the Selçuk Seldjonkides, who after their victory at Manzikert in 1071 gained a permanent foothold in Asia Minor. The Comnenus dynasty (1081–1185) pursued a pro-Western policy and made persistent efforts to retain its territory, but before long Constantinople's power was weakened by the repeated attacks of the Turks and Venetians. The Venetian victory at Myriokephalon in 1176 precipitated the empire's decline, and it vanished altogether with the sack of Constantinople by the Crusaders in 1204.

THE BREAK-UP OF THE BYZANTINE EMPIRE, 1204–1453. Four independent Greek states emerged from the ruins of the Roman Empire: the empires of Trebizond and Nicaea and the despotates of Morea (the Peloponnese) and Epirus. The reconquest of Constantinople in 1261 and the restoration of Emperor Michael Paleologus (1261–82) provided only a short respite. The Ottoman Turks took Epirus in 1349 and Gallipoli in 1354. They failed to capture Constantinople in 1422, but returned to lay siege to it in 1453. On May 29, 1454, Constantinople, the capital of the Byzantine Empire for a thousand years, succumbed to the forces of Sultan Mehmet II. Mehmet subsequently offered the Greek savant Gennadios Scholarios the patriarchal throne, giving him spiritual and temporal authority over all the Christians within his empire. This allowed the Greek Orthodox Church to preserve a sense of national identity.

GREEK CULTURE IN THE WEST. During the 15th century many Greeks fled to the West. Among these were intellectuals, many of whom settled in Italy, bringing with them their cultural heritage. This led to a revival of interest in ancient texts, which later animated the Humanist movement all over Europe. The first works printed in Greek appeared in Milan, Florence, Rome and Venice in the late 15th century. Venice became the principal center for Greek publications.

1054
The Great Schism.

11TH CENTURY
Construction of the monasteries of Daphni and Hosios Loukas.

1082
Venice gains the right to free trade.

1096
The First Crusade.

1204–61
Nicaean Empire.

1261–1453
Empire of Constantinople.

1540–70
The Ottomans master all of Greece.

1645–69
Venetian–Turkish wars. Ottomans conquer Crete.

1687
Venice reconquers the Peloponnese. The Parthenon bombarded.

GREECE IN EXILE, 16TH–18TH CENTURIES

The Venetian Republic offered asylum to many exiled Greeks, who eventually took over an entire district of Venice, the *Campo dei Greci*. During this period Cyril Loucaris (1572–1638), the Patriarch of Alexandria and later Constantinople, promoted learning and introduced the art of printing into Greece. In Crete, occupied by the Venetians since 1271, there were also many exiled Greeks, and the meeting of the two cultures produced a rich harvest. Greek writers, inspired by the Italian

Church of the Kapnikarea.

example, produced much original work. The Cretan school of religious painting was, with that of Macedonia, one of the most accomplished in the history of Western art.

THE PHANARIOTS. The aristocrats living in the Greek quarter of Constantinople, the Phanar, founded schools and printing houses and instigated social and economic reforms. The growing volume of trade with the West in the 18th century brought about a revival of Hellenism. In 1774 the Treaty of Kutchuk-Kainarji with Russia allowed Greek ships freedom of navigation between the Mediterranean and Black Seas.

THE GREEK NATIONALIST MOVEMENT, 1770–1821. The scholar Eugene Vulgaris (1716–1806), who traveled all over western Europe and translated Voltaire, was the instigator of the Greek Luminaries movement. Started by Phanariot princes in the 18th century on the pattern of enlightened despotism, this movement was soon taken up by the bourgeoisie. Between the Treaty of Karlowitz in 1699 and the Treaty of Kutchuk-Kainarji in 1774, the Ottoman Empire was forced to relinquish territory to Russia and Austria. The Greeks' desire to free themselves from Turkish domination was reawakened by emissaries of Catherine the Great of Russia, who encouraged rebellion in the Balkans. This desire was undaunted by the failure of Count Orlov's expedition to the Peloponnese in 1770. Adamantas Coraës (1748–1833), a celebrated Hellenist and philosopher, became a leader of the Greek revival. A republican who had participated in the French Revolution, Coraës became the main spokesman for Greek independence. Constantine Rhigas of Velestino (1757–98), author of literary and scientific works and revolutionary pamphlets, founded Greece's first newspaper, *Ephimeris*, in Vienna in 1790.

THE "SEVEN ISLES". After the retreat of the French army from the Ionian islands (1797–8) and the signing in 1800 of a treaty between Russia and the Ottoman Empire, the "Seven Isles" acquired the freedom to form their own government under their own constitution.

Portrait of Constantine Rhigas (1757–98).

1715
Turkish reconquest of the Peloponnese.

1748
Adamantas Coraës born in Smyrna.

1769–70
Russo-Turkish War; uprising in the Peloponnese.

Death of Lambros Tzavellas, anon.

1790
Vienna, the Austrian capital, becomes the center of the Greek diaspora.

1800
The Ionian Republic.

1823
Solomos composes his Hymn to Liberty.

View of Athens from the Hill of Philopappos, by Richard Bankes Harraden, 1830.

Portrait of Ioannis Kapodistrias (1828–31) on the old 500 drachma note.

In the 19th century a number of Greek secret societies were formed. The most influential, the Philiké Hetairia, appeared in Odessa in 1814; financed by exiled Greek merchants, it took an active part in the propagation of revolutionary ideas and collected funds for the armies of liberation. After the appearance of the first Greek newspaper, published 1790–98, many other publications followed. Between 1811 and 1821 they provided a link between Greeks in exile and those back home.

Greek warship during the War of Independence.

THE PHILHELLENES. From its beginnings in the late 18th century as a symbol of Western European intellectual interest in ancient Greece, philhellenism became a political force in the two decades before the Greek War of Independence. In the wake of Chateaubriand and Lord Byron, many writers, philosophers, savants, politicians and soldiers became sympathetic to the Greek cause and brought their influence to bear on their often reluctant governments. Committees were formed to support the war effort, and many philhellenes enlisted as volunteers to fight alongside the Greek rebels.

THE WAR OF INDEPENDENCE, 1821–27. The war began in March, 1821 with offensives in the Danube provinces and in the Peloponnese. The armed forces, for the most part made up of irregular Klepht and Armatole soldiers, at first made rapid headway, setting up local governments as they advanced. The Chios Massacre in 1822 outraged international opinion and inspired the painter Delacroix to one of his most moving compositions. Byron disembarked at Missolonghi in December, 1823. From 1823 to 1825 disagreements between the various factions led to vicious infighting among the Greeks, which delayed liberation. The armies of independence suffered several heavy reverses in 1826, including the loss of Missolonghi and the fall of the Acropolis in Athens. But on October 20, 1827, the combined fleets of England, France and Russia annihilated the Turkish-Egyptian fleet off Navarino.

IOANNIS KAPODISTRIAS, 1828–31. Seven months before the victory of Navarino the Third Greek National Assembly elected Greece's first governor, Ioannis Kapodistrias, an aristocrat from Corfu and former minister of Czar Alexander I. In 1829 the Treaty of Adrianople recognized Greek autonomy, which was confirmed by a protocol signed in London in February, 1830. Kapodistrias set about the organization of the new state, giving priority to education. But his refusal to apply the constitution provoked opposition; his assassination, on October 9, 1831, plunged Greece into anarchy and obliged the allies to step in and impose a monarch of their own choosing.

1827
Victory of the allied fleets of England, Russia and France at Navarino.

1831
Assassination of Kapodistrias.

1833
Accession of King Otto.

1834
Athens chosen as capital of Greece.

1837
Foundation of the University of Athens.

King Otto and his wife, 1854 (engraving).

1843
Uprising for the re-establishment of the Constitution.

1863
Accession of George I.

Arrival of George I in Athens, *Illustrated London News*, November 28, 1863.

German ME 110 warplanes

Eleftherios Venizelos.

1864
Annexation of the Ionian islands.

1881
Annexation of Thessaly.

The Battle of the Five Wells: Greeks and Turks, 1912.

1912–13
Assassination of George I, accession of Constantine I.

OTTO, KING OF GREECE. The son of Ludwig I of Bavaria, Otto (1833–62) became King of Greece before he was 18 years old. He abolished the 1827 Constitution and reigned as an absolute monarch until 1843. Despite the reorganization of certain institutions, the proclamation of the autocephalous church and in 1837 the foundation of a university, discontent spread. The Greek people were offended by the constant interference of French, Russian and English envoys and were in the throes of an economic crisis. Insurrection broke out on September 3, 1843 in Athens, where citizens joined forces with political and military leaders to restore the Constitution. After a brief resistance, Otto capitulated. Nonetheless, foreign interventions into Greece's affairs continued to fan the passions of anti-dynastic liberals. Between 1854 and 1857, the occupation of Piraeus harbor by the French and British armies exacerbated the discontent which eventually led to the expulsion of the king and queen in 1862.

GEORGE I, KING OF THE HELLENES. The reign of George I (1863–1913) coincided with Greek expansion into Thessaly in 1885, the Ionian islands in 1864 and into Crete, Epirus, Macedonia and the islands of the Aegean in 1912. Prime Minister C. Tricoupis (1882–95) introduced economic reforms and launched major public works projects, among them the canal through the Isthmus of Corinth (1882–93), which prompted a major development of Greek trade and of the Greek merchant fleet.

Bad News, contemporary postcard.

THE 20TH CENTURY

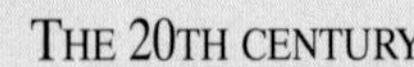

1917–20
Constantine I exiled, Venizelos becomes Prime Minister.

1922
Constantine abdicates.

1926
Proclamation of the Republic.

1928–32
Venizelos recalled to the Government.

General Metaxas and George II (1936).

ELEFTHERIOS VENIZELOS. A former minister of Justice and Foreign Affairs in Crete, and the leader of the 1905 uprising which brought about Crete's liberation, Eleftherios Venizelos (1864–1937) was called to mainland Greece following the 1909 coup d'état. Appointed Prime Minister in 1910, he based his policies on the support of the liberal bourgeoisie and intellectuals. In 1912, Greece joined the Balkan Alliance against the Turks, gaining more territory which was confirmed by the Treaty of Bucharest in 1913.

WORLD WAR ONE AND WORLD WAR TWO. In 1914, disagreement between Venizelos, who favored the Allies, and Constantine I, who wished Greece to give support to the German

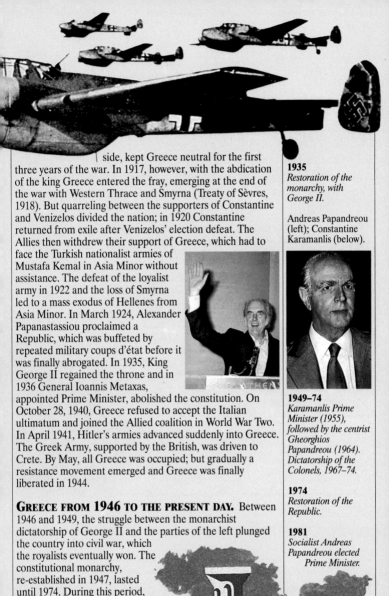

side, kept Greece neutral for the first three years of the war. In 1917, however, with the abdication of the king Greece entered the fray, emerging at the end of the war with Western Thrace and Smyrna (Treaty of Sèvres, 1918). But quarreling between the supporters of Constantine and Venizelos divided the nation; in 1920 Constantine returned from exile after Venizelos' election defeat. The Allies then withdrew their support of Greece, which had to face the Turkish nationalist armies of Mustafa Kemal in Asia Minor without assistance. The defeat of the loyalist army in 1922 and the loss of Smyrna led to a mass exodus of Hellenes from Asia Minor. In March 1924, Alexander Papanastassiou proclaimed a Republic, which was buffeted by repeated military coups d'état before it was finally abrogated. In 1935, King George II regained the throne and in 1936 General Ioannis Metaxas, appointed Prime Minister, abolished the constitution. On October 28, 1940, Greece refused to accept the Italian ultimatum and joined the Allied coalition in World War Two. In April 1941, Hitler's armies advanced suddenly into Greece. The Greek Army, supported by the British, was driven to Crete. By May, all Greece was occupied; but gradually a resistance movement emerged and Greece was finally liberated in 1944.

GREECE FROM 1946 TO THE PRESENT DAY. Between 1946 and 1949, the struggle between the monarchist dictatorship of George II and the parties of the left plunged the country into civil war, which the royalists eventually won. The constitutional monarchy, re-established in 1947, lasted until 1974. During this period, Greece's wounds began to heal; the nation's will to regain its political and economic balance was guided by the ambition to join the European Common Market. But ideological conflicts persisted and the political instability caused by these conflicts led to the seizure of power by a military junta in 1967. The Dictatorship of the Colonels lasted until 1974; in December of that year the abolition of the monarchy was voted in a referendum. Thereafter, Greece made giant strides forward in both economic and social terms, and was finally voted into the Common Market in 1986.

1935
Restoration of the monarchy, with George II.

Andreas Papandreou (left); Constantine Karamanlis (below).

1949–74
Karamanlis Prime Minister (1955), followed by the centrist Gheorghios Papandreou (1964). Dictatorship of the Colonels, 1967–74.

1974
Restoration of the Republic.

1981
Socialist Andreas Papandreou elected Prime Minister.

NAVARINO, THE LAST SEA BATTLE OF THE AGE OF SAIL

In 1827, six years after the start of the War of Independence, the outcome of the Greek revolution still hung in the balance. For two years the forces of Ibrahim Pasha had been rampaging through the Peloponnese. After seizing Missolonghi and the Acropolis, the Turks were now once again masters of mainland Greece. Spurred by the pressure of public opinion and the need to protect their commercial interests, France, England and Russia demanded that the sultan immediately sign a treaty granting autonomy to the Greeks. The refusal of the Sublime Porte to submit to this demand led to the Battle of Navarino, on October 20, 1827, between a Turkish-Egyptian naval force and the allied fleets.

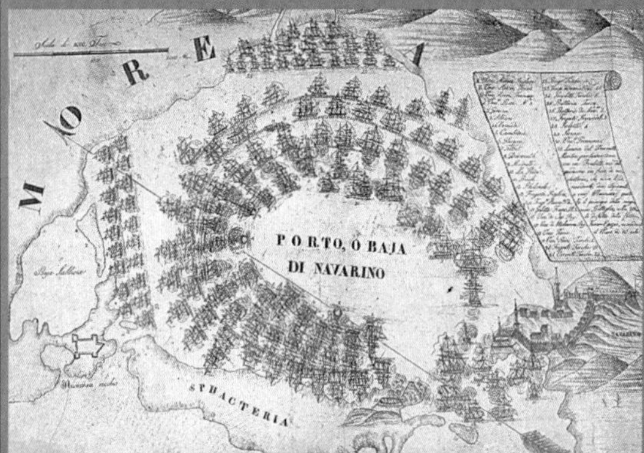

The Turkish forces lay along the eastern shore of the bay. The two fleets deployed in a crescent formation from north to south, from the point of the citadel to the end of the roadstead. The French squadron formed the left wing of a three-deep crescent. The British admiral advanced slowly, and at 1.35 am passed the forts defending both sides of the roadstead.

"ON MY ARRIVAL, I FOUND THE EGYPTIAN FLEET AT ANCHOR; I AM KEEPING IT UNDER OBSERVATION."
VICE ADMIRAL SIR EDWARD CODRINGTON

Admiral de Rigny

Rear Admiral Heiden

THE IMPACT OF NAVARINO Engravings were produced to influence public opinion in favor of the Greeks. This Epinal print shows the Greek *Hellas*, commanded by Admiral Miaoulis, in company with the flagships *Asia* (British), *La Syrène* (French) and *Azov* (Russian).

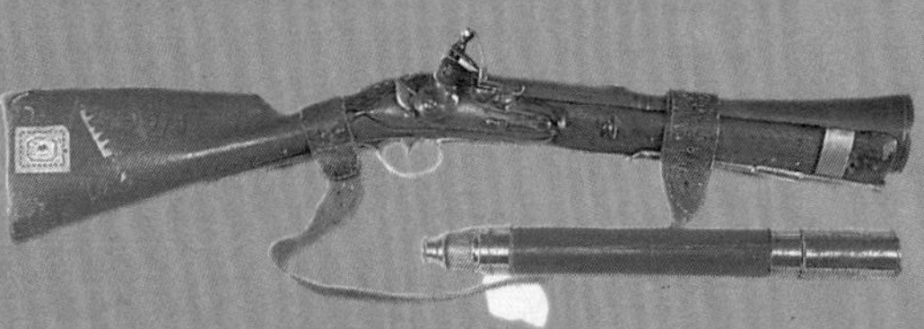

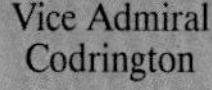

Vice Admiral Codrington

ADMIRAL MIAOULIS' WEAPONS Admiral Miaoulis commanded the Greek naval forces engaged in the War of Independence (1821–7). This blunderbuss and telescope were used by him during the war.

THE BATTLE OF NAVARINO This painting by Louis Garneray was commissioned by the French government. On the left is the flagship of the Turkish admiral, Tahir Pasha, with its raised poop, gold paint and crimson pennant at the mainmast. The frigate of Moharem Bey flies a green pennant with crescent and stars, the flag of the commander-in-chief of the Egyptian fleet. HMS *Dartmouth*, in the foreground, is obstructed by an Egyptian fireship; a musket ball fired from this vessel killed the *Dartmouth*'s commander, Captain Fellowes. The *Dartmouth* is shown responding with a broadside. In all, eighty-seven allied warships were involved in the battle. Scarcely had the first shots been fired than action erupted all over the bay. The result: sixty-five Turkish warships were burned and sunk by the end of the day, and the naval power of Turkey was utterly broken. Indeed, the outcome of the Greek War of Independence was effectively settled at Navarino.
In 1829, the sultan was forced to sign the tready of Adrianople which recognized Greek autonomy. A year later, the Protocol of London confirmed Greek independence, under the protection of France, Russia and Great Britain.

Bory de Saint-Vincent was a dedicated naturalist, born at Agen in France in 1778. In his youth he took part in a scientific expedition to the South Seas, and during the campaigns of Napoleon's Grande Armée reached the rank of lieutenant colonel. Stripped of his rank and forced into exile with the restoration of the Bourbons (1816–19), he turned to journalism and politics, scraping a living writing works of popular science, and several times narrowly escaping imprisonment for debt. Finally, thanks to Mastignac, a former school friend, Saint-Vincent was appointed to direct the scientific section of the Peloponnese Expedition. His Parisian colleagues on the Expedition, however, were distinctly cool toward this short, inquisitive and glib Napoleonic veteran, who was entirely self-taught.

MAPS OF THE PELOPONNESE
The kind of map current before the Peloponnese Expedition (left). This one is by the Dutch cartographer William Blaueu of Alkmaar (17th century). In spite of surveys made of the coastline in the early 19th century the interior remained little known, and a triangulation survey was urgently needed. The information gathered by the French officers made it possible to draw up a precise grid, etched in stone on a scale of 1:200,000. The resulting map (detail below) covered twenty sheets and was published in 1852.

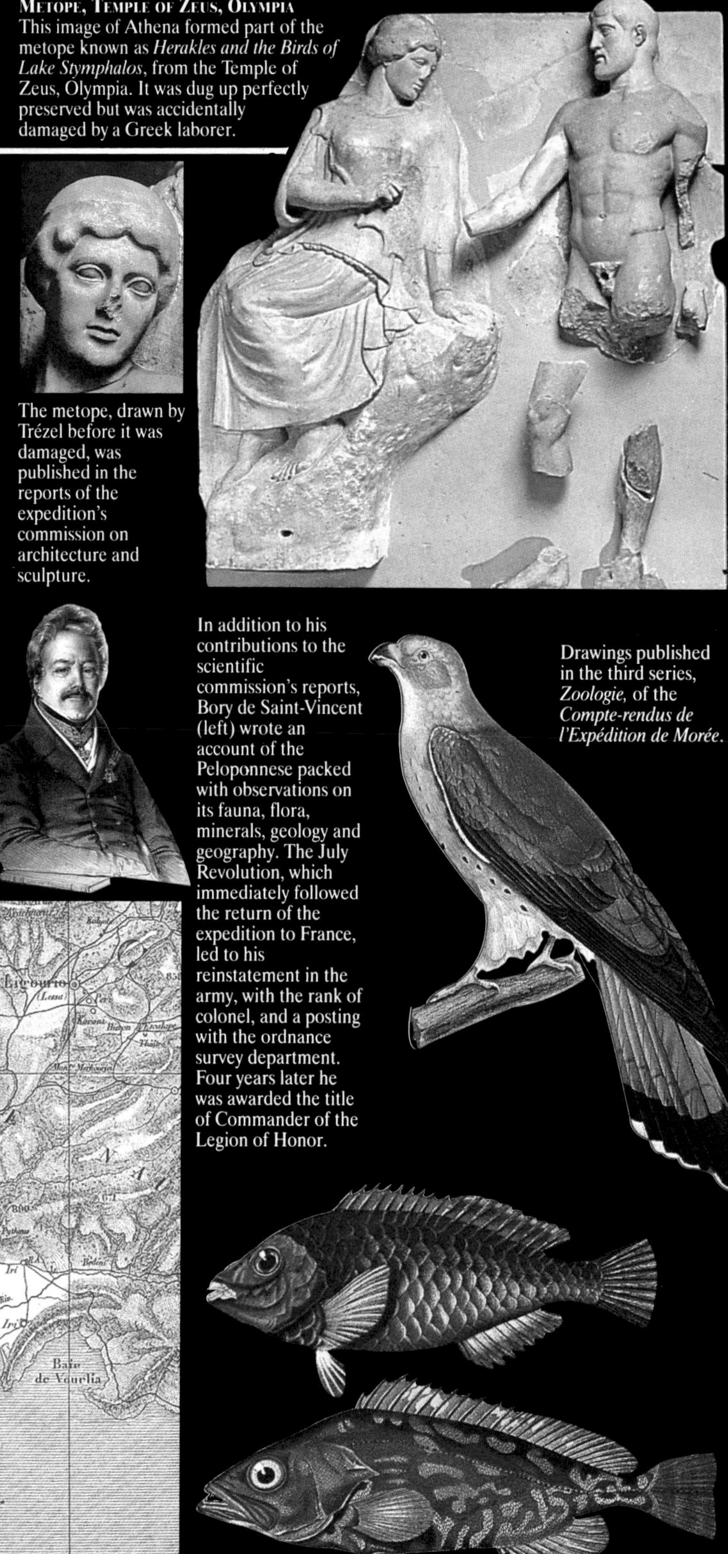

Metope, Temple of Zeus, Olympia
This image of Athena formed part of the metope known as *Herakles and the Birds of Lake Stymphalos*, from the Temple of Zeus, Olympia. It was dug up perfectly preserved but was accidentally damaged by a Greek laborer.

The metope, drawn by Trézel before it was damaged, was published in the reports of the expedition's commission on architecture and sculpture.

In addition to his contributions to the scientific commission's reports, Bory de Saint-Vincent (left) wrote an account of the Peloponnese packed with observations on its fauna, flora, minerals, geology and geography. The July Revolution, which immediately followed the return of the expedition to France, led to his reinstatement in the army, with the rank of colonel, and a posting with the ordnance survey department. Four years later he was awarded the title of Commander of the Legion of Honor.

Drawings published in the third series, *Zoologie,* of the *Compte-rendus de l'Expédition de Morée*.

View of the Port of Modon. Modon was used (with Navarino and Coron) by the French expeditionary corps as a supply port for troops stationed in the Peloponnese. Several ships are seen at anchor. In the margin are the words "Minaret in which Jesus has supplanted Mahomet". The liberation of Greece was in many respects a crusade against Islam.

The scientific commission en route. The Peloponnese had been devastated by the war, and its villages burnt to the ground. Those of the population who had not been massacred or sold into slavery had been scattered far and wide, many to the islands. Consequently, open bivouacs proved to be the least uncomfortable lodgings for the expedition.

Ithome and Evan. The heights dominating ancient Messina, seen from the southeast, near one of the sources of the Pamisos. The scientists are pictured resting under a tree, with their mules turned loose in the marshes. The size of the mountains has been somewhat exaggerated by the painter Baccuet, who was a member of the expedition.

"At the entrance to the roads, against the rockface, the wrecked walls of Navarino with their loopholes, blackened doors and mounds of debris, looked like a country cemetery." Edgar Quinet

Arrival of the commission in a Greek village. At Kardamyli, on the eastern shore of the Gulf of Messina at the foot of Mount Taygetos, four armed soldiers escorted six scientists, formally dressed for their reception by the local authorities. The French press reported that "everywhere the French were greeted with gratitude and enthusiasm".

The commission's arrival at Tripolitza. This town suffered heavily from the effects of the war. The Greeks seized control of it in the first year of the uprising, massacring every Turk within its walls. The compliment was returned with interest by Sultan Ibrahim when he recaptured Tripolitza in 1825.

The Rock of Monemvasia seen from the mainland. Protected as it was by a narrow strait, Monemvasia was one of only two strongholds in the Peloponnese to hold out against Sultan Ibrahim's reconquest.

The philhellenic movement, which came into being at the start of the War of Independence, was much strengthened in 1825 by a combination of events. The death of Byron at Missolonghi, the town's two-year resistance to the Turks, the final heroic death of its defenders and horrifying reports of the selling of women and children into slavery outraged world opinion and provoked a surge of international support for the Greeks. A huge array of works of art and more mundane everyday objects were manufactured and sold to further their cause: clocks, vases, china plates, commercial labels, etc. The subject matter of these objects was often taken from paintings by masters such as Eugène Delacroix, Ary Scheffer or Horace Vernet and generally depicted heroic episodes or personalities from the struggle for independence.

Philhellenic plates were extremely popular. The one on the right shows the Greek Committee presided over by Chateaubriand. Around the edge, encircled by laurel wreaths, are the names of three prominent philhellenes linked to those of three heroes of the fight for independence:

Canaris/Favier, Miaoulis/Byron and Botsaris/Eynard, with the legend *Croix et Liberté*. The two plates below illustrate key events in the war: the Greeks receiving the Benediction at Missolonghi (left) and Mavrokordatos capturing a fort from the Turks (right). These plates were manufactured in Montereau.

LORD BYRON
This wallpaper panel, after a composition by J-J Deltil entitled *Lord Byron in Greece*, was made by Zuber at his factory in Rixheim in 1828. As president of the Mulhouse Philhellenic Committee (1825–30), Zuber also produced a huge color panorama, c. 50 feet long and 10 feet high, entitled *The Wars of the Greeks*.

THE HEROIC THEME
This painting entitled *Young Greek Defending His Father*, after Ary Scheffer, occupies the top part of the surround of a pier glass.

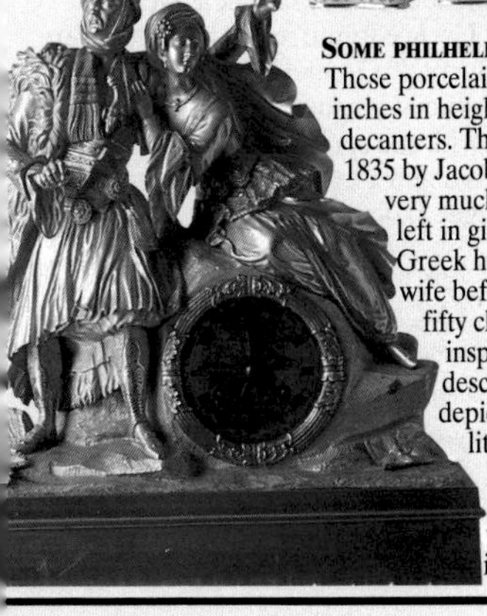

SOME PHILHELLENIC OBJECTS
These porcelain figurines, ranging from 7 to 13 inches in height, were in fact liqueur decanters. They were manufactured around 1835 by Jacob Petit. Clocks, too, were very much in vogue; the one on the left in gilded bronze (1830) shows a Greek husband taking leave of his wife before going off to war. About fifty clock patterns were inspired by feats of arms described in the press or depicted in popular lithographs. The *Seated Greek* design on the right was used to decorate a variety of artefacts, including inkstands.

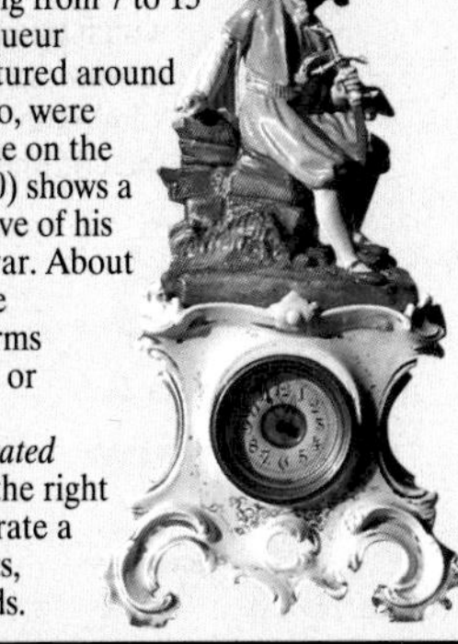

THE PROBLEM OF GREEK

The Greek language of today has evolved from the spoken tongue, and from a series of linguistic reforms undertaken since the creation of the Greek state. For two centuries the question of the language was a central issue for intellectuals, and between 1780 and 1820 (just before the War of Independence) there was considerable debate about the choice of a language for the new nation of the Hellenes. Throughout these years the defenders of classicism, led by the Patriarchate of Constantinople, found themselves in direct opposition to the new urban classes, who favored a simplification of the language.

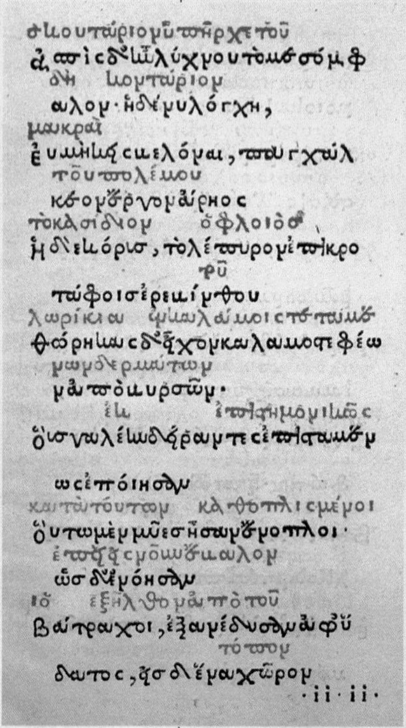

THE INFLUENCE OF CORAËS. A group of intellectuals influenced by Adamantas Coraës, a Greek writer living in Paris, proposed a compromise between the language of the Church and that of the bourgeoisie and merchants in the cities. Taking the view that the Greeks were direct descendants of the Hellenes of antiquity, Coraës concluded that the new Greece should grow in the fertile soil of Hellenic culture; and hence that the language spoken by ordinary people since the Byzantine era should be supplanted by a language purged of foreign words and nourished by the glorious past of the Hellenes. Moreover, for the nation to raise itself from its state of servitude, educating people in this new language was a priority.

The War of the Frogs and the Mice, one of the first Greek books printed in Venice, 1486.

LINGUISTIC DUALISM (DIGLOSSIA) IN GREECE

In the years following independence Coraës' ideas were adopted in full. As a result Greece found itself with what were virtually two languages: "purified" Greek (*katharevoussa*), which became the written, official language, and "demotic" (*dhimotiki*), which evolved with the spoken language. This "diglossia" was by no means a new phenomenon in Greece: the common Byzantine tongue (*koine*) had already developed

Α	Β	Γ	Δ	Ε	Ζ
Alpha. A	Béta. B	Gamma. G	Delta. D	Epsilon. E	Zeta. Z
Ν	Ξ	Ο	Π	Ρ	Σ
Nu. N	Xi. X	Omicron. O	Pi. P	Rho. R	Sigma. S

> "THE RIVER OF THE GREEK LANGUAGE HAS ABSORBED THE WATERS OF MANY FOREIGN STREAMS ALONG THE WAY; YET EVEN NOW IT STILL SPRINGS FROM THE SAME SOURCE."
>
> JACQUES LACARRIÈRE

independently of the official language of the Church and State, the purists having sought to establish it as a symbol of the Christian empire's indestructibility. In modern Greece linguistic dualism reflected the classic division between the common people and the elite. Practically, the learning of *katharevoussa* – in effect a simplified form of ancient Greek that anyone with any intellectual or professional aspirations has to master – is only possible at school. Until the 1970's the laws, administrative documents, newspapers and radio news were all produced in *katharevoussa*, the vehicle *par excellence* of Greek thought, science and ideas; but, in contrast to civil servants, lawyers, doctors and priests, the farming people, small traders and manual workers tended to use the popular language, *dhimotiki*.

ADAMANTAS CORAËS (1748-1833). A celebrated Hellenist and philosopher, Coraës was one of the leaders of the independence movement.

LITERATURE

Linguistic dualism was also present in Greek literature. Throughout the post-Byzantine period popular Greek was confined to oral traditions. With the exception of one or two popular novels and some theological treatises published in Venice and the Ionian islands, literature written in the popular language was rare before the close of the 19th century. The writer and literary critic Roïdis (1836–1904), for example, defended the spoken language, but still used *katharevoussa* for his own work. "The present state of our language," he wrote, "is such that writers are unable to express one idea in every five in a manner sufficiently precise, without recourse to some word or grammatical form that has either been banished from our written language because of its vulgarity or is archaic – and hence non-functional – in terms of the spoken tongue...the issue is not one of a people's language versus an academic one, but of both being used by the same people, who possess a living language that they use to express their feelings and passions, but who are compelled to use another for writing and speechmaking, even though it is absolutely impossible for them to express either feelings or passions

This theological treatise in Greek was published during the Turkish occupation.

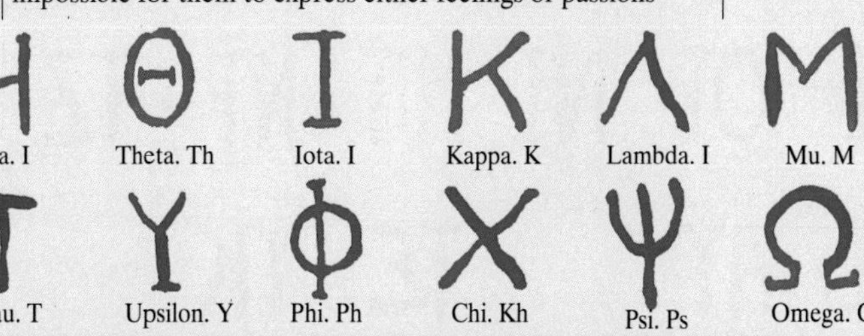

THE ILIAD
The founding masterpiece of Greek literature was first published in modern Greek in 1488, in Florence. This beautiful illustrated edition of Homer's *Iliad* was printed by "Demetrios the Cretan".

therewith..." (Preface to *Parerga*, 1885). In 1886 the first collection of poems by Kostas Palamas appeared in demotic Greek; 1888 saw the publication of Psichari's *Voyage*, a work which was half essay and half novel and which relaunched the linguistic controversy. Psichari championed the immediate adoption of demotic Greek in every field of national life and originated the intellectual movement of the turn of the century that became known as *Dhimotikimos*. Men of letters fought for the recognition of the popular language through a number of organizations. The Ethniki Ghlosa (National Language Association) and Ekpedheftikos Omilos (Education Association), among others, were at the root of the linguistic reform of 1917, which lasted only three years. The traditionalists considered the partisans of *dhimotiki* to be rank socialists, even anarchists. This political twist to the question came from the fact that the socialist and communist movements had adopted demotic Greek as a platform. The linguistic status quo was reinforced in 1920; and it was not until 1975 that the neo-Hellenic language, as it was then renamed, became Greece's official means of expression.

A NEW GENERATION OF WRITERS. Two writers were overwhelmingly responsible for this change: the novelist Papadiamadtis and the poet Cavafy, who fashioned their own language halfway between *katharevoussa* and *dhimotiki.* Between the two world wars a new generation of authors began to develop a literary language broadly based on spoken Greek: among these were Kazantzakis, Sikelianós, Varnalis, Karíotákis, Seferis, Embirikos, Elytis, Ritsos and Venezis. The system of diglossia nevertheless remained in place until the 1970's, when the regime of the colonels – whose pretensions to strict correctness were constantly exposed as ludicrous by semi-literate errors – stripped *katharevoussa* of its last shreds of credibility. In his *Essays* the Nobel laureate George Seferis neatly stated the problem: "In Greece it is as if we are moved by mortal hatred of our own language. This evil has now reached such a pitch that we cannot explain it in any other manner than as the symptom of some kind of collective alienation. It may be that our contemporary neuroses are the natural result of centuries of repression by prigs and pedants: but don't forget, the question today is no longer whether or not we are to write in demotic or *katharevoussa*. No, ours has become a tragic dilemma: shall we write in Greek, or shall we prefer some kind of Esperanto masquerading as such?"

DIPHTHONGS
A grouping of two simple vowels forms a diphthong (from the Greek *diphthongos*, a double sound) – a complex vowel sound used only in speech. Certain consonants are also joined to represent "hard" consonants, such as English b, d and g, which are not in the modern Greek alphabet.

ΕΥ ΗΥ ΟΥ, Ʊ

ΑΙ ΟΙ ΝΙ ΜΠ ΝΤ ΤΖ

ΕΙ ΑΥ ΤΣ ΥΚ

rch comprises the feast of the Resurrectio
Christ and the rebirth of all living things. It
ulated by Byzantine orthodoxy, rich in colo
charged with emotion. The Greek
hodox Church, ever traditionalist in matter
concerning ritual, uses the Gospe
in their original form, still
understood in Greece, and
psalms that are more than

Anastasis

Christ risen is borne away toward the light, symbolized here by a gilded vault. He leads Adam and Eve and all the rest of humanity out of the Kingdom of Death, the gates of which lie broken at his feet. Dressed in the robes of Byzantine emperors of the Macedonian dynasty, the Hebrew kings Solomon and David are seen paying homage to the Messiah.

The Paschal Lamb

The lamb, Christ's emblem, is embroidered on the priestly garment shown here. The name *ovelias* is given to the lamb roasted on a spit for Easter lunch, recalling the burnt offerings of the ancients.

Red eggs

For Wednesday in Holy Week, the women paint eggs in the joyous color red, representing the blood of Christ. These eggs are exchanged as symbols of the message of the Resurrection: *Christos Anesti*.

Easter candles

White, symbolizing purity, is omnipresent: houses and streets are whitewashed, and the candles burning with the flame of the Resurrection are always white. A special privilege of children, Easter candles covered in decorations and ribbons are sold in every shop.

In contemporary Greek society, an individual's identity is defined by his belonging to a family group. The term *ikoghenia*, which means family, comes from *ikos* (house) and *genos* (ancestry). The family is a group of relatives bearing the same name and living in the same house, which is the focus of their social being. In modern Athens a number of customs descend from much older traditions. One example is the dowry system, a legacy of the Aegean Islands, where the family house constitutes the dowry, or *prika*, which is the property of a woman and is given with her at her marriage.

FAMILY NAMES
According to the traditional system, men are born and die within the same family group; solidarity between men of the same blood is the absolute rule. For women the case is different: their social identity is defined by their relationship with men. A woman is the daughter or the wife of a man, and the grammatical form of family names in Greece reflects this. The wife of O Kirios Mikros (Mr Little), for example, is known as I Kiria Mikrou (meaning the wife of Mr Little).

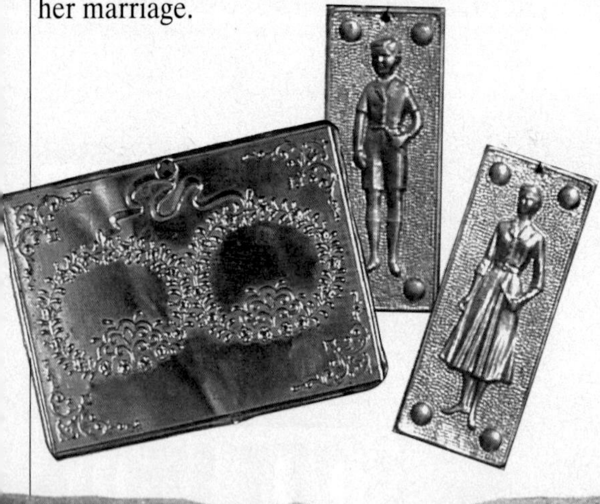

The Five Brothers
The shop sign of a grocer, underlining the proprietors' family solidarity.

Wedding dress
This superb 1930's wedding dress includes a chasuble and a delicate silk veil, both woven with fine gold thread; the jewelry, which includes gold pieces, is extremely sumptuous. A girl's wedding dress was handed down from mother to daughter and was an essential part of her trousseau, along with other clothes woven and embroidered by the bride-to-be herself.

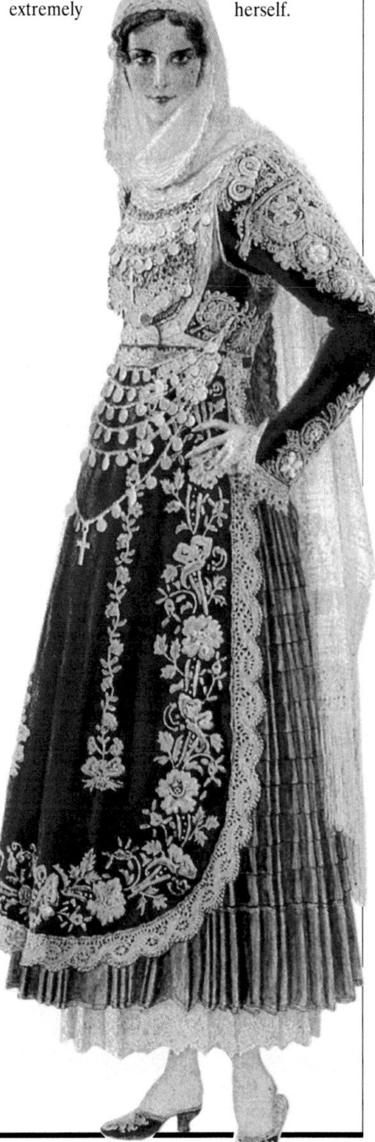

Islanders and townsmen
In Athens, as on the islands, sisters tend to live together in the same house, with female cousins for neighbors. The ground floor serves as the family home: the first floor becomes the apartment of the first daughter to marry, followed by the second and third. In working neighborhoods you will notice scores of small unfinished buildings, new floors being added to keep pace with the marriages of the family's daughters.

Distaff

Marriage procession in the early 1900's
With musicians leading the way, the bride's family and wedding guests arrive at the village of Itea for a wedding.

Greek costume is very diverse, partly because of its antique and Byzantine legacy, and partly on account of its influences, notably Turkish. Each region of Greece takes pride in the details of its costume, which are emblematic of cultural and geographical identity. Male costumes are generally sober in effect, preferring pure, beautiful lines to mere adornment. The clothes of the women, on the other hand, are full of highly contrasted colors with intricate, skillfully executed embroidery and accessories that include coif, shawl and abundant jewelry. In the 19th century a bride's wedding dress was embroidered with gold thread, her headdress being covered in pearls or gold and silver coins.

FESTIVAL AT MEGARA, ATTICA
On feast days women put on their traditional costumes. Until very recently they not only embroidered and adorned their own clothes but wove their own fabrics on hand looms.

REGIONAL COSTUMES (FROM THE BENAKI MUSEUM)

Athens region

The "Maina"

Arcadia

Hydra

Albania

Athens

1 2 3 4

Women's costumes 1. Psara, 19th century. The headdress is a rigid oval frame, around which scarves are wound, the longest embroidered. Under the black paletot and apron are a white blouse and embroidered skirt. 2. Bride from Amorgos, 18th century. The coat is embroidered with gold, the skirt made from rich fabric. (Collection of the National Museum, Athens)

Men's costumes 3. Cyprus, 19th century. In the islands the most widespread costume consisted of baggy trousers with a short waistcoat. 4. Costume of the Primate of Hydra, 19th century. The long robe was customarily worn by the more prominent citizens. The pleated skirt (the fustanella), which has become so well known, was of Albanian origin and became fashionable during the 19th century, after being adopted by King Otto.

Sleeveless coat (19th century) The sleeveless coat, a traditional part of female costume, is worn over a dress that is open at the front and sides, which is itself worn over a light blouse.

Two main periods marked the development of Greek folk music: the Acritic period (9th–11th centuries), when songs reflected the life and warlike deeds of the Acrites, who guarded the frontiers of the Byzantine Empire, and the Klephtic period, when the songs were about the Klephts, the bandit-heroes who fought the Turkish occupying forces. Each region has its own musical style, more rustic in the mountain districts, more lyrical in the islands, but everywhere *dhimotiko* music reflects the longing of the Greek people for liberty, their joys, sorrows and attitude to death. The urban folk songs (*rebetika*) now inspire many composers. A small museum in Plaka ▲ *178* exhibits the musical instruments collected by the great musicologist Anoyanakis.

THE ZOURNAS This double-reed instrument of the oboe family has a piercing sonority that can sound either martial or sweet, depending on the way it is blown. Popular at village fairs and festivals, it is usually accompanied by the *daouli* (small drum).

Shepherds used to make a type of pastoral flute, the *floyera*, out of reeds, wood, iron or hollow bones from a bird of prey.

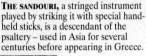

THE SANDOURI, a stringed instrument played by striking it with special hand-held sticks, is a descendant of the psaltery – used in Asia for several centuries before appearing in Greece.

GREEK SINGERS The lute played by the musician in the center and the *tambouras* held by the figure on the right are the ancestors of the *bouzouki* and the *baghlamas* respectively. Their strings are plucked with a plectrum; here they accompany a Klepht singer. Instruments such as these became immensely popular during the War of Independence, at which time they were used to accompany epic revolutionary songs. The *tambouras* used by General Macriyannis is now in the National Museum in Athens.

Traditionally fashioned in the form of amulets, the bells which Greek shepherds hung around their animals' necks gradually evolved into musical instruments tuned to harmonize with the shepherd's *floyera*.

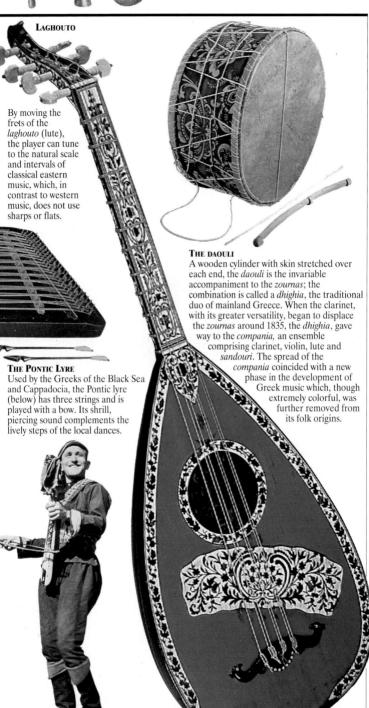

Laghouto

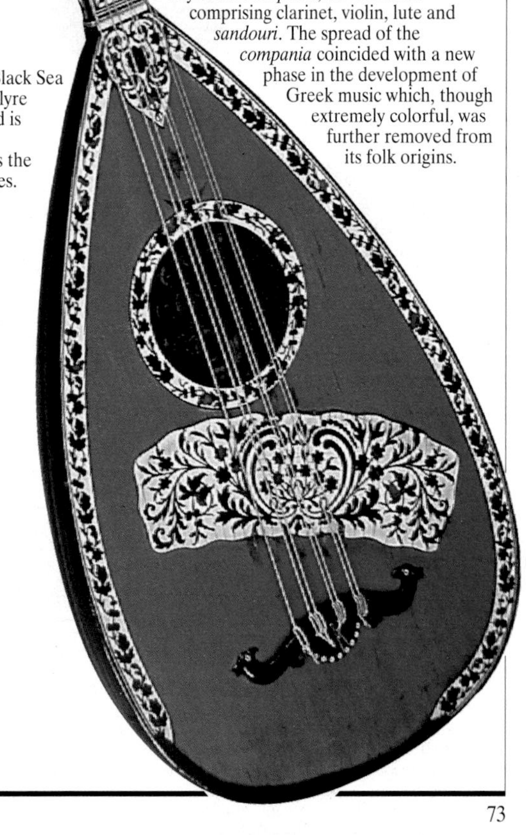

By moving the frets of the *laghouto* (lute), the player can tune to the natural scale and intervals of classical eastern music, which, in contrast to western music, does not use sharps or flats.

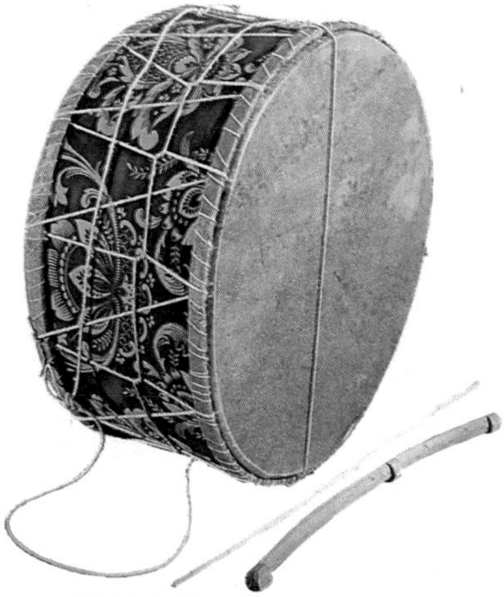

The daouli

A wooden cylinder with skin stretched over each end, the *daouli* is the invariable accompaniment to the *zournas*; the combination is called a *dhighia*, the traditional duo of mainland Greece. When the clarinet, with its greater versatility, began to displace the *zournas* around 1835, the *dhighia*, gave way to the *compania,* an ensemble comprising clarinet, violin, lute and *sandouri*. The spread of the *compania* coincided with a new phase in the development of Greek music which, though extremely colorful, was further removed from its folk origins.

The Pontic Lyre

Used by the Greeks of the Black Sea and Cappadocia, the Pontic lyre (below) has three strings and is played with a bow. Its shrill, piercing sound complements the lively steps of the local dances.

FILET OF BEEF, MARINATED AND ROASTED
CHERRY PILAF

Roasted, marinated beef filet is a traditional Sunday dish in Greece. It is usually accompanied by rice cooked with dried fruit such as raisins, prunes, apricots or wild cherries, soaked in advance in apple or orange juice. Fresh or tinned cherries may be used.

3. Chop the bay leaves, grind the pepper and coriander and chop the garlic finely.

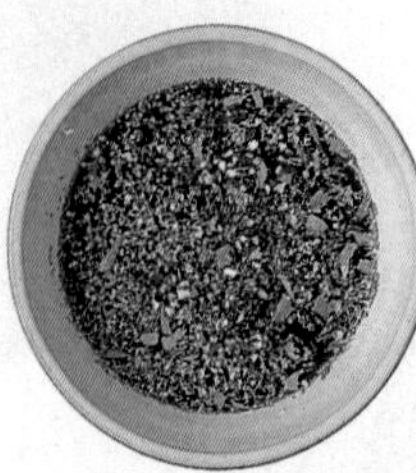

4. Mix the red wine, cherry brandy, bay leaves, garlic, thyme, coriander and pepper in a large bowl.

5. Immerse the meat in this mixtur cover and leave in the refrigerato to marinate for 12 hours. Turn the meat 2 or 3 times.

8. Rinse and drain the rice.

9. Add the remaining 2 tbs of olive oil to the saucepan, followed by the rice and the parsley.

10. Sauté until the rice becomes translucent.

13. Sauté gently for several minutes, then add the cherry juice and 3 cups of water.

14. Cook gently over a low heat for 20 minutes.

18. Place the beef filet on a grill in a roasting dish and cook for 25 minutes in a preheated oven at 230° C (445° F).

19. Check periodically. When done, the juice of the roast should still be pink. Leave the roast in front of the open oven door for a few minutes to yield some of its juice.

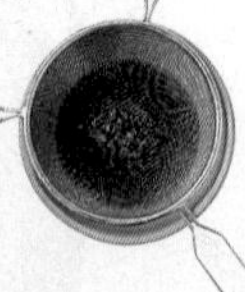

20. Deglaze the roasting pan with the strained marinade. Reduce by half.

1. Ingredients: ⅔ cup cherry brandy, ⅔ cup red wine, 2lbs trussed beef filet with the fat removed, 2 bay leaves, 2 tsp olive oil, 10 peppercorns, 1 tsp coriander seeds, 1 tsp thyme, 2 garlic cloves, a pinch of salt.

2. For the pilaf: One bunch parsley, 3 oz hazelnuts, 6 oz wild cherries, 1 lb basmati rice, 5 tbs olive oil, 1 medium onion, 3 tbs cherry juice, pepper.

6. In the meantime, prepare the pilaf. Finely chop the parsley, onions and hazelnuts.

7. In a large saucepan, sauté the onions gently in 3 tbs of olive oil.

11. Add the chopped hazelnuts.

12. Stir in the pitted cherries; set aside the cherry juice. Season with salt and pepper.

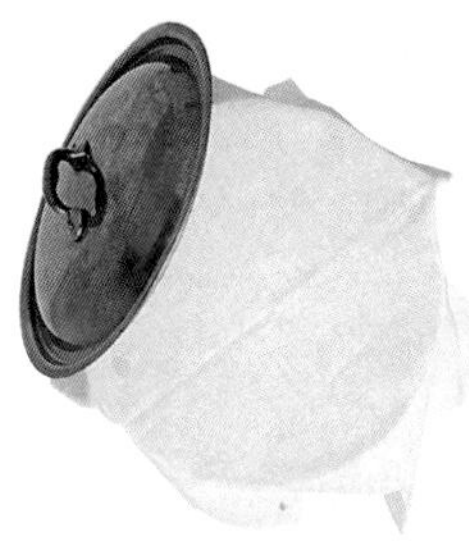

15. Remove the saucepan from the heat, cover with a tea towel and a saucepan lid. Leave the rice to steam for 15 to 20 minutes.

16. During this time, remove the meat from the marinade and dry it with a paper towel.

17. Sear the meat in a deep frying pan which has been oiled with olive oil and sprinkled with salt.

21. Carve the roast. Pour over the sauce and serve with the cherry pilaf.

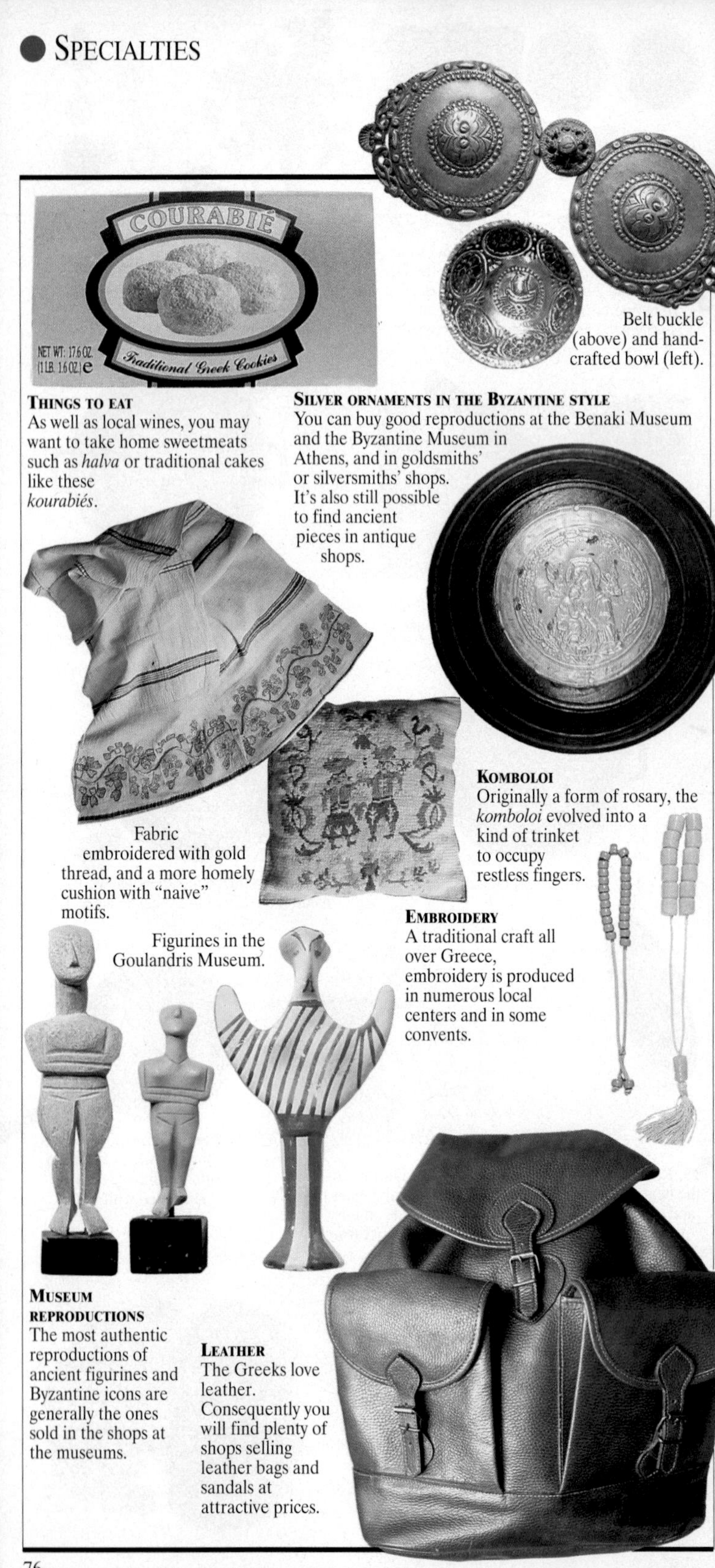

Belt buckle (above) and hand-crafted bowl (left).

Things to eat
As well as local wines, you may want to take home sweetmeats such as *halva* or traditional cakes like these *kourabiés*.

Silver ornaments in the Byzantine style
You can buy good reproductions at the Benaki Museum and the Byzantine Museum in Athens, and in goldsmiths' or silversmiths' shops. It's also still possible to find ancient pieces in antique shops.

Komboloi
Originally a form of rosary, the *komboloi* evolved into a kind of trinket to occupy restless fingers.

Fabric embroidered with gold thread, and a more homely cushion with "naive" motifs.

Embroidery
A traditional craft all over Greece, embroidery is produced in numerous local centers and in some convents.

Figurines in the Goulandris Museum.

Museum reproductions
The most authentic reproductions of ancient figurines and Byzantine icons are generally the ones sold in the shops at the museums.

Leather
The Greeks love leather. Consequently you will find plenty of shops selling leather bags and sandals at attractive prices.

Architecture

Greek civilization was basically urban. The urban habitat of the classical Greeks, the *asty* (city), functioned in harmony with the rural habitat of the *komai* (villages). The relationship between the two was clear: the city, which was fortified, was there to control the plains around it. To deserve the title of city, it had to fulfill political, economic and religious purposes, maintaining public buildings and open areas: a city was not complete without an acropolis, an agora, and a gymnasium. But urban development is not always easy to trace. The Greek colonies were planned as complete cities from the start, but the early stages in the construction of cities like Athens are barely discernible from excavations. Only their evolved forms are clear as their early forms developed gradually over several centuries with no coherent plan.

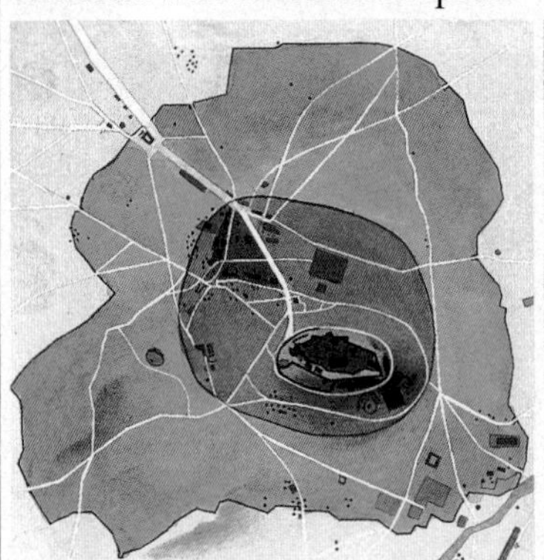

CONCENTRIC GROWTH OF ATHENS. Athens was organized around two key points: the Acropolis and the Agora. The city's principal axis was the Panathenaic Way, which ran from the west slope of the Acropolis to the Kerameikos, cutting across the Agora.

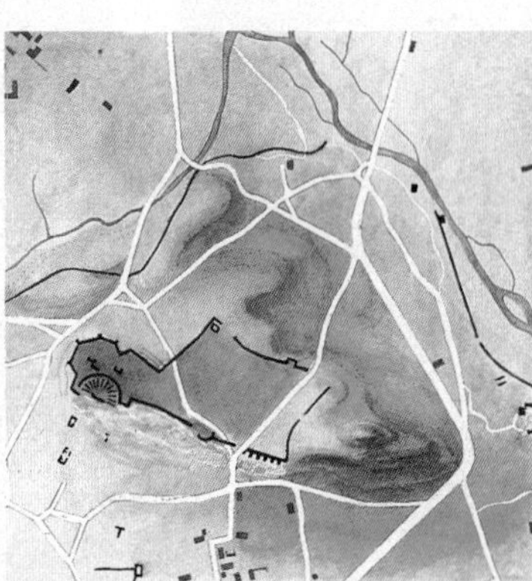

SPARTA Although Sparta was one of Greece's most important cities, it was not typical: it was not made up of a city governing the surrounding territory, for centuries it had no defensive walls, and it maintained only a minimum of public buildings.

MILETOS. A new, more modern pattern for urban development appeared in the 5th century BC, thought to have been invented by Hippodamos of Miletos. Supervising the rebuilding of his city after it was devastated in 494, he devised an orthogonal plan based on simple mathematical principles and functional zoning.

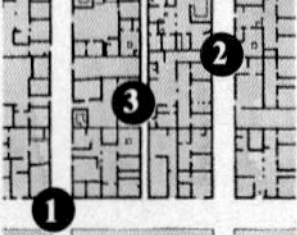

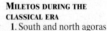

THE 4TH-CENTURY CITY OF OLYNTHOS. The houses gave on to an inner courtyard surrounded by a peristyle. The *insula* (block), which formed the basis of the Hippodamian system, comprised ten square plots. The streets were graded according to function: main street (1), access to the *insulae* (2) and access to individual plots (3).

MILETOS DURING THE CLASSICAL ERA

1. South and north agoras
2. Theater
3. Bouleuterion (council building)
4. West agora
5. Stadium
6. Delphinion and temple of Athena
7. Naval port
8. Trading port
9. Residential district
10. Surrounding wall
11. Gymnasium.

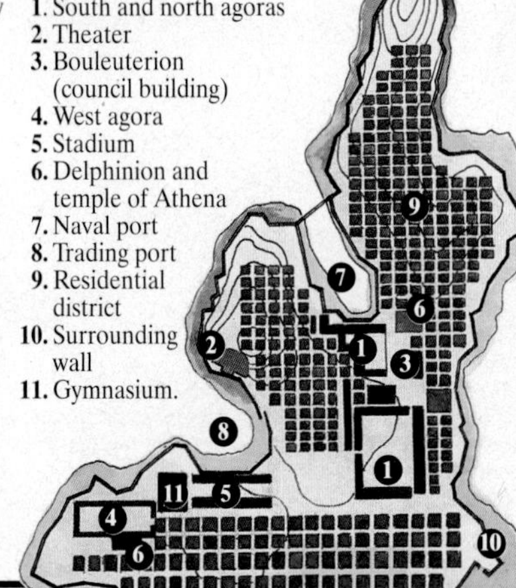

“MAN IS BY NATURE A BEING DESTINED TO LIVE IN CITIES.”
ARISTOTLE

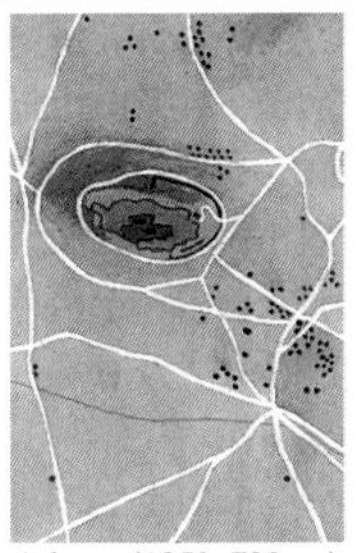
Athens (1050–700 BC)

GEOMETRIC PERIOD
Athens was built around two key centers: the Acropolis, originally called the “city”, which simultaneously served as a defensive position and a sanctuary, and the lower city, *asty*, around the Agora. The only significant relics are the tombs.

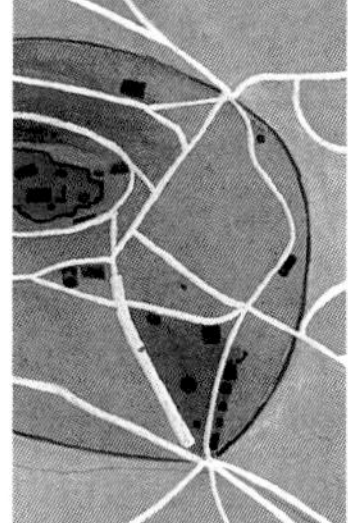
Athens (700–510 BC)

ARCHAIC PERIOD
The architectural development of the area parallelled the general development of the city and the complexity of its political institutions. The western part of the Agora is the site of the tribunal and *prytanikon*, which are in their original state.

A THOUSAND YEARS IN THE HISTORY OF THE ATHENIAN AGORA

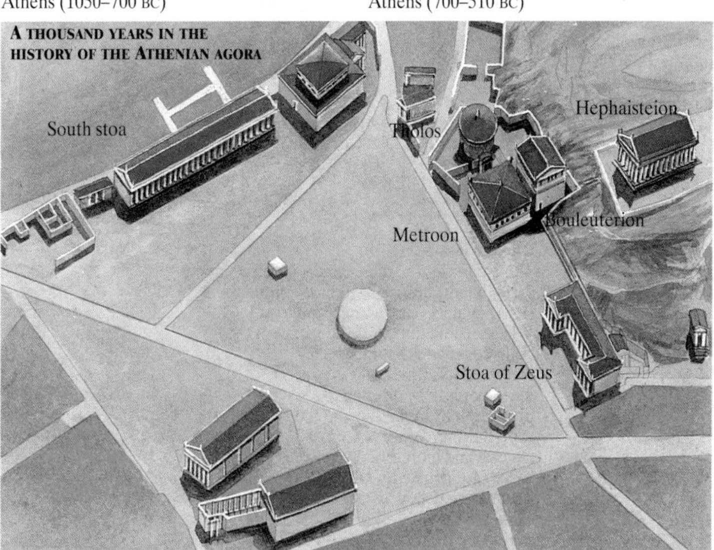

END OF THE 6TH CENTURY BC. The stoas appeared – that of Zeus Eleutherios ▲ *192* on the western side and the long south stoa. The democratic nature of Athenian institutions required meeting places: old and new *bouleuterions* ▲ *193* for council members; the *tholos*, in which the city fire always burned; and the *strategeion.* The Agora also retained its function as a forum for social gatherings and festivities, as well as for the horse-racing contests of the Panathenaic Games.

4th century BC

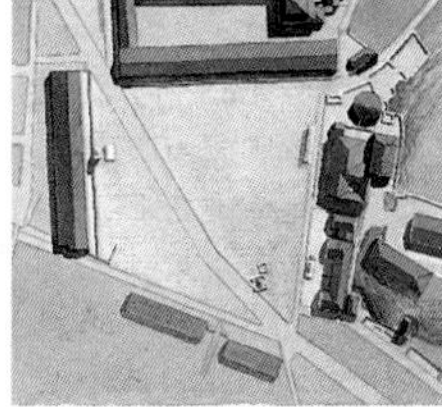
2nd century BC

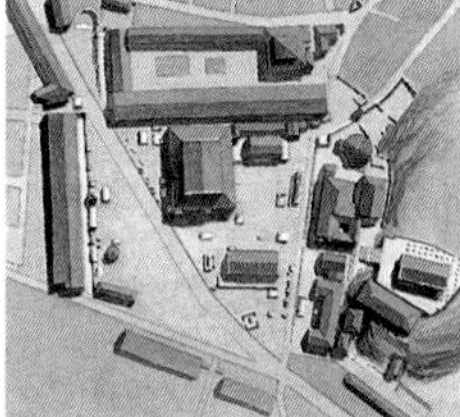
2nd century AD

4TH CENTURY BC. The Temple of Apollo Patroos was rebuilt next to the Stoa of Zeus and the northeast corner was adorned with a square peristyle.

HELLENISTIC PERIOD
The Agora became an orderly, closed site, dominated by stoas. The stoa in the east, a gift from the King of Attalos, towering over 360 feet high and now restored, was modelled on the stoa of Eumenes on the south side of the Acropolis. The Middle Stoa, 525 feet long with 160 Doric columns, closed the site to the south.

ROMAN PERIOD
The model for urban planning was no longer that of Athens, but that of major cities of the Empire, such as Pergamon and Ephesus. The city continued to grow, adorned by gifts from the emperors. The the Odeon of Agrippa used up much of the available space. In the 1st century, the old Panathenaic Way was re-laid.

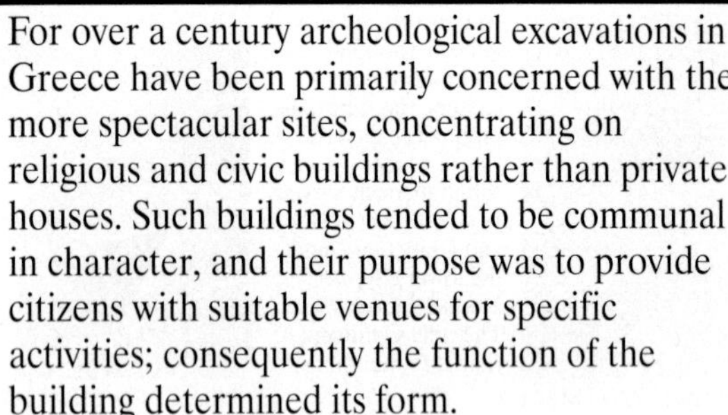

For over a century archeological excavations in Greece have been primarily concerned with the more spectacular sites, concentrating on religious and civic buildings rather than private houses. Such buildings tended to be communal in character, and their purpose was to provide citizens with suitable venues for specific activities; consequently the function of the building determined its form.

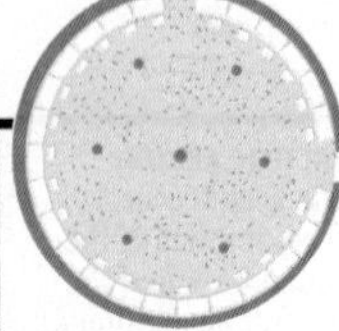

PLAN OF THE THOLOS
Built of tufa in 470–460 BC, the Tholos ▲ *193* housed the *prytaneis* (magistrates), who took turns to keep vigil there day and night. They ate reclining on couches arranged around the outer wall; in the center burned the inextinguishable flame of Athens.

THE STOA OF ZEUS ELEUTHEROS ▲ *192*
Built c. 430 BC of marble and tufa, with two projecting wings, this was the first of many stoas in the Athenian Agora.

BANQUETING HALL
The agora was the most important place in the social life of the Greeks. They went there to stroll, to meet one another, and to talk. When a community had the means, it built stoas for its agora, which increased its attractiveness as a meeting place by offering protection from the sun and the rain. But there were other less general and more ritualized forms of social intercourse for which banqueting halls provided a focus. Banquets could be public or private, but they were invariably all-male affairs in which the object was not only the pleasures of eating and drinking but also to act out the symbolism of sharing and exchange.

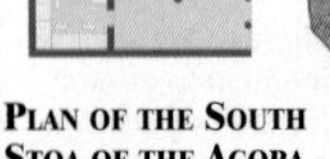

PLAN OF THE SOUTH STOA OF THE AGORA
This Doric stoa was over 250 feet long. Behind the colonnade, which opened onto the South Square ▲ *195*, there were banqueting rooms with couches arranged around the walls.

Fortress with watchtowers at Aigosthena
In most Greek city-states all or part of the territory was defended by fortifications, the cities themselves being the most rigorously fortified points.

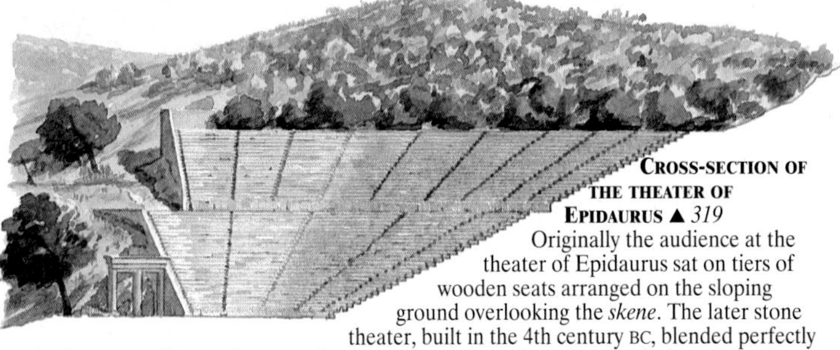

Cross-section of the theater of Epidaurus ▲ *319*
Originally the audience at the theater of Epidaurus sat on tiers of wooden seats arranged on the sloping ground overlooking the *skene*. The later stone theater, built in the 4th century BC, blended perfectly with the surrounding landscape and was renowned throughout the classical world for its geometrical perfection.

Plan of the Odeon of Pericles in Athens ▲ *173*
Less common and more elitist than the open-air theater was the covered *odeon*, or concert hall, where music contests were held.

Bouleuterion
Partial reconstruction of the council chamber at Priene. Buildings were needed for civic meetings and political debates. An open-air site was provided for the thousands of participants in the people's assemblies, while for the one hundred members of Priene's Boule (council) there was a roofed building, backing on to the hillside, with tiers of seats. At the center of the chamber was an altar where sacrifices were made to invoke the help of the gods in the debates.

Cross-section of the Pnyx
In the 6th century BC the hill of the Pnyx in Athens ▲ *207* was adapted into a venue for meetings of the Ecclesia (people's assembly). A semicircular terrace was built on the hill to place the listeners at the same level as the orators on the tribune. The greater number of citizens involved and the need for comfort during the assembly's sessions explain the alterations made at the close of the 5th century and in the time of Alexander.

Plan of the Pnyx
The semicircular design was similar to that of Greek theaters.

The history of Greek architecture began with the Myceneans, around the start of the 15th century BC. Initially they were influenced by the still flourishing Cretan civilization, though this was limited to certain technical and decorative characteristics of Minoan palaces. The settlement of the Myceneans in mainland Greece in places unprotected by the sea forced them to build citadels rather than palaces. Their penchant for monumental architecture, encouraged by the military character of their buildings and their taste for symmetry, as expressed in the central megaron with its columns and pillars, defined the basic principles of Greek architecture.

ROOF STRUCTURE OF THE PALACE AT MYCENAE
The column (**1**), which widens at the top, supports the architrave (**2**); the rafters (**3**) of round poles jointed together show the Minoan influence. The painted décor echoes the Cretan palaces at Knossos and Malia. The poles, wedged at the corners by a beam (**4**), support a second level of beaten earth, which constitutes the roof terrace.

FAÇADE OF THE MEGARON AT MYCENAE ▲ *304*
The façade testifies to the Mycenean taste for symmetry and sobriety. The base consists of cut-stone blocks with irregular joints (**5**); these support courses of unfired brick (**6**) held together by ties of wood (**7**), which help stabilize the building and inject rhythm into the façade. The entrance has a covered vestibule (*prodomos*), entirely fronted with wood and framed by the walls (**8**) of the *domos* (main chamber). This arrangement later emerged as an integral aspect of the design of Greek temples. Windows with wooden grilles (**9**) admitted daylight into the *domos*.

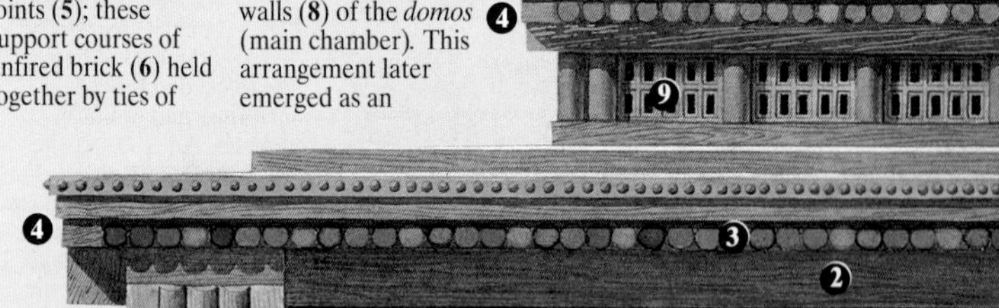

The citadel of Mycenae. During the Mycenean era the citadel, which contained only the prince's palace (**1**), served as a refuge for people living outside the walls (**2**). The regular pillaging of extra-mural houses proved an obstacle to economic development. A solution was found in the Archaic era when an outer wall was added. Thereafter the acropolis lost its primacy in community life and was replaced by the public square, or agora.

The domed Treasury of Atreus
▲ *303*
Beehive-shaped *tholos* tombs and corbeled domes had been a feature of Cretan burial places. The Myceneans rejected clay mortar, instead adopting and perfecting the technique of cut stone, which allows perfectly adjusted blocks to stabilize themselves without any mortar. The broad circular chamber has a dome covered with earth; this forms a tumulus, into which the *dromos* (entryway) was cut. The size of the dome, 40 feet high and over 45 feet in diameter, was not surpassed until the construction of the Pantheon in Rome 1,400 years later.

The Lion Gate
▲ *302*
The relieving arch (**2**) directs the vertical load to the sides of the gate, thus reducing the pressure on the lintel (**1**).

Gateway at Messene
Here the lintel (**1**) supports both its own weight and that of the stones above. The breadth of the gate depended on the builders' ability to manhandle blocks of such huge size.

Doorway of the Treasury of Atreus
The massive corbeled stone blocks (**3**) are assembled so that no stone is needed within the relieving arch, which is here left empty. Instead the load is directed down either side of the huge lintel (**1**), which therefore needs only to support its own weight.

Gateway at Elaios
Here the corbeling (**3**) dispenses altogether with the need for a lintel. In contrast to arch construction – to which the Myceneans and the Greeks assigned a secondary role – the excessive load bearing down on the sides made it impossible to build wide spans.

The two principal orders of Greek architecture were the Doric (developed in the Peloponnese, western Greece and Magna Graecia) and the Ionic (mainly found in Asia Minor and the Aegean Islands). These stone buildings did little more than reproduce the proportions and elements of earlier wooden structures. The two orders are characterized by their lack of gratuitous ornament and their formal purity; only the Ionic order, with its scroll-shaped capitals, retains a hint of oriental decoration.

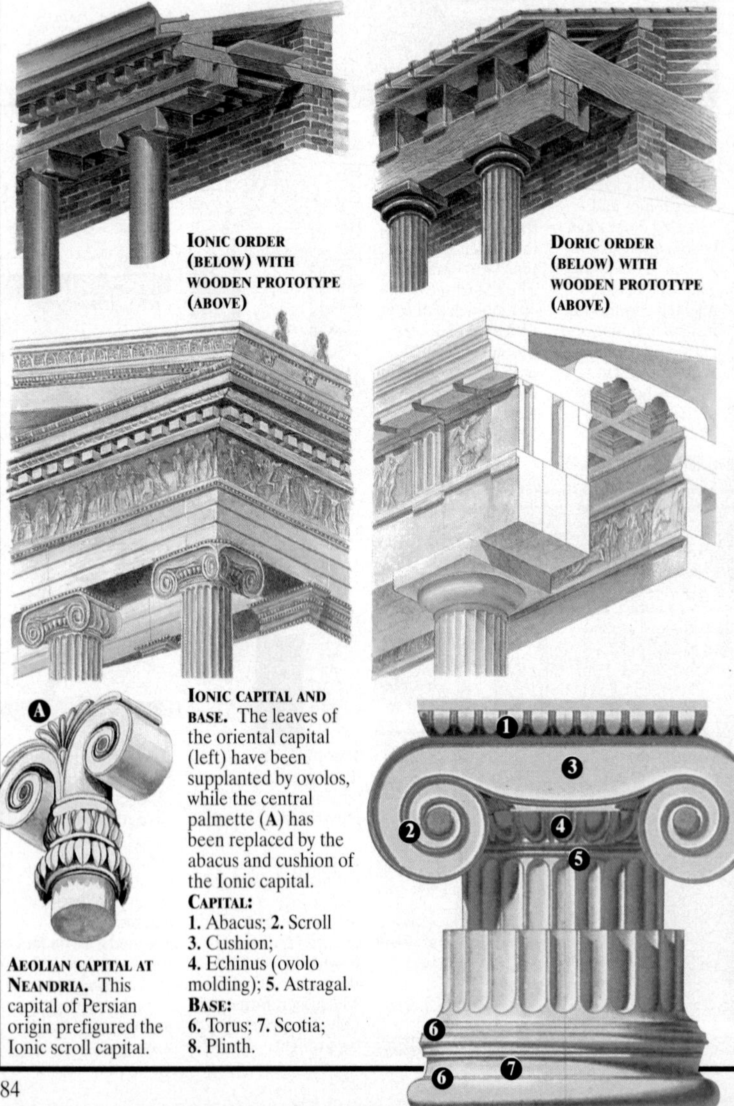

IONIC ORDER (BELOW) WITH WOODEN PROTOTYPE (ABOVE)

DORIC ORDER (BELOW) WITH WOODEN PROTOTYPE (ABOVE)

AEOLIAN CAPITAL AT NEANDRIA. This capital of Persian origin prefigured the Ionic scroll capital.

IONIC CAPITAL AND BASE. The leaves of the oriental capital (left) have been supplanted by ovolos, while the central palmette (**A**) has been replaced by the abacus and cushion of the Ionic capital.
CAPITAL:
1. Abacus; **2.** Scroll
3. Cushion;
4. Echinus (ovolo molding); **5.** Astragal.
BASE:
6. Torus; **7.** Scotia;
8. Plinth.

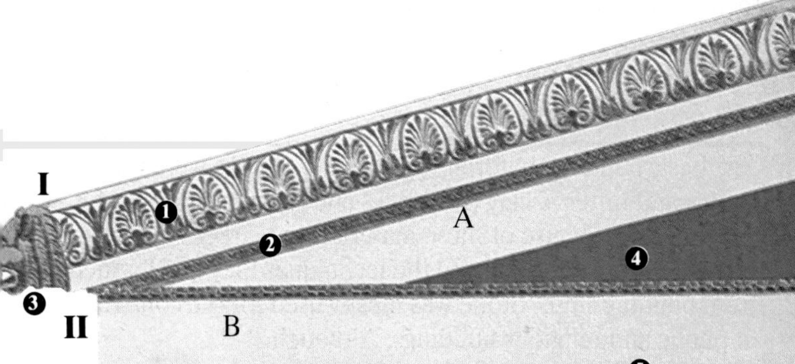

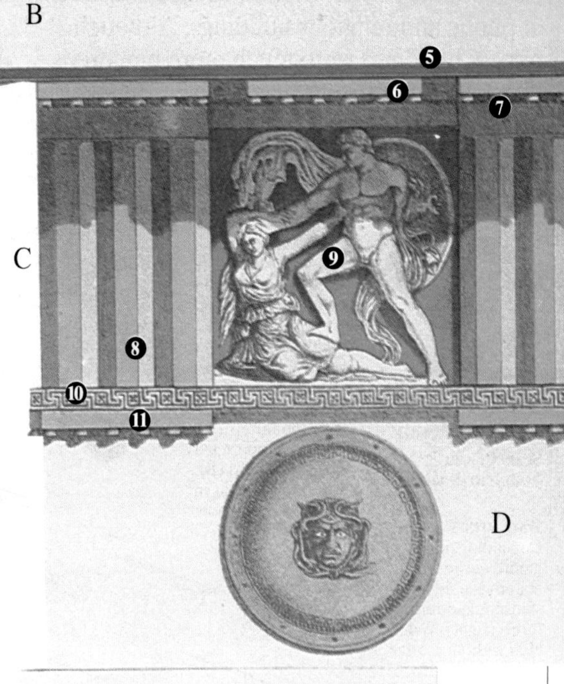

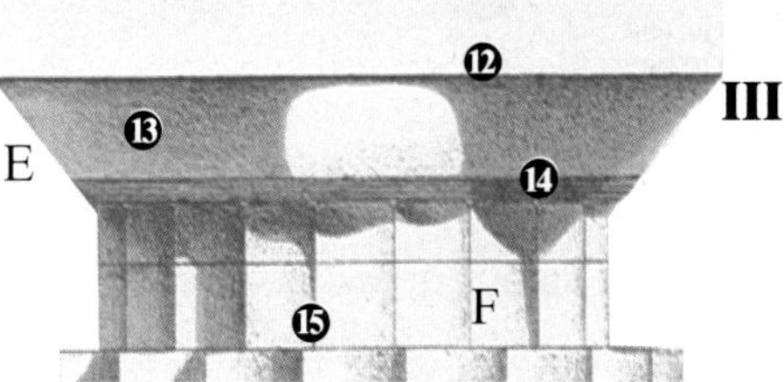

Elements of the Doric order
Every element of the original wooden prototype of the Doric order was reproduced in stone, the austerity of the result being relieved by polychrome decoration.

I. Pediment
A. Roof slope
1. Cyma **2.** Cornice
3. Gargoyle
4. Tympanum.
II. Entablature
B. Cornice
5. Dripstone consisting of mutules (**6**) and guttae (**7**).
C. Frieze
composed of triglyphs (**8**) and metopes (**9**); **10.** listel; **11.** regula.
D. Architrave
with medallion.
III. Column
(composed of capital, shaft and base)
E. Capital
composed of abacus (**12**), echinus (**13**) and rings (**14**).
F. Shaft
with fluting (**15**).

Corinthian capital
Invented in the second half of the 5th century BC, the Corinthian order is an extension of the Ionic. The column and entablature are identical, but the capital is shaped like an upside-down bell, decorated with acanthus leaves. Callimachus, the Athenian sculptor and goldsmith, is said to have devised the first Corinthian capital: legend has it that a basket surrounded by acanthus leaves, placed on a tomb in Corinth, was his inspiration. Although it originated in Greece, the Corinthian order only attained its definitive form during the Roman era, eventually becoming the preferred order of Roman architecture.

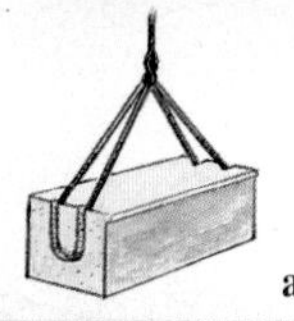

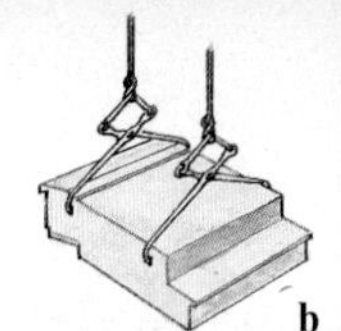

The basic building materials used by the Greeks were wood (for beams and rafters), clay (for bricks and tiles), metal (for studs) and stone. In the use of these materials the Greeks surpassed all other civilizations, thanks to the techniques they had learned from building ships. Stone was mostly used for the construction of public and religious buildings. Although private buildings were much more numerous, they were of unfired brick, which accounts for the relative absence of visible remains.

SPARTAN AND CORINTHIAN TILES

ROOF MATERIALS
When tiles were used, to avoid slippage they were placed on a bed of clay (*dorosis*) and rushes, the latter being laid criss-cross or fixed with metal pins. Pine or fir were most commonly used for the rafters (**A**), which supported a system of laths (**B**); more rarely oak, as in the Parthenon.

WALL STUDS
Depending on the nature of the materials used, wall studs took different forms (right). Walls built without mortar required great precision when cutting the stone, and the blocks had to be bonded with studs.

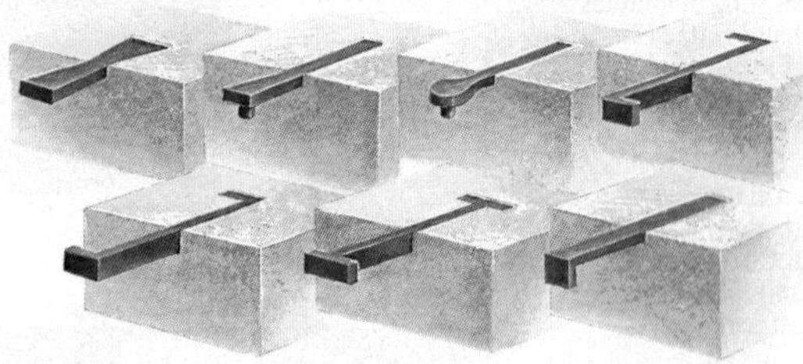

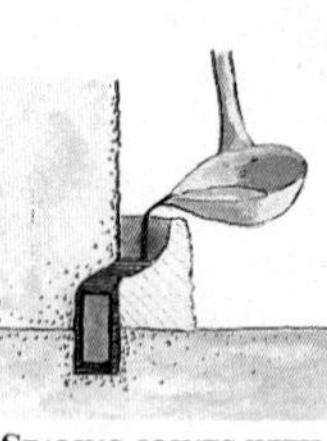

SEALING JOINTS WITH LEAD
The jointing of stone blocks was carried out on the spot, either by pouring lead directly into the cavities or by inserting metal studs prepared in advance. Hardwoods such as cypress were sometimes used for jointing, in place of metal.

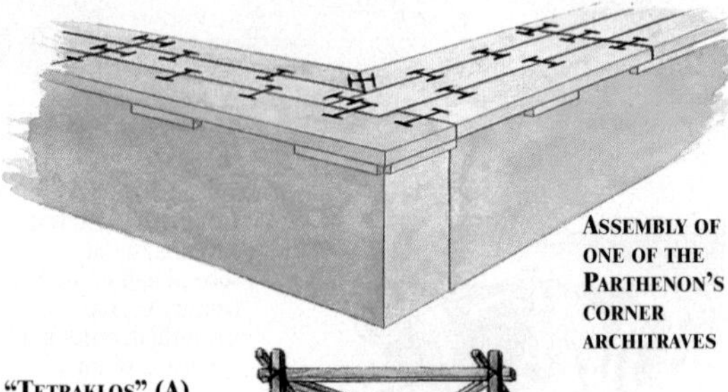

ASSEMBLY OF ONE OF THE PARTHENON'S CORNER ARCHITRAVES

"TETRAKLOS" (A) AND "DIKLOS" (B)
These two lifting mechanisms, described by the Roman architect Vitruvius (1st century AD), enabled the Greeks to hoist blocks weighing several tons.

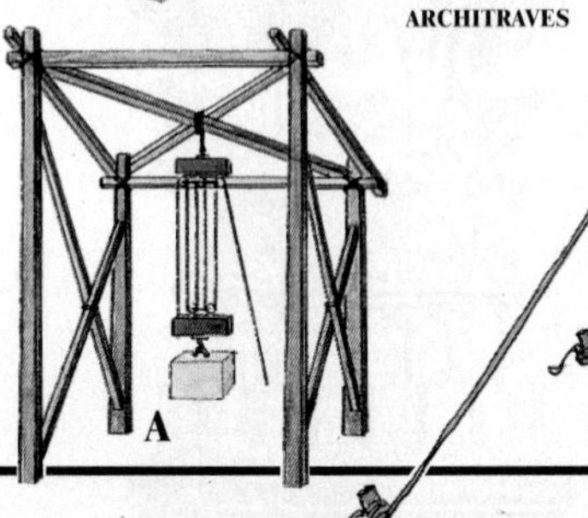

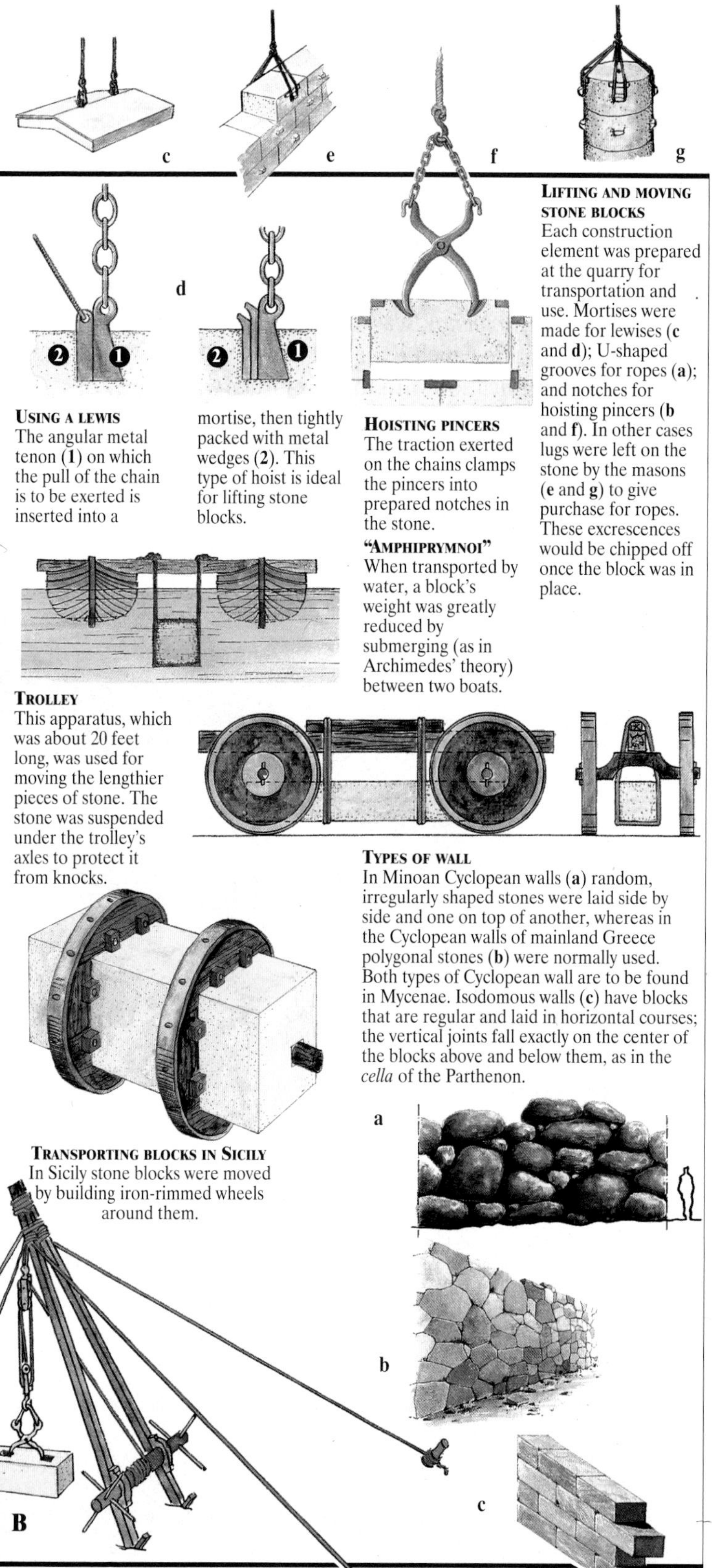

Lifting and moving stone blocks
Each construction element was prepared at the quarry for transportation and use. Mortises were made for lewises (**c** and **d**); U-shaped grooves for ropes (**a**); and notches for hoisting pincers (**b** and **f**). In other cases lugs were left on the stone by the masons (**e** and **g**) to give purchase for ropes. These excrescences would be chipped off once the block was in place.

Using a lewis
The angular metal tenon (**1**) on which the pull of the chain is to be exerted is inserted into a mortise, then tightly packed with metal wedges (**2**). This type of hoist is ideal for lifting stone blocks.

Hoisting pincers
The traction exerted on the chains clamps the pincers into prepared notches in the stone.

"Amphiprymnoi"
When transported by water, a block's weight was greatly reduced by submerging (as in Archimedes' theory) between two boats.

Trolley
This apparatus, which was about 20 feet long, was used for moving the lengthier pieces of stone. The stone was suspended under the trolley's axles to protect it from knocks.

Types of wall
In Minoan Cyclopean walls (**a**) random, irregularly shaped stones were laid side by side and one on top of another, whereas in the Cyclopean walls of mainland Greece polygonal stones (**b**) were normally used. Both types of Cyclopean wall are to be found in Mycenae. Isodomous walls (**c**) have blocks that are regular and laid in horizontal courses; the vertical joints fall exactly on the center of the blocks above and below them, as in the *cella* of the Parthenon.

Transporting blocks in Sicily
In Sicily stone blocks were moved by building iron-rimmed wheels around them.

THE SANCTUARY AND SACRIFICIAL RITES

The basic features of Greek religious life were communal, and most of the rituals had a social or political context. While every aspect of Greek existence was marked to some extent by the divine, consecrated places were set aside for religious functions. The sanctuary, or *temenos*, was a defined space dedicated to one or more gods, within which their cult was celebrated. The usual means of communication with the immortals was by way of sacrifice; hence, while a temple was in no way indispensable to the *temenos*, the altar was an essential element. The layout of the space and the architectural choices within the sanctuary were dictated by the nature of each separate liturgy.

BUCRANE
Bucranes (ox-skull ornaments) were a reminder of former sacrifices, attached to the temple columns or sculpted on the metopes.

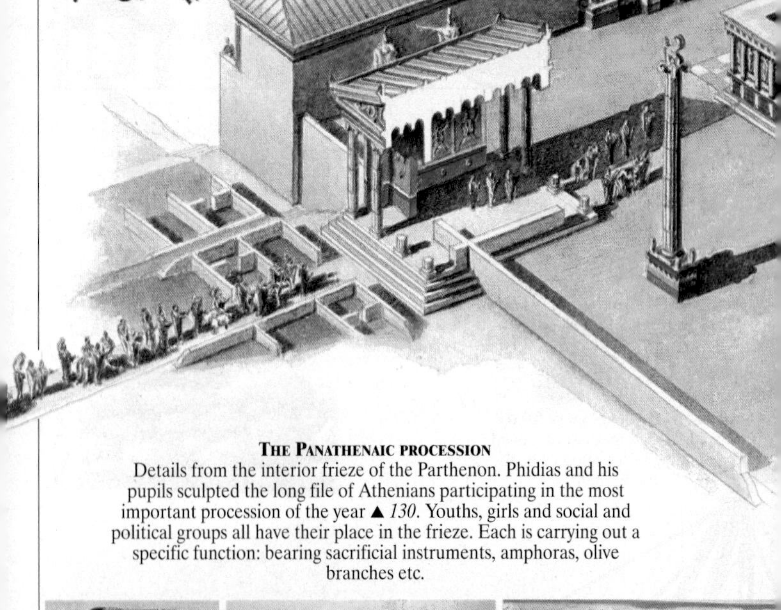

THE PANATHENAIC PROCESSION
Details from the interior frieze of the Parthenon. Phidias and his pupils sculpted the long file of Athenians participating in the most important procession of the year ▲ *130*. Youths, girls and social and political groups all have their place in the frieze. Each is carrying out a specific function: bearing sacrificial instruments, amphoras, olive branches etc.

Scenes of sacrifice
A number of painted vases depict officiators at sacrifices and illustrate their ritual actions. The death of the animal is seldom shown.

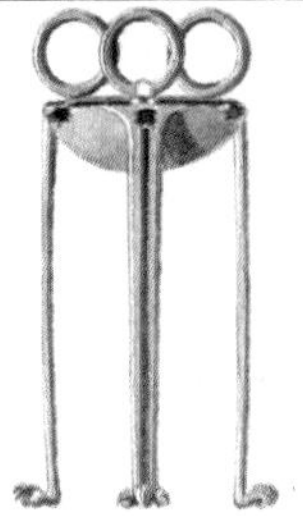

Tripod and altar
The tripod had symbolic significance: the meat of the sacrificed animals was cooked in it, scented with aromatic herbs. The altar could take many different forms, from the crudest heap of stones or ashes to the most majestic carved monument, depending on the cult it served.

Religious festival
Imaginative reconstruction of the Temple of Athena Polias at Priene. The men are paying a formal visit to the goddess, bringing an offering. The long, orderly procession approaches the precinct by the Sacred Way, which leads to the *temenos*. Although its composition may vary a little, its religious function – to bring animals to the place of sacrifice – is always the same. After entering the *temenos* by way of the *propylaea*, it proceeds to the sacrificial area on the east side of the temple. There the animals, carefully selected to be in perfect condition, are sprinkled with water, fed with grains of barley thrown by the participants, then knocked on the head. Their bones and fat are grilled on the fire of the altar (which faces the rising sun), while the flesh is shared out among the citizens present and then boiled. The gods are content with the odor wafting up to them, which also penetrates to the statue of the goddess in the temple's inner sanctum. According to myth, Prometheus cheated Zeus of his share of the sacrifice by tricking him into choosing the worst portion (bones covered with fat), while keeping the meat for mortals.

Although the temple was not an indispensable element of the sanctuary, it was its principal edifice during the classical era. First and foremost it was the abode of the god, who was present in the form of a statue. Religious statuary and temple architecture therefore evolved simultaneously. The Archaic era (8th century BC) witnessed a change from coarser materials such as wood and brick to limestone and finally marble. From the 5th century BC onward the temple became a focus for the most advanced architectural theories, which greatly benefited Greek architecture as a whole.

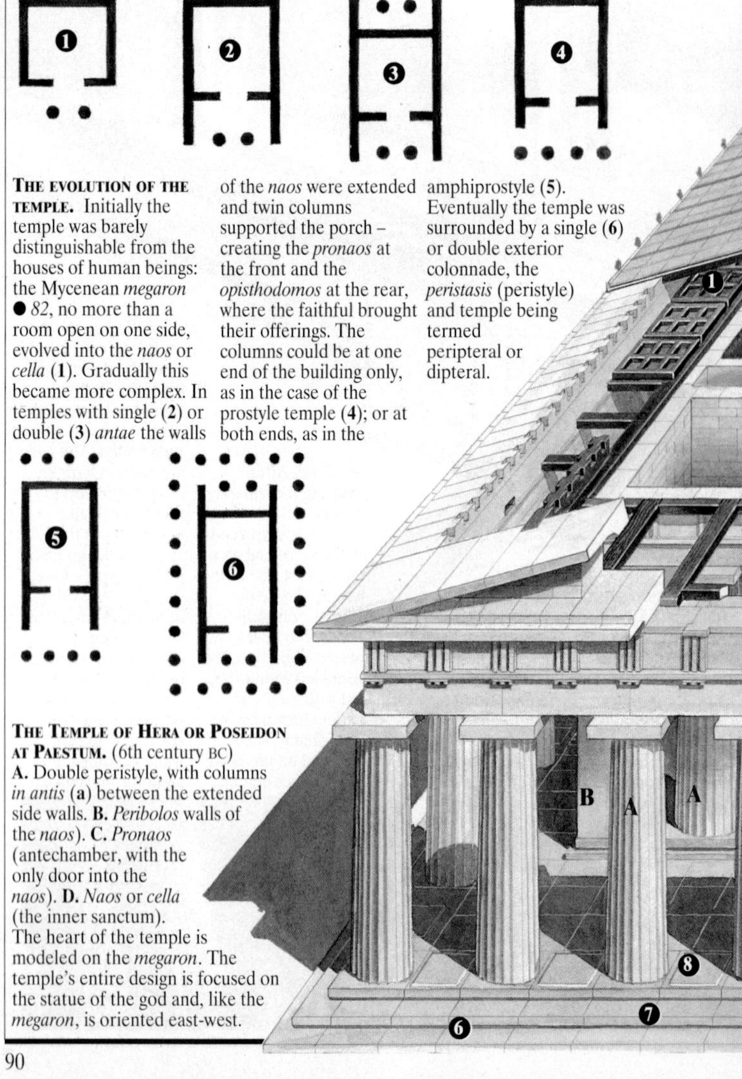

THE EVOLUTION OF THE TEMPLE. Initially the temple was barely distinguishable from the houses of human beings: the Mycenean *megaron* ● *82*, no more than a room open on one side, evolved into the *naos* or *cella* (**1**). Gradually this became more complex. In temples with single (**2**) or double (**3**) *antae* the walls of the *naos* were extended and twin columns supported the porch – creating the *pronaos* at the front and the *opisthodomos* at the rear, where the faithful brought their offerings. The columns could be at one end of the building only, as in the case of the prostyle temple (**4**); or at both ends, as in the amphiprostyle (**5**). Eventually the temple was surrounded by a single (**6**) or double exterior colonnade, the *peristasis* (peristyle) and temple being termed peripteral or dipteral.

THE TEMPLE OF HERA OR POSEIDON AT PAESTUM. (6th century BC)
A. Double peristyle, with columns *in antis* (**a**) between the extended side walls. **B.** *Peribolos* walls of the *naos*). **C.** *Pronaos* (antechamber, with the only door into the *naos*). **D.** *Naos* or *cella* (the inner sanctum).
The heart of the temple is modeled on the *megaron*. The temple's entire design is focused on the statue of the god and, like the *megaron*, is oriented east-west.

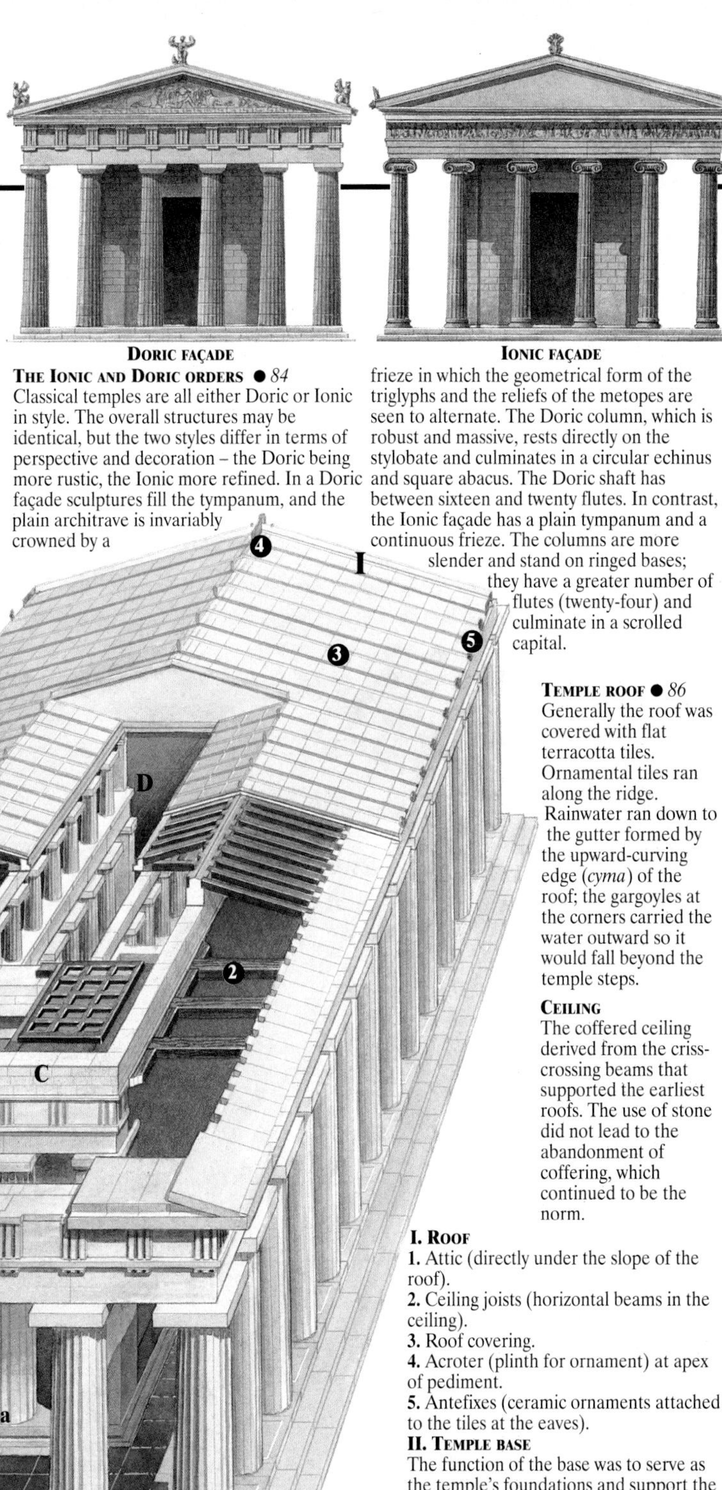

The Ionic and Doric orders ● *84*
Classical temples are all either Doric or Ionic in style. The overall structures may be identical, but the two styles differ in terms of perspective and decoration – the Doric being more rustic, the Ionic more refined. In a Doric façade sculptures fill the tympanum, and the plain architrave is invariably crowned by a frieze in which the geometrical form of the triglyphs and the reliefs of the metopes are seen to alternate. The Doric column, which is robust and massive, rests directly on the stylobate and culminates in a circular echinus and square abacus. The Doric shaft has between sixteen and twenty flutes. In contrast, the Ionic façade has a plain tympanum and a continuous frieze. The columns are more slender and stand on ringed bases; they have a greater number of flutes (twenty-four) and culminate in a scrolled capital.

Temple roof ● *86*
Generally the roof was covered with flat terracotta tiles. Ornamental tiles ran along the ridge. Rainwater ran down to the gutter formed by the upward-curving edge (*cyma*) of the roof; the gargoyles at the corners carried the water outward so it would fall beyond the temple steps.

Ceiling
The coffered ceiling derived from the criss-crossing beams that supported the earliest roofs. The use of stone did not lead to the abandonment of coffering, which continued to be the norm.

I. Roof
1. Attic (directly under the slope of the roof).
2. Ceiling joists (horizontal beams in the ceiling).
3. Roof covering.
4. Acroter (plinth for ornament) at apex of pediment.
5. Antefixes (ceramic ornaments attached to the tiles at the eaves).

II. Temple base
The function of the base was to serve as the temple's foundations and support the upper parts of the building. It included:
6. Euthynterion (the transition between the foundations and the first step).
7. First step.
8. Stylobate (the "top step", on which the walls and columns stood).

HORSEMAN'S HEAD
Marble, c. 560 BC. The head and beard are typical of the Archaic period.

Greek statuary began to develop in the 7th century BC, concomitant with religious architecture. The *naos* had to contain an image of the god or goddess worthy of his or her house. The Greeks had an anthropomorphic idea of the divine which led sculptors to fashion the gods in the image of humans. Sculpture evolved continually throughout the Archaic era (7th to 6th centuries BC), the classical era (5th to 4th centuries BC) and the Hellenistic era (late 4th century BC to the Roman epoch), retaining remarkable unity, yet gaining diversity from regional schools and the wide variety of materials.

THE ARCHAIC ERA. The first sculptures were monumental in style. As a rule they represented naked youths (*kouroi*) or girls (*korai*). These figures tended to be hieratic and conventional.

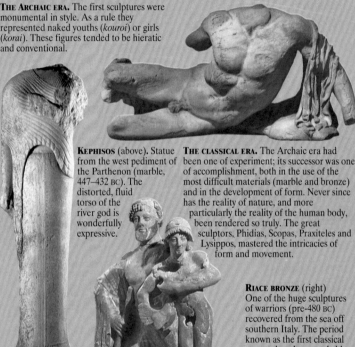

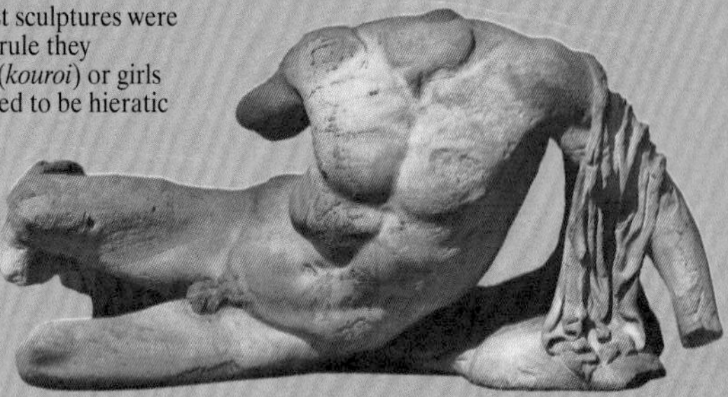

KEPHISOS (above). Statue from the west pediment of the Parthenon (marble, 447–432 BC). The distorted, fluid torso of the river god is wonderfully expressive.

THE CLASSICAL ERA. The Archaic era had been one of experiment; its successor was one of accomplishment, both in the use of the most difficult materials (marble and bronze) and in the development of form. Never since has the reality of nature, and more particularly the reality of the human body, been rendered so truly. The great sculptors, Phidias, Scopas, Praxiteles and Lysippos, mastered the intricacies of form and movement.

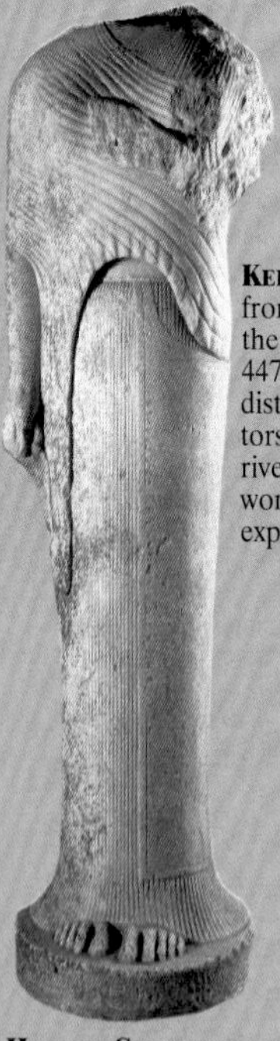

RIACE BRONZE (right)
One of the huge sculptures of warriors (pre-480 BC) recovered from the sea off southern Italy. The period known as the first classical era produced a remarkable series of bronzes of very high quality, such as the Poseidon of Artemision ▲ *238* and the Auriga of Delphi ▲ *267*.

HERA OF SAMOS
Body of the goddess Hera (marble, c. 560 BC). It looks like a column-statue, with its unobtrusive forms (like those of other contemporary *korai*) and the simple parallel folds of the clothes.

ZEUS ABDUCTING GANYMEDE
This *ex voto* group (left) depicts the erotic abduction of the youth by the god (polychrome terracotta, c. 480 BC). The smile and vigorous movement of the adult contrast strongly with the expressionless immobility of the boy in his arms.

"NATURE HAS BESTOWED UPON US MARBLE IN ABUNDANCE...WITH WHICH WE CREATE STATUES THAT ARE WORTHY OF THE GODS' MAJESTY."
XENOPHON

NIKE REMOVING HER SANDAL. Temple of Athena Nike (marble, 411–407 BC). The evolution of the treatment of drapery – which is transparent and suggestive here to emphasize the movement of the body – is clearly evident.

THE HELLENISTIC ERA.
The city-states of classical Greece were succeeded in the art of statuary by those of Asia Minor and Rhodes. Their sculptural expression was characterized by a taste for strong sentiment and a penchant for the theatrical portrayal of movement.

LAOCOÖN
This group from Rhodes (marble, probably from the 2nd century BC) demonstrates the virtuosity and power of Hellenistic sculpture.

The Byzantine era, which started with the foundation of Constantinople in AD 350 and ended with its fall to the Turks in 1453, served as a link both between antiquity and the Middle Ages and between East and West. Byzantine architects, masters of the use of brick, became superb builders of cupolas and arches in their religious architecture. In Greece the Byzantine style was characterized by the adoption in the 10th century of the Greek-cross plan for churches and by the influence of the classical period, which led to a preference for stone over brick, although the latter was invariably used for cupolas and for the decoration of exterior façades.

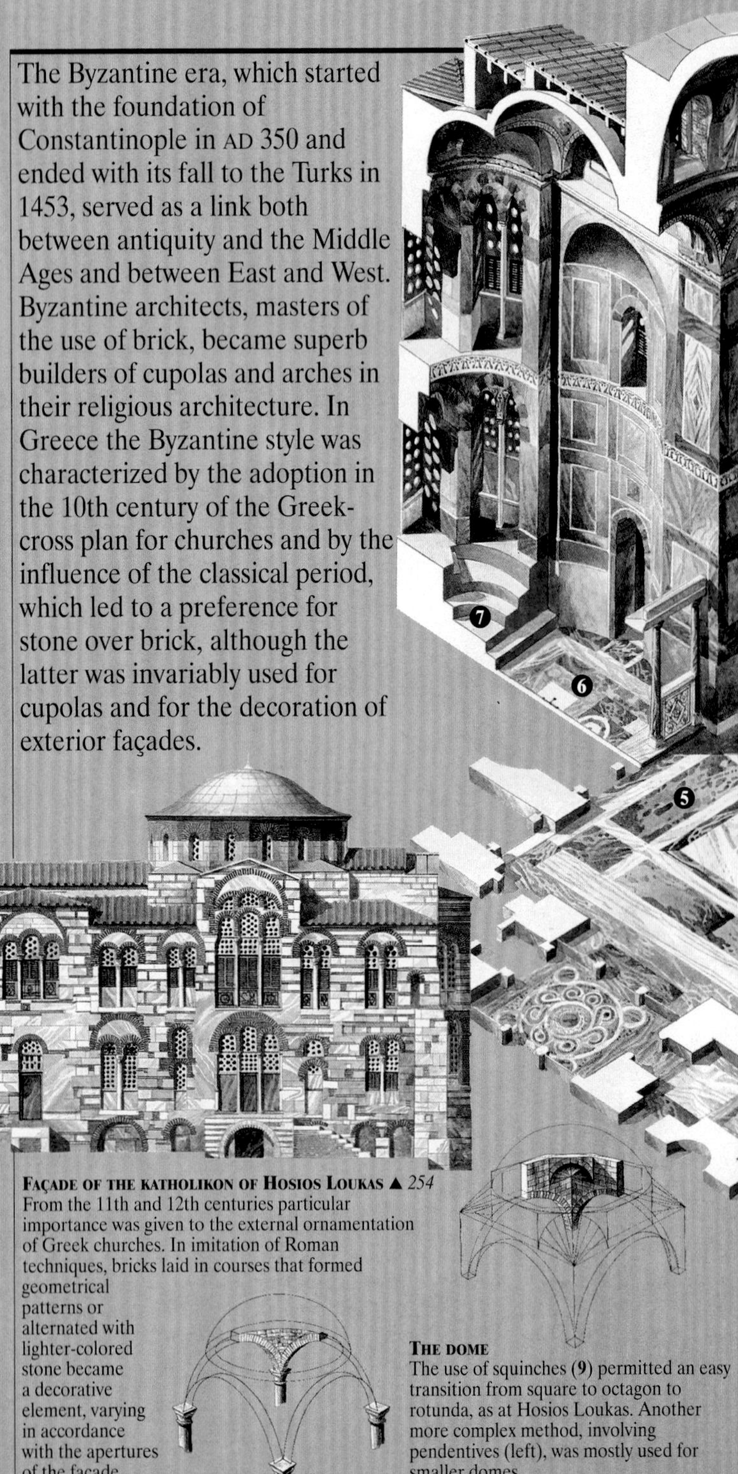

FAÇADE OF THE KATHOLIKON OF HOSIOS LOUKAS ▲ *254*
From the 11th and 12th centuries particular importance was given to the external ornamentation of Greek churches. In imitation of Roman techniques, bricks laid in courses that formed geometrical patterns or alternated with lighter-colored stone became a decorative element, varying in accordance with the apertures of the façade.

THE DOME
The use of squinches (**9**) permitted an easy transition from square to octagon to rotunda, as at Hosios Loukas. Another more complex method, involving pendentives (left), was mostly used for smaller domes.

Mosaics. Cubes of glass paste (*smalto*), colored with metal oxides, were set into a bed of fresh cement. These were often covered with a thin layer of gold or silver leaf, symbolizing eternity, protected by a veneer of glass. The 9th-century mosaics of the dome of the katholikon were damaged in 1593 and replaced by paintings, but the magnificent mosaics of the narthex are still *in situ*.

Frescos. In the painting technique known as *a fresco*, colors were applied to fresh plaster and incorporated into it by the rapid drying process. Like the mosaics, the frescos of the katholikon are painted in a severe, conventional style that has great expressive power.

The katholikon of Hosios Loukas
Greek-cross plan church, 11th century.
1. Narthex (portico or vestibule at the entrance, containing portraits of saints and scenes from the life of Christ.)
2. Tomb
3. Baptistry
4. Philopation
5. Solea (passageway leading to the main entrance)
6. Bema (site of the altar)
7. Conch (apse with shell-shaped vault)
8. Treasury
9. Squinch
10. Dome.

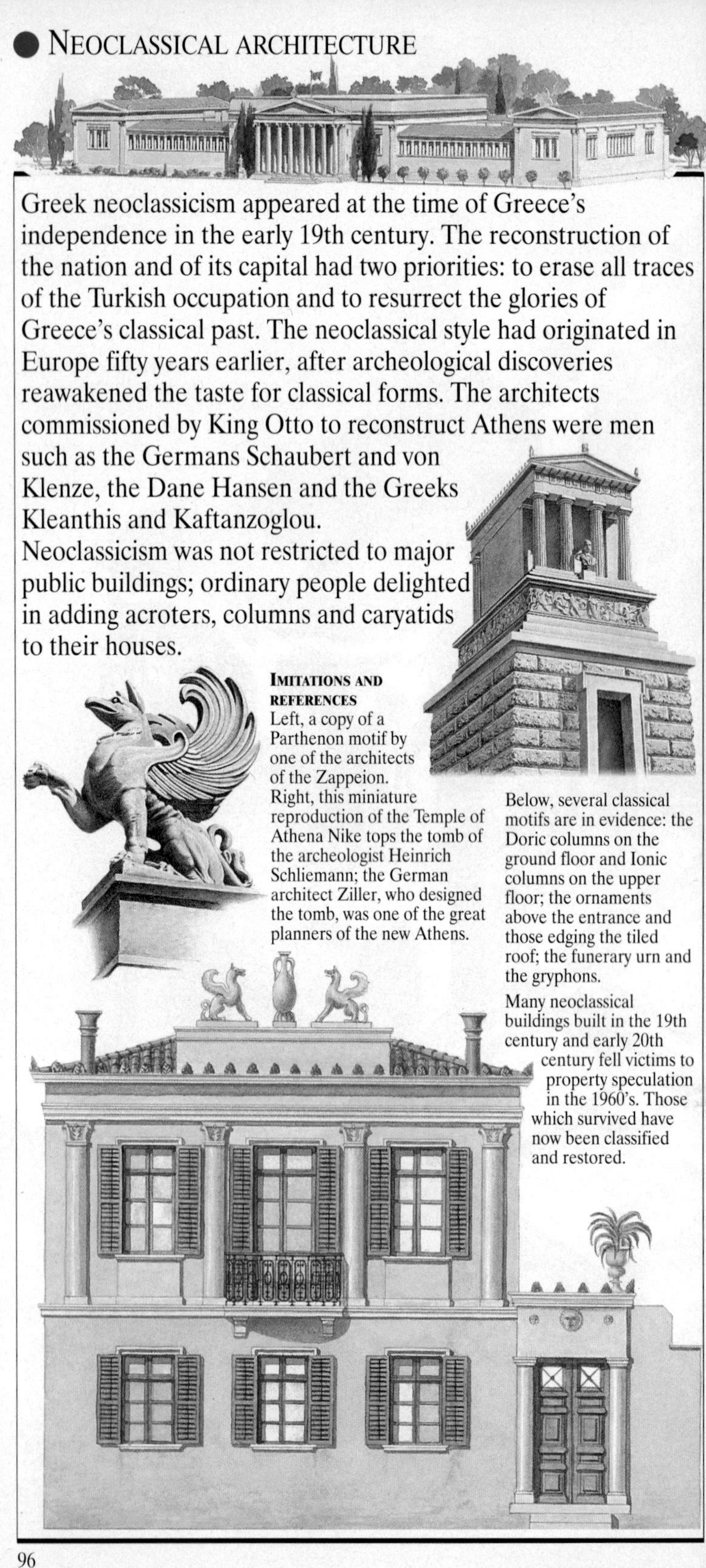

Greek neoclassicism appeared at the time of Greece's independence in the early 19th century. The reconstruction of the nation and of its capital had two priorities: to erase all traces of the Turkish occupation and to resurrect the glories of Greece's classical past. The neoclassical style had originated in Europe fifty years earlier, after archeological discoveries reawakened the taste for classical forms. The architects commissioned by King Otto to reconstruct Athens were men such as the Germans Schaubert and von Klenze, the Dane Hansen and the Greeks Kleanthis and Kaftanzoglou.
Neoclassicism was not restricted to major public buildings; ordinary people delighted in adding acroters, columns and caryatids to their houses.

IMITATIONS AND REFERENCES
Left, a copy of a Parthenon motif by one of the architects of the Zappeion.
Right, this miniature reproduction of the Temple of Athena Nike tops the tomb of the archeologist Heinrich Schliemann; the German architect Ziller, who designed the tomb, was one of the great planners of the new Athens.

Below, several classical motifs are in evidence: the Doric columns on the ground floor and Ionic columns on the upper floor; the ornaments above the entrance and those edging the tiled roof; the funerary urn and the gryphons.
Many neoclassical buildings built in the 19th century and early 20th century fell victims to property speculation in the 1960's. Those which survived have now been classified and restored.

GREECE AS SEEN BY PAINTERS

"BEHOLD WHERE ON THE AEGEAN SHORE A CITY STANDS BUILT NOBLY, PURE THE AIR, AND LIGHT THE SOIL, ATHENS THE EYE OF GREECE, MOTHER OF ARTS AND ELOQUENCE..."

JOHN MILTON, *PARADISE REGAIN'D*

The years 1850 to 1860 saw the appearance of the first artists of modern Greece. At that time European art in general tended to be heavily academic: the unbridled Romanticism of Delacroix was a thing of the past. Greek artists, too, were broadly conservative and most had studied in Munich; they painted grandiloquent pictures in the Western style, favoring battle scenes inspired by the 1821 national uprising, allegorical canvases and interiors and genre scenes, all treated with close attention to detail and no regard at all for social reality.

NICOLAS GHYZIS (1842–1901) reflects an idealized vision of Greece in the late 19th century. His scenes of daily existence, such as *The Children's Betrothal* (2) and *Woman and Child* (3), though purporting to be taken from life, were painstakingly composed in his studio, hence their technical perfection.

THEODORE VRYZAKIS (1814–78) painted pictures glorifying the national uprising (especially military engagements with the Turks), such as *Episode from the War of Independence* (4). His battle scenes and portraits of revolutionary heroes have a certain value as historical documents. Greek painters using the sea as subject matter had a somewhat freer approach, and produced a number of superb seascapes worthy of Bonnington or Courbet.

CONSTANTINE VOLONAKIS (1837–1907), as a young man, was painter to the Imperial Court in Vienna. A great traveler, he painted seascapes (1) reflecting the beauty and serenity of fishing ports and scenes from the lives of fisher folk. His style has much in common with Late Romantic artists, coupled with a perfection of mood reminiscent of Boudin.

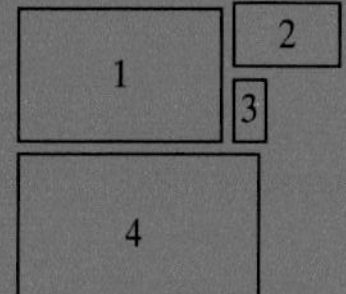

Important changes took place between 1910 and 1920 in the world of Greek art. Greek painting was closely associated with the trends originating in France. **CONSTANTINE PARTHENIS** (1878–1967) exerted great influence on his pupils and friends, among whom were D. Diamantopoulos, Tsarouchis and Ghikas. A number of very different personalities profited directly from the new artistic climate: Photios Kontoglu rediscovered the beauty of the icon, while **YANNIS TSAROUCHIS** (1910–89) in *Neon Café* (below), painted in 1965, deals with the subject matter of ports and cafés in the manner of a naive icon-painter. These artists also had links with other creative fields, mainly theater and architecture. Between the 1930's and the 1960's, just before World War Two and in the period following the Greek Civil War, the development of Greek art was very rapid. N. Bouzianis (who was closely allied to the German Expressionists of the 1930's), Spyropoulos, A. Koutopoulos and Fassianos also contributed, to mention only a few.

"The house, cafés, neighborhoods which I see and where I walk; for years and years I have created you in joy and in sorrows: out of so many circumstances, out of so many things. You have become all feeling for me." Cavafy

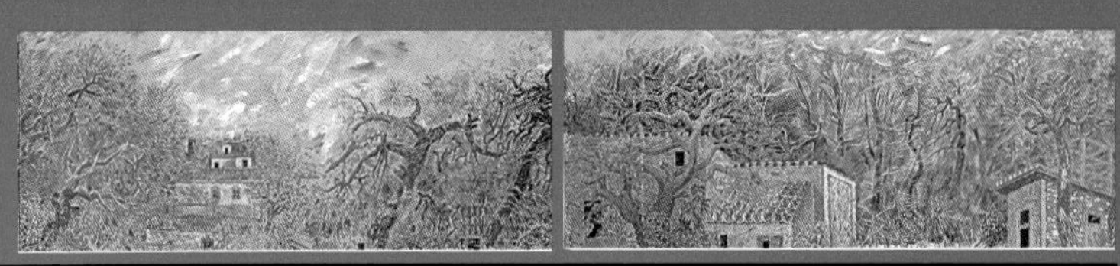

NICO GHIKAS was born in Athens in 1906. He left the city in 1922 to study literature at the Sorbonne, where he attended the Académie Ranson. A man of means and a member of an influential Greek family, Ghikas traveled extensively in France, where he met Pablo Picasso and Henri Matisse on the Côte d'Azur. He acquired an intimate knowledge of Cubism and Fauvism, and was involved in new trends in modern art. Painting in France between 1930 and 1935 represented a totally new departure for young Athenian artists; Ghikas, who was strongly influenced by Picasso, worked on a series of brightly colored canvases, in particular his *Athenian Balcony* (5), painted in 1955. At the same time he suffused his pictures with a peculiarly Greek light, an intense chiaroscuro that was common to many of his contemporaries. Later Ghikas designed costumes and sets for Shakespeare's *As You Like It*, introducing powerful innovations, as did Tsarouchis in the sphere of costume. After 1960 he turned to sculpture and completed a number of imaginary drawings of the poet Cavafy. Ghikas continued to work in oils – for example his *Hydra* (1) and *Kifissia* series (2, 3 and 4) painted in 1973 – and was renowned as one of the greatest teachers at the Athens Polytechnic. Many of his large, subtly composed pictures can now be seen in a room named after him in the Athens Pinacotheca ▲ *228*.

2 3
4
1
5

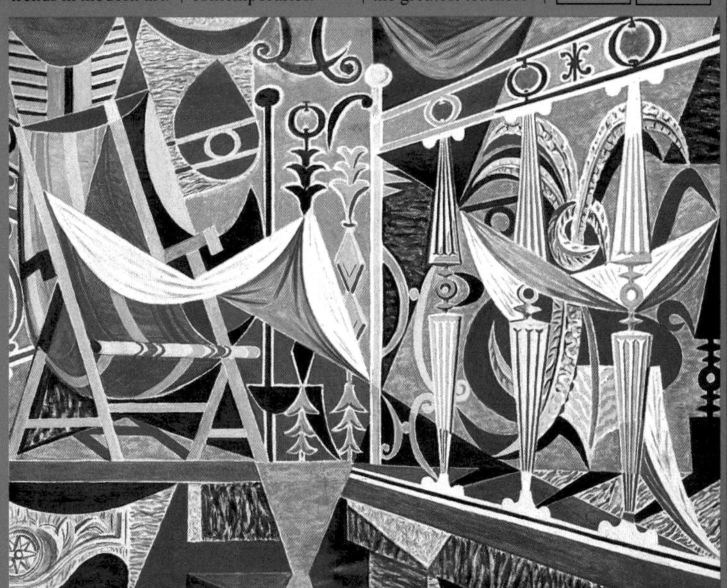

PIERRAKOS – LANDSCAPE AND ICONS

ALKIS PIERRAKOS, who was born in 1920, produced his first pictures at a very early age. Between 1941 and 1944 he began painting marble quarries and stony landscapes, creating light-filled compositions that were a kind of eulogy to the arid land of Attica. Such themes were to become a perennial feature of his work. From 1956 onward he produced a series of *Icons*, with rigid structures and forms echoing traditional Byzantine art, but with very different subject matter. Indeed the hard, grimacing faces in thickly applied polychrome paint are far removed from the iconography of the Orthodox Church, and his subjects (Constantine and Theodora, army colonels, prostitutes) express a contempt for the faith. Nevertheless, the pictures he paints today, such as *Windows* and seascapes, have reverted to the original inspiration of his art, the landscape of Greece. His work has a contained energy, with sensitive, imaginative lines. Thus canvases which at first sight seem to be expressionist and emotional in their view of the world turn out to be a perfect marriage between graphics and color. *Seascape* (1), *The Birds* (2), *Still Life* (3).

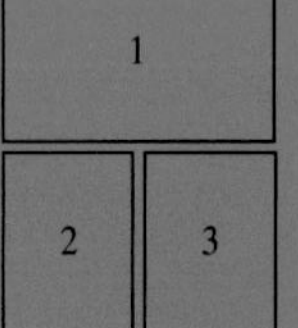

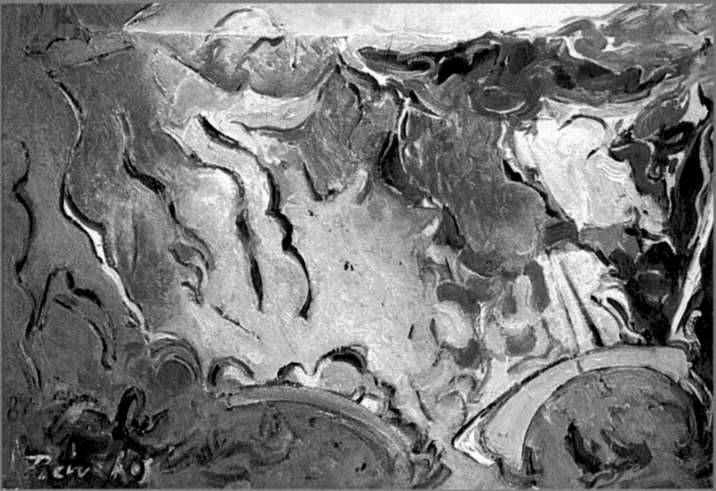

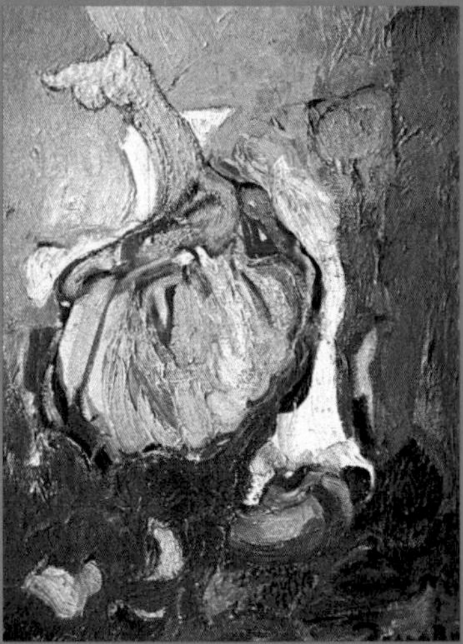

GREECE
AS SEEN BY WRITERS

ANCIENT GLORIES

A DIVINE WORK

In his long political "Ode to Liberty", Percy Bysshe Shelley (1792–1822) devoted the fifth verse to the building of the city of Athens.

"Athens arose: a city such as vision
Builds from the purple crags and silver towers
Of battlemented cloud, as in derision
Of kingliest masonry: the ocean-floors
Pave it; the evening sky pavilions it;
Its portals are inhabited
By thunder-zonèd winds, each head
Within its cloudy wings with sun-fire garlanded, –
A divine work! Athens, diviner yet,
Gleamed with its crest of columns, on the will
Of man, as on a mount of diamond, set;
For thou wert, and thine all-creative skill
Peopled, with forms that mock the eternal dead
In marble immortality, that hill
Which was thine earliest throne and latest oracle."

SELECTED POETRY, ED. NEVILLE ROGERS,
PUB. OXFORD UNIVERSITY PRESS, 1912

THE ACROPOLIS AND THE PARTHENON

Gustave Flaubert (1821–80) wrote to his friend Louis Bouilhet on December 19, 1850, of his first impressions of the city.

"I have been here since yesterday – we are being kept in quarantine until Sunday. I'm reading Herodotus and Thirlwall. The rain falls in torrents, but at least it's warmer here than in Constantinople, where these last few days the snow was covering the houses. I was truly happy yesterday when I caught sight of the Acropolis, shining white in the sun under a sky heavy with clouds. . . .
The Parthenon is the color of brick, with, in places, tones of bitumen and almost of ink. The sun shines on it almost constantly, whatever the weather. It gleams gloriously. Birds come and perch on the dismantled cornice – falcons, crows. The wind blows between the columns; goats browse amid pieces of white marble, fragments that shift under your feet. Here and there, in holes, piles of human bones: reminders of the war. Small Turkish ruins amid the great Greek ruin; and then, in the distance and always, the sea!

Among the pieces of sculpture found on the Acropolis I noticed especially a bas-relief representing a woman fastening her shoe. There remains only a fragment of the torso, just the two breasts, from the base of the neck to above the navel. One of the breasts is draped, the other uncovered. What breasts! Good God! What a breast! It is apple-round, full, abundant, widely spaced from the other; you can feel the weight of it in your hand. Its fecund maternity and its love-sweetness make you swoon. The rain and sun have turned the white marble to yellow, a tawny color, almost like flesh. It is so calm, so noble! It seems about to swell; one feels that the lungs beneath it are about to expand and breathe. How well it wore its sheer pleated drapery! How one would have rolled on it, weeping! How one would have fallen on one's knees before it, hands joined! . . . A little more and I'd have prayed.❞

The Letters of Gustave Flaubert, 1830–57,
Selected, edited and translated by Francis Steegmuller,
pub. Faber & Faber, London, 1981

Ruined sculpture

The Parthenon by moonlight both impressed and unnerved the innocent traveler described by Mark Twain (1835–1910).

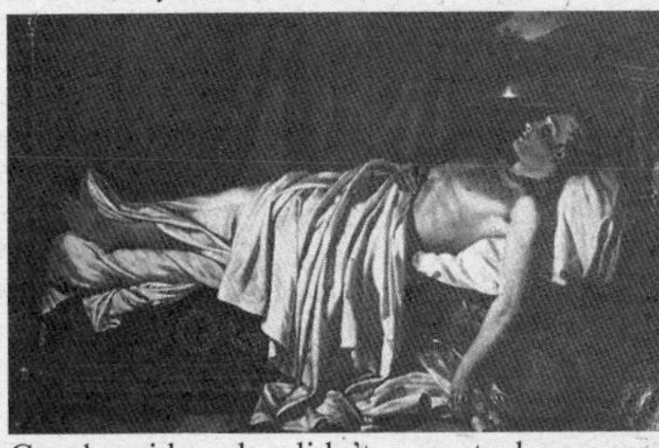

❝We crossed a large court, entered a great door, and stood upon a pavement of purest white marble, deeply worn by foot-prints. Before us, in the flooding moonlight, rose the noblest ruins we ever looked upon – the Propylaea; a small Temple of Minerva; the Temple of Hercules, and the grand Parthenon. (We got these names from the Greek guide, who didn't seem to know more than seven men ought to know.) These edifices were all built of the whitest Pentelican marble, but have a pinkish stain upon them now. Where any part is broken, though, the fracture looks like fine loaf sugar. Six caryatides, or marble women, clad in flowing robes, support the portico of the Temple of Hercules, but the porticos and colonnades of the other structures are formed of massive Doric and Ionic pillars, whose flutings and capitals are still measurably perfect, notwithstanding the centuries that have gone over them and the sieges they have suffered. . . .

Most of the Parthenon's imposing columns are still standing, but the roof is gone. (It was a perfect building two hundred and fifty years ago, when a shell dropped into the Venetian magazine stored here, and the explosion which followed wrecked and unroofed it.)

As we wandered thoughtfully down the length of this stately temple, the scene about us was strangely impressive. Here were floors of vast flags of cut marble, neatly fitted together and perfectly level; cut into this floor were two semi-circular grooves which the casters of the great doors used to traverse; here and there, in lavish profusion, were gleaming white statues of men and women, propped against blocks of marble, some of them armless, some without legs, others headless – but all looking mournful and sentient, and startlingly human! They rose up and confronted the midnight intruder on every side – they stared at him with stony eyes from unlooked-for nooks and recesses; they peered at him over fragmentary heaps far down the desolate corridors; they barred his way in the midst of the broad forum, and solemnly pointed with handless arms the way from the sacred fane; and through the roofless temple the moon looked down, and banded its floor and darkened its scattered fragments and its broken statues with the slanting shadows of its columns.

What a world of ruined sculpture was about us! Stood up in rows – stacked up in piles – scattered broadcast over the wide area of the Acropolis – were hundreds of crippled statues of all sizes and of the most exquisite workmanship; and vast fragments of marble that once belonged to the entablatures, covered with bas-reliefs representing battles and sieges, ships of war with three and four tiers of oars, pageants and processions – everything you could think of. History says that the temples of the Acropolis were filled with the noblest works of Praxiteles and Phidias, and of many a great master in sculpture besides – and surely these elegant fragments attest it.

We walked out into the grass-grown, fragment-strewn court beyond the Parthenon. It startled me, every now and then, to see a stony white face stare suddenly up at me out of the grass with its dead eyes. The place seemed to be alive with ghosts. I half expected to see the Athenian heroes of twenty centuries ago glide out of the shadows and steal into the old temple they knew so well and regarded with such boundless pride. . . .

The full moon was riding high in the cloudless heavens, now. We sauntered carelessly and unthinkingly to the edge of the lofty battlements of the citadel, and looked down – a vision! . . . Athens by moonlight! . . . It lay in the level plain right under our feet – all spread abroad like a picture – and we looked down upon it as we might have looked from a balloon. We saw no semblance of a street, but every house, every window, every clinging vine, every projection was as distinct and sharply marked as if the time were noonday; and yet there was no glare, no glitter, nothing harsh or repulsive – the noiseless city was flooded with the mellowest light that ever streamed from the moon, and seemed like some living creature wrapped in peaceful slumber. On its further side was a little temple, whose delicate pillars and ornamented front glowed with a rich lustre that chained the eye like a spell; and nearer by, the palace of the King reared its creamy walls out of the midst of a great garden of shrubbery that was flecked all over with a random shower of amber lights – a spray of golden sparks that lost their brightness in the glory of the moon, and glinted softly upon the sea of dark foliage like the pallid stars of the milky-way. Overhead the stately columns, majestic still in their ruin – under foot the dreaming city – in the distance the silver sea – not on the broad earth is there another picture half so beautiful!❞

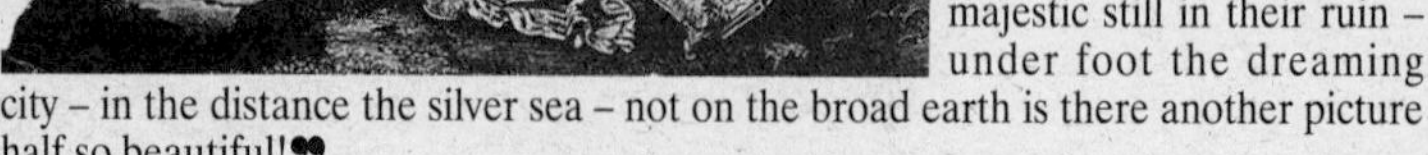

MARK TWAIN, *TRAVELING WITH THE INNOCENTS ABROAD*,
ED. DANIEL MORLEY MCKEITHAN, PUB. UNIV. OF OKLAHOMA PRESS, 1958

DAZZLING WHITE

Edward Lear (1812–1888) wrote to his elder sister Ann in June 1848 of the strong sense of history he perceived in Athens, and the ancient colors.

❝June 3rd, 1848, I have risen as early as I could this morning, & surely never was anything so magnificent as Athens! – far more than I could have had any idea of. The beauty of the temples I well knew from endless drawings – but the immense sweep of plain with exquisitely formed mountains down to the sea – & the manner in which that huge mass of rock – the Acropolis – stands above the modern town with its glittering white marble ruins against the deep blue sky is quite beyond my expectations. The town is all new – but the poorer part of it, what with awnings, & bazaars & figures of all possible kinds is most picturesque. There are some very good shops, & a sort of air of progress about the whole place. The weather is getting rather hot. . . .

“A PLACE WHICH I THINK I PREFER ON THE WHOLE TO ANY I HAVE SEEN.”

LORD BYRON, ON ATHENS, 1810

Sunday, June 4th, Yesterday afternoon we all went to the Acropolis – which is really the most astonishing monument of a great people I have yet seen. Poor old scrubby Rome sinks into nothing by the side of such beautiful magnificence. No words can give any idea of the appearance of such a vast mass of gigantic ruins all of dazzling white marble, of the most exquisite proportions – & overlooking such splendid tracts of landscape. It is difficult to keep away from that part of the city, but unfortunately we are at the other end. The King's palace is a very ugly affair – though built of white marble also. . . .

Today – 8th – has been extremely hot. There is *no* shade whatever – no, not a bush near Athens – & as the roads are very dusty it is not an agreeable residence. The King wears the full Greek dress & rides about often with the Queen. I wish you could see the temple of the Parthenon, or the Acropolis by sunset – I really never saw anything so wonderful. Most of the columns being rusty with age the whole mass becomes like gold & ivory – & the polished white marble pavement is literally blue from the reflection of the sky. You walk about in a wilderness of broken columns – friezes etc. etc. Owls, the bird of Minerva, are extremely common, & come & sit very near me when I draw. . . .

The Areopagus – or Mars hill, where St. Paul spoke – (Acts 17th.) – is a long ridge of rock below the Acropolis – & was once the centre of town – though now only inhabited by sheep & goats. A flight of steps leads to the top & these St. Paul must have ascended – as there is no other way up; the Acropolis, with its temples must have looked much then as it now does, & perhaps no spot in Europe is more interesting.”

EDWARD LEAR, *SELECTED LETTERS*
ED. VIVIEN NOAKES,
PUB. CLARENDON PRESS, OXFORD, 1888

PINKISH BROWN

Evelyn Waugh (1903–66) described the colors of the Acropolis in rather more mundane terms.

“I did not revisit the Tower of Winds or the Temple of Theseus or the Acropolis, and will say nothing about them here, except to remark about the last that it is not 'snow-white,' as I have seen it described by quite responsible observers, but a singularly beautiful tone of very pale pinkish brown; the nearest parallel to it in Nature that I can think of is that of the milder parts of a Stilton cheese into which port has been poured.”

EVELYN WAUGH, *LABELS – A MEDITERRANEAN JOURNEY,*
PUB. DUCKWORTH, 1930

LANDSCAPES

Edmund Wilson (1895–1972) describes the colors of Greece as indefinite and changing.

“It has been shown that the classical Greeks had a rather uncertain sense of color. They used the same word for yellow and green, and they seem to have confused red with purple. It was the Romans who brought color into European poetry with the Italian landscapes of Virgil – as well as the sense of materials, of hardness and tightness and weight, with the marbles and bricks and bronzes that Horace and Virgil both describe in their verse and imitate by its structure. The Greeks lacked this feeling for matter, for their very mountains seem immaterial, and they worked in Pentelican marble, which gives the effect of solidified light. As soon as one arrives in Greece, one understands how a native of this country who had never seen anything else might have had no conception of a world that was painted in definite colors. The olive trees, the pepper trees, the tiny firs are indeterminately blue, green and gray; the yellow of the earth is a neutral tint which is always turning pink or brown, and the pinks and browns themselves sometimes deepen or brighten to red. What the Greeks did have highly developed – besides the architectural sense of proportion – was an appreciation of the light and shade that are the main features of visible Attica. You find it in the choruses of the plays, where things are always darkling or gleaming, and in the settings of Plato’s dialogues, when they take place on sunny days in the shade; and you find it exploited in the most masterly way in the colonnades and porches of the temples. You still have to learn in Athens to appreciate everything in terms of light.”

EDMUND WILSON, *EUROPE WITHOUT BAEDEKER*,
PUB. RUPERT HART-DAVIS, 1967

THE LIGHT

Greek poet and novelist Nikos Kazantzakis (1885–1957) describes the light of his homeland.

“Crowded in among clamoring, sweating, newspaper- and basket-laden householders, I watch Attica slipping away behind me, dematerialized in the light. In every Greek landscape, but even more so here in Attica, the light is the protagonist-hero. The mountains, the valley and the sea form the arena in which he struggles, or the couch on which he reposes. The mountains, the valley, the sea play a secondary role. The light is the resplendent Sober Dionysos who is dismembered and suffers, then rejoins his parts and triumphs. . . .

High noon. The light falls vertically, this is the most Greek of hours. The perfectly classic. A little later the dusk will bring romantic shadows, will envelop the pure, severe nudity of the Greek earth in chiaroscuro effects, and break the steady, certain lines. This meridian sun is the true ancient Greek. Dusk, the night and the moon all belong to the sorceresses of Thessaly and Thrace, and to far-northern romantics.”

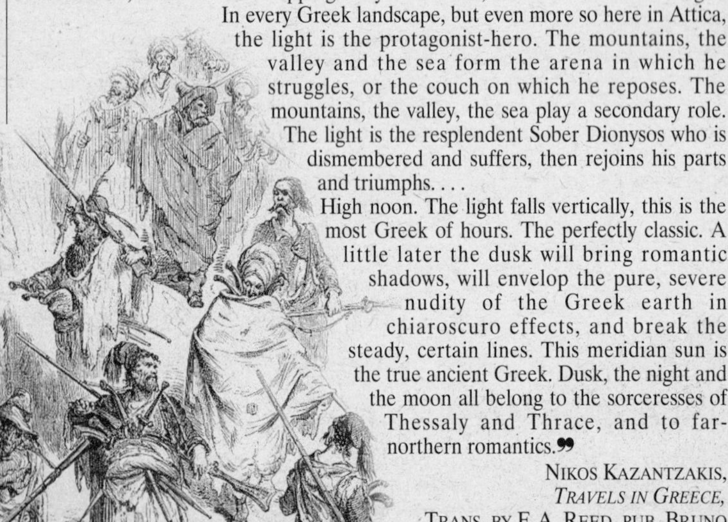

NIKOS KAZANTZAKIS,
TRAVELS IN GREECE,
TRANS. BY F. A. REED, PUB. BRUNO CASSIRER, OXFORD, 1966

Unhappy times

Athenians enslaved

A French naval officer named La Borderie wrote to his mistress in Lyons in 1537 of the misery of the Athenians under Turkish domination.

❝Athens, once worthily called the flower of the world, has now, under heavy servitude, sunk to being the poorest and most miserable of cities. The wonderful buildings and great theaters are ruined, and are turned into small dwellings. The wretched Greeks pay heavy taxes and *haratch.* Every household pays one *soultani* per head, and the Athenians, once considered the noblest inhabitants of Greece, are enslaved and have lost the privileges of their nobility, and are devoted by necessity to manual labor. The great tyrant rules them by arbitrary laws, humbles them by fear, and governs them like slaves. I had only half a day's leave to gratify my curiosity, to see the relics of this once splendid city all grown over with grass. Its size and extent, however, are revealed by traces that remain. I saw one theater that time has not managed to level, supported on marble columns, sixteen on the sides, and six at the ends. The Athenians have turned it into a church of St Andrew, erecting a curved wall inside, that seems of later date.❞

Quoted in Demetrios Sicilianos,
Old and New Athens,
Trans. Robert Liddell, pub. Putnam, 1960

The Republic

The unrest of the years from 1924 to the restoration of the monarchy in 1935 was witnessed by Evelyn Waugh during a visit in January 1927, but does not seem to have disturbed him unduly.

❝We went to the National Museum in the morning and for a walk after luncheon. Wherever we went Greek soldiers appeared and shot at us. There is a nice café called the Pine Tree, underground. They dance Pyrrhic dances there. I get tired of the restaurants where we have our meals. I am afraid I have inherited much of my father's homely sentiments. The truth is that I do not really like being abroad much.❞

The Diaries of Evelyn Waugh,
ed. Michael Davie,
pub. Weidenfeld & Nicolson, 1976

After World War Two

Edmund Wilson describes the post-war shortage of commodities in the Greek capital.

❝In any case, one realizes, as one walks in the streets, that Greece now is really the country where nobody has anything at all. In Italy there are still many commodities that are being produced and sold – striped neckties, pink silk slips and lace brassières, new books in crisp bright covers, perfume and candy and cakes – and that revive some of the brilliance of the shops in places like Milan and Rome. But in Greece there is not much beyond remnants of old stocks that must predate the war, and, in clothing, a scanty supply that only meets rudimentary needs. No woman in the streets wears make-up, and they have only rather dreary cheap dresses, mostly of the national blue; none of the men has a necktie on, even when his shirt collar is buttoned. If you go to a better-class restaurant, you can get little but a slice of fish, a dish of cut-up tomatoes, a bottle of resinated wine and a slice of watermelon. The people are not riding bicycles, as they are in Italy and England; but this fact is due, I am told, not so much to the difficulty of getting them as to the scornful aversion that the Greeks have always felt toward bicycle-riding. They regard it, it seems, as undignified. The one thing that the Athenians have that the Romans and Neapolitans don't have is quite enough light at night. They defended their electric plant and saved it when the Germans were evacuating; and it is very cheerful, coming from cities where the streets are murky and blind, to find Athens twinkling among its hills under the dry clear summer sky.”

EDMUND WILSON, *EUROPE WITHOUT BAEDEKER,*
PUB. RUPERT HART-DAVIS, LONDON 1967

CHANGE

English journalist Dilys Powell also noted the postwar changes in Athens.

“In 1945 I knew what the capital had undergone since I last saw it. But I could not rid myself of my romantic ideas. I still thought of Athens as a place of sun, friendly, elegant, cosmopolitan; a place of chattering cafés, smart parties and sophisticated argument; a place to sit on a summer evening amidst the murmur of crowds and the glimmer of bright dresses. Intellectually I recognized that Greece was living with savaged nerves. Yet I could not bring myself to look on it except as the easy, welcoming country I had known before the war. When I thought of Greece I thought of swimming off hot, voiceless, deserted bays, rousing at dawn to walk all day through mountains, coming at night to a village with the scent of charcoal braziers. I thought, to be honest, of Perachora.

Now everything was changed. I came back to a country full of rage. After the long, cold, hungry war, after the relief of liberation, the Greeks had found themselves in the trap of yet another battle. And it was not their fault; they were sure of this. As a matter of fact, said some of my old friends, it was the fault of the British.”

DILYS POWELL, *AN AFFAIR OF THE HEART,*
PUB. HODDER & STOUGHTON, 1957

"ATHENS, THE MARVELLOUS CITY THAT IN ALL THINGS RAN AHEAD OF HER ENVIOUS AND SULLEN CONTEMPORARIES."

THOMAS DE QUINCEY

FOOD AND DRINK

A COMFORTABLE LIFESTYLE

The twenty-two-year-old Lord Byron (1788–1824) was largely content with his domestic arrangements in Athens during his visit in January 1811.

❝I am still in Athens making little tours to Marathon, Sunium, the top of Hymettus, and the Morea occasionally to diversify the season . . . I am living in the Capuchin Convent, Hymettus before me, the Acropolis behind, the Temple of Jove to my right, the Stadium in front, the town to the left; eh, Sir, there's a situation, there's your picturesque! nothing like that, Sir, in Lunnun, no not even the Mansion House. And I feed upon Woodcocks and Red Mullet every day, and I have three horses (one a present from the Pasha of the Morea), and I ride to Piraeus, and Phalerum, and Munychia, which however don't look quite so magnificent after the harbours of Cadiz, Lisbon, Constantinople and Gibraltar, not forgetting Malta. I wish to be sure I had a few books, one's own works for instance, any damned nonsense on a long Evening.❞

LORD BYRON'S CORRESPONDENCE,
ED. JOHN MURRAY, PUB. JOHN MURRAY, 1922

WINE AND HONEY

E. D. Clarke (1769–1822) was not so happy with the food, complaining particularly about Hymettus honey and retsina.

❝We dined with Signor *Lusieri* and the artists who were his fellow-labourers in the *Acropolis*, upon a boiled kid and some rice. Honey from Mount *Hymettus* was served, of such extraordinary toughness and consistency, although quite transparent, that the dish containing it might be turned with its bottom upwards without spilling a drop; and the surface of it might also be indented with the edge of a knife, yielding to the impression without separation, like a mass of dough. As an article of food, it is reckoned very heating; and persons who eat much of it are liable to fever. We tasted the wine of *Athens*, which is unpleasant to those who are not accustomed to it, from the quantity of resin and lime infused as substitutes for brandy.❞

E. D. CLARKE,
TRAVELS IN VARIOUS COUNTRIES OF EUROPE AND ASIA, VOL. VI,
PUB. T. CADELL & W. DAVIES, 1818

"THE GREEK RITZ"

English composer and suffragette Ethel Smyth (1858–1944) toured Greece between March and May 1925, and stayed in a hotel in Karditza she called "the Greek Ritz".

❝The famous hotel turned out to be a pretentious, plush-lined, stucco palace covered with appalling decorative *motifs* and crowned by a gigantic dome.

Afternoon tea, served in a huge bare café to the sound of astonishing fireworks executed on the cracked piano by a stray traveller, filled us with hope, for it consisted of butter – a thing almost unknown outside Athens – marmalade, and white bread. On the other hand, the bedrooms, each furnished with two beds, one chair, and scarcely any other furniture, rather shook us. We had ordered dinner for 7pm in the restaurant, which turned out to be another huge room just like the café, only be-hung with brewers' advertisements and mercifully *minus* piano. A wait of forty-five minutes elapsed, during which time all we could do was begin on a bottle of really good wine; no bread, no bell, no response to our spirit-rappings; only two men sipping beer at a table a mile off, and noting our fruitless efforts to attract attention with surprise and pity. At last appeared odd hunks of the eternal lamb, and instead of potatoes and greens, a vegetable-dish full of hot buttered toast; and that was the whole dinner at this Greek Ritz.❞

ETHEL SMYTH, *A THREE-LEGGED TOUR IN GREECE*,
PUB. WILLIAM HEINEMANN LTD, 1927

TAVERNAS

Peter Mayne is much more complimentary about Greek food, and wrote lyrically about a meal at Costi's restaurant in Athens, calling it "excellent" and "a positive pleasure". Here he describes a typical taverna.

❝Rents are lower underground and the cellar could be in almost any little side-street of Omonia Square at the wrong end of Athens – or even off Kolonaki Square at the elegant right end of Athens, as far as that goes. But from the outside in the street, standing at the top of the stone steps that lead down to the cellar, very little of it would be visible – only the legs of men sitting round tables. It is an eating-place, primarily: a 'taverna' – though not a taverna in the now-fashionable sense of the term, all spruced up and done over, where visitors from abroad could drop in for an evening of local colour. This one, and dozens of others like it, is where people try to feed for seven or eight drachmas a time, keeping something in hand for more wine. It would probably be bean soup, with plenty of garlic and olive oil in the preparation of it, or perhaps stewed octopus, and bread of course. Possibly there would be a little of that sheep's-milk cheese for which Mount Parnassus is famous – Feta. Or else a cabbage salad. The wine is *retsina*, the resinated wine of the people. Barrels of it on racks line one side of the cellar. There is a thing in the corner like a collapsed summer-house with a kitchen stove visible through the glass panes, also an array of big copper saucepans with food. A conical chimney over all this takes some of the fumes away. The lighting is the cruel and brilliant white of neon tubes, the floor is cracked concrete, there is a pick-up and radio, the latter dressed in a little frilly cretonne cover to conceal the tuning knobs, and it is difficult to guess why. The tables are apt to have covers of American cloth patterned with roses and the men's feet under them are heavy and for the most part down at heel. There may be a woman or two in the place, a man may have brought his wife or his fiancée for example, but if so then she sits with her eyes commendably downcast, picking at her food as if she were not hungry at all. Sometimes she may lean her head against the man's shoulder, formally romantic. But it is not boots or American cloth roses or formal romance that cause the stranger to stop dead in his tracks and stare down into the cellar: it is the rippling, metallic, enveloping, quicksilver music of the bouzouki, flowing over everything and up the stone steps and out into the street to drag men in by the ears. It was so strange to mine when first I heard it that it took me weeks before I could distinguish the rhythms and succumbed to them.❞

PETER MAYNE, *THE PRIVATE SEA*,
PUB. JOHN MURRAY, 1958

NIGHTLIFE

Evelyn Waugh sampled the delights of several different kinds of clubs.

❝We went back to the *Stella* for dinner and then returned to see the night life. First we went to an underground café decorated with pseudo-Russian frescoes. Here we saw most of the English colony, engaged in those fervent intrigues, part social, part political, part personal, which embellish and enrich Athenian life more than that of any capital in Europe. But the entertainment was confined to one pianist in Georgian peasant dress. We asked if there was to be no cabaret. 'Alas,' said the manageress. 'Not to-night. Last night there was a German gentleman here, and he bit the girls so terribly in the legs that to-night they say they will not dance!' From there we went to the Folies Bergère, which was very chic and Parisian; the waiter tried to induce us to order champagne, and a Hungarian Jewess performed Oriental dances in a Chu-Chin-Chow slave market costume, modestly supplemented with pink cotton tights. Mark's boredom soon became uncontrollable, so we called for our bill, paid them half what they demanded (which they accepted with every manifestation of gratitude), and left. 
We walked across the gardens to the poorer part of the town. Of the many smells of Athens two seem to me the most characteristic – that of garlic, bold and deadly like acetylene gas, and that of dust, soft and warm and caressing like tweed. It was in this dusty smell that we walked in the garden, but garlic met us at the bottom of the steps which led from the street to the door of the Bar Thellatoë; it was garlic sweetened, however, by the savour of roast lamb. There were two lambs impaled horizontally on spits, sizzling over an open charcoal fire. The atmosphere was one of Dickensian conviviality. Only men were present, most of them peasants come up from the country for the night. They all smiled greetings to us, and one of them sent three mugs of beer across to our table. This began a tremendous round of ceremonious health-drinking which was still going on by the time we left. It is the commendable practice of the Greeks never to serve drink without food, usually a little bit of garlic sausage, or bad ham on the end of a match; these appear in little saucers, and our table was soon strewn with them.
Two men in the corner were playing guitars of a kind, and others were dancing, with very severe expressions on their faces but a complete lack of self-consciousness. They were Pyrrhic dances of indefinable antiquity. Four of them danced together, going through the various figures with great solemnity. If one of them made a false move it was as though he had dropped a catch in an English cricket match; they accepted his apologies in as sporting a spirit as they could assume, but it clearly was a grave wrong, not lightly to be dismissed or expiated except by prodigies of accuracy in the future.❞

EVELYN WAUGH, *LABELS – A MEDITERRANEAN JOURNEY*,
PUB. DUCKWORTH, 1930

SELF-INDULGENCE

Athenian writer Katsimbalis is described by Henry Miller (1891–1980) eating dinner at a taverna in Piraeus.

❝*The food* . . . food was something he was passionate about. He had been enjoying good food since childhood and I guess he will go on enjoying it until he dies. His father had been a great gourmet and Katsimbalis, though perhaps lacking some of his father's sensual refinements and accomplishments, was following the family tradition. Between great carnivorous gulps of food he would pound his chest like a gorilla before washing it down with a hogshead of *rezina*. He had drunk a lot of *rezina* in his time: he said it was good for one, good for the kidneys, good for the liver, good for the lungs, good for the bowels and for the mind, good for everything. Everything he took into his system was good, whether it was poison or ambrosia. He didn't believe in moderation nor good sense nor anything that was inhibitory. He believed in going the whole hog and then taking your punishment. There were a lot of things he couldn't do any more – the war had bunged him up a bit. But despite the bad arm, the dislocated knee, the damaged eye, the disorganized liver, the rheumatic twinges, the arthritic disturbances, the migraine, the dizziness and God knows what, what was left of the catastrophe was alive and flourishing like a smoking dung-heap. He could galvanize the dead with his talk. It was a sort of devouring process: when he described a place he ate into it, like a goat attacking a carpet.❞

HENRY MILLER, *THE COLOSSUS OF MAROUSSI*,
PUB. SECKER & WARBURG, 1942

ANTIQUITIES

IN ATHENS

Ethel Smyth found the masterpieces in Greek museums very moving but was disturbed by their organization.

❝The least expert haunter of such places must surely feel the difference between other museums and those of Athens, which contain hardly anything but masterpieces exhumed on or near the spot where they took life. You may not be a connoisseur, but in presence of original marbles undishonoured by the proximity of even excellent copies, your eye becomes cleansed and sharpened, and you see as you never saw before. Nothing, I think, can wrench one more violently out of the present than that roomful of archaic Athena statues, high-bosomed and inscrutably smiling, now mere museum pieces on the Acropolis where once they fashioned destiny. Surely John Knox himself would shrink from the thought of the stone company on the roof of St. John Lateran coming to be nothing but specimens of

“The Greeks are strong, & skilful to their strength,
Fierce to their skill and to their fiercenesse Valiant.”

William Shakespeare,
Troilus and Cressida, c. 1601–2

Christian sculpture in some collection in the heart of Africa, or wherever the next civilisation is going to spring up! There has been much discussion as to whether these votive statues represent the goddess or the worshipper, but as the disagreement of doctors is unanimity compared to that of archaeologists, one is free to adopt the theory one prefers. In any case the plight of dethroned Athena poignantly affected E. and me.

The national indifference to organisation is nowhere more manifest than in these magnificent museums, where the insane numbering of the exhibits seriously interferes with one's pleasure. For instance, the numbers on a given shelf or wall run 1325, 72, 125, 1, 1470, and so on; and as in such poor catalogues as there are nothing is put down numerically, and as they shift the exhibits from room to room every three months or so, often giving two numbers to each, the result on the temper of the painstaking and earnest-minded admirer of the beautiful can be imagined. It is provoking, too, that these cool resorts should be closed, as are all the shops, between twelve and three – just the time when no one is in the mood for constitutionals.”

Ethel Smyth, *A Three-legged Tour in Greece*,
pub. William Heinemann Ltd, 1927

Care and custody

Virginia Woolf (1882–1941) noted in her diary that the Greeks should take better care of their inheritances.

“We went to the hill which the driver called Phillipappos [Philopappos], all in one gulp, but it was wired off, & we therefore turned back & went on to the theatre [of Dionysos], with its curved marble seats each cut with the name of a priest seat holder as they stick cards on the boxes at Covent Garden. One, the pawed one, the lion one, was for the priest of Dionysos, & had a carving of goats prancing & vines pendant. Here L. sat & we said that Sophocles Euripides and Aristophanes must have sat here & seen – Anyhow the hills were before them, as before us. And if the 2000 years have laid a few light rubbishy stucco houses on the earth, in the way, very little has been done to damage the view – nothing solid & immense & lasting has been built. Poverty & war & misery have prevented any obliteration – here or elsewhere. Indeed one might ask for more care, & more custody, not less. This afternoon the Greek ragamuffin boys were shying stones at a marble ruined arch, & pitting it, so that in some years it will be irrecoverably damaged. And the graves are nettled, tin-canned, dirty, dissolute, though the Greeks made the tombs with their own hands – no the land is too exhausted even to guard its own interests any longer – no doubt Lord Elgin's excuse for stealing the statues from the Parthenon & the pillars from the tomb of Agamemnon at Mycenae.”

The Diary of Virginia Woolf,
ed. Anne Oliver Bell
with Andrew McNeillie,
pub. Harcourt Brace Jovanovich, 1982

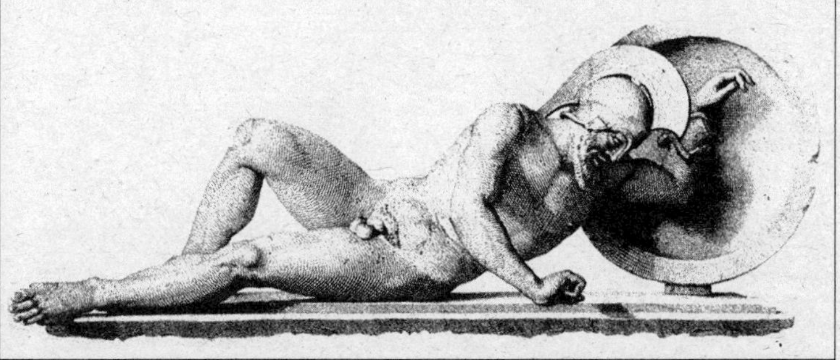

THE METEORA

Eric Newby (b. 1919) remarks on another Greek antiquity which was acquired for the British Museum in London.

❝Of all the strange, exotic and outlandish sights to be seen in any of the lands bordering on the Mediterranean few have created a greater impression on travellers than the astonishing rock formations of various shapes and sizes that soar into the air in closely massed clumps above the valley of the River Peneus near the place where it emerges into the Thessalian Plain from the gorges of the Pindus in what is still the territory of the Vlachs.

The majority of these columns, pilasters, stalagmites, giant mushrooms, needles, pinnacles, islands, spikes, cylinders, drums, stacks, obelisks and tusks, which are just a few of the similes that have been attributed to them, were made more remarkable by the fact that the largest number of them, and the most inaccessible, had monasteries built on them, to which there was no access except by rope, drawbridge or ladder and, in the earliest times, by scaffolding pegged to the rock.

'Twelve sheets would not contain all the wonders of Meteora, nor convey to you an idea of the surprise and pleasure which I felt in beholding these curious monasteries planted like eagles' nests, on the summits of high and pointed rocks,' wrote the architect, traveller and explorer of remote and wild places, Charles Robert Cockerell, on a journey which off and on kept him in the Mediterranean lands for seven years, in the course of which, among other notable works of ancient art, he discovered the reliefs forming the frieze of the temple of Apollo in Arcadia, which was bought by the British Government and now forms one of the more spectacular adornments of the British Museum.❞

ERIC NEWBY, *ON THE SHORES OF THE MEDITERRANEAN,*
PUB. HARVILL PRESS, 1984

CITY LIFE

INVADERS

English writer Robert Byron (1905–41) details the perils of life in an Athenian apartment in high summer.

❝Howe's flat, situate in a basement, was cool even in the days that followed – the August tail of the hottest summer within living memory. At first I lay prostrate in the breeze of a fan, unable to move till the evening. At the back, a vine-covered courtyard gave access to numerous other households, whose washing and common

idiot enlivened the scene. Lurked also, in its recesses, a tribe of lean and tawny cats, who came speeding day and night through the open doors and windows in horrible battle. Heedless of ground glass, arsenic, and entanglements of electric wires, their objective was the kitchen, where platters, cups, and lids of casseroles were flung remorselessly to the floor in their efforts to disinter the few provisions we could afford. Such was the savagery of their onslaughts that every night we stealthily deposited the more decomposed, and therefore magnetic, of the day's refuse in a near-by street. To these enemies were added gigantic insects, an inch and a half long, and clad in orange armour, that emerged from every crack in the plaster, rendering each doze and bath a period of suspense.❞

ROBERT BYRON, *THE STATION,*
PUB. DUCKWORTH, 1931

CATS

English travel writer Patrick Leigh-Fermor (b. 1915) observed a creature of habit.

❝The cats of Athens, like the citizens, are very intelligent. Just after the war I used to eat almost every night in an open-air taverna in the Plaka. One end of the garden was separated by a high wall from an outdoor cinema, and at the same moment every night, a huge black and white tom-cat stalked over the tiles to sit with his back towards us on this wall, intent and immobile except for the slow rhythmic sway of his hanging tail. After exactly five minutes he would saunter away again over the roofs. The waiter's verdict on this procedure was obviously correct: 'He comes for the Mickey Mouse every night,' he explained. 'You could set your watch by him.'❞

PATRICK LEIGH-FERMOR, *MANI – TRAVELS IN THE SOUTHERN PELOPONNESE,*
PUB. JOHN MURRAY, 1958

FISHING

Virginia Woolf describes a trip to the island of Aegina in April 1932.

❝Oh the rain, the rain! That was the next day at Aegina. That lovely shelving island with the baked narrow path, the sea & the beach, the little pink & yellow houses, the thyme, the steep hillside, the Temple, skeletal, dominant, the bays flowing filled with sea – all this was nothing but chill, mist, rain, Americans clustering round a thin professor; & we cowering under a pine tree which let the rain on us. Even so – Roger said awfully swell; this is superb – a sandstone temple better than Sunium. Marvellous what genius can do in a little space – here's the perfectly moving proportions – & the rain drove us down to our boat as soon as we could. They had caught red fish & octopus. How? Well they put onions, bread & so on down, & the fish settle on them, then they drop a charge & pouf! – it goes up like that, & the fish come to the top dead, & they spear them. It's not allowed. But nobody can see you, round there. Such was the account given by the stoker with the lovely Greek smile – the smile the muleteers have & the taximen. For R. & M. were mounted, & very queer they looked, jolting up the hill – the polie makria [*far distant*] hill, as the bright faced girl called it. For the people are desperately poor, & come, offering flowers, & are given the remains of lunch.❞

THE DIARY OF VIRGINIA WOOLF,
ED. ANNE OLIVER BELL WITH ANDREW MCNEILLIE,
PUB. HARCOURT BRACE JOVANOVICH, 1982

STREET CRIERS

Back in Athens, Robert Byron writes about the noise of the streets.

“In the narrow Athenian streets, every doorstep and lintel of Pentelic marble, every cornice serrated with the acroteria that have descended uninterrupted from before Christ to the meanest hovel of the 20th century, where is Europe? Before the sun is up the vendors are about, uttering the ‘cries of Athens’ in the piercing semi-tones of a people who, like the Jews, are of no continent:
‘Figs, fresh figs!’
‘Pots and casseroles!’
‘I buy old boo-oots!’
‘Chairs to mend!’
‘Lovely lace one drachma an ell!’
‘Ice! I-ice!’
Every morning at eight o’clock the ice-man delivered his block. And, as he put it in the chest, still, almost beneath his breath, he wailed the chant, ‘Ice! I-ice – Π∂gos, o Π∂gos,’ as though mesmerised with the beauty of his calling.”

ROBERT BYRON, *THE STATION,*
PUB. DUCKWORTH, 1931

THE GREEK CHARACTER

Henry Miller observed the people as he walked around the Zapion.

“Seeing lovers sitting there in the dark drinking water, sitting there in peace and quiet and talking in low tones, gave me a wonderful feeling about the Greek character. The dust, the heat, the poverty, the bareness, the containedness of the people, and the water everywhere in little tumblers standing between the quiet, peaceful couples, gave me the feeling that there was something holy about the place, something nourishing and sustaining. I walked about enchanted on this first night in the Zapion. It remains in my memory like no other park I have known. It is the quintessence of park, the thing one feels sometimes in looking at a canvas or dreaming of a place you’d like to be in and never find. It is lovely in the morning, too, as I was to discover. But at night, coming upon it from nowhere, feeling the hard dirt under your feet and hearing a buzz of language which is altogether unfamiliar to you, it is magical – and it is more magical to me perhaps because I think of it as filled with the poorest people in the world, and the gentlest. I am glad I arrived in Athens during that incredible heat wave, glad I saw it under the worst conditions. I felt the naked strength of the people, their purity, their nobility, their resignation. I saw their children, a sight which warmed me, because coming from France it was as if children were missing from the world, as if they were not being born any more. I saw people in rags, and that was cleansing too. The Greek knows how to live with his rags: they don’t utterly degrade and befoul him as in other countries I have visited.”

HENRY MILLER, *THE COLOSSUS OF MAROUSSI,*
PUB. SECKER & WARBURG, 1942

THE FACE OF GREECE

Nikos Kazantzakis sees the imprint of history on the people of today.

“The face of Greece is a palimpsest bearing twelve successive inscriptions: Contemporary; the period of 1821; the Turkish yoke; the Frankish sway; the Byzantine; the Roman; the Hellenistic epoch; the Aegean; and the Stone Age.
Pause on a patch of Greek earth and anguish overcomes you. It is a deep, twelve-leveled tomb, from which voices rise up calling to you. Which voice should you choose? Every voice, every spirit longs for its body; your heart is shaken and cannot decide. For a Greek, the journey through Greece is a fascinating, exhausting ordeal.”

NIKOS KAZANTZAKIS, *TRAVELS IN GREECE,*
TRANS. F.A. REED, PUB. BRUNO CASSIRER, OXFORD, 1966

Itineraries

▲ The Acropolis.

▼ Athens (center, the Zappeion and Olympieion).

▼ Aerial view of the port of Pira

▲ Basketmaker near the Church of the Taxiarchs, Plaka.

▲ Bric-a-brac dealers, Avicinas Square.

▼ Fish stall, Athinas Market.

▲ Antique dealer, Avicinas Square, Monastiraki.

▲ Shoe vendor, Plaka.

▼ Lottery enthusiast

▲ Monastery of Ioannis Prodromos, Arcadia.

▲ Fortress of Acrocorinth.

▼ Mist

THE ACROPOLIS

▲ ATHENS

1. SALAMIS
2. ASPROPYRGOS
3. DAPHNI
4. PIRAEUS
5. CENTRAL PORT AREA
6. NAVAL MUSEUM
7. MOUNT PARNES
8. AKHARNAI
9. NORTH STATION AND SOUTH STATION
10. AGORA
11. OMONOIA SQUARE
12. ACROPOLIS
13. PLAKA
14. SYNTAGMA SQUARE
15. MOUNT LYCABETTUS
16. MONUMENT OF PHILOPAPPOS
17. PANATHENAIC STADIUM
18. KIFISSIA
19. KAISARIANI
20. MOUNT HYMETTUS
21. AIRPORT

EUBOEA
GULF OF NOTIOS EVOIKOS
18
15
9
11
10
12
13
14
17
16
19
20
21
SARONIC GULF

ORIGINS

Archeologists have uncovered house foundations, wells, tombs and pottery indicating that the Acropolis and its slopes were inhabited throughout the Bronze Age (3000–1125 BC) until the beginnings of recorded history. During the ascendancy of the Mycenean civilization (c. 1500–1125 BC) the kings of Athens occupied a palace inside a ring of fortifications.

THE PANATHENAIC FESTIVALS. During the Mycenean era the people of Attica began to celebrate the Panathenaic festivals in honor of Athena. There were major and minor events of this kind; the minor ones took place every three years on May 21, while the major ones were held every four years. In general this festival remained the principal public celebration in Greece until the end of antiquity. Its climax was a procession which began at the outer Kerameikos and crossed the Dipylon, the inner Kerameikos and the Agora before ascending the west side of the Acropolis, where it paused for a while. During the festival a *peplos* (tunic) woven by a group of young Athenian girls during the previous year – described by Euripides as the "saffron-tinted veil of Athena in her gorgeous chariot" – was hoisted to the masthead of a float so the crowd could see it.

THE OWL OF ATHENA
"To carry owls to Athens" was a well-known proverb among the ancient Greeks, an owl being the emblem of Athens. People came from all over Attica to pay homage to the goddess. The olive branch symbolized the region's greatest source of wealth.

INACOTHECA
HELLENISTIC PEDESTAL
SANCTUARY OF ARTEMIS BRAURONIA
PROPYLAEA
TEMPLE OF ATHENA NIKE
BEULÉ GATE

The float was then moved on hidden wheels to the Areopagus, where the *peplos* was taken down by girls and carried to the Parthenon. The final stage of the procession led along the Sacred Way. The frieze that decorated the upper part of the *cella* of the Parthenon ● *88* illustrated this procession. After the abolition of the monarchy the seat of the government was transferred to the lower city of Athens, and the Acropolis was abandoned to the sanctuaries of Athena. The most ancient monuments there date back to the Archaic era (700–480 BC), by the end of which Athens had gained primacy over the other city-states of Greece, having managed to persuade the Hellenes to defend their liberty against the Persian invasions between 490 and 480–479 BC ● *45*. During the Second Persian War the Athenians abandoned their city to the invaders, who destroyed the sanctuaries of the Acropolis.

PERICLES' ACROPOLIS. In 447 BC Phidias was commissioned by Pericles to reconstruct the buildings on the Acropolis. He formed a team of architects, sculptors, painters and artists and worked out a design for the Parthenon, which was built between 447 and 432 BC. Work on Pericles' Propylaea (entrance porticos) was begun in 437, but was interrupted by the Peloponnesian War in 432. Although the Athenians

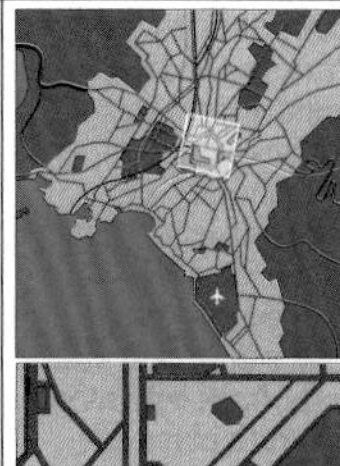

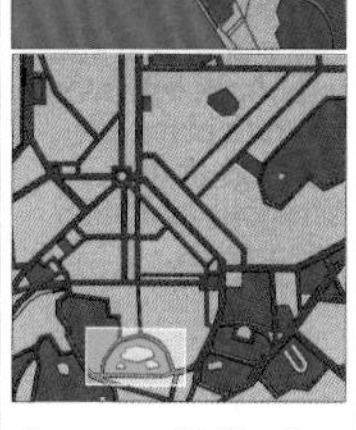

Half a day

THE ACROPOLIS
These drawings by Marcel Lambert illustrate the monuments "side by side as they were formerly, on their different levels." By including both the details and the overall plan, he sought to construct a complete reference for the Parthenon. Like all the other architects of his time, Lambert affirmed that "the Parthenon offers a chance to study all the principles which make Greek architecture the most perfect in the world." The first cross-section shows the restored Acropolis; the second (on the same east-west axis) shows the Acropolis in 1877.

PLAN OF ATHENS
Prior to the 17th century drawings of Athens were rudimentary and often misleading. The travelers of the late 17th century were better informed and came back with more accurate plans and drawings of the Acropolis and other monuments.

BOMBARDMENT OF THE ACROPOLIS
Vernedon left this record of the bombardment by the Venetian army on September 26, 1687. The explosion destroyed half the Parthenon, knocking down the roof and opening a breach between the two pediments.

THE TURKISH OCCUPATION
The Acropolis was used as the headquarters of the Turkish governor, and houses were built there for Ottoman soldiers and their families.

eventually converted the Acropolis into a fortress following the invasion of the Goths in AD 267, the Parthenon remained a temple until the 6th century AD, at which time it became a church dedicated to the Virgin.

THE ARCHEOLOGICAL SITE

The Sacred Way, a footpath punctuated by steps, leads to the site's main entrance. This is the Beulé Gate, named for the French archeologist Ernest Beulé, who discovered it buried under a Turkish bastion in 1852. It consists of two large towers on either side of a gate, and its axis is aligned with the Propylaea, the monumental classical entrance to the Acropolis. The Beulé Gate was probably erected by the Byzantines following the sack of Athens by the Heruli, a Germanic tribe, in AD 267 ● *47*. Beyond the Beulé Gate a broad stairway, built by the Romans in the 3rd century AD, leads to the Propylaea. The Temple of Athena Nike stands on a platform at the southwest corner of the plateau, to the right of the steps.

"WE SHALL STORE IT IN THE ACROPOLIS, UNDER SEAL, JUST AS THEY STORE GOLD."

PLATO

THE MONUMENT OF AGRIPPA. The plinth of the Monument of Agrippa is of blue-grey Hymettus marble. The marks at the top of the plinth show how it was crowned by different quadrigas on two separate occasions. The monument was originally placed here in 178 BC by King Eumenes II of Pergamum and his brother Attalos, to commemorate their winning of a chariot race at the Panathenaic Games that year. Their quadriga was eventually supplanted by statues of Antony and Cleopatra in 39 BC. Shortly after, Antony and the Egyptian queen were defeated at Actium by Octavian. When the latter became Emperor, under the name of Augustus, he made Agrippa his chief minister; accordingly a statue, probably mounted on a bronze chariot, was erected here in his honor in 27 BC. Although the inscription is difficult to decipher today, it was copied earlier by Stuart. It reads: "The people give honor to their benefactor, Marcus Agrippa, son of Lucius."

In 1492 Hartmann Schedel described Athens in his *Liber Chronicarum* as "an unexceptional city whose name he did not rightly know"; in an engraving (left) he called it Setines.

FAUVEL, BY DUPRÉ
Fauvel, antiquarian and French consul to Athens, collaborated on Choiseul-Gouffier's *Voyage pittoresque de la Grèce*. His house, which lay between the Theseion and the Stoa of Attalos, had a view of the Acropolis.

THE TEMPLE OF ATHENA NIKE, OR NIKE APTERA
The platform of the temple is reached by way of the south wing of the Propylaea. Nike, the personification of Victory, was at first represented as a figure in flight. When the Athenians assimilated their religion with that of their protectress they called her Athena Nike, but since the goddess had never been represented with wings she became Nike Aptera (Wingless Victory). Wags sometimes claim that the Athenians took away the wings of Victory so that she would remain with them forever; in fact, from that time Athena was usually portrayed with winged Victories hovering around her.

THE TEMPLE OF ATHENA NIKE ★

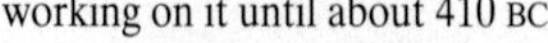

THE LEGEND. This small temple is one of the most memorable monuments here. Pausanias mentions seeing it on the way up to the Propylaea: "The Temple of Athena Aptera stands to the right of the Propylaea. The sea is visible from this spot, and the story goes that Aegeus flung himself from here when he saw the ship which had borne the young Athenians to Crete returning with black sails aloft. Theseus had left Athens in the hope of killing the Minotaur and had promised his father that he would hoist white sails in the event of success. But he forgot his promise and Aegeus, thinking he had been slain, leapt to his death from the citadel."

HISTORY. The Temple of Athena Nike was begun in 427 BC, two years after the death of Pericles. The building was completed three years later, but the sculptors continued working on it until about 410 BC.

ON THE ACROPOLIS
View of the Erechtheion and the Parthenon.

THE FIRST RECONSTRUCTION. In 1676 Spon and Wheler viewed the temple intact on its outcrop, but within eleven years it had been demolished during the siege of the Acropolis by the Venetians. In 1835 the architects Schaubert and Hausen rediscovered nearly all the blocks and reconstructed the temple on its original foundations, which had remained intact. Ionic in style, this small temple of Pentelic marble is about 23 feet high, 27 feet long and 18 feet wide. Both the front façade and the back have a four-column portico. The *cella*, or main room of the temple, has unadorned walls, except for the east wall where two rectangular pillars stand between the *antae*. Originally it housed a statue of the goddess that was a copy of the *xoanon* (wooden image) burned during the Persian occupation. The Ionic triple architrave is supported by the porticos and the long walls of the *cella*.

THE SCULPTURES OF THE FRIEZE. A sculpted frieze runs around all four sides of the building. The only surviving original panels *in situ* are those on the east side; all the others are castings taken from the originals, which are in the British Museum. The figures on the frieze of the east wall have been damaged by pollution; but Athena, with her shield, and Zeus (beside her) are easily recognizable, with a throng of gods and goddesses around them. Illustrated on the other friezes are battles against the Persians, notably the 5th century BC Battle of Plataea ● *45*, on the north wall. Because the temple is so close to the edge of the platform there is a parapet on every side except the east. The balustrade, about 3 feet high and built of marble, supports a bronze grille. The marble slabs are

THE FRIEZE
The north and south sides illustrate battles between the Greeks and the Persians, identifiable by their costumes.

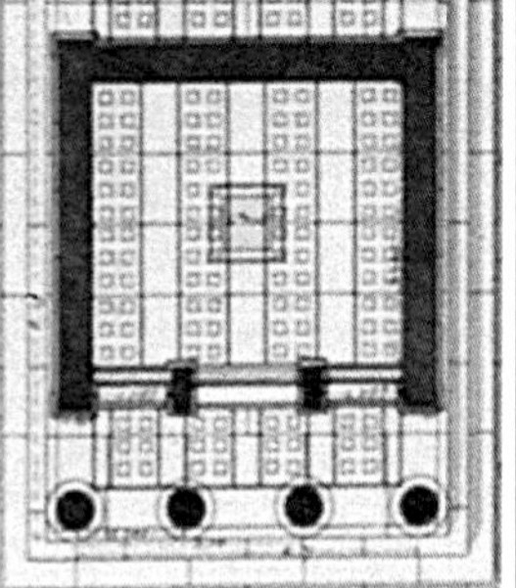

AN IONIC TEMPLE
The elegant little temple dedicated to Athena Nike is "amphiprostyle tetrastyle", meaning that it has two rows of four columns on each façade. Its stylobate rests on three steps, and a marble balustrade adorned with reliefs surrounds it. Above, floorplan by Boitte, 1876.

THE PROPYLAEA
After the excavations conducted by Ernest Beulé in 1852, L.-F. Boitte proposed to the French Académie des Beaux-Arts in 1864 that the monument should be re-erected, incorporating remains from every era (such as the Frankish Tower) and a restored cross-section of the west façade.

The monumental entrance to the Acropolis, photographed in the early 20th century.

decorated with reliefs on the outside. At the center of the west side of the balustrade, the most decorative panel of the ensemble depicts Athena receiving the homage of two processions of winged Victories. Some of these sculptures are on display in the Acropolis Museum ▲ *150*.

RESTORATION OF THE TEMPLE. The program of restoration now under way involves the complete dismantling of the temple and the treatment of each stone individually. The concrete foundation dating from the 1938 restoration will be demolished and its iron girders replaced; the plinth will then be reconstructed and the temple restored to include newly identified architectural elements, secured with titanium studs.

THE PROPYLAEA

CONSTRUCTION. The architect of the Propylaea was Mnesicles, a colleague of Phidias. His original plan covered the western side of the Acropolis. As well as the central gate and the two wings that extend it to the northwest and southwest, Mnesicles also planned two great halls, on the northeast and southeast sides. The main work was completed in 432 BC, just before the outbreak of the Peloponnesian War. The gate with its two wings at right angles had been built, but two porticos were still just foundations and were never finished. The Propylaea complex is made up of a central building with two wings at right angles built on a limestone base. The central building is a rectangle divided in two by a partition wall pierced by five doorways, with the highest and broadest in the middle and a pair of smaller ones on

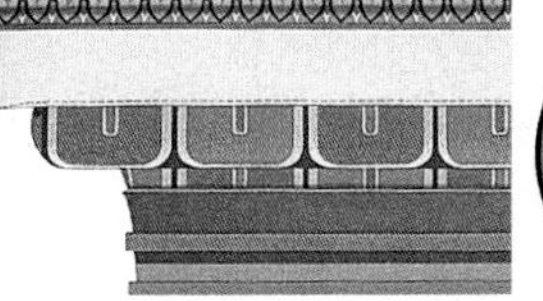

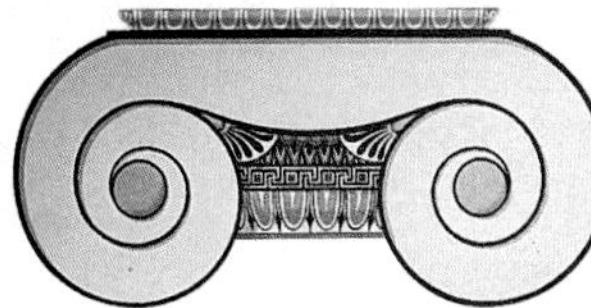

Restored architrave and Ionic capital Blue and yellow colors have been used to soften the light.

each side. The roof of the porches was adorned by a pediment, and the exterior porticos were flanked by two wings. Processions, chariots and sacrificial animals entered the Acropolis by the Sacred Way.

The porticos. Pedestrians walked up four steps to enter the Acropolis through the outer portico, then negotiated a second flight of steps to reach a portico with gateways at each side leading to the buildings. The façades of the two porticos included six columns. The space between the two middle columns was greater than that separating the others, in order to provide enough room for the broad flight of steps.

The vestibules. The flight of steps was flanked by three pairs of tall columns which supported the ceiling of the western vestibule overlooking the lower town. The western vestibule was twice the length of the central columns, and these formed the base of a coffered ceiling decorated with golden stars against a blue background. The inner vestibule was also adorned with such a ceiling. The two wings of the Propylaea were built at right angles to the central gateway; their stylobate and the steps leading to it forming an extension of those of the western vestibule. The façades had three Doric columns between the projecting parts on one side of the lateral walls. The north wing served as a portico to a rest room; by way of the northwest portico, visitors to the Acropolis came through a door to relax on the beds awaiting them there.

Work in progress. Today a wooden staircase leads to the Propylaea to save the original marble steps from further wear. A superb Ionic capital crowns the last column on the left of the central colonnade. Part of the coffered ceiling has been replaced. From here the visitor moves on to the plateau of the Acropolis proper, and is confronted by the Parthenon, framed by the central columns of the eastern vestibule of the Propylaea.

The original stone blocks have been complemented with Pentelic marble dressed by marble cutters from the island of Tinos, where traditional techniques are still preserved.

In 1869 Charles Garnier wrote: “Sit on the threshold of the Parthenon or below the Propylaea and you will remain there for hours, gazing at the same columns again and again.”

▲ THE PARTHENON: RECONSTRUCTION BY BENOÎT LOVIOT, 1881

After the proclamation of Independence, the Greek government and the Archeological Service set about the long-term preservation of the Acropolis. Restoration work began in 1884. Whole sectors were cleared, modern buildings were demolished and the restoration of the monuments was begun. Throughout the 19th century, both Greeks and foreigners started on major archeological digs in the precinct, especially between 1885 and 1890, when many of the pieces now shown in the museum were unearthed.

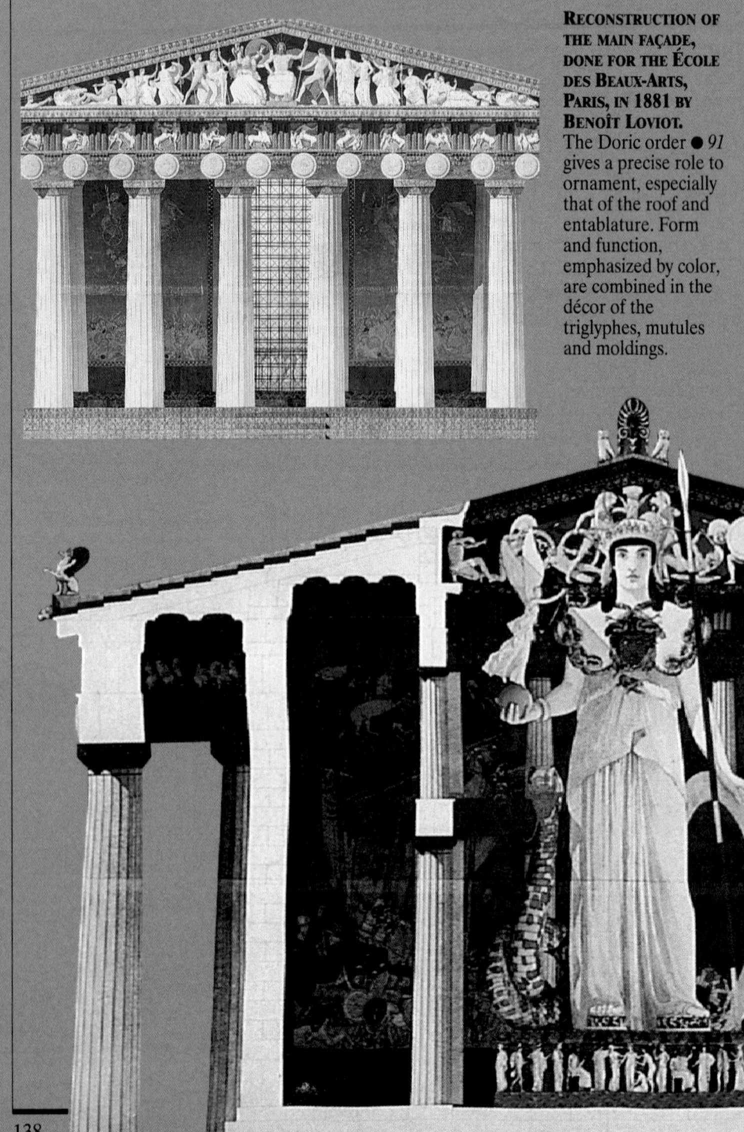

RECONSTRUCTION OF THE MAIN FAÇADE, DONE FOR THE ÉCOLE DES BEAUX-ARTS, PARIS, IN 1881 BY BENOÎT LOVIOT. The Doric order ● *91* gives a precise role to ornament, especially that of the roof and entablature. Form and function, emphasized by color, are combined in the décor of the triglyphes, mutules and moldings.

The exterior peristyle
The proposed reconstruction concentrated on the esthetic aspects of the peristyle, which make the temple a truly monumental construction. The columns rest directly on the top step, which is the stylobate. Above the main beam, the stone slabs of the triglyphs mark the seats of the joists. Painted slabs, or metopes ● *85*, fill the spaces in between. The roof begins with a dripstone projecting above the frieze, on which the guttering rests.

Athena Parthenos
This Roman copy of the statue by Phidias, in the Louvre, and the reconstruction below reproduce the chryselephantine (gold-and-ivory) statue which the Athenians gave as an offering to their protectress.

Ionic capital, with volutes

Gargoyle
The temple is surrounded by a gutter, the rainwater being drained off by gargoyles, mostly in the shape of lions' heads.

The Parthenon (cross-section)
In the center is Phidias' statue of Athena Parthenos in chryselephantine with polychrome details. The sculptor handed his work to a painter, "whose job was to add the final touch of perfection and endow the statue with religious meaning."

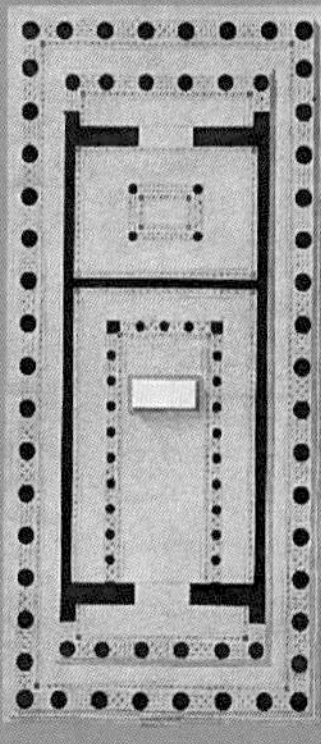

Plan of the Parthenon by Benoît Loviot

The committee for the preservation of the Acropolis and Manolis Korres, the architect responsible for the works, emphasize that the overall form of the Parthenon will not be changed by its restoration. The proposed additions only involve the rebuilding of about 10 percent of the temple. The aim of making the monument more accessible means it will be restored to be recognizable to visitors and historically accurate. The new blocks of marble are specially patinated to lessen the contrast with those of antiquity, but as recommended in the 1964 Venice Charter, there is a slight difference of color between the new and old blocks, so that visitors can see which is which.

SAFEGUARDING THE MONUMENTS
Over a period of three years Manolis Korres and his assistants identified and stockpiled hundreds of marble blocks from all around the temple. The blocks were often broken in pieces and scattered among about seven thousand stones from other monuments on the Acropolis or from medieval Turkish buildings. Now the architect is proposing to carry out a partial restoration of the *cella*, by adding several hundred ancient stone blocks.

A SCIENTIFIC INVENTORY
The committee has a broad spectrum of possibilities for the completion of the monument. In 1986 the pediment of the façade and its entablature were dismantled. In the following two years the components of the pediment, the corner friezes and the marble of the architrave were reassembled. The restorers compiled a file describing each displaced block along with recommendations regarding the best way to preserve it.

Techniques. Titanium tenons have been inserted, secured with cement. The holes for them are made with small traditional drills. The cutting and polishing of the new blocks is being carried out by marble cutters from Tinos, who are trained in classical methods of working with this kind of stone. Fissures in the marble are repaired by joints and grouting. Fragments of white marble are added to damaged blocks, identical to the original stone and even quarried from the same place: Mount Pentelikon.

Work in progress
A crane has been set up inside the Parthenon, along with scaffolding and a whole series of machines and instruments. About 150 elements of the original architecture have been dismantled, moved to the workshops, treated by specialists and replaced precisely in their original positions.

The construction of the 5th-century BC temple
Some elements, such as the column drums and capitals and the sculptures of the pediment, were put in place with a crane or other hoisting mechanism. Drawing by Manolis Korres.

RESTORATION AND CLEARING OF THE SITE
The first restoration work was begun in 1834. Above, Orlandos' restoration project, 1940.

THE PARTHENON

THE SANCTUARY OF ARTEMIS BRAURONIA. You are now facing the Parthenon. The Sanctuary of Artemis Brauronia ▲ *260* is on the right. The cult of Artemis as bear goddess appeared in the time of Pisistratus ● *40* and was celebrated at five-yearly intervals: young Athenian girls retreated to the sanctuary and disguised themselves as she-bears. The temple was made up of a stoa, with a back wall parallel to the southern rampart of the Acropolis, with two porticos. The largest of these contained the *xoanon* of the goddess and a statue of her by Praxiteles.

THE CHALKOTHEKE. Adjoining the sanctuary are a number of limestone blocks, still in their original positions, as well as the foundations of walls cut into the rock; one of these overlaps the steps on the west side of the Parthenon. These are the

THE ROCK OF THE ACROPOLIS
The plateau on the hilltop, several times leveled by man's agency, forms a polygon approximately 1,000 feet long, while its greatest width is slightly less than 450 feet and its circumference exceeds 2,500 feet.

The west façade of the Parthenon in 1819.

Restoration of the Parthenon
Between 1923 and 1933 Balanos rebuilt the north colonnade and part of the south colonnade. His efforts were something of a disaster, because he cut holes in the marble and inserted steel tenons that later rusted. Orlandos, his associate, was against the restoration of the south colonnade without a similar restoration of the walls of the *cella*. On Balanos' death, in 1942, Orlandos took over the work, guided by the conviction that restoring the monument as closely as possible to its original form would allow visitors to appreciate its beauty properly.

remains of the Chalkotheke, the building where the bronze dishes and votive offerings to Athena were stored. At the beginning of the 4th century a stoa was added to the northern façade, the northeast corner of which still encroaches on the steps to the Parthenon.

The ramparts. You are now approaching the area near the southwest corner of the Parthenon where two ditches, surrounded by parapets, have been left open so visitors can see the ramparts that formerly ran along the southern side of the plateau. The oldest of these date from the 13th century BC, the remainder from the second quarter of the 5th century BC. The latter were completed under Pericles, who had the top terrace of the plateau filled in and leveled before the construction of the Parthenon was begun.

The old Parthenon. The excavations of 1885 led to controversy about the temples found here that predated the Parthenon. It was felt that the huge 6th-century temple whose foundations were uncovered on the site must have been pulled down shortly after the victory over the Persians at Marathon in 490 BC, to make way for a new marble sanctuary dedicated to Athena; and that this temple was still unfinished by the time the Persians sacked Athens. Many components from this temple, known as the Old Parthenon, were subsequently re-utilized.

The work of restoration
Throughout the 19th century both Greeks and foreigners applied themselves to the work of restoration, but the Parthenon as we see it today was mostly reconstructed at the turn of the century. The intensive excavations on the Acropolis between 1885 and 1890 yielded many of the unique works of art now on view in the museum.

The Temple of Athena at Athens, 1725.

THE EAST PEDIMENT
By the time Carrey made this sketch of the rear pediment (facing page), only seven figures and the heads of four horses remained on it.

THE WEST PEDIMENT
The theme here was Zeus' presentation of Athena to the gods of Olympus. The sculptures of Hercules, Hestia, Dione and Aphrodite are now in the Elgin Rooms at the British Museum.

THE TEMPLE PROJECT. In the time of Pericles all Athens was willing to contribute to the building and ornamentation of a great new temple, in addition to a number of other monuments. Plutarch commented: "The monuments were imposing in their unrivaled grandeur, beauty and grace; the artists vied with one another in the technical perfection of their work, but the most admirable thing was the speed of execution." Pericles entrusted the overall management of the project to the sculptor Phidias, who "presided over everything" especially the décor, for which he employed Athens' greatest artists. The architects Ictinos and Callicrates were commissioned to draw up and execute the plans. Construction began in 447 BC and was completed nine years later, the last of the sculptures being set place in 432. Pericles and his architects decided from the start to build the new sanctuary on the foundations of the Old Parthenon. Apart from the limestone foundations and the ceilings and wooden

HEAD OF A YOUNG MAN
This head comes from one of the temple's metopes. Brönsted found two heads (one being that of a centaur) in the Copenhagen Museum; these had been brought back to Denmark by Captain Hartmand, who was present with Koenigsmark at the siege of the Acropolis in 1687.

doors, the temple was built entirely of marble, even its roof tiles. The stone came from the quarries of the Pentelic Mountains, Parian marble being reserved for the sculptures. The temple was opened to the public the moment it was finished, and was formally dedicated to the goddess during the Panathenaic Games of 438 BC ▲ *130*.

The temple. The Parthenon rests on a plinth three steps high. The upper level of the plinth measures about 225 x 85 feet. It is a peripteral temple (surrounded by a single row of columns). The peristyle consists of eight Doric columns on the west and east sides and seventeen along the north and south sides (if you count the corner columns twice). The shafts consist of twelve fluted drums and are about 33 feet high, including the capitals, with diameters tapering from 6 feet 3 inches at the base to 4 feet 9 inches at the top. There is a perceptible bulge two fifths up each column; the Greeks knew the principle of the outward curvature of a column (*entasis*), which compensates for the optical effect that makes columns seem thinner in the middle when viewed from below. The corner columns were thicker, reducing the space between them and their neighbors: because they received more sunlight, they would otherwise have appeared thinner than the rest. Finally, to give the impression of absolute perfection, the plinth gradually increased in height, by about 4 inches in the middle of the long sides and by about 3 inches at the center of the façades.

Pediments
In 1674 the Marquis de Nointel had two hundred drawings made by Jacques Carrey of the relief sculptures decorating the pediments. Since these sculptures were later destroyed by the Venetian bombardment, his drawings are of unique importance.

Sculpture on the Archaic pediment
Painted in blue and red, this statue with a triple human torso and a Triton's lower half was part of the pediment of the 6th-century temple.

Lapiths and centaurs
Each metope featured a different scene, consisting of two figures in high relief. The metopes along the east side of the temple represented the struggle between the gods and the giants; those of the west side, an Amazonomachy; those of the south side, the battle between the Lapiths and the Centaurs; and those of the north side, scenes from the Trojan War. The theme common to all is the triumph of the Greeks and their gods over their human or mythical adversaries.

THE SACRED OLIVE
The north portico opens onto the Pandroseion, or Temenos (precinct) of Pandrosos (one of the daughters of Cecrops), wherein grew the sacred olive of Athena.

THE ERECHTHEION ★

THE SACRED OLIVE TREE OF ATHENA. The Erechtheion is one of the most astonishing buildings of Greek architecture. Its name means the "house of Erechtheus", the latter being one of the legendary heroes of Athens who was either the offspring of Hephaistos and Earth, or else of Pandion I and Xeuxippe, and hence one of the early Athenian kings. Subsequently he became identified with Poseidon: the god, who had decided to appropriate Athens for himself, was said to have created a saltwater spring on the Acropolis with a blow of his trident, and Athena planted an olive tree nearby. Both acts were carried out in the presence of the serpent-king Cecrops, who was appointed by Zeus to arbitrate between the two. Cecrops testified that Athena had been the first to stake her claim, and that the olive was more useful than a saltwater well – so Poseidon was obliged to share the shrine with her.

THE ERECHTHEION
The temple is famous for the elegance of its architectural details. The architect Polycles took charge of its construction in the final two years, but we don't know if he was the author of the original plan. Its slender Ionic columns are garlanded at the base and have capitals that are among the loveliest ever built.

THE TEMPLES. The Erechtheion was built in stages between 421 and 406 BC. It consists of two Ionic temples, one facing east and one facing west. The first, which was the largest, was dedicated to Athena Polias and contained a wooden statue of the goddess, which was clothed in the *peplos* during the Panathenaic Games. The second temple was dedicated to Poseidon-Erechtheus. At the eastern end of it was a *pronaos* adorned with six Ionic columns that supported the pediment and the entablature. The floor at the western end of the building is almost 10 feet lower, with the result that the façade here has two levels with a supporting wall below and four Ionic columns between the *antae*; it is crowned with a pediment and entablature, and the Ionic columns are decorated at the base with garlands. Note also the sculpted band which begins at the

“ERECHTHEUS, CALLED THE SON OF EARTH, HAS A TEMPLE INSIDE THE CITADEL, WHEREIN ONE MAY CONTEMPLATE AN OLIVE TREE AND A SALTWATER SPRING.”

HERODOTUS

the temple, with alternating palm and lotus motifs, emerging at regular intervals from clumps of acanthus, with volutes and ovoids. Traces of color are still discernible here. On the east side the *pronaos* originally had a coffered marble ceiling, much like those of the Parthenon and the Propylaea. The western ends of the two long sides both open onto porticoes. The larger north portico, built slightly lower than the south one, extends beyond the westernmost point of the *secos* (the interior).

THE PORCH OF THE CARYATIDS. This was originally called the “Porch of the Korai”, on account of the statues of girls in Ionic tunics which serve instead of columns to support the entablature and coffered ceiling. These figures bear capitals of a distinctive decorative form; they stand four in front and two behind, on their own parapet.

CONSERVATION WORK ON THE ERECHTHEION. The restoration project completed in 1987 made use of new marble components, with a view to creating stability wherever the original stone was defective. During the work a number of errors committed by earlier restorers were corrected, in particular regarding the ceiling of the north porch and the walls of the sides of the sanctuary, where computer analysis of the stones made it possible to pinpoint their original locations. Basically the Porch of the Caryatids has now reverted to its original form; the crosspieces that held the statues at fixed distances apart have been removed, and the east façade is once again complete, the northeast corner having been reconstructed with copies of the column and epistyles removed by Lord Elgin (now in the British Museum). From here, make your way to the belvedere at the northeast corner of the Acropolis, from which there is a magnificent panorama of Athens and its surroundings.

THE PORCH OF THE CARYATIDS
According to Vitruvius, the sculptors took as models the girls of Caryai, in Laconia, who danced with burdens on their heads in honor of Artemis.

The construction of the Erechtheion (built to the north of the Parthenon) was probably started in 421 BC and finished in 406. It was made up to two sanctuaries. A statue of Athena stood in the first sanctuary, which opened eastward with a six-columned portico. A second portico, to the north, led into a smaller sanctuary, dedicated to Pandrosa, the daughter of Cecrops, one of the mythical kings who founded Athens. The sanctuary is roofless because the cult olive (the sacred tree given to Attica by Athena) was planted here. The restoration of the Erechtheion by Martin Tétaz in 1851 still prevails over later versions and serves largely as the basis for the project of restoring the east façade. The pastel shades reflect the colors discovered on the capitals of the Erechtheion.

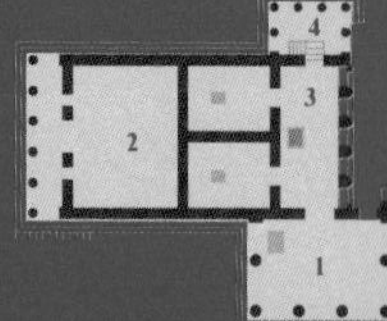

1. North portico
2. Cella of Athena
3. Cella of Poseidon Erechtheus
4. South portico (portico of the caryatids).

POLYCHROMATIC DECORATION
The decoration proposed by Tétaz and above all his treatment of the friezes, painted in bright colors against a dark background, seem more in keeping with Pompeii than classical Greece. Polychromy has always been a highly controversial subject, but since the 19th century, due to finds made by archeologists and research carried out by architects, traces of color found on some blocks of stone leave no doubt as to the painting techniques employed by the ancient Greeks.

Wooden statue of Athena Polias

Sacred olive

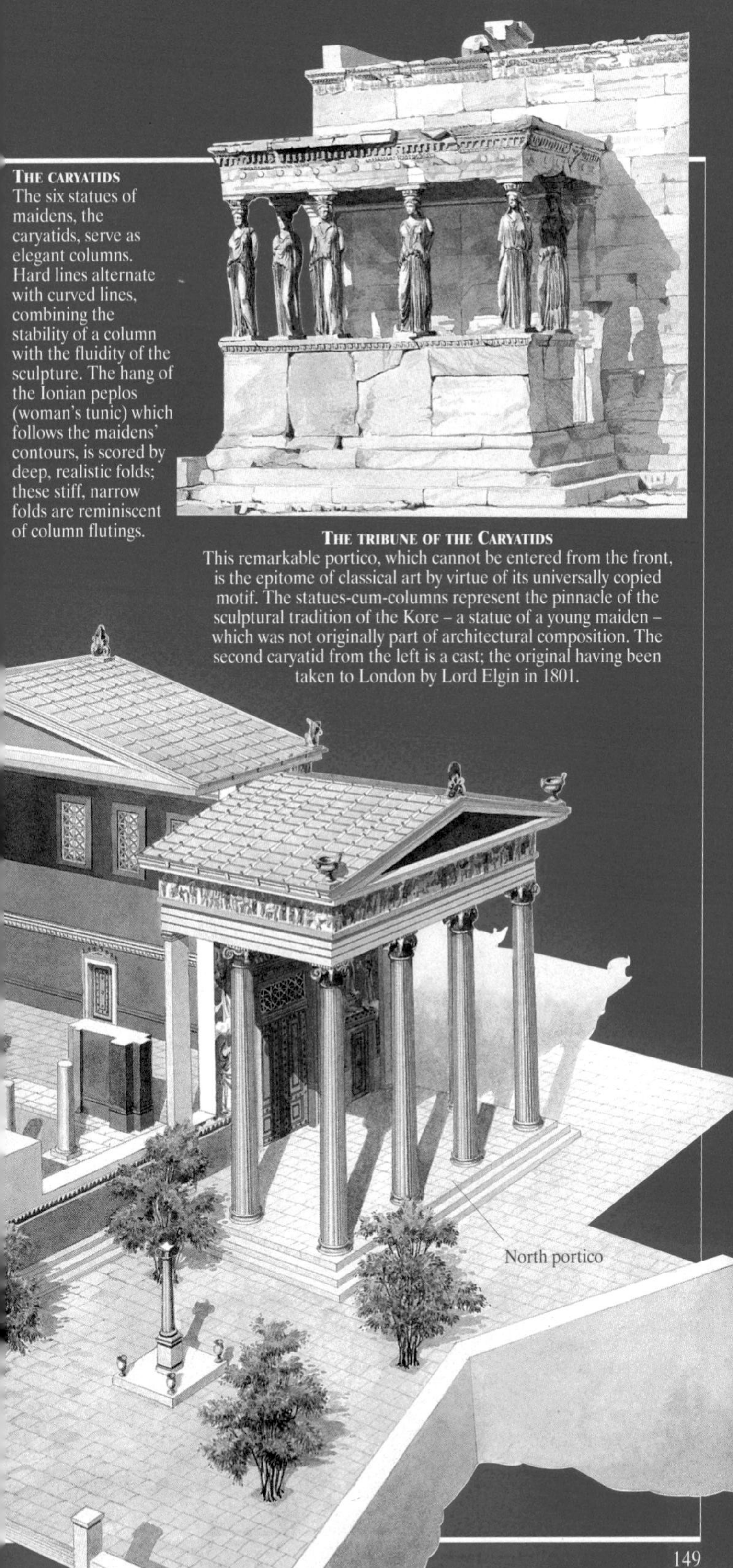

The caryatids
The six statues of maidens, the caryatids, serve as elegant columns. Hard lines alternate with curved lines, combining the stability of a column with the fluidity of the sculpture. The hang of the Ionian peplos (woman's tunic) which follows the maidens' contours, is scored by deep, realistic folds; these stiff, narrow folds are reminiscent of column flutings.

The tribune of the Caryatids
This remarkable portico, which cannot be entered from the front, is the epitome of classical art by virtue of its universally copied motif. The statues-cum-columns represent the pinnacle of the sculptural tradition of the Kore – a statue of a young maiden – which was not originally part of architectural composition. The second caryatid from the left is a cast; the original having been taken to London by Lord Elgin in 1801.

The museum is on the southeast edge of the Acropolis. It contains only items found on the site. In 1834, a year after the departure of the Turks, the modern buildings on the Acropolis were demolished to make way for preliminary restoration work and the assembly of the collections destined for the museum. Several fragments of the Parthenon frieze that escaped the eye of Lord Elgin constitute some of the museum's greatest treasures. The construction of the museum was completed in 1874; between 1885 and 1891 its collections were enriched by a number of Archaic sculptures (6th–5th century BC) excavated by P. Kavvadias.

HEAD OF THE "BLOND BOY"
The crestfallen expression is typical of the Attic style shortly before 480 BC. The hair was originally painted a dark yellow.

"MOURNING ATHENA", C. 480 BC
The goddess Athena in pensive mood, contemplating the boundary mark of the sanctuary built for her by the Athenians. She is wearing her helmet and leaning on a spear; her clothes are the *apoptygma peplos* and a short tunic, the *palla*, held by brooches at the shoulders.

PEPLOPHORE KORE (MAIDEN WEARING A PEPLOS), 530 BC
(left) The work of one of the greatest anonymous sculptors of the Archaic period.

CHIOT KORE, C. 510 BC
(center) This kore, attributed to an artist from the island of Chios, retains much of its original painted surface.

KORE, C. 500 BC
(right) The most recent of the three figures.

Moschophoros (calf bearer), c. 570 BC
One of the earliest examples of antique marble statuary in Greece, this sculpture depicts a citizen named Rhombos carrying on his shoulders a calf for sacrifice to Athena. Rhombos was doubtless the donor of this work, which itself was an offering to the goddess.

PHIDIAS (C. 490–431 BC)
The pupil of Hegias and follower of Myron and Polycletos, Phidias achieved fame with the chryselephantine statue of Zeus in the Temple of Zeus at Olympia. He was then commissioned by Pericles to decorate the Parthenon and was responsible for the frieze, pediments and metopes, as well as the chryselephantine statue of Athena, a replica of which is in the National Archeological Museum.

THE FRIEZE OF THE PARTHENON
Here the sculptor innovated by crowning a Doric ensemble with an Ionic frieze. This series originally decorated the *cella* and the entrance to the *pronaos*; it ran from south to north, beginning on the east side of the temple. The subject matter is the procession of the Panathenaic Games, celebrated annually in honor of Athena.

THE PROCESSION
The movement of the procession is perfectly conveyed by the rhythmic progression of the figures' postures; first come horsemen about to mount, and then horsemen riding away; the horses progress from a walk, to a trot, to a canter, as the cloaks of their riders begin to flutter behind them. The scene culminates, around the central panels of the east side, with a horse rearing up high. Phidias was the first Western sculptor to give such a degree of suppleness and life to his work.

The restoration of the Parthenon

by

Manolis Korrès
Chief Architect

The restoration of the Parthenon has provoked a number of interesting reactions, some more dogmatic than others. Indeed, it is certainly true that the theoretical grounds for restoring any monument are largely relative; each generation has its own ideas, which often vanish with it, only to reappear many years later in some other form. Each point of view has its value – apart from the blinkered conviction that one theory and one alone has universal validity. Our work on monuments is just like every other human enterprise: the results are never exactly what we set out to achieve, and the gains we achieve are inevitably accompanied by losses. The ultimate goal of any restoration should not be to avoid all losses (that would be impossible), but to minimize them while maximizing the gains.

Reconstruction of the interior
A two-level colonnade originally divided the interior into two parts: a central area and a perimeter. This supported the full weight of the roof. The central space was lit from the 30-foot-high doorway, while the perimeter was lit by two great windows on either side of the doorway. This chiaroscuro light entering from the side gave extra emphasis and effect to the colossal gold-and-ivory statue of Athena in the center.

The large honorific monument at the northeast corner
The life-size bronze quadriga (178 BC) hid part of the temple. On the architrave of the east side of the temple, there are large votive shields from the Hellenistic period and an epigraph from the Roman era with letters in metal; the architrave on the north side has somewhat smaller votive shields.

To judge the cases for and against restoring the Parthenon requires a thorough evaluation of all aspects of the dilemma. Clearly, when additions are made to an authentic but partly destroyed building, some aspects of the building's value will be greatly improved, while other areas will lose out. A good illustration of this is the removal of the Parthenon sculptures: when irreplaceable features of a monument have to be replaced on the monument itself by replicas, the originals being taken to a museum in order to preserve them, opinions are bound to differ. The desire to preserve the sculptures clashes with the desire to preserve the original relationship they had with the Parthenon. Similarly the desire to safeguard the authentic form of the monument as a ruin clashes with the desire to improve our perception of it and to show to greater advantage its many valuable aspects as a work of art. By comparing different monuments, it soon becomes evident that some have a value that is chiefly historical, while in others the principal value is artistic. Some monuments possess extremely interesting architectural features; others have none to speak of. In the case of the Parthenon, despite the overpowering presence of history, such as the melancholy scars left on it by fire and sword, one aspect dominates all the rest, namely the building's priceless value as a classical temple. From this point of view, what we stand to gain from restoring even the least prominent column that has suffered damage far outweighs anything that may be detracted from the monument's more general historical character as a result of the restoration.

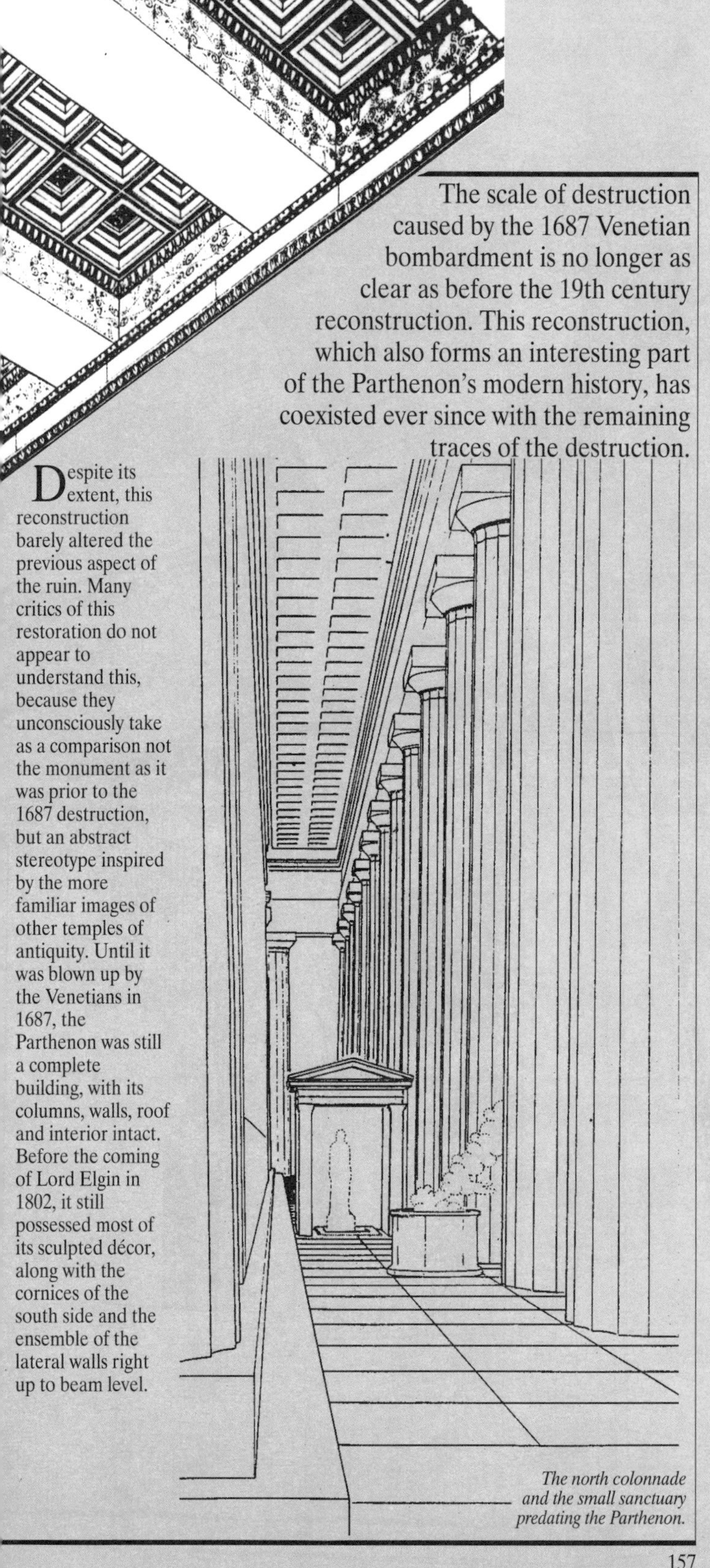

The scale of destruction caused by the 1687 Venetian bombardment is no longer as clear as before the 19th century reconstruction. This reconstruction, which also forms an interesting part of the Parthenon's modern history, has coexisted ever since with the remaining traces of the destruction.

Despite its extent, this reconstruction barely altered the previous aspect of the ruin. Many critics of this restoration do not appear to understand this, because they unconsciously take as a comparison not the monument as it was prior to the 1687 destruction, but an abstract stereotype inspired by the more familiar images of other temples of antiquity. Until it was blown up by the Venetians in 1687, the Parthenon was still a complete building, with its columns, walls, roof and interior intact. Before the coming of Lord Elgin in 1802, it still possessed most of its sculpted décor, along with the cornices of the south side and the ensemble of the lateral walls right up to beam level.

The north colonnade and the small sanctuary predating the Parthenon.

THE EAST SIDE OF THE PARTHENON'S RECESS, AS IT WAS FROM THE 12TH CENTURY TO 1687. *The semi-hexagonal apse took the place of a circular paleo-Christian one. From the sumptuous marble roof, destroyed by fire in AD 267, a few beams remain in place, along with nearly all the frieze. Only the central stone has been removed, as well as the corresponding part of the architrave, most of which was used as a sill for the window in the center. Above, on the left, one of the windows of the pronaos was still in place.*

"THE SUNSHINE OF GREECE SHEDS A GOLDEN SHEEN ON THE MARBLE OF MOUNT PENTELIKON; IT IS THE SHEEN OF RIPE CORN."

CHATEAUBRIAND

Never before has a restoration program like the Parthenon project, which involves putting authentic marble blocks back in place, been attempted on such a large monument. For the first time, however, we can be certain that each block will be replaced in its original position with absolute precision; because of this the objection that reconstruction obliterates the historical character of the monument is no longer valid. In effect, thanks to an exhaustive study of all the surviving architectural material, we who are working on the Parthenon are for the first time able to reconstruct not only the previously unknown forms of the east entrance to the Roman building, but also those of the throne of the Christian sanctuary, and a number of other elements from more recent phases in the Parthenon's history. If it proves necessary for some reason to undo what we have done, that is perfectly possible: the work has been carried out on the principle that it can always be reversed. Drawings on a scale of one to ten have been made to pinpoint each new addition, each seal, each hidden bar of titanium. A means of dismantling the metal supporting framework has also been devised. For organizational reasons the restoration project has been subdivided into twelve programs, most of which are entirely independent. They correspond to a logical division of the restored part of the monument and are solidly based on architectonic criteria. The elements in urgent need of protection have been dealt with as a priority, while the others, especially those due to be restored with authentic and/or modern blocks, were only tackled after a long period of discussion and careful planning.

The greater part of the reconstruction concerns the interior of the temple. The new blocks of marble are specially patinated to diminish the contrast with those of antiquity. According to Korres, "It is important that there should be a slight difference of color between the two versions of marble, so that the visitor can see which is which, but it must not be too obvious." A distinction of this kind is recommended for the restoration of historic monuments in the Venice Charter which was signed by fifteen countries, including Greece, in 1964.

"THROUGHOUT ITS LENGTH THE SYMMETRICAL FLUTING OF THE COLUMNS SOARED FREELY TOWARD THE SKY LIKE RIVERS OF SOME DARK FIRE, ONLY TO CULMINATE IN GLISTENING, MANGLED, WRETCHED SUMMITS." CHARLES MAURRAS

Korres plans to re-erect several columns inside the temple (which were brought down by a fire, probably during the sack of Athens by the Goths), in addition to reopening the side portals of the paleo-Christian basilica, which at present are walled up.

Among Korres' proposals for the pronaos is that of revealing the base of a Byzantine apse, along with the restoration of part of the threshold built toward the end of the Roman period.

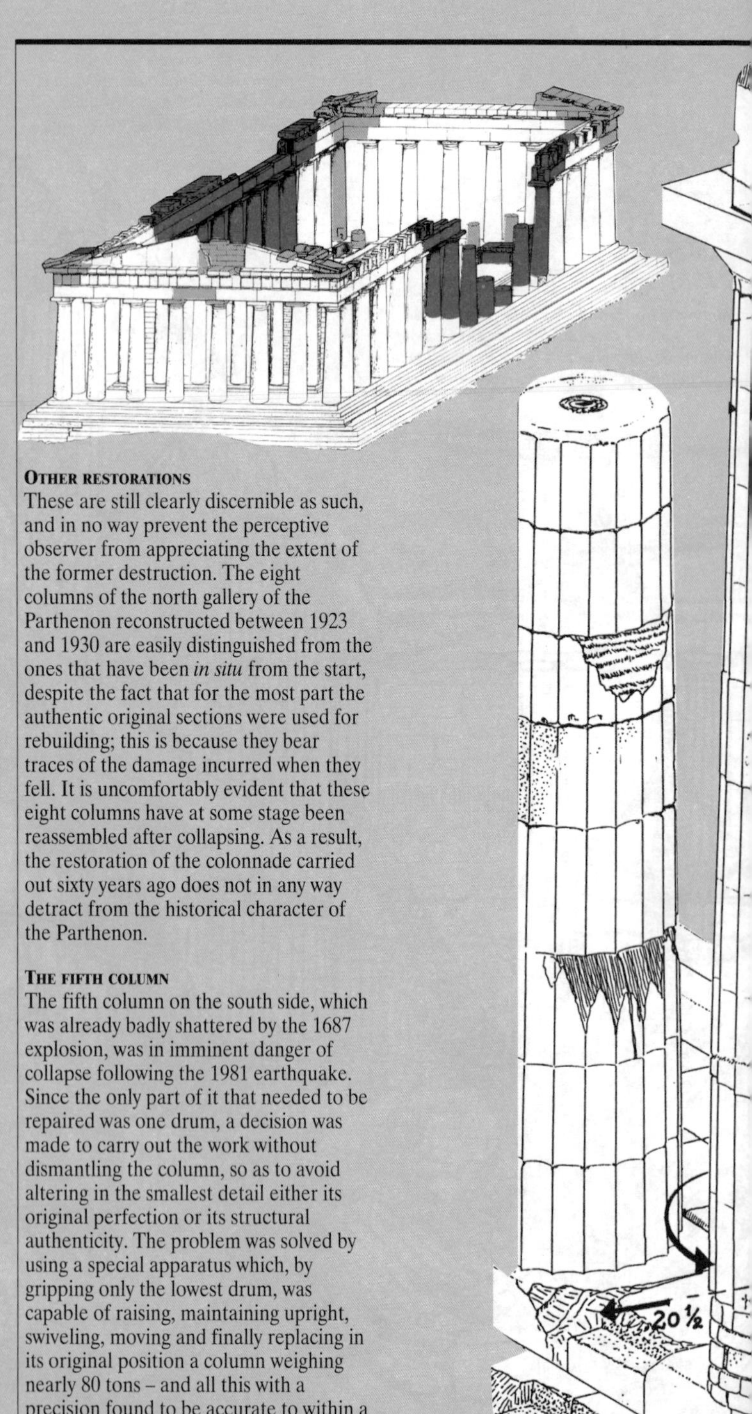

Other restorations
These are still clearly discernible as such, and in no way prevent the perceptive observer from appreciating the extent of the former destruction. The eight columns of the north gallery of the Parthenon reconstructed between 1923 and 1930 are easily distinguished from the ones that have been *in situ* from the start, despite the fact that for the most part the authentic original sections were used for rebuilding; this is because they bear traces of the damage incurred when they fell. It is uncomfortably evident that these eight columns have at some stage been reassembled after collapsing. As a result, the restoration of the colonnade carried out sixty years ago does not in any way detract from the historical character of the Parthenon.

The fifth column
The fifth column on the south side, which was already badly shattered by the 1687 explosion, was in imminent danger of collapse following the 1981 earthquake. Since the only part of it that needed to be repaired was one drum, a decision was made to carry out the work without dismantling the column, so as to avoid altering in the smallest detail either its original perfection or its structural authenticity. The problem was solved by using a special apparatus which, by gripping only the lowest drum, was capable of raising, maintaining upright, swiveling, moving and finally replacing in its original position a column weighing nearly 80 tons – and all this with a precision found to be accurate to within a fraction of an inch.

.06
7°

The new work on the Parthenon began with the east façade, which was judged to be in most danger after the damage caused by the 1981 earthquake. The pediment, the right-hand dripstone, fourteen metopes (plus three more on the eastern end of the north side), thirteen triglyphs, several dozen filler blocks and buttresses, fifteen epistyle blocks, a capital and a half-drum of a column were taken down. In the course of the provisional dismantling of the entablature, several hundred antique iron clamps, pins and armatures were removed; these had already burst the marble. The reattachment and reinforcement of the fragments of the epistyle posed specific problems. In order to place them in their correct positions on the capitals, it was imperative that the original alignment of the blocks should be perfectly matched to within a fraction of an inch. Each block weighed about 10 tons and measured 14 or 15 feet in length.

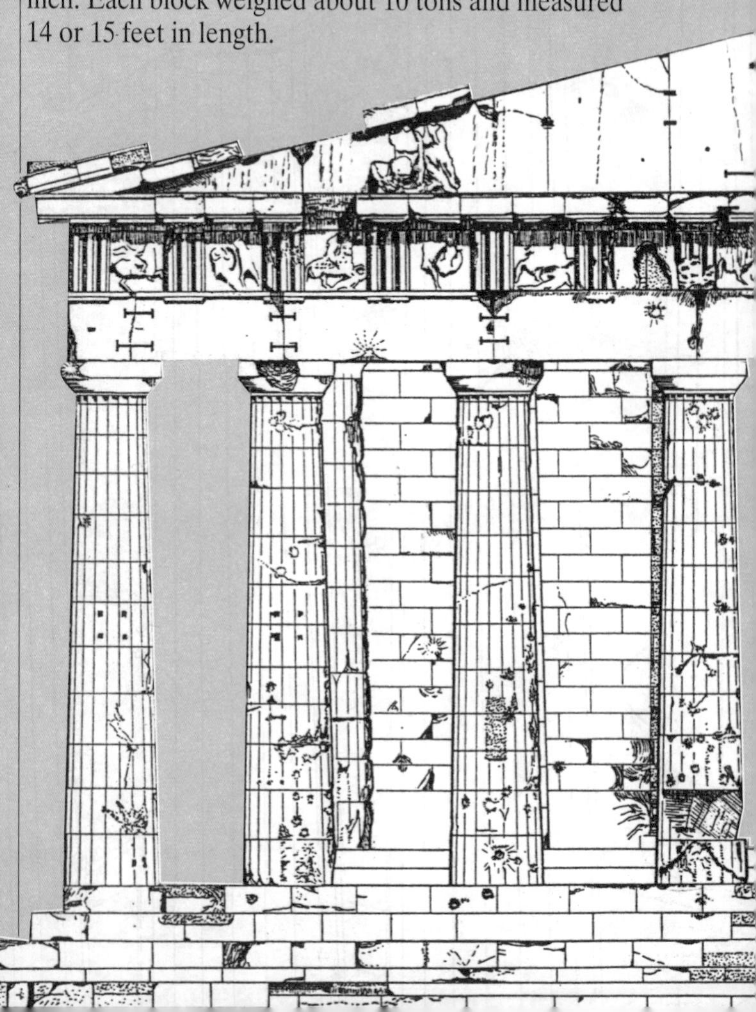

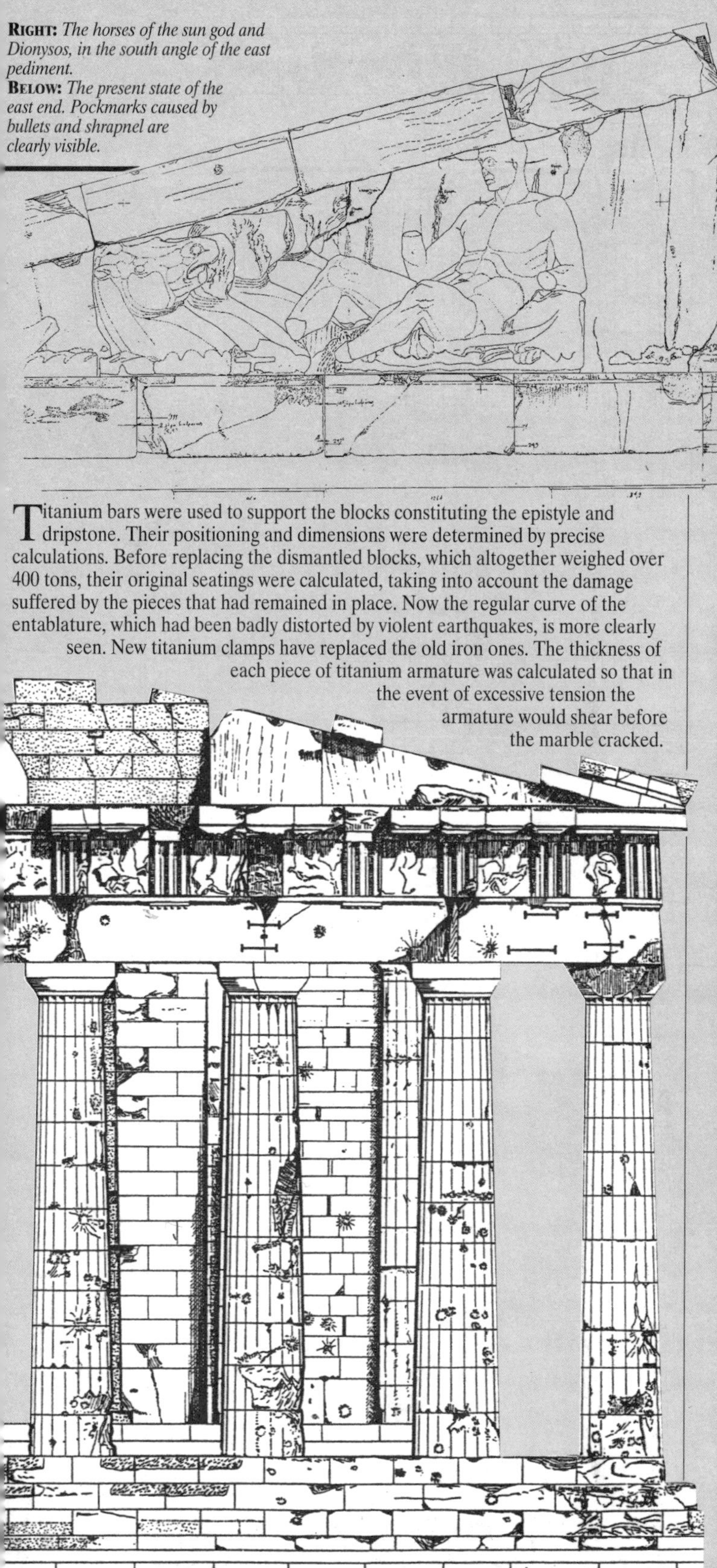

Right: *The horses of the sun god and Dionysos, in the south angle of the east pediment.*
Below: *The present state of the east end. Pockmarks caused by bullets and shrapnel are clearly visible.*

Titanium bars were used to support the blocks constituting the epistyle and dripstone. Their positioning and dimensions were determined by precise calculations. Before replacing the dismantled blocks, which altogether weighed over 400 tons, their original seatings were calculated, taking into account the damage suffered by the pieces that had remained in place. Now the regular curve of the entablature, which had been badly distorted by violent earthquakes, is more clearly seen. New titanium clamps have replaced the old iron ones. The thickness of each piece of titanium armature was calculated so that in the event of excessive tension the armature would shear before the marble cracked.

From 1992 to 1993 a very delicate operation was performed on the west side of the *cella*. The ceiling beams and the blocks below the entablature of the *opisthodomos* (back chamber) were lowered to the ground, and the portion of the frieze hitherto *in situ* – seventeen blocks of marble with a sculpted surface some 80 feet long – was taken to the museum. The original sculptures will eventually be replaced by casts, once the columns and blocks making up the epistyle have been fully restored.

By the year 2000, up to 50 percent of the side walls of the Parthenon will have been restored. The calculation of the exact position of each block of marble has been made easier by the use of a specially devised computer program. The final stage will be the dismantling, repair and precise reconstruction of the part of the north colonnade restored between 1922 and 1930, and of the part of the south colonnade that was restored between 1930 and 1933. The most extensive and innovative work, subject to approval, will be the restoration of much of the *pronaos* with marble blocks, 70 percent of which will be original. Today the majority of specialists are in favor of the most extensive possible restoration of this important part of the Parthenon.

ABOVE: *Proposal for a partial restitution of the pronaos, alternative no. 2.*
BELOW: *Proposal for a partial restitution of the pronaos, alternative no. 4. About 70 percent of the original materials will be preserved.*

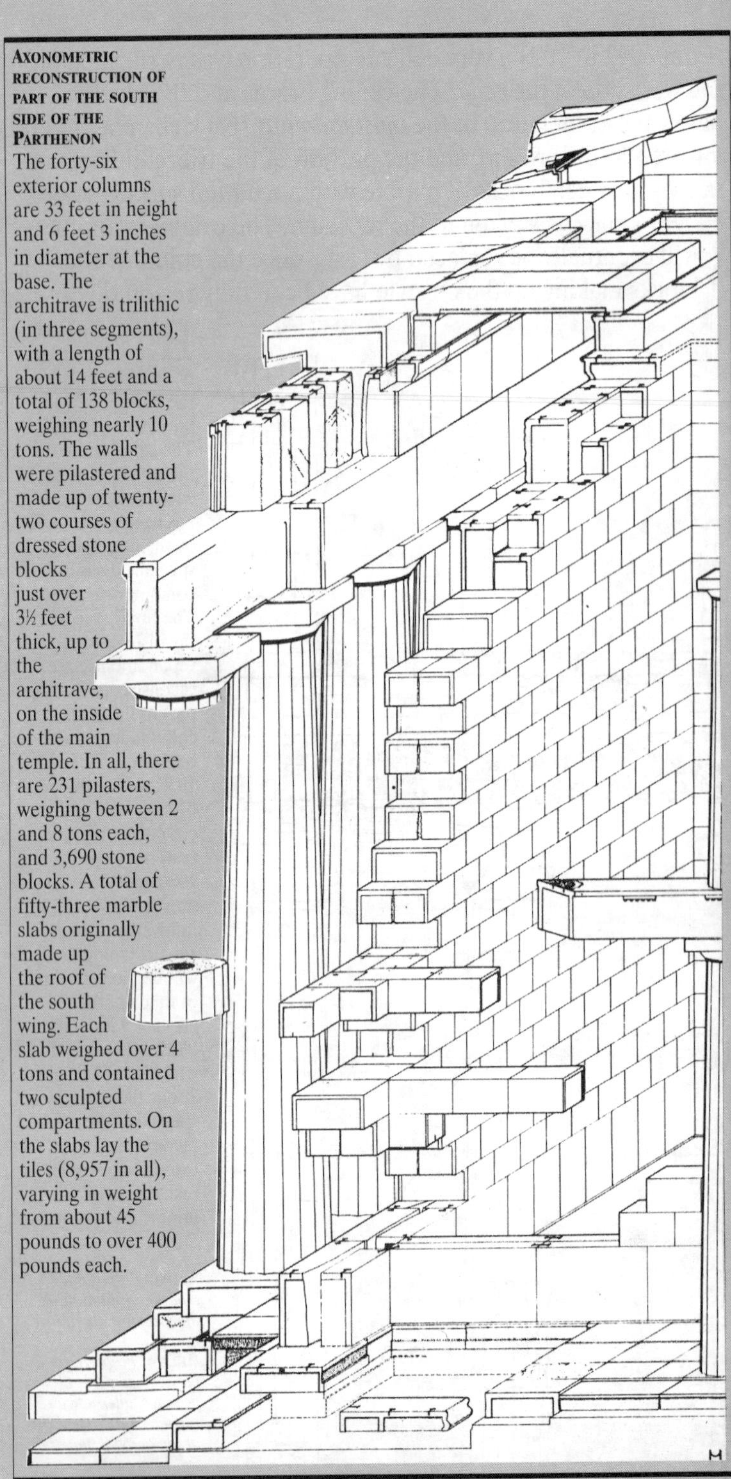

AXONOMETRIC RECONSTRUCTION OF PART OF THE SOUTH SIDE OF THE PARTHENON
The forty-six exterior columns are 33 feet in height and 6 feet 3 inches in diameter at the base. The architrave is trilithic (in three segments), with a length of about 14 feet and a total of 138 blocks, weighing nearly 10 tons. The walls were pilastered and made up of twenty-two courses of dressed stone blocks just over 3½ feet thick, up to the architrave, on the inside of the main temple. In all, there are 231 pilasters, weighing between 2 and 8 tons each, and 3,690 stone blocks. A total of fifty-three marble slabs originally made up the roof of the south wing. Each slab weighed over 4 tons and contained two sculpted compartments. On the slabs lay the tiles (8,957 in all), varying in weight from about 45 pounds to over 400 pounds each.

The south side of the Acropolis

▲ The south side of the Acropolis

Odeon of Herodes Atticus
Stoa of Eumenes
Peripatos
Sanctuary of Dionysos
Sanctuary of Asklepios
Theater of Dionysos

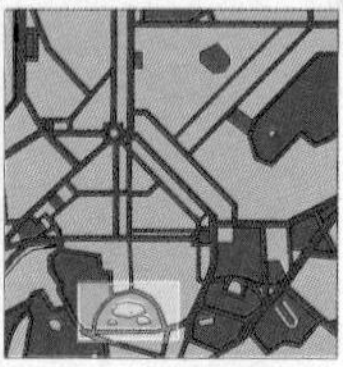

Half a day

The main access to the south side of the Acropolis is by way of Avenue Dyonisiou Areopaghitou.

The sanctuary of Dionysos Eleutheros

This sanctuary, dedicated to the god of wine and nature, owes its name to Eleutherai, a village in Boeotia from which Pegasus is said to have brought back the statue of Dionysos.

The temenos. The ruins of a long Doric stoa built by Lycurgus in 330 BC stand between the theater of Dionysos and the remains of the sacred precinct, or *temenos*, of the sanctuary. Demarcated by a stone *peribolos* (wall), part of which is still visible, the *temenos* enclosed the *thymele* (altar) on which sacrifices were offered to the god.

The temples. The first temple, which backs on to the Stoa of Lycurgus, was built during the reign of Pisistratus (561–527 BC). Only the foundations are still standing today. On the south side of these remains are those of a later sanctuary, built by Nikias around 420 BC. This larger temple was about 70 feet long and 30 feet wide; its *pronaos* ● *90* was made up of a four-column porch on the façade and a pair of columns on each corner. Foundations are the only surviving features: southeast of these stands the marble altar which probably once occupied the center of the *orchestra* of the Theater of Dionysos.

The Temple of Dionysos
Only the foundations are visible today.

The Altar of Dionysos
This altar dating from the 2nd century BC is beautifully sculpted with ornamental festoons and alternating rosettes and masks of satyrs.

Choregic monument of Thrasyllos
Parthenon
Acropolis Museum
Erechtheion

Dionysos
If the popularity of a god is to be measured by the number of his likenesses, Dionysos was unquestionably one of the favorites in the Greek pantheon.

The Theater of Dionysos

The birth of Greek tragedy. The art of dramatic tragedy originated in Athens ● *40*. The Agora ▲ *190* was its birthplace, the first known drama being performed there in 536 BC. Its author, Thespis, was the first to associate an actor with a chorus (composed of actors, singers and dancers). In his time the theaters were still rough-and-ready wooden affairs; the one in the Agora eventually collapsed under the weight of the spectators, and a new edifice was built in the 5th century BC on the south slope of the Acropolis dedicated to Dionysos, whose temple stood close by. The plays of Aeschylus, Sophocles, Aristophanes and Euripides were all performed here for the first time, when their authors competed in dramatic contests over the three final days of the Great Dionysia festival ● *40*.

Aeschylus
This Roman bust represents Aeschylus (525–456), one of the greatest of the Athenian tragic poets. Out of some eighty plays written by him, only seven have survived; among these are *The Persians*, which recounts the triumph of the Greeks at the Battle of Salamis ● *45* (at which Aeschylus was present), and the author's principal work, the *Oresteia* trilogy (458 BC). According to Pausanias, Dionysos appeared to Aeschylus in a dream, urging him to write his first play.

Dionysos and tragedy
On this stele *Skene* (the female personification of the dramatic arts) offers Euripides a tragic mask. Behind them, Dionysos is shown holding a cup used for libations.

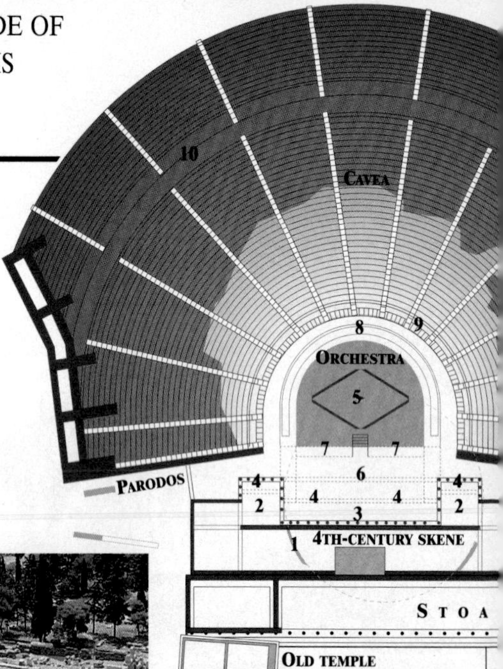

THE THEATER OF DIONYSOS
The drawing (right), based on the work of the late 19th-century archeologist Dörpfeld, shows the various different periods in the construction of the theater. Only a part of the *cavea* is shown. The original stalls ascended right to the foot of the rock of the Acropolis, as the topography of the site might suggest.

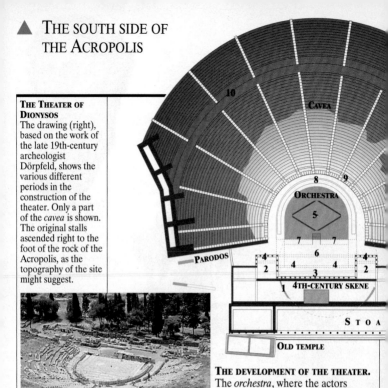

10
CAVEA
8
9
ORCHESTRA
5
7
7
6
PARODOS
4
4
4
4
2
2
3
1
4TH-CENTURY SKENE
STOA
OLD TEMPLE

THE DEVELOPMENT OF THE THEATER. The *orchestra*, where the actors appeared, began as nothing more than a circular area of beaten earth; and the *skene*, from which our word "scene" derives, was a simple, unadorned wooden structure. The building of the stone theater began around 400 BC but was not completed until the time of Lycurgus, in about 330 BC. At that time classical tragedy and comedy gave way to the new comedy form, and a number of other Greek cities built theaters for these highly popular spectacles. The ruins we see today mostly date from Roman times, but their basic architectural structure is Greek.

THE SKENE. During the classical period of Greek dramaturgy, the chorus and the actors performed at the same physical level on the *orchestra,* in front of the *skene*. This word basically means "hut" or "tent"; hence the *skene* began as a precarious structure of wood and canvas, housing the actors' dressing rooms. Little by little the *skene* increased in importance; and before long it was decorated, to provide a backdrop to the play. The first dramatic work played before a full-fledged theater décor was probably Aeschylus' *Oresteia* trilogy. The theater completed under Lycurgus was provided with a monumental stone *skene*, consisting of a hall nearly 150 feet long and 13 feet high. Two wings (called the *paraskenia*) stood on either side of the *proskenion*, the platform on which the actors spoke their lines. During the Hellenistic era this

THE FRIEZE OF DIONYSOS
Completed during the reign of Nero (1st century AD), this relief depicts scenes from the myth of Dionysos. On the far left are Zeus (seated) and Hermes (standing upright), carrying the newborn Dionysos.

The head of the aged, bearded Silenus, a disciple of Dionysos, has been preserved thanks to the figure's crouched position; he seems to be supporting the weight of the stage on his shoulders.

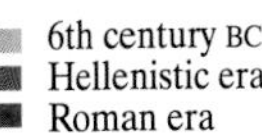

6th century BC
Hellenistic era
Roman era

1. *Orchestra* (6th century BC)
2. *Paraskenia*
3. *Proskenion* (4th century AD)
4. *Proskenion* and *paraskenia* (1st century BC)
5. *Thymele*
6. Nero's *proskenion*
7. Phaidros' *proskenion*
8. Throne of the High Priest of Dionysos Eleutheros
9. Imperial box
10. Lower *diazoma*

ODOS

area was edged by colonnades. The visible remains of the stage were built much later, dating from the early 4th century AD. The frieze in high relief which decorates its base was taken from an older structure, probably erected in the time of Nero (AD 54–68), and recut to fit the new site. The scenes represented describe the life of Dionysos, from his birth to his triumphal arrival in Attica. Behind the stage, an open porch offered shelter to the public in case of bad weather.

THE CAVEA. This public area was enclosed on its west side by massive walls. It could seat about seventeen thousand spectators, in three sections separated by *diazomata*. The two lower sectors were made up of thirty-two rows of seats, and the upper one of fourteen rows. The upper *diazoma* was an extension of the *peripatos*, the public way cut into the flank of the Acropolis. The front row consisted of sixty-seven thrones of Pentelic marble, reserved for high dignitaries; sixty of these are still in place. They carry inscriptions (usually the titles of the people permitted to sit in them) and, although they date from the first century AD, they are nonetheless exact copies of those of the theater built by Lycurgus. During the reign of Hadrian an Imperial box was built behind the throne of the high priest, and statues of the emperor were erected at different points around the structure.

THE THRONE OF THE HIGH PRIEST OF DIONYSOS
The central throne on the front row, much more imposing than the others, was reserved for the priest of Dionysos, with an inscription to that effect. Its feet and armrests are sculpted with reliefs inside and out.

NEAR THE THEATER

During the Roman era a stone barrier was erected facing the auditorium to protect spectators from wild beasts, during the circus games introduced by the Romans. The *orchestra* of the theater, which was originally an area of beaten earth, was eventually paved in marble and surrounded by a stone drain to lead off rainwater. At its center stood the *thymele*, or altar of Dionysos.

THE ODEON OF PERICLES ● *81.* To the west of the theater of Dionysos stood a rectangular odeon, constructed in 445 BC by Pericles. This building received musicians and athletes during the Great Dionysia and the Panathenaic Festival. Three rows of seventy-two columns ran around its four sides, the performers occupying a broad central area. The odeon was destroyed when Sulla sacked Athens in 86 BC; then was rebuilt twenty-five years later, to the original plan, by Ariobarzanes II, king of Cappadocia, who had studied in Athens as a young man. Only the foundations of this edifice are visible today.

THE PANAGHIA SPILIOTISSA
Above the Theater of Dionysos is a cave closed off by an iron grille. In antiquity this was sacred to Artemis; later, at the beginning of the Byzantine era, it was converted into a Christian chapel and called the Panaghia Spiliotissa (Our Lady of the Cave).

THE CHOREGIC MONUMENT OF THRASYLLOS. To the left of the chapel stand a pair of Corinthian columns. These constitute the only standing remains of the Monument of Thrasyllos (erected in 320–319 BC), dedicated to a wealthy citizen who financed a chorus in the drama and poetry competitions.

THE STOA OF EUMENES II. This 535-foot stoa connected the Theater of Dionysos with the Odeon of Herodes Atticus. Eumenes II, king of Pergamum (197–159 BC), gave it to Athens, where both he and his younger brother Attalos had studied as young men. The stoa had two levels, with sixty-two Doric columns along the façade and thirty-two Ionic ones at the center. According to Vitruvius, spectators sometimes sheltered in it.

THE CHOREGIC MONUMENT OF NIKIAS. At the southeast corner of the stoa are the foundations of the monument of Nikias, built in 320–319 BC. This structure was a prostyle temple ● *90*, with a *pronaos* with six Doric columns facing west. After it was pulled down by the Heruli in AD 267, the stones of this monument were used to build the Beulé Gate ▲ *132*, the main entrance to the Acropolis.

This engraving shows the two columns of the Monument of Thrasyllos where they are still to be seen today.

THE ODEON OF HERODES ATTICUS

STRUCTURE. This small theater, consisting of a semicircle 125 feet wide, was constructed in AD 161 by Herodes Atticus. It had a cedar roof, which sheltered the audience and made it possible to stage concerts of vocal and instrumental music in all seasons (the word *ode*, from which "odeon" derives, means "song" in Greek). The façade, with its semicircular arches and rectangular niches, contained a number of statues. It had two levels in its central part, flanked by two three-level wings which give onto the *parodoi* (side passages) and the sides of the stage. Inside, stairways served the different levels. At the center of the façade, with its back to the stage structure, was a vaulted porch which had three entrances communicating with three other doors leading to the stage.

THE STAGE. This was raised 3 or 4 feet above the ground. It was about 100 feet long and 30 feet deep, and the back and sides were adorned with colonnades. These supported a kind of balcony or upper stage, probably used by the actors playing the roles of gods. Above this a line of semicircular window embrasures is the only surviving part of the structure. The *orchestra* in front of the stage has retained its floor of alternating white and onion marble.

THE STOA OF EUMENES
The back wall of this stoa was held up by forty buttresses and included a line of semicircular window embrasures. It was uncovered during the construction of the Wall of Valerian (AD 253–60), which necessitated the stoa's demolition.

This 18th-century engraving purports to be one of the first reconstitutions of the "Theater of Bacchus", but is in fact a representation of the Odeon of Herodes Atticus. Travelers and scholars were apt to confuse the two monuments, because the Theater of Dionysos mentioned in old texts was buried underground.

THE CAVEA. With buttresses of its own, the *cavea* consists of thirty-two rows of stalls with a capacity of five thousand spectators. A walkway, communicating with the stairways of the wings, runs around the upper part of the hemicycle.
THE ATHENS FESTIVAL. Every summer (June to September) the Athens Festival ◆ *372, 396* recreates the tradition of classical tragedy at the Odeon of Herodes Atticus, which has now been restored. These performances attract large numbers of spectators. The festival also puts on concerts, ballet performances and operas.

THE ASKLEPIEION

A small terrace overlooks the northwest corner of the theater; here are the ruins of a temple to Asklepios, founded in 419–418 BC by a certain Telemachus. The site, which measures about 165 feet long and 80 feet wide, once enclosed a sanctuary, an altar and a stoa in the Doric order with two stories.
THE CULT OF ASKLEPIOS. This cult spread throughout Greece after the 4th century BC, eventually comprising more than three hundred shrines. One of the best preserved is the shrine at Epidaurus ▲ *316.* The god of medicine, recognizable by his emblems of a staff and twin serpents, was often associated with his daughter Hygieia, who personified health.
THE SANCTUARY. The entrance to the site is by way of the ruins of its *propylon* ● *89*, a monumental gate dating from Roman times. To the right are the ruins of a Roman portico; and to the left are those of a Doric stoa built in the 4th century BC, at the foot of the Acropolis, which served as a dormitory for the patients at the Asklepieion. This was nearly 165 feet long and just over 30 feet deep.

Two actors in the costume of antiquity, acting in a tragedy at the Odeon of Herodes Atticus.

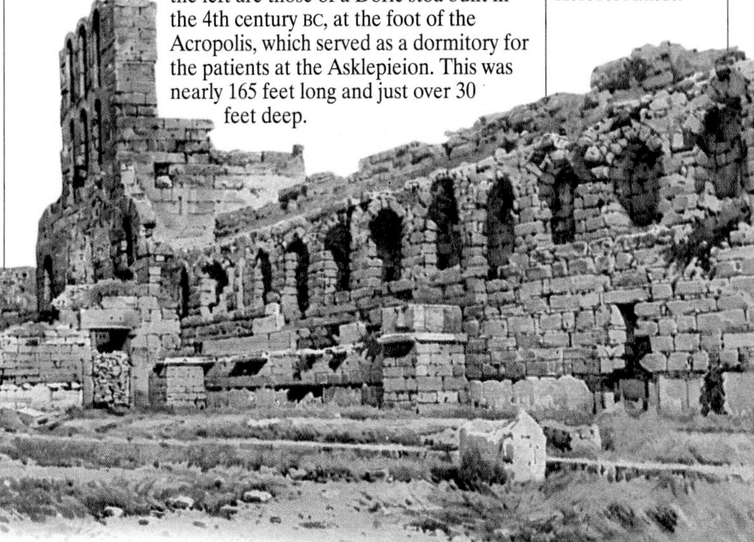

THE SANCTUARY OF ASKLEPIOS
This sanctuary was consecrated in 420 BC.

Originating in Epidaurus, the cult of Asklepios was introduced into Attica following the plague of 429 BC.

ASKLEPIOS AND HYGIEIA
On this funerary stele Asklepios and his daughter receive votive offerings from mortals. The latter are recognizable by their small size in comparison to the gods.

The two levels included seventeen Doric columns on the façade and six Ionic columns positioned along the central axis. At the eastern end of the stoa, the rock was mined to a depth of 13 feet to create a large room. In the floor one can see a pit where the sacred serpents of Asklepios were probably kept. The foundations of a small temple dedicated to the latter and his daughter Hygieia have been excavated at the western end of the stoa; investigations have also revealed the presence of a large altar at the center of the Asklepieion. Most of the marble fragments here formed part of a Christian basilica built on this site in the mid 5th century AD. This church was dedicated to Saints Cosmas and Damian, known in Greece as the *Haghii Anargyroi* (the penniless saints) because they refused to accept money from the poor people they had cured of their ills. The west side of the Asklepieion sanctuary extends to an outcrop, while the ruins of the north side represent the only known remains of a pre-400 BC Ionic stoa. At the back of this are four rooms with a pebble-mosaic floor: facing these there used to be a porch of twelve Ionic columns. This stoa also served as a ward for patients. Just to the west is the site of a warm-water bath dating from the 6th century BC, of which only one piece has survived. This was built around a sacred spring dedicated to the nymph Alkippe. The ancients attributed to naiads (nymphs that inhabited springs and rivers) the power of conferring medicinal properties on water. The curative powers of sulphur, in particular, lay behind their belief. But these often irresistibly attractive divinities were not always benevolent to humans: it was said that if a mortal had the ill-luck to catch a glimpse of a naiad bathing, he would immediately go stark mad.

From Plaka to Monastiraki

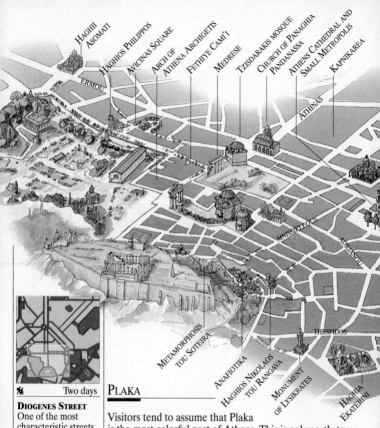

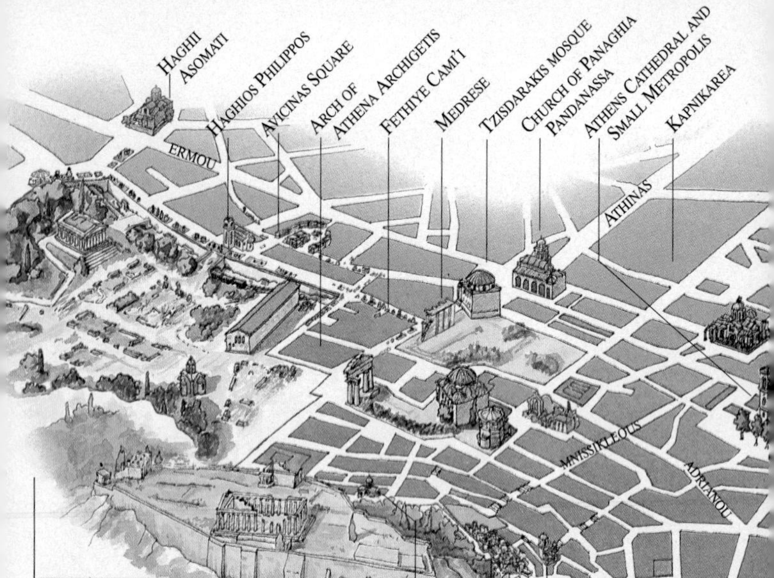

Haghii Asomati
Haghios Philippos
Avicinas Square
Arch of Athena Archigetis
Fethiye Cami'i
Medrese
Tzisdarakis Mosque
Church of Panaghia Pandanassa
Athens Cathedral and Small Metropolis
Kapnikarea
Ermou
Athinas
Mnissikleous
Adrianou
Thespidos
Metamorphosis tou Soteira
Anafiotika
Haghios Nikolaos tou Rangava
Monument of Lysikrates
Haghia Ekaterini

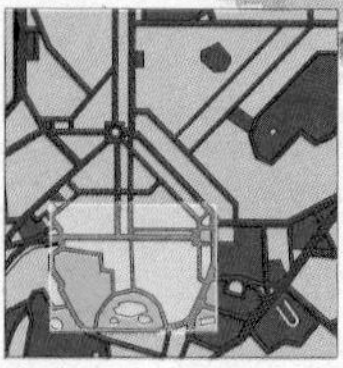

Two days

Plaka

Diogenes Street
One of the most characteristic streets of Plaka, flanked by low houses with multicolored façades. The details are often remarkable: heavily ornamented doors and plaster statues in niches proclaim the locals' pride in their district.

Visitors tend to assume that Plaka is the most colorful part of Athens. This is only partly true; nevertheless, this district is the only one in the city which escaped the galloping urbanization of the 1960's and 1970's. But, having escaped the demolition workers, it nearly succumbed to unbridled tourism; fortunately the authorities acted in time to help, and a program of restoration launched in 1983 has gradually brought back the color and luster of Plaka's 19th-century buildings. Phony *bouzouki* bands no longer fill the streets with deafening amplified music. Plaka has rediscovered itself, and the old spirit is once again abroad – among the silver reliquaries of Byzantine churches filled with *ex voto* offerings, in the stones of ancient monuments, in the courtyards of small white houses with wooden balconies, in the steep alleys, and in the dark recesses of underground taverns where *retsina* flows.

Plaka's origins. Plaka is supposed to mean "the flat" – as opposed to the rising ground of the Acropolis, which overshadows it. But the many steep alleys here would seem to deny this explanation; a more plausible theory is that the word comes from the Albanian word *pliaka*, meaning old. Whatever the truth of the matter, if you get tired of interminable dead-straight avenues and right-angled intersections, you can always come here to sample a different side of Athens.

The formation of the district. Looking down on the city from the summit of Lycabettus or the slopes of Mount Hymettus, it is hard to imagine that at the beginning of the

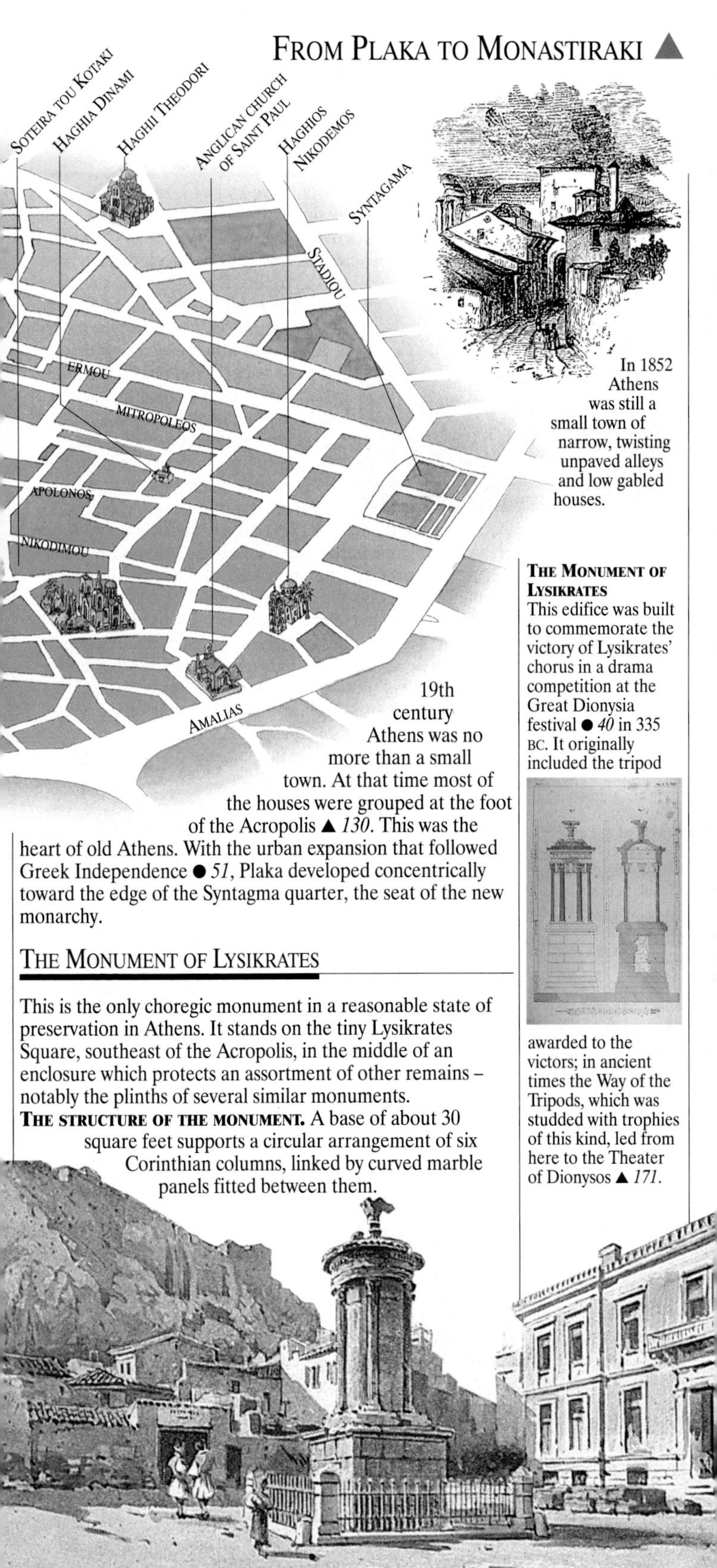

In 1852 Athens was still a small town of narrow, twisting unpaved alleys and low gabled houses.

19th century Athens was no more than a small town. At that time most of the houses were grouped at the foot of the Acropolis ▲ *130*. This was the heart of old Athens. With the urban expansion that followed Greek Independence ● *51*, Plaka developed concentrically toward the edge of the Syntagma quarter, the seat of the new monarchy.

THE MONUMENT OF LYSIKRATES

This is the only choregic monument in a reasonable state of preservation in Athens. It stands on the tiny Lysikrates Square, southeast of the Acropolis, in the middle of an enclosure which protects an assortment of other remains – notably the plinths of several similar monuments.

THE STRUCTURE OF THE MONUMENT. A base of about 30 square feet supports a circular arrangement of six Corinthian columns, linked by curved marble panels fitted between them.

THE MONUMENT OF LYSIKRATES
This edifice was built to commemorate the victory of Lysikrates' chorus in a drama competition at the Great Dionysia festival ● *40* in 335 BC. It originally included the tripod awarded to the victors; in ancient times the Way of the Tripods, which was studded with trophies of this kind, led from here to the Theater of Dionysos ▲ *171*.

FAMOUS GUESTS
Lord Byron, during his first visit to Athens in 1811, wrote to his friend Francis Hodgson: "I am lodged in a Capuchin convent. Mount Hymettus is before me, the Acropolis behind, the Temple of Jupiter to my right, the Stadium in front, the city to my left. What a site this is, and how picturesque!" Chateaubriand also stayed for a while at the Capuchin convent.

PLATEIA FILOMOUSOU ETAIREIAS
The square named for the "association of the Friends of the Muses" is one of Plaka's most charming backwaters.

A street at the heart of Anafiotika.

At the top, a tripartite architrave and a frieze showing scenes from the myth of Dionysos are capped by a dome made from a single marble block, carved with foliage motifs. Crowning all is a stone finial of acanthus-leaf carving, which was the base for the tripod. The inscription on the architrave reads: "Lysikrates of Kikyna, son of Lysitheides, was *choregos*; the tribe of Akamantis won the victory with a chorus of boys; Theon played the flute; Lysiades of Athens trained the chorus; Euainetos was archon."

A CAPUCHIN MONASTERY. For many centuries this monument was known as the "Lantern of Demosthenes". A diminutive reading room was built into the rotunda and until the 17th century it was thought that the great orator came here to prepare his speeches. After being absorbed into a Capuchin monastery (founded in 1669), it served for a while as the monks' library. The monastery precinct was burned to the ground at the start of the War of Independence, but the Monument of Lysikrates remained practically undamaged; the surrounding rubble was cleared away, and its restoration was paid for by France in 1845.

HAGHIOS DIMITRIOS. Epimenidou Street, one of the oldest thoroughfares in Plaka, begins at the monument of Lysikrates; on it stands the small chapel (*paraklissi*) of Haghios Dimitrios. The chapel has a modern façade, but the interior is original, dating from the beginning of the Ottoman period.

AROUND THE ACROPOLIS

ANAFIOTIKA. At the top of Epimenidou Street, take Stratonos Street along the edge of the Acropolis to Anafiotika, which overlooks Plaka. This small village has a strong character that has always distinguished it from the rest of the quarter. Its name is derived from its first inhabitants, who came from Anafi, a small island in the Cyclades east of Santorini. These people arrived as refugees in Athens in 1821 and created a village exactly like the one on their island, with low houses and walled gardens along a labyrinth of marble-paved alleys. Despite a law of 1834 forbidding all construction in this part of the city, Anafiotika grew immensely over a few years, keeping pace with Athens' rapid expansion following the War of Independence. However, the Anafiots preserved the identity of their ghetto.

HAGHIOS NIKOLAOS TOU RANGAVA. Hard by Anafiotika, at the end of Epicharmou Street, is the Church of Haghios Nikolaos tou Rangava. This building, which dates from the 18th century, was rebuilt and enlarged at the start of the

The Museum of Musical Instruments ● 72 This small museum (on Pelopida Street, near the Tower of the Winds) houses the collection of the Greek musicologist Anoyanakis. Earphones are available in front of each display case, so you can listen to

20th century. The original church was built along traditional cruciform lines, but at the time it was rebuilt the nave was extended westward, thereby doubling its size, while a lateral chapel prolonged the north side. Note the inclusion in the walls of antique columns and capitals.

The Canellopoulos Museum. Two fine neoclassical buildings at the foot of the Acropolis house the large and eclectic collection of Paul and Alexander Canellopoulos. Protohistoric ceramics, Coptic fabrics and Byzantine antiques of a very high quality are exhibited here in buildings of surpassing elegance. Note, in particular, the magnificent icons, along with three portraits dating from the Roman era; painted on wood, these treasures were found in sarcophagi excavated in the Fayum region of Egypt.

The Aerides

The Aerides are the winds, as represented on the panels of the eight sides of the Tower of the Winds ▲ *214*. By extension their name has been adopted by the surrounding quarter, which straddles Plaka and Monastiraki.

The Roman Market ▲ *212*. Between the Tower of the Winds and the Gate of Athena Archegetis is the Roman Market. Here the Turkish occupants established a wheat exchange, where the merchants used antique marble measures that were recently discovered *in situ*. The houses are constructed around closed courtyards fronting narrow, winding alleys; most of them were built with materials salvaged from the surrounding ruins.

The Fethiye Mosque. Overlooking the Roman Market stands the Fethiye Cami'i, or Victory Mosque, which is the oldest mosque in Athens. This was built in 1458, two years after the taking of the city by Mehmet the Conqueror, fresh

Church of the Metamorphosis tou Soteira
The Byzantine Church of the Transfiguration of the Savior dates from the 14th century. Inside is a cave containing a chapel dedicated to Haghia Paraskevi (Saint Friday). A proto-Christian capital is used here in lieu of an altar.

Logothetis House
A door and an entryway to the inner courtyard are all that remain of the luxurious mansion of the Logothetis family, who were powerful in Athens under the Turkish regime.

The Medrese
Perceived as a symbol of Turkish oppression, the Medrese was razed in 1919.

from his seizure of Constantinople in 1455. The Greeks rechristened the building Cami tou Staropazoron, the "grain-market mosque". The building occupies an area of about 50 feet by 50 feet. Its shallow dome rests on a low rectangular drum, with half domes on all four sides. The façade consists of five domed bays opening onto an inner courtyard through four semicircular arches. Now used as an archeological workshop, the Fethiye Cami'i is closed to the public.

Church of the Taxiarchs. This building, which dates from the 11th century, stands just to the north of the Roman Market. It was completely rebuilt after the War of Independence ● *51*, and has recently been restored again.

The Medrese. Opposite the Tower of the Winds is the site of the Medrese, a Turkish Koranic school founded in 1721 by Mehmet Fakri, a dignitary of the court of Sultan Ahmed III. Theology students here occupied cells built around a central courtyard. From time to time the school was the scene of assemblies of the Turkish authorities. Seriously damaged during the two sieges of the Acropolis, it served as a prison during the last years of Ottoman rule and continued to do so under the Greek monarchy until 1911. Razed to the ground in 1919, today all that remains of it is a ruined gateway.

Toward Syntagma Square

Haghia Ekaterini. A short way up Lysikratou Street is the small Church of Haghia Ekaterini next to the ruins of a Roman bath. The church dates from the 12th century and possesses some fine icons with sculpted marble frames.

Soteira tou Kotaki. This church is situated at the intersection of Kodrou and Kidathineon streets. Founded in the 11th or 12th century, it was rebuilt by the Russians in 1834 and subsequently enlarged at the beginning of the 20th century.

Haghios Nikodemos. On the east side of Plaka is the Russian Church of Athens, built in the first half of the 11th century. Its original name was Soteira (the Savior) Lykodimou; the building served as a chapel for a monastery which was destroyed in the 18th century. Damaged by a Turkish bombardment in 1827, it was left derelict after the War of Independence until Czar Nicholas I offered to buy it from the Greek government on behalf of the Russian community in Athens, in exchange for its restoration. The work was begun in 1850 and completed five years later.

The Museum of Greek Popular Art
Situated at 17 Kidathineon Street, this museum displays objects ranging from the 17th century to our own time – clothes, embroidery, wood carvings, and works by the naive painter Theophilos Hadjimichali (1868–1934). The artist kept his brushes and colors in this box, which he decorated himself.

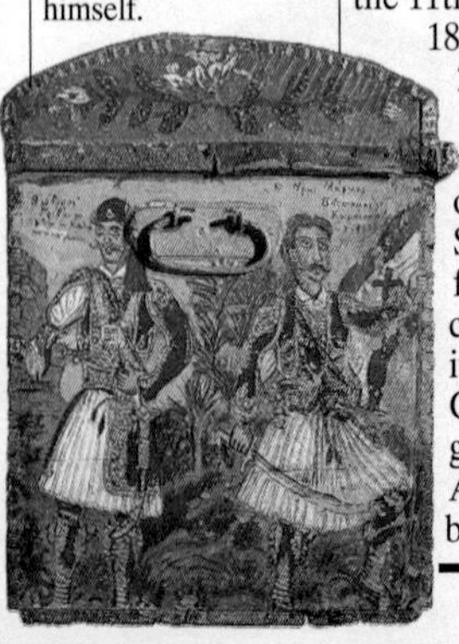

Haghios Nikodemos
The church's belfry was paid for by Czar Alexander II; the interior was decorated by the German painter Thiersch.

Center for Folk Art and Traditions. This municipal art center, at 6 Hadjimihali Street, possesses a collection devoted to Greek crafts and the Greek rural heritage. Assembled by the anthropologist Angeliki Hadjimihali, it includes reconstructions of interiors, along with examples of embroidery, weaving, woodcarving and costumes etc.

Cathedral Square

Continue up Diogenes Street and turn left along Evangelistrias Street to the cathedral, which is the seat of the Metropolitan Archbishop of Athens.
Athens Cathedral. The Metropolis is the most imposing building on Mitropoleos Square. It was designed by Theophil von Hansen, Franz Boulanger and Dimitrios Zezos, and the first stone was laid on Christmas Day 1842 by King Otto and Queen Amalia. However, it took twenty years to complete the cathedral, and it was not until May 21, 1862, that the king and queen dedicated it to the Annunciation of the Virgin.
The Small Metropolis ★. The Small Metropolis is beside the cathedral; it is dedicated to the Panaghia Gorgoepikoös, "the Madonna who Swiftly Hears", a miraculous icon that is the church's most precious treasure.

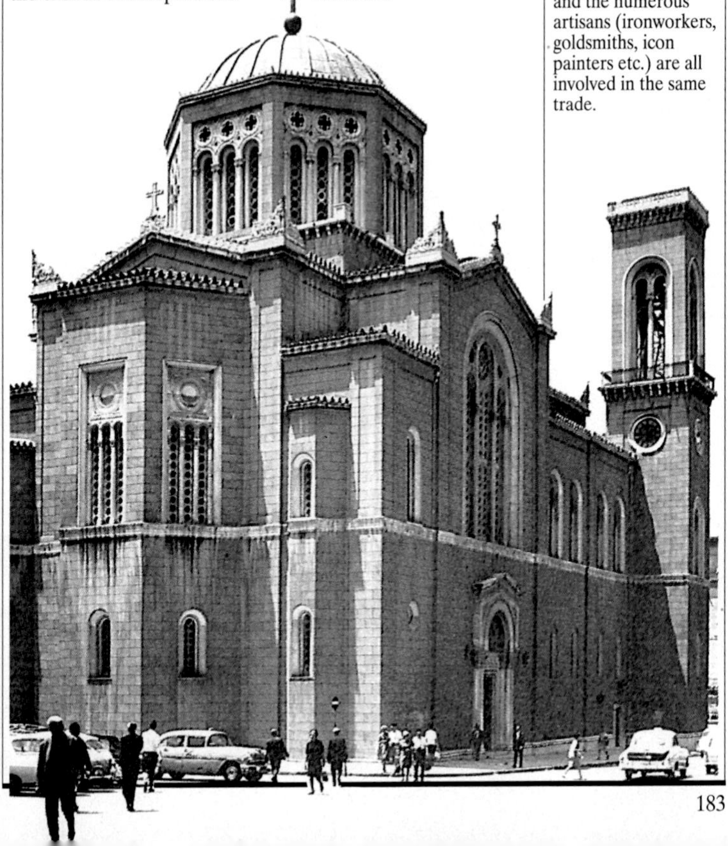

Evangelistrias Street
The atmosphere and name of this street

are strongly evocative of Greek piety. The shops here sell nothing but icons and other religious items, and the numerous artisans (ironworkers, goldsmiths, icon painters etc.) are all involved in the same trade.

The Byzantine Church of Panaghia Gorgoepikoös ("The Madonna who Swiftly Hears") was formerly the cathedral of Athens. It was built in the 12th century of materials from sundry Greek, Roman, paleo-Christian and Byzantine structures; other names for it are Haghios Eleutherios and the Small Metropolis (Mikri Mitropolis). During the Ottoman occupation this building was the seat of the Metropolitan Archbishop of Athens.

ANCIENT GREEK BAS-RELIEFS
Some of the bas-reliefs at the Small Metropolis come directly from ancient structures. The reuse of such ornaments was no doubt due to the presence in Athens of the scholar and antiquarian Michael Choniates at the close of the 12th century.

This painting of the interior of the Small Metropolis is based on a 19th-century engraving. The paintings which at that time covered the nave, the transept and the inside of the dome have since been covered by whitewash.

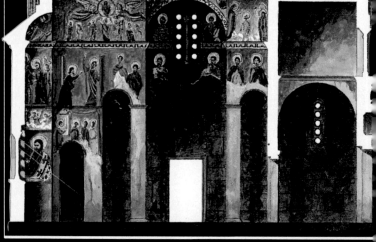

church, cruciform with a
e and narthex, remains
as it was, except for the
columns on which
ome rests; these
replaced in
by four
pillars.

The foundations consist of blocks of marble taken from ancient monuments. Their upper parts are decorated with bas-reliefs, the most recent of which date from the late 12th century.

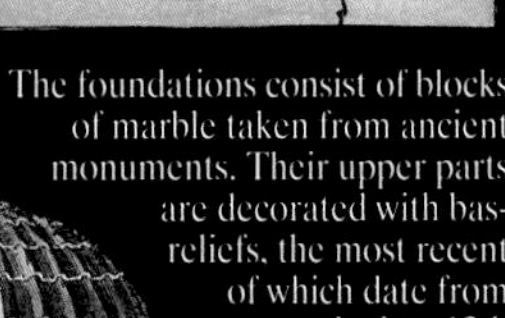

Bas-reliefs
The façade of the Small Metropolis is a veritable museum of Byzantine architectural ornament. The upper part is covered with bas-reliefs of different themes: a calendar in the form of a frieze, a labyrinth inside a square, Byzantine crosses, funerary stelae and animal motifs.

THE KAPNIKAREA
This 11th-century church, dedicated to the Virgin of the Dormition, stands on the edge of Plaka on a square at Ermou and Kapnikarea streets. The cruciform plan, the dome seated on an octagonal drum, the toothed decoration and semicircular windows on the brick façade, and the sculpted capitals of the small columns make the church a model of the

classical Byzantine style. The frescos in the nave were painted in the 1950's by Photios Kontoglu.

Although the Small Metropolis was built during the 12th and 13th centuries (replacing a church dating from about 600) and some of the sculpted marble blocks date from that period, the multitude of inscriptions and reliefs on the façade make the building a museum of the classical, Byzantine and Roman epochs. Abandoned during the War of Independence, the church was used as a library prior to its reconsecration in 1868. Since then it has been restored along its original lines.

MONASTIRAKI

Monastiraki means "little monastery"; the name was given to the Panaghia Pandanassa or "Mother of the Universe", the church which stands on the central square of the district. Under the Ottomans this square, on which seven shopping streets converge, already constituted the lower sector of a bazaar extending as far as the Roman market. Since then it has been the exclusive preserve of street vendors, fruit and vegetable stalls, and traders selling items such as sponges, leather goods, coconuts, dried fruit and

Museum of Decorative Arts
This museum has been housed in the Tzisdarakis Mosque since its restoration following an earthquake in 1981. It contains the important Kyriazopoulos collection of ceramics and a variety of craftwork.

peanuts. At present the construction of the new metro obscures its center, and for the time being the railings are used for displaying all manner of merchandise.

The Panaghia Pandanassa. The origins of this church, which is dedicated to the Dormition of the Virgin, go back to the 10th century, though the first mention of its existence dates from 1678. Formerly it was part of a convent, also founded in the 10th century, which was partly demolished during construction of the first metro line. The building we see today was renovated, rather unsatisfactorily, in 1911.

Church of the Haghii Assomati. The hexagonal Church of the Haghii Assomati (at the intersection of Ermou and Assomatou streets) is dedicated to the "immaterial saints" and dates from the second half of the 11th century.

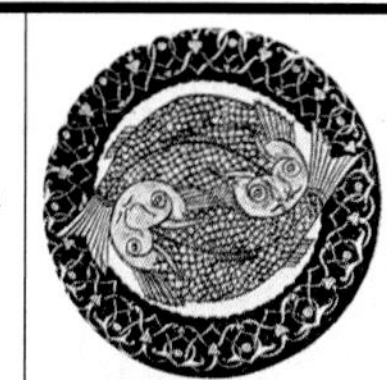

Contemporary Ceramics
Professor Kyriazopoulos assembled one of the most important collections of early-20th-century ceramics from Greek and Cypriot workshops.

The Flea Market

The millions of tons of concrete unleashed on Athens over the last few decades have not submerged her oriental spirit. To appreciate this you need only take a stroll around Monastiraki on a Sunday – when traders are present in huge numbers, yelling to attract the attention of customers above the general hubbub. In Ifestou, Kynetou and Adrianou streets, or around the square dominated by the Church of Haghios Phillipos, you have to be patient – and robust in the use of your elbows – if you mean to make your way through. With the profusion of items on sale, it is very difficult to separate the good from the bad. The influx of tourists over the last twenty years has nourished a cheap trade in plastic Parthenons, keyrings in the shape of satyrs with giant penises, and diminutive *tsaroukhis* (red leather shoes with pompoms) as worn by the *evzones* (Greek guardsmen) on parade. Some people like to hang these on the rearview mirrors of their cars. Nevertheless, if you take the trouble to look between the ranks of so-called works of art you may make out something of the social mosaic of the city and its recent history. One area, for example, is predominantly Russian, while another is Albanian; yet another is apparently reserved for Greeks from the islands; and survivors of the hippie era, strumming guitars and sitars, still haunt the west wall of the Library of Hadrian ▲ *210*. Curiosities are manifold; bargains rare. Gone are the

Barriers around the future Monastiraki metro station, wire fences protecting the Agora, the perimeter fence around the archeological dig at the Library of Hadrian – all are legitimate vending sites for dealers who have no fixed stalls.

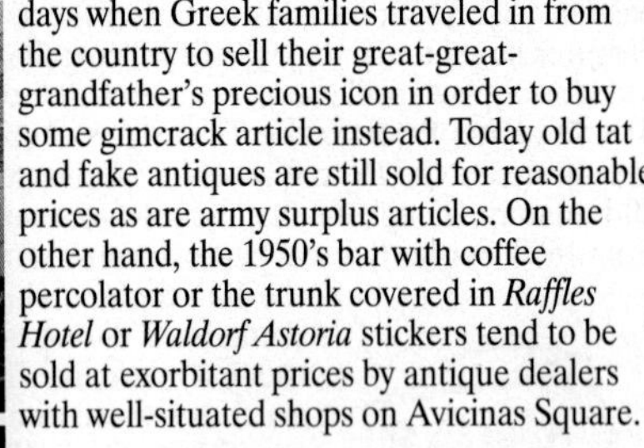

days when Greek families traveled in from the country to sell their great-great-grandfather's precious icon in order to buy some gimcrack article instead. Today old tat and fake antiques are still sold for reasonable prices as are army surplus articles. On the other hand, the 1950's bar with coffee percolator or the trunk covered in *Raffles Hotel* or *Waldorf Astoria* stickers tend to be sold at exorbitant prices by antique dealers with well-situated shops on Avicinas Square.

AVICINAS SQUARE ★

On the intersection of Ifestou and Kynetou streets, this enclave sandwiched between modern buildings has been a haven for junk dealers for many decades. This is the real heart of the Athens flea market. After jostling your way through the crowds, you will be glad to come to rest on the terrace of a small café facing a stall selling old iron, before you set about buying a gramophone which is, if anything, just as ancient as its owner. Here, more than anywhere else, the visitor will find plentiful supplies of local color. The middle of the square is reserved for bric-a-brac dealers, who arrive at the crack of dawn to unpack their curious wares – piles of non-matching plates, trinkets, old iron, etc., all artistically arranged on the ground. Around these sit the vendors of furniture and domestic appliances, the hardware merchants and the authentic antique dealers, with whom bargaining is often an uphill task. Just a short walk from here is the site of the Agora ▲ *190*.

The Agora

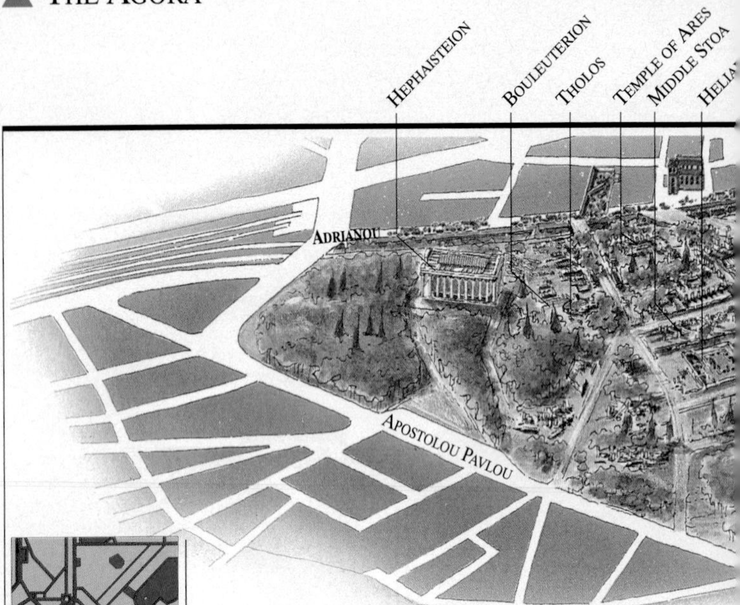

HEPHAISTEION
BOULEUTERION
THOLOS
TEMPLE OF ARES
MIDDLE STOA
ADRIANOU
APOSTOLOU PAVLOU

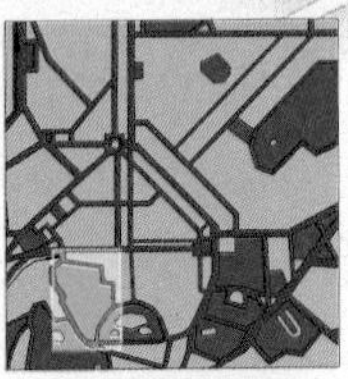

Half a day

HISTORY

The Agora of a Greek city was the focus of public life, fulfilling many different purposes – political, religious (in that it was itself a sanctuary and sheltered many temples), economic and commercial. In addition to being the market square, the Agora was where the Assembly sat and where Athenians met, gathering in the central square or in the shade of the stoas (open colonnades) to indulge their favorite pastime: conversation. People came to the Agora to hear the latest news, to sit at the feet of philosophers or invite friends to dinner. The development of Athens eventually led to specialization within the districts and the Assembly held its meetings on the Pnyx ▲ *207*. Nevertheless, the Agora still retained most of its public buildings.

Once the first stage of the excavation had been completed, the American School undertook a major landscaping scheme for the Agora. Trees and shrubs were planted not only to embellish the site, but also as a reminder of the greenness of Athens in antiquity.

A THOUSAND YEARS OF ARCHITECTURE ● *79*. The site of the Agora was inhabited from the 3rd millenium BC; but it was at the beginning of the 6th century BC, in the time of Solon, the initiator of Athenian democracy, that the Agora acquired its pre-eminent place in the city's life. Cleisthenes, who after 510 BC carried on the work of Solon, launched a huge program of construction on the Agora, which was carried on after his death by Pericles. The works continued for nearly 1,000 years thereafter. In 480 BC the religious and civic buildings on the west of the Agora were badly damaged during the sack of Athens by the Persians. They were eventually restored, and in the late 5th and early 4th centuries were complemented with new public buildings on the north and south. By the 2nd century BC the Agora had acquired its definitive site. In 86 BC Roman troops under Sulla destroyed some of the south side. From the close of the 1st century BC to

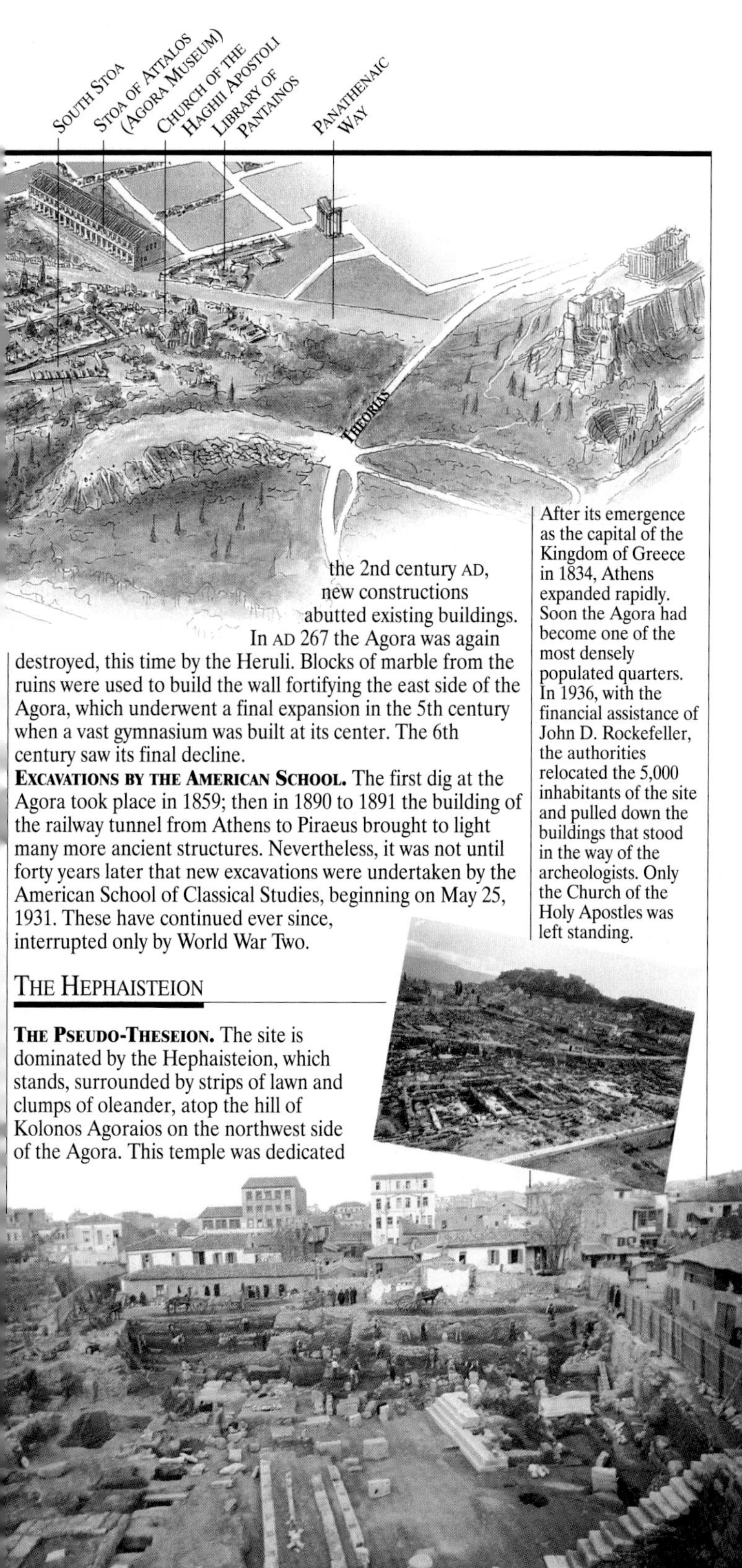

the 2nd century AD, new constructions abutted existing buildings. In AD 267 the Agora was again destroyed, this time by the Heruli. Blocks of marble from the ruins were used to build the wall fortifying the east side of the Agora, which underwent a final expansion in the 5th century when a vast gymnasium was built at its center. The 6th century saw its final decline.

Excavations by the American School. The first dig at the Agora took place in 1859; then in 1890 to 1891 the building of the railway tunnel from Athens to Piraeus brought to light many more ancient structures. Nevertheless, it was not until forty years later that new excavations were undertaken by the American School of Classical Studies, beginning on May 25, 1931. These have continued ever since, interrupted only by World War Two.

After its emergence as the capital of the Kingdom of Greece in 1834, Athens expanded rapidly. Soon the Agora had become one of the most densely populated quarters. In 1936, with the financial assistance of John D. Rockefeller, the authorities relocated the 5,000 inhabitants of the site and pulled down the buildings that stood in the way of the archeologists. Only the Church of the Holy Apostles was left standing.

The Hephaisteion

The Pseudo-Theseion. The site is dominated by the Hephaisteion, which stands, surrounded by strips of lawn and clumps of oleander, atop the hill of Kolonos Agoraios on the northwest side of the Agora. This temple was dedicated

to Hephaistos, the blacksmith god, and his sister Athena. Two lateral stairways lead up to it, and to the belvedere where an orientation map shows the position of the various ancient buildings on the site. For many years this temple was assumed to be a sanctuary dedicated to Theseus, whose exploits are featured on its metopes. In fact the real Theseion, built by Kimon in 475 BC, stood on the east side of the Agora, at the foot of the Acropolis. The Hephaisteion by contrast was built in about 449 BC, two years before work began on the Parthenon, and its architect is unknown. Having escaped destruction several times, the temple remained practically intact until the mid 7th century AD, when it was converted into a Christian basilica dedicated to Saint George. Damaged during the War of Independence, this church was restored and reconsecrated after the foundation of the monarchy.

STRUCTURE OF THE TEMPLE. The Hephaisteion is a Doric hexastyle temple ● *90.* Its stylobate and superstructures are of Pentelic marble. The front and rear porches are distyle, *in antis*. The inner colonnade originally included two levels of Doric columns, surmounted by a wooden entablature. A monumental door separated the *pronaos* from the *naos*, which was dominated by a colossal statue of Hephaistos.

SCULPTED DÉCOR
The reliefs of the frieze, along with the metopes of the temple, are sculpted in Parian marble and

represent the labors of Hercules and the exploits of Theseus. Only eighteen of the sixty-eight metopes were sculpted; the fifty others were probably painted. The pediments were adorned with sculptures, of which only the smallest traces remain. The frieze of the *pronaos* illustrates the mythical contest of the Athenians and Lapiths against the Centaurs. Theseus is included in the group on the right, bearing a large round shield.

THE PUBLIC BUILDINGS OF DEMOCRATIC ATHENS

At the foot of the hill of the Agora is a line of foundations that shows where the main public buildings of ancient Athens stood.

THE STOA OF ZEUS ELEUTHERIOS ● *80.* Completed in the last thirty years of the 5th century BC, this stoa was used for both lay and religious purposes and was dedicated to Zeus Eleutherios, god of liberty. It was a popular meeting place for Athenians. Nothing remains of it today except its foundations, but originally it was composed of a long portico flanked by projecting wings, both resembling the porch of a temple. The north wing is now buried beneath a railway line. The museum of the Agora possesses a statue of Nike (Victory) in Pentelic marble that was discovered against the north wall of the stoa.

THE TEMPLE OF APOLLO PATROÖS. About 30 feet from here are the foundations of a small Ionic temple built in 330 BC; this was the sanctuary of Apollo Patroös, father of Ion, the founder of the Ionian race.

SANCTUARY OF ZEUS AND ATHENA. North of the Temple of Apollo Patroös are the remains of a tiny sanctuary, dating from mid 4th century BC, dedicated to Zeus Phratrios and Athena Phratria, the tutelary divinities of the fraternities (*phratriai*) into which citizens were grouped. Each of the Attic tribes was made up of three fraternities, which were in turn divided into clans (*gene*).

THE METROÖN. This building was a sanctuary dedicated to the goddess Rhea, mother of the first gods (*Meter Theon*). Constructed in the 2nd century BC, it was also a repository of state archives; its four rooms, all of different sizes, opened onto a colonnaded porch. The religious sanctuary probably occupied the second room in from the south. The north area, which had two levels, was used as a reading room; in the center of the building stood an altar.

THE BOULEUTERION ● *81*. Built in the early 5th century BC, the Bouleuterion (Council Building) was the oldest of the Agora's public buildings. It was here that the Boule, or Council of the Five Hundred, met. It became a council representing the citizens of Athens following the democratic reforms of Solon in 594 BC. Cleisthenes defined its manner of recruitment, extended its powers and increased its members to five hundred. These members were elected by lot every year from the newly created ten tribes of Attica. They worked out proposals for new laws, which were then submitted to the vote of the Ecclesia (the people's assembly), which met first in the Agora and then on the Pnyx ▲ *207*. A first Bouleuterion was erected to the north of the Tholos at the beginning of the 5th century BC; its foundations are still visible, in the southwest corner of the Agora. At the end of the century, a new building was built just west of the old one: the two coexisted for over three centuries. The old Bouleuterion served as the archive of the Boule until it was demolished in the 2nd century and replaced by the Metroön.

THE THOLOS ● *80*. South of the Metroön, circular foundations mark the site of the Tholos, or Prytaneum, built in 465 BC. This was the seat of a reduced committee of the Boule. The nerve center of the government, this council was made up of the fifty *boulentes* of a clan. They each sat for one tenth of the year, alternating with the fifty representatives of each of the other nine clans. A limited council remained on hand night and

MONUMENT OF THE EPONYMOUS HEROES
In front of the Metroön one can distinguish the foundations of a pedestal. On this stood the ten statues of the *eponymoi*, the mythical heroes who gave their names to the ten tribes of Athens formed by Cleisthenes. The long base of these monuments was hung with whitewashed wooden tablets on which public notices were inscribed.

This instrument was used for drawing lots to select members of the tribunals.

STATUE OF HADRIAN
This torso stands near the Metroön. The emperor's breastplate shows Athena, crowned by winged Victories, with her owl and serpent emblems on either side.

▲ THE AGORA

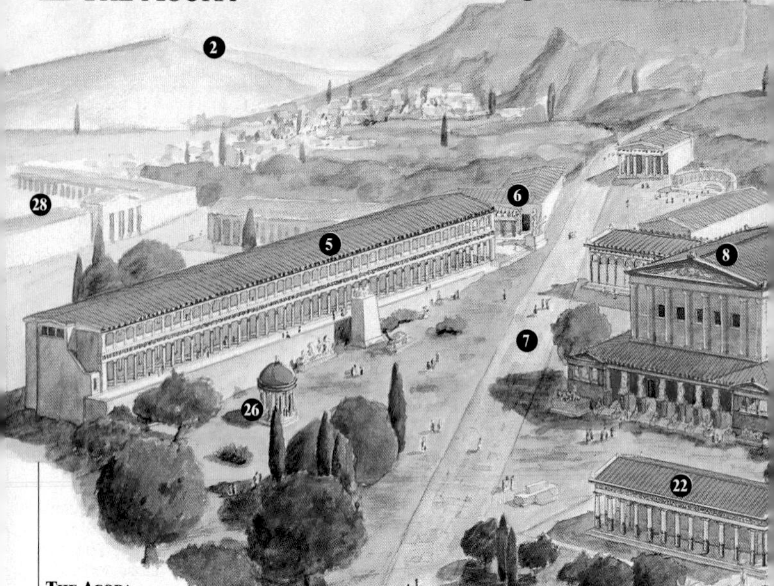

THE AGORA
1. The Acropolis
2. Mount Hymettus
3. Monument of Philopappos
4. Areopagus
5. Stoa of Attalos
6. Library of Pantainos
7. Panathenaic Way
8. Odeon of Agrippa
9. Middle Stoa
10. South Square
11. Heliaea
12. Southwest Fountain
13. Tholos
14. Bouleuterion
15. Hephaisteion
16. Arsenal
17. Metroön
18. Temple of Apollo Patroös
19. Stoa of Zeus Eleutheros

day so that there was no power vacuum at any time. Every day the *prytaneis* drew lots to select their president (*epistates*), who then headed the Prytaneum, the Ecclesia and the Boule for the next twenty-four hours. The *prytaneis* were fed by the city and performed libations and sacrifices. The Tholos also housed the standard weights and measures of the state.

THE MAIN SEWER. About 50 feet east of the Tholos is a ditch partly covered with stone flags, which marks the junction of the two channels of Athens' main sewer in ancient times.

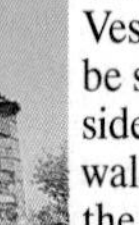

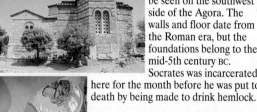

THE STATE PRISON
Vestiges of this prison may be seen on the southwest side of the Agora. The walls and floor date from the Roman era, but the foundations belong to the mid-5th century BC. Socrates was incarcerated here for the month before he was put to death by being made to drink hemlock.

THE CHURCH OF THE HOLY APOSTLES IN THE AGORA
The Church of the Haghii Apostoli, adjoining the southwest fountain, was built in the 10th century on the foundations of a nymphaeum. Altered in the 19th century, it was restored to its original state by the American School of Classical Studies. The frescos on its dome date from the 18th century.

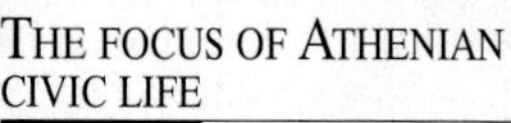

THE FOCUS OF ATHENIAN CIVIC LIFE

Stoas (*stoai*), long porticos occupied by stallholders and merchants, were a characteristic feature of all Greek agoras. Their name and social function still survive in modern Athens.

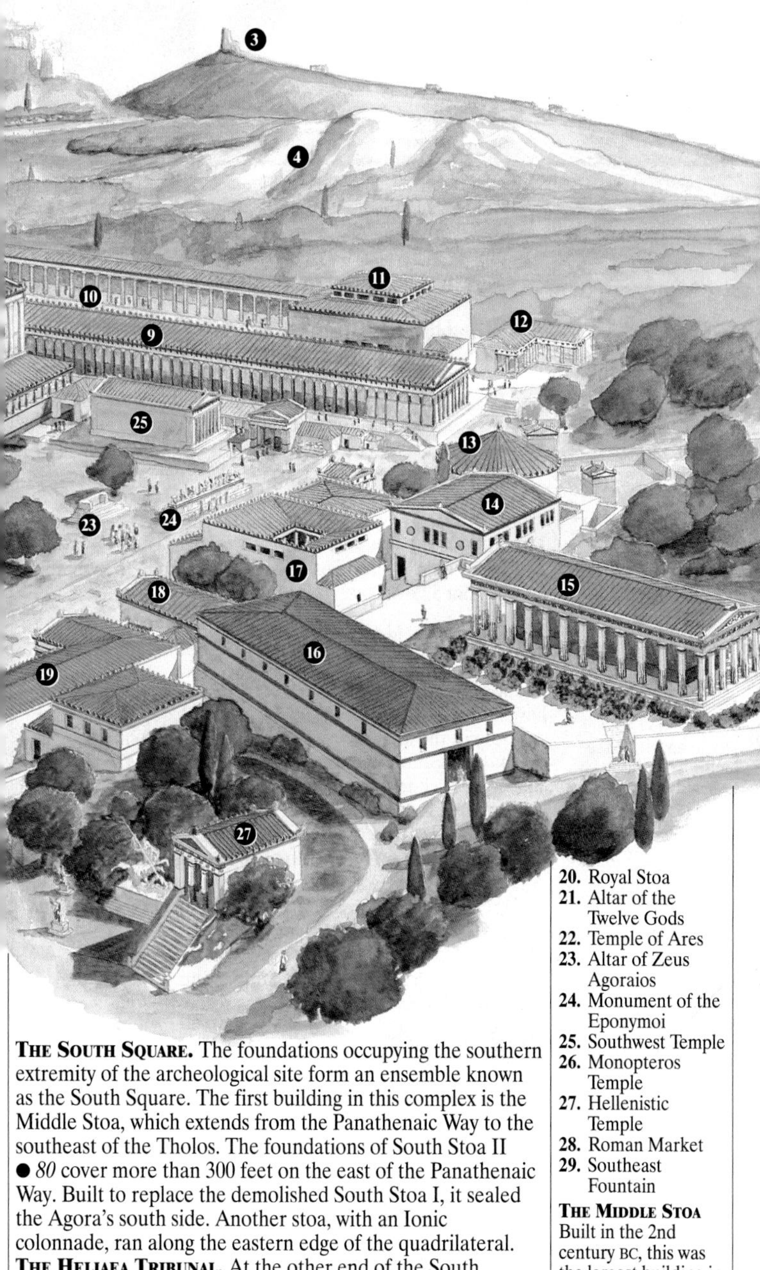

20. Royal Stoa
21. Altar of the Twelve Gods
22. Temple of Ares
23. Altar of Zeus Agoraios
24. Monument of the Eponymoi
25. Southwest Temple
26. Monopteros Temple
27. Hellenistic Temple
28. Roman Market
29. Southeast Fountain

THE SOUTH SQUARE. The foundations occupying the southern extremity of the archeological site form an ensemble known as the South Square. The first building in this complex is the Middle Stoa, which extends from the Panathenaic Way to the southeast of the Tholos. The foundations of South Stoa II ● *80* cover more than 300 feet on the east of the Panathenaic Way. Built to replace the demolished South Stoa I, it sealed the Agora's south side. Another stoa, with an Ionic colonnade, ran along the eastern edge of the quadrilateral.

THE HELIAEA TRIBUNAL. At the other end of the South Square are the foundations of a large rectangular building, with the ruins of the Southwest fountain beside it. This was the site of the Heliaea, the largest and most important of the judicial buildings in ancient Athens. The tribunal was made up of 6,000 "heliasts" (jurors), chosen from among the citizens without regard for rank or fortune. As a people's tribunal, it gradually became an instrument used by demagogues to eliminate their political adversaries. Aristophanes, in his play *The Wasps*, wrote a satire on

THE MIDDLE STOA
Built in the 2nd century BC, this was the largest building in the Agora, at 480 feet long by 55 feet wide.

THE TRIAL OF SOCRATES
A steadfast enemy of all tyranny, Socrates ultimately fell victim to a democratic government. Having refused the chance to recant, he drank the hemlock for two reasons: first, out of respect for the laws of Athens, and second, to demonstrate the injustice of those laws when in the wrong hands.

the Athenian system of justice. Socrates fell victim to the tribunal when the heliasts, manipulated by politicians who were worried about his growing influence as a philosopher, accused him of corrupting the morals of Athens' youth and condemned him to death, after a show trial, in 339 BC.

THE LIBRARY OF PANTAINOS. The traces visible just to the south of the Stoa of Attalos are those of the library founded by T. Flavius Pantainos during the reign of Trajan (98–117). The building included a courtyard surrounded on three sides by porticos, the main library being to the east of this.

THE ARGYROKOPEION. The remains behind the nymphaeum and the Southeast Temple are the foundations of the mint, or Argyrokopeion, built in 400 BC.

THE SOUTHEAST FOUNTAIN. Directly to the west of the Argyrokopeion are vestiges of the southeast public fountain, dating from 525–500 BC.

THE STOA OF ATTALOS

Founded by the philhellene sovereign Attalos II, king of Pergamum from 159 to 138 BC, this stoa took up most of the east side of the archeological site. A popular promenade and commercial center near the Panathenaic Way, the stoa was a convenient venue for artisans and merchants, who occupied it continuously for four centuries until it was virtually obliterated by the Heruli in AD 267.

Twenty-one shops occupied the west side of the lower gallery. Some of them have been reconstructed.

AN EXEMPLARY RECONSTRUCTION. The ruins of the stoa were identified and excavated by Greek archeologists in the second half of the 19th century. In 1931 the American School of Classical Studies continued this work and the monument was reconstructed in 1953–6 according to plans drawn up by the archeologist Jean Travlos.

THE BUILDING. About 180 feet long and 65 feet wide, the stoa's two levels of galleries stand on a three-stepped platform. The capitals of the colonnades belong to four orders. On the lower floor, the outer colonnade is Doric in style and the central one is Ionic. Above, double Ionic capitals crown the exterior half-columns, while on the inside an adaptation of the Egyptian palm-tree capital adorns the colonnade.

THE AGORA MUSEUM. All the architectural fragments, sculptures and objects discovered on the site of the Agora are kept in the Stoa of Attalos. The ground-floor portico contains marbles, statues, tombstones, votive reliefs and sarcophagi, ranged against columns and along walls. The Agora Museum

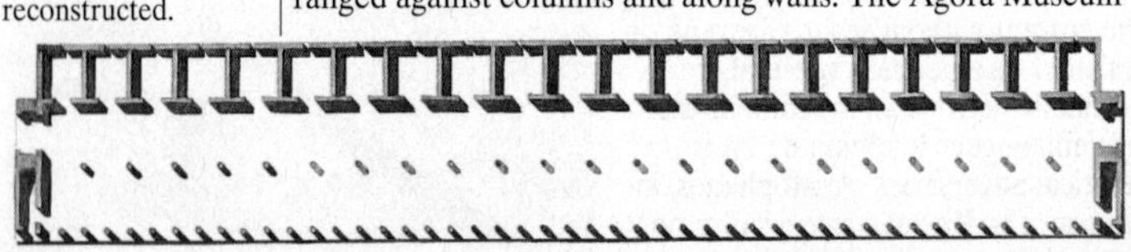

On the lower level, a Doric colonnade supports a coping decorated with triglyphs and metopes. Above, a double row of fluted half-columns, linked one to the next by smooth sections of stone, supports the architrave. A marble parapet runs the full length of the gallery. The roof is covered by Roman tiles (*tegula*) joined together by small convex covering tiles (*imbrex*).

occupies the site of some of the original shops. The collection here covers a period extending from the Neolithic era (c. 3000 BC) to Roman times. Among the works of art on display is a head of Nike (Victory) in bronze from 420 BC, which was originally covered in gold and formed part of a winged statue. At either end of the museum is a stairway leading to the upper level of the stoa. Here, close to the offices of the American School, is a small museum showing a collection of objects and inscriptions that illustrate daily life in ancient times, in addition to various reliefs, statues and architectural fragments. There are also models showing how the Acropolis, Agora and Pnyx must have looked in their heyday.

These ostracism counters bear the name of Themistocles, the statesman who built part of the walls of Athens and played a decisive role in the victories of Marathon and Salamis. He was ostracized (exiled) in 472 BC for misappropriating public funds.

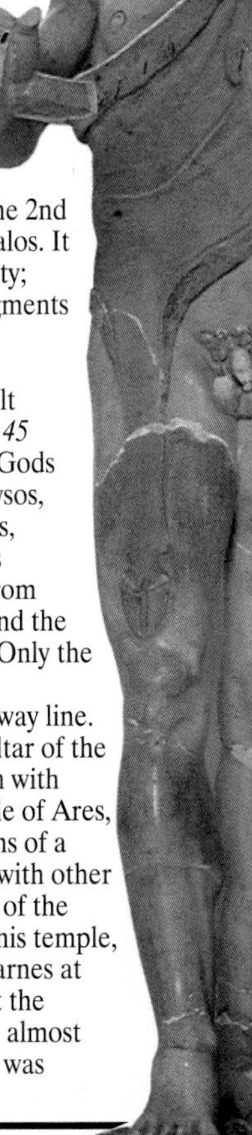

Ivory statuette of a young satyr, 2nd century AD.

The center of Attica

The Monopteros Temple. This small circular monument, which had eight green-marble columns topped by a brick dome, was built in the 2nd century AD just west of the stoa of Attalos. It probably contained a statue of a divinity; nothing remains of it except a few fragments of a decorated cornice and some odd columns.

The Altar of the Twelve Gods. Built during the archonship of Pisistratus ● *45* (522–521 BC), the Altar of the Twelve Gods (Zeus, Hera, Poseidon, Athena, Dionysos, Demeter, Ares, Aphrodite, Hephaistos, Apollo, Artemis and Hermes), with its surrounding *peribolos*, was the point from which the distances between Athens and the other cities of Attica were calculated. Only the southwest part of it is still visible, the remainder being buried under the railway line.

The Temple of Ares. South of the Altar of the Twelve Gods, a broad rectangle strewn with stones designates the site of the Temple of Ares, god of war, built in 430 BC. The remains of a marble altar dedicated to Ares, along with other substantial remains at the eastern end of the foundations, can still be seen today. This temple, originally built at the foot of Mount Parnes at Acharnai, was brought to the Agora at the beginning of the Roman era. It was an almost exact copy of the Hephaisteion, which was designed by the same architect.

THE STOA OF THE GIANTS
This portico, added to the north wall of the Odeon of Agrippa in AD 150–75, was known as the Stoa of the Giants because of the six gigantic statues that supported its architrave. Three members of the original group of three giants and three Tritons remain beside the main entrance to the site. The giants, who were monsters of the earth, had human heads and torsos, with serpents' tails in lieu of legs. The sea-monster Tritons were half men, half fish. During the construction of the gymnasium, these giants were moved into position as ornamentation for the new building's façade.

THE ODEON OF AGRIPPA. Erected in 15 BC by Marcus Vipsanius Agrippa, this colossal covered theater was larger than the Parthenon; it was burned down by the Heruli when they sacked Athens in AD 267, and its ruins were used to build the last Roman defensive wall. At the beginning of the 5th century a large gymnasium was built on the site, which was both an athletes' training place and a school.

THE ALTAR OF ZEUS AGORAIOS. Between the Odeon of Agrippa and the Monument of the Eponymous Heroes lie the remains of an altar, dating from the late 4th century BC, dedicated to Zeus Agoraios, inspirer of eloquence. This building was originally constructed on the Pnyx.

This head of Hermes was unearthed close to the Royal Stoa. It belonged to one of the phallic figures guarding the entrance to the Agora. These were mutilated by the Hermokopidai (defacers of Hermes) the night before the expedition against Sicily sailed in 415 BC.

THE NORTH SIDE OF THE SITE

The digging of the Athens–Piraeus railway tunnel in 1890 to 1891 severed the north side of the Agora from the archeological perimeter. The foundations of the two main monuments on this part of the site, the Royal Stoa and the Stoa Poikile, were excavated only in 1971. The remains are visible from Adrianou Street; but since excavations are still in progress, the site is not open to the public.

THE ROYAL STOA. Nest to the railway line are the foundations of the Basileios Stoa (Royal Stoa). This contained the seat of the archon-king. After the reforms of Cleisthenes, this magistrate assumed judicial functions regarding religious matters. Thus he was in charge of the celebration of the mysteries and presided over both the Areopagus Council and the tribunal of senior magistrates called Ephetai who tried cases of homicide.

THE STOA POIKILE. According to Pausanias, the Stoa Poikile (Painted Stoa) was one of the most famous monuments in ancient Athens. Built toward the middle of the 5th century BC, it owed its name to the scenes of battle painted on its walls by celebrated artists. A favorite haunt of poets and philosophers, it was occasionally used as a court of justice.

KERAMEIKOS AND THE CITY WALLS

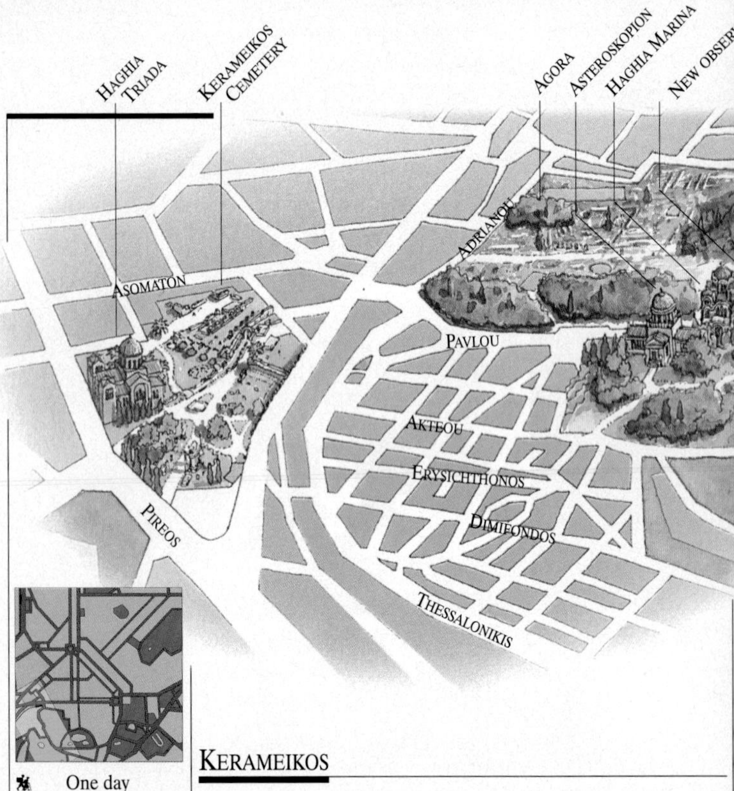

One day

Commercial opportunities offered by the area, together with the presence of a river (the Eridanos) promoted growth in Kerameikos of a thriving pottery industry. The production of ceramics continued here until the middle of the 20th century.

KERAMEIKOS

Kerameikos is one of the original quarters of ancient Athens. According to Pausanias, its name comes from Keramos, son of Dionysos and Ariadne, who was the patron of potters. Located just northwest of the Agora, across Ermou Street, this district was cut through by the Wall of Themistocles ▲ *206* at the end of the Persian Wars ● *44*. The part outside the walls contained the largest necropolis in the city; from early in the 6th century BC Athenians, like the people of other Greek cities, stopped burying their dead within the city limits. The part of Kerameikos within the walls included the Agora. **THE ARCHEOLOGICAL SITE.** Situated between Pireos, Ermou and Melidoni streets, this represents only a fraction of the

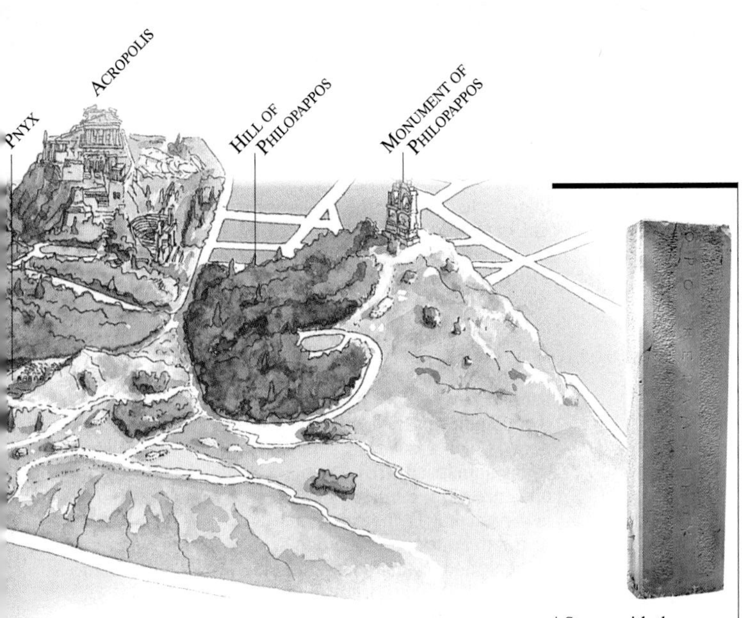

ancient quarter. Kerameikos was a burial place as early as the post-Mycenean era (12th century BC) and remained the principal cemetery of Athens until the city was sacked by Sulla in 86 BC. Subsequently abandoned, it gradually disappeared under mud deposits, up to 35 feet deep, from the Eridanos River. Excavations were begun here by the Greek Archeological Society in 1871, and after 1913 continued under the auspices of the German Archeological Institute.

The Oberländer Museum. The museum stands at the left of the entrance to the site, and is named after the patron who helped to finance the excavations. It houses a collection of objects found on the site, apart from those now in the National Museum. In the entrance hall is a series of funerary monuments, while around the courtyard behind glass are objects discovered in the tombs. These are arranged in chronological order, and represent a period extending from the Mycenean era to Roman times.

A major intersection. Two of the ancient city's most important streets pass through Kerameikos: the Dromos and the Sacred Way (*Hiera Odos*). The former starts at the Academy, traverses the cemetery, passes through the Dipylon Gate and then crosses the Agora to the Acropolis. The second passes through the Sacred Gate and leads to Eleusis. It rejoins the Street of Tombs at the Tritopatreion ("shrine of the ancestors"), of which nothing remains but a triangular wall in which were found boundary stones bearing the inscription *Horos Hieron Tritopatreion Habaton* ("boundary of the shrine of the ancestors, entry prohibited."). The Panathenaic procession ● *88*, which took place at the conclusion of the athletic games, went along the Dromos on its way to the Acropolis via the Agora. The procession included animals later sacrificed to Athena and carried to the Parthenon the *peplos* (tunic) woven by young girls of prominent Athenian families to adorn the image of the goddess ▲ *130*.

Stones with the inscription *Horos Kerameikou* ("boundary of Kerameikos") marked the border between the quarters of Kerameikos and Kolonos Agoraios.

The Dipylon Vase
This amphora was found in one of the geometric tombs near the Dipylon, hence its name. It dates from the first half of the 9th century BC. Vases of this kind were decorated with lines and geometric designs; some of them also included friezes of stylized animals and human figures.

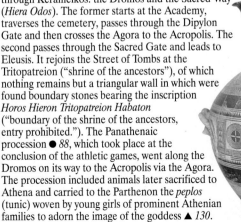

Pilgrims heading for the Mysteries at Eleusis ▲ *292* in honor of Demeter and Persephone took the Dromos, then joined the Sacred Way.

THE GOLDEN AGE OF FUNERARY ART. By the 4th century BC funerary art had reached an extremely high standard thanks to a prosperous clientele who commissioned sculptors of genius to carve bas-reliefs, stelae, statues and stone vases or urns for their tombs. The latter might be a *kotylos* (a two-handled cup used for mixing wine and water), *loutrophoros* (two-handled vase) or *lekythos* (with one handle and a narrow neck), which was usually kept for the tombs of virgins and young unmarried girls. Athenians prided themselves on the opulence of their funerary monuments, until the sumptuary laws passed by Demetrios Phaleros in 317 BC imposed restraint. Pottery continued to be used for tomb decoration in Hellenic and Roman times, but funerary art never again reached the heights of the preceding era.

THE STREET OF TOMBS ★. Each plot of land was reserved for a different wealthy family, whether Athenian or from outside, and the tombs took many different forms: small aedicules with pediments and carved reliefs, stelae surmounted with palmettes, pedimented rectangular stones and large urns with or without bas-reliefs. On the south side of the street a crescent-shaped tomb contains a cast of the memorial of Dexileos (the original is in the Oberländer Museum). Further on, the tomb of the brothers Agathon and Sosikrates contains a small aedicule with traces of a painting on it as well as a stele carved with a particularly touching scene, showing Agathon's wife Korallion taking leave of her husband. The tomb of Dionysos of Kollytos stands out due to the bull above its aedicule, a copy of a sculpture in Pentelic marble. Among others that should not be missed is the tomb of Lysimachos, with its bas-relief of Charon, the ferryman of the underworld, and a Molossian dog in Hymettian marble. At the back of this enclosure, which overhangs the

LOUTROPHOROS
A distinctively shaped urn, often placed on the tomb of a bachelor.

LEKYTHOS
A vessel used to carry water for funeral rites.

A parting scene depicted in relief on a funerary urn.

FRIEZE OF HORSEMEN
The marble base of a funerary monument from the Archaic era was reused in one of the towers of the Dipylon Gate. It is now in the Oberländer Museum.

street, stelae of all kinds bristle like spikes on the sloping ground – among them plain columns, tombs in the form of slabs, *loutrophoroi* and *lekythoi*, and tombs shaped like couches. Also on this hill is the precinct traditionally dedicated to Hekate, with its two altars. As you leave the enclosed part of the site, on the north side of the street is the plot of Eubios, with its Stele of Euphrosyne and Column of Bion, which has a *loutrophoros* on top. In the nearby plot of Koroibos of Melite, in addition to his own stele, there is the *loutrophoros* of Kleidemos, his grandson, and a copy of the famous monument to Hegeso, his wife, showing the daughter of Proxenos choosing a jewel from a box proffered by a servant (the original is in the National Museum).

COMMUNAL TOMBS. Crossing the wide grassy expanse of the Church of Haghia Triada (which was moved and rebuilt to the north of the site in the 1930's), the visitor reaches the Dromos. The unusual width of this road is explained by the events that used to take place there. Each winter the *Epitaphia* was held here, a funeral ceremony in honor of Athenians and their allies who had fallen in battle. The ashes of the dead were placed in a communal tomb, known as the *Demosion Sema*. Its exact location has not been identified, but along the Dromos between the church and the end of the site can be seen communal graves, including that of some Spartans.

MEMORIAL OF DEXILEOS
This young soldier, who died at the age of twenty in 394 BC fighting the Corinthians, was interred in a large communal tomb. A memorial was erected by his parents in their family plot.

THE GATEWAY TO ATHENS

To the east of the site is the Dipylon Gate, the "double gate", rebuilt in the 4th century BC, through which the Dromos and the Sacred Way both passed. It stood at the end of a large court which was closed on three sides and had a tower at each corner. There are two openings, hence the name Dipylon. It is the largest gateway known in ancient Greece.

These small columns (below), modest memorials from Hellenic and Roman times, often commemorated dead slaves.

THE STREET OF TOMBS
Lined with the tombs of rich Athenian families, the Street of Tombs is dominated by the imposing bull marking the grave of Dionysos of Kollytos.

The many images of death that abound in ancient history, the objects that were placed carefully in tombs with the bodies, and the meticulous care with which funerary likenesses were made, are all evidence of a firm belief in an afterlife – a concept that gained general acceptance in the 6th century BC. From that time on it was regarded as a base infamy not to give a dead body a tomb, so condemning it to a hundred years roaming the banks of the Styx, the dreaded river of the underworld.

EKPHORA
The decoration on this monumental *krater* from the Dipylon necropolis features a corpse laid out on a chariot, surrounded by friends and relations; the figures in the frieze below the handles have their arms raised heavenward in lamentation. The bowl, dating from 740 BC and decorated in pure geometric style, is one of the earliest depictions of *ekphora*, the ritual of carrying the body of the deceased to the necropolis outside the city walls. The ceremony took place before dawn, to spare the sun the sight of the funeral.

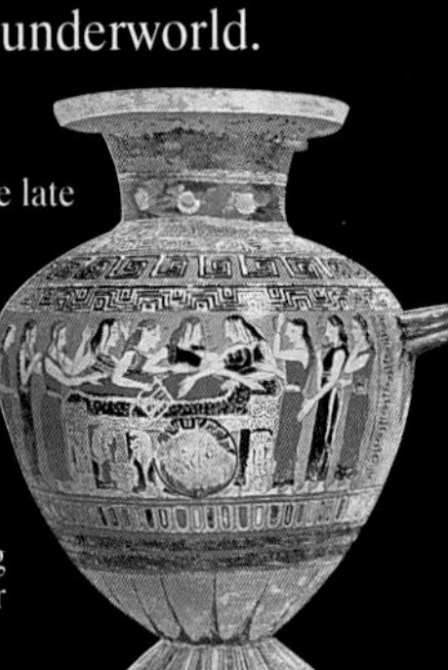

PROTHESIS
On this Corinthian ewer of the late 6th century BC the body of Achilles is shown undergoing the rite of *prothesis* (laying out on a funeral couch) which prepared it for the journey to the underworld. The arms of the great hero have been placed beside him, while the Nereids surrounding the corpse weep and tear their hair.

The sumptuary laws passed by Solon in the 6th century BC, which deprived artists of much of their livelihood, were partially repealed in the 5th century, restoring a certain amount of freedom in the decoration of tombs. The imposing stelae sculpted in high relief from this period often feature figures grouped around the deceased. On this one the dead woman, accompanied by a servant, is depicted taking leave of her son.

PENTATHLETE
This fragment of a stele reused as part of the Wall of Themistocles shows the head of a pentathlete. The high quality of the workmanship indicates that this masculine head in profile, dating from around 540 BC, was produced during the classical age.

FUNERARY OBJECTS
It was customary to place a variety of objects in the tomb that the deceased might need during his journey to the underworld – such as this terracotta perfume brazier dating from the 7th century BC. It comes from one of the tombs in the Dipylon necropolis at Kerameikos.

FUNERARY STELE
This reconstruction of a stele combines a variety of stylistic elements. The sphinx probably signifies a hero's death; the warrior, carrying a sword, and the bas-relief of the Gorgon both come from Kerameikos. The image of the deceased (most often a man) is shown in profile and carved in bas-relief on a long narrow marble plaque in the style typical of the Archaic period. After the sumptuary laws of Solon, representational ornament disappeared in favor of simple epitaphs.

CHARON THE FERRYMAN
It was Charon's task to ferry the souls of the dead across the Styx (the river of the underworld) in his boat. From the 6th century BC it became the custom to place a silver coin in the mouth of the corpse to enable the deceased to pay the fare. This stele from the plot of Lysimachos at Kerameikos shows four people feasting, watched by Charon from his boat.

THE PUBLIC FOUNTAIN
Standing close to the entrance to the city, the fountain had a reservoir at the rear and a portico in front where women came to fetch water.

In time of peace the courtyard was a popular meeting place and also a useful assembly point. In wartime aspiring invaders would naturally be drawn to this spot, only to find themselves caught in a trap. To the left of the gate are the remains of a public fountain.

THE POMPEION. Behind the wall between the Dipylon and the Sacred Gate, the remains of three buildings are superposed. The oldest, the Pompeion, built at the beginning of the 4th century BC, was a rectangular structure set in a cloister-style courtyard, off which were a few rooms. Entrance from the city side was through a monumental gateway. Important processions were prepared here, as the building also served as a storehouse for the heavy vehicles and other equipment used in them. Destroyed in 86 BC, it was replaced in the 2nd century AD by a two-story building divided into three on the ground floor by two rows of columns. This was destroyed in AD 267; two porticos were built on the west side in the 4th century, joined by a triumphal arch at the city end.

THE GATES OF ATHENS

1. Sacred Gate
2. Dipylon Gate
3. Sacred Way (to Eleusis)
4. Eridanos River
5. Pompeion (4th century BC)
6. Building from 4th century AD
7. Dromos (leading to the Agora)
8. Public fountain
9. Tower
10. Wall of Themistocles
11. Ditch
12. Heroön (Tomb of the Heroes)

Further along, on the left are the ruins of the Sacred Gate, also in the form of a courtyard and with a double entrance, one on the left for the Eridanos River, the other for the Sacred Way. Its different phases of construction and rebuilding, and also those of the section of wall leading back up to the museum, are clearly identifiable, enabling the different techniques employed to be compared.

THE CITY WALLS

In the 5th century BC, at the end of the Persian Wars, Athens was surrounded by a new rampart known as the Wall of Themistocles. This was connected to the Long Walls, which consisted of a pair of walls built in the time of Pericles between Athens and Piraeus to protect access to the sea.

At the end of the 4th century BC another wall, the Diateichisma, was erected, which crossed from the Hill of the Nymphs to the Hill of the Muses, passing just behind the Pnyx. The most important remains of these defenses can be seen between Kerameikos and the Monument of Philopappos, south of the Acropolis. On leaving the archeological site, take the bridge over the railway track; then turn right into Thessalonikis Street and left into Erysichthonos Street. Part of the walls are visible at the junction with Heracleidon Street; and there are further remains at 29 Erysichthonos Street, visible through a grille at pavement level. This is close to the Peraic Gate. Further on, steps lead to Galatias Street, which then becomes Akamandos Street. The Demian Gate was situated here, just south of where the northern Long Wall rejoined the Wall of Themistocles. On the right, Amphictyonos Street leads to the square of Haghia Marina: in ancient times there was a shrine to Zeus where the church now stands. A road climbs up the hill to the garden of the observatory. The area opposite, where the new telescope now stands, has an excellent view of the Acropolis.

The Pnyx ● *81*. To the south of the observatory is the site of the Pnyx, where there is seating for the *son et lumière* on the Acropolis ▲ *130*. The Pnyx is an immense semicircular terrace where the Ecclesia, or Assembly of citizens, was formerly held (the name signifies a place where people are packed tightly together).

The Pnyx
The Assembly of citizens used to meet on this rocky esplanade overlooking the Acropolis.

Part of the Wall of Themistocles can be seen at the junction between Heracleidon Street and Erysichthonos Street.

The Asteroskopion
The old observatory was built between 1843 and 1846 by Danish architect Theophilus von Hansen with money from Baron Simon Sinas ▲ *229*. Its garden was formerly the Sanctuary of the Nymphs.

In the rear wall votive niches have been carved in the rock, indicating the site of a shrine to Zeus Hypsistos ("the most high"). In the middle of the wall is the three-stepped platform, or tribune, from which great orators such as Aristides, Themistocles, Pericles and Demosthenes addressed the Assembly in the 5th and 4th centuries BC. The people listened from the shallow-sloped auditorium below the tribune. At the back of the upper terrace, which is closed in by a wall, can be seen the foundations of two porticos, bordered on the south by the Diateichisma wall. From the enclosure of the new observatory, a path (on the left) leads to the little Church of Haghios Dimitrios Loumbardiaris; here and there among the grass are fragments of the ancient wall.

HAGHIOS DIMITRIOS LOUMBARDIARIS
This chapel is named for a Turkish cannon used against the Greeks in 1656.

THE MONUMENT OF PHILOPAPPOS ★. Opposite the church a track climbs up to the Monument of Philopappos, which is at the top of the Hill of the Muses. The route virtually follows the remains of the Diateichisma, and part of the foundations are still visible. In 294 BC Demetrios Poliorketes built a fortress on the summit, overlooking the western approaches and the corridor between the Long Walls. Here, between AD 114 and 116, the Athenians erected a funerary monument to honor C. Julius Antiochus Philopappos, the last prince of Commagene (northern Syria), who was a prominent Athenian citizen. The monument was 40 feet high and rectangular, with a slightly concave façade; behind this was a burial chamber containing the prince's sarcophagus.

THE MONUMENT OF PHILOPAPPOS
The lower bas-relief (detail below) is of a procession with Philopappos, wearing a toga, in a quadriga (chariot) preceded by lictors. The upper part of the monument has three niches with statues: Philopappos himself, in the center; his grandfather Antiochus IV, on the left; and Seleucus I (Nicator), founder of the dynasty, on the right. The monument was much admired by visitors to Athens after Cyriac of Ancona, the first "modern" traveler, copied its inscriptions in the 15th century.

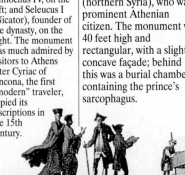

Roman Athens

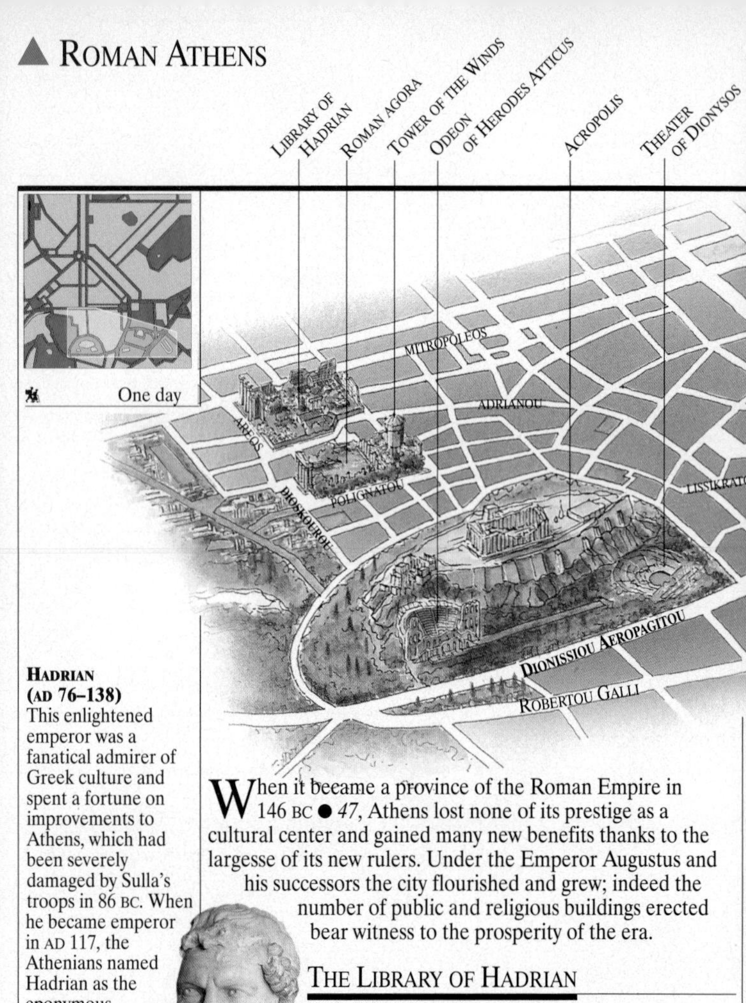

HADRIAN (AD 76–138)
This enlightened emperor was a fanatical admirer of Greek culture and spent a fortune on improvements to Athens, which had been severely damaged by Sulla's troops in 86 BC. When he became emperor in AD 117, the Athenians named Hadrian as the eponymous founder of one of the tribes of Athens. Thus deified, he entered the city in 122, calling himself Olympian Zeus. During his twenty-one year-reign he came to the city several times and enlarged it around the Olympieion, on the eastern side, by building the elegant suburb of Adrianopolis and extending the city limits beyond the Wall of Themistocles ▲ *206*.

When it became a province of the Roman Empire in 146 BC ● *47*, Athens lost none of its prestige as a cultural center and gained many new benefits thanks to the largesse of its new rulers. Under the Emperor Augustus and his successors the city flourished and grew; indeed the number of public and religious buildings erected bear witness to the prosperity of the era.

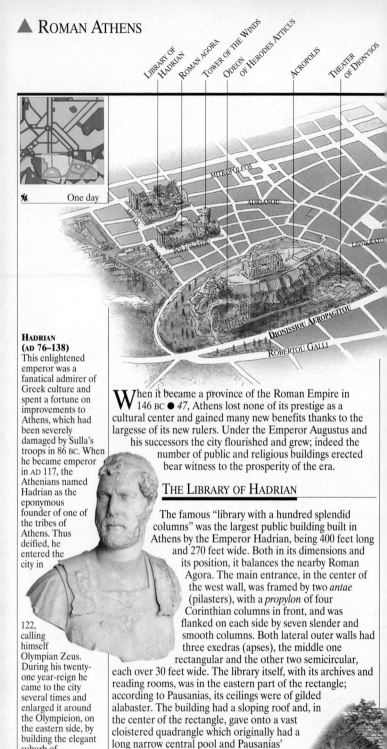

THE LIBRARY OF HADRIAN

The famous "library with a hundred splendid columns" was the largest public building built in Athens by the Emperor Hadrian, being 400 feet long and 270 feet wide. Both in its dimensions and its position, it balances the nearby Roman Agora. The main entrance, in the center of the west wall, was framed by two *antae* (pilasters), with a *propylon* of four Corinthian columns in front, and was flanked on each side by seven slender and smooth columns. Both lateral outer walls had three exedras (apses), the middle one rectangular and the other two semicircular, each over 30 feet wide. The library itself, with its archives and reading rooms, was in the eastern part of the rectangle; according to Pausanias, its ceilings were of gilded alabaster. The building had a sloping roof and, in the center of the rectangle, gave onto a vast cloistered quadrangle which originally had a long narrow central pool and Pausanias' "hundred splendid columns". In the early 5th century AD a large building with four apses and a mosaic floor was erected in the eastern half, only to be replaced in the following century by a paleo-Christian

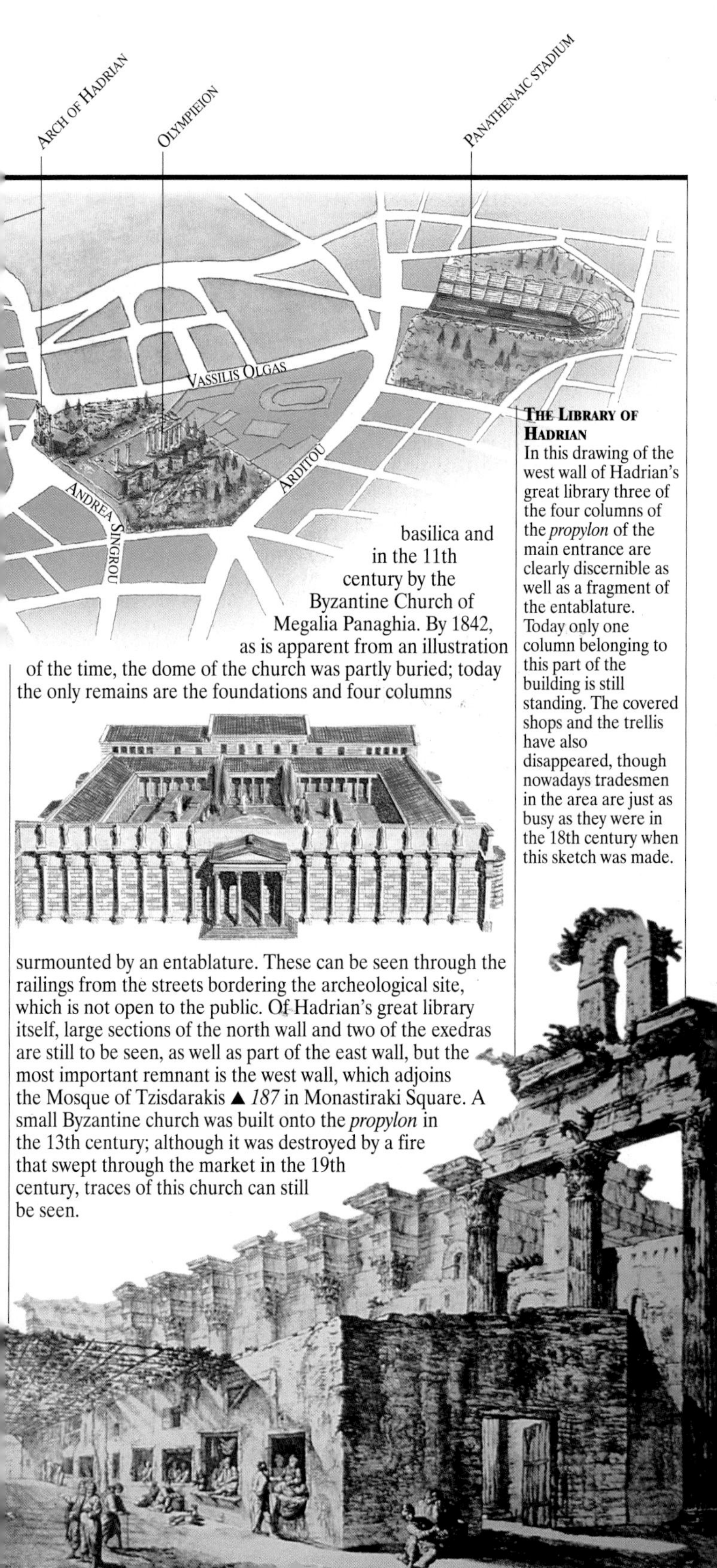

basilica and in the 11th century by the Byzantine Church of Megalia Panaghia. By 1842, as is apparent from an illustration of the time, the dome of the church was partly buried; today the only remains are the foundations and four columns surmounted by an entablature. These can be seen through the railings from the streets bordering the archeological site, which is not open to the public. Of Hadrian's great library itself, large sections of the north wall and two of the exedras are still to be seen, as well as part of the east wall, but the most important remnant is the west wall, which adjoins the Mosque of Tzisdarakis ▲ *187* in Monastiraki Square. A small Byzantine church was built onto the *propylon* in the 13th century; although it was destroyed by a fire that swept through the market in the 19th century, traces of this church can still be seen.

THE LIBRARY OF HADRIAN
In this drawing of the west wall of Hadrian's great library three of the four columns of the *propylon* of the main entrance are clearly discernible as well as a fragment of the entablature. Today only one column belonging to this part of the building is still standing. The covered shops and the trellis have also disappeared, though nowadays tradesmen in the area are just as busy as they were in the 18th century when this sketch was made.

THE ROMAN MARKET
The huge courtyard of the ancient Roman market stretches out in front of the Byzantine Fethiye Cami'i or Victory Mosque.

PLATANOS TAVERNA
This is a pleasant place to rest, in the shade of a huge plane tree, near the Roman market. Below the terrace are the foundations of a monumental pantheon, probably destroyed by the Heruli in AD 267. Pausanias attributes the building to Hadrian.

THE "BAZAAR GATE"
The Gate of Athena Archegetis stands at the center of an area extensively damaged during the War of Independence ● *51*. Under Turkish rule the old Roman marketplace became a commercial market once again. Consequently, the gateway became known as the "Bazaar Gate".

THE ROMAN AGORA

The existence of a market here is affirmed by a marble slab in a house beside the gateway to the Agora, carved with an edict of the Emperor Hadrian about the sale of oil. Its origins go back to the reign of Augustus.

THE GATE OF ATHENA ARCHEGETIS. This monumental gateway formed the entrance to the Roman marketplace. A *propylon* with coping supported a pediment adorned by statues. On the lintel an inscription stated that the monument was erected by the people of Athens thanks to the generosity of Julius Caesar and Augustus, between 10 BC and AD 2, and that it was dedicated to Athena Archegetis ("Athena who governs"). Between the columns of the gateway were three openings leading to the marketplace, the central one being for wagons and horses, and the side ones for pedestrians.

THE ROMAN MARKET. The paved marble square, dominated by the Tower of the Winds, is about 370 feet long and 315 feet across. Around the edge was a double peristyle. The shops were in covered colonnades, some of which can still be seen on the south and east sides. The colonnades supported an architrave, a cornice with lion's-head gargoyles and a double-pitched roof. On the south side there was an older Doric colonnade, within the peristyle but separated from it by a step. At the center of the marketplace was a fountain. To the right of the entrance of the site are the square foundations of the city's first public lavatories.

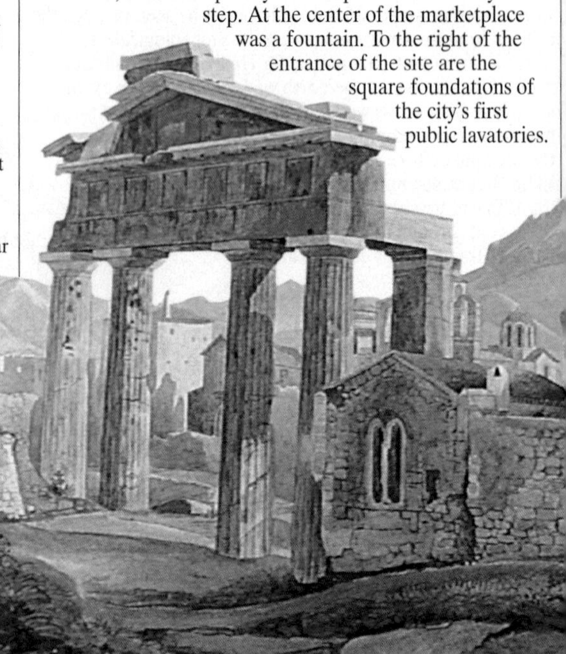

“GREECE, TAKEN CAPTIVE, CAPTURED HER SAVAGE CONQUEROR AND CARRIED FORTH HER CULTURE TO RUDE ITALY.”

HORACE

Detail of a capital with acanthus leaves from the Corinthian columns on the upper part of the Arch of Hadrian. As is the case on other monuments in Athens, the deterioration of the internal pins that hold the drums together has necessitated the use of iron retaining bands to prevent the columns from breaking up.

THE ARCH OF HADRIAN

This arch of Pentelic marble, which was erected in honor of the Emperor Hadrian, stands at the boundary of ancient Athens and “Adrianopolis, Novae Athenae”. The inscriptions on its frieze make this division quite clear, with “This is the ancient city of Athens, the city of Theseus”, inscribed on the side facing the Acropolis and “This is the city of Hadrian, not Theseus” inscribed on the other. The impressive gate is 45 feet wide and 60 feet high; its semicircular arch sits upon Corinthian pilasters, which were formerly flanked by Corinthian columns with rectangular bases and attached to the wall by consoles that are still visible. The attic, or upper part of the gateway, had three openings framed by Corinthian columns which supported the architrave. The middle opening had a pair of Corinthian pilasters, one on each side, which jutted out slightly giving extra support to the architrave as well as to the pediment which crowned the central section.

In this drawing of 1751, with the ruins of the Olympieion in the background, the Arch of Hadrian is shown surrounded by countryside. Such pastoral visions of the banks of the Ilissos were far from accurate. The marble panels covering the upper part of the arch, fragments of which can be seen in the picture, no longer exist: Queen Amalia had them removed to enhance the elegance of the monument.

Weather vane, water clock and sundial combined, the Tow
the Winds stands on the east side of the Roman Agora. It w
built by the Syrian architect Andronikos Kyrrhestes in the
century BC. In the Middle Ages the tower was believed to b
tomb of Socrates. When the Turks ruled Athens it was occ
by a community of dancing dervishes.

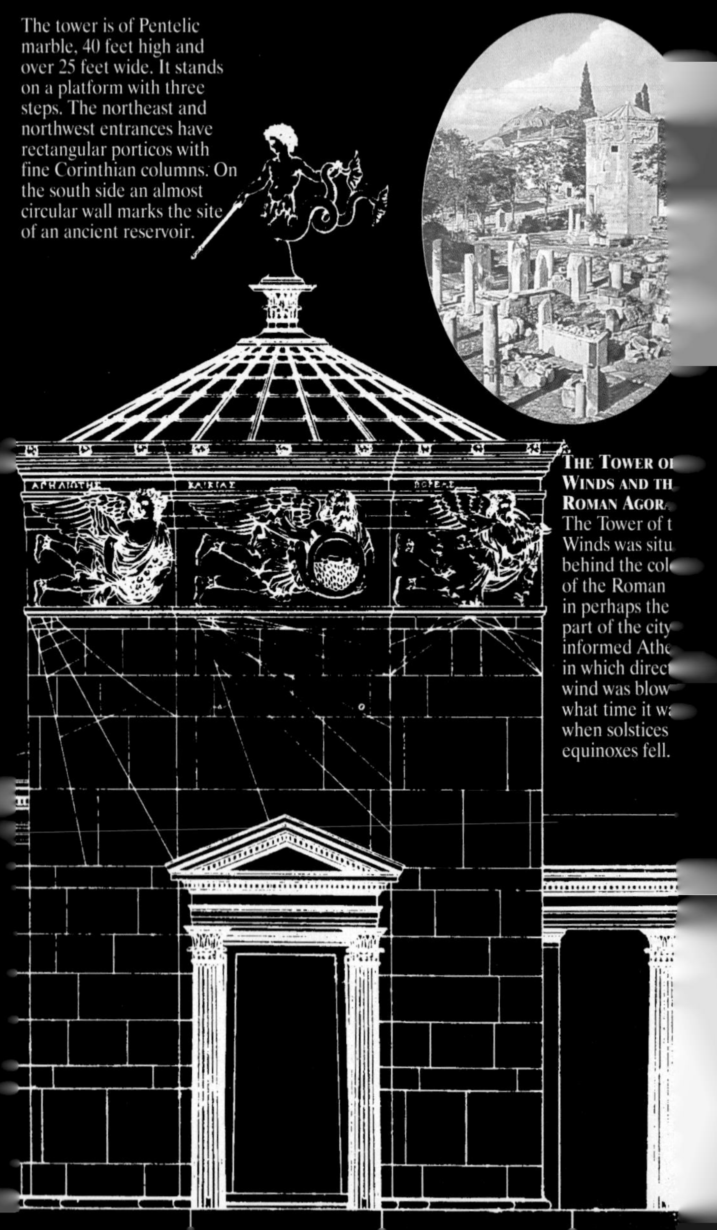

The tower is of Pentelic marble, 40 feet high and over 25 feet wide. It stands on a platform with three steps. The northeast and northwest entrances have rectangular porticos with fine Corinthian columns. On the south side an almost circular wall marks the site of an ancient reservoir.

The Tower o Winds and th Roman Agor
The Tower of t
Winds was situ
behind the col
of the Roman
in perhaps the
part of the city
informed Athe
in which direc
wind was blow
what time it w
when solstices
equinoxes fell.

The Winds

Each of the eight bas-reliefs of the frieze on the upper section of the tower represents a mythical figure personifying one of the winds.

1. Boreas, the North Wind, represented by a bearded man with a conch shell.

2. Kaikias, shown emptying a shield full of hailstones.

3. Apeliotes, a youth personifying the East Wind. His tunic is filled with fruits and spices.

4. Euros, depicted as an old man wrapped in a great cloak.

5. Notos, the South Wind and bringer of rain, symbolized by a youth emptying an urn.

6. Lips holds the stern light (*aplustre*) of a Roman ship – a good omen for a voyage.

7. Zephyros, the West Wind, introduces Spring by sprinkling blossoms kept in a fold of his robe.

8. Skiron is on the point of upturning a vessel – a potent symbol of the season of floods.

Under Turkish domination an order of dervishes took over the Tower of the Winds as their *tekke* or monastery. In their graceful, whirling dance the dervishes sought the state of *sema*, a unity with the divine spirit, to the accompaniment of drums and the melody of the *ney*, a Turkish flute. The ceremony took place each Friday at the conclusion of midday prayers. During the early years of King Otto's reign ● *52* the Tower of the Winds housed a Catholic order.

Together with the Acropolis ▲ *130* and the Hephaisteion ▲ *191*, the Olympieion is one of the Athenian monuments that has fired the imagination of travelers, artists and writers. The French author Chateaubriand was struck by the grandeur of its columns as he stood on the vast esplanade: "How isolated they seem now, scattered here and there on the bare ground, but what an effect they make: they look like the palm trees you see among the ruins of Alexandria." The engraving by Turner (above) shows three columns still standing, before one was blown over in the great storm of 1852.

THE OLYMPIEION

If Thucydides is right, the Olympieion (Temple of Olympian Zeus) is one of the oldest sanctuaries in the city. According to legend it was built near the spot where the last waters of the Flood drained away. Pisistratus wanted a monument comparable in size to the massive Archaic temples of oriental Greece, such as the Heraion of Samos and the Artemision of Ephesus. Although construction began in the second half of the 6th century BC, the building – in the style of a dipteral temple with ranks of columns to either side – was not completed until 650 years later. Indeed, at the time when Hippias, the son of Pisistratus, was exiled in 510 BC, bringing the dynasty of these benevolent tyrants to an end, only the stylobate and possibly some columns were in place. Work began again in 174 BC, at the instigation of the Seleucid king Antiochus IV (175–163 BC) who called in the Roman architect Cossutius. The latter chose the Corinthian order of columns but kept the dimensions of the temple virtually unchanged, with a stylobate approximately 355 feet long and 135 feet wide. The 104 Corinthian columns were arranged in two ranks of twenty columns on each side, with three ranks of eight columns (octastyle) at either end. According to Vitruvius it was a *cella* temple, with the main body of the building left open. From his description as well as from other sources, it would seem that the Olympieion was still unfinished when Hadrian

commissioned its refurbishment during his second visit to Athens, in AD 125, nearly three centuries after the death of Antiochus. Whatever work remained to be done, one fact is certain: it is to Hadrian that the Olympieion owes the impressive *peribolos* surrounding the esplanade on which the temple stands. This supporting wall, a massive structure built of poros, 676 feet by 423 feet, is reinforced at intervals of approximately 17 feet by a hundred buttresses. Work was finally completed around AD 132. Soon afterwards Hadrian revisited Athens for the consecration of the temple and the huge chryselephantine (gold-and-ivory) statue of Zeus. After this the architectural history of the Olympieion becomes confusing. Part of the surrounding wall was demolished to fill the new line of defenses put up by the Emperor Valerian between 253 and 260. The temple then sustained serious damage in a raid by the Heruli in 267 ▲ *132*. It is most unlikely that it was rebuilt afterwards, since Athens went into a decline towards the end of the Roman Empire. The Olympieion was anyway in ruins at the beginning of the Byzantine era. When Cyriac of Ancona visited Athens in 1436 he found only 21 of the 104 columns still standing; today only 15 remain. In medieval times a stylite lived on the section of architrave at the western end of the line of 13 columns that still stand together. On April 27, 1759, the Turkish governor Tzisdarákis blew up one of the columns to make lime for the construction of the mosque ▲ *187* that bears his name in Monastiraki Square (now the Museum of Decorative Arts); for this act of vandalism, at which the Athenians were justifiably outraged, Tzisdarakis was fined by the Pasha of Euboea. The weather has also contributed to the temple's destruction: the column now lying on the ground was blown over during a storm in 1852.

The Baths of Hadrian
Close by the entrance to the site are the foundations of a long building in the shape of a basilica, with an apse that has a marble mosaic. These belong to the Baths of Hadrian. The brick construction to the rear is the hypocaust, or Roman underfloor heating system.

Festivals near the Olympieion
Athenians have always revered the Olympieion, and until recent times gathered near the temple to celebrate the festivals held on the first Monday in Lent and the third day after Easter. In 1838 Christian Perlberg painted this romantic vision of the festival of *Koulouma* (the last Monday of Carnival), when Athenians came here to sing and dance and to eat a simple meal of bread and olives.

Between 1869 and 1879 Ernst Ziller organized excavations at the Panathenaic Stadium, which was later restored according to the original plans and using the same materials. While still unfinished, the stadium managed to accommodate the vast crowd that arrived on April 5, 1896 to attend the first Olympic Games of modern times. When the last stone was laid in place in 1906, the games held to celebrate its completion drew fifty thousand spectators.

OTHER REMAINS OF ANCIENT ROME

THE PANATHENAIC STADIUM. Situated at the end of the Avenue Vassileo Konstantinidou, this was probably built during the reign of Lycurgus, in 330–329 BC. It lies neatly in a valley between two low hills on the left bank of the Ilissos, with tiered seating carved out of the earth, plus a number of marble seats for important personages. The stadium was originally the venue for athletic contests held as part of the Panathenaic Festival ● *130*. After AD 132 it was used for contests and spectacles in the Adriana Olympia, a quinquennial festival inaugurated by Hadrian. There were events like those in the amphitheaters at Rome, such as fights between gladiators or with wild beasts, which were virtually unknown in Greece before the Roman occupation. At the opening of the Panathenaic Festival in AD 140 Herodes Atticus promised to build a new stadium in time for the next games. He was as good as his word: a new stadium clad throughout in Pentelic marble was officially opened at the Panathenaic Festival of AD 144.

THE ODEON OF HERODES ATTICUS ▲ *174*. This wealthy Athenian, who was a friend of the Emperor Hadrian, commissioned the huge odeon on the south slope of the Acropolis. Pausanias states that he built it in memory of his wife, Regilla, who died in AD 160 or 161. Concerts and theatrical performances are given here throughout the year.

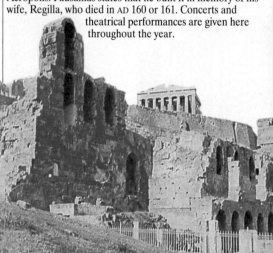

ODEON OF HERODES ATTICUS
The theater's semicircular *orchestra*

is paved with marble and is 95 feet in diameter. The auditorium is surrounded by a supporting wall, and its thirty-four rows of seats can hold five thousand spectators. At the bottom are the remains of a *skene*, pierced with arcades.

Syntagma and its museums

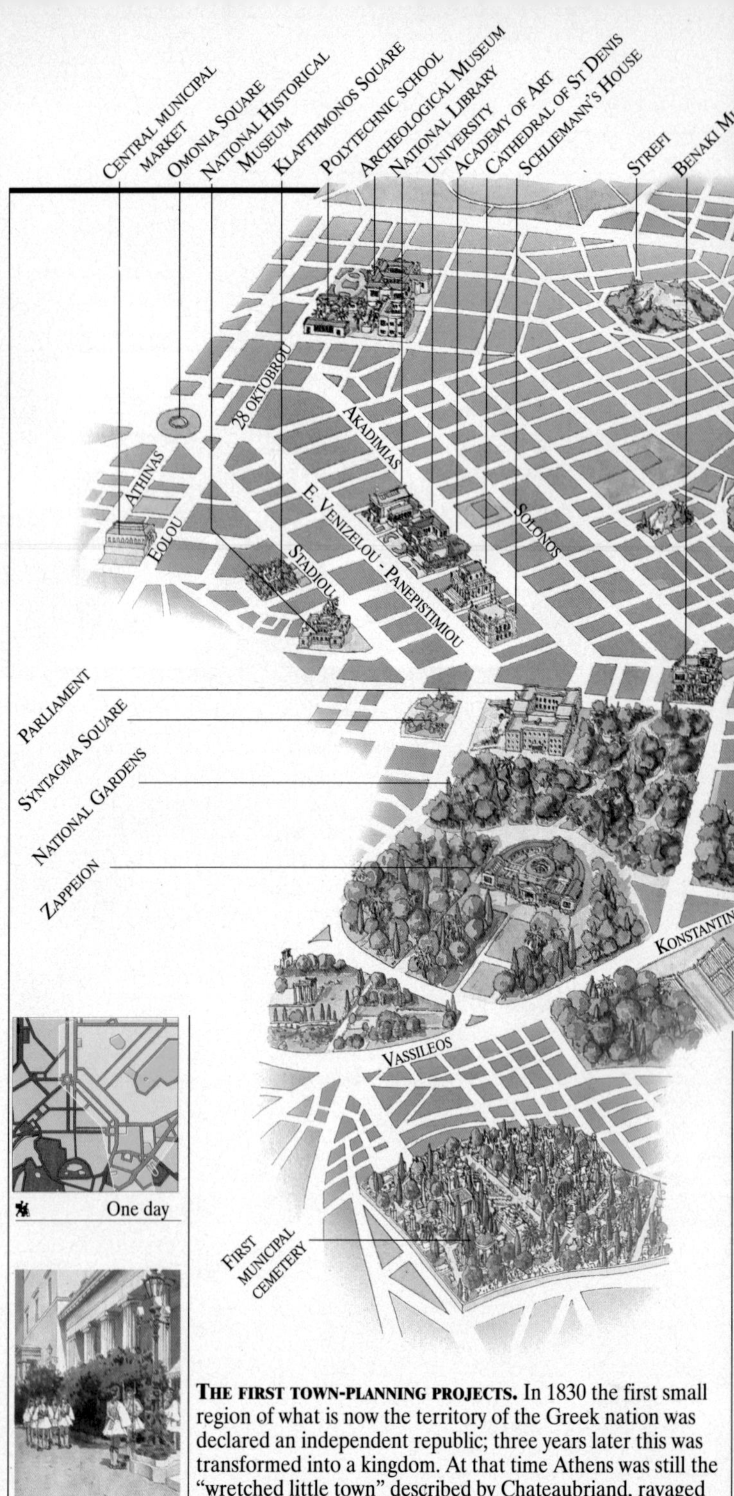

One day

Changing the guard in front of the presidential palace.

The first town-planning projects. In 1830 the first small region of what is now the territory of the Greek nation was declared an independent republic; three years later this was transformed into a kingdom. At that time Athens was still the "wretched little town" described by Chateaubriand, ravaged and ruined by ten years of warfare. Nevertheless, the first town-planning projects for the new city – proposed in 1883 by Kleanthis and Schaubert – were never realized, because they ran counter to the interests of landowners and required more money than the state could afford.

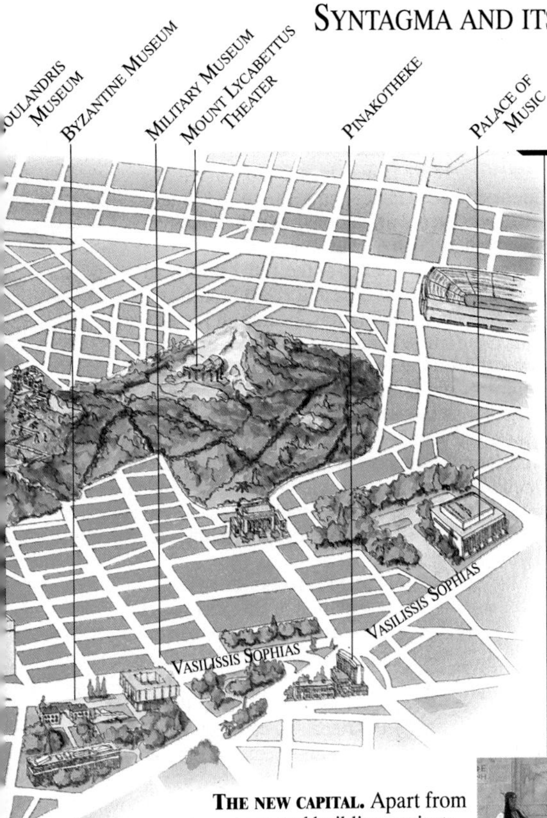

GOULANDRIS MUSEUM
BYZANTINE MUSEUM
MILITARY MUSEUM
MOUNT LYCABETTUS THEATER
PINAKOTHEKE
PALACE OF MUSIC
VASILISSIS SOPHIAS
VASILISSIS SOPHIAS

In 1834 Athens became the capital of the new Kingdom of Greece. In the same year a state archeological department was founded; and the city, formerly a "pile of ruins", was transformed into a hive of activity. Scores of foreign architects arrived, bringing with them the neoclassical style – paradoxically, as the buildings they designed to symbolize the modern Greek state were mostly inspired by the legacy of the past.

THE NEW CAPITAL. Apart from one or two concerted building projects, the new city of Athens grew up in a completely anarchic fashion, without any overall plan or concerted vision of the future. The military government that ruled Greece between 1847 and 1860 introduced summary measures which allowed it to appropriate land without compensation, simply by decree; in this way the army was able to evacuate entire districts of the city to make way for new roads. In the second half of the 19th century successive governments resorted to foreign technical advisers, notably from France. These advisers arrived, drew up complicated projects and then hastily departed, leaving puzzled local architects to wrestle with unrealistic plans. The ambitious building works that were to have burnished the prestige of

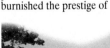

EVZONES
King Otto created the vogue for the fustanella (pleated skirt ● 71) and chose the uniform of the *evzones* (national guard).

THE ACROPOLIS, FROM OLGAS AVENUE
The German architect Schinkel suggested to King Otto that his palace should be built on the Acropolis, the home of the first Athenian monarchs. The project was never realized.

SYNTAGMA
The Syntagma quarter as it is today; and George I Street as it was at the turn of the century.

Athens were soon abandoned, and a more modest town plan defined between 1876 and 1879 was eventually adopted. Several hundred major changes to the city were carried out during the final quarter of the 19th century. At that time (between 1882 and 1889) French engineers built Alexandras Avenue, at the end of which the sun sets, and Syngrou Avenue stretching away toward the sea. These two roads were a great improvement to the city.

NEOCLASSICISM ● *96*. At this time the whole of Europe was engrossed with the classical style. To begin with, romantic classicism was imported into Greece, but later on Greek architects began to draw on the ancient architecture they saw around them to create an original classicism of their own, which was clearly distinguishable from the French and German schools.

THE NEO-HELLENIC STYLE. The Greek adaptation of classicism (Greek neoclassical) is a shrewdly balanced blend of the architectural styles developed in Greece since the fall of Constantinople with the Western classicism that emerged from the Renaissance. With its leaning toward dignity and elegance, even austerity, this style of architecture, more than any other form of cultural or artistic expression, bears the imprint of 19th-century Greek society. Virtually every style assimilated from Greece's past of influenced by foreigners contributed to the neo-Hellenic style in some way – ranging from Doric to Renaissance, Byzantine and Gothic.

A SKIN OF MARBLE. Many of the buildings dating from the period following the War of Independence have disappeared in the welter of a city forced to provide living space for a mushrooming population. Two million Greeks from Asia Minor were repatriated during the 1920's, and the civil war was followed in the 1950's by a massive influx from country

THE NATIONAL GARDENS
■ *34*. The park of the royal residence was laid out in 1839 by the architects Kalkos and Barauld and planted by Queen Amalia's head gardener (the queen herself having instigated the idea). Initially it was filled with 150,000 flowers and shrubs imported from Italy. Soon after, in 1841, Greek flora were added.

areas. The buildings still to be seen bear out the opinion of most 19th-century travelers, who felt on entering Athens that here was a city "lovingly built". The new capital became the intellectual hub of the nation, attracting politicians, administrators, civil servants, historians and teachers. The quarries had been reopened, and once again the gleaming white marble of Mount Pentelikon clothed public buildings, covered the cornices of great private houses, and graced long flights of steps. Magnificent gardens, filled with fountains, burgeoned in the center of Athens.

THE ZAPPEION
The Zappeion exhibition hall stands in a garden full of pines, plane trees and cypresses behind the Acropolis and facing the Panathenaic Stadium. It was built between 1874 and 1888 to plans by the architects F. Boulanger and T. Hansen.

SOUTH OF SYNTAGMA SQUARE

PARLIAMENT. Following King Otto's accession his father, Ludwig I of Bavaria, financed the building of the huge palace which today dominates Plateia Syntagma (Constitution Square). Built between 1836 and 1840, to plans by the Bavarian architect F. von Gärtner, the palace was modified in 1930 to become the Parliament building.

THE NATIONAL GARDENS ■ *34.* A number of Roman remains were uncovered during the laying out of the gardens, notably a villa with a mosaic pavement and fragments of columns from the original walls erected by Hadrian. These add to the attraction of this immense park, much loved by Athenians, who come here for quiet and repose.

THE ZAPPEION MEGARON. In the southern section of the National Gardens stands the Zappeion exhibition hall, named for its founder, Zappas. The dream of this great man was to revive the Olympic Games: he was the inspiration of the four first Olympiads, as the sporting and commercial events that took place in Athens were known prior to the first fully fledged Olympic Games held in 1896 ▲ *358.*

THE CEMETERY. Situated on the southeastern fringe of Ardettos, the precinct of the Church of Lazarus became the first municipal cemetery of the new capital in 1838. An edict pronounced that "the burial ground should be laid out at a sufficient distance from the city and township, and planted with trees and hedges".

Funerary monuments in the municipal cemetery.

The mansion of the Saripolos family dates from the second half of the 19th century, a period of transition in Athens when a number of cultural and artistic tendencies existed side by side and the political class set about modernizing the Greek state. An enlightened bourgeoisie contributed to the forming of a new Athenian society. It left its esthetic mark on the city by importing foreign architectural trends, both sophisticated and mundane, including classical, Romantic and neoclassical styles. The Saripolos family was typical of this development.

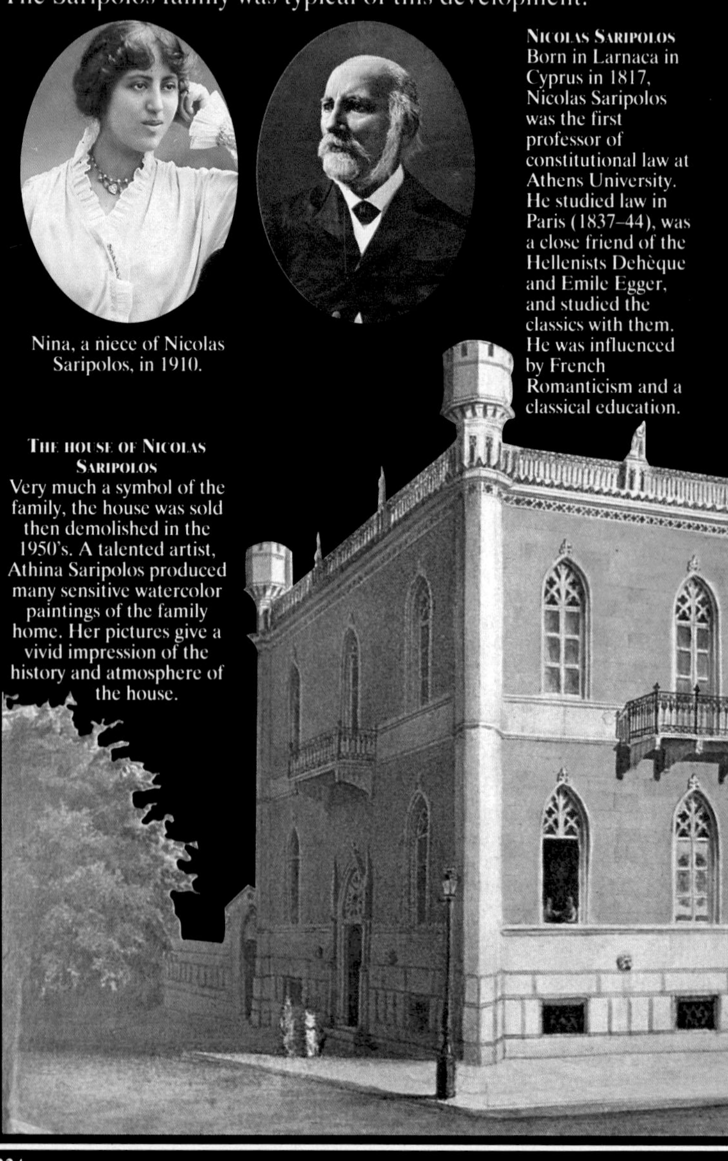

Nina, a niece of Nicolas Saripolos, in 1910.

NICOLAS SARIPOLOS
Born in Larnaca in Cyprus in 1817, Nicolas Saripolos was the first professor of constitutional law at Athens University. He studied law in Paris (1837–44), was a close friend of the Hellenists Dehèque and Emile Egger, and studied the classics with them. He was influenced by French Romanticism and a classical education.

THE HOUSE OF NICOLAS SARIPOLOS
Very much a symbol of the family, the house was sold then demolished in the 1950's. A talented artist, Athina Saripolos produced many sensitive watercolor paintings of the family home. Her pictures give a vivid impression of the history and atmosphere of the house.

A sideboard with shelves, an armchair, a simple table and ordinary chairs furnish the dining room. The small pedestal table among the sofas and armchairs in the salon (right) is a reminder of the past in a modern house.

Walls and ceilings with moldings, antique columns, marble paving – with his love of classical culture, Nicolas Saripolos wanted his house to reflect the past. Both the furniture and the architecture are imbued with this sense of nostalgia.

Bedroom One of the family's bedrooms, with its brass 19th-century bedstead and homely furniture. The presence of the occupants is hinted at by the coat and boater lying on the bed and the umbrella and boots.

THE GENNADION LIBRARY
Founded by J. Gennadios, this library has a collection of some 24,000 works on Greek-related topics.

THE BENAKI MUSEUM
The museum building has been altered on three occasions since its construction (in 1965, 1968 and 1973). Further changes are currently under way to improve the display facilities for the various collections, which include exquisite jewelry, Byzantine and post-Byzantine works of art, and some fine examples of more modern craftwork, especially traditional handmade costumes.

To this labyrinth of marble and foliage, studded with small antique temples and elegant sculptures, the Athenians of the last century were brought to rejoin their ancestors. Here, beneath the neoclassical jumble, lies the dust of scholars, politicians, bankers, architects, poets and merchants, united in the timeless honor of having died in Athens.

THE PRESIDENTIAL PALACE. The new palace, which stands on the corner of Herodes Atticus Street and George II Street, was built between 1891 and 1897 for Crown Prince Constantine, then newly married to Princess Sophia of Russia. The architect Ernst Ziller, who directed the works, used plans drawn up by T. Hansen in 1887 for a summer residence. At the request of Princess Sophia, Ziller placed special emphasis on the private nature of the house. Later it served as the home of Kings Constantine I, Alexander, George II, Paul II and finally Constantine II (until he was deposed in 1967). Today the Greek President resides here.

VASILISSIS SOPHIAS AVENUE

THE BENAKI MUSEUM. This establishment occupies a private mansion built at the turn of the century by Anastasios Metaxas, the architect who worked on the restoration of the Panathenaic Stadium. It was subsequently embellished and enlarged by Metaxas in 1910, following its purchase by the Benaki family, recently arrived in Athens. Though a relatively late example of the Greek neoclassical style, it is nevertheless a typically elegant 19th-century aristocratic residence. In 1930, Antoine Benaki, a rich collector based in Cairo, transformed it into a museum; today it contains an eclectic mix of art treasures of widely different origins and periods. These include Egyptian antiquities; antique, Hellenistic, Byzantine and Venetian jewelry; T'ang-dynasty Chinese porcelain (7th–9th century); icons and manuscripts; superb Turkish and Venetian fabrics (16th–18th centuries); and two paintings by El Greco. The museum also has a library of some eighty thousand volumes, along with extensive archives of contemporary Greek history.

MUSEUM OF CYCLADIC AND ANCIENT GREEK ART, GOULANDRIS FOUNDATION ▲ *240*. After leaving the Benaki Museum, continue along Vasilissis Sophias Avenue, then turn left into Neofitou Douka Street until you come to the museum founded by Dolly Goulandris in memory of her husband. The collections here, which span Greek history from the early Bronze Age to the end of antiquity, are rich in examples of the most ancient art of the Cyclades, the islands in the center of the Aegean.

The first floor contains some two hundred and thirty Cycladic pieces dating from the 3rd millenium BC, the finest of which are the marble idols found buried with votive offerings. They represent the goddess of fertility, who was worshipped around the Aegean and in Anatolia from the Neolithic era to the close of the Bronze Age. The second floor is reserved for nearly three hundred items dating from about 2000 BC to about the 4th century AD. Particularly fine is a collection of pottery from the classical period, and a series of works of art in gold, silver, bronze, marble and glass.

THE BYZANTINE MUSEUM. One of the oldest private mansions on this avenue is that of the Duchesse de Plaisance, the wife of the third French consul, Charles François Lebrun. A convinced philhellene, this lady went to Greece for the first time at the end of the War of Independence. On the death of her daughter in 1837 she settled in Athens for good, building herself a large residence between 1840 and 1848. This Byzantine-inspired edifice, designed by Kleanthis, was a favorite meeting place for Athenian high society under King Otto. Today it is the home of the Byzantine Museum.

THE MILITARY MUSEUM. On leaving the Byzantine Museum, continue along Vasilissis Sophias Avenue to the next street, which contains the Military Museum, with its displays of weapons and other items relating to the many wars of the Greeks, from ancient times to the present century.

MODERN AND CONTEMPORARY ART AT THE PINAKOTHEKE

The works by Volonakis ● *99*, Lytras, Buyzis and Iakovidis in the Pinakotheke (National Gallery) represent the period when Greek art was absorbing Western influences unchecked. The artists who came after managed to create a more characteristically Greek style; those best known today include the painters Ghikas ● *103*, Parthenis, Kontoglu and Theophilos Hadjimichali, and the sculptors Prosalentis and Halepas.

THE PALACE OF ILION Schliemann's house, built by the architect Ernst Ziller in 1878, now harbors the National Numismatic Collection. Formerly it housed Greece's Supreme Court, the Areopagus.

Stadiou Avenue.

THE NATIONAL GALLERY (PINAKOTHEKE). On the corner of Vasileos Konstantinou Avenue and Rizzari Street, near the Hilton Hotel, is the Ethniki Pinakotheke. The permanent collections here are mainly devoted to Greek paintings and sculptures of the 19th and 20th centuries, though the museum possesses works by great European artists too – among them a sculpture by Rodin and paintings by Bruegel, Caravaggio, Delacroix, El Greco, Picasso and Utrillo. There are also a number of pictures, by both Greek and foreign artists, depicting Athens at the end of the Turkish occupation and during the first years of King Otto's reign.

The equestrian statue of Theodore Kolokotronis in front of the National Historical Museum (right).

Philhellinon Avenue at the beginning of this century.

KOLONAKI

The best way back to Syntagma Square is across the Kolonaki quarter, which extends along the north side of Vasilissis Sophias Avenue. Many Athenians consider this the most pleasant part of the city, with a cosmopolitan population of intellectuals and professional people. The district lies at the foot of Mount Lycabettus (the view from the top extends from the Acropolis to the island of Salamis). It is primarily an area of shops, art galleries, cafés, restaurants, fashion agencies, embassies and bookshops, in addition to being the home of the French, British and American schools of archeology. The name Kolonaki refers to a column that once stood in Dexamenis Square (meaning "Cistern Square"), where Hadrian's aqueduct began. This tiered square tucked into the side of the hill, with its open-air cinema, restaurants and cafés, in many ways constitutes the

St Denis
The plans for this basilica were drawn up by Leo von Klenze, the architect of Ludwig I of Bavaria.

heart of the capital's night-time existence. During the day a similar role is assumed by Philikis Eterias Square: any Athenian worthy of the name feels obliged to spend an occasional moment or two in one of the cafés there. Today Kolonaki is still one of Athens' principal meeting places, even though pollution has driven many of its former inhabitants to the northern suburbs or to Kifissia.

Street vendor selling *koulourias* (Greek croissants).

Stadiou and Eleftheriou Venizelou avenues

The National Historical Museum ▲ *234*. This institution occupies the former home of the Greek parliament, built between 1858 and 1871 to plans by F. Boulanger. The museum's collections range from the Byzantine period to the 19th century – with rich documentation on the War of Independence, including portraits and souvenirs of the combatants, figureheads of Greek warships, and much more.

An Athenian trilogy. The National Library, the University and the Academy form an exemplary triad of 19th-century Athenian neoclassicism. The materials used for the three buildings are identical: Piraeus stone for the ground floor, and Pentelic marble for the upper stories, the colonnades and the staircases.

Akademias and Stadiou avenues
These two roads are named for the two institutions that symbolize the heritage of Athens – the university, temple of the mind, and the stadium, temple of the body.

The University. The National University was designed by C. Hansen and was built between 1839 and 1864, with donations from philhellenes and Greeks of the diaspora. A sober, rather elegant piece of architecture, which is still seen as the modern city's first monument, it remains the most interesting building constructed in Athens during King Otto's reign. It is H-shaped and directly inspired by antiquity; its façade is decorated with an Ionic colonnade and sculptures by I. Kossos and G. Fytalis, among them effigies of Rhigas Velestinlis and the Patriarch Gregory V, who were among the first victims in the uprising against the Turkish occupation. Inside is a huge mural painting by K. Rahl and E. Lebiedzky of a chorus of muses dancing around Otto's throne – an allegory of the rebirth of the arts and sciences in liberated Greece.

Museum of the City of Athens
This building on Klafthmonos Square was the residence of King Otto in 1836. Since 1980 the museum has used it to display its splendid collections tracing the history of Athens, including a huge scale model of Athens in 1842.

The Academy. To the right of the university building stands the Academy (1859–85). T. Hansen's original plans for this were to some extent altered by Ernst Ziller, who was in charge of the construction. The cost of the Academy (three million drachmas) was paid by Baron Simon Sinas, a Greek banker ennobled in Austria. Although the overall design is Ionic, like that of the public buildings of ancient Greece, the Academy is otherwise typically neoclassical. Its frieze is decorated with murals by K. Rahl representing scenes from mythology, while statues of Apollo and Minerva on tall columns enliven its façade.

The National Library. Immediately adjoining the university, on the left, this edifice was also designed by T. Hansen and built by Ernst Ziller. A somewhat ponderous Doric building,

STADIOU AVENUE
Several public buildings were erected along this avenue during the 19th century, notably the Royal Printworks (1834) and the City Hospital (1836–42). Belle, a 19th-century traveler, recounts the patriotic pride and fervor of the Athenians, who filled their capital with enough schools and charity foundations to supply a city six times larger.

completed in 1903, it contains a fine Renaissance double staircase – and a statue of M. Valianos, the eldest of the three brothers who financed its construction.

OMONIA SQUARE

A café in a shady spot on Amalias Street (right).

PLATEIA OMONIAS (Concord Square) has probably suffered more from the radical changes of the last fifty years than any other part of Athens. At the beginning of the century it was the hub of Athenian life, with cafés, restaurants and a large underground station; today it is a gathering point for the city's paupers and vagrants. The four 19th-century hotels on Omonia Square that were internationally famous during the Belle Époque – the Excelsior, the Carlton, the Alexander the Great and the Baguion – are now dilapidated and are lost among the undistinguished buildings erected during the 1950's and 1960's. Nowadays Athenians only go to Omonia in the daytime and in their cars; at best they might stop there briefly in the early morning to buy the first newspapers and discuss the news with their anonymous fellow citizens.

THE UNIVERSITY
Most of the monumental constructions in the center of Athens were built by private subscription, as were most of the major public buildings.

SOUTH OF OMONIA SQUARE

CITY HALL SQUARE. Only a few hundred yards from Omonia, in the liveliest quarter of the capital, is City Hall Square, still known to Athenians as "the Agora". About twenty years ago extensive archeological discoveries were made here during the construction of a municipal parking lot, which led to the full-scale excavation of the square. It has nevertheless retained much of its original charm; the best old buildings here are the National Bank and the Melas mansion, on the east side.

THE NATIONAL BANK. This institution occupies what was once the mansion of G. Stavros, who founded the bank in 1841

KORAIS AND UNIVERSITY STREETS
One of Athens' oldest cafés, the Gambetta, named for the French statesman who served as a model for Greek liberals and radicals, stood at the intersection of these two main thoroughfares. It was demolished during the rebuilding program of the 1950's.

The Academy.

along with the old Hôtel d'Angleterre. Restoration work on it was undertaken in 1900 by the architects N. and A. Balanos, who opted for the Renaissance style. The Melas mansion, which for many years served as Athens' main post office, was likewise purchased by the bank and is now used as an annex for exhibitions.

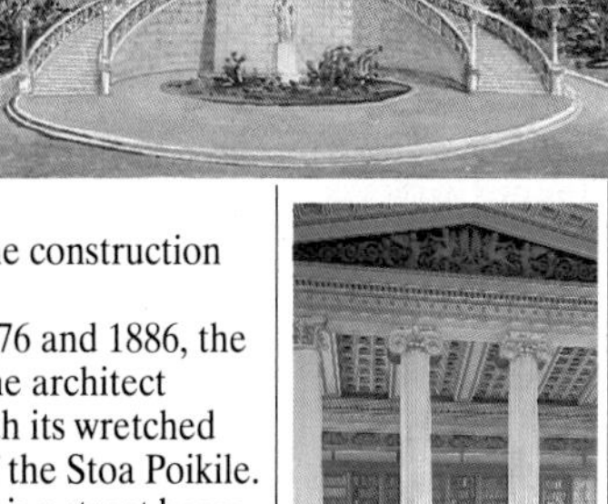

Façade of the National Library.

City Hall. On the west side of the square is the City Hall, a heavy, barrack-like edifice typical of the late 19th century. It was built between 1872 and 1878, to plans by P. Kalkos. Initially the City Hall occupied the first floor only; the shops and workshops on the ground floor were rented out by the city in order to repay the 130,000 drachmas borrowed to finance the construction work.

The municipal market. Erected between 1876 and 1886, the present market buildings were designed by the architect Koumelis. They replaced the old market "with its wretched sheds", built by the Ottomans on the ruins of the Stoa Poikile.

Eolou Street. This narrow, winding pedestrian street bears the name of Aeolus, the god of the winds. In addition to a series of small shops, there are two churches on Eolou Street, the one designed by Zezos and the other by Ziller. Much of the Greek administration was concentrated within this district in the early days of the monarchy, and many prominent figures, both Greeks and foreigners, built town mansions here. Among the principal buildings are the Prokesh von Osten Palace (1836), which is now the Conservatoire; the Serpieris Palace (1880), now occupied by the

The pediment and Ionic columns of the National Library.

THE OLD MARKET IN ATHENS
The central covered market is still one of the city's great attractions. During the day it is thronged by shoppers, while at night it is frequented by people dining out and also by the homeless. The market has several restaurants that serve Greek delicacies hard to find elsewhere.

Agricultural Bank; and the Limnios Palace, which soon became the Hôtel Grande-Bretagne.

NORTH OF OMONIA SQUARE

THE NATIONAL THEATER. Until the later part of the 19th century Athens possessed only one stone-built theater: this was the Athens or Boukouras Theater, which was inaugurated in 1840. The actors performed in the open air, in the vicinity of the Royal Gardens and Omonia Square. However, the Municipal Theater, built between 1873 and 1888 to plans by Ernst Ziller, answered the city's growing need for theatrical entertainment. Ten years later King George I used a donation of one million drachmas from a wealthy Greek merchant in London to build a third theater. This Royal Theater, which was constructed between 1895 and 1901 to plans by Ziller, was originally reserved for the Court. Built in the Renaissance style, its décor and interior layout were inspired by the People's Theater in Vienna. Viennese engineers supervised the work, and the result included the most modern heating, lighting and scene-shifting arrangements available at the time. Today the Royal Theater has been renamed the National Theater.

THE NATIONAL ARCHEOLOGICAL MUSEUM ▲ *237*. The protection of Greece's archeological heritage was one of the principal concerns of the Kingdom of Greece from the moment of its inception. The twenty years immediately preceding the War of Independence had witnessed the transfer of large quantities of priceless antiquities to the museums of Paris, London, Munich and Berlin. For more than thirty years, those masterpieces that

"THE BROAD SQUARE IN FRONT OF THE PALACE IS CALLED SYNTAGMA, OR CONSTITUTION SQUARE. THE CHARM OF IT IS ENTIRELY ATTRIBUTABLE TO DEMOCRACY."

DAVID HOGARTH

remained were assembled and exhibited either inside or outside major venues such as the Parthenon, the Stoa of Hadrian and the Hephaisteion, while they awaited the construction of a proper museum. An initial proposal, by the architect Leo von Klenze, surfaced in 1835. Broadly inspired by one of von Klenze's earlier commissions, the Pinakothek in Munich, the building was to be a kind of "temple of the arts", noble and imposing in spirit, but austere and inward-looking in aspect. But only the idea of a European-style central museum was acceptable. After several other proposals by Western European architects had also been rejected, an international contest was organized in 1858. The jury put together by the Munich Academy was unable to reach a decision; although the various projects displayed at Athens were much admired, they were felt to be unrealistic. Several years elapsed before the government finally entrusted this difficult commission to a Greek architect, P Kalkos, who proceeded with the construction of the museum between 1866 and 1880.

THE POLYTECHNIC SCHOOL. Adjoining the Archeological Museum are the neoclassical buildings of the Polytekhneion (Polytechnic School). These were erected between 1862 and 1884 to plans by the Greek architect Lyssandros Kaftantzoglou, who endowed them with elegant Ionic and Doric colonnades. The sponsors of the school, three merchants named Stournaris, Averof and Tasitsas, gave it the name of Metsovion, in honor of Metsovo, their native village in Epirus. The Polytekhneion, which includes a Fine Arts section and several engineering schools, was a late-19th-century symbol of the renewal of Greek arts and sciences, and of the westernization and modernization of Greek society. It trained large numbers of engineers who were later to supervise the transformation of the landscape of Attica. Between 1923 and 1956 the three original buildings were complemented by two multistory annexes. It was at the Polytekhneion that the first mass demonstration against the dictatorial regime of the Colonels took place.

The Polytechnic School.

Omonia Square.

THE EXPANSION OF ATHENS IN THE 19TH CENTURY

Houses and palaces were built and boulevards laid out, and political parties emerged and salons flourished. By the turn of the century the poets, scholars and politicians of Athens were on a par with the elite of Europe.

The National Theater (left). The National Archeological Museum (below).

The museum has occupied the former parliament building since 1960. It contains the collections of Greece's Historical and Ethnological Society, founded in 1882, and covers Greek history from the Fall of Constantinople to modern times. Above all it is a memorial to the great actors in the emergence of Greece as a nation-state, with portraits, flags, arms and armor, costumes and objects associated with the leaders of the struggle for independence, along with a collection of souvenirs of the generals and the first monarchs of the new nation.

CRETAN ARMOR (16TH CENTURY)
The Ottoman conquest of Greece was completed in the 16th century under Suleyman the Magnificent and Selim II, who expelled the Knights Hospitalers, the Venetians and the Genoese from the eastern Mediterranean. Crete was taken from the Venetians in 1699.

REGIMENTAL BANNER
This banner dates from the 1912–13 Balkan War; it bears the image of Saint George, together with the names of the battles in Macedonia at which the regiment fought.

CUTLASS OF GEORGAKIS OLYMPIOS
Olympios was a member of the masonic Philiki Eteria, founded at Odessa in 1814 by three Greek merchants. This was the largest secret society involved in preparing the national revolution.

SEAL OF THE AREOPAGUS
This seal is made up of four parts, assembled on an iron base screwed to a wooden handle. Each member retained one section, while the president kept the base and the screw.

LONG RIFLE (EARLY 19TH CENTURY)
The property of Theodore Kolokotronis, hero of the War of Independence.

The National Historical Museum occupies a palace in Stadiou Street built in 1871 to designs by the French architect Boulanger.

Figurehead of the "Leonidas"
In the War of Independence, Greek warships often bore the names of heroes from ancient times.

Watercolor of the ships that took part in the Battle of Navarino. The museum possesses large numbers of lithographs of episodes from the War of Independence.

George Ainian's ring
This ring was used by George Ainian, a member of the Society of Friends, to indicate his identity when making contacts in Greece in 1820. It bears the symbols of the secret society: the cross for faith, the flame for liberty and the anchor for resolve.

Admiral Canaris
Dinner plate from a set sold by French society ladies to raise money for the Greek cause.

The Fall of Constantinople
The museum possesses eight of the twenty-four paintings by Zografos that were commissioned by General Makriyannis, a hero of the revolution who learned to read and write expressly to record his memoirs of the War of Independence.

The Mask of Agamemnon
This gold funeral mask was discovered at Mycenae by Schliemann, in Tomb V of the first circle. The archeologist believed it belonged to the legendary King of Mycenae and Argos, hence its name. It dates from the 14th century BC.

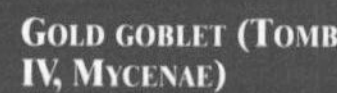

Gold goblet (Tomb IV, Mycenae)
This goblet is remarkable for the originality of its form with fine woven fillets of gold linking the foot to the two handles, on which birds are perched.

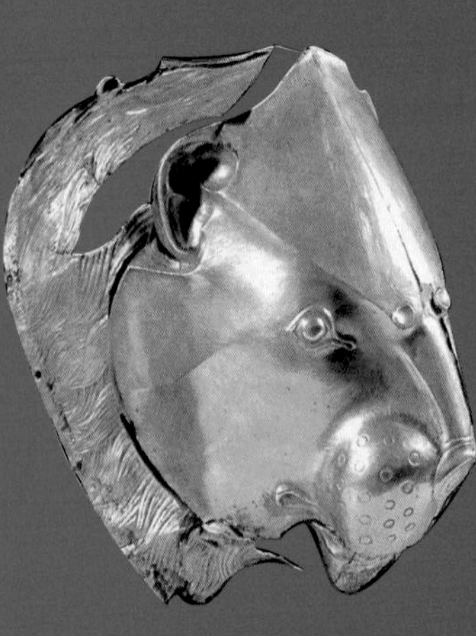

Gold cup (Kyatos type)

Rhyton shaped like a lion's head
This gold cup was found in Tomb IV of the first circle of the acropolis of Mycenae; it dates from the 16th century BC. The symmetry and schematization of detail are extraordinarily original.

Gold goblet (15th century BC)
This masterpiece of Mycenean goldwork came from a *tholos* tomb at Vaphio in Laconia.

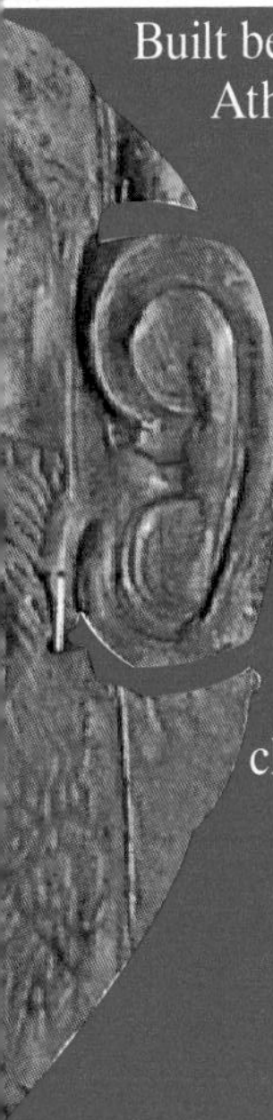

Built between 1850 and 1889, the archeological museum in Athens is the oldest institution of its type in Greece. In 1891 all the antiquities previously dispersed around the country were assembled here. The rapid accumulation of works of art from excavations all over Greece obliged the authorities to add another wing in 1939. A complete reorganization of the collections was carried out by Christos Courousos just after World War Two. Today the museum exhibits objects from all over the Hellenic world and from every epoch from ancient Greece to the Roman period. These are displayed in chronological order, according to the materials used, and by private collections where applicable.

Gold signet rings
Rings like these had a practical use – in that they enabled people to stamp their personal mark on possessions, packages or jars – but the ingenuity of their creators gave them value as jewelry and even as talismans. These three signet rings from Mycenae offer a sample of the themes with which they were engraved: scenes of combat between two, three or four figures; hunting, fishing and bullfighting scenes; and religious vignettes, in which the figures tend to be feminine – in this case, two priestesses.

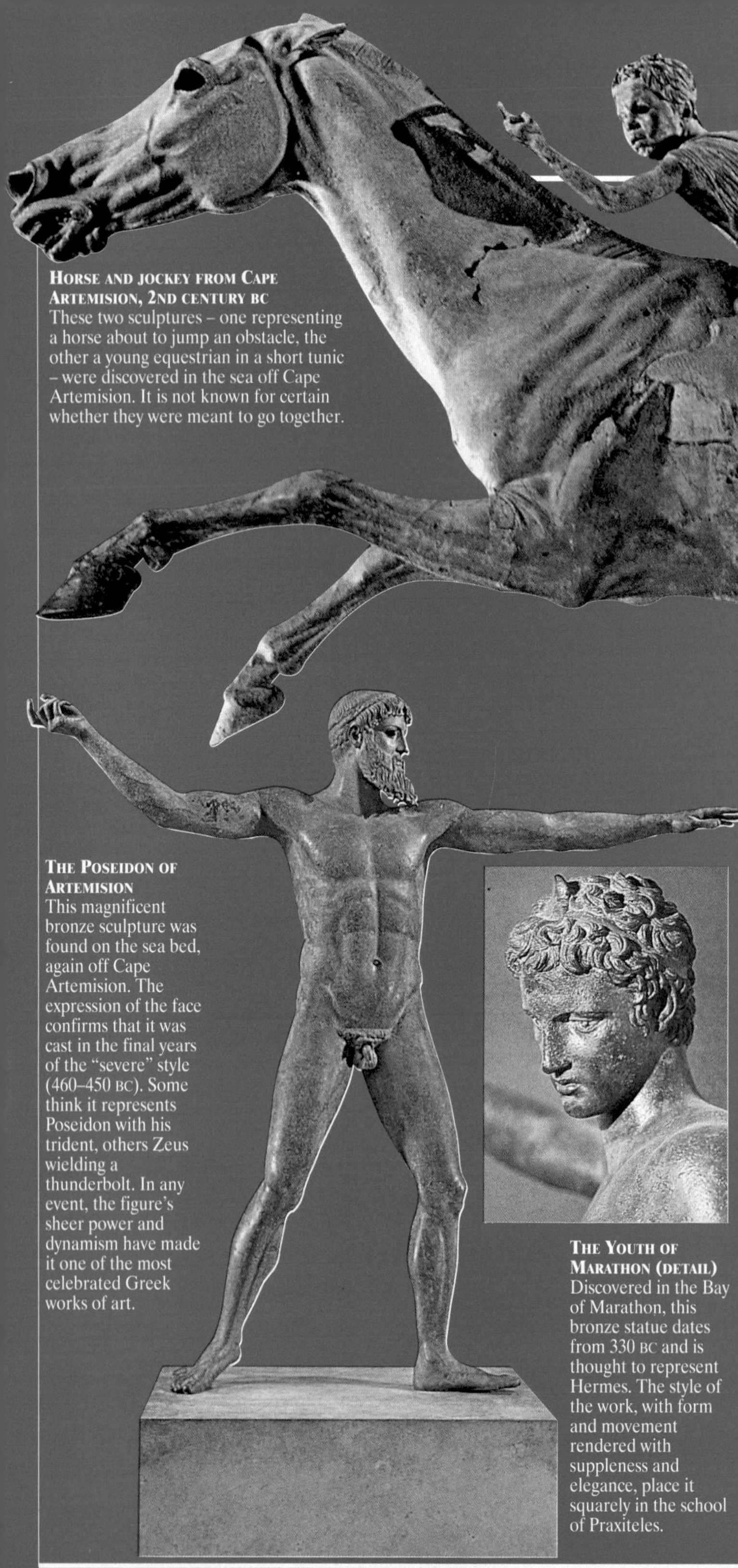

Horse and jockey from Cape Artemision, 2nd century BC
These two sculptures – one representing a horse about to jump an obstacle, the other a young equestrian in a short tunic – were discovered in the sea off Cape Artemision. It is not known for certain whether they were meant to go together.

The Poseidon of Artemision
This magnificent bronze sculpture was found on the sea bed, again off Cape Artemision. The expression of the face confirms that it was cast in the final years of the "severe" style (460–450 BC). Some think it represents Poseidon with his trident, others Zeus wielding a thunderbolt. In any event, the figure's sheer power and dynamism have made it one of the most celebrated Greek works of art.

The Youth of Marathon (detail)
Discovered in the Bay of Marathon, this bronze statue dates from 330 BC and is thought to represent Hermes. The style of the work, with form and movement rendered with suppleness and elegance, place it squarely in the school of Praxiteles.

The museum's collection of sculptures contains original works of extraordinary quality from the great temples and principal cities of ancient Greece. It offers a complete overview of the development of Greek sculpture.

BUST OF PRIAPUS
Phallic sculptures of this kind would be placed at the entrance of a domain to ensure its prosperity.

KOUROS, 525 BC
An epigram engraved on the base of this *kouros* indicates that it was placed on the tomb of Croesus. It was discovered at Anavyssos in Attica.

HOPLITES RELIEF (DETAIL), 490 BC
This fragment came from the base of a *kouros* incorporated into the Wall of Themistocles. It represents a procession of hoplites, headed by a two-horse chariot.

Museum of Cycladic and Ancient Greek Art

The especially mild geophysical conditions prevailing in the Cyclades encouraged the emergence of one of Greece's earliest civilizations, between 3200 and 2000 BC. Marble, which is abundantly available in these islands, is the basic material for Cycladic art, with its uniquely streamlined, near-abstract forms. Nicolas P. Goulandris began collecting Greek antiquities in 1961; before long he developed a special passion for Cycladic art, assembling a collection of over two hundred separate pieces. On the ground floor and first floor of the museum, which opened in 1986, are displayed marble figurines and obsidian blades, along with vases and other vessels in terracotta or marble.

Male figurine
This marble figurine (10 inches high) probably represents a hunter or warrior, given the chevron bandoleer across the chest.

Dish in the shape of a frying pan
This dish in the form of a frying pan (10 inches in diameter) is part of a group found at Kampos. Its complex decoration consists of curvilinear drawings cut into the clay before firing.

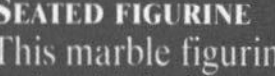

Seated figurine
This marble figurine (6 inches high) is seated on a stool, a cylindrical goblet in one hand. The stool and the body are slightly inclined, while the almond-shaped head is tilted backward.

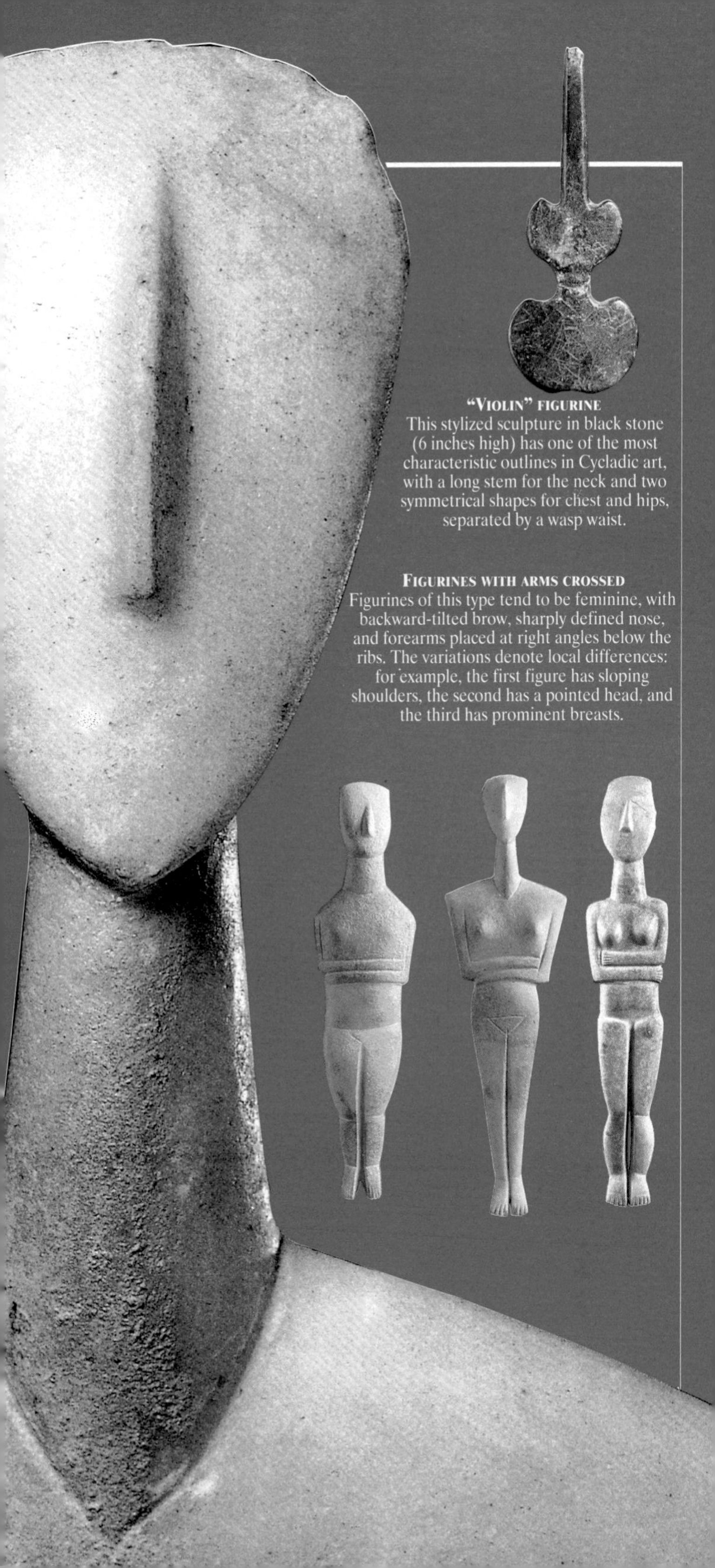

“Violin” figurine
This stylized sculpture in black stone (6 inches high) has one of the most characteristic outlines in Cycladic art, with a long stem for the neck and two symmetrical shapes for chest and hips, separated by a wasp waist.

Figurines with arms crossed
Figurines of this type tend to be feminine, with backward-tilted brow, sharply defined nose, and forearms placed at right angles below the ribs. The variations denote local differences: for example, the first figure has sloping shoulders, the second has a pointed head, and the third has prominent breasts.

Museum of Cycladic and Ancient Greek Art

Geometrical kylix
A *kylix* was a low, wide-mouthed bowl used for drinking, usually painted inside and out. This one dates from about 730 BC.

The collection of ancient Greek art is exhibited on the second floor of the museum. The pieces here, which date from 2000 to 400 BC, are arranged by epoch. The five sections comprise Minoan and Mycenean ceramics; Geometric art; Archaic art; black-figure ceramics; red-figure ceramics; and bronzes. This unique collection, which today includes more than three hundred items, has been enriched on several occasions, both by new Goulandris acquisitions and by other private donations, such as that of Lambros Evtaxias.

Black-figure amphora
This amphora, made between 540 and 530 BC, was decorated by the painter Polyphemus. It features two lions and a sphinx (a mythical creature with the body of a winged lion and the breasts and head of a woman).

Black-figure amphora, 515–510 BC
Here the motif is the battle between the gods and the giants. Poseidon, with his trident, is shown confronting the armed Polybotes.

Red-figure ceramics
Greek vases of the classical period were painted with red figures against a black background. The one on the left, which dates from about 460 BC, shows a satyr working with a hoe. On the right is a *krater* made in Apulia, southern Italy, between 350 and 340 BC.

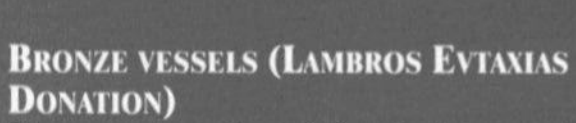

Bronze vessels (Lambros Evtaxias Donation)
The vessel on the left is a *hydria*, used to draw water, with two small horizontal handles and a large vertical one; it dates from about 450 BC and probably came from the Temple of Zeus at Dodona. On the right is a two-handled pail in the Macedonian style (4th century BC); the rim and the area below the handles are decorated with finely wrought engraving.

PIRAEUS

PHILIPS' PLANISPHERE
SHOWING THE PRINCIPAL STARS
VISIBLE FOR EVERY HOUR
IN THE YEAR.
FEBRUARY
MARCH
MAY
JUNE
AUGUST
SEPTEMBER
OCTOBER
NOVEMBER

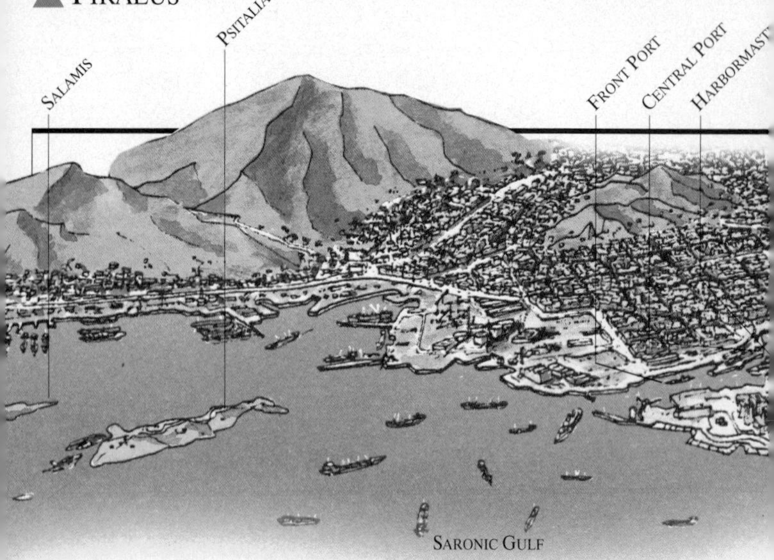

SALAMIS
PSITALIA
FRONT PORT
CENTRAL PORT
HARBORMAST
SARONIC GULF

The city of Piraeus and its various port installations are situated on the Akti Peninsula, on the Aegean. From Athens, some 6 miles away, there is fast and easy access to Piraeus by the Kifissia-Piraeus electric train, which leaves from the stations in Omonia Square and Monastiraki ▲ *178*.

Half a day

PIRAEUS AND ATHENIAN MARITIME POWER

From ancient times Piraeus has been the principal port of Athens and the focus of its trade. At the beginning of the 5th century BC Athens had neither a fleet nor a port worthy of the name. After the Battle of Marathon ● *44*, ▲ *260*, Themistocles persuaded his fellow citizens to build a war fleet and a maritime complex on the Akti Peninsula. This replaced the indifferent anchorage of Phaleron. The money required for the work came from the Laurion silver mines, which began producing in 483 BC. Themistocles envisaged three ports: to the north Kantharos, a trading port the site of which corresponds to today's central harbor, and to the south two naval ports, one in the Zea roads and the other at Munychia (today's Mikrolimano). The Athenian democracy had sizable needs but few resources: since Attica produced little in the way of wheat, minerals and wood, the Athenians were obliged to buy these products from their colonies or to try to import them from abroad. To ensure that the fleet could move about unhindered, Pericles set up

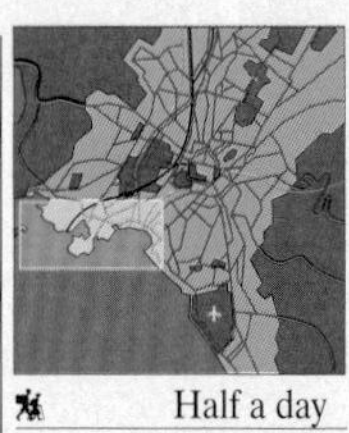

THE WALLS OF ATHENS AND THE PORTS
Considerable stretches of the walls which formerly protected the Akti Peninsula on the seaward side are still visible today. These walls were built by Conon in 394 BC. About sixty-five years before Themistocles had surrounded Athens itself with similar walls.

The port and the Greek fleet at the turn of the century.

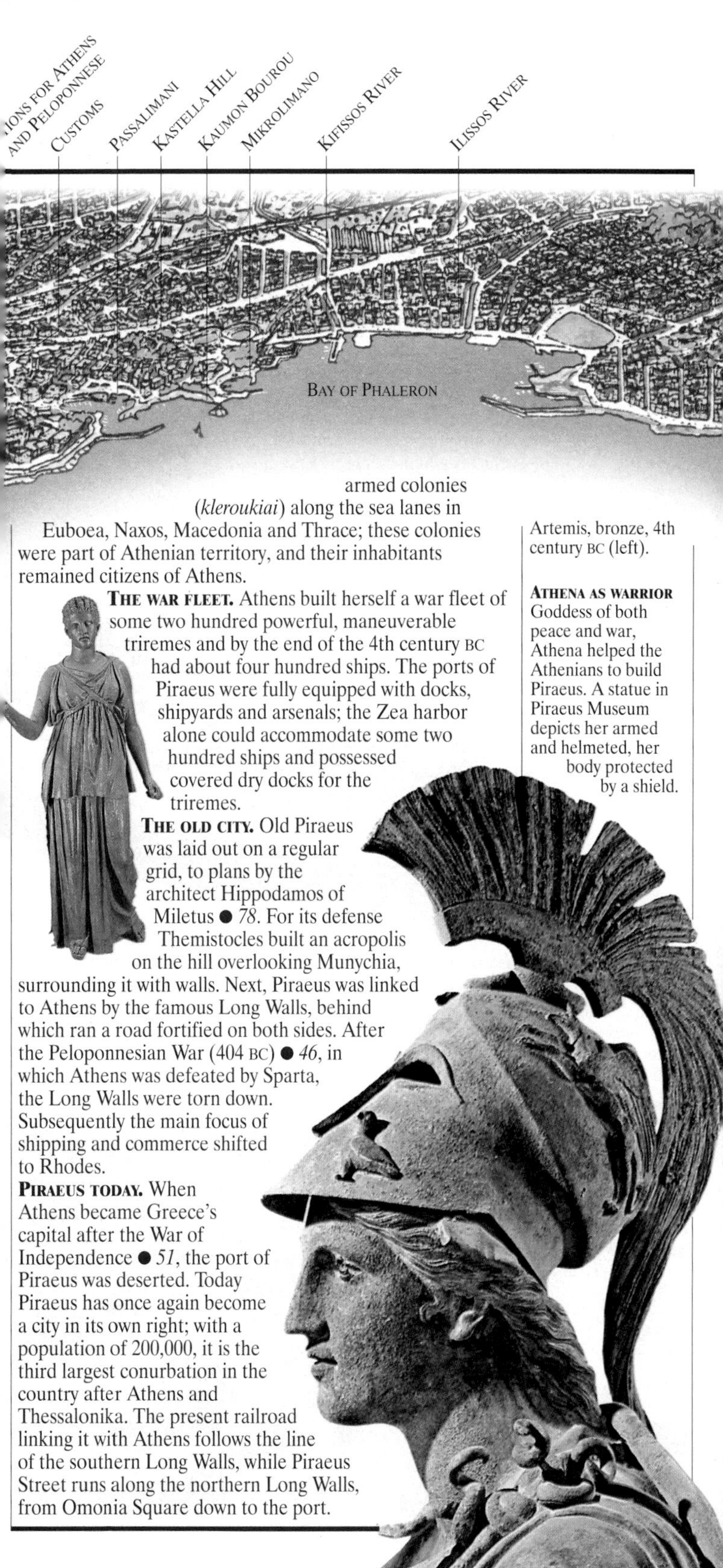

armed colonies (*kleroukiai*) along the sea lanes in Euboea, Naxos, Macedonia and Thrace; these colonies were part of Athenian territory, and their inhabitants remained citizens of Athens.

THE WAR FLEET. Athens built herself a war fleet of some two hundred powerful, maneuverable triremes and by the end of the 4th century BC had about four hundred ships. The ports of Piraeus were fully equipped with docks, shipyards and arsenals; the Zea harbor alone could accommodate some two hundred ships and possessed covered dry docks for the triremes.

THE OLD CITY. Old Piraeus was laid out on a regular grid, to plans by the architect Hippodamos of Miletus ● *78*. For its defense Themistocles built an acropolis on the hill overlooking Munychia, surrounding it with walls. Next, Piraeus was linked to Athens by the famous Long Walls, behind which ran a road fortified on both sides. After the Peloponnesian War (404 BC) ● *46*, in which Athens was defeated by Sparta, the Long Walls were torn down. Subsequently the main focus of shipping and commerce shifted to Rhodes.

PIRAEUS TODAY. When Athens became Greece's capital after the War of Independence ● *51*, the port of Piraeus was deserted. Today Piraeus has once again become a city in its own right; with a population of 200,000, it is the third largest conurbation in the country after Athens and Thessalonika. The present railroad linking it with Athens follows the line of the southern Long Walls, while Piraeus Street runs along the northern Long Walls, from Omonia Square down to the port.

Artemis, bronze, 4th century BC (left).

ATHENA AS WARRIOR
Goddess of both peace and war, Athena helped the Athenians to build Piraeus. A statue in Piraeus Museum depicts her armed and helmeted, her body protected by a shield.

Emblem of the Greek navy.

Vestiges of these walls are visible from the Phaleron Station, just before Piraeus, between Piraeus Street and the new stadium. The main part of the city is built on the Akti Peninsula, where one can walk around the ruins of Conon's fortifications.

THE CENTRAL PORT DISTRICT. From Piraeus underground station it is a short walk to the north shore and the main port area (the Kantharos of the ancients). The inner part of the port is now used exclusively by ferries serving the islands of the Saronic Gulf and the Aegean, Crete and the various countries of the Mediterranean. In the morning the quays swarm with vehicles and passengers. East of Karaiskakis Square is Poseidonos Quay, which leads to the Dimarchion (city hall) of Piraeus. Not far from here is the Haghia Triada Cathedral, the main landmark for sailors navigating into the port.

MODEL OF A STEAMSHIP
In 1827 the newly appointed governor of Greece, Ioannis Kapodistrias ● *51*, endowed the nation with a modern fleet built in Britain. The Naval Museum in Piraeus displays a collection of models of the principal vessels.

PASSALIMANI AND THE ZEA MARINA. The narrow neck of the peninsula is occupied by Passalimani (the Pasha's port). At the time of the Turkish occupation this little harbor was the main anchorage for the Ottoman fleet. Today it is a yacht marina. The front of the port is taken up by the installation known as the Zea Marina, used by some of the island ferries.

THE MODERN CITY
Modern Piraeus dates for the most part from the 19th and early 20th century. The cafés lining the quays overlook a spectacular array of ships and boats.

"ONCE WITHIN, THE OARSMEN CAN LEAVE THEIR VESSELS WITHOUT ANY MOORINGS, AS SOON AS THEY HAVE REACHED THE LINE OF THE ANCHORAGE."

HOMER

Bird's-eye view of Mikrolimano and the Zea Marina.

THE MERCHANT FLEET
Since the end of World War Two the commercial port has grown steadily. The Athens docks of Piraeus and Eleusis can accommodate huge tankers; they are backed by a major industrial zone including naval shipyards and petroleum refineries.

MIKROLIMANO. About half a mile to the southeast of here is Turkolimano ("the Turkish harbor"), which was called Munychia in classical times. It has now been renamed Mikrolimano ("the small harbor") and is much favored by the Athenians, who come here in the evenings to stroll around the crescent-shaped bay. There is a solid line of fish restaurants (mostly excellent) along the quayside, with tables spread out under the bowsprits of moored yachts and fishing boats.

ARCHEOLOGICAL MUSEUM. Situated on Trikoupis Street, next to the Zea Theater, the museum possesses a rich collection of statues, reliefs and funerary stelae. It is particularly noteworthy for four bronze sculptures salvaged from the sea off Piraeus in 1959: a late classical statue of Athena, two statues of Artemis (4th century BC) and a *kouros*-type statue of Apollo (late 4th century BC).

NAVAL MUSEUM. The maritime museum, situated on the Zea Marina quayside, below Phreatidos Street, traces the history of the Greek navy from ancient times right up to the present day. Among the oldest exhibits are carved obsidian artefacts, some of them dating from 8000 BC. The mythical travels of Odysseus and the great naval engagements of antiquity are represented on vases, bas-reliefs and frescos, the most celebrated being the fresco found at Akrotiri on the island of Thera (Santorini). Other exhibits include models of various types of Greek ship, from the triremes of ancient times, with their three banks of oars, to modern frigates. There are also drawings and maps of important naval battles such as Salamis ● *45*, ▲ *366*, Lepanto and Navarino ● *54*. In the museum's gardens visitors can inspect artefacts such as cannons, shells and torpedoes. Parts of the Wall of Themistocles are still visible on Themistokleous Quay and within the museum precinct.

MARINAS
The ports of Zea and Mikrolimano are now havens for pleasure boats; they occupy the south end of the peninsula. Kantharos, to the north, is the principal commercial port.

PIRAEUS

Nowadays Piraeus is one of the world's busiest ports, receiving some 25,000 ships and around 16,000 tons of goods in transit annually. The greater part of Greece's industrial and economic activity is concentrated within the Piraeus-Athens-Eleusis triangle, hence the high pollution levels here. Nevertheless, the cosmopolitan, shifting atmosphere of this great port is still as captivating as ever, with the ceaseless comings and goings of sailors and travelers from all over the world, the reverberating sound of ships' horns and sirens, and the stiff breeze blowing off the sea. Piraeus is huge and multifaceted. There is the industrial character of the docks and arsenals, the bustle of the quays where fifty thousand passengers embark every year, and the carefree atmosphere of the markets and tavernas; and around the small harbor of Mikrolimano there are dozens of restaurants serving freshly caught fish and octopus, which is regarded as a great delicacy in Greece.

Byzantine Monasteries and Churches

THE MONASTERY OF KAISARIANI

Nestling in a valley on the slopes of Mount Hymettus 3 miles from Athens, Moni Kaisariani is a virtually unaltered Byzantine monastery dating from the Middle Ages. Its remarkable state of preservation allows us to form a picture of how the monastery – with its monks' cells, refectory, kitchen, bathhouse and fountain – was organized and how it could be defended; the purpose of each building is very clear. Several 13th-century documents mention the Monastery of Kaisariani. It flourished under the Ottomans when its monks were renowned for their erudition. The katholikon, which is dedicated to the Presentation of the Virgin, stands in the center of the courtyard. It dates from the early 12th century and is in a state of perfect preservation; designed in the shape of a cross, it is crowned by a dome resting on four columns. The narthex too is topped by a dome, and flanked on its south side by a chapel dedicated to Saint Anthony. The katholikon is remarkable for its sobriety: the dome is underpinned by a simple cornice, decorated with cut stones separated by horizontal courses of bricks. The arch in the north façade is a superb example of the skilled stonemasonry of the Middle Ages. Christ Pantocrator is represented at the center of the dome, the Holy Liturgy on the walls of the apse, and the principal feasts of the Orthodox Church on those of the nave. The frescos of the narthex were executed in 1682 by the painter Ioannis Hypostos, a native of the Peloponnese, according to the inscription above the entrance.

DAPHNI
The katholikon and façade of the 10th-century monastery.

MONI KAISARIANI
The monastery stands at the foot of a wooded valley.

Buildings at Daphni, half-hidden by greenery.

The frescos. On the inside, the original structure is still visible, as is its décor, which also dates from the 12th century. But the frescos of that era have vanished: they were replaced in the mid 16th century by magnificent paintings.

The Monastery of Daphni

The Monastery of Daphni is the most important Byzantine monument near Athens, due as much to its superb Byzantine mosaics as its excellent state of architectural preservation. It is situated about 7 miles from the city center, beside the ancient road linking Athens to Eleusis which is now the N8.

History. The monastery's origins are unknown, but its scale suggests that it was an Imperial foundation dating from the 5th century. The site was once occupied by a temple dedicated to Apollo – one of whose symbols was the laurel, called *daphni* in Greek. This temple was destroyed by invading Goths in 395, when Theodosius split the empire in two. All that remains of it is an Ionic column. The monks made use of this column by placing it in the middle of the south entrance of the exonarthex. Among the structures still visible and dating from the 5th and 6th centuries are the remains of a quadrangular surrounding wall, against which the cells were built; fortified in the Middle Ages, this wall had no towers or buttresses. The church which was built during the reign of Justinian, and was larger than the one we see today, disappeared in the 8th century. In the 7th and the 8th centuries, a time of major migrations all over Europe, Byzantium was gripped by quarrels about succession and religion ● *48* and the region lost many of its inhabitants during this period. The monastery was reconstructed in the 9th century under the Comnenus dynasty, in such a way that some historians have speculated that it may have been linked to the Monastery of Daphni at Constantinople; this would certainly explain its name more satisfactorily than the tenuous link with the cult of Apollo.

The Nativity
The Virgin and Child before the grotto.

Byzantine mosaics
Mosaic subjects had to be immediately identifiable. Their colors, like the rendering of their figures, obeyed precise guidelines. Before the crucifixion Christ's clothes are blue and gold; after the Resurrection he wears purple and gold.

The south side of the katholikon of the Monastery of Daphni.

THE CISTERCIAN MONKS. Precise information exists about the monastery from 1211 onward, when it was occupied by the Cistercians. In 1205 the Franks of the fourth Crusade, who had partitioned Greece after seizing Constantinople, came to pillage Daphni. The Duke of Athens, Otho de la Roche, who had ties with the Abbey of Bellevaux in Burgundy, gave the monastery to the Cistercians around 1211. The de la Roche family, and after them the family of Gautier de Brienne, were buried here. The Cistercians added the Gothic exonarthex and built a floor above the narthex to house a library, a treasury and probably a lodging. This can be reached by way of a staircase on the north side. It seems probable that the abbey lost its importance in the years following the arrival of the Franks, because in 1412 the last abbot was buried elsewhere. At the time of the Turkish invasion in 1458, the Cistercians left altogether. The monastery was reoccupied in the 16th century by Orthodox monks, who built the cloisters and cells of the square courtyard.

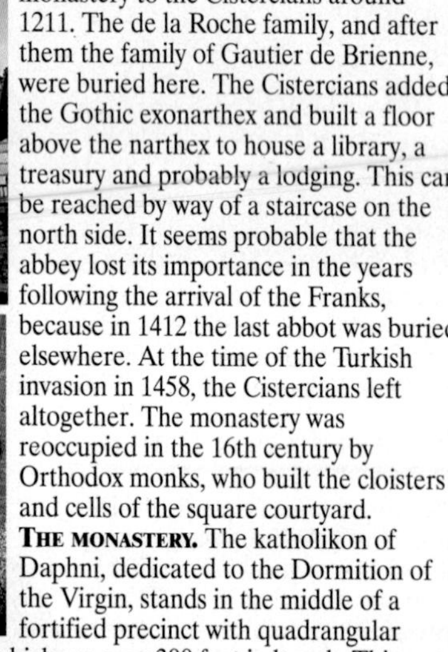

THE MONASTERY. The katholikon of Daphni, dedicated to the Dormition of the Virgin, stands in the middle of a fortified precinct with quadrangular walls, the sides of which are over 300 feet in length. This precinct is thought to be older than the church itself, and probably dates from the reign of Justinian. To the north of the katholikon are the ruins of the monastery refectory, built at the same time as the church in the 11th century. In the restored cells of the monks, marble fragments of architectural elements are displayed.

THE CHURCH
Seen from the outside it is clear that the massive rectangular blocks of the foundation are laid out in the form of a cross, at regular intervals, up to window level. The windows, with their fine red-brick arches, form an equilateral triangle. On the west side, the elegance of the triple arcature is emphasized by the presence of two slender cypresses planted on either side, which rise up to the level of the dome. Their dark foliage contrasts with the light grey of a small olive tree next to them.

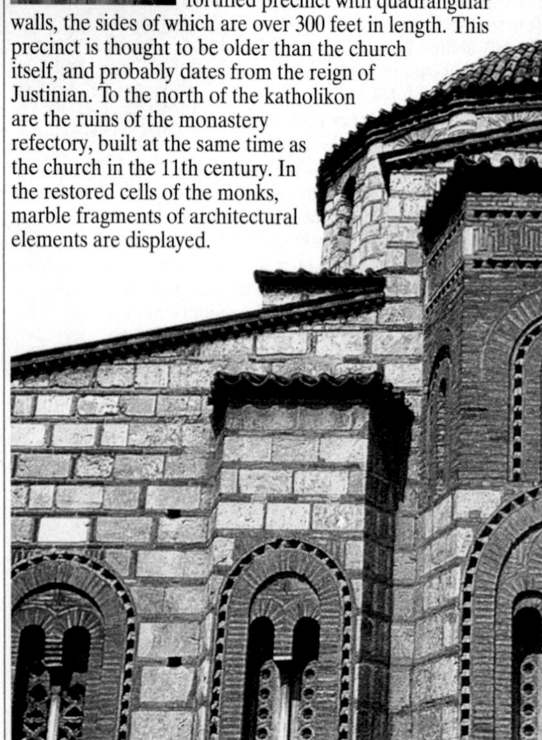

"HARD BY THE SMILING SLOPES OF FLOWERY HYMETTUS IS A SACRED FOUNTAIN; A SOFT GREEN SWARD CLOTHES THE EARTH...THE AIR IS SCENTED WITH ROSEMARY, LAUREL AND DARK MYRTLE".

OVID

FOLIAGE AND INTERTWINING PATTERNS
By banning images the iconoclasts encouraged the spread of a decorative style featuring geometrical, animal and vegetable motifs. The richness of the materials and color combinations used for interior decorations of this kind gave a new dimension to church sculpture.

THE MUSEUM. Damaged during the War of Independence, the Monastery of Daphni is no longer used by monks as a working monastery. In 1955 it was restored and converted into a museum, but its church and outer walls were severely damaged by the 1981 earthquake.

THE CHURCH. The katholikon is octagonal in form, with a dome, and is very much characteristic of mainland Greece. Its archetype is the church of the Monastery of St Luke at Phocis. The dome is very broad, resting on four arches and four corner squinches ● *94*. At the corners of the building are four chapels, whose presence completes the structure in a most harmonious manner. The katholikon is entered from the south, by way of the cloister. The marble facing at the base of the walls has disappeared, but the fine mosaics in the upper areas are in a good state of preservation. They are considered to be one of the most representative ensembles of the entire Byzantine Renaissance, comparable to the mosaics of Hosios Loukas ▲ *254* (on the road to Delphi) and to those of Nea Moni on the island of Chios. They are thought to have been crafted by artists specially brought in from Constantinople; the refinement of the design, the elongated bodies reminiscent of antique statuary (notably *The Baptism of Christ*) and the

A GIANT DOME
The church is built on the pattern of a Greek cross (which has four branches of equal length) with a broad dome over its center, on the same lines as St Sophia in Constantinople. Chapels and side rooms have been built on the corners. The outside is decorated with intertwining motifs, done in brick, and with moldings: these may also be seen around the arched windows in the tambour of the dome.

CHRIST PANTOCRATOR
This masterpiece of Byzantine art adorns the center of the main dome of the Church of the Dormition of the Virgin at Daphni. The majestic image of Christ in Judgment depicts him as the Master of the Universe, surrounded by his prophets. The dome itself represents heaven.

dancing attitudes of the figures standing on tiptoe in the crowd scenes, have led some experts to compare them with illuminated manuscripts. At the center of the dome is a huge Christ Pantocrator, surrounded by sixteen prophets, from Isaiah to David. This "Christ in Judgment" is handled in a strongly abstract manner; his eyes are distant, he holds the Bible against his heart, and his thumb is pressed against the cross on the binding, which echoes that of his shining halo. Art historians have speculated that the oriental aspect of his face is evidence of the presence at Daphni of mosaic artists from Constantinople. Most of the figures in the other frescos have peaceful expressions. In the apse, the Virgin is flanked by the archangels Gabriel and Michael. On the corner squinches of the dome the twelve liturgical feast days are illustrated, as at Hosios Loukas: the Annunciation, the Nativity, the Baptism (with the hand of God and a dove) and the Transfiguration. Thirteen other scenes adorn the central nave, some of which are adapted to the curve of the vault, along with various saints and angels with gigantic wings against a gold backdrop. In the south transept are illustrations of *The Coming of the Magi, Christ Descending into Limbo* and *The Presentation of Christ in the Temple*. The north transept shows *The Nativity of the Virgin,* a *Crucifixion* in which the Virgin and St John are seen grieving, *Christ's Entrance into Jerusalem* and *The Raising of Lazarus*. At the entrance to the central nave, opposite the apse, is a deptiction of *The Dormition of the Virgin*, the event to which the church is dedicated. Various scenes from the life of Mary follow, among them *The Presentation in the Temple*, and *The Prayer of St Anne*; these are balanced, within the narthex by representations of *The Last Supper, Christ Washing the Feet of the Faithful* and *The Betrayal of Judas*. The exonarthex is undecorated. Experts have compared these compositions with the mosaics of St Mark's in Venice, the construction of which began in the second half of the 11th century. The mosaics of St Mark's were created shortly after those of Daphni, and respect the same iconographic tradition codified by the monks of Mount Athos. Another interesting comparison is with contemporary churches in Kiev, notably St Sophia. In the light of these comparisons, the décor at Daphni has been dated around 1100.

THE NATIVITY
The images here have the depth and naturalness of illuminated illustrations, as witness the wealth of detail, graceful gestures and supple drapery. The range of colors used and the profusion of gold are also reminiscent of illuminated books.

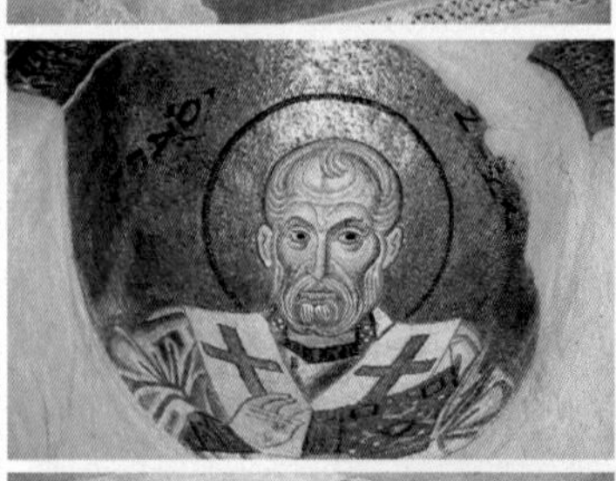

HOSIOS LOUKAS ● 94

The domed church at the Monastery of St Luke at Phocis, an Imperial foundation dating from the 11th century,

is dedicated to Hosios Loukas, an ascetic hermit who accomplished a series of miracles and prophecies. Hosios Loukas is one of the loveliest of all surviving Byzantine churches. Situated about 95 miles from Athens and 25 miles from Delphi, it is justly famous for its mosaics, which are typical of the second golden age of Byzantine art.

STRUCTURE OF THE CHURCH. The exterior is simple and imposing. Inside, the central nave supports a broad dome; square at the base, it becomes octagonal by the addition of four arches cutting across each corner to form smaller half-domes, or squinches. To emphasize the vertical lines of the building the architects used columns and pilasters, and buttresses on the outside. Light filters into the church through apertures in the tambour of the dome. The system of vaults and countervaults plays a fundamental role in the static strength of the structure.

THE DÉCOR OF THE INTERIOR. Every detail of the mosaics, with their exquisite gold background, draws the onlooker's eye upward to the dome surmounting the four equal arms of the Greek-cross floor plan. Here imagery is used as a teaching aid: the golden hues of the mosaics are symbolic of light and affirm the domination of the celestial world. The whole of Orthodox doctrine is encapsulated in images according to an immutable iconographic program, which enables the faithful to read their church like a holy book. The organization of the mosaics of Hosios Loukas is a fine illustration of this program.

THE NARTHEX. Above the central doorway is the image of Christ Pantocrator, holding a Bible open at the words "I am the Light of the World". To the right of the Pantocrator are representations of a *Crucifixion* and *The Descent into Hell*. On the far right of the narthex, in a niche, is a rendering of *Christ*

CROSS-SECTION OF THE DOMED CHURCH OF HOSIOS LOUKAS
The cross-section above (published in 1901 in the *Monastery of St Luke in Phocis*) clearly shows the rich interior decoration, with its polychrome marble floors and sculpted marble iconostasis. The squinches of the great central dome, the smaller dome of the sanctuary, the nave and the narthex are all entirely decorated with mosaics against a gold background. The hierarchy of images begins with the floor, which illustrates the terrestrial world and the saints inhabiting it. Then come the nave, the sanctuary, the squinches and the apse, where Mary, the mother of God, is pre-eminent. The cycle is completed by the dome itself, which symbolizes heaven.

HOSIOS LOUKAS
The monastery stands in the shadow of Mount Pleistos, at an altitude of about 1,200 feet.

The tall columns and buttresses emphasize the elegance of the monastery's façade.

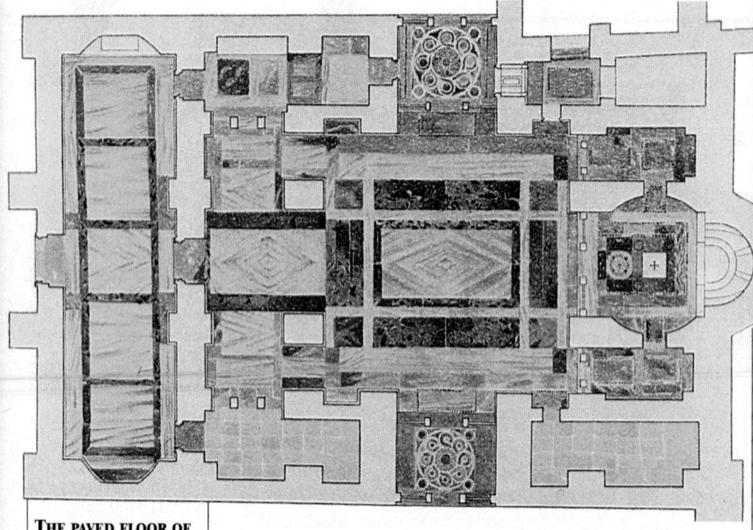

THE PAVED FLOOR OF HOSIOS LOUKAS
The paving is made of red, grey and ocher marble.

THE MOSAICS
The church is adorned with more than one hundred and forty portraits of saints (among them, of course, Saint Luke). In the arches of the dome, the artists who decorated the interior placed images of Saint Gabriel and Saint Theodore of Thiro.

and the Apostles, with Saint Thomas sitting at the Savior's feet. To the left of the main entrance is a mosaic of *The Crucifixion*: beneath the cross can be seen the grieving figures of Mary and Saint John, the apostle; above Christ's figure, there are depictions of the moon and sun, shown with human faces. At the far left of the narthex is a scene of *Christ Washing the Feet of Saint Peter*.

THE CENTRAL NAVE. The squinches are covered with mosaics narrating the twelve episodes from the life of Jesus that make up the twelve great feast days of the church year – among them *The Presentation of the Virgin, The Nativity* and *The Baptism of Christ.* On one of the squinches John the Baptist is shown conducting the baptism in the waters of the Jordan; above, the hand of God points to Jesus, with the inscription "This is my Beloved Son".

THE MOSAICS IN THE SANCTUARY. In the apse, we come face to face with a world of symbols. Above the altar, on the ceiling of the little dome, is a rendering of the scene of Pentecost; the Holy Spirit descends on the apostles in the form of a dove. The center of the apse is occupied by the images of the Virgin and Child. On the half-dome of the apse is the image of Mary, seated, holding in her arms the infant Christ, whose hand is held up in blessing.

THE CENTRAL DOME. In the middle of the central dome there used to be a mosaic of Christ Pantocrator, but this was destroyed long ago. The image of Christ becoming God, the Master of the Universe, was the final lesson given to the faithful before the Last Judgement. The mission of the Byzantine Church, which adhered to the old forms of Christianity, was to convince and guide mankind within the Orthodox faith.

Around Cape Sounion

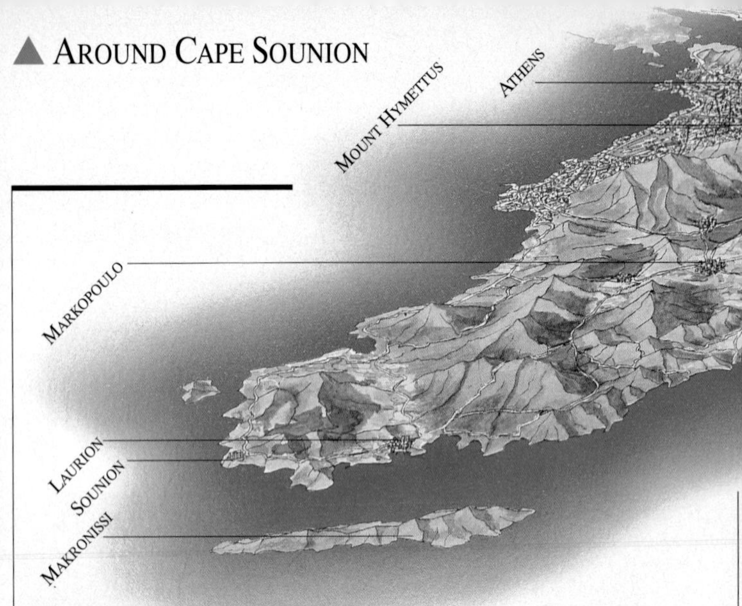

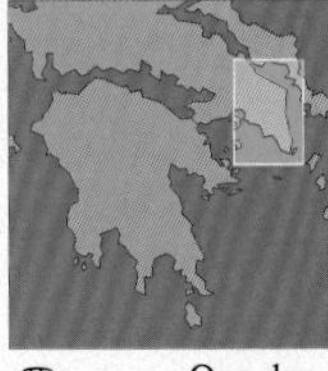

Cape Sounion

Heading out of Piraeus ▲ *244*, the road leads along the coast of the Saronic Gulf to Cape Sounion (formerly known as Cape Colonna), some 40 miles from Athens. Cape Sounion, the southernmost point of Attica, rises like a sheer cliff out of the sea. It is a place of great beauty, especially at sunset when the hills, the water and the surrounding islands are bathed by the waning light. Sounion is crowned by a temple dedicated to Poseidon, and no doubt worship of the sea god was practiced here from the earliest times. The cape was well known to sailors, who rounded it in both directions, from the Aegean to the Saronic Gulf and vice versa. Homer knew it as the "sacred cape": when Nestor tells Telemachos about the journey home from Troy, he mentions "Sounion, the sacred promontory of Athens".

Mariners rounding the cape
An 18th-century engraving.

Lord Byron
The poet carved his name on one of the columns of the Temple of Poseidon.

The century of Pericles. Archeological excavations show that the cult of Poseidon goes back to the 6th century BC. The present temple was built in the time of Pericles, shortly after the middle of the 5th century BC, when Athens was rich and powerful. The architect who drew up the plans was a pupil of Ictinos, and the sculptures were crafted by pupils of Phidias. The architecture and dimensions of the building are identical to those of the Hephaisteion ▲ *191* in the Agora at Athens, which was completed in 440 BC. The historian William Bell has concluded that the two buildings were designed by one architect.

The archeological site. The shrine is entered by way of the *propylaea*. This area was actually a portico divided by two columns. At its center were two flights of steps and a broad stone ramp; of these, only the bases remain.

The Temple of Poseidon

The temple was a peripteral Doric construction, with six columns on its façade and thirteen along

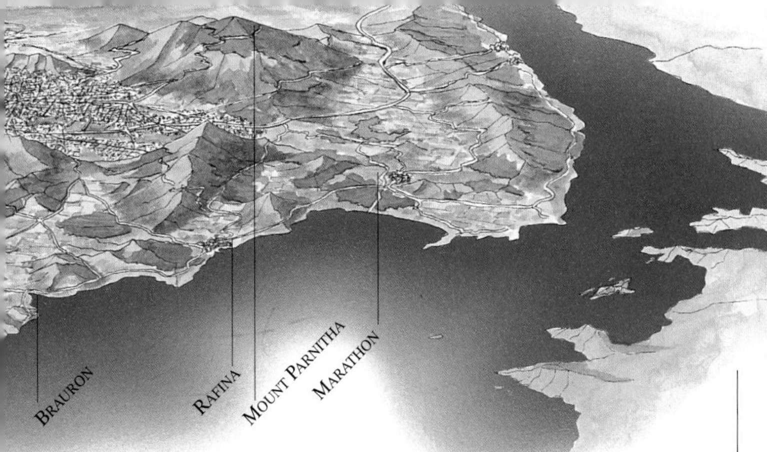

each side. Of the thirty-four columns of the original peristyle, fifteen remain (nine on the north side and six on the south); four were discovered during restoration work in 1958–9. The columns are made of marble from the quarries of Agrileza and are more slender than those of the Hephaisteion. Nearly 20 feet high, they have a fairly constant diameter of just over 3 feet. There are fewer flutings than usual (sixteen instead of twenty), probably so that their ridges would be less vulnerable to erosion by the salt-laden sea breezes.

THE BEAUTY OF SOUNION
The gleaming white columns of the Temple of Poseidon have inspired many poets.

THE BASE. The temple is built on a foundation of two terraces, one on top of the other. The stylobate has two parts, an original base on the north side and a more recent foundation dating from the 5th century BC. The building consisted of a *cella* with *pronaos* and *opisthodomos* ● *90*, with two columns *in antis*. The marble flooring has not survived.

THE METOPES OF THE FRIEZE. The architrave of the *pronaos* had a frieze in white Parian marble, decorated with sculptures in lightly carved relief depicting the battle of the Lapiths and the centaurs, scenes of giant-killing, and the exploits of Theseus. Fourteen of the slabs, all badly eroded by time and weather, are now displayed in a small shed near the *propylaea*.

THE MINES OF LAURION. After Sounion the coast road leads up to Laurion, which was famous in antiquity for its lead and silver mines. These made Athens rich in the 5th century BC: according to Plutarch, they were a "fountain of wealth" and a "treasure of the earth". In 484 Themistocles used the revenues of the mines to build the Athenian fleet ▲ *244*. They continued to be exploited by Greek and French mining companies until the last century. The mining works of the classical era are now open to the public.

BETWEEN THE COLUMNS
The façade of the *pronaos* is visible here, along with the one remaining column between the walls of the *cella*.

SIDE VIEW OF THE TEMPLE OF POSEIDON
Reconstruction by Louvet for the Ecole des Beaux Arts, 1855.

THE PLAIN OF MARATHON
Marathon is hemmed in by mountains; in the background are the sea, the peaks of Euboea and the summit of Mount Ókhiorós.

LEKYTHOS
This oil jar, in the form of a long-necked vase with a single handle, can be seen at the entrance of Marathon Museum.

HELMET
The hoplite (ancient Greek infantryman) wore a helmet with two metal wings to protect his face.

BRAURON

A little less than twenty miles from Laurion, near the sea, Brauron (the modern Vravrona) has a charming setting in the midst of vineyards. This was the high place of the cult of Artemis, and the great Doric portico of the Temple of Artemis Brauronia, probably built by Pisistratus in the 6th century BC, has been completely restored. The museum near the site contains sculptures, ceramics and reliefs dedicated to the goddess, and a variety of Cycladic, Mycenean and Geometric artefacts unearthed nearby.

MARATHON

Today Marathon is no more than a flat plain with an artificial lake; but its name still evokes the great victory won by the Greeks against the invading Persians.

THE BATTLE OF MARATHON. In 490 BC the war fleet of Darius, 600 ships strong, appeared in the Bay of Marathon. The Persian army intended to march on Athens, 25 miles away. Sparta prevaricated; only Plataea immediately sent its entire force of one thousand hoplites to aid the Athenians, who with eight or nine thousand men met and defeated the Persian army of 24,000. Herodotus describes the battle as follows: "The Persians, seeing their foes charging at the double, awaited the shock of battle. Due to the Athenians' inferior numbers, and the way they were running toward them, they believed them to be seized by a madness that would shortly bring them to utter ruin… But on the left and right wings the Athenians and Plataeans gained the upper hand, driving their opponents before them; then they joined forces to cut to pieces the Persian troops that had broken through the Athenian center. The victory of the Athenians was total."

“THESE MEN DISPLAYED INDOMITABLE COURAGE WHEN THEY ATTACKED THE ENEMY OUTSIDE THE WALLS.”

INSCRIPTION

THE BURIAL MOUND. The Athenians buried the ashes of their 192 dead beneath a tumulus, which can still be seen on the battlefield. Excavations of the site have turned up fragments of vases and *lekythoi* from the early 5th century BC. The Marathon Museum displays the objects found on the battlefield – mostly vases, statues and inscriptions. Today the village of Marathon holds an annual foot race in memory of the Greek messenger who ran from Marathon to Athens to bring news of the victory over the Persians. On leaving Marathon, head for Grammatiko and then Haghia Marina: half way between these two towns look for the sign to Rhamnus (locally called Rhamnunda).

CAPITAL FROM THE TEMPLE OF NEMESIS AT RHAMNUS
Two archeologists, Gell and Gandy, made a study of the monuments at Rhamnus in the early 19th century. As this reproduction of the capital of an *anta* shows, they paid particular attention to the techniques used for engraving and painting the moldings, roofs and coffered ceilings of the temple.

RHAMNUS

The acropolis and ancient fortress of Rhamnus occupy a beautiful, unspoiled site on a hill overlooking the Gulf of Euboea. Close to the ancient town, at the foot of its acropolis, was a port at the river mouth.

POLYGONAL STONES
Details of the foundations and walls of the Temple of Nemesis.

THE TEMPLE OF THEMIS. Rhamnus is organized around a terrace, reached by a ramp. This small Doric temple was probably used as a treasury; in its *cella*, archeologists have discovered three statues, one of them representing Themis. The massive polygonal stones at the base of the temple's walls date from the 6th century BC.

THE TEMPLE OF NEMESIS. In addition to the reconstruction of the Acropolis, Pericles' program ● *45* included the building of temples dedicated to Hephaistos and Dionysos in Athens, the temple to Poseidon at Sounion and a temple to Nemesis at Rhamnus. This last is in the peripteral Doric style ● *90*, built on a three-step stylobate. It dates from the mid 5th century BC. Pausanias states that there was a statue by Phidias in the *cella*, but all that remains of this today is the base.

Attic peasant costume, c. 1910.

THE AMPHIAREION OF OROPOS

To reach Oropos, go back to Grammatiko, then follow the signs to Varvanas, Kapandriti, Kalamos and Markopoulos.

THE SANCTUARY. This shrine straddles a small tree-lined river. In antiquity it depended upon Oropos, a small fishing port about 6 miles away, which at various times was part of Boeotia and part of Attica. The sanctuary was dedicated to Amphiaraos, one of the seven chiefs that laid siege

ANCIENT CITADELS
The acropolises of Orchomenos and Rhamnus possess some of the finest remains of fortifications in Greece.

THE THEATER
The small theater attached to the sanctuary of Oropos stands behind the stoa. The tufa seats are badly eroded, but the walls of the stage, the half-columns of the *proskenion* and a single *skene*, about 13 feet deep, are still visible.

ORCHESTRA STALLS
The only seats that remain are the five marble thrones of the *proedria*, decorated with reliefs and inscribed with the name of the priest of Amphiaraos.

to Thebes, who was subsequently revered as a god with special powers of healing. Pilgrims came here from all over Greece; the oracles propounded by the priests of Amphiaraos were so celebrated that Croesus himself once came to consult them. The site is reached by way of a path along the left bank of the river. The Temple was built in the early 4th century in the Doric style ● *91*; its *cella* is divided into two parts, with a *pronaos* edged by eight columns. The foundations have been restored. In front of the temple is an altar, with a sacred spring nearby which was reputed to have healing powers.

THE MUSEUM. Among the museum's collections are various inscriptions and fragments from the Enkoimetrion and temple, which are kept in the inner courtyard.

THE ENKOIMETRION. This stoa was about 425 feet long, with a bench running along it on which the sick were treated by *enkoimisis*, or "incubation", a gruesome procedure whereby they first sacrificed a goat, then spent the night wrapped in its bloody skin. In the morning the priests would appear to interpret their dreams and prescribe therapies for their ailments.

THE ANCIENT THEATER. Behind the stoa is a small, fairly well preserved theater which could seat three thousand spectators. The *orchestra* was only 40 feet across; the *proskenion* of the stage was decorated with eight Doric half-columns, to which were fixed scenes painted on wooden panels. The acoustics of the site were considered excellent. Opposite, by the river, are the ruins of *sanatoria* and hotels where visiting patients were housed. On leaving the Amphiareion, go back the same way you came, as far as Kapandriti; from there you can rejoin the Athens road by way of Kifissia. This town, with its charming Kefalari Square and its streets lined with fine 19th-century houses, gardens, restaurants and luxury shops, is a pleasant place to spend the night before continuing back to the capital.

DELPHI

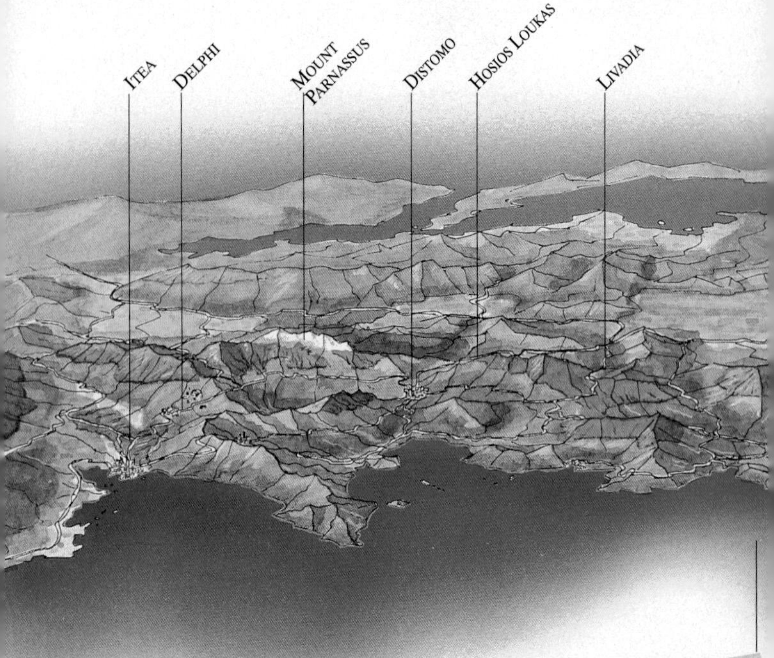

ITEA
DELPHI
MOUNT PARNASSUS
DISTOMO
HOSIOS LOUKAS
LIVADIA

THE CASTALIAN FOUNTAIN
Here travelers would carve their names. The spring flows into a pool in the gorge of the Phaedriades.

ALBERT TOURNAIRE
The French architect on the excavations from 1892 to 1901.

EARLY VISITORS

The ancient site of Delphi has never fallen into oblivion. Although the village built on the ruins was named Kastri, it was always remembered that the oracle of Apollo had dwelt in this rugged and awesome place, close to the sacred Castalian Spring which rises between the Phaedriades, the shining rocks. These are undercliffs of Mount Parnassus, which overshadows the Pleistos Valley. Some remains have always been visible, such as the stadium, the Castalian Fountain and the Argive exedras, exciting the notice of generations of travelers as far back as the 15th century when the earliest recorded visit of modern times was made by Cyriac of Ancona ▲ *208*.

THE FRENCH SCHOOL OF ATHENS

It was not until the last century, however, when archeology began to flourish and foreign institutes were set up in Greece for its encouragement, that serious interest was taken in the Shrine of Apollo. After a few exploratory digs, some of them quite extensive, carried out by lone French and German archeologists, the French School of Athens obtained a ten-year concession on the site from the Greek government in order to carry out a thorough investigation. The negotiations alone had

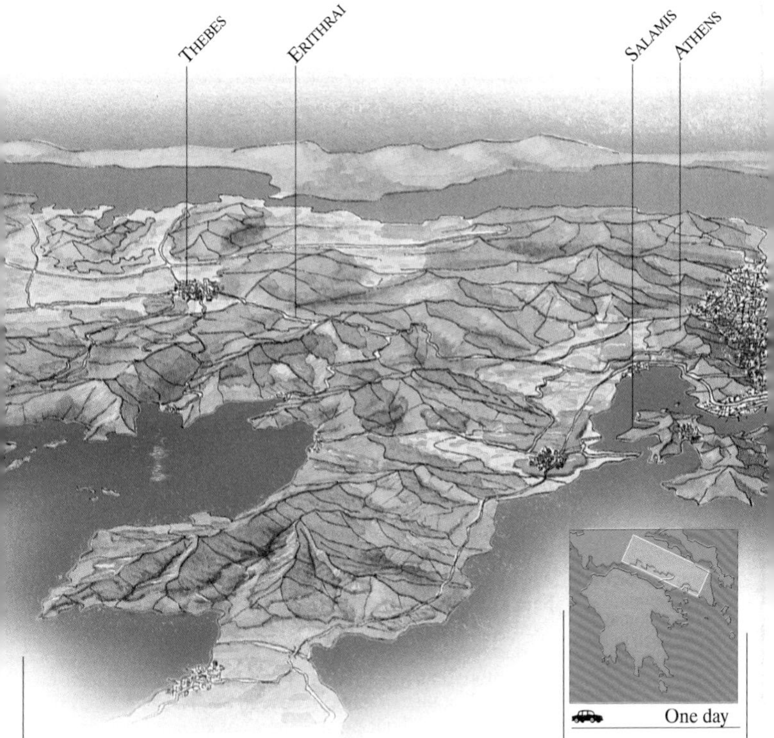

THEBES ERITHRAI SALAMIS ATHENS

One day

taken more than ten years, with the two French directors, Paul Foucart and Théophile Homolle, having to overcome stiff competition from German and American contenders. Before granting them the concession, the Greeks extracted a number of diplomatic and commercial favors, such as an agreement that France would import Greek currants. The French government shouldered the costs of the huge venture, which included demolishing and rebuilding an entire village to gain access to the various archeological levels. A sum of 400,000 French francs was made available to cover the compensation that had to be paid, as well as the expenses of the dig itself. But the prestige of such an enterprise justified the cost: French archeologists now had the chance to rival the Germans, who fifteen years earlier had made such exciting discoveries at Olympia.

The village of Kastri
The houses of the village of Kastri seen when the dig first started in 1892, and the unearthing in 1893 of the polygonal wall beneath the Stoa of the Athenians.

Major excavations

The enormously ambitious excavations began in 1893, on a scale seldom witnessed in archeological history. The village of Kastri was razed to the ground, and over a mile of railway line was constructed to transport the thousands of tons of excavated material. Several hundred men were employed to work in shifts under the French team. One can still see a

IVORY INLAY
Fragments of an ivory inlay, carved in relief, found in 1939. It shows the sons of Boreas chasing off the Harpies – an episode from the Argonauts' quest for the Golden Fleece.

CLEOBIS AND BITON
The first *kouroi* ▲ *274* were found in a modern wall to the northwest of the Treasury of the Athenians on May 30, 1893.

THE "BIG DIG"
The massive French excavations began with the building of a railway line at the lower end of the village. Thirty wagons were bought from the company that had just built the Corinth Canal.

magnificent drawing, a conjectural reconstruction of the site, by the architect Albert Tournaire, who was closely involved in the excavations, in the site museum. Work began by following the Sacred Way, and soon led to the discovery of the Treasury of the Athenians, which confirmed the high hopes of the experts. The Treasury of the Siphnians, the Theater and the Temple of Apollo were gradually uncovered, along with a considerable number of statues, including the famous bronze charioteer, unearthed in April and May of 1896. They also found more than three thousand inscriptions, so informative and revealing that Delphi can be read almost like a "book of stone". It is one of our prime sources of knowledge of ancient Greek civilization. Lastly the Shrine of Athena at Marmaria, below that of Apollo, was excavated. A French journal gave this account of the excavations in 1896: "The fall will see work continuing on a number of different archeological sites. The excavations last spring brought bountiful results. Homolle himself described to us the discovery of a beautiful bronze figure of a chariot driver. He and his colleagues have also found numerous inscriptions. Work has continued on the site of the Stadium, and near to the center, more than 15 feet beneath the surface, they have uncovered a marble tribune on which the judges of the games used to stand." In 1903 the site was handed back to the Greeks, a museum was built to house the treasures that had been found, and Homolle declared the excavations officially closed.

"DELPHI, I SHOULD THINK PERHAPS THE GREEKEST THING OF ALL. IT COMES NEAREST TO BEING SERIOUS, AND IS CHARMING."

HENRY ADAMS, 1898

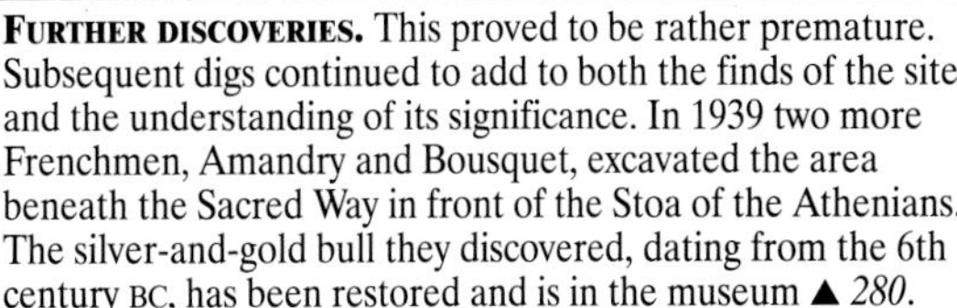

FURTHER DISCOVERIES. This proved to be rather premature. Subsequent digs continued to add to both the finds of the site and the understanding of its significance. In 1939 two more Frenchmen, Amandry and Bousquet, excavated the area beneath the Sacred Way in front of the Stoa of the Athenians. The silver-and-gold bull they discovered, dating from the 6th century BC, has been restored and is in the museum ▲ *280*.

DELPHI TODAY. Recently an immense amount of work has been done at Delphi. Between 1990 and 1992 excavations were carried out in a part of the shrine that had been left undisturbed by the early French dig, just below the temple terrace, beneath the foundations of the Chariot of Helios. Modern methods enabled a much more accurate chronological account of the earliest occupation of the site to be made. Enormous strides have been taken in the field of archeology, undreamt of in the 19th century. Work progressed simultaneously on deciphering the inscriptions and restoring the structures and sculptures, including the piecing together of thousands of fragments. The giant jigsaw puzzle has now been all but completed.

A SACRED PLACE

Before embarking on a tour of the site it is important to understand its history. Delphi has always fascinated archeologists because it was one of the cornerstones of Greek civilization. For the ancients it was the "navel of the world", ever present in their literature and central to their perception of the world. Its importance was primarily due to its oracle which was particularly influential during the 7th and 6th centuries BC.

POLITICAL INFLUENCE. No important political decision could be made without consulting the Pythia (priestess of Apollo). During

THE DISCOVERY OF THE BRONZE CHARIOTEER
In April 1896 the lower half of a bronze statue was uncovered.

THE CHARIOTEER
The charioteer formed part of a bronze chariot group, offered by Polyzalos of Gela, around 475 BC, in honor of his victory in the Pythian Games. The young man stands holding the reins in his right hand; he is wearing a long tunic and the headband of victory. It is among the most famous of all Greek sculptures.

RESTORING THE THOLOS
Christos Kaltsis was supervisor of the 1936 excavations. He was responsible for assembling what was needed for the restoration of the tholos and the *cella* of the Temple of Apollo.

the Persian Wars (490–480 BC) Themistocles ● *44* was one of the last to make such use of it, understanding the "wooden rampart" that the oracle mentioned as the salvation of the Greeks to be a naval fleet, which needed to be prepared in great haste. For such enigmatic utterances, Apollo had come to be known as Loxias ("the Oblique"). The fame of the oracle spread far beyond Greece: the Pharaohs and the kings of Persia made offerings, and Delphi became one of the spiritual centers of the world. Colossal riches accumulated there during the classical period, and Socrates drew upon the words of wisdom engraved upon the temple walls, borrowing such aphorisms as "Know thyself" and "Beware of excess".

THE AMPHICTYONIC LEAGUE. The shrine was administered by an international association (made up of cities and independent Greek leagues) called the Amphictyonic League. The representatives of these member states, twenty-four in number, met twice a year. Every four years they organized the Pythian Games. These were much like the Olympic Games – but, as they were dedicated to Apollo, more prominence was given to music and drama. In addition, although the League had an exclusively religious function at the outset, the institution gained such prestige that it became an international tribunal, establishing a code of war and other laws. Consequently it has been compared, with some exaggeration, to modern international organizations. Its main function remained the protection and administration of the possessions of Apollo, in particular the sacred land (the valley

of the Pleistos and Mount Cirphis, which formed the south side of the valley); and when the need arose, it would wage a "sacred war" on the impious. The city of Delphi, otherwise of no importance, was a member of the Amphictyonic League. Although the association denied the city possession of the sacred precinct, it nevertheless retained control of the oracle. Only some relatively recent houses have been removed, mostly dating from the Roman and Byzantine periods.

DELPHI'S GOLDEN AGE

The golden age of the Shrine of Apollo, like that of Zeus at Olympia ▲ *354*, was during the preclassical era. It remained active and important until the Roman conquest. During this period several attempts were made to carry off the treasures (by the Persians in 480 BC, and the Gauls under Brennus in 279) or to take over the shrine through control of the Amphictyonic League. The Thessalians in the 5th and 4th

THE TEMPLE OF APOLLO
In this reconstruction Albert Tournaire enlivened his view of the temple with figures. He proposed that there were two levels of columns inside, Ionic then Doric, framing a huge statue of Apollo. He gave the temple an opening in the roof, basing his assumption on Justinus, who wrote in AD 278 that God came down into the temple "through the opening above".

centuries BC, Philip and Alexander of Macedonia in 346 and 323 and the Aetolian League in the 3rd century all, in turn, made such an attempt – for whoever controlled Delphi had prestige and considerable authority throughout Greece. From the 2nd century BC onward, however, the shrine, having lost its political status, went into a steady decline, and in the days of the Roman Empire pilgrims visited Delphi more out of historical interest than as an act of faith. Eventually the Amphictyonic League faded out of existence in the 3rd century AD, not long before paganism disappeared altogether.

THE THOLOS
Artist's impression by Gottlob (May, 1962) of the marble Tholos, with a view of the Delphic shrines as they might have appeared in antiquity.

TOUR OF THE SITE

There are two distinct shrines at Delphi: the larger one to the northwest, dedicated to Apollo, and the smaller one consecrated to Athena Pronaia. The association of these two cults has never been fully explained, and our knowledge of the site remains far from complete. Many of the monuments have not yet been identified with certainty; and, although the identity of some is now known, it is uncertain on which foundations they stood, so it has not been possible to restore them to their original positions. Due to the geological peculiarities of the terrain and to frequent earthquakes, the topography of the

THE TEMPLE OF APOLLO AND THE THEATER
The theater was built in the 4th century BC, with seating for five thousand people. It lies above the Temple of Apollo, where oracles were given, and overlooks Delphi's magnificent natural amphitheater.

earthquakes, the topography of the site has been much disturbed. With regard to the Shrine of Apollo itself, Pausanias' account of a visit in the 2nd century AD, in his work *The Periegesis,* is very helpful. The remains visible today form a much mutilated image of the shrine which corresponds most closely to its state under Roman Imperial rule. Most of the ancient monuments were still visible at that time, but many more recent structures had also been added. So we are left with a historically compressed view of the shrine, without any sense of chronological perspective. During its nine centuries of existence the sacred precinct changed in appearance, but its overall area, topography and main features had been defined by the end of the 6th century BC. One should imagine it crowded with buildings and brightly colored statues, giving an impression of disorder and abundance. It is best to follow the route most commonly taken in ancient times: pilgrims could arrive on the road from Thebes or from the northwest, over Mount Parnassus and Mount Amfissa, but they mostly entered through the gate near the modern town of Itea.

MARMARIA

This area is called Marmaria because the inhabitants of Kastri used it as a quarry, taking away the ancient marble blocks that were still visible. Some of these were found farther up the hill

– which gives some idea of the problems that a site like Delphi presents to archeologists.

THE SHRINE OF ATHENA. The shrine built here is dedicated to the goddess Athena, whose duty it was to protect the sacred precinct of her half-brother Apollo. She performed her task well, for Herodotus recounts that it was here, in 480 BC, that the Persians were stopped in their tracks by an earthquake on their way to pillage Delphi.

THE TEMENOS OF THE HEROES. Pausanias provides little information on the monuments in this part of the site, and identifying them has proved extremely difficult. Lower down there are the foundations of two smaller 6th-century structures, probably dedicated to the local heroes Phylakos and Autonoos, mentioned by Herodotus.

THE CASTALIAN FOUNTAIN
“From Parnassus a torrent rushes down a fissure between two sheer-sided mountain peaks, Nauplia and Hyameia. From the latter it is said that Aesop, the writer of fables, was thrown to his death by the inhabitants of Delphi. The racing water pours out of its narrow course into a vaulted passage whence it runs into a square pool formed naturally in the rock, although slightly enlarged by man. The pool is about 30 feet long and 10 feet wide, and contains the famous Castalian Fountain, in which the Pythia would bathe before making her oracular utterances.”
Extract from a 19th-century guide to Greece

GENERAL VIEW OF DELPHI (1803)
Colored aquatint by W. Walker.

FRAGMENT OF GUTTERING WITH LOTUS AND PALMETTES
Watercolor by Albert Tournaire.

PALMETTE ANTEFIX
Painted red and cream, this came from the roof of the *leskhe* (assembly room) of the Cnidians, built c. 470 BC, which contained murals by Polygnotus of Thasos. Watercolor by Tournaire, 1893.

1938 RESTORATION
"The reconstruction partially completed in 1938 is still standing. The drums that made up the column shafts were broken into many pieces and were so precisely made that an architect had to be called in to solve the puzzle. It turned out that five blocks were needed rather than the usual four, which made the columns more slender and graceful than others of the Doric order dating from the 5th century BC or even the early 4th century. A 1991 reappraisal of the fragments revealed that the two pieces of guttering had the same curvature, and must have lain side by side on the Tholos."
From *La redécouverte de Delphes* (French School of Athens)

THE TEMPLE OF ATHENA PRONAIA. Next comes the main temple, which is of the Doric order and built from tufa. It had six sets of twelve columns; two of the columns are still standing. The building was dedicated to Athena toward the end of the 6th century BC. It was in such good condition at the time of the French excavations that it was possible to re-create the peristyle, but a landslide in 1905 (the rocks can still be seen amid the ruins) destroyed the work. This temple was preceded by another, smaller, temple that stood in the same place, serving the same purpose. Some of its Doric capitals survive, now sitting at the western end of the stylobate ● *91* on which the colonnade stood; their remarkable outlines, with very flat quarter-rounds, go back to the 7th century BC, when they were the capitals of one of the very oldest stone temples known in the Greek world.

THE ALTARS OF ATHENA AND ZEUS. On the eastern side of the temple are altars which were found in the area, though not where they are now. From their 5th-century inscriptions it is known that they were dedicated to Athena and to Zeus. On the supporting wall can be read the names Eilythyia (goddess of childbirth) and Hygieia (goddess of health).

TWO TREASURIES. To the west of the temple are the foundations of two marble treasuries. A treasury was usually a four-cornered structure with an opening guarded by two columns *in antis* ● *90*. Cities built these treasuries at Delphi to house their offerings, rivaling each other to create the finest structures as symbols of their wealth and power;

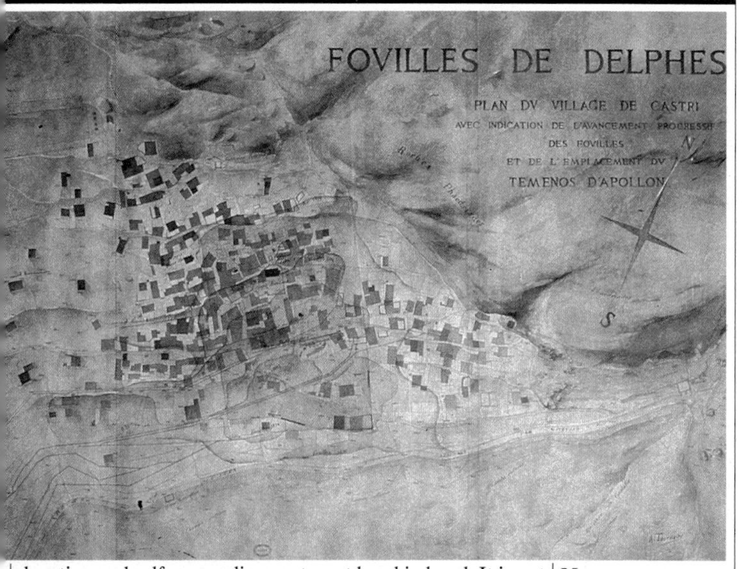

devotion and self-aggrandizement went hand in hand. It is not known who built the first of these two treasuries, which is of the Doric order and dates from the 5th century BC. The second, standing to the west, is of the Aeolian order and dates from the 6th century; its capitals, carved with palms, are on show in the museum, next to the Naxian Sphinx ▲ *280*. The fine carving of this treasury can still be seen in the fluted torus and the frieze of pearls in the remaining sections of wall.

The tholos ★

The next monument is the tholos ● *80* (a generic name signifying a round stone chamber), which was partially restored in 1938. Its marble came from Attica. The order is Doric on the outside, with twenty columns; the original number of Corinthian columns inside is unknown, despite the evidence of early reconstructions. The building dates from around 380 BC and is one of the architectural wonders of the world – an incredible feat of mathematics involving the precise calculation of ratios based on the golden number, represented by the blocks of the stylobate. The algebraic complexity of the structure is matched in detail and perfection by its decoration. The moldings are delicate; and the carving, both in bas-relief and in the round, is masterly. There were two magnificent friezes (badly damaged but partially restored): an exterior one and another around the top of the *cella* wall, each with forty metopes. It is the most beautiful and mysterious building in Delphi. There are no inscriptions, and nowhere in literature do we find any hint as to its origin or purpose.

The limestone temple. This is contemporary with the tholos, but completely different in material, form and style. Here there are neither sculptural decorations nor fine moldings, but the stonemasonry is extremely skillful.

Map of the village of Kastri
Tournaire's map (1896) shows the position of the Shrine of Apollo and indicates the progress of the excavations, advancing roughly from south to north.

Exterior frieze of the tholos (detail)
The frieze is of a battle between Amazons and centaurs. The Amazons' attire consists of a short tunic and an animal skin knotted at the shoulder.

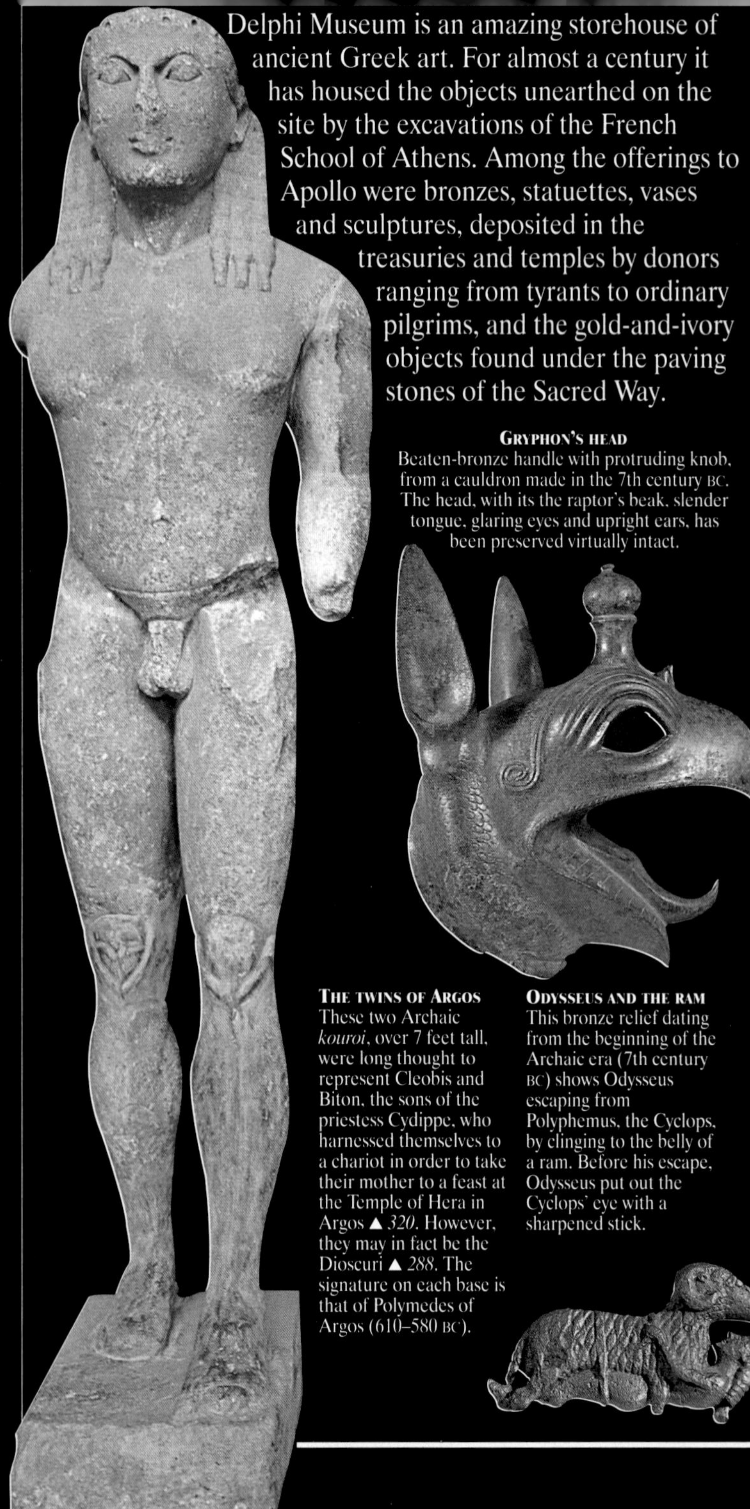

Delphi Museum is an amazing storehouse of ancient Greek art. For almost a century it has housed the objects unearthed on the site by the excavations of the French School of Athens. Among the offerings to Apollo were bronzes, statuettes, vases and sculptures, deposited in the treasuries and temples by donors ranging from tyrants to ordinary pilgrims, and the gold-and-ivory objects found under the paving stones of the Sacred Way.

Gryphon's head
Beaten-bronze handle with protruding knob, from a cauldron made in the 7th century BC. The head, with its the raptor's beak, slender tongue, glaring eyes and upright ears, has been preserved virtually intact.

The twins of Argos
These two Archaic *kouroi*, over 7 feet tall, were long thought to represent Cleobis and Biton, the sons of the priestess Cydippe, who harnessed themselves to a chariot in order to take their mother to a feast at the Temple of Hera in Argos ▲ *320*. However, they may in fact be the Dioscuri ▲ *288*. The signature on each base is that of Polymedes of Argos (610–580 BC).

Odysseus and the ram
This bronze relief dating from the beginning of the Archaic era (7th century BC) shows Odysseus escaping from Polyphemus, the Cyclops, by clinging to the belly of a ram. Before his escape, Odysseus put out the Cyclops' eye with a sharpened stick.

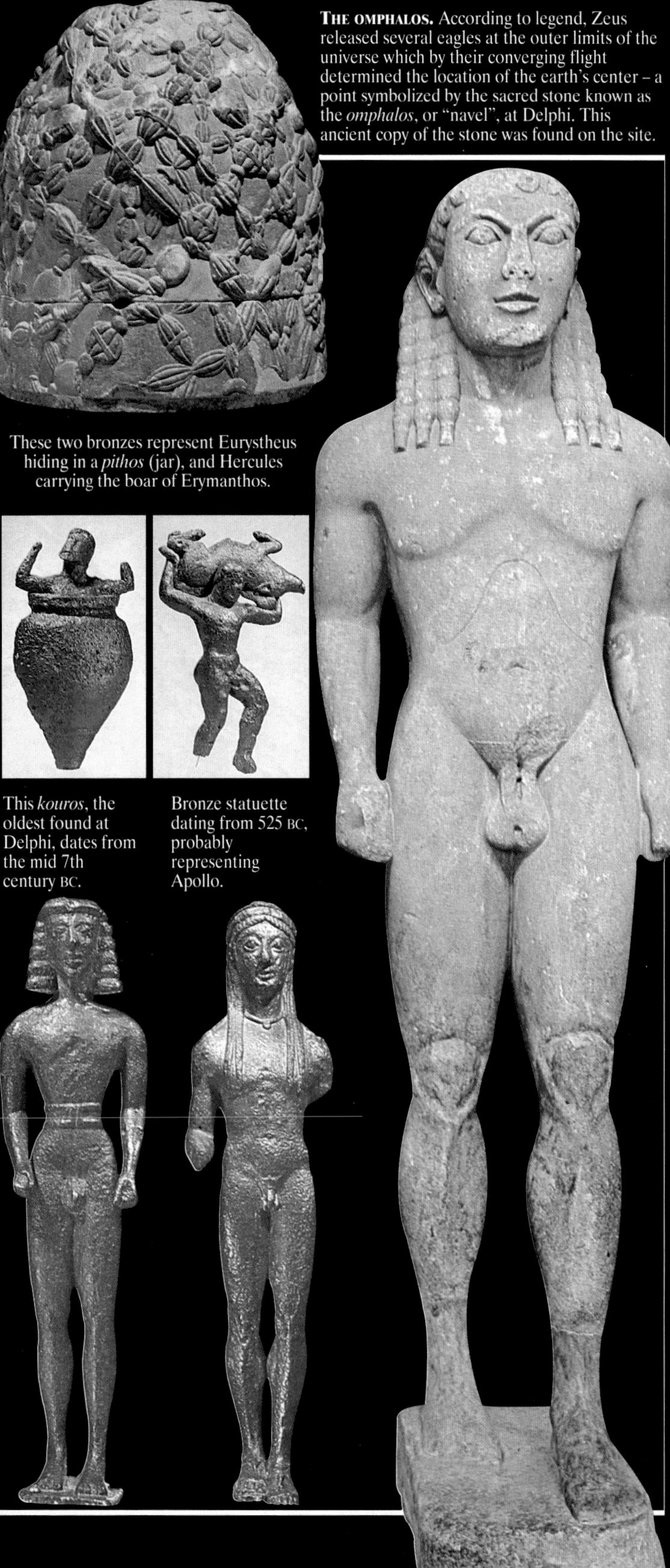

The omphalos. According to legend, Zeus released several eagles at the outer limits of the universe which by their converging flight determined the location of the earth's center – a point symbolized by the sacred stone known as the *omphalos*, or "navel", at Delphi. This ancient copy of the stone was found on the site.

These two bronzes represent Eurystheus hiding in a *pithos* (jar), and Hercules carrying the boar of Erymanthos.

This *kouros*, the oldest found at Delphi, dates from the mid 7th century BC.

Bronze statuette dating from 525 BC, probably representing Apollo.

The Delphi Museum was built in 1903 at the conclusion of the major excavations conducted by the French School of Athens. Restored and enlarged between 1950 and 1960, the museum has been reorganized by its curators with the aim of achieving a coherent and esthetically pleasing display. Although devoted exclusively to objects found on the site of Delphi, it is nevertheless one of Greece's most important archeological museums, along with those in Athens and Olympia.

Head of Apollo
This ivory head formed part of a chryselephantine statue dating from the 6th century BC. The hair is represented by leaves of silver plated with gold.

Plaque with gryphon
This embossed gold plaque was probably worn as a pendant.

Statue of a bull (silver and gold) 6th century BC
This *ex voto* figure, discovered in 1939 in a pit beside the Stoa of the Athenians, has been displayed in the museum since 1978. The bull's body consisted of wood covered with silver, and parts of it were plated in gold. The figure was damaged when the stoa was destroyed by fire.

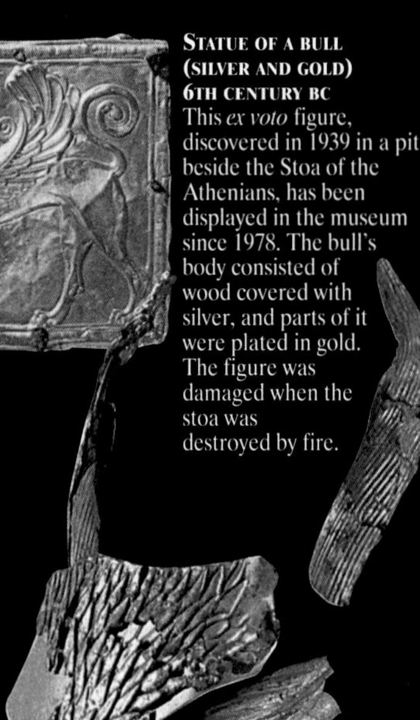

The Naxian Sphinx
Sculpted in marble, the sphinx has the body of a lion, the wings of a bird, the head of a woman and feet with huge claws. It stood on top of an Ionic column, 30 feet high, with a cylindrical base.

Attic cup with white background (c. 480 BC)
Apollo is shown sitting on a stool with lion's paws, with a blackbird perched in front of him. He is wearing sandals, a white *peplos* and red *himation*, and a myrtle wreath. The god is pouring a libation of wine with his right hand, and holding a lyre in his left.

Statue of Antinoüs
Famed for his beauty, Antinoüs was the favorite of Hadrian. After his death, the emperor deified him: hence the presence of his statue in many shrines of the ancient world.

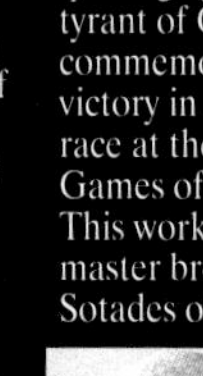

Charioteer ▲ *267*
This famous statue belonged to a quadriga given by the tyrant of Gela to commemorate his victory in a chariot race at the Pythian Games of 476 BC. This work is by the master bronze-caster Sotades of Thespiai.

Bronze perfume censer with cover

Dancers ▲ *285*
Tambour of a sculpted column (335–325 BC) in the form of an acanthus stem, decorated with three female figures.

Dionysos
This marble statue representing the god Dionysos, dressed in a flowing tunic, was the central figure of the west pediment of the Temple of Apollo at Delphi. It dates from between 340 and 330 BC.

Equestrian statue of Paulus Emilius.

THE GYMNASIUM. Investigations are not yet completed in this area which, strictly speaking, is not a part of either sacred precinct. Nevertheless, the gymnasium is an important annex to the cult, since it was here that contestants prepared for the Pythian Games. Although it was built by the Amphictyonic League around 330 BC, making it one of the earliest "sporting complexes" known in ancient Greece, the gymnasium was also used by the city of Delphi. The entrance was at the far northwest end of the Shrine of Athena.

THE PALESTRA. Entrance is by the lower terrace, which is about 200 feet long; the *palestra* lies on the southern side. At first wrestlers were trained here, but subsequently it came to be used for all kinds of exercise. Beyond is the *loutron* (bathhouse). The upper terrace of the gymnasium is longer, and on it stood the *xystos* or covered track. Runners trained under this colonnade in bad weather. On the far wall painted inscriptions reserving places for the athletes can be seen. In front of and parallel to the *xystos* is the *paradromis*, where training took place out of doors.

THE CASTALIAN FOUNTAIN. The sacred fountain of Apollo cannot be visited at present. Works to shore up rocks threatening to topple from the Phaedriades make access impossible. In ancient times pilgrims had to purify themselves in the fountain before consulting the oracle. The lower pool dates from about the 6th century BC; later, in the Hellenistic period, it was superseded by a rocky pool positioned further upstream. There are a number of niches that once contained statues.

THE SHRINE OF APOLLO

Nowadays entrance is through the Roman agora – a square dating from the time of Roman Imperial rule, once bordered on three sides by porticos containing shops. The shrine itself begins at the western edge of this square and is surrounded by a massive wall (*peribolos*). This is trapezoid in shape, its longest side measuring over 600 feet. There were a number of gates to the east and west. The method of construction varies (sometimes polygonal, sometimes isodomic ● *87*), evidence of construction and repairs at different periods extending from the 6th century BC (when the basic layout was established) to the 4th century.

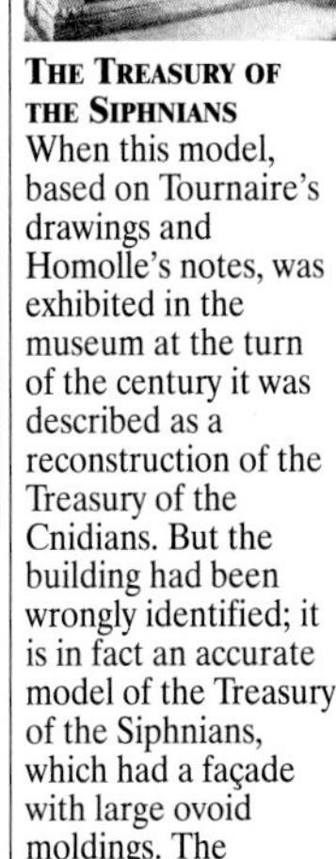

The Treasury of the Siphnians
When this model, based on Tournaire's drawings and Homolle's notes, was exhibited in the museum at the turn of the century it was described as a reconstruction of the Treasury of the Cnidians. But the building had been wrongly identified; it is in fact an accurate model of the Treasury of the Siphnians, which had a façade with large ovoid moldings. The dimensions of the base are also correct.

The Sacred Way. The Sacred Way winds through the precinct; the paving stones of the second section date from the Roman Empire. The ancient level of the first section was much higher than today, as can be seen by a rock that has been left in front of the Treasury of the Sicyonians. Since then the route of the Sacred Way has altered little, except beyond the Treasury of the Athenians. Along the first part of the way are some structures that once supported statues: on the right are the bases of statues offered by the Arcadians; on the left stood a monument dedicated by Lysander, celebrating the Spartans' defeat of the Athenian fleet in 405 BC toward the end of the Peloponnesian War ● *46*. This part of the sacred precinct is something of a muddle, and identification has been based on Pausanias' description rather than firm archeological evidence. Further on are two exedras erected by the city of Argos: on the left stood statues of the heroes of the war of the Seven against Thebes, on the right the city's mythical kings.

The Treasury of the Sicyonians. The original treasury was rebuilt twice. Most of the blocks from the first building were subsequently used for foundations. Erected c. 580 BC, it was a Doric *tholos* ● *80* with a frieze that was not centered over the columns. Circular fragments can be seen amid the remains. The second edifice (c. 560 BC) had a single row of columns on all sides, forming a sort of Doric canopy; its metopes, now in the museum, depict Jason and the Argonauts, and Europa being carried off by the bull. The third structure (c. 525 BC) was a Doric treasury building.

The east frieze
The frieze dates from c. 525 BC. Aphrodite, Zeus, Artemis, Ares and Apollo are assembled for battle.

Reconstruction of the gymnasium
The gymnasium looked like a long stoa. Its Doric columns were replaced under Hadrian by a crude Ionic colonnade.

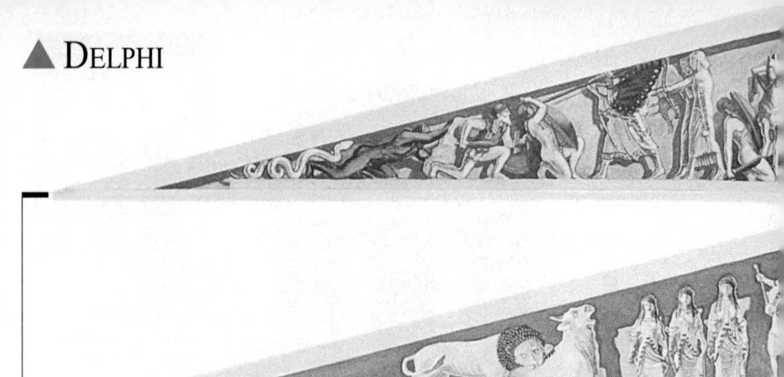

THE POLYGONAL WALL
This is a gigantic limestone puzzle, erected to create a stable base for the Temple of Apollo when it was rebuilt at the end of the 6th century BC. Eight hundred inscriptions are engraved upon it – including decrees of the city of Delphi and the Amphictyonic League, and acts emancipating slaves.

THE TEMPLE OF APOLLO
The architect Henri Ducoux, overseeing the raising of the columns of the southeast corner of the temple.

THE TREASURY OF THE SIPHNIANS. Built around 525 BC, the Treasury of the Siphnians was considered one of the jewels of the shrine. It faced west. The moldings were richly decorative and caryatids replaced columns on either side of the entrance. A sculpted pediment showed Herakles and Apollo fighting for the sacred tripod (the key to the Pythia's powers), while inside friezes ran around all the walls, depicting heroes, gods, processions and famous events.

THE TREASURY OF THE ATHENIANS. It is thought that this treasury was erected at the end of the 5th century to celebrate the victory of Marathon ● *44*. It was restored between 1903 and 1906. A sculpted Doric frieze (now in the museum) illustrated the deeds of Herakles and Theseus ▲ *192*. The south wall is a carved page of history, with fascinating inscriptions, many decorated with crowns honoring citizens. Most extraordinary of all are the two hymns to Apollo, preserved in the museum. Their musical notation constitutes the key to our slim understanding of the music of ancient Greece. On the south *anta* is a small Apollo with a lyre at the center of an inscription.

THE STOA OF THE ATHENIANS. The building of the Ionic order standing a little higher up was erected to house the spoils taken at the naval defeat of the Persians, according to the monumental inscription engraved on the top step. At the western end of the stoa, behind the Rock of the Sibyl, lie some of the drums of the Column of the Naxians; the upper part of the column and the sphinx ▲ *280* that surmounted it are in the museum. Between the stoa and the next bend in the Sacred Way lies an open space upon which stand votive monuments. On the other side of the way is the base of the Tripod of Plataea, celebrating the Greek victory over the Persians in 479 BC: the bronze pedestal that supported

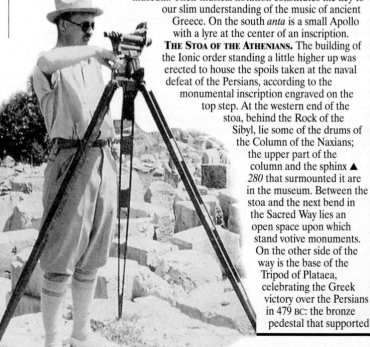

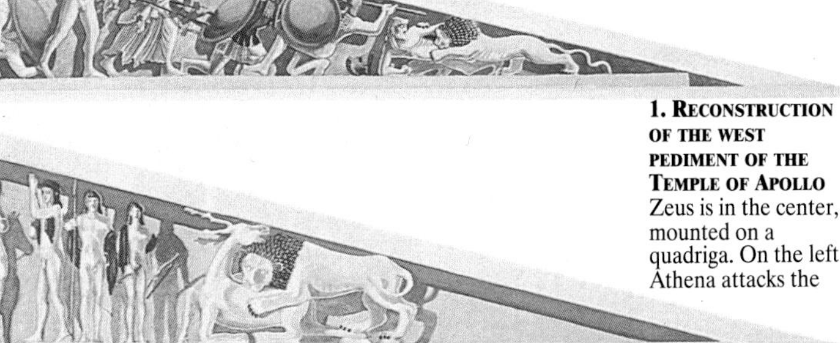

1. Reconstruction of the west pediment of the Temple of Apollo
Zeus is in the center, mounted on a quadriga. On the left Athena attacks the giant Enceladus; on the right Poseidon fights two giants.
2. Artist's impression of the east pediment
Apollo is in the center, mounted on a chariot. Symmetrical groups on either side show a lion attacking a bull and another devouring a stag.

the bowl (now missing) is in Istanbul. Just below the temple terrace can be seen the circular bases of ancient Syracusan tripods. Higher up is the base of the Acanthus Column; its dancing girls ▲ *281* are now in the museum. Further east stands the base of the Column of Attalos.

The Temple of Apollo

This great temple, of the Doric order, went through various incarnations. After the ancient wooden temple was destroyed by fire in 548 BC, a new temple was financed by an Athenian family, the Alcmaeonids (marble and tufa blocks from it can be seen in the museum). This building was in turn destroyed by a landslide in 373 BC and rebuilt thanks to a subscription raised by the Amphictyonic League. Work was completed in 327, having been interrupted for ten years by the sacred war against the Phocians. The building costs were inscribed on the stone itself, giving a fascinating insight into the details of such a massive construction project. The plan of the temple respected the previous one, and made use of some of the old stone, such as the recut columns in the foundations at the southwest corner. The materials are varied: limestone and marble, and poros for the columns that were partially

The offering of Krateros
Northwest of the temple is a large rectangular niche with a Doric façade. This is known from Plutarch's description and its inscription (of the 4th century BC) to have held an offering made by the son of Krateros, Alexander the Great's general. Sculpted by the artists Leochares and Lysippos, it showed Krateros saving Alexander's life during a lion hunt.

Cross-section of the temple by Tournaire
In this 1894 drawing, Tournaire put a statue of Apollo in the center of the temple. In fact a golden statue of the god stood in the inner sanctum that housed the sacred tripod and the *omphalos* (navel stone).

DELPHIC FESTIVALS
The poet Anghelos Sikelianos and his wife Eva Palmer organized Delphic Festivals in May of 1927 and 1930. The programs included performances of Greek tragedies such as Aeschylus' *Prometheus Bound* and *The Suppliants*, modern dance in the style of Isadora Duncan, and gymnastics competitions. The photographs on the right show modern dancers and actors in costumes inspired by antiquity.

HYMNS TO APOLLO (2ND CENTURY BC)
Two hymns to Apollo are carved on the south-facing wall of the Treasury of the Athenians: "Hark, all ye who inherit the sacred grove of Mount Helicon, fair-limbed maidens, daughters of Zeus! Hasten with your sweet voices to charm your golden-haired brother Phoebus."

re-erected in 1941. The interior of these columns show marks of a fire that took place during the period of Roman Imperial rule. Attached to the metopes of the frieze were shields taken from the Persians and the Galatians when, on different occasions, they were prevented from plundering the shrine. Traces of one of these shields can still be seen on a metope on the north side of the temple. The ramp leading up to the temple was a fairly common feature. Between the *pronaos* and the *opisthodomos*, the *cella* had a colonnade of the Ionic order (a capital from it is visible lower down in the southeast corner), protecting within it the prophetic Pythia on her tripod. No trace of a geological fault has been found corresponding to the chasm in the *adyton* (inner sanctum) which was said to have sent up hallucinogenic vapors.

THE THEATER ▲ *270*. Musical and dramatic contests took place in the theater. No trace of the *skene* ▲ *172* remains *in situ*, but it is possible that in Roman times it was decorated with the frieze illustrating the labors of Herakles now in the museum. The tiers of seats and the *orchestra* were built in the Hellenic and Roman periods.

THE STADIUM. Although built in the 4th century BC, the stadium was altered twice. The stone seating, which could accommodate 6,500 spectators, was provided by Herodes Atticus ▲ *218* in the 2nd century AD. The track is 550 feet long. At the eastern end stood a triumphal arch with three semicircular arches; beneath it a number of tiers were hewn into the rock. The southern supporting wall bears an ancient inscription, forbidding the use of wine in the stadium except for libations.

From Athens to Corinth

ACROCORINTH
CORINTH
LOUTRAKI

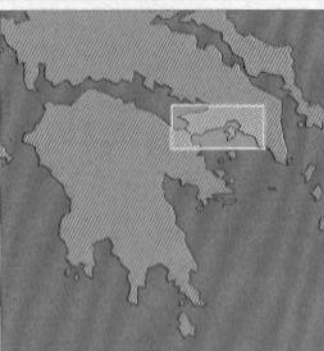

Half a day

PLATO'S ACADEMY ▲ 290

For about half a mile the road from Athens to Eleusis follows the route taken by Plato's disciples on their way to the Academy. Here, close to Sophocles' birthplace, Kolonos, was the Shrine of Akademos. This mythical local hero, who gave his name to the Academy, is known for his alliance with the deities Castor and Pollux ▲ *274*, the Dioscuri or twin sons of Zeus, who were often represented riding horses. In the classical era a gymnasium stood here, surrounded by gardens and woods. Among the woodland walks (walking, according to Plato, was particularly conducive to reflective thought) were sacred olive trees said to be the descendants of the olive planted by the goddess Athena on the Acropolis ▲ *146*. Plato believed that the world was not ruled by chance; nor was it by chance that he bought a piece of land in this region in 388 BC. Here he established his famous school modeled on the ideal society of Pythagoras, who proposed a community in which each pupil lived in conformity with the philosophical doctrine of his master. Plato's school was more a place of study than a forum for discussion (in contrast to the methods of Socrates, Plato's master, who used conversation as a means of enquiry); indeed it was not unlike a modern research center. Plato, the founder of idealism, postulated another world, the world of ideas, that was only attainable by thought. Ideas, he argued, are eternal and unvarying, whereas objects are in a constant state of flux. Aristotle, who was one of Plato's pupils, defied him by asserting that ideas only have reality in so far as they are materialized in the form of

GENERAL VIEW OF ATHENS
The Greek capital at the beginning of the 20th century.

The Acropolis and the Olympieion ▲ *216* at the beginning of the 20th century, by the Greek painter K. Maleas.

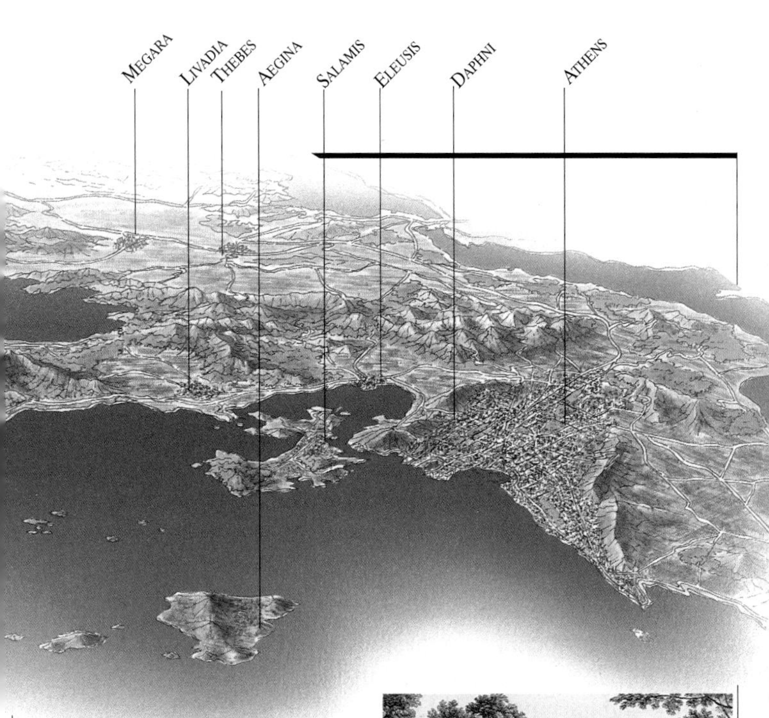

individual objects. For Plato, whose main concern was moral education, virtue was one of the objectives of the pursuit of knowledge and was a quality that could be learned, in the same way as a craft such as shoemaking; if people learned to appreciate moral values, he theorized, they would eventually put them into practice in their everyday lives. According to Plato, dialectic (the term denoting philosophical enquiry by the method of question and answer) led to true knowledge and had to be preceded by the study of mathematics, logic and political science. Plato himself attempted a career in politics, but gave it up in disgust when Socrates was sentenced to death ▲ *194*. Thereafter he was convinced that the only salvation for the Greek city-states would be to make philosophers their rulers, or alternatively to turn their rulers into philosophers. Plato taught at the Academy until his death, and was buried there in 347 BC. The Academy continued to function, without interruption, until AD 529, when the Christian emperor Justinian closed down all the schools of philosophy in Athens.

DAPHNI ▲ *251*. Protected from the road by a high crenelated wall, the Byzantine monastery at Daphni is now a museum. The original institution was founded in the 5th century and dedicated to the Dormition of the Virgin; today it is celebrated for its remarkable Byzantine mosaics. It owes its name to a sanctuary of Apollo that once stood on the site, close to a gorge through which the Sacred Way passed, linking Eleusis and Athens (just over 6 miles away). The laurel, *daphni* in Greek, was dedicated to Apollo. Every year from July 15 to September 30 a night-time wine festival is held in the pine groves of the monastery grounds, at which all the principal wines of Greece are represented – and sampled.

PLATO'S ACADEMY
The "Garden of the Philosophers" (once a wood sacred to Athena) used to be a favorite walking place for Athenians.

HEAD OF A PHILOSOPHER
Bronze, 240 BC. In Greek sculpture philosophers were often depicted as bearded men.

The Greeks were the first to define a purely esthetic ideal. But in Plato's philosophy the question of what is beautiful does not only apply to the esthetic domain: it also concerns the fundamental aspirations and questions of human life. For Plato beauty is not merely a characteristic of a work of art or a person, but a complete way of being: it is the reflection of excellence, harmony and perfection. Significantly the expression used in Greek to mean "good men" translates literally as "the good and the beautiful". Beauty, so far as Plato was concerned, was only comprehensible in terms of its relationship with goodness and truth. It may be that the Greeks felt a conflict between their aspirations to greatness and their regard for beauty: the problem was how to reconcile their yearning to leave a mark on history with the possibility that balance and harmony might be destroyed in the process.

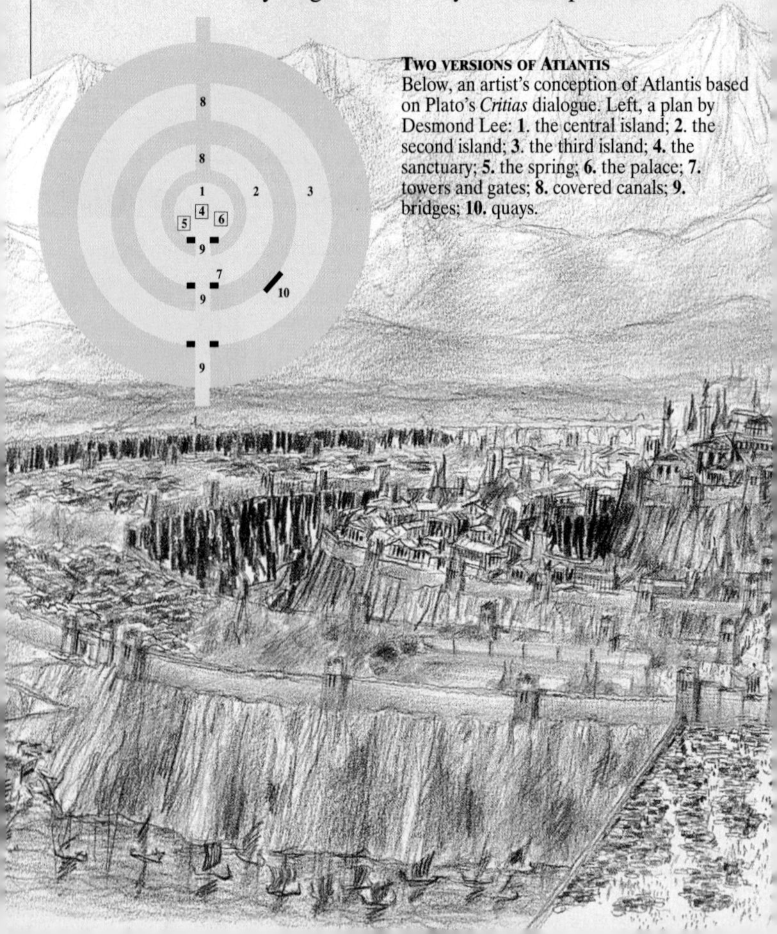

TWO VERSIONS OF ATLANTIS
Below, an artist's conception of Atlantis based on Plato's *Critias* dialogue. Left, a plan by Desmond Lee: **1**. the central island; **2**. the second island; **3**. the third island; **4.** the sanctuary; **5.** the spring; **6.** the palace; **7.** towers and gates; **8.** covered canals; **9.** bridges; **10.** quays.

Plato with his pupils on Cape Sounion
Plato's description, in his *Critias* dialogue, of the Temple of Poseidon on Atlantis could well fit the temple on Cape Sounion.

Atlantis – fact or fiction?
Few topics have had so strong a hold on the human imagination as Atlantis. The people of this great mythical island near the Strait of Gibraltar were supposed to have attempted to rule the world, a goal thwarted by the Athenians. The name Atlantis came from Atlas, the giant son of Athena's rival Poseidon, who reigned there on his father's behalf. Plato gives the first literary account of Atlantis, in which its civilization is portrayed as having been the ultimate of which mankind was capable – and yet it is suddenly cut short (like the text of the *Critias* dialogue itself), swallowed up by earthquakes and floods. Plato used the myth of Atlantis to remind his civilized, cosmopolitan contemporaries of their cosmic insignificance: no doubt he intended the story as a warning to the Athenians, who in his own time were displaying dangerous longings for historical immortality. Atlantis is neither fact nor pure fiction, but something else: a myth firmly based in human history.

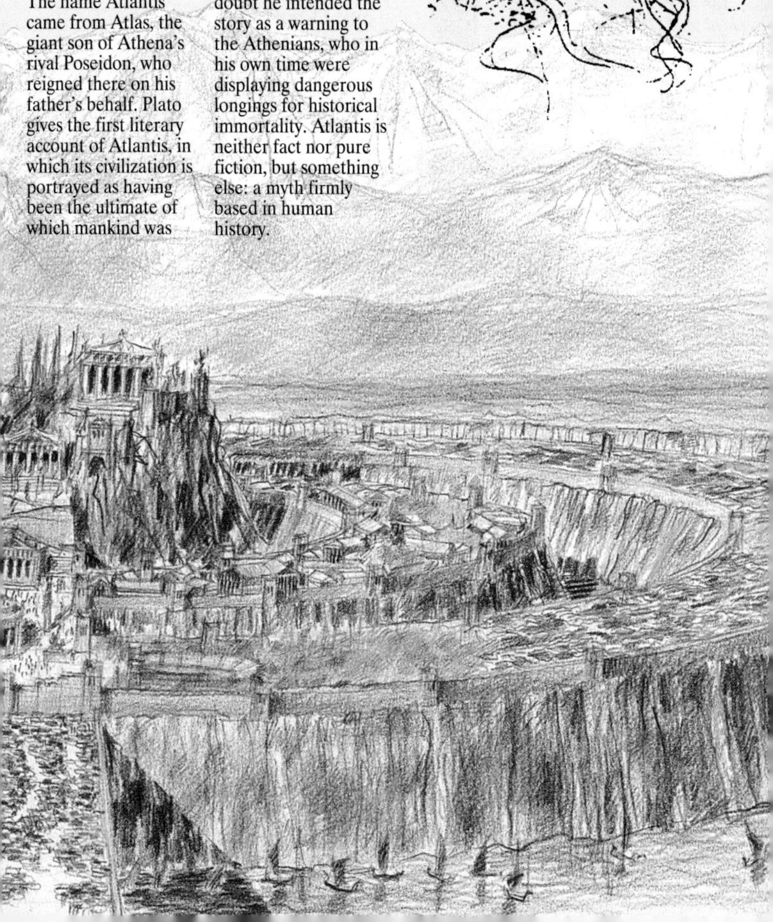

THE CITADEL OF CORINTH
This was occupied successively by the Byzantines, the Franks, the Venetians and the Turks. Whoever controlled it dominated the Peloponnese.

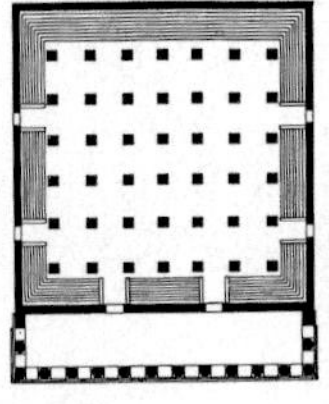

PLAN OF THE TELESTERION
A hypostyle building with a ceiling supported by columns, the Telesterion dates from the 5th century BC. It was intended as a kind of indoor theater. Here, initiates experienced the revelation of the sacred objects kept at the center of the hall. The portico of the façade was built by Philon in the 4th century BC.

CROSSING THE ISTHMUS OF CORINTH
In ancient times ships were moved from one sea to the other over land by a special road, the Diolkos. The canal, completed toward the end of the 19th century, still provides ships from Marseilles, Genoa and Naples with a short cut to Piraeus.

ELEUSIS

To reach Eleusis, about 7 miles from Daphni, take the main road to Thebes, turn off past Aspropyrgos and continue on the old Sacred Way toward Corinth.

THE GREEK AND ROMAN SANCTUARIES At the entrance of the site is a paved esplanade dating from the 2nd century BC, with the ruins of two temples dedicated to Artemis Propylaea and Poseidon Pater. Both were built in Roman times on foundations dating back to the 8th century BC. Close by stood a triumphal arch (there was a matching arch to the northwest) and a fountain where pilgrims purified themselves. The white marble *propylaea* were built in the reign of Antoninus Pius, the adoptive son of the emperor Hadrian. Below the esplanade is the Well of Callichoros, where Demeter was said to have met the daughters of King Celeus, and where the women of Eleusis sang and danced in her honor.

THE PLOUTONEION. To the right of the Sacred Way are two caverns surrounded by a sacred precinct dedicated to Pluto. These were supposed to give access to the Underworld, and it was here that Demeter's daughter Persephone (also called Kore) was said to have reappeared after her abduction by Pluto.

THE TELESTERION. The Sacred Way continues up to the Telesterion, the main building of the Shrine of the Mysteries. Roughly square in shape, this edifice served as a backdrop to the initiations into the Mysteries of Demeter and Kore. Some three thousand people could be accommodated in the tiers of seats. The most sacred part of the Telesterion was the *anaktoron*, a kind of chapel in the center of the building.

CORINTH
To the 18th-century traveler, the acropolis of Corinth appeared to be an intact medieval town in which the constructions of various epochs were hard to tell apart.

On the southeast façade Philon built a twelve-column portico of Pentelic marble, whose whiteness contrasted with the Eleusinian grey-blue marble used to face the walls of the hall.

THE FESTIVALS. The religious festival of Eleusis were distinct from the Mysteries. Contests in August preceded the games on the Isthmus. The victors were awarded a prize of barley harvested near the acropolis of Eleusis, where the festival of the sacred ploughing was held. Pausanias states that in the 2nd century AD, not far from the sanctuary but outside the walls, an area with an altar was reserved for the youthful god Triptolemos; barley and wheat were sown here and later used to bake offerings of bread.

THE MYSTERIES. The study of ancient paintings and sculptures has only given us a rough idea of what took place during the celebration of the mysteries. They were based on the myth of Persephone's re-emergence into the light of day, and on Demeter's attempt to make Demophon immortal. For initiates, the idea was to acquire some hope of a happy existence in another world after death; they were convinced that if they missed the chance of initiation in this world they were condemned in the next. Men, women, and children – even slaves – were all entitled to initiation, provided they were able to utter the sacred formulae. Apart from this, as Aristophanes wrote ironically, "...all that was needful was an obol for the priest and three drachmas to buy a suckling pig for sacrifice."

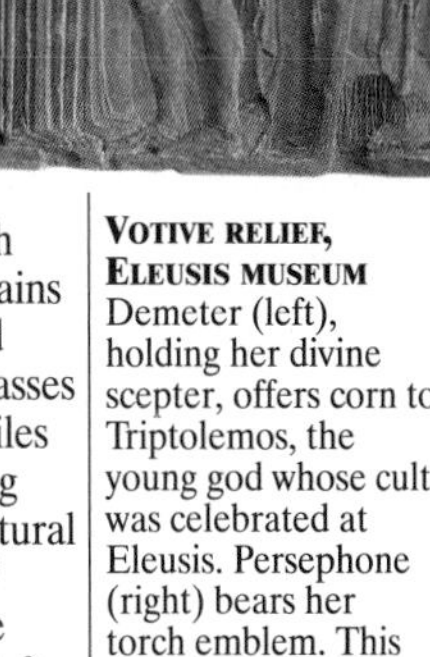

VOTIVE RELIEF, ELEUSIS MUSEUM
Demeter (left), holding her divine scepter, offers corn to Triptolemos, the young god whose cult was celebrated at Eleusis. Persephone (right) bears her torch emblem. This magnificent relief dates from the late 5th century BC.

MEGARA. Leaving Eleusis, the Corinth road skirts the north slope of the acropolis and continues toward the sea. The plains of Eleusis and Megara are separated by hills which descend from the Kitheron Mountains down to the bay. The road passes through vineyards, olive groves, pines and myrtles for 10 miles or so between Eleusis and Megara, which is now a sprawling town. It was originally built on a site resembling a broad natural amphitheater, with two acropolises overlooking the bays of Eleusis and Salamis. Now that Megara has merged with the suburbs of Athens, there are few ancient remains. Little is left of the city's glorious past, apart from the ruins of its aqueduct and so-called Fountain of Theagenes. Today's main square is probably built on the site of the former agora; like its predecessor, it is a marketplace and meeting point for locals.

SARCOPHAGUS
Displayed in the museum's garden, this beautiful mid 2nd-century AD sarcophagus is decorated with reliefs depicting the legendary hunt at Calydon, a city in Aetolia on which Artemis unleashed a giant boar.

Corinth museum
The museum's Roman collections comprise reliefs, statues, busts and magnificent intricately-worked mosaics in bright colors which paved the rooms of Roman villas and public buildings.

Corinthia and the Argolid

This north-south corridor of land has probably been crossed by man since the stone age. Traces of 25,000-year-old human habitations have been found near Epidauros in the Franchthi caves.

The isthmus of Corinth. After Megara, the coast road continues to the canal and the city of Corinth ▲ *296*. At several points in history, Corinth has vied with Athens to be capital of Greece.

The fortress of Acrocorinth. This stronghold dominates the Gulf of Corinth, the narrow rocky spit leading to continental Greece, and the Saronic Gulf. From its walls there is a fine view of the mountains inland, many of which exceed 6,000 feet in altitude.

The museum of the isthmus. This museum displays a number of objects discovered during the excavation of the isthmus and the ancient port of Keuchreai – including ceramic panels unearthed by American archeologists in 1964. Among the architectural remains is a lion's head between the palmettes of the Temple of Poseidon ▲ *296*.

The Peloponnese. The Peloponnese is the broad peninsula which forms the southern end of Greece; its shape on the map resembles a blackberry leaf, hence the name of "Morea" by which it was known until the 19th century. Since then the region has re-adopted its ancient name, which associated it with the mythical hero Pelops, King of Elis and founder of the family of the Pelopides. Elis, along with Argos, Sparta, Messenia, Achaia and Arcadia, is one of the political divisions of the modern Peloponnese. This is a country of myth: it was successively occupied by Carians, Achaeans, Aeolians and Ionians. The Peloponnese also saw the birth of Mycenean civilisation in the second millennium BC. Remains of classical Greek temples and theaters, traces of the Roman occupation, Byzantine churches, Frankish fortresses and Venetian buildings make this peninsula one of the great treasures of Greece. Spring and fall are the best seasons to explore the Peloponnese. In summer, plan visits to the ancient sites for as early as possible in the morning; don't imagine you can do much more than lie on the beach in the afternoon.

Corinthian sphinx
This smiling sphinx, made of baked clay in the 6th century AD, has traces of polychrome decoration on its wings.

FROM CORINTH TO ARGOS

ARGOS
NEMEA
MYCENAE
NAUPLION
TIRYNS
ACROCORINTH
CORINTH
CORINTH CANAL
EPIDAURUS

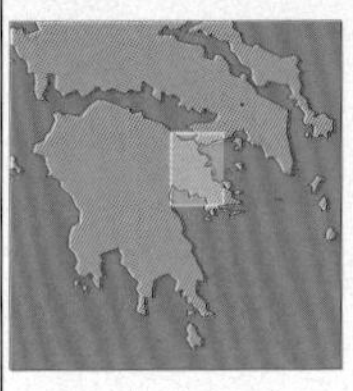

Two days

CORINTHIA
Mountains, in places stripped bare of trees, surround the narrow plains of Corinth – which now, as in ancient times, are planted with vines and orchards and (to the south) with market gardens and olive groves ■ *24*.

Polychrome gutter decorated with lion's head. Now restored and on display in the Corinth Museum.

CORINTH

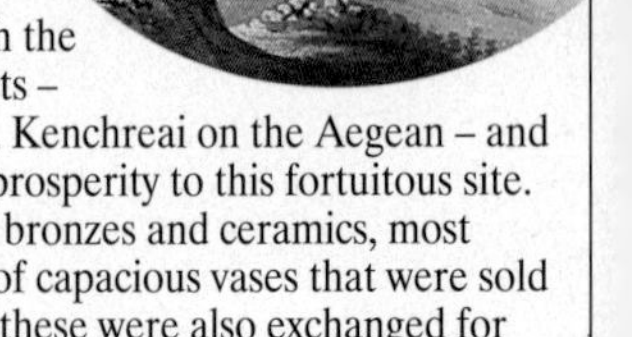

The ancient city of Corinth stood at the intersection of the sea and land routes that linked mainland Greece with the Peloponnese. It had two ports – Lechaion on the Ionian Sea, Kenchreai on the Aegean – and the Corinthians owed their prosperity to this fortuitous site. Their artisans specialized in bronzes and ceramics, most notably in the manufacture of capacious vases that were sold all over the Mediterranean; these were also exchanged for wheat, which was stored at Corinth and from there distributed throughout Greece. Otherwise, the city was a byword for luxury and for the beauty of the courtesans at its Temple of Aphrodite. In 146 BC Corinth was captured and destroyed by the Roman general Mummius. However, architectural

remains dating from the Roman colony founded by Julius Caesar in 44 BC have survived, and vestiges from antiquity are to be seen at Palaia Korinthos (about 4 miles from New Corinth, on the plateau which separates it from Acrocorinth ▲ *294*). The American School of Archeology has excavated the more important areas of the site.

CORINTHUS
Woodcut dating from the 15th century.

THE TEMPLE OF APOLLO. The most imposing monument here is the Temple of Apollo: its seven remaining Doric columns ● *85* are still linked by part of the original architrave. The temple once had a peristyle of thirty-eight columns, with six visible at each end and fifteen at each side.

THE FOUNTAIN OF PIRENE. The two most celebrated fountains in Corinth are situated just below the temple. The Fountain of Pirene yielded water from two springs from the earliest times; its supply was channeled from the hill by way of a tunnel and stored in six reservoirs. It was remodeled by Herodes Atticus ▲ *218* in the 2nd century, with the addition of an upper level, a double colonnade and vaulted apses on three sides with niches for statues. Nearly all the other vestiges visible today date from the Colonia Laus Julia Corinthus, which Julius Caesar dreamed of making the capital of Greece.

ACROCORINTH, ENTRANCE TO THE FORT
This limestone outcrop is some 1,900 feet high. The ruins are covered with thyme and thistles. From here there is a spectacular view over the Saronic Gulf, part of Attica, the Peloponnese and the Gulf of Corinth.

THE AGORA. Among the most remarkable ruins here is the Agora (over 500 feet long and 300 feet wide), one of the largest ever built in a Roman city. It was subdivided into two terraces, the upper one being fronted by administrative buildings and the lower one by shops and booths. The *bema*, the tribune from which the governor habitually addressed the citizens, was situated between the two levels, in the center of the Agora's south side. Behind it stood the South Stoa, one

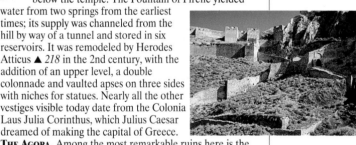

The city of Corinth, 18th-century engraving.

of the most imposing constructions of its kind in Greece, which included some sixty bedrooms designed to house visiting delegates from the Hellenic League.

THE MARKET SQUARE. The square was once overlooked on its west side by several Roman temples. Where the Lechaion Way entered the Agora, the Romans built a triumphal arch topped by a double quadriga, which took the place of a gateway with *propylaea*. The shops on this street were shaded by a colonnade, with their backs to a large building, perhaps a basilica, whose pediment was embellished with four sculptures called "the façade of the captives" which are now in the museum.

THE CORINTH CANAL. To avoid the hazards of sailing round Cape Malea, Periander, tyrant of Corinth, began the excavation of a canal across the isthmus in 602 BC. Much later Nero continued the construction of the canal, but was eventually forced to abandon it. Traces of this Roman effort still remain. The line of the canal was so perfectly planned by the emperor's engineers that it was adopted unchanged by the French team which revived the project in 1882. After the French company went bankrupt, the Greeks finally completed it themselves in 1893. Today the Corinth Canal is a narrow waterway nearly 4 miles long; at the

THE SANCTUARY OF NEMEA
In ancient times the sacred grove of olive and plane trees was a shrine for pilgrims.

THE TEMPLE OF ZEUS
In the center of a small valley stand three Doric columns – two of them still joined by an architrave, the third standing alone.

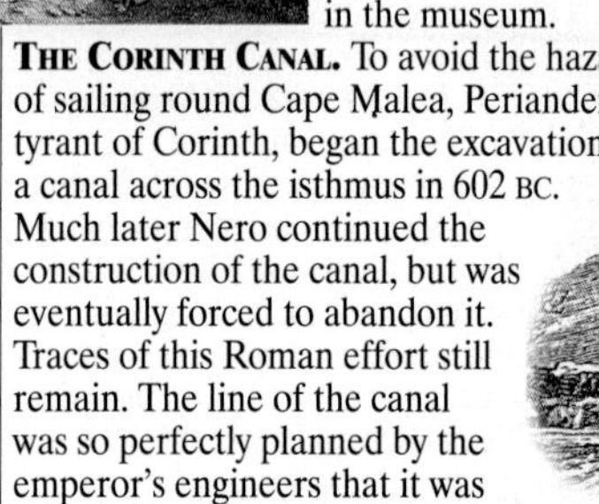

NEMEA MUSEUM
A broad gallery inside the museum exhibits objects excavated from the site of Nemea, among them this rendering of Asklepios and Hygieia. The physician-god, like his daughter, has a serpent as his principal emblem. He wears a simple *himation* which leaves his chest bare; in his left hand is a short baton.

NEMEAN WINE
The vines of the village of Philionte produce a wine known as "Blood of Hercules" which has been famous since ancient times.

"AT NEMEA THERE IS A REMARKABLE TEMPLE DEDICATED TO NEMEAN ZEUS, BUT WHEN I SAW IT THE ROOF HAD FALLEN IN AND NO STATUES REMAINED."

PAUSANIAS

surface it is 80 feet wide (about the same width as the Suez Canal). The depth of the water is approximately 25 feet: and its banks, which in places exceed 250 feet in height, stand between 150 and 200 feet apart. The cruise ships that call at Loutraki, on their way to Piraeus, are towed through the canal by tugs. (Leave Corinth by way of the Argos freeway; after 2½ miles you will come to the archeological site of Nemea.)

NEMEA

The site of Nemea, famous in mythology as the scene of Herakles' triumph over the lion, lies at the entrance of the defile of Dervinaki, where in 1822 Kolokotronis inflicted a bloody defeat on the Turkish army of Dramali Pasha ● *51*.

THE SANCTUARY OF ZEUS. What remains of this Doric peripteral temple ● *90* stands a mile or so outside the modern village of Nemea. With its long, slender columns, this building has a distinctive style, characteristic of Greek art at its apogee. The two columns still linked by a section of architrave belonged to the first room of the *cella*. The third one still standing is situated at the far end of the outer portico, which was six columns wide and twelve long (with two more columns for the *pronaos* and no *opisthodomos*). The peristyle was about 140 feet long and 70 feet wide. The interior columns were Corinthian in style; and the temple possessed a crypt, at the bottom of some steps on the inside. It is known that this building was constructed at the time of the 110th Olympiad, c. 344 BC. The walls must have been destroyed at some stage by an earthquake, since the fallen columns discovered here were all found precisely aligned with their bases.

THE THEATER. Recently the *cavea* and *skene* ▲ *174* of a theater have been excavated close to the temple. South of this theater stood a large rectangular building, the four sides of which consisted of porticos with Doric columns, surrounding an open courtyard. The building, which dates from the 5th century BC, appears to have been destroyed and rebuilt on at least one occasion, and to have served as an *agora* (assembly place and market area) remaining in use until the 4th or 5th century AD. In general the site is rather grand, nestling as it does amid vineyards and orchards.

DECORATIVE MOTIF
An *akroterion* (ridge tile) of the 4th-century temple, now displayed in the museum courtyard.

THE TEMPLE OF ZEUS
At the north and east sides of the site is an eminence nearly 3,000 feet in height, the top of which has been leveled; this is Mount Apesas, mentioned by Pausanias. Aspens and young cypresses frame the three slender columns still standing here; the components of the others lie nearby among the rocks and weeds.

LAKE STYMPHALOS
According to myth, birds that ate human flesh lived in the marshes of Stymphalos, not far from Nemea.

▲ Mycenae

Mycenae stood on a hilltop between two higher mountains.

The tomb circle
The site was excavated by archeologists between 1952 and 1955. In addition to jewels and gold masks, a number of figurines were discovered.

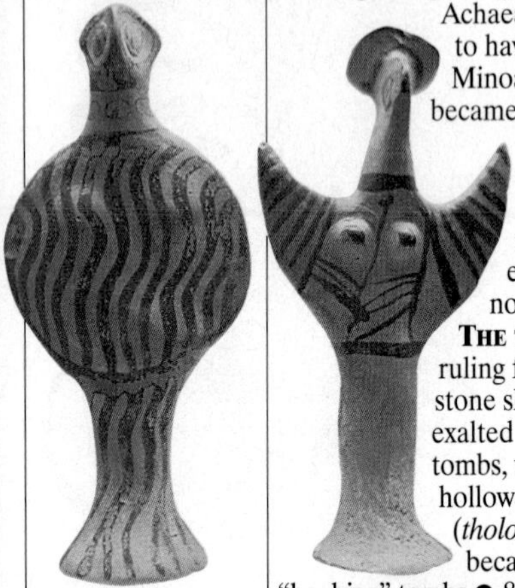

Origins

Mycenae stands on a site overlooking the plain of Argos. Once there was a large bay here, but over the millennia it filled up with alluvial soil, so that the sea is now 10 miles from the archeological site. Only a cemetery survives from the Neolithic era, in which crude pottery has been discovered. The beginning of Mycenean civilization ● *43* – meaning the Achaean society mentioned by Homer – seems to have been roughly contemporary with the Minoan civilization ● *42* in Crete, which became established around 1600 BC.

Monuments outside the citadel
Mycenae gradually spread beyond its citadel. Numerous private houses, surrounded by graves, have been excavated on all the hills to the north and northwest of the Acropolis.

The tomb circle. The shaft graves of the ruling family were surrounded by a circle of stone slabs in the 17th or 16th century BC; less exalted people had to be content with cist tombs, vertical stones, or else simple cavities hollowed out of the hillside. Later, circular (*tholos*), oval and rectangular burial chambers became the norm. The domed, circular "beehive" tombs ● *83* of the ruling family had an entry shaft (*dromos*), driven directly into the rock. The outer entrance was closed by a wooden door, with a lintel and relieving triangle above it. The corbeled courses of masonry rose to a height of about 35 feet, and the diameter of the burial

"PART OF THE CITY WALL REMAINS, AND A GATEWAY CROWNED BY STATUES OF LIONS."

PAUSANIAS

THE NORTH GATE

THE ACROPOLIS
Shaped like a long, somewhat irregular triangle, the Acropolis of Mycenae has Cyclopean walls ● *87* built of roughly hewn square blocks and polygonal stones of varying size.

chamber was roughly the same. Offerings would be placed around the body of the deceased, which was placed either in a cist tomb or on the ground. Four *tholos* chambers at Mycenae are particularly famous: the Treasury of Atreus, built around 1250 BC; the Lion Tomb ● *83*, near the gate of the same name; and, dating from the mid 14th century BC, the Tomb of Aegisthus (as Pausanias calls it), whose beehive roof has collapsed but which would seem to predate the so-called Tomb of Clytemnestra (1220 BC) by two or three centuries. The French statesman Chateaubriand claimed that he discovered the latter, between 1803 and 1810, in his *Itinéraire de Paris à Jérusalem:* "On my way back to the Corinth road, I heard the ground echoing hollow under the hooves of my horse. I dismounted and discovered the vaulting of a tomb beneath me. Pausanias says that there are five great tombs at Mycenae: those of Atreus, Agamemnon, Eurymedon, Teledamus, Pelops and Electra. He adds that Clytemnestra and Aegisthus were buried outside the city walls; might not this tomb that I had stumbled upon be that of Clytemnestra and Aegisthus? I indicated its location to M. Fauvel, who will seek it on his next trip to Argos. How strange is destiny, which brought me from Paris to discover the ashes of Clytemnestra!"

THE LION GATE
The lintel is topped by a relieving triangle, a tufa slab carved with two lions facing each other. The heads of the lions were made of bronze or of steatite, a stone that did not weather well.

THE ACROPOLIS ● *83*. Mycenae's Acropolis stands on a hill between two mountain peaks. On the north and south sides are deep ravines, the gorge of the Chavos (nearly 900 feet deep) separating it from the goat pastures of Mount Zara. The workmen therefore had to bring the massive rectangular limestone blocks for the walls up very steep terrain. The two faces of the blocks, which vary in height, conceal a filling of rubble and clay. Although the blocks were cut and dressed without iron tools, the courses of masonry are almost horizontal. The walls of the Acropolis define a triangle whose base is oriented toward the north. In places they are more than 26 feet thick; the area they enclose measures nearly

ACROPOLIS PLAN

1. Lion Gate
2. Tomb circle
3. Wace Building
4. Tsountas' House
5. Ramp
6. Propylon of the palace
7. Main courtyard
8. Megaron
9. Artisans' quarters
10. Cisterns
11. North gate

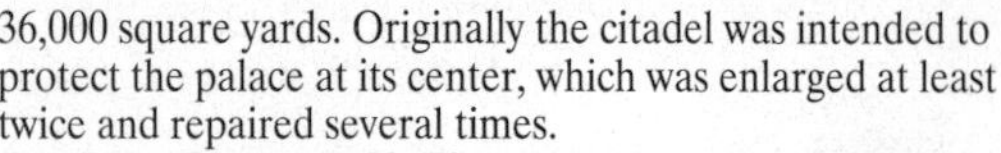

36,000 square yards. Originally the citadel was intended to protect the palace at its center, which was enlarged at least twice and repaired several times.

THE LION GATE ★ ● *83*. The western entrance to Mycenae, through the famous Lion Gate, was defended by a bastion jutting out from the rampart. This arrangement, which dates from the 13th century BC, was known as *skaaipulai* or "left-handed gates". Once an attacking force had entered this passageway of stone blocks laid in horizontal courses, it could be showered with missiles on its right-hand (unshielded) side by defenders on the bastion. The gateway itself, which consists of four massive dressed stones jointed without mortar, is a little over 10 feet high and almost as wide. The threshold paving is scored to prevent animals from slipping, and has grooves for chariot wheels and to facilitate drainage. The lintel, made of a single block weighing at least 100 tons, framed the gates, which could not swing outward. The projecting stones of the rampart support it at each end. Above the lintel is a triangular stone slab adorned by a relief of two lions, whose front paws rest on two altars; between the lions is a column with a capital of three rings. This bas-relief is the oldest known monumental sculpture in Europe. It is thought to be the emblem of the palace and may represent the arms of the dynasty of Atreus, mythical king of Mycenae, given that the Lion Gate was said to date from his reign. The bronze-covered wooden gates were reinforced at the back by a rectangular

THE PALACE
"Here architecture goes back farther even than poetry, for these monuments represent times known to history by a few outlines of one or two races still intact, tribes, castes, priesthoods and symbols."
Edgar Quinet

THE TREASURY OF ATREUS
The chamber is circular, with a domed vault. The vaulting is formed by thirty-three concentric courses of masonry, each overlapping the one below it.

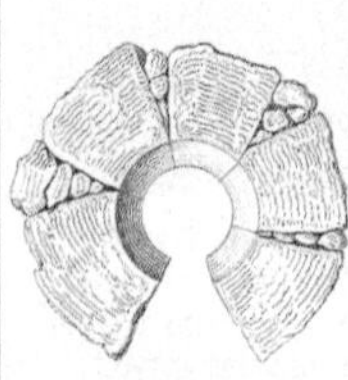

An open passage leads to the doorway of the main chamber, which has a smaller chamber off it to the right, cut into the rock.

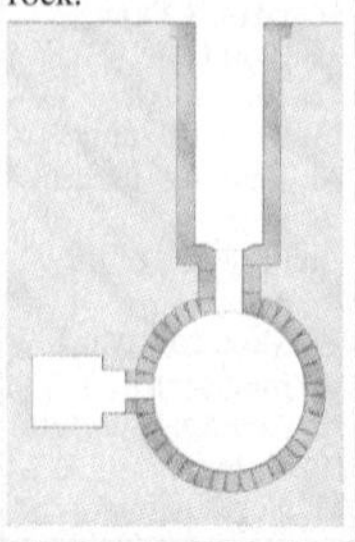

bar, the sockets for which are still visible. Two vertical grooves cut into the walls on the inside allowed the gates to be wedged open. Beyond the gateway is a small square courtyard; from here a flight of steps leads to a broad ramp running around the walls to the palace. In a storehouse nearby, known as the granary, jars of carbonized wheat and barley seeds were found. The positions of the tombs were probably marked by limestone stelae, some of which have been unearthed; the ones sculpted with chariots, men, lions and horses are now in the National Archeological Museum in Athens ▲ *236*, along with the famous gold masks and burial furnishings.

The houses of Mycenae. To the south and west of this precinct the foundations of several houses have been excavated: the House of the Warrior Vase, The Wace Building, Tsountas' House, the Priest's House, and one called the Oil Merchant's House, in which sealed oil jars were found, along with tablets listing consignees and shippers on one side and plants and aromatic essences on the other. This house appears to have burned down in the 13th century, and it is possible that it was a perfume factory catering to princes rather than an oil merchant's shop.

The palace ● *82*. Mycenean civilization was highly complex, and its innovative architecture reflects this. The palace was both the economic and religious focus of the city – both an administrative center and place of worship.

The Treasury of Atreus
Among the buildings he saw at Mycenae, Pausanias mentions "the underground chambers in which Atreus and his children hoarded their treasure". The massive lintel of this "treasury" is capped by a relieving triangle, but its decoration has now disappeared. The National Archeological Museum in Athens displays fragments of green porphyry half-columns and a gypsum flagstone decorated with spirals that once formed part of this structure.

Gold signet ring
▲ *237*. This treasure was found in Tomb IV by Schliemann during the first excavations of Mycenae.

The tomb chamber of the Treasury of Atreus
Archeologists believe the tomb chamber was decorated with bronze panels or plaques. The *tholos* is over 40 feet high, and its diameter over 45 feet. It was the largest dome in existence until the building of the Pantheon in Rome in AD 118. On the north side is a low door to a small room, the presence of which led to the edifice being called a "treasury", its tomb function forgotten. Like the Lion Gate, it dates from around 1250 BC.

Decorative alabaster frieze, from the palace.

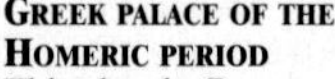
GREEK PALACE OF THE HOMERIC PERIOD
This plan, by Perrot and Chipiez, is based on the *Odyssey*. The royal residence described by Homer was probably inspired by the palace of the Achaean princes in the Argolid.

THE MAIN ENTRANCE. The entrance (*propylon*) was on the northwest side; to the southeast a monumental staircase led to the courtyard containing the guests' apartments. The palace was constructed on several terraced levels, supported on their south side by the rampart. Today an almond tree grows on the highest of these terraces. The buildings themselves were burned to the ground long ago, but from the west courtyard there is a magnificent view of the plain of Argos. The southeast corner of the palace looked out across the mountains on the far side of the ravine. In general, excavations have revealed the influence of the Cretan system of palace design.

THE MEGARON ● *82*. The social focus of the palace was the Megaron, a covered rectangular hall that was a specifically Mycenean innovation. It consisted of a two-column porch, preceding a light well (*aïthousa*), a vestibule (*prodomos*), where

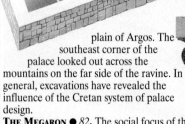

The last ramparts to be built were those of the northeast extension, which included postern gates. In 1963 excavations revealed that the work was undertaken to improve the water supply: an underground cistern existed here, into which a subterranean aqueduct spilled water from springs on the Mountain of the Prophet Elijah.

TREASURY OF ATREUS
Geometric patterns on a capital and column shaft in green breccia.

Palace of the Homeric period, as described in the "Odyssey" - Reconstruction
1. Main entrance
2. Outer courtyard
3. Servants' and guests' quarters
4. Stables and cattle stalls
5. Altar of Zeus Herkeios
6. Vestibule leading to the Megaron, *aïthousa* and *prothyron* (furnace room)
7. Tholos
8. Megaron
9. Hearth of the Megaron
10. Women's Megaron
11. Storehouse
12. Arsenal and treasury
13. Bridal chamber
14. Guest bathrooms

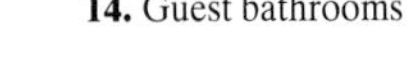

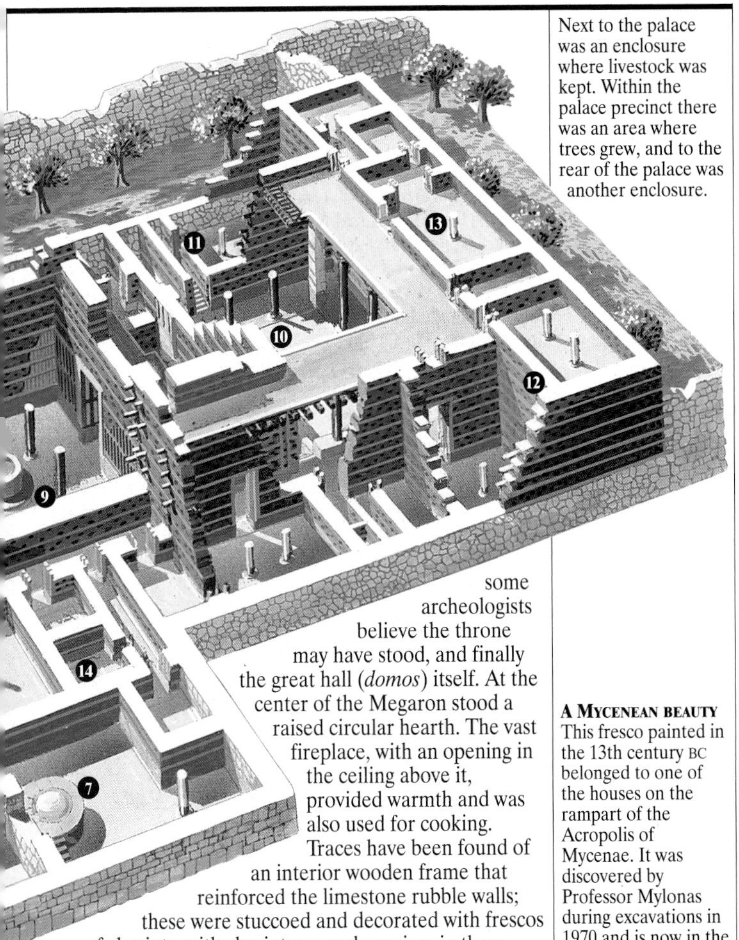

Next to the palace was an enclosure where livestock was kept. Within the palace precinct there was an area where trees grew, and to the rear of the palace was another enclosure.

some archeologists believe the throne may have stood, and finally the great hall (*domos*) itself. At the center of the Megaron stood a raised circular hearth. The vast fireplace, with an opening in the ceiling above it, provided warmth and was also used for cooking. Traces have been found of an interior wooden frame that reinforced the limestone rubble walls; these were stuccoed and decorated with frescos of chariots, with charioteers and warriors in them.

Corridors separated the reception rooms from the apartments of the princes and women, some of which were on the floor above. The porticoed central courtyard was paved with gypsum. The private apartments included bathrooms (water conduits have been unearthed here). The palace's guest rooms, workshops, quarters for artists and artisans, and a house with columns similar to those in Odysseus' house on Ithaca as described by Homer have also been excavated. To the north of the citadel is a gate of roughly similar dimensions to the Lion Gate, which provided access to the surrounding countryside.

A Mycenean beauty
This fresco painted in the 13th century BC belonged to one of the houses on the rampart of the Acropolis of Mycenae. It was discovered by Professor Mylonas during excavations in 1970 and is now in the National Archeological Museum in Athens.

SCHLIEMANN
From 1876 onward Schliemann was deeply involved with the excavations at Tiryns. In 1884, together with W. Dörpfeld, he returned to the site. Today the German School of Archeology continues research.

THE FORTIFICATIONS
All the defenses of Tiryns, which was a massive, unscalable fortress, were planned to deal with attacks from the sea. The outer walls are nearly a mile around and may have had brick crenelations, as this 19th-century reconstruction suggests.

HISTORY

From the Gulf of Argos the citadel of Tiryns is clearly visible, standing on the summit of a rocky knoll 60 feet high. During the Mycenean era ● *43* the fortifications defended a palace comparable to that of Mycenae itself. The ramparts, which run from north to south, are nearly 300 yards in length. Strabo, in his *Geography*, recounts the legend of the founding of Tiryns by the mythical King Proitos, adding that the city "served as a military stronghold for Proitos, who had the Cyclops surround it with walls". The site of Tiryns, which is very close to Mycenae, was inhabited from Neolithic times, the first village here having been established between 2500 and 2200 BC. Traces have been found on the Acropolis of a round building, some 54 feet in diameter, dating from the early Bronze Age. During the Mycenean era a fortification of irregular stone blocks was erected, around 1400 BC, prior to the construction of the palace. This citadel was severely damaged in the second half of the 13th century BC, before being completely destroyed by a second attack around 1200 BC. When, in the late 19th century, Heinrich Schliemann undertook his archeological excavation to clear away the debris covering the walls, no remains of any kind were visible.

THE ACROPOLIS. Up the slope of the outer wall runs a track which passes between two ramparts and a gateway 15 feet wide, before continuing to the top of the Acropolis, entering the fortified perimeter by way of massive *propylaea*. The perimeter walls are between 18 feet and 32 feet thick, the south wall being the thickest of all, with galleries and chambers incorporated into it. The surface area of the Acropolis is naturally divided into three plateaux: the highest of these, onto which the *propylaea* open, is on the south side.

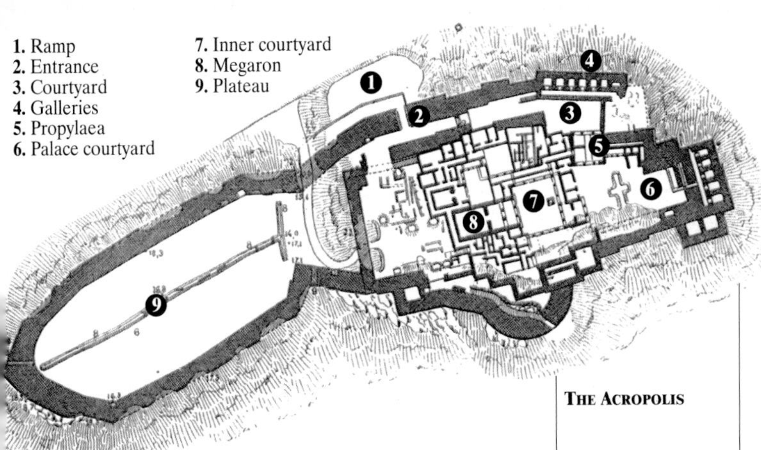

The Acropolis

The Mycenean palace. Beyond the entrance is a small outer courtyard closed off by the main *propylaea* of the palace: two exterior and interior porticos, of which the threshold still remains. These were the ancestors of the monumental temple entrances of the classical era, most notably the one on the Acropolis at Athens ▲ *136*. On the north side of this courtyard stood a second, smaller *propylaea* – which opened onto a passageway leading to the private apartments of the palace – followed by the central courtyard, which was closed in on three sides by a portico. The five casemates here were probably used as storehouses; a gallery below the level of the central courtyard led to further rooms and a postern. To the north two vestibules preceded the Megaron ● *82*. Near the entrance to it a low, round altar and a pit used for sacrifices show that the palace had a religious as well as a secular role. The Megaron is characteristic of Mycenean architecture ▲ *304*, with its central hearth surrounded by four columns, the bases of which are still visible.

The décor. The building was adorned with murals, painted on stucco made with lime. The west wall bore a frieze of alabaster and lapis lazuli, with alternating rows of embossed rosettes and half-circle designs. Remains of these can be seen in the National Archeological Museum in Athens.

The galleries of the citadel
These galleries were incorporated, like casemates, in the body of the wall. Ogival in shape, they are made up of five or six courses of stone, each projecting inward over the last, with a keystone at the top.

A Cyclopean fortress
The huge blocks of Tiryns' Cyclopean walls ● *87*, dragged here from the quarries and cut on the spot, were as amazing to the ancients as they are to us.

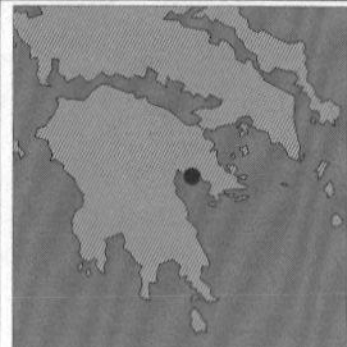

One day

HISTORY

THE MYCENEAN ERA. Nauplion has been inhabited since prehistoric times, but the original settlement – on top of a rocky promontory, 280 feet above the sea – is now buried beneath later constructions. From the Mycenean era the only survivals are tombs, discovered in the present suburb of Pronia, to the northeast and east of the highest fortress.

THE FRANKISH CONQUEST. From the Middle Ages to modern times, Nauplion has played a vital role in the history of Greece. The Byzantines restored the city's fortifications, gave it the dignity of a bishopric, and administered it until about 1200. After the capture of Constantinople by the crusaders in 1204, the King of Salonica ceded to William Champlitte and Geoffrey de Villhardouin the right to annexe the Peloponnese. Setting out from the Gulf of Corinth, the Frankish expeditionary force followed the Ionian shoreline, taking the coastal cities one by one but making certain that it kept its ships constantly in sight. When the peninsula had been subdued and divided up among the Frankish knights and barons, strongholds were built at key sites, including Nauplion. A cultivated society, speaking the best Parisian French, grew up among the emigrants from France, and for seventy years the Peloponnese prospered to the advantage of both conquerors and conquered. Later the suzerainty of the region passed to the kings of Naples, the successors of Charles d'Anjou, who allowed the Venetians and Spaniards to make such extensive inroads that within a short time French domination was brought to an end ● *49*.

NAPOLI DI ROMANIA. The coastal plain was marshy and fever-ridden; not until the 11th century were the first attempts made to drain it. Beginning in 1389 the Venetians undertook major drainage works near Nauplion (which they called "Napoli di Romania"), with a view to installing refugees from the island of Euboea (Chalcis) who had been

ISLET OF BOURDZI

NAUPLION: THE TOWN AND PORT IN 1907
A small, elegant town with sunny houses painted white, Nauplion had paved streets from the end of the 19th century. Under King Otto, it was briefly the capital of Greece.

THE PORT IN 1864
Engraving by A. Sargent.

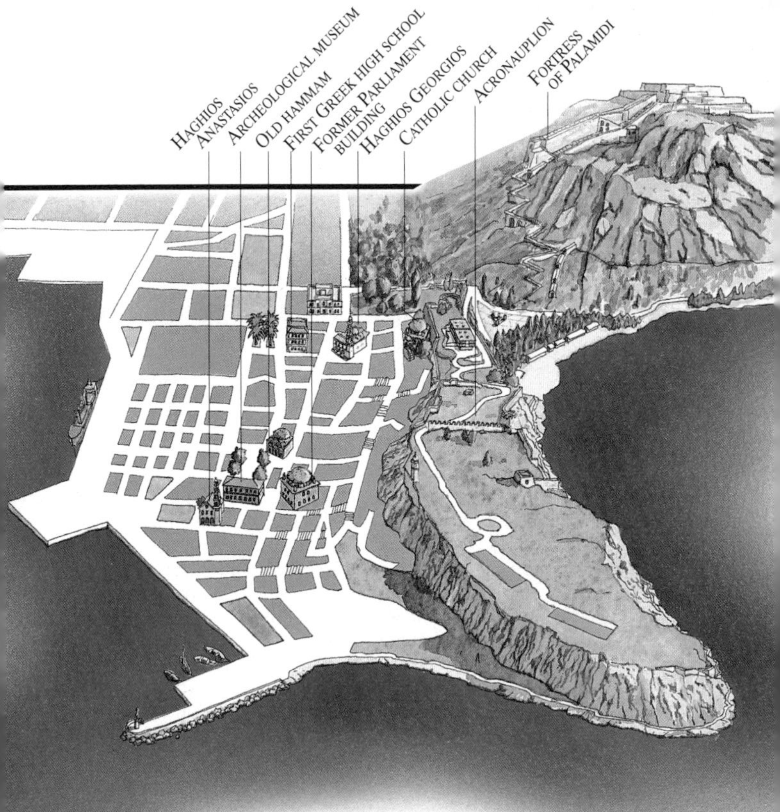

driven from their homes by the Turks. They built the first houses of the lower town on pilings, and developed the port to such effect that Nauplion quickly became Venice's principal possession in the Orient. After 1460 the Turkish armies of Mehmet II conquered the Peloponnese, but the Venetians were able to hang on to Nauplion until 1540. They won it back again between 1684 and 1715, partly thanks to the Greeks, who supplied them with *stradioti* (soldiers). But the surrounding plains remained in Turkish hands, and the Turkish pasha, who was tolerant of Christians, lived in Nauplion. Earlier, in 1656, Capuchin monks had founded a church and a school in the town.

NAUPLION IN THE 19TH AND 20TH CENTURIES. Although there are only 10,000 inhabitants, Nauplion is tightly compressed by fortifications and is built on an orderly plan, very like that of Patras ▲ *360*. The streets are straight, and the neoclassical houses possess a certain elegance. Nauplion has three main areas of interest: the port, the historic old town, and on the crags high above it the castles – Greek, Frankish and

NAPOLI DI ROMANIA
The bastions built by the Venetians are emblazoned with inscriptions and bas-reliefs featuring the Lion of St Mark.

Nauplion is situated on the east side of the Gulf of Argos, on a narrow spit of land.

SYNTAGMA SQUARE AND THE FORTRESS OF PALAMIDI Drawing of the entrance to the fortress, 1896. In the foreground, a *palikare* dressed in the fustanella (Greek kilt) ● *71* is talking to soldiers from the garrison.

IOANNIS KAPODISTRIAS The first governor of Greece organized the administration, economy, army and public education of the new state during his period in office. Kapodistrias was assassinated in Nauplion on October 9, 1831, by the Mavromichalis brothers.

STAIKOS STAIKOPOULOS A hero of the War of Independence, memorialized in Nauplion.

Venetian – that make up Acronauplion and the Fortress of Palamidi. On Plateia Syntagma (Constitution Square) there is a monument to the French volunteers commanded by General Maison who took part in the War of Independence. The former Vouleftiko Mosque, the first seat of the Greek parliament, is at the southwest corner of the square. This is a lively shopping area with cafés filled with people in the evenings. The houses around it are neoclassical in style, with picturesque iron balconies.

THE WAR OF INDEPENDENCE. During the War of Independence, the Greek revolutionaries took Nauplion with the celebrated cry of "*Eleftheria i Thanatos*!" (Liberty or Death!) In 1821 the Greek heroine Bobolina blockaded Nauplion by land and sea for fourteen months, laying siege to the castle and citadel and repelling the sorties of the Turkish garrison. When they finally surrendered, the Turks used Bobolina as an intermediary during their negotiations with the Greek leaders. Nauplion then served as the capital of Greece for several years. The first Greek National Assembly met here in 1822, in the grey-and-white 16th-century Vouleftiko Mosque. After his election as first governor of the new Greek State, Ioannis Kapodistrias ● *51*, a descendant of the Venetians who arrived with the Franks, entered Nauplion in January 1823 amid wild jubilation. Eight years later he was assassinated in St Spiridon, a small white 18th-century church which can still be seen in the old town. When, after a period of anarchy, Otto (son of Ludwig I of Bavaria) was elected King of the Hellenes in 1833, he made the

> "I plan to rise with the sun so I can at last set eyes on the Gulf of Argos, Argos itself and Nauplion, the real capital of Greece."
>
> Alphonse de Lamartine

Fortress of Palamidi his palace. In a street in the center of the old town are several houses in the neo-Hellenic style; one of these, an austere two-story building, was occupied by Otto's regent, Von Armansperg. The capital was moved to Athens in 1834.

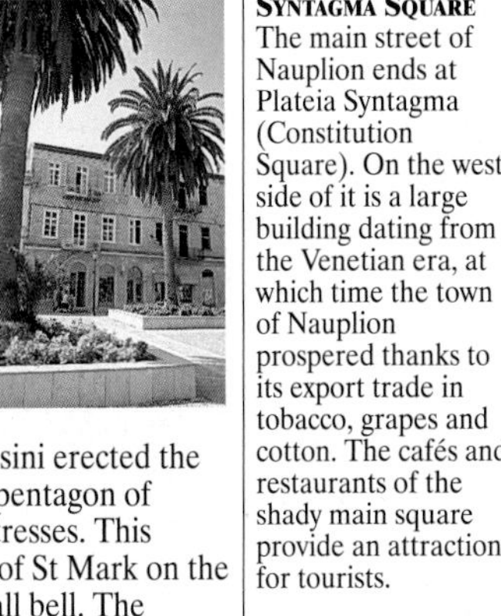

Syntagma Square
The main street of Nauplion ends at Plateia Syntagma (Constitution Square). On the west side of it is a large building dating from the Venetian era, at which time the town of Nauplion prospered thanks to its export trade in tobacco, grapes and cotton. The cafés and restaurants of the shady main square provide an attraction for tourists.

The Fortress of Palamidi

This stronghold was built by the Venetians in the 18th century 700 feet above sea level. The Venetian admiral Morosini erected the ramparts, which can still be seen, forming a pentagon of outworks connecting seven independent fortresses. This explains the presence of a magnificent Lion of St Mark on the main gateway, which is surmounted by a small bell. The complex was built in four years, in 1711–14, by the French colonel La Salle, to plans by a Dalmatian engineer, Giaxich. The courtyards are now deserted and even the most recent buildings, constructed by the Turks and later used as a prison, have been demolished. The best time to visit the fortress is early in the morning, by way of the nine hundred steps from Nikitara Square; however, the climb is exhausting, and the fortress can also be reached by car via a turning off the Epidaurus road.

The Bavarian Lion. On the way up to the fortress you can see the sculptor Siegel's bas-relief of a lion, cut from the rock, which symbolizes the arms of the royal house of Bavaria and is dedicated to the memory of the Bavarian soldiers killed defending the rights of King Otto in 1833 and 1834. But the real reward for the arduous climb is the view of the Bay of Nauplion and, on the landward side, of the mountains and the Argolic plain with the Inachos River flowing through it.

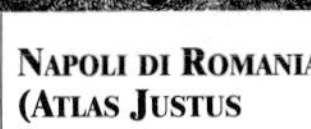

Napoli di Romania (Atlas Justus Dankerts)
Nauplion fell into Venetian hands in 1686. The construction of the small fortress in the bay dates from this time.

Early travelers
This pretty, busy little port has always been a magnet for travelers. The private houses were elegant, while the shops built by the Venetians and Kapodistrias' government palace gave the town the aura of a genuine capital.

The old Venetian arsenal on Syntagma Square is now the Nauplion Archeological Museum. The ceramics, vases, statuettes, frescos and bronzes on display are derived from the great palaces of the Mycenean world: Mycenae itself, Tiryns, Mideia and Asine. These palaces were inhabited by warriors, as shown by the suit of armor found at Mideia and the many weapons found here. The art of the period is most notable for the vases decorated with figures, which replaced geometrical patterns.

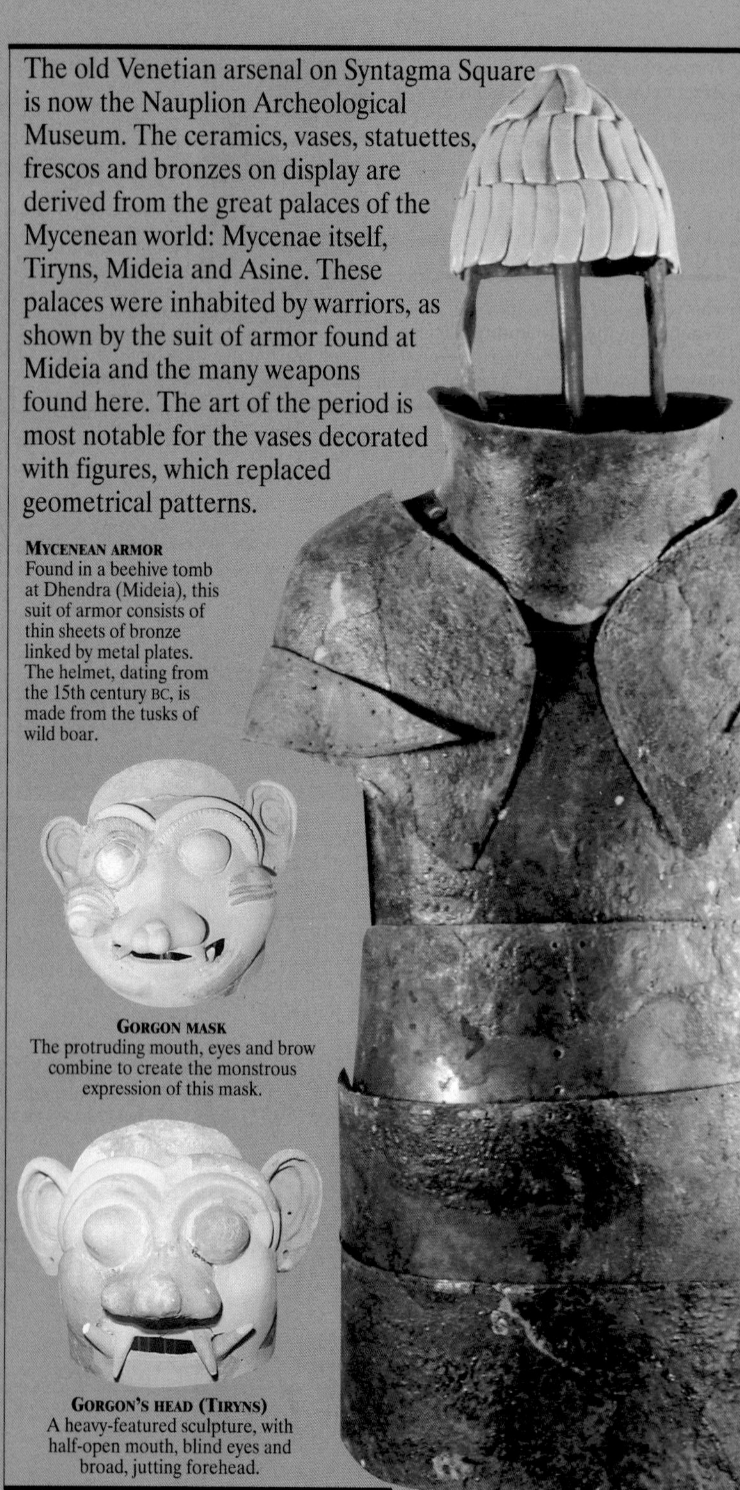

MYCENEAN ARMOR
Found in a beehive tomb at Dhendra (Mideia), this suit of armor consists of thin sheets of bronze linked by metal plates. The helmet, dating from the 15th century BC, is made from the tusks of wild boar.

GORGON MASK
The protruding mouth, eyes and brow combine to create the monstrous expression of this mask.

GORGON'S HEAD (TIRYNS)
A heavy-featured sculpture, with half-open mouth, blind eyes and broad, jutting forehead.

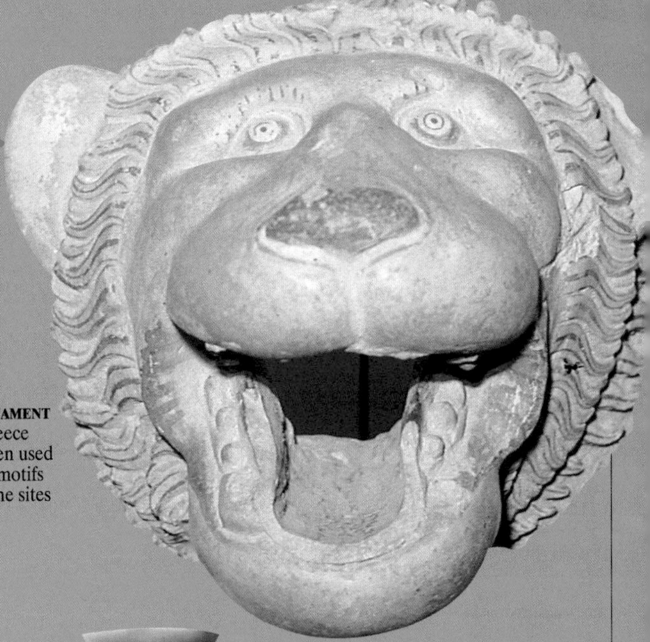

Lion's head, fountain ornament
In ancient Greece lions were often used as decorative motifs and to mark the sites of tombs.

Black-figure amphora
In the 7th century BC, artists began to paint pottery with humans and animals, using the black-figure technique.

"Bell-shaped" krater
A vase decorated with the red-figure technique, showing heroes and gods in sophisticated perspective.

A Mycenean princess
This fresco, found at Mycenae, dates from the 13th century BC. The woman is wearing a royal head dress, of blue edged with red, and holds a small sheaf of wheat. The bright colors closely resemble those of the fragment of fresco ▲ *305* found in 1970 in a house on the western rampart of the Acropolis of Mycenae, now in the National Archeological Museum in Athens.

THE STREETS OF NAUPLION
In general Nauplion's streets are narrow; and those close to the sea are steep as well, many of them connected to each other by flights of steps. Here you will find old houses with overhanging upper stories, and fountains built by the Turks.

GETTING TO NAUPLION
"There are three ways to reach Nauplion, in the Argolis, the houses of which may be seen to the northwest from the height of Palamidi. The first is by carriage along the royal thoroughfare; the second is on horse-back along the coast, skirting the bay as far as Myli, whence Argos is but one hour's ride; the third by sea to Myli, and thereafter by horse. At five in the morning we left the port in a deckless boat; the breeze blowing off the coast filled our square sail, rigged to the mast on the diagonal, a characteristic of Greek vessels."
H. Belle, 1874

"PEOPLE OF NAUPLION, TAKE COURAGE!"

THE ARCHEOLOGICAL MUSEUM

The Archeological Museum ▲ *312* on Nauplion's Syntagma Square makes a fitting conclusion to any tour of the Mycenean sites. It is installed on two floors of a handsome yellow-stucco Venetian arsenal building, which dates from the early 18th century. The collections are displayed chronologically.

MUSEUM OF THE PELOPONNESIAN FOLKLORE FOUNDATION. Nauplion's other small museum (off Ypsilantou Street, between the port and Syntagma Square) belongs to the Folklore Foundation. Here the emphasis is on traditional crafts, fabrics, costumes and jewelry. From the Mycenean era onward the weaving of linen and wool was one of the great contributions of women to the economy, as is clear from tablets discovered at Pylos. Historians believe that in ancient times fabrics and carpets were probably exported from this area. Later, cotton and silk were among the major products of the Peloponnese. During the 19th century travelers invariably praised the beauty and richness of the clothes worn by Greeks on feast days, and to this day many Greek women remain highly skilled in embroidery.

THE CITADEL OF ACRONAUPLION

The citadel stands at the end of the promontory, below the Fortress of Palamidi, and may be reached from Nikitara Square. The only ancient remains here are the original walls of polygonal stones. These were successively built upon by the Byzantines and the Franks, the latter developing a coherent defense system here shortly before 1210. In the 15th century the Venetians built a two-towered castello and in the 18th century strengthened the Byzantine works to the north, adding a monumental gateway; at about the same time the castle defenses were augmented by the Grimani bastion, which completed the link with the town walls and the

nine-hundred-step stairway leading to the Fortress of Palamidi up above. The citadel of Acronauplion included a barracks, a prison and a hospital; but today the most impressive thing is the view. To provide additional military support the Venetians built a small fort on the islet of Bourdzi, so they would have warning of seaborne attacks and could catch enemy ships in their crossfire. Like its neighbor, the citadel of Acronauplion has beautiful panoramic views.

The port and the Islet of Bourdzi

Today Nauplion is a naval base and a lively local center, with cafés and shops lining the waterfront. The port area has much to recommend it, with tavernas that serve freshly caught fish, and bustling cafés from which you can watch the sunset beyond the Castel da Mar, on Bourdzi, built by the Venetians in the 15th century. This fort lies some 400 yards offshore and is now one of the most picturesque hotels in Greece.

Beaches on the Gulf of Argos. Nauplion has only one small beach, at Arvanitia; but about 2 miles further along the road out of town, past the Fortress of Palamidi, is the magnificent Karathona beach, bordered with eucalyptus trees. About 5 miles beyond this there is another fine beach, at Tolon, on a narrow peninsula projecting into the Gulf of Argos. With such facilities nearby and its pleasant sea breeze, it is not surprising that Nauplion is a popular holiday resort. Byron lingered here during his grand tour of the Peloponnese; and nowadays travelers tend to use Nauplion as a base where they can stay for a few days in order to explore the great sites of Mycenae, Argos, Tiryns and Epidaurus.

Bourdzi
Designed to shield Nauplion from attack from the sea, the fortress on Bourdzi was linked to the land by a jetty. On the ruins of the Venetian walls, the Turks built a stronghold where ships were obliged to halt in order to pay their harbor dues. In the 19th century the public executioner was lodged here, kept well away from the town out of superstition. The plain surrounding Nauplion is marshy and covered with nurseries, vineyards and wheatfields. In contrast to the dryness and bareness of the nearby mountains, ranks of poplars, rushes and fruit trees form a green belt around the bay.

The port of Nauplion in 1928

The site
The site includes the theater and the principal buildings of the sanctuary. Today it is entered from the south, though in ancient times the entrance was on the north side.

The sanctuary of Epidaurus ★

One of the most beautiful sites in Greece, about 5 miles inland from the coast and less than 20 miles from Nauplion, can be reached by taking the road which runs along Mount Araknaion.

The Temple of Asklepios. A temple dedicated to Apollo Maleatas, a god invoked by convalescents, was built in the 7th century BC on a Mycenean holy site on Mount Kynortion, close to the future theater. Apart from a few steps surrounded by bushes, practically nothing remains of this today, although it was still in use in Roman times. The temple was supplanted in the 6th century by the sanctuary of Asklepios, whose cult originated in Thessaly. This god was reputed to have succeeded in bringing the dead to life, for which crime he was smitten with a thunderbolt by Zeus and transformed by Apollo into the constellation of Serpentaria. The emblems of Asklepios were a snake coiled around a rod, bay leaves, a dog and pine cones. His cult gave birth to a school of medicine run by the priests at his sanctuary and to the creation of a hospital with a dormitory where the sick were treated.

The sacred fountain. Arriving by the Sacred Way, pilgrims entered the *propylaea* and offered sacrifices in goods or in coin. They purified themselves at the sacred fountain, and then submitted to special diets, baths and magic rituals. The medical instruments in the museum show that surgical operations were performed here, at least in Roman times.

The Tholos. A *tholos* was built behind the temple around 360 BC. Larger than the one at Delphi ▲ *273*, it had twenty-six exterior columns in the Doric style and fourteen interior ones, with capitals embellished with acanthus leaves, in the

The Temple of Asklepios
This reconstruction by Alphonse Defrasse of 1891–3 offers a general view of the *hieron* (sanctuary) of Asklepios (5th and 6th centuries BC), with sculptures in Pentelic marble. The tufa cornice and painted ornaments have been restored from traces of color found at the site.

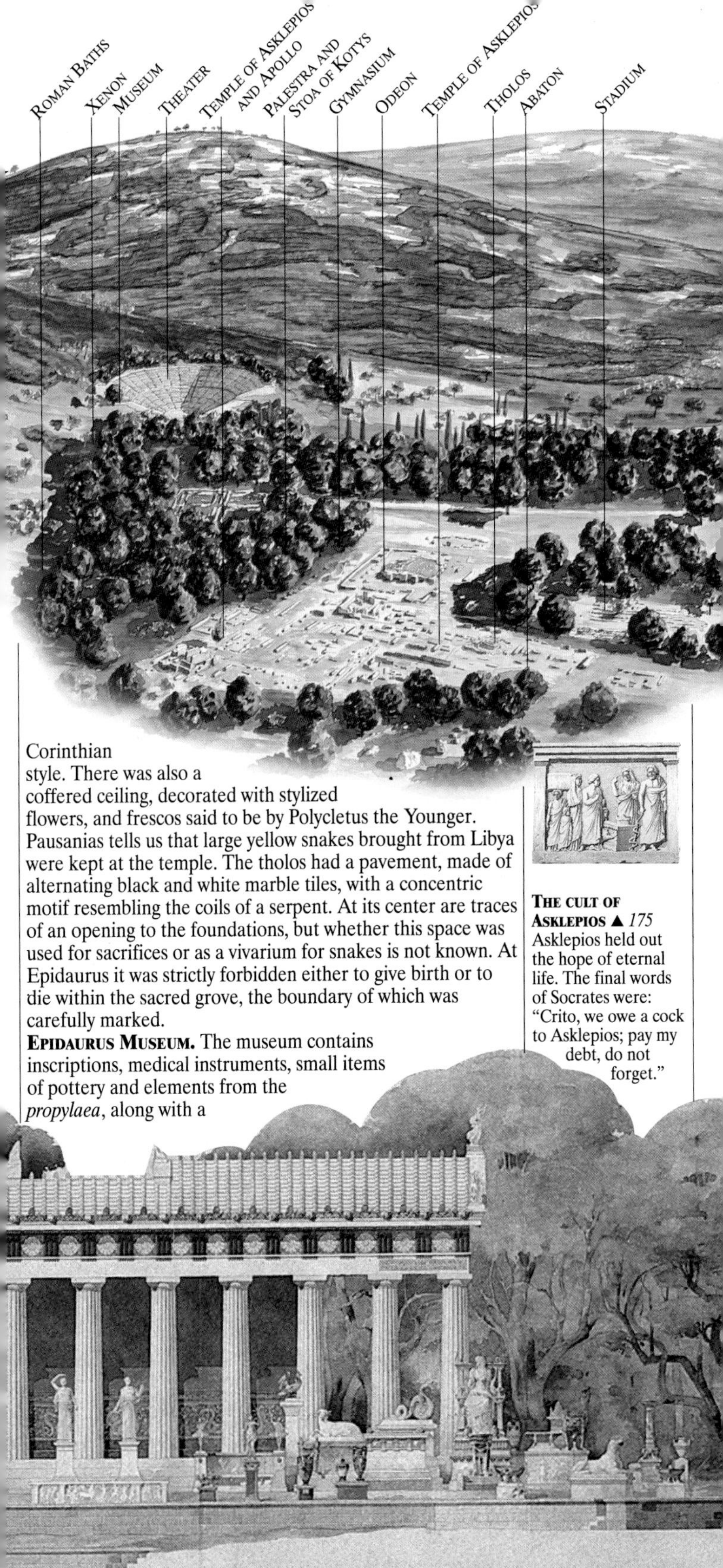

Corinthian style. There was also a coffered ceiling, decorated with stylized flowers, and frescos said to be by Polycletus the Younger. Pausanias tells us that large yellow snakes brought from Libya were kept at the temple. The tholos had a pavement, made of alternating black and white marble tiles, with a concentric motif resembling the coils of a serpent. At its center are traces of an opening to the foundations, but whether this space was used for sacrifices or as a vivarium for snakes is not known. At Epidaurus it was strictly forbidden either to give birth or to die within the sacred grove, the boundary of which was carefully marked.

Epidaurus Museum. The museum contains inscriptions, medical instruments, small items of pottery and elements from the *propylaea*, along with a

The cult of Asklepios ▲ *175*
Asklepios held out the hope of eternal life. The final words of Socrates were: "Crito, we owe a cock to Asklepios; pay my debt, do not forget."

THE COFFERING OF THE THOLOS
The painted coffering of the ceiling was decorated with plant motifs. The archives of the temple mention the work of gilding some of these features.

THE THOLOS
Inside there were Pentelic-marble Corinthian columns, a black-and-white pavement of Eleusis marble, and tufa walls. The tufa foundations rested on a solid-rock base.

partial reconstruction of the tholos and of one of the original Corinthian capitals, which make it easier to appreciate the site. The finest pieces unearthed at Epidaurus are now in the National Archeological Museum in Athens: these include acroters and floral sculptures from the façade, as well as nereids on horseback, a statue of Hygieia (the daughter of Asklepios and goddess of health) and one of Penthesileia, Queen of the Amazons, who helped the Trojans after the death of Hector and was slain by Achilles, to his great regret.

THE GYMNASIUM AND THE PALESTRA. In ancient times, every four years and nine days after the Isthmian Games, athletes gathered at Epidaurus to celebrate the Asklepieia. For this festival they had at their disposal a gymnasium, the *palestra* and Stoa of Kotys, and from the 5th century AD a stadium, where you can still see the starting lines, the race lanes (just under 200 yards long) and tiers of seats cut into the rock. After attending the various athletic events, horse races and poetry competitions, the pilgrims repaired to the theater.

THE THEATER ● *81*. In designing a theater for more than thirteen thousand spectators, the architects (who included Polycletus the Younger) based their calculations on the Golden Section. They maintained a ratio of 0.618 between the upper and lower tiers, so the ratio between the smaller and larger of these two areas would be the same as that between the larger area and the whole. The *orchestra* ▲ *172*, or stage, which is more than 30 feet in diameter, forms a full circle, a rarity in Greece. The rows of seats are built around it, while the two aisles dividing the fifty-five rows of the *cavea*, with twenty-one rows above and thirty-four below, both have a width of 4 ells (the ancient Greek measurement of an ell is

Reconstruction of the monument "as it would be if its component parts were put back in their original places". A. Defrasse, 1893

"I HAD TO GO TO EPIDAURUS TO DISCOVER THE TRUE MEANING OF PEACE."

HENRY MILLER

THE THEATER
"It was the work of Polycletus", writes Buchon, "at about the time of the 90th Olympiad; and it surpassed all others by its elegant and generous proportions and the beauty of its building materials. Most of the tiers of seats still survive. The beautiful marble of which they are made covers the flank of the hill, amid a wealth of greenery."

just over 1½ feet). The spectators (who sat on the first wooden steps from around 550 BC) watched as a storyteller recited a tale punctuated by the comments of the chorus. Over the years they saw tragedies by Aeschylus, Sophocles and Euripides, who drew their heroes – Agamemnon, Orestes, Electra, Andromache and Oedipus – from Greek myths and Homer. Comedy, chiefly represented by Aristophanes, satirized contemporaries and contemporary political morality, as in *The Wasps*. In the earliest tragedies the *koryphaios* (leader of the chorus) carried on a dialogue with the principal characters, while the chorus supplied a running commentary and drew a moral from the events as they unfolded. The chorus' function was to transcend the preoccupations of ordinary mortals; sometimes it acted as a mouthpiece for the gods, who would intervene in the lives of their protégés or of those they meant to punish. The sanctuary and theater of Epidaurus were in constant use until the 4th century AD. The cult of Asklepios, which had become an obstacle to the spread of Christianity, was abolished under Emperor Theodosius the Great (346–95).

THE FESTIVAL OF EPIDAURUS. Since 1955 the annual Festival of Epidaurus (June to September) has been continuously successful. The great Greek soprano Maria Callas contributed to this success by coming here to sing in Bellini's *Norma*. The beautiful amphitheater, with its extraordinary acoustics, owes its survival to the pinewoods that covered it for centuries.

(Make your way back to Corinth, about 45 miles, either by the corniche road around the Saronic Gulf or by the inland highway via Argos.)

THE GODDESS ATHENA
This statue is displayed in the Epidaurus Museum.

THE PLAIN OF ARGOS
A majestic landscape, with vineyards, olive trees and gray-tinted hills running down to the sea.

ARGOS

Argos, along with the smaller towns of Mycenae, Tiryns and Nauplion which it subjugated, was founded by the Dorians. The town lies in a fertile plain at the foot of Mount Chaon, which is the site of a Byzantine, Frankish and Turkish fortress built on the ancient ramparts of two acropolises. These acropolises, Aspis and Larissa, may be reached by a road leading from the center of the modern city. Largely destroyed during the War of Independence ● *51*, Argos was rebuilt during the 19th century, with broad streets fronted by private houses and shops. Today the population stands at about twenty thousand people, and the town remains much the size it was in ancient times.

THE ACROPOLIS
Argos was one of the settlements perched high in the hills that appeared at the start of the Bronze Age and were later fortified (around the 13th century BC).

THE THEATER. Argos' principal monument is its ancient theater. Located just outside town on the road to Tripolis, it was excavated by the archeologists of the French School of Athens. It dates from the end of the 4th century BC. Much larger than those at Delphi and Epidaurus, it could accommodate twenty thousand spectators and was cut into the side of Mount Chaon. On the main square of Argos is the town's museum, with a rich collection of Mycenean objects.

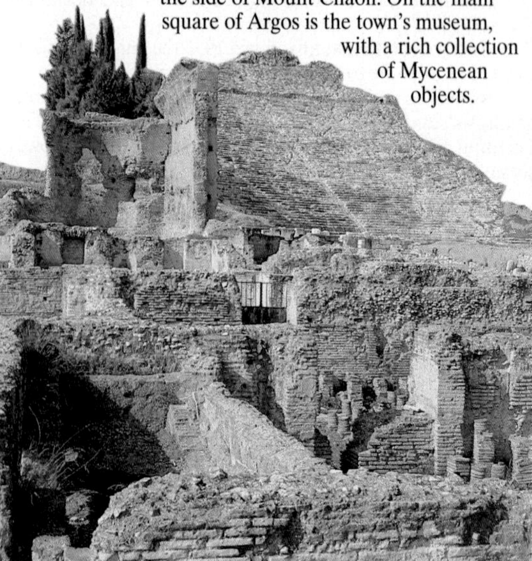

THE THEATER AND BATHS AT ARGOS
The baths date from the Roman era. The theater, cut into the flank of the mountain, is the largest in Greece. It was restored during the reign of Hadrian, and today is dominated by the citadel of Kastro, which can be reached from the Odeon (near the Roman aqueduct) by way of a footpath.

From the Argolis to Arcadia

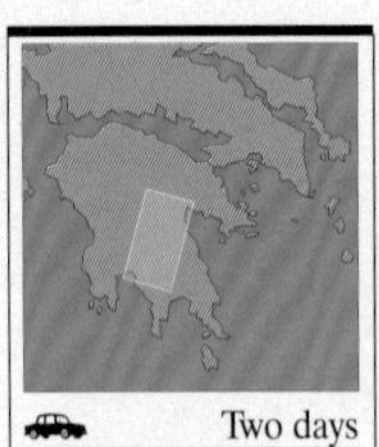

Two days

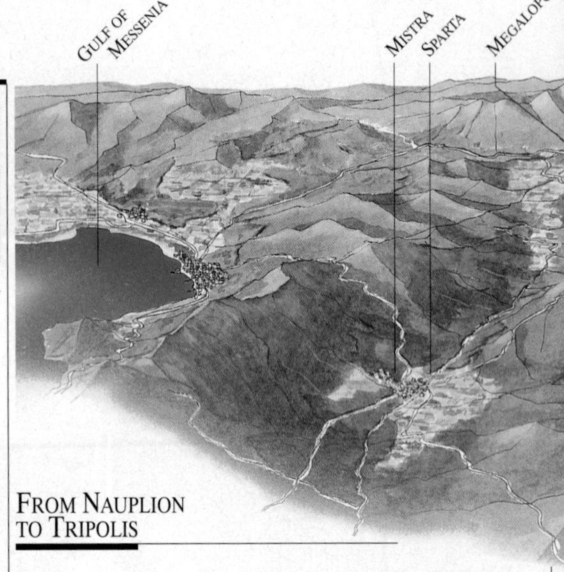

FROM NAUPLION TO TRIPOLIS

The coast road from Nauplion runs along the northernmost bay of the Gulf of Argolis, by way of Nea Kios and Myli, to Lerna.

LERNA. The ancient site of Lerna was discovered on a hill to the south of the village of Myli, by the sea. It was occupied from the 4th millennium BC until the end of the Mycenean era. Excavations, undertaken by the American School in the 1950's, brought to light many significant finds, the most important of which was a large building which predates the coming of the Greeks and has been dated to the middle period of the Bronze Age (2600–2200 BC). This is the House of the Tiles, so called because its gently sloping roof was covered with slates and terracotta tiles set in lime. To judge by its size (about 82 x 40 feet), it may have been the abode of a prince: in addition to a suite of three ground-floor rooms, it had an upper floor and was fortified against attackers.

It appears to have been burned down, then rebuilt in the late period of the Early Bronze Age. Trojan pottery has been unearthed on the site and on the strata corresponding to the Middle Bronze Age (2000–1580 BC). Shards of pottery from the Balkans, Crete and the Cyclades have been found. Around 1650 BC the entire structure was buried under a mound in which two royal tombs were dug by the Myceneans. Tombs from the Geometric period (1000–800 BC) have also been excavated on the southwest side of the site.

TRIPOLIS. A little to the south of Myli, the main road runs inland to Tripolis, the capital of Arcadia. Tripolis ("three towns") corresponds to the territories of the three ancient fortresses of Tegea, Mantinea and Pallantion and all the surrounding plain.

TRIPOLIS
Under the Venetians, Tripolis became the principal town of the Morea, known as Tripolitsa. Then in 1770 it was made the capital of the Turkish *pashalik* of the Peloponnese. Taken by the Klepht leader Theodore Kolokotronis at the head of the Greek army (1821), it was burnt to the ground by Ibrahim Pasha in 1827. Three years later, after Independence, the town was entirely rebuilt.

EASTER ● *66*
In the Orthodox Church it is customary to color Easter eggs red and eat them after the

SPARTA, CAPITAL OF LACONIA

Leaving Tripolis, drive due south to Sparta, about 37 miles away. The dearth of fine monuments here – a dearth which visitors were already complaining about even in ancient times – reflects the ideal of austerity that Sparta cultivated from her earliest origins. Lycurgus, the great Spartan lawgiver, believed that the ornamentation of public buildings distracted the attention of citizens when they gathered to deliberate.

THE MENELAION. Any disappointment in Sparta may be alleviated by a visit to the Menelaion hill at sunset. The view from this spur at the end of the chain of mountains overlooking the city from the east gives a clear idea of Sparta's natural site, the valley of the Eurotas River ■ *28*, whose bed winds among the hills blanketed with olive groves beneath the Taygetos Mountains.

SHRINE OF HELEN AND MENELAUS
This structure, now razed to the ground, once towered more than 30 feet above the hilltop.

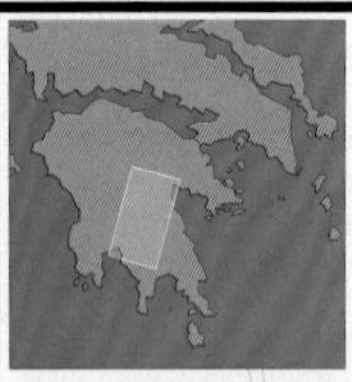

Two days

Mount Taygetos
The tallest mountain in the Peloponnese (almost 8,000 feet high), Mount Taygetos dominates the entire plain of Sparta.

The shrine of Helen and Menelaus. The Menelaion Hill owes its name to the shrine of Helen and Menelaus, built by the Spartans during the Archaic period in memory of the legendary royal couple – to which this place was already dedicated at the time of the Geometric era, as is proven by the many *ex votos* in bronze, lead and terracotta found here: a bronze perfume bottle, for instance, is inscribed "to Helen and Menelaus". The shrine, rebuilt in the 5th century BC, was in use until the Hellenistic era, and its ruins have remained visible ever since. It was excavated several times between 1839 and 1977; it consisted of a small temple of white tufa built on a platform. This was surrounded by an exedra in bluish limestone, resting on high supporting stone walls. The entrance, from the west, was by way of a steep ramp. It was no accident that the Spartans chose this spot to honor the memory of the heroes whose heirs they claimed to be; for it appears that several centuries earlier the Menelaion lay at the center of the Mycenean sphere of influence. Moreover, it is known that the heroic cults which emerged in Greece at the end of the Geometric era tended to take root in the places where heroes were thought to have lived or been buried.

Sparta Museum
The neoclassical museum, built in the town center between 1875 and 1876, exhibits objects and implements found at sites in the region.

The palace. Less than 100 yards northeast of the Shrine of Helen and Menelaus, recent excavations have uncovered the principal architectural ensemble of the Mycenean era. This proved to be a huge building dating from about the middle of the 15th century BC, which had to be rebuilt shortly afterward, probably as a result of an earthquake. It was altered to some extent to limit damage from further tremors, though the main features were retained: these were a central unit made up of a porch, a vestibule and a spacious inner hall, framed by two wings subdivided into several more rooms. This *megaron*-type design was clearly a forerunner of the palaces of Tiryns ▲ *307*, Mycenae ▲ *304* and Pylos, predating them by about a hundred years. No doubt the Menelaion was the administrative center for the area and the residence of the chief. Did the Spartans from the later, historic epoch know it as the Palace of Menelaus, or his tomb, when they came here to found the sanctuary which bears his name? Or might there have been another such palace built in the vicinity roughly a hundred years later, which has now vanished without trace?

Archaic amphora (late 7th century BC)
This large terracotta funerary amphora is on display at the Sparta Museum. It is decorated in relief with a hunting scene and a procession of chariots.

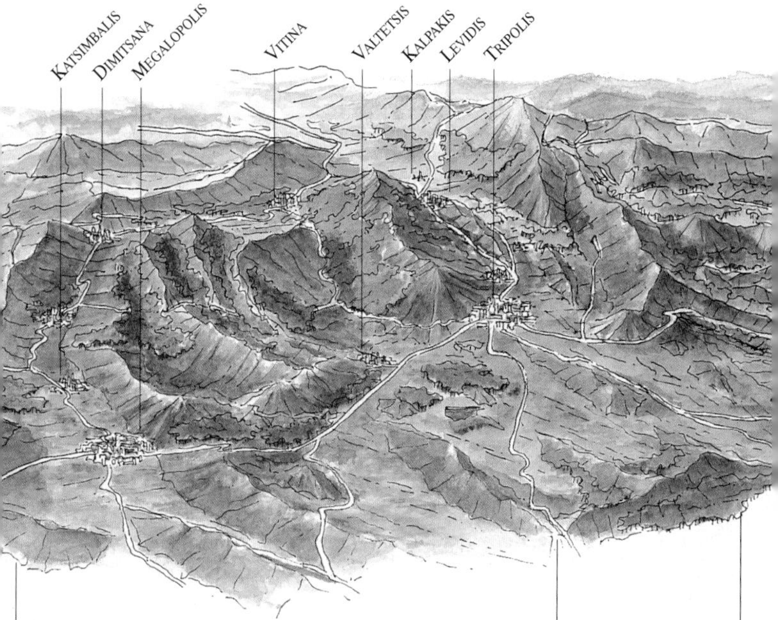

KATSIMBALIS DIMITSANA MEGALOPOLIS VITINA VALTETSIS KALPAKIS LEVIDIS TRIPOLIS

FROM TRIPOLIS TO ANDRITSAINA

From Tripolis, take the road to Megalopolis (situated about 22 miles to the southwest).

MEGALOPOLIS. With only five thousand inhabitants, the "Great City" no longer quite deserves its name. The ruins of the ancient town cover a wide area north of the modern one; it was founded by the Theban Epaminondas three years after his victory over the Spartans at Leuctria (371 BC) ● *46*, with a view to creating a capital city for the Pan-Arcadian League. Its theater was the biggest in Greece. The Romans added a stone stage (*proscenium*), and a wall and overhanging cornice. During the festivals held on August 15 each year, tragedies are performed here. The Pan-Arcadian Assembly of the Ten Thousand customarily met at the adjoining Thersilion to elect its fifty-member federal council. The Thersilion, dating from the foundation of Megalopolis, remained in use until the sack of Megalopolis by the Spartans in 223; it was never rebuilt and today nothing remains of it save its foundations and the bases of one or two columns. Past the shrine of Zeus Soter ("Zeus the Savior") and the Portico of Philip, likewise in ruins, the way leads on to the market place on the west side of the city, which was also named after Philip of Macedon. To the east of the Agora the Myropolis Stoa, built for Aristodemos, led through to Megalopolis' celebrated perfume market. Of the ancient city's many other temples, variously dedicated to Demeter, Persephone, Dionysos and Asklepios, nothing has survived to the present day but a few altars.

MEGALOPOLIS TO ANDRITSAINA. Halfway between Megalopolis and Andritsaina is the village of Karitaina, perched nearly 2,000 feet above the gorge of the Alpheios River. Karitaina is dominated by the ruins of a Frankish castle. The view from here is stunning.

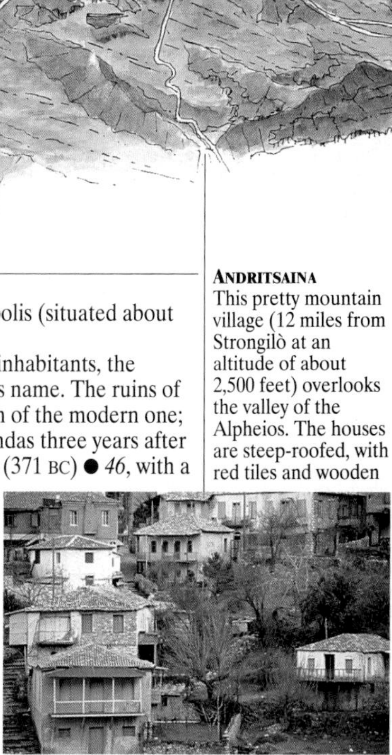

ANDRITSAINA
This pretty mountain village (12 miles from Strongilò at an altitude of about 2,500 feet) overlooks the valley of the Alpheios. The houses are steep-roofed, with red tiles and wooden balconies; the village's pride and joy is a library of over 25,000 books, some of them very rare, which was founded in 1840 by Agatrophos Nikolopoulos, a former assistant at the library of the Institut de Paris. Andritsaina also has a museum containing artifacts found on neighboring archeological sites.

THE TEMPLE OF BASSAE

Andritsaina is the best departure point for a visit to the Temple of Apollo Epikourios, 9 miles to the south, at Bassae. This is one of Greece's best preserved shrines. It was built in about 450 BC to a design by Ictinos, one of the architects who later contributed to the Parthenon. He was in charge of the works here until 447 BC. Construction was halted at that time, and it was not until 425 BC that the temple was completed, by another architect who modified Ictinos' original plan.

The interior of the *cella* has two rows of five slender half-columns with eleven flutings each, standing on broad bases. The engaged columns back onto quadrangular pillars, which are fixed to the walls with T-shaped metal studs. The four front columns on either side are topped by Ionic capitals, but the last pair were Corinthian in style – as was a third, isolated, column that served as a separation between the *cella* and the *adyton* and is the earliest known example of a Corinthian column ● *85*.

STRUCTURE OF THE TEMPLE. The floor plan is oriented north-south (as opposed to the traditional east-west). The *cella* has no back wall; instead it opens onto a rectangular room and also has an opening to the east. In all probability this *adyton* replaced an earlier chapel that was oriented eastward, and the doorway faced east so the morning sun shining through it would illuminate the statue of Apollo. On the outside, this peripteral ● *90*, hexastyle temple belongs to the Doric order. 125 feet long by 48 feet wide, it has six sets of fifteen columns, as well as the usual columns *in antis* of the *pronaos* and *opisthodomos*. The drums of the fallen columns have been re-erected, so today the only missing column is the one at the southeast corner of the building.

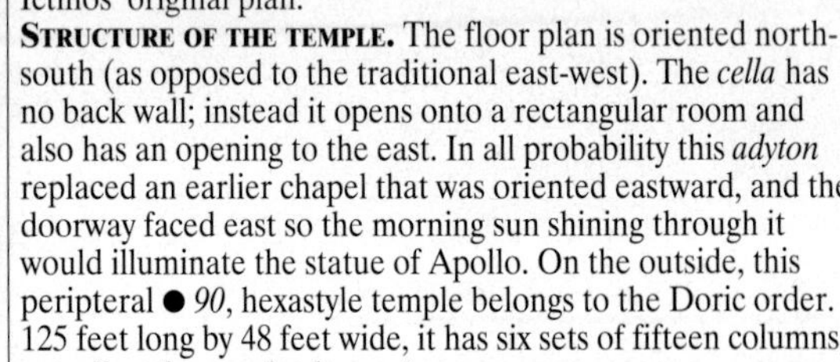

DECORATION. The frieze was unique for its time in style: the surviving fragments are in the British Museum. There was once a monumental bronze statue of Apollo, which was later replaced by a wooden one with marble head, hands and feet. Six metopes, adorned with bas-reliefs, embellished the coping of the *pronaos* and *opisthodomos*, but nothing remains of these save a few damaged fragments. It would seem that the pediments were prepared to accommodate sculptures, but none have been found here.

Arcadia, the mythical backdrop for Theocritus' *Idylls* and Virgil's *Bucolics*, is also "a closed, mountain country, where night and day the sky swoops low" (George Seferis). In spring Arcadia is lush with a rich mantle of oak and ivy, olive groves and fruit orchards; and the soft meadows and terraced hills attest to man's patient conquest of the land. Nevertheless, Arcadia has its hard, ruthless side: the men of this region, descendants of the ancient Achaeans, figured prominently in the hard-fought War of Independence against the Turks in the early 19th century.

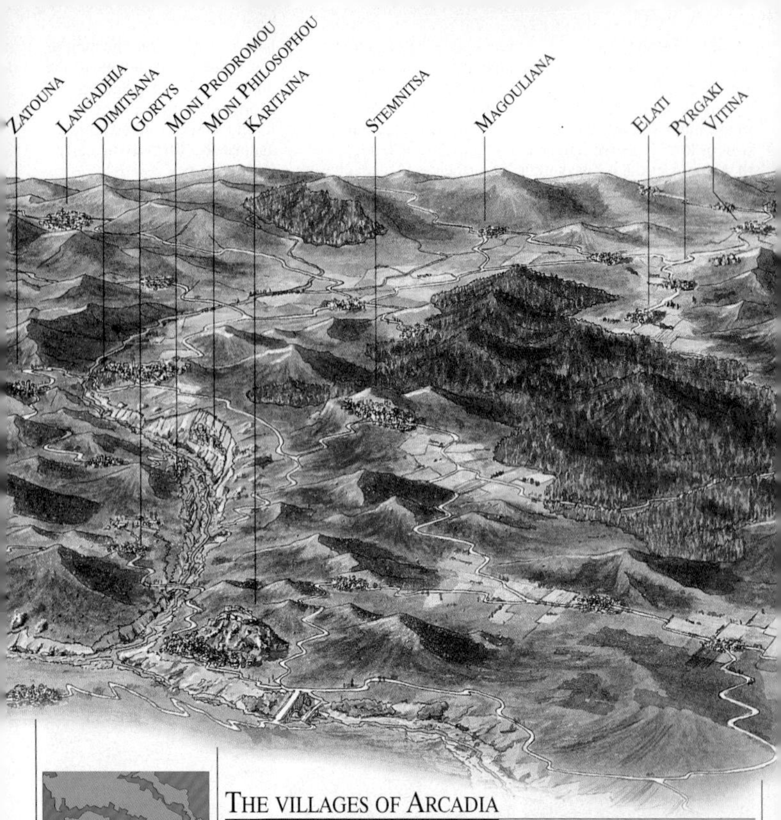

Zatouna
Langadhia
Dimitsana
Gortys
Moni Prodromou
Moni Philosophou
Karitaina
Stemnitsa
Magouliana
Elati
Pyrgaki
Vitina

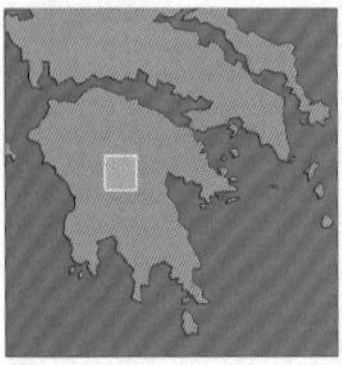

Two days

Western Arcadia, or Kynouria, was a wholly pastoral region until recently; there are still very few tourists here. The wild mountain landscape is a blend of pine forest, pasture, deep gorges, cultivated plains and valley bottoms. This is a country of scattered villages, with massive stone houses built hard against steep slopes, and monasteries on cliff tops overlooking the Loussios.

The villages of Arcadia

In the heart of Arcadia there are a number of small towns and villages, which are semi-deserted in the winter but full of people in the summer. Religious festivals, notably Easter ● *66*, are the traditional occasions for family reunions, here as elsewhere in Greece.

Langadhia. About 45 miles from Tripolis, on the road to Pyrgos, is the mountain town of Langadhia, overlooking a deep valley. The economic center of the region and a magnet for tourists, Langadhia is also one of the nomes (administrative sectors) of Arcadia. It has four churches, around which are clustered small groups of carefully painted, lovingly maintained houses. Their modest aspect contrasts with the imposing Arcadian mansions built by the village's stonemasons, whose skill was a byword throughout Greece. The shops, cafés and restaurants are grouped on either side of the main street, which cuts through the middle of the village.

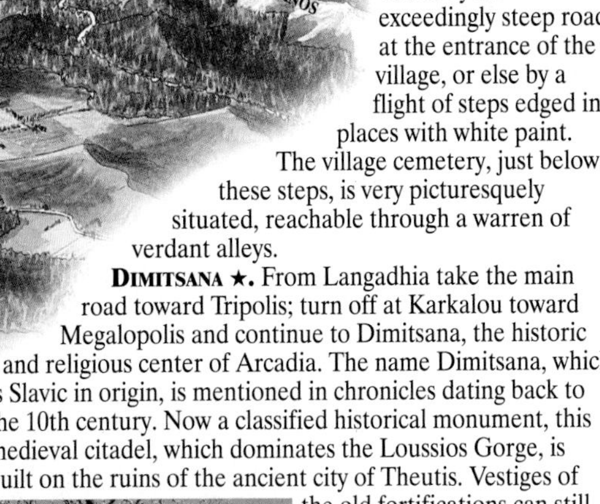

You can reach the high part of Langadhia either by an exceedingly steep road at the entrance of the village, or else by a flight of steps edged in places with white paint. The village cemetery, just below these steps, is very picturesquely situated, reachable through a warren of verdant alleys.

DIMITSANA ★. From Langadhia take the main road toward Tripolis; turn off at Karkalou toward Megalopolis and continue to Dimitsana, the historic and religious center of Arcadia. The name Dimitsana, which is Slavic in origin, is mentioned in chronicles dating back to the 10th century. Now a classified historical monument, this medieval citadel, which dominates the Loussios Gorge, is built on the ruins of the ancient city of Theutis. Vestiges of the old fortifications can still be seen; elsewhere there are three distinct eras of construction. The oldest is the ancient acropolis, in the Kastro quarter; then comes Platza, just below, which is medieval and Venetian; and finally there are the "modern" quarters, dating from the 18th and 19th centuries. Around the main square, with its shops and cafés, a maze of streets leads through the medieval Venetian district. A small ecclesiastical museum exists in the house where a hero of the Independence struggle, the Patriarch of Constantinople, Gregory IV, was born; it contains a number of icons and religious objects from all over the region. Two illustrious revolutionary families, the Kolokotronis ▲ *234* and Deligiannis families, originally came from Dimitsana; indeed there is hardly a village in the whole area that does not honor the memory of its own particular hero of the War of Independence.

ZATOUNA. The village of Zatouna, opposite Dimitsana, has been virtually abandoned by its people, most of whom emigrated to Australia or America to seek their fortunes. Those who succeeded have paid for the restoration of the village's fountains and churches, as their inscriptions attest. Geese and chickens have colonized magnificent buildings that are gradually falling into ruin, and the narrow alleys are completely silent.

SOUVENIR VENDOR AT LANGADHIA
Here there are no postcards of the Parthenon by night and no hoplites' helmets made of tin – only a craftsman at the entrance to the village, who will try to sell you a shepherd's crook and handmade wooden spoons.

DIMITSANA
The main square of Dimitsana has changed little since this photograph was taken.

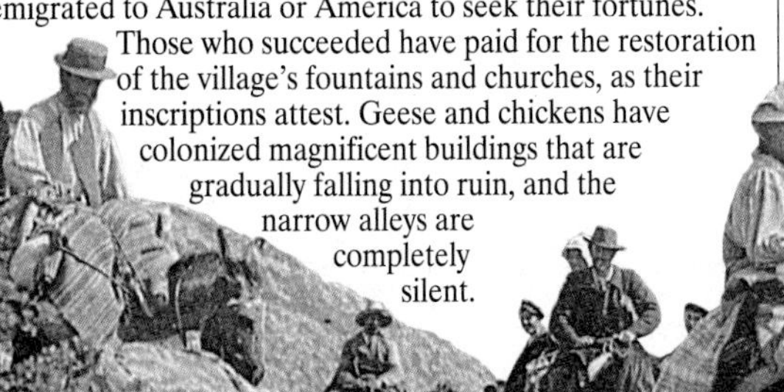

In the last century it was hazardous to travel through Arcadia; nowadays there is a scanty but sufficient infrastructure of hotels, and the road network has improved immeasurably.

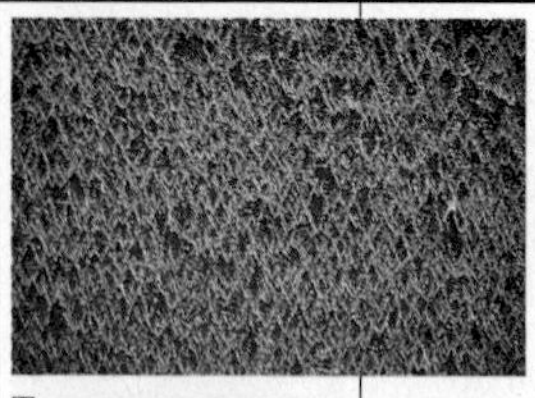

THE ROAD THROUGH THE PINES.
Nearly 8 miles from Stemnitsa toward Tripolis, a road to the left passes through a forest of Cephalonian pines at an altitude varying between 2,500 and 5,000 feet. During the War of Independence the partisans of the Arcadian general Kolokotronis took refuge here. Kolokotronis himself was born in the vicinity, in the village of Magouliana to the north.

The Loussios is a tributary of the River Alpheios that runs through the valley of Olympia and that Hercules is said to have diverted to clean the Augean stables.

In the eyes of the few remaining people, tourists seem like travelers from another world.

STEMNITSA. Just over 6 miles south of Dimitsana, on the road to Megalopolis, is Stemnitsa, still known locally as Ipsounda or Ipsos. This village stands at the bottom of a deep gorge; above it is a rocky spur, crowned by a monument to the dead. There is a fine view from the belvedere, across the Loussios Valley and the plain surrounding Megalopolis. The village has an interesting ethnographic museum in one of its spacious traditional houses.

THE LOUSSIOS GORGE

Dimitsana is an excellent point of departure for an excursion along the rocky and picturesque Loussios Gorge. On the way out of the village, take the road to Stemnitsa (Ipsounda) and then to Palaiokhora, just under 2 miles farther on. As you come into this small town, turn right along an unpaved road, which leads to three interesting monasteries: Moni Aimyalou, Moni Ioanni Prodromou and Moni Philosophou. At the next fork, the track on the left leads to Moni Prodromou and the one on the right to Moni Philosophou. These two monasteries face each other across the Loussios Gorge.

MONI PHILOSOPHOU ★. This monastery, which is dedicated to the Virgin Mary, was named after its founder, Ioannis Lambardopoulos – a secretary at the court of the Byzantine Emperor Nikephoros II Phokas – who was nicknamed "the philosopher". There are two groups of monastic buildings here; pictured below is the more

recent of the two, which is currently being restored, dates from the end of the 17th century and contains several splendid icons attributed to Victor the Cretan. The older wing, which is now in ruins, was founded in 963. Under the Ottomans this group of buildings was known as the "Hidden School": concealed as it was in a hollow of the rocks, it was one of the centers where Greek traditions and the Orthodox religion were secretly taught and preserved. The monastery itself is a twenty-minute walk along a rough path, indicated by a sign. The path begins with a flight of stone steps set against the steep rockface, before plunging through the underbrush to a tumble of rocks, above which the buildings stand. Although it has been abandoned for centuries, the monastery still has its tiny chapel, crowned by an octagonal dome, and a highly defensible entrance built right into the cliff face, from which it is barely distinguishable. A few walls are all that remain of the convent buildings themselves, but the atmosphere of former grandeur and austerity combined with desolation is very powerful. From here, take the path that leads down to the gorge, crossing the Loussios river by a small bridge, and then continuing through low woods and meadows to Moni Ioanni Prodromou. This pleasant walk should take about three quarters of an hour.

Moni Prodromou. Founded in 1167 by Manuel I Comnenus ● *49*, the monastery of Ioannis Prodromos (John the Baptist) still harbors a substantial monastic community. It possesses a pair of churches, the smaller and older of the two being built against the rockface. Around this church the monastery buildings were gradually assembled over time, with balconies projecting over the edge of the cliff, suspended above a heart-stopping drop straight into the Loussios Gorge. The second of the two churches, which is of more recent construction, is less interesting architecturally. It stands outside the monastery precinct on a hill overlooking the entire area. Moni Prodromou is above all a place of prayer and contemplation: visitors are therefore asked to observe a few rules, in particular to dress modestly and conduct themselves with decorum while visiting the monastery.

"Ex voto" shrines
These proofs of Greece's religious fervor are to be seen everywhere along the roadsides. Every village has one or more of these miniature churches, extravagantly shaped and colored, at its entrance. Within, a small oil lamp illuminates the icon of a saint, around which are assembled various objects put there by villagers as tokens of gratitude.

This old signpost (at ground level) once marked the road to Moni Philosophou.

Isolated by its mountains, Arcadia brings its own reward. You meet few people on its roads, few of which are surfaced.

The site at Gortys will appeal to those with a special interest in archeology; other visitors may be more impressed by the atmosphere of this isolated spot, and by the elegant Byzantine church close to the ancient remains.

THE FORTRESS OF KARITAINA
This stronghold stands on a crag 1,200 feet high, commanding an impressive panorama of the gorge of the Alpheios and the plain of Megalopolis.

THE BRIDGE AT KARITAINA
On the road out of the village leading to Bassae ▲ *326*, below the modern bridge across the Alpheios is a three-arched medieval bridge with a chapel at one end.

GORTYS. From Dimitsana, drive to Stemnitsa, then Karitaina. In the village of Helleniko a sign points the way to Gortys, which can be reached by way of an earth road opposite the bridge over the Loussios. Situated on an oblong summit, the east side of which falls sheer to the river, this ancient site, which has been excavated by the French School of Athens, includes among other things a fortified Acropolis, which controlled the pass into the plain of Megalopolis, and a terrace along the Loussios. Here, at one time, there was a shrine dedicated to Asklepios ▲ *175*; it contained lodgings for pilgrims and three monuments: an "incubation" portico ▲ *262*, a temple and a thermal spa. The spa building (situated on the left after the bridge) was constructed in the second half of the 4th century BC; it took the form of a large house with a central courtyard and a bathing pool. During the Hellenistic era, a circular sweating room (traces of which are still visible) was added near the entrance, along with a small rotunda with nine sitting baths and a large rectangular room with three apses which served as an immersion bath. The foundations of the great temple beside this edifice are still in place; they indicate that this was a peripteral temple ● *90*, with a *cella* and a *pronaos in antis*, and that it was probably never completed. Some of the foundation stones were reused for the adjacent bathhouse. (From Helleniko, continue on to Karitaina.)

KARITAINA. This village, one of the nomes (administrative sectors) of Arcadia, is dominated by a crag on which are perched the ruins of a castle built by the Franks in the 13th century. At the foot of the fortress is a chapel dedicated to the Virgin. After the seizure of Constantinople by the Crusaders in 1204 ● *49*, Arcadia was one of the strategic points of the Frankish occupation (a fact reflected in many of the local place names), and Karitaina became the capital of an important barony of twenty-two fiefs, ruled by Hugo and Geoffroy Bruyère. It was these two barons who built the stronghold.

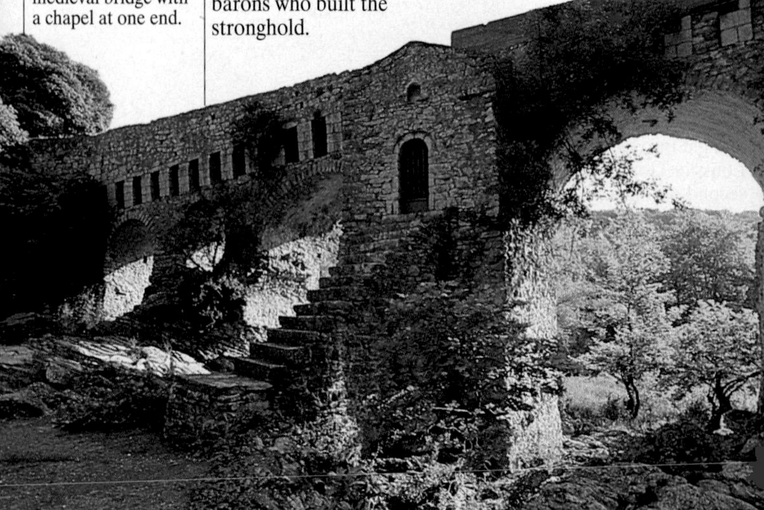

Mistra

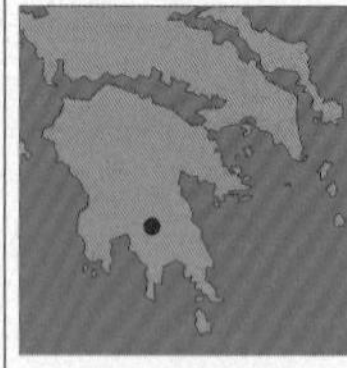

Four hours

MISTRA, A FRANKISH STRONGHOLD

Mistra was probably no more than a simple fortified outpost when in 1259 William de Villehardouin, Prince of Achaea (1246–78), made it one of the major strongholds of Laconia, along with those of Monemvasia ▲ *406* and the Mani ▲ *349*, ▲ *350*, thereby securing his control of southwestern Morea.

A CULTURAL CENTER. Under the Paleologi (1348–1460), Mistra was the brilliant center of the cultural renaissance of

THE FRANKISH TOWN
The steep hill on which 13th-century Mistra was built stands at the foot of the Taygetos Mountains, from which it is separated by deep gorges. The houses rise one above the other right up to the walls of the citadel. Today Mistra is deserted, and little more than a museum.

1. Entrance
2. Metropolitan Church
3. The Evangelistria
4. Church of the Haghii Theodori
5. Afendiko Church
6. Monemvasia Gate
7. Church of St Nicolas
8. Despot's Palace
9. Church of St Sophia
10. Frankish castle of Villehardouin
11. Convent of the Pantanassa
12. Mansion of Frangopoulos
13. Perivleptos Monastery
14. Church of St George
15. Church of St Christopher
16. Mansion of Laskaris

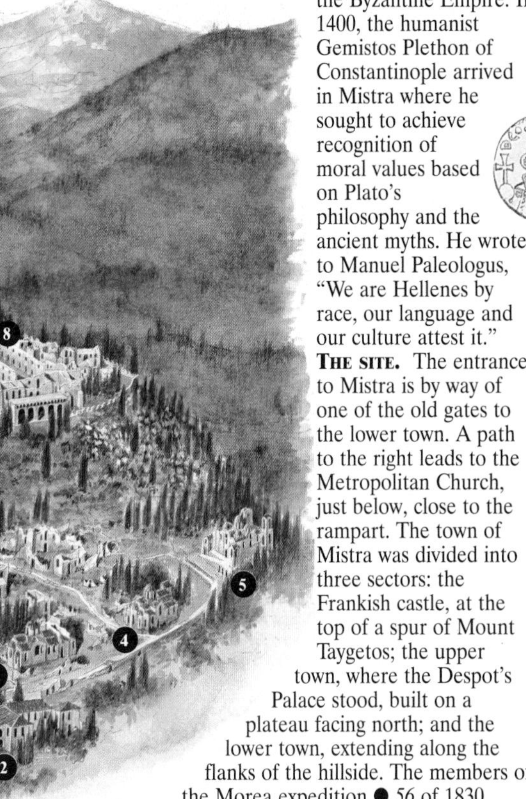

the Byzantine Empire. In 1400, the humanist Gemistos Plethon of Constantinople arrived in Mistra where he sought to achieve recognition of moral values based on Plato's philosophy and the ancient myths. He wrote to Manuel Paleologus, "We are Hellenes by race, our language and our culture attest it."

The site. The entrance to Mistra is by way of one of the old gates to the lower town. A path to the right leads to the Metropolitan Church, just below, close to the rampart. The town of Mistra was divided into three sectors: the Frankish castle, at the top of a spur of Mount Taygetos; the upper town, where the Despot's Palace stood, built on a plateau facing north; and the lower town, extending along the flanks of the hillside. The members of the Morea expedition ● *56* of 1830 described it as follows: "The lower town, where several church towers are to be seen, along with minarets and cypresses that form pyramids of greenery, is crowned by a castle built by the Franks atop a high, nearly conical rock. This is the final foothill of Mount Taygetos.

The Metropolitan Church. Two inscriptions bear witness to the foundation of this cathedral church in 1291 by Nikephoros, bishop of Sparta. Originally, the church was shaped like a basilica; its transformation dates from the early 15th century, when a bishop had the wooden roof of the nave removed and built the upper gallery and a dome resting on four pillars, supported by the columns of the lateral naves. The frescos date from the late 13th century and the first half of the 14th century.

The museum. Mistra's museum occupies two floors of the west wing of the Episcopal Palace, built in 1754, to the north of the church. Here one may see sculptures and architectural elements from the churches of Mistra, portable mosaic icons

A great town
Geoffrey of Villehardouin founded a mint at Mistra. The small Greek state which grew up around the Frankish castle grew in importance and had many intellectual and political links with Constantinople.

The Metropolitan Church
After 1262, when Mistra had developed into a true town, the people of Sparta sought refuge there. Monasteries were founded, the castle was enlarged and the Metropolitan Church was built and dedicated to Saint Demetrios. The seat of the bishops of Sparta was moved to Mistra.

Icons are more than religious art: as theophany (a manifestation of "the likeness of God") they possess a sacred dimension. The renaissance of the genre after the iconoclastic period reached its climax under the Comnenus dynasty (1057–1155) and the Paleologus dynasty (1261–1453). After the fall of Constantinople Byzantine art survived in the great monasteries of Greece and in Venetian-occupied Crete (1204–1669). The Cretan School, which initially consisted mainly of Greek artists who had fled Constantinople, Mistra or Thessalonika, dominated from the 15th to the 17th century; it perpetuated the Byzantine and Greek stylistic tradition, into which Italian influences were gradually integrated. The Cretan model, which became the standard, was adopted on the mainland, though executed more crudely.

St John the Evangelist (17th century) Traditionally Saint John was portrayed as an old man with a long white beard.

St Christopher Kynocephalos (1685 An Egyptian-influenced image.

Ss. Peter and Paul (17th century) Presentation of bread ar wine at the Eucharist.

St John Chrysostom and the translation of his relics (17th century). He was onc of the three great teachers of the Greel Church.

St John Prodromos (16th century). Prodromos means "precursor", signifying John the Baptist.

The Prophet Elijah
(17th century)

The hieratic and sensitive styles
Two opposing stylistic tendencies are perceptible in the development of the icon. The one "sensitive", with expressive faces and colors; the other "hieratic", with severe faces and geometrical lines.

Sacred and miraculous icons
Some icons were reputed to be miraculous. This belief was based on the Christian theology of images. Thus St John of Damascus wrote that "In their lifetimes the saints were filled with the Holy Spirit. After their deaths this grace remains attached not only to their souls but also to their mortal remains in the tomb, to their names and to their holy images."

King David
(15th century)

St Demetrios
(17th century)
Like St George, St Demetrios is traditionally represented with the features of a young and handsome prince, mounted on a horse with magnificent trappings. In many icons the two saints are shown facing each other – St George striking down the dragon in an allegory of the battle between Good and Evil, and St Demetrios personifying the Church Militant. This type of icon was very popular.

THE DESPOT'S PALACE
This was built in 1249 by Guillaume de Villehardouin, who occupied it with about eighty knights from Burgundy and Champagne. Villehardouin's castle was modified by the Byzantines and then by the Turks. The largest part of it, the northwest wing, consists of a ground floor with a vaulted ceiling, a first floor with eight apartments and a second floor containing a Byzantine throne room. The east side features a series of Gothic window embrasures, plus a second row of six windows.

THE CITADEL
The path to the castle is very steep. This stronghold was successively defended against the Franks, the Albanians, the Venetians and the Turks.

A MYTHICAL TOWN
Mistra is a ghost town: its ramparts, churches, monasteries and houses now lie deserted amid the encroaching countryside.

and fragments of frescos. This collection was assembled by Gabriel Millet, who made Mistra known in Western Europe with his works on Byzantine art.

THE EVANGELISTRIA. Along the same road is a church dating from the end of the 14th century. Built in the form of a Greek cross, it has a dome supported by an octagonal tambour resting on two columns and two pillars. There is a gallery for women above the narthex. The frescos date from the Paleologus dynasty.

THE CHURCH OF THE HAGHII THEODORI. Farther on are two of Mistra's most imposing churches, the Haghii Theodori and the Aphentiko, or Panaghia Hodigitria, beside the northern rampart. Both were part of the Monastery of Brontokhion, built between 1290 and 1322. The most striking exterior elements of Haghii Theodori are its dome, which has a central octagon with sixteen windows, and the décor of its walls, which are framed by courses of narrow bricks alternating with ceramic tiles and carefully dressed rectangular stones. Inside, the tambour rests on corner squinches ● *94* and barrel vaults. The frescos are thought to date from the 14th century.

“THIS MOUNTAIN IS CONSTITUTED LIKE A HUMAN MIND. THE DEBRIS OF EVERY ERA AND OF WIDELY DIFFERENT RACES MERGE INDISTINGUISHABLY.”

MAURICE BARRÈS

THE CHURCH OF THE HODIGITRIA. From the outside this building looks like a two-story Greek cross, with a central cupola surrounded by four small corner domes. But once inside you discover that its base is built on a basilical plan with three naves separated by two rows of three columns, while the upper level is laid out according to the Greek-cross plan, with four columns. The galleries run around three sides of the building, as far as its eastern corners. The west gallery is built over the narthex, which is crowned at its center by a sixth cupola. The numerous frescos, most of them extremely well preserved, date from the first half of the 14th century.

THE MONEMVASIA GATE. Going back toward Haghii Theodori, take the track leading to the upper town; after passing a series of ruined houses, you will come to the magnificent Monemvasia Gate into the citadel. On the left are the Church of St Nicholas and a house dating from the 15th century. The main square, which overlooks the valley of the Eurotas, is flanked on two sides by the massive ruin of the Despot's Palace.

THE DESPOT'S PALACE. The palace consists of two wings built at right angles: these are rectangular in shape and together form the north side of the square. The first stage of the palace's construction involved the northeast wing, which stands on the far right of the square. The broken arches of its windows are reminiscent of the Crusader castles of the Peloponnese. The northeast wing is believed to have been built by Guillaume de Villehardouin between 1249 and 1259; the two other parts probably date from roughly the same period. The first of these contains kitchens and water tanks on the ground floor, while the other was the baron's residence. The residence had six huge rooms on each floor, plus a porch at the end and a balcony from which there was a view along the entire valley as far as Sparta; on the upper floor was a chapel decorated with frescos. The northwest wing of the palace, a rectangular two-story edifice about 130 feet long by 30 feet wide, was built after 1400 for the Paleologi; the second floor was reserved for the Chrysotriklinon, an audience room modeled on the one in the palace at Constantinople.

THE SMALL PALACE. The square to the south is overlooked by the Small Palace. This is one of the most imposing baronial buildings of the Byzantine era. It has three floors and consists of two separate buildings, the oldest of which is the donjon. The path to the

ST NICHOLAS
Situated close to the Monemvasia Gate and the Small Palace, the Church of St Nicholas dates from the period of the Turkish occupation.

THE PERIVLEPTOS MONASTERY
This small monastery, situated on the edge of the cliff close to the outer ramparts, is unusual in that it is partially built into the rockface. It has some remarkable frescos, including the *Procession of Angels* (in a small apse) and *Christ in Judgement Surrounded by the Prophets* on the dome.

Byzantine house near the Church of St Sophia

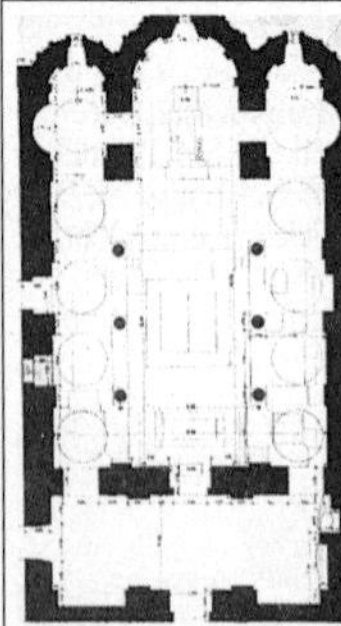
PLAN OF THE CHURCH OF THE PANTANASSA

THE CHURCH OF ST SOPHIA
The magnificent detached bell tower is in the Champenois style, brought to Mistra by Villehardouin. It once had a spiral staircase, and was used as a minaret during the Turkish occupation.

BYZANTINE CAPITAL
One of the exhibits in the museum at the Metropolitan Church.

MISTRA FROM THE FOOT OF THE ROCK
Villehardouin himself selected the rocky site of Mistra, where he built a fortress and a virtually impregnable town. In the old French dialect Mistra meant "the mistress town", but the Greek name for the town was *mizithra* – which, puzzlingly, is a kind of soft cheese.

left leads to the Church of St Sophia (Haghia Sophia).
HAGHIA SOPHIA. The Church of St Sophia was founded between 1350 and 1365 by Manuel Cantacuzene, the first despot of Morea (1348–80), who dedicated it to Christ. Built to the Greek-cross design, it doubled as the palace chapel and the katholikon of the Zoïllotos monastery. One or two frescos survive in the apse and chapels (among them a *Christ in Majesty*), along with a polychrome marble pavement.
THE PANTANASSA. From Haghia Sophia, walk down to the Monemvasia Gate and take the path leading to the Convent of the Pantanassa. An inscription commemorates its foundation by John Frangopoulos, prime minister of the despot Theodore II Paleologus. The church, which is a three-nave basilica, has some original frescos in the two arms of the cross, but the paintings on the lower part of the walls date from the 17th and 18th centuries. The entrance, on the north side, is fronted by a four-arched portico. The Gothic western bell tower is four stories high. As you walk from here toward the lower town, note the 15th-century Byzantine house along the way.

THE PERIVLEPTOS MONASTERY. The path continues to the southeast corner of the lower town, where there is a small monastery dating from the end of the 14th century. The church is built to the usual Greek-cross plan, with a trefoil apse; its dome rests on two columns and two pillars. The frescos, executed by painters from the court of Constantinople, are among the earliest examples of the scheme of iconography formulated at Mount Athos. They illustrate four cycles: *The Eucharist, The Twelve Feasts, The Passion* and *The Life of the Virgin.* In the apse is *The Divine Liturgy*, one of the great masterpieces of Byzantine art. From here, return to Mistra's main entrance.

The Mani

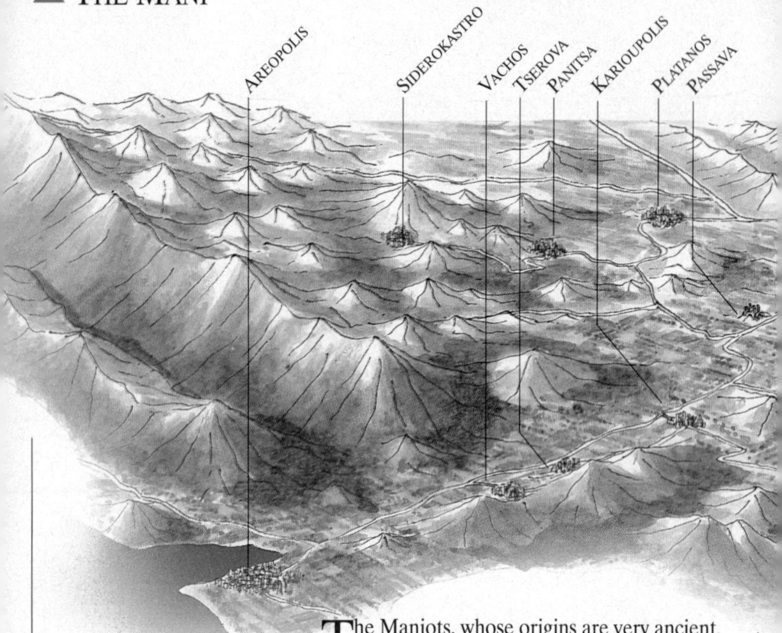

AREOPOLIS
SIDEROKASTRO
VACHOS
TSEROVA
PANITSA
KARIOUPOLIS
PLATANOS
PASSAVA

The Maniots, whose origins are very ancient, have survived in the southern Peloponnese partly thanks to geography. Their customs date back for millennia and their language, the Tsaconian dialect, is descended from a pre-Dorian tongue ● *43*. Moreover, since they live in a relatively closed society, the Maniots have been able to preserve their ethnic identity, despite the domination of Romans, Byzantines, Franks, Venetians and Ottomans. Because of the arid soil they inherited, they have traditionally depended less on agriculture than on the sea. Before the end of the age of sail, opportunities for seaborne trade were abundant on account of the numerous small ports and anchorages around the coast of the Mani; furthermore, the region served as a staging area for any vessel passing the southern Peloponnese. After the conquest of the Peloponnese by the Ottomans in 1461, the Mani entered an era of prosperity. In exchange for an annual tribute, the Maniots were spared Turkish military occupation and were allowed to remain independent. Isolated by land from the rest of the peninsula, they naturally turned to the sea at a time when piracy and buccaneering were the order of the day. The coastline of the Mani, together with the island of Kythera and, farther south, the western end of Crete, formed a bottleneck through which all shipping between the eastern and western Mediterranean had to pass. Ships cruising in these sea lanes were easy prey for the Maniots, who operated in collusion with the neighboring Sphakiot pirates based in Crete. In times of war between the

GYTHEION
Above the port of Gytheion are remains of an ancient acropolis, and a Roman theater.

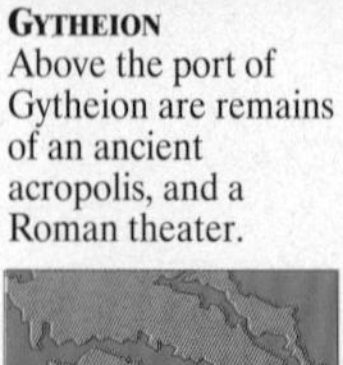

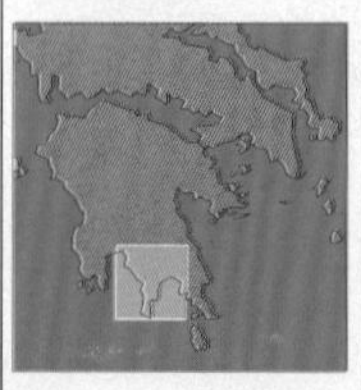

Two days

great powers, they privateered on behalf of one side or the other: this happened during the Seven Years' War between England and France, and later during the Russo-Turkish War.

THE INTERIOR OF THE MANI

From the Middle Ages to the beginning of the 18th century this region was totally unsafe for travelers. The Maniot villages were situated along the ridges of Mount Taygetos and around the Gulf of Scutari. The Frankish and Turkish invaders occupied the stronghold of Passava, on the east side of the Mani, in turn. After 1780 the Maniots moved to the plains and coastal areas, as far as the new frontier of Trinissa. The ports of Gytheion and Mavrovouni nearby were developed on the initiative of Tzanetbey Grigoraki (1742–1813).

GYTHEION. Slightly to the north of its port, the town of Gytheion has preserved the elegant neoclassical architecture of the late 19th and early 20th centuries. The main square, with its cafés and tavernas, is a magnet for holidaymakers, who come to eat the local specialty, *sigglina*, a kind of pork sausage flavored with orange. Facing the port, on the islet of Kranae, is a fortress and mansion built by Tsanetaki, son of Tzanetbey. Now restored, it contains the new Historical and Ethnological Museum of the Mani.

PASSAVA. The "Passe-Avant" of the Crusaders ● *49* is perched on a rock commanding the narrow defile into Maniot country. It was built in 1250 by the Franks, and occupied by the Turks from 1481 to 1780. From 1685 to 1715, during the second period of their domination, the Venetians virtually demolished it. In its central part, the ruins of a mosque are still visible. From Passava, a road leads to the heights of Mount Taygetos across a landscape of hills. Among the towns of the region are Panitsa, Pilala, which overlooks the fortress of Khatzakos, and Siderokastro and Polyaravos in the mountains behind.

KARIOUPOLIS. The town of Karioupolis still has its fortifications, built by the Phoca-Kavallieraki family on a hilltop, which controlled the main defile into the Mani and commanded the small fertile valley of Dikhora fronting the sea anchorage of Kato-Vathy. The two fortified areas are completed by a tower and a bastion, along with a chapel dedicated to Saint Peter and the much larger church of the Presentation of the Virgin.

Signs outside Maniot cafés.

PETRO MAVROMICHALIS
Bey from 1815 to 1821, Mavromichalis also gloried in the title of "Chief of the Maniots or former Spartans". The proud Maniot mountaineers claimed descent from the warriors of Leonidas, King of Sparta.

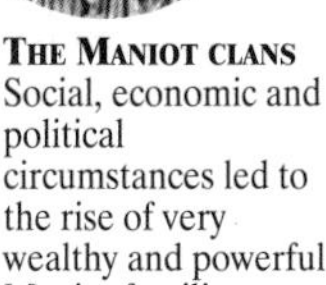

THE MANIOT CLANS
Social, economic and political circumstances led to the rise of very wealthy and powerful Maniot families, which operated as united clans.

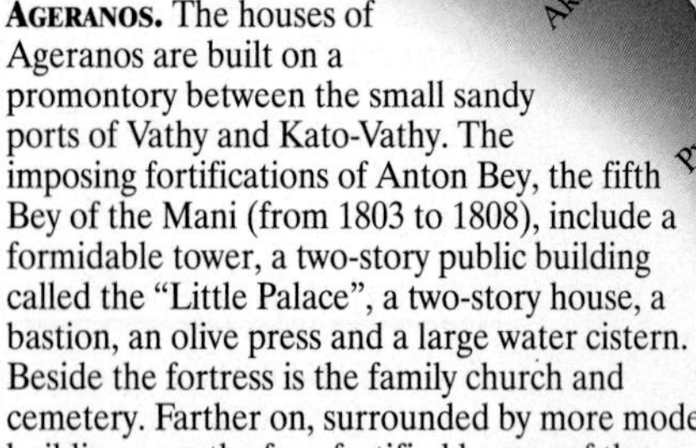

ARCHITECTURE
In the north of the Mani (around Areopolis, Kotronas and Pyrgos Dirou) the architecture of the houses and other types of building has a very particular form which lies midway between the northern and southern styles of the region. The Mani is littered with ruins of towers, churches and old farms.

AGERANOS. The houses of Ageranos are built on a promontory between the small sandy ports of Vathy and Kato-Vathy. The imposing fortifications of Anton Bey, the fifth Bey of the Mani (from 1803 to 1808), include a formidable tower, a two-story public building called the "Little Palace", a two-story house, a bastion, an olive press and a large water cistern. Beside the fortress is the family church and cemetery. Farther on, surrounded by more modest buildings, are the four fortified houses of the nephews of Anton Bey.

SCUTARI. The town of Scutari, on its hill near the coast, is likewise dominated by a tower and fortifications. Around it stand the ruins of several towers, churches and old houses.

TSEROVA. From this mountainous village the view stretches uninterrupted to the sea as far as the Eurotas ■ *28* and inland toward the picturesque village of Vakhos. Beside it, on a hill, stands the ancient Kastro and the village of Palea-Karyoupoli, with tower, paleo-Christian and Byzantine churches, and medieval houses.

LIMENI IN THE 1930'S
The palace of Petro Mavromichalis, overlooking the bay, symbolized the power of his clan.

AREOPOLIS AND THE SOUTH

From Gytheion the road follows the Gulf of Laconia and the east side of the peninsula as far as Kotronas. According to medieval sources, the southern part of the peninsula was not only more isolated and wilder than it is today but also more populous. At Flomokhori the fortified towers are as tall as the cypress trees that surround them.

VATHIA. This village stands on a hilltop about 6 miles to the south. All around, the ruins of old houses are visible, although Vathia was once busy and prosperous. It was divided into four quarters, each of which belonged to a different clan. Since 1975 the Greek National Tourist Organization has encouraged the establishment of inns, restaurants and other tourist facilities here.

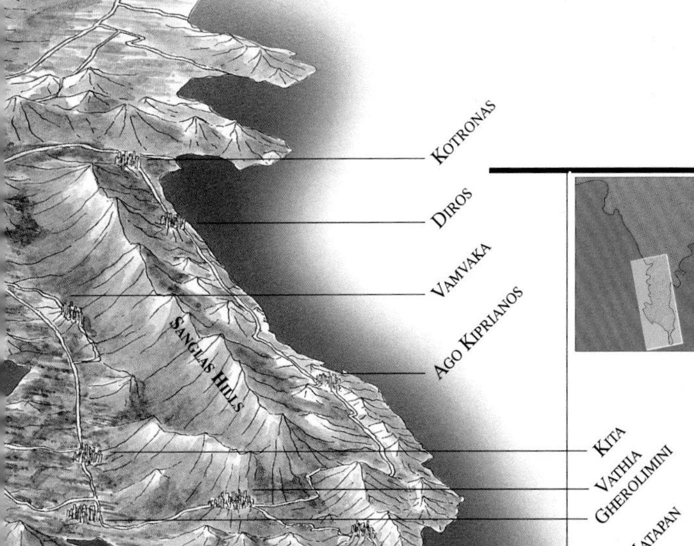

Cape Matapan. For many years the presence of the Maniots around Cape Matapan made it possible for them to control the movements of shipping in the strait between the Peloponnese and Kythera. In the Gulf of Psamathos one can still see the remains of the Psychopompeion, the sacred precinct of the Temple of Poseidon and the ancient buildings surrounding it, which date from the preclassical era to Roman times.

Porto Kagio. Overlooked by the dark outline of Cape Matapan, the beaches of the village of Porto Kagio (which the Franks called "Le Port aux Cailles") and Marmari are delightful places for bathing. On the south slope of Porto Kagio is a Turkish-built stronghold dating from 1670. From Vathia continue to the small, picturesque port of Gherolimini by way of Alika, which is close to the site of the ancient city of Kiparissos, known for its paleo-Christian basilicas.

Tigani. Perched on a rocky promontory, Tigani is visible from the port of Mezapos. Even in ancient times there was a small stronghold here; this was enlarged by the Byzantines, who made it their headquarters for the administration of the southern Mani. On the highest point of the small peninsula are traces of a paleo-Christian basilica, houses and water cisterns.

Kita. This is one of the most substantial villages in the region. Kita is subdivided into six areas, corresponding to its six principal families; these areas consist of between fifteen and fifty buildings, many built of huge stone blocks, along with military towers and churches.

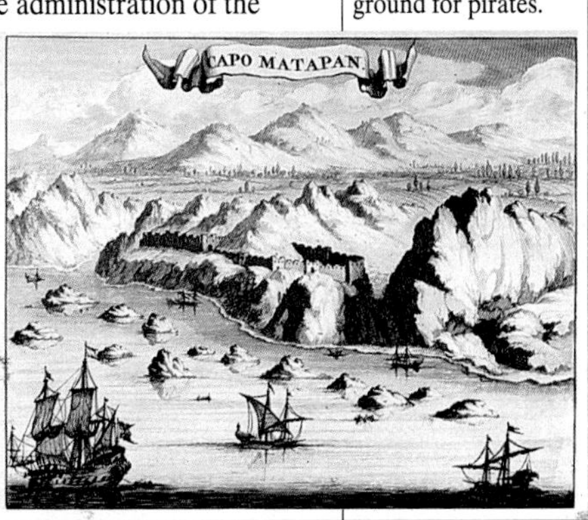

Maniot villages
The bare landscape of the Mani is in perfect harmony with the architecture of its buildings. Here time has come to a halt, allowing one to wander among buildings that have remained unchanged for centuries and follow the slow progress of local architectural history.

Cape Matapan
From Vathia you can see Cape Matapan reaching out into the Mediterranean. This was where the ancients reckoned the gates of Hades were located; in more recent history it was a celebrated cruising ground for pirates.

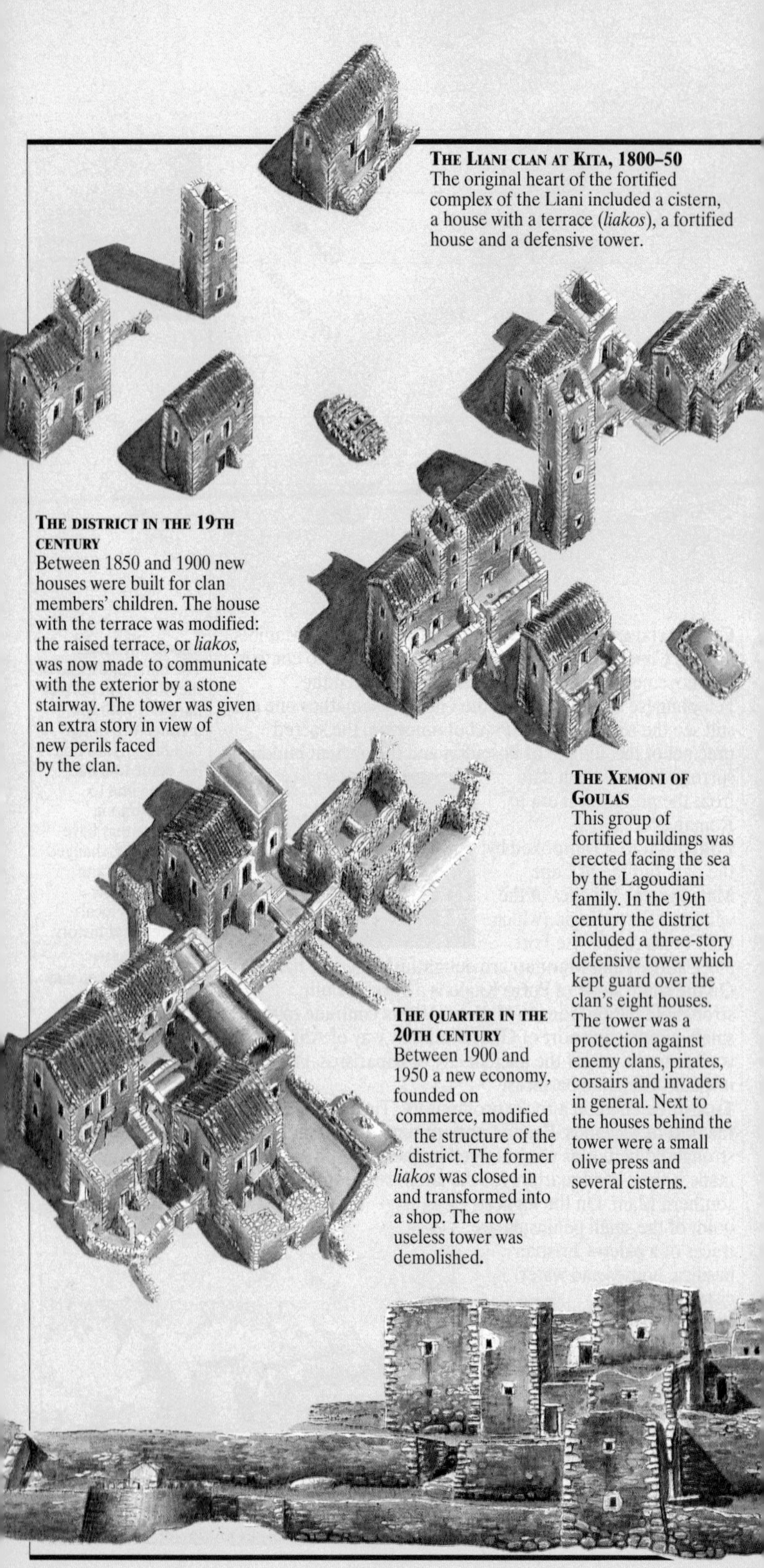

The Liani clan at Kita, 1800–50
The original heart of the fortified complex of the Liani included a cistern, a house with a terrace (*liakos*), a fortified house and a defensive tower.

The district in the 19th century
Between 1850 and 1900 new houses were built for clan members' children. The house with the terrace was modified: the raised terrace, or *liakos*, was now made to communicate with the exterior by a stone stairway. The tower was given an extra story in view of new perils faced by the clan.

The Xemoni of Goulas
This group of fortified buildings was erected facing the sea by the Lagoudiani family. In the 19th century the district included a three-story defensive tower which kept guard over the clan's eight houses. The tower was a protection against enemy clans, pirates, corsairs and invaders in general. Next to the houses behind the tower were a small olive press and several cisterns.

The quarter in the 20th century
Between 1900 and 1950 a new economy, founded on commerce, modified the structure of the district. The former *liakos* was closed in and transformed into a shop. The now useless tower was demolished.

The power of a clan was measured by the number of buildings, palaces, towers and churches it possessed. The clan would choose an elevated site and there build a defensive tower, houses, olive presses and water cisterns. Around these would be grouped the individual houses of the members of the clan. The church was flanked by a cemetery and by the *rouga*, a square used for assemblies that was the center of social life. An access road linked the district with the outside world, while an unoccupied strip insulated it from other clan strongholds. Poorer families, or *phanegi*, lived in humble houses which were often built with aid from the clan's chieftain.

THE COMMUNAL TOWERS OF THE MANI
From ancient times until the late 19th century these towers were the emblem of the Mani. They testify to the evolution of construction techniques, four stages of which are illustrated here. Between the Megalithic age and 1750 (**1** and **2**) large stone blocks were used for building and strengthening the lower walls. Between 1750 and 1850 (**3**) the towers had two or sometimes three stories; then from 1850 until the end of the 19th century (**4**) the evolution of the towers paralleled that of the local houses. The space inside the towers was extremely restricted. Some of them had seven floors and were as much as 60 feet high.

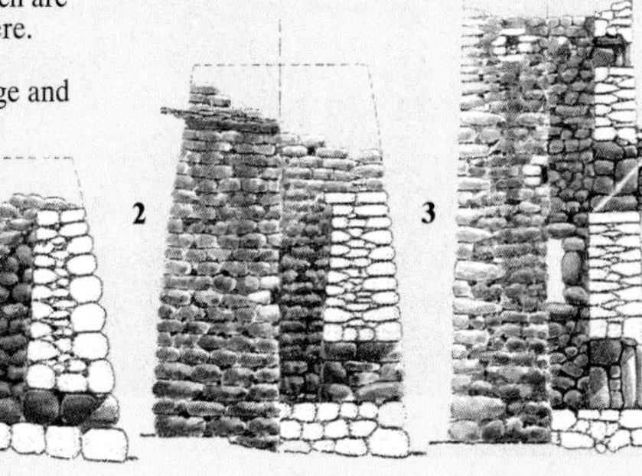

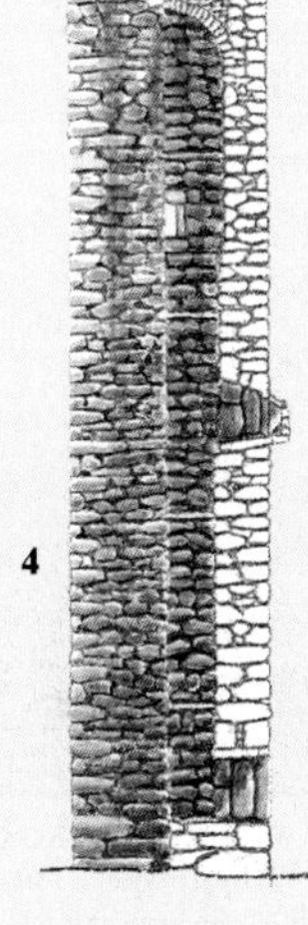

These vases are made from pine cones.

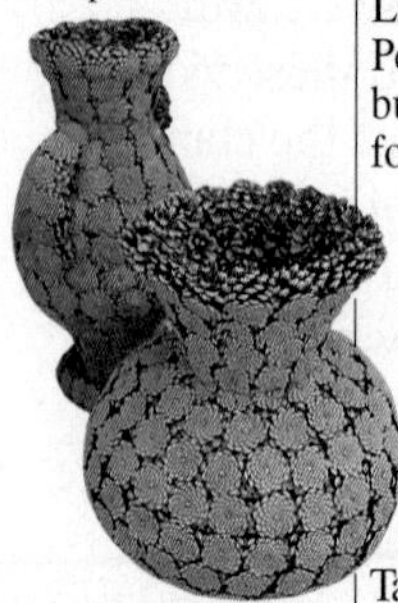

DIROS. In the summer of 1826 the Maniots repelled the Egyptian army at Diros.

LIMENI. Fronting the port of Areopolis, at Limeni, stands the 19th-century palace of Petro Mavromichalis, consisting of a huge building, long and narrow, with a square four-story tower.

AREOPOLIS. The town developed considerably under the influence of the Mavromichalis family, which fostered its trade. In 1836 Areopolis was designated as the region's administrative center. The town possesses two churches built by the family at the beginning of the 18th century, the Church of St John and the Church of the Taxiarchs. The latter was restored in 1798 and contains splendid frescos from the 13th and 14th centuries. One may also admire the imposing fortified buildings, the residence of Stylianos and Kyriacouli Mavromichalis, and the Tower of Kapetanakos.

KALAMATA

ALMIRON

CAVES AROUND THE GULF OF DIROS
The caves of Glyfada and Alepotrypa have now been equipped to receive visitors. At Glyfada the tour is conducted by boat over about a mile of underground river. The cave at Alepotrypa was inhabited during the Paleolithic and Neolithic ages.

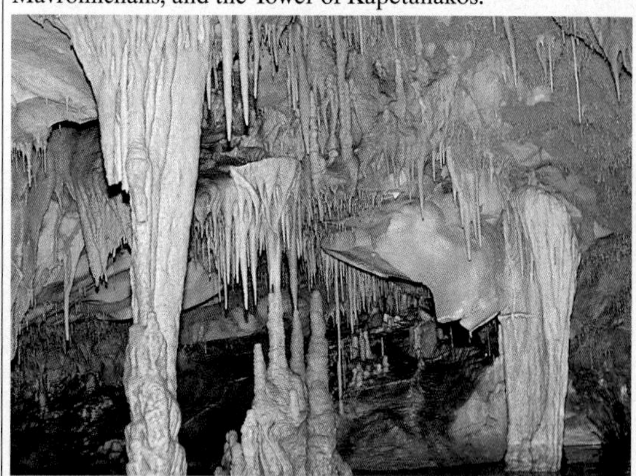

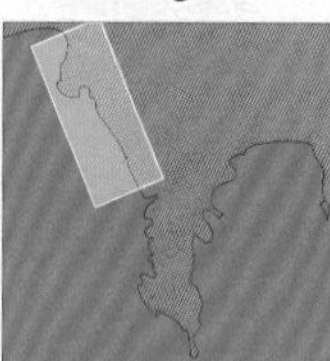

THE TOWERS OF KITA
The most typical are those of Voudikhari (1763) and Lazzaroggona (1850), both on the old Foulia Square.

THE OUTER MANI

During the Byzantine era the despots and princes of Mistra possessed huge, rich properties in this region. However, the outer Mani was exposed to periodic Turkish invasions. Several aristocratic clans with hereditary chieftans were established here; their social organization, which was feudal to all intents and purposes, can be read in the architecture of their buildings.

ITYLO. This spot has been inhabited since the earliest times. Perched at an altitude of 750 feet on the steep side of Kako Langadi, the town is sited on what was once the acropolis of Oetylos. Toward the end of the 18th century a number of very old families, such as the Medicis and the Stefanopolis family, were forced to emigrate to Italy and Corsica. The central square, the houses huddled together, the fountains, churches and monasteries (18th-century Dekoulos Monastery is an example) all testify to Itylo's long history.

Several tower houses of more recent construction emphasize the verticality of the architecture.

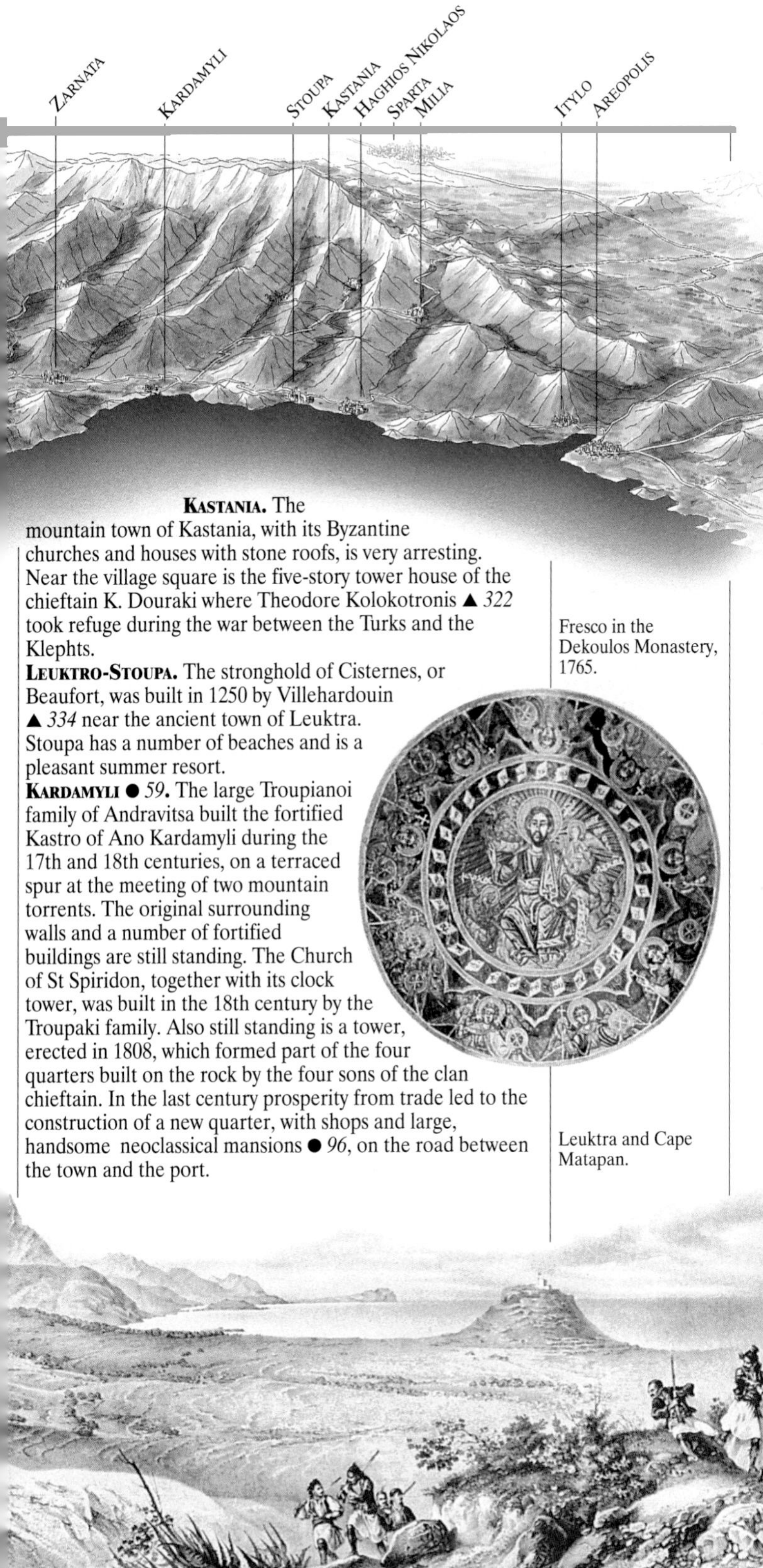

KASTANIA. The mountain town of Kastania, with its Byzantine churches and houses with stone roofs, is very arresting. Near the village square is the five-story tower house of the chieftain K. Douraki where Theodore Kolokotronis ▲ *322* took refuge during the war between the Turks and the Klephts.

LEUKTRO-STOUPA. The stronghold of Cisternes, or Beaufort, was built in 1250 by Villehardouin ▲ *334* near the ancient town of Leuktra. Stoupa has a number of beaches and is a pleasant summer resort.

KARDAMYLI ● *59.* The large Troupianoi family of Andravitsa built the fortified Kastro of Ano Kardamyli during the 17th and 18th centuries, on a terraced spur at the meeting of two mountain torrents. The original surrounding walls and a number of fortified buildings are still standing. The Church of St Spiridon, together with its clock tower, was built in the 18th century by the Troupaki family. Also still standing is a tower, erected in 1808, which formed part of the four quarters built on the rock by the four sons of the clan chieftain. In the last century prosperity from trade led to the construction of a new quarter, with shops and large, handsome neoclassical mansions ● *96*, on the road between the town and the port.

Fresco in the Dekoulos Monastery, 1765.

Leuktra and Cape Matapan.

ZARNATA
This small town occupies a dominant hilltop position in the middle of a fertile valley. Plenty of interesting remains have been found here, some from Neolithic times, others from the classical and Byzantine eras.

ZARNATA. During the Venetian era Zarnata became the capital of the region (Alta Maina). Around its fortress were gathered four different suburbs with churches, monasteries, shops, wells and gardens. At the top of the castle there is still a three-story house which belonged to the Koutifari chieftains (1776–9) and later to Koumoundouros (1798–1803).

DOLI. This village, with its fine houses, interesting churches and lush surrounding countryside and farmland, was made famous all over Europe by an engraving published by the French expedition to the Morea in 1829 ● *56*.

TRIKOTSOVA. The Kapetanakis family erected this hilltop fortress between 1795 and 1821. Within its square walls are two long, narrow buildings, a fortified tower, a chapel, main and secondary gates, and several water cisterns.

MARKET STALLS AT KALAMATA
Kalamata has a reputation for its excellent olives, dried figs and bananas.

MILI. On the shores of the bay of Mili-Almiron the Kapetanakis family owned four watermills and a fortified tower, adjoining an administrative building that has survived. The fortified Verga-Almirou line defended the northwest frontier of the Mani; it consisted of a wall with loopholes and two towers, one round, one square. Here, between June 21 and June 24 of 1826, the Maniots repelled the Egyptian forces of Ibrahim Pasha ● *54*. Prior to the War of Independence the frontier of the Mani was the Saint Zion River. Beyond it are Messenia and Kalamata. The Kastro of Kalamata was built by Villehardouin in 1208 ▲ *334*. The mainly 19th-century town, which is just over 2 miles from the river, has a number of hotels and makes a good base for visitors to the Mani.

Jetty near Kalamata. In the background is Mount Taygetos.

Olympia and Patras

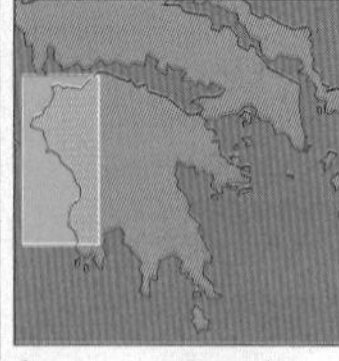

One day

Zeus in gold and ivory
Pausanias wrote that a statue of the god "made of gold and ivory is seated on a throne here; he wears a wreath of olive leaves and holds a gold-and-ivory Victory." This engraving dates from the 18th century.

The valley and Altis (shrine) of Olympia
One of the most venerated sites in all Greece. The Olympic Games were held here every four years.

From Messenia to Elis

Kiparissia. Surrounded by vineyards and olive groves, Kiparissia is the largest resort on the west coast of the Peloponnese as you drive from Messenia to Elis. The houses of the upper town cluster around a Frankish castle built by Guillaume de Villehardouin. This agglomeration was demolished by Ibrahim Pasha ● *54* in 1825, then rebuilt and extended as far as the seashore during the reign of King Otto, when it took the name of Kiparissia ("city of cypresses"). Several Mycenean centers, among them Peristeria and Nestor's Amphigeneia, can be visited in the vicinity.

The road to Olympia. Once you have crossed the Nida, the Elis region begins about 10 miles farther on. Beyond the town of Zacharo the coast road passes between the sea and sulphurous Lake Kaiafa; a causeway across the lake gives access to the island of Haghia Ekaterini and the spa of Loutro Kaiafa, which has been in use since ancient times. After this, the road cuts inland around the western spur of Mount Kaiafa (the altitude of the summit is almost 2,500 feet). After skirting Lake Agoulinitsa, turn right to Kristena (1 mile). Here, on the left, is the beginning of the road to Olympia, which crosses the Alpheios River before leading to the great shrine. The ruins of Olympia fill the peaceful valley where the Alpheios and Kladeos rivers meet.

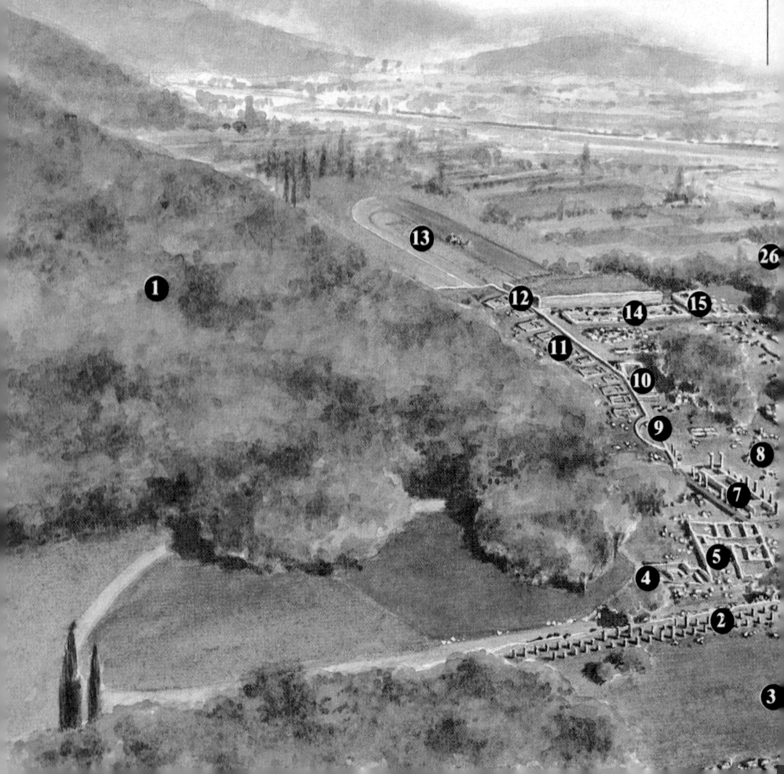

THE SITE OF OLYMPIA

The French expedition to the Peloponnese ● *58* carried out the first excavations in 1829 and brought back the three metopes from the Temple of Zeus that are now in the Louvre. More thorough research, funded by Germany, was initiated by the Greek government in 1874 and continued until 1881 under the direction of Ernst Curtius and Friedrich Adler. The German Institute of Archeology undertook farther excavations from 1936 to 1941, and from 1952 to the present. Access to the site is by way of the northwest corner, between the Kladeos and Mount Kronion. The first remains (which are on your left) are of Roman baths, followed (to the south) by the Prytaneum, where the counselors of Elis used to give a banquet for the victors at the end of the Olympic Games. Farther on, at the foot of Mount Kronion, is the northwest corner of the wall surrounding the Altis (shrine).

THE BOULEUTERION ● *81.* The entrance to the Bouleuterion, where the Council of Elis met and deliberated, is outside the Altis near the house which Nero built for his visits to Olympia. The Bouleuterion consisted of an Ionic portico, on the east façade, and a square, open area flanked on the north and south sides by buildings. These wings communicated with an Ionic portico of twenty-seven columns, which had a façade of three Doric columns.

THE ALTIS
Reconstruction by Victor Laloux, 1883.

OLYMPIA MUSEUM
"In the Heraion is a marble statue by Praxiteles of Hermes carrying the infant Dionysos." Pausanias

Praxiteles' *Hermes* (left) and a pediment sculpture from the Temple of Zeus.

1. Mount Kronion
2. Stoa
3. Gymnasium
4. Roman baths
5. Hestiatorion
6. Philippeion
7. Heraion
8. Pelopion
9. Exedra of Herodes Atticus
10. Metroön
11. Treasuries
12. Stadium entrance
13. Stadium
14. Stoa Poikile
15. Hellanodikeion
16. Temple of Zeus
17. Bouleuterion
18. South Stoa
19. Southern baths
20. Leonidaion
21. Roman bedrooms
22. Christian basilica
23. Heroön
24. Roman baths
25. Palestra
26. Racecourse

THE PHILIPPEION AND THE PALESTRA
This circular edifice was built by Philip of Macedon after his victory over the Greeks at Chaeronea. It contained statues of Philip himself, of his son Alexander, and of his wife Olympias, all by Leochares.

Foot-race, depicted on a vase.

THE PALESTRA
This was the part of the gymnasium used for wrestling exercises.

THE TEMPLE OF OLYMPIAN ZEUS. Huge drums from the columns of the Temple of Zeus lie strewn everywhere, although many of the shafts are still *in situ*. Archeologists have been unwilling to restore or rebuild the temple, which was built for the Olympic Games of 468 BC, though not consecrated until those of 460 or 456. According to Pausanias, it was the work of the Elian architect Libon. The building rested on a stylobate ● *91* some 210 feet long by 90 feet wide, which made it the second largest Doric temple in Greece after the Parthenon. On the east façade, as at the Temple of Aphaia on Aegina ▲ *365*, a ramp led up to a terrace. The building was peripteral in form ● *90*, with six columns on the façades and fourteen at the sides, plus two small columns *in antis* in the *pronaos* and *opisthodomos*. The interior consisted of two rows of seven columns on two levels. The pediments were decorated with statues of Parian marble (the ones now in the museum were found at the end of the last century by researchers from the German Institute). The statues on the east

> “TRACES OF HUGE WALLS, MASSIVE STONES, THE BASE OF A FLUTED COLUMN – THIS IS ALL THAT REMAINS OF OLYMPIA.”
>
> GUSTAVE FLAUBERT

pediment were described in detail by Pausanias: they represented the mythical chariot race, presided over by Zeus, in which Pelops, the son of Tantalus, outwitted the Aetolian King Oenomaus. The west pediment was decorated with a scene of centaurs. Friezes ran above the columns of both porches; and the twelve labors of Herakles were depicted in relief on the temple’s metopes.

THE HERAION. Situated beyond the fountain, near the northeast corner of the Altis, this temple was built around 600 BC. Originally it was dedicated to Zeus and Hera, but after the completion of the Temple of Zeus it was devoted to the cult of Hera exclusively. The Heraion stands on a two-step plinth; it is a peripteral, hexastyle temple ● *90* in the Doric manner ● *91*, with six columns in front and sixteen at the sides, plus two columns *in antis* for the *pronaos* and *opisthodomos*. The original wooden columns were gradually replaced by stone ones. Sections of thirty-four have survived, enabling two columns to be re-erected in 1905 and a third in 1970. The walls of the *cella* are of limestone up to a height of three feet and of sundried bricks above. Apart from the roof tiles, the rest of the building was made of wood.

THESEUS AND THE MINOTAUR
By observing naked athletes in action Greek sculptors were able to study the complex play of their muscles. Here Theseus and the Minotaur are locked together, like wrestlers, in a pyramidal composition.

THE ZANES
Bronze statues representing Zeus lined the roadside from the Altis to the stadium, along with offerings in his honor. Seen here (left) are the stone bases of the statues.

STADIUM ENTRANCE
The official entrance of the athletes and the Hellanodices was by way of the *krypte* (left) ▲ *356*.

THE METROÖN. To the west, after the Zanes and below the Terrace of the Treasuries, stood the Metroön, a temple dedicated in the 4th century BC to Rhea, mother of the gods. Small and peripteral in design, it had six Doric columns by eleven, plus two columns *in antis* for the *pronaos* and *opisthodomos*, and Corinthian columns ● *85* along the two *cella* walls. After the proclamation of the Roman Empire the Metroön was dedicated to the cult of Rome and Augustus, and thereafter to the other deified emperors.

THE HELLANODIKEION. At the southeast corner of the Altis are the foundations of the Southeast Building, or Hellanodikeion. Archeologists speculate that this was the shrine of Hestia, goddess of the home, mentioned by Xenophon; if so, it dates from at least the 4th century BC. The building consisted of four rooms with a Doric colonnade of nineteen columns on the west side and eight on the north and south sides. It was demolished in 67 BC and replaced by a peristyle villa for the Emperor Nero, traces of which may still be seen. A little farther on stood the octagonal central hall of the Roman baths.

PALEO-CHRISTIAN BASILICA
This was built on the foundations of Phidias’ studio.

OFFERINGS AT OLYMPIA
The museum possesses a very rich collection of bronzes from the Geometric period (late 8th century BC). This elegant bronze decoration features two figures holding a tripod.

THE STOA POIKILE, OR ECHOING COLONNADE. Still on the east side of the Altis, but north of the Shrine of Hestia, are the remains of the Stoa Poikile ("painted portico"). According to Pausanias, the walls of this building were covered with frescoes. In front of the stoa ● *80* are numerous statue bases and a long plinth that once supported two Ionic columns 30 feet tall, on top of which stood statues of Ptolemy II Philadelphos (285–246 BC), King of Egypt, and Queen Arsinoë.

THE KRYPTE. At the northeast corner of the Altis is the stadium entrance, or *krypte*, a vaulted tunnel used by the athletes and officials of the Olympic Games. This dates from the 1st century AD and is about 12 feet wide by 100 feet long. Its eastern end was restored at the same time as the stadium, between 1958 and 1962. On the outside, on twelve pedestals aligned east to west, rested the Zanes, bronze statues of Zeus (*Zan* in Archaic Greek) paid for by fines inflicted on those who dishonored the games. The largest was the statue of Zeus Orkios, before which the athletes traditionally swore their oaths on the first day of the games.

THE STADIUM. The restored stadium has regained much of its 4th-century BC appearance, when it witnessed the exploits of runners, wrestlers, pugilists and jumpers. It could hold twenty thousand spectators on the steep surrounding bank. In the 2nd century BC wooden benches were placed on the north side, probably for the Council of Elis and important guests. The rectangular stadium was just over 360 yards long, while the race track was about 230 yards in length, the distance separating the starting and finishing lines (both still visible) being almost exactly 210 yards. The stone edging and, on the south side, the paved section where the judges' marble box once stood can also still be seen.

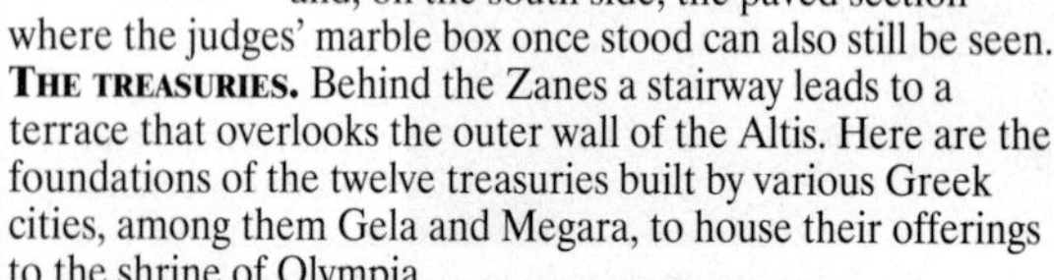

Bust of a priest from the Temple of Zeus.

THE TREASURIES. Behind the Zanes a stairway leads to a terrace that overlooks the outer wall of the Altis. Here are the foundations of the twelve treasuries built by various Greek cities, among them Gela and Megara, to house their offerings to the shrine of Olympia.

STONE LION
This tufa lion (7th century BC), now exhibited in the museum at Olympia, was once part of a fountain.

The Olympic Games

The ancient tradition was that the games were founded in 776 BC and were held at regular intervals of four years, or Olympiads. The contests of each Olympiad began at the full moon following the summer solstice. At the start of this sacred month the Elians sent out heralds throughout Greece to proclaim the *ekecheiria*, inviting athletes and spectators to come from all over Greece, Asia Minor and Sicily to Olympia. All the great states sent their delegations, and the tradition of the Olympic Games continued without interruption for over a thousand years. During the Roman era Nero delayed the games for two years so that he could find time to take part in them; when he did so in 67 BC he had a total of six prizes allotted to himself. The Olympic Games regained some of their original rigor under Hadrian, in the 2nd century AD, before the shrine was pillaged by the Heruli in 267. In 392 a decree of Theodosius forbidding pagan practices throughout the Eastern Empire led to the closing of the shrine and the cessation of the games. In the 6th century two successive earthquakes demolished many of the buildings, one of them causing a landslide from Mount Kronion that buried the Temple of Zeus. The Alpheios river then overflowed its banks and covered the west side of the sanctuary with silt.

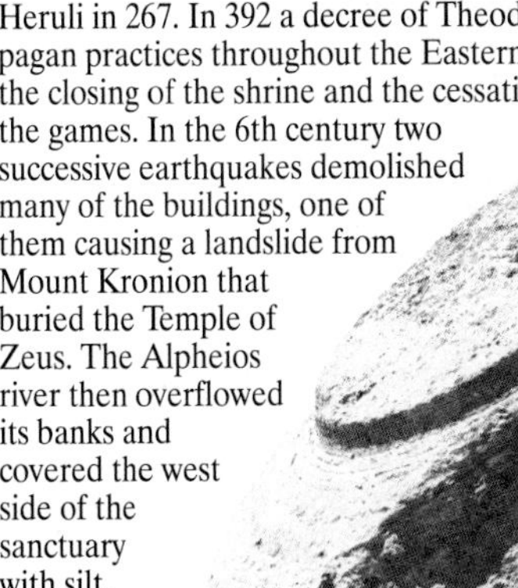

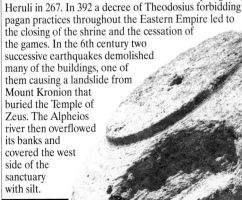

The plain of Olympia and the Alpheios
Karl Rotthmann painted this view of Olympia in 1855 before the German Institute of Archeology began to excavate the site and its shrines.

The Temple of Hera
Founded in the 6th century BC, the Temple of Hera was originally surrounded by a simple wooden colonnade. The masonry was of rough brick, and the stone foundations can still be seen.

The Metroön
Only part of the stylobate and entablature are now visible. The shafts of the columns are still present on the site.

Feasts in honor of Olympian Zeus marked the opening of the Olympiads. The first day was reserved for athletic contests. On the second day a herald proclaimed the names of the participants in the chariot races, horse races and pentathlon, all of which were scheduled for the following day. On the fourth day young men competed at running unencumbered, running in full armor, the high jump, boxing, wrestling and *pankration* (a combination of the two). The games culminated on the fifth day with sacrifices and, in the evening, a banquet for the victors, who wore crowns of olive leaves.

PUGILIST
Boxers wore strips of leather to protect their hands, and sometimes their forearms too. There were also bare-fisted boxing contests and *pankration*, which involved both boxing and wrestling.

Diskobolos
The young athlete (below) is about to throw his discus. The mattock and pair of dumb-bells indicate that this scene is set in the *palestra*.

Ball game
Athletes trained under the porticos of the *palestra*. Here (above) they are divided into three-man teams for a ball game.

Zeus, the warrior god
Zeus, who was venerated at Olympia, was said to aid the Greeks in the games (*stater* from Elis, 4th century BC).

Throwing contests
These contests originally involved hurling a stone, which was eventually replaced by the javelin and the discus.

Poster for the first modern Olympics
The Panathenaic Stadium ▲ *218* in Athens was excavated between 1869 and 1879, and then restored. On April 5, 1896, the first Olympic Games of modern times were held there.

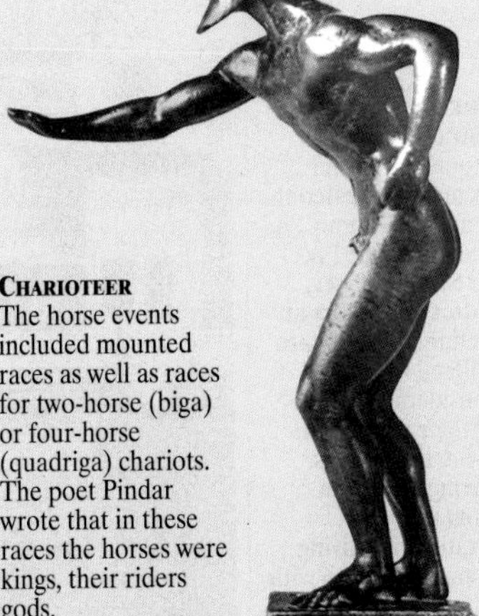

Charioteer
The horse events included mounted races as well as races for two-horse (biga) or four-horse (quadriga) chariots. The poet Pindar wrote that in these races the horses were kings, their riders gods.

PATRAS

The road from Patras to Corinth completes the tour of southern Greece. Patras is the largest port in the Peloponnese; with its 140,000 inhabitants, it is also the capital of the nome of Achaea. In ancient times the Acropolis of Patras stood about half a mile from the port, access to which was protected by long walls. Today all that remains of the old town are one or two vestiges of the Frourion (fortress) on the Acropolis; the Byzantine constructions here have Frankish and Turkish additions. About 300 yards farther is a Roman odeon, of which the *skene* ▲ *174* wall has been restored. The modern town was built in the time of Ioannis Kapodistrias ● *51*, in the 19th century; its straight streets, neo-Hellenic architecture and broad squares are reminiscent of that time.

THE CHURCH OF HAGHIOS ANDREAS. At this neo-Byzantine church close to the harbor, part of the cross of Saint Andrew, who was crucified at Patras, has been preserved. A gold reliquary containing his skull was taken to Rome by Thomas Paleologos five centuries ago and finally returned to Patras by the Pope in 1964. The church occupies the site of an earlier Byzantine basilica, destroyed in 1821. The celebration of the Patras carnival, or *apokreos*, which is the most famous in Greece, involves masked balls and processions in classical and medieval costume.

THE PORT. Patras is an important commercial port. Built during the 19th century, it has developed on a scale similar to that of Piraeus. Ferries ply between here and Italian ports all year round.

THE TOWN AND PORT OF PATRAS
At the beginning of the 20th century Patras was already the second port of Greece (after Piraeus), exporting currants and wine from the Peloponnese. The modern town, with its spacious squares, was built in 1830 under the first government of Ioannis Kapodistrias.

Kalavrita Street, in Patras.

THE ROMAN COLONY
Patras returned to prominence after Octavian defeated the armies of Antony and Cleopatra in 31 BC. As Strabo relates, "After the victory at Actium, the Romans billeted a considerable portion of their army in the town; thus Patras, having become a Roman colony, acquired a thriving population to go with its excellent harbor".

“After a voyage of sixteen hours, we awoke this morning off Patras. This is the true Greece.”

Comtesse de Gasparin

The main square of Patras
All 19th-century Greek towns were organized around a main square, the center of local activity.

From Patras to Corinth

A few miles from Patras, at the entrance to the Gulf of Corinth, the small town of Rhion is the embarkation point for Andirrhion, in Aetolia. Nearby is a fortress dating from 1499, restored in 1713 by the Venetians.

Aigion. Nearby is Aigion, one of the oldest towns in the Peloponnese. Excavations at this site have revealed its prehistoric origins. Here Agamemnon is said to have assembled the chiefs of Achaea before the siege of Troy. Aigion was one of the first towns liberated from the Turks in 1821.

The Vouraikos Gorge. From Diakapto you can take the rack-and-pinion railway in the magnificent Vouraikos Gorge up to Megaspilaion and Kalavrita.

Moni Megaspilaion. Halfway up (at Zakhlorou station) is the celebrated Monastery of Megaspilaion, established during the Byzantine era in a “great cavern” on Mount Khelmos. Destroyed by fire in 1934, the original buildings were replaced by a seven-story construction, built against the vertical side of the mountain. Among the ancient icons in the katholikon the most revered is that of the Virgin, which is supposed to have been painted by Saint Luke. The discovery of this icon in AD 342 by a shepherdess named Euphrosyne led to the founding of the religious community here by two monks from Salonica, Theodore and Simeon.

The Gulf of Patras

Tornese Castle
Built in 1220, this *kastro* at Kyllene is the largest in Achaea.

AIGION
The large modern seaport, exporting the produce of the Peloponnese, principally currants, olive oil and wine, was built on the foundations of the ancient one. Aigion still has a number of fine neoclassical houses.

KALAVRITA. Kalavrita stands at an altitude of nearly 2,500 feet, on the site of the ancient city of Kynaithes. From 1941 to 1945 resistance against the occupying Germans was active here; in reprisal the Germans shot 1,436 men and youths aged over fifteen, and burned the town to the ground. A twenty-four-foot-high cross was raised to the victims' memory, and the church clock was stopped at the time of execution: 2.34.

MONI HAGHIA LAVRA. This monastery, about 4 miles from Kalavrita, was founded in 961. Here Archbishop Germanos of Patras, raised the revolt on March 21, 1821 ● *51*. The present monastery dates mostly from 1839, but the katholikon, dedicated to the Dormition, is much older. The museum contains objects from the Mycenean and classical eras, and manuscripts from the 11th and 12th centuries. On the road skirting the Gulf of Corinth, don't miss the site of Aegira (ancient Hyperesia), which is being excavated by the Austrian Institute of Archeology. A Hellenistic theater and Roman baths have been uncovered; on the Acropolis vestiges of Mycenean buildings and pottery have been brought to light, and foundations from the 7th century BC, which may be those of the Temple of Artemis Iphigenia referred to by Pausanias. At Mavra Litharia ("black rocks") the region of Corinth begins; from here the freeway leads to Sikea, where the home of the poet Angelos Sikelianos (1884–1951) ● *64* has been made into a museum. From Xylokastron a road leads to the site of Sicyon: there are remains of a theater (3rd century BC), a Doric temple (4th century BC) and a Hellenistic gymnasium. To complete your circuit of the Peloponnese, continue to Corinth ▲ *296*, about 13 miles farther on.

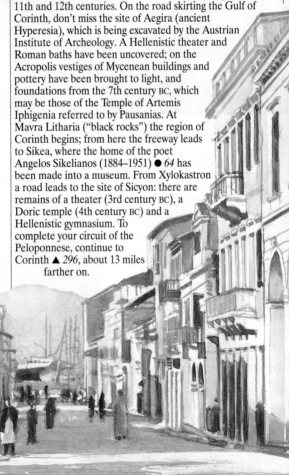

Islands of the Saronic Gulf

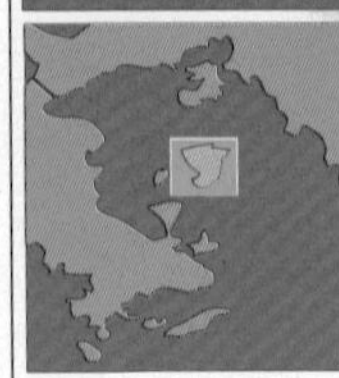

One day

In the 14th century a twin-domed chapel dedicated to Saint Nicholas was built on one of the piers of the port. Behind the masts of the vessels at anchor stand an array of fine 19th-century houses, clustered around the cathedral. Aegina's museum, which was installed in the Eynardion in the 19th century, has three rooms devoted to its archeological collections: these include Mycenean vases, sculptures such as the famous Sphinx of Aegina, geometrically decorated ceramics, terracottas and Byzantine sculptures.

AEGINA

The Aeginetans distinguished themselves at a very early date by their excellent ships and seamanship. Diodorus Siculus claimed in the 1st century BC that they were among the score or so of tribes which had mastered the sea, and created a government based on that mastery. They had outposts at Miletus, on the Black Sea, in Cyprus and in Egypt, while to the east they maintained commercial relations with Umbria, in Italy, and mainland Spain.

AEGINA AND ATHENS. Because of its strategic position, Aegina was viewed as a threat by Athens; indeed Pericles called the island "the eyesore of Piraeus". At the start of the 5th century BC, at the urging of Themistocles, Athens equipped two hundred ships for war with Aegina, which had formed an alliance with its trading partner, Persia. But when Xerxes invaded Greece in 480 BC Aegina took the side of Athens, sending thirty triremes to the Battle of Salamis ● *45*. In 431 BC the Peloponnesian War ● *46* broke out between Athens and Sparta, to whom the Aeginetans were allied. After a nine-month siege, the city of Aegina surrendered; its fortifications were immediately dismantled, its fleet destroyed, and its inhabitants expelled. The final defeat of Athens in 405 BC allowed the Aeginetans to return to their island, but they never regained their former prosperity.

Coinage of Aegina
The wealthy shipowners of Aegina minted the island's first coins, with the emblem of a sea turtle.

Temple of Aphaia

Haghia Marina

Ancient sites on Aegina

To the north of Karantina is the Kriptos Limen ("hidden port"), built in classical times, where the piers and docks, capable of holding sixty triremes, are still visible below the surface of the water.

Column of Apollo. This first site is on the hill of Kolona, above the "hidden port". The Myceneans who settled here between the 16th and the 12th centuries BC erected major fortifications. The column, still standing, that gave its name to the spot belonged to the *opisthodomos* of a Doric peripteral temple ● *90*, dedicated to Apollo around 500 BC; this replaced a 7th-century BC shrine. Several sculptures from these temples have been unearthed, as well as marble bas-reliefs from a monument dedicated to Ajax, dating from about 500 BC, which is mentioned by Pausanias.

Temple of Aphaia. The second site is about 8 miles to the northeast. It can be reached by bus or boat, both of which stop at the fine beach of Haghia Marina, a thirty-minute walk from the main site. The temple, on a pine-covered hillside, is the most famous on any Greek island, except perhaps Delos, due to its position and excellent state of preservation. Objects found nearby show that it must have been founded in about the 3rd millennium BC. From the 13th century BC it was dedicated to an ancient local goddess, Aphaia (the "Invisible One"). In the 6th century it was rebuilt along the lines of the Mycenean *megaron* ● *82*. At that time it consisted of a *cella* preceded by a *pronaos* bounded by lateral walls, and the pediment was supported by two simple columns. Around 490 BC it was rebuilt again, in locally quarried limestone and marble. It is about 95 feet long and 45 feet wide. During the Athenian occupation the temple was reconsecrated to Athena; twenty years later its east pediment of Parian marble was struck by lightning, and its damaged sculptures were buried in the sacred precinct. The sculptures of the west pediment date from the end of the Archaic period, whereas those which replaced the original sculptures on the east pediment were installed around 480 BC, heralding a new classical style.

Temple of Aphaia
This Doric peripteral temple is six columns wide and twelve long. Its double interior colonnade of five columns – of different orders, placed one on top of the other – is unique. It divided the *cella*, the main room of the temple, which contained the statue of the goddess, into three parts.

The sculptures of the east pediment were discovered in April of 1811 by four architects and painters from Germany and Britain: Cockerell, Foster, Haller von Hallerstein and Linck. They were sold to the King of Bavaria for 130,000 gold francs. The most famous of them (now in Munich) were a head of Athena, a kneeling Hercules and a dying warrior.

Four hours

PALAIOKHORA. At the summit of the Oros is the ghost town of Palaiokhora, once the refuge of islanders fleeing from the coast when pirates were sighted. The ruined houses, dating from the 9th and 10th centuries, were protected by a medieval stronghold. Although destroyed by the Turks in 1537 and by the Venetians in 1634, Palaiokhora was inhabited until the early 19th century. Steep alleys lead up through the houses clustered on the hilltop. The most famous of the churches, the Omorphi Ekklesia ("beautiful church"), built in 1239, has remarkable frescos.

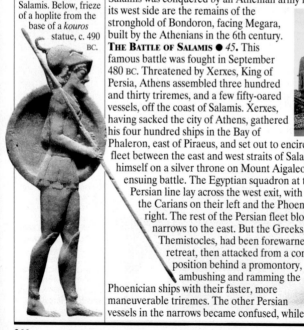

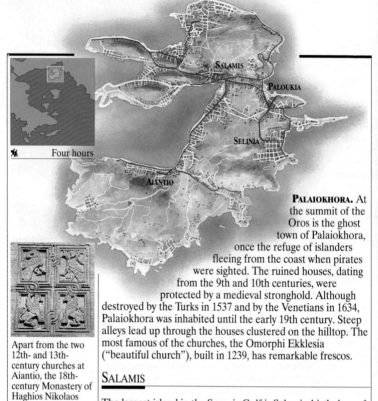

Apart from the two 12th- and 13th-century churches at Aiantio, the 18th-century Monastery of Haghios Nikolaos and the 17th-century Convent of Phaneromini, there are few Byzantine monuments on Salamis. Below, frieze of a hoplite from the base of a *kouros* statue, c. 490 BC.

SALAMIS

The largest island in the Saronic Gulf is Salamis, birthplace of the Homeric hero Ajax. Its first inhabitants were Phoenician colonists. Archeologists have uncovered vestiges of an acropolis and a port dating from the Mycenean era. In 612 BC Salamis was conquered by an Athenian army led by Solon. On its west side are the remains of the stronghold of Bondoron, facing Megara, built by the Athenians in the 6th century.

THE BATTLE OF SALAMIS ● *45*. This famous battle was fought in September 480 BC. Threatened by Xerxes, King of Persia, Athens assembled three hundred and thirty triremes, and a few fifty-oared vessels, off the coast of Salamis. Xerxes, having sacked the city of Athens, gathered his four hundred ships in the Bay of Phaleron, east of Piraeus, and set out to encircle the Greek fleet between the east and west straits of Salamis. He installed himself on a silver throne on Mount Aigaleos to watch the ensuing battle. The Egyptian squadron at the center of the Persian line lay across the west exit, with the Ionians and the Carians on their left and the Phoenicians on their right. The rest of the Persian fleet blocked the narrows to the east. But the Greeks, commanded by Themistocles, had been forewarned; they feigned retreat, then attacked from a concealed position behind a promontory, ambushing and ramming the Phoenician ships with their faster, more maneuverable triremes. The other Persian vessels in the narrows became confused, while

their Greek adversaries had the advantage of fighting with the shore behind them. After the first encounter, the Greeks beached as many wrecks as they could on the island and prepared to fight a second time. But the Persians had had enough. Xerxes formed a pontoon of ships between the mainland and Salamis to create a screen while the remains of his fleet made for the open sea. Messengers were sent to Persia with news of the defeat and orders that the bridge of ships across the Hellespont should be cut to prevent the Greeks from hindering Xerxes' retreat. A few months later the Greeks won the Battle of Plataea, and by the following year the Persian threat had melted away.

HYDRA

Hydreia (the "well-watered" island) only acquired a significant population after 1460, with the arrival of refugees from Mistra fleeing the Turks; after 1730 there were several waves of Albanian immigrants. Maritime commerce, smuggling and piracy brought wealth to the Hydriots; wealthy captains and shipowners built Hydra's tall, grey-stone Italianate houses, the pride of the port. When, on March 25, 1821, the War of Independence ● *51* broke out, of the 290 Greek warships, 190 were Hydriot; and the Hydriot commanders Boundouridis, Miaoulis ● *55*, Tombatsis and Tsamados played a leading role in the war. By the end of the conflict, Hydra had been reduced to a ships' graveyard. Shortly afterward George Kountouriotis, one of the Hydriot leaders, became the head of the Greek government.

PLACES OF INTEREST. On the quayside stands a 17th-century monastery with a marble bell tower and a fine cloister. On its west side the port is overlooked by the remains of a medieval citadel, to which fortifications were added after 1821. In the north of the island stands the isolated Monastery of Zourvas. At Kalo Pigadi there are 17th-century houses, some tiny, exquisite chapels and a magnificent view. To the south, a three-hour climb (on foot or by mule) will bring you to the Monastery of the Prophet Elijah, where Kolokotronis ▲ *322* and his companions were imprisoned in 1825 before being amnestied. The Convent of Haghia Efpraxia nearby is worth a visit, for its church and for the embroidery and weaving still practiced by the nuns.

HYDRA TODAY
Traffic is strictly limited on Hydra, and the yachts that anchor there have spawned luxury shops and a thriving nightlife in summer. The narrow streets winding up the hill between the whitewashed houses, the tiny squares and the flower-filled gardens have always attracted painters, whose work is sold in local galleries. The School of Fine Arts in Athens now owns the magnificent villa occupied by Admiral Iakovos Tombatsis in 1820.

Five hours

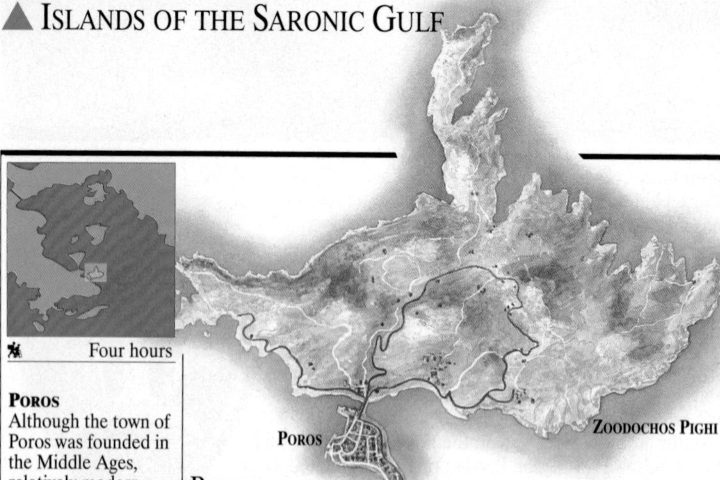

Four hours

POROS
Although the town of Poros was founded in the Middle Ages, relatively modern whitewashed houses, with blue shutters and tiled roofs, line the road all the way up the hill dominated by the elegant bell tower of the church.

POROS

Poros means "strait" in Greek, the two joined islands here being barely a quarter mile from the mainland. Poros was the main naval base in the region from the 18th century onward. Its shrine to Poseidon, common to several other Greek maritime cities and islands (among them Aegina), was founded in the 6th century BC close to a Mycenean settlement. It may be reached by taxi, or else by a walk (about an hour) along a path that skirts the island's south coast before cutting inland, through the pines, to a hilltop some 650 feet high. Along the way, visit the Zoodochos Pighi, a 17th-century monastery which has a fine gilded wood iconostasis.

SPETSAI

The island of Spetsai (ancient Pityoussa, meaning "pine-clad") is very green, and suffused with the resinous odor of Aleppo pines. Its coast is dotted with beaches, and traffic is largely banned from the harbor area. Spetsai was the first island to commit to the cause of Independence ● *51*. The houses of Laskarina Bouboulina ▲ *310* and Katzigiannis-Mexis (now a museum) are well worth visiting. Also to be seen are the 18th-century frescos in the Church of the Dormition, and the iconostasis in the 18th-century Haghia Triada. From the highest point in the island there is a fine view across the sea to the Peloponnese.

BOUBOULINA, HEROINE OF SPETSAI
One day when the Turks threatened Spetsai, and all the men were away at sea, Laskarina Bouboulina ▲ *310* had fezes put on every seafront plant. The Turks, believing a large force was awaiting them, sailed away.

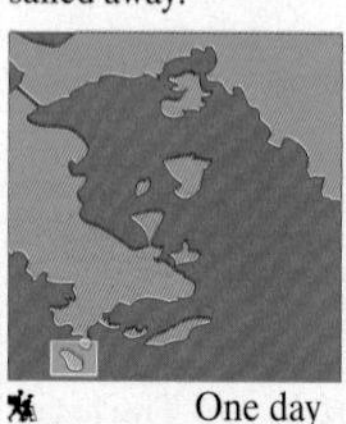

One day

Practical Information

As Greece has been a member of the EC since 1981, there are no entry restrictions for citizens of other EC member states. U.S. citizens do not need a visa to visit Greece. Due to its popularity as a tourist location, Greece is well represented by travel agents, who offer a wide choice of competitive package holidays, as well as a large number of charter flights.

INFORMATION

IN THE U.K.
GREEK TOURIST AGENCY
Morley House,
314-20 Regent Street
London W1
Tel. 071 437 0218

IN THE U.S.
GREEK TOURIST OFFICE IN NEW YORK
Olympia Towers
645 Fifth Avenue,
5th floor
New York, NY 10022
Tel. (212) 421 5777

GREEK TOURIST OFFICE IN CHICAGO
168 North Michigan
Avenue, Suite 600,
Chicago, IL 60601
Tel. (312) 782 1084

GREEK TOURIST OFFICE IN LOS ANGELES
611 West 6th Street,
Suite 2198
Los Angeles,
CA 90017
Tel. (213) 626 6696

FORMALITIES

For short stays, a current passport is adequate. If you want to stay longer than three months, you must obtain a visa.

CUSTOMS

EC regulations apply. You can bring out objects worth up to a maximum of £300/$200 per person, but this sum cannot be divided: a higher amount cannot be split between several people.

CURRENCY

There is no upper limit to the amount of foreign currency you can take into Greece. You can take100,000 drachmas in Greek currency. The maximum you can bring out is 25,000 drachmas per person.

HEALTH

You will need a doctor's prescription in order to take certain medications into Greece.

ANIMALS

You can take pets into Greece so long as you have a recent health certificate for them (six months for cats, a year for dogs), stating that they have been vaccinated against rabies. However, many hotels do not permit pets; and quarantine regulations apply in some countries (including the U.K.) when you return home.

U.K. AND U.S. EMBASSIES IN GREECE

AMERICAN EMBASSY
91 Vassilisis Sophias
Avenue
10160 Athens
Tel. (1) 721 29 51

BRITISH EMBASSY
1 Ploutarkhou Street
Kolonaki, Athens
Tel. (1) 723 62 11

DRIVING

If you are traveling in your own vehicle, you will need your registration papers and insurance certificate, as well as a current driving licence, which will also have to be produced when hiring a car in Greece.

MAJOR AIRLINES WHICH FLY TO GREECE

AMERICAN AIRLINES
For flight information
Tel. (800) 228 8356

BRITISH AIRWAYS
For flight information
Tel. 081 759 2525

OLYMPIC AIRWAYS
11 Conduit Street
London W1R
Tel. 071 409 2400
or 071 409 3717

TWA
For flight information
Tel. (800) 221 2000

UNITED AIRLINES
For flight information
Tel. (800) 241 6522

General view of the city of Athens, with Mount Lycabettus in the background.

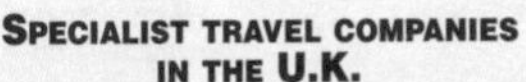

SPECIALIST TRAVEL COMPANIES IN THE U.K.

ADELPHI TRAVEL
16 Kennington Road
London SE1
Tel. 071 620 4455

ATHENA EXPRESS
308 Regent Street
London W1
Tel. 071 637 2057

KUONI TRAVEL LTD
84 Bishopsgate
London EC2
Tel. 071 374 6601

SIMPLY SIMON HOLIDAYS
1-45 Nevern Square
London SW5
Tel. 071 373 1933

CALENDAR OF SEASONAL EVENTS

SPRING — March to May

Spring revolves around the lavish celebration of Easter, a festival which forms the high point of the Orthodox Christian calendar.

FIRST MONDAY IN MARCH	**LENT**, PUBLIC HOLIDAY
MARCH 25, INDEPENDENCE DAY	**NATIONAL HOLIDAY** PUBLIC HOLIDAY
EASTER FRIDAY AND SATURDAY PUBLIC HOLIDAYS	**PROCESSIONS**, accompanied by folk dancing in some villages
EASTER SUNDAY	**RESURRECTION MASS**, in Tripolis the pascal lamb is roasted and carved in the market place after the Mass
EASTER MONDAY	**PUBLIC HOLIDAY**
MAY 1	**LABOUR DAY**, PUBLIC HOLIDAY

★ Easter hymns in the Small Metropolis in Athens.

MARCH 46°-58° · APRIL 52°-68° · MAY 61°-77°

SUMMER — June to August

Summer is the great season for festivals, as well as for crowds of tourists and sizzling temperatures. It is perfect for devotees of watersports, but spring or fall are better for visiting the major ancient sites.

MAY TO SEPTEMBER	**FOLK DANCING** at the Philopappos Theater, Wednesday and Friday evenings
JUNE, JULY, AUGUST, SEPTEMBER	**FESTIVAL OF ATHENS** PERFORMANCES OF CLASSICAL DRAMA, OPERA, BALLET AND CONCERTS at the Odeon of Herodes Atticus and the Lycabettus Theater
AUGUST 15	**ASSUMPTION**, PUBLIC HOLIDAY
END OF JUNE TO END OF AUGUST	**FESTIVAL OF EPIDAURUS**, PERFORMANCES OF CLASSICAL DRAMA
JUNE TO SEPTEMBER	**FESTIVAL OF PATRAS**, DRAMA, MUSIC, DANCE AND ART EVENTS

★ Open-air theater in Epidaurus.

JUNE 68°-86° · JULY 81°-91° · AUGUST 73°-91°

FALL — September to November

The season of the grape harvest. Several wine festivals, vestiges of time-honored tributes to Dionysos, take place in the fall.

SEPTEMBER	**WINE FESTIVAL** at Daphni
END AUGUST-EARLY SEPTEMBER	**WINE FESTIVAL** at Patras
SEPTEMBER 8-9	**REGATTA IN SPETSES** celebrating the victory over the Ottoman fleet in 1882
SEPTEMBER-OCTOBER	**INTERNATIONAL FAIR IN THESSALONIKI**, CINEMA, SINGING, DIMITRIA FESTIVAL

★ Sunset off Cape Sounion.

SEPTEMBER 66°-84° · OCTOBER 59°-75° · NOVEMBER 53°-66°

WINTER — December to February

The Greek winter is liberally dotted with religious festivals.

DECEMBER 25	**CHRISTMAS**, PUBLIC HOLIDAY
JANUARY	**BLESSING OF THE WATERS AT PIRAEUS**
JANUARY 5	**EPIPHANY**, PUBLIC HOLIDAY
FEBRUARY	THREE WEEKS BEFORE ORTHODOX LENT, **CARNIVAL IS CELEBRATED THROUGHOUT GREECE**. THE FIRST DAY OF LENT IS THE FEAST OF THE PURIFICATION

★ Carnival in Plaka.

DECEMBER 46°-59° · JANUARY 43°-55° · FEBRUARY 45°-57°

Sunny and hot · Changeable to overcast · Rainy · Cold, possible snow

Minimum and maximum temperatures are shown in degrees Fahrenheit.

When to go: The best times to visit Athens and the Peloponnese

Opt for spring (May-June) or fall (September-October), so you avoid the extreme temperatures and summer crowds. The quieter atmosphere will enhance your appreciation of the sites and museums, the surrounding countryside is particularly beautiful at these times of year, and the sea is warm enough for swimming.

Clothing suggestions

In summer:
lightweight clothing, a hat, sunglasses.
In spring or fall:
a jacket and sweater for the evenings and days when the *meltemi* blows in.
All year round:
a formal, even dressy, outfit for shows and smart restaurants. You will need flat, comfortable shoes for visits to archeological sites.
When visiting churches women must cover their arms: do not be caught out – take a shirt, cardigan, or shawl with you wherever you go.

Maps of Athens

The Falk Map of Athens, with an exhaustive index of streets (scale 1:23,000), is available from good bookstores.

Maps of Greece

On sale everywhere:
Map of Greece, Michelin No. 980 (1:700,000).
Map of Greece, Kümerly-Frey, more accurate though more expensive (1:500,000).
Map of the Peloponnese and Attica, Hallwag (1:400,000).

Weather from May to October

May	June	July	Aug	Sept	Oct
Daytime temperature					
77°	86°	91°	91°	84°	75°
Nighttime temperature					
61°	68°	73°	73°	66°	59°
Number of hours of sunshine per day					
9	11	12	12	9	7
Number of days of rain					
4	1	1	1	2	6
Daytime temperature of the sea					
79°	88°	93°	93°	86°	75°
Nighttime temperature of the sea					
63°	70°	73°	73°	68°	61°

What to take

During the summer, remember to take a good sunscreen and an effective insect-repellent cream. As medication is more expensive in Greece, it is a good idea to stock up with your usual first-aid and toiletry products – as well as anti-sunstroke medication if you are particularly sensitive to the sun. Buy films before you go: they are more expensive in Greece, and it is virtually impossible to find slide film.

Reading suggestions

As the ancient seat of Western culture, Greece has inspired many writers and artists. You will find their accounts and novels are excellent as an introduction or traveling companions:

You can relive Odysseus' travels with Homer's *Odyssey*.

Zorba the Greek (1946) by Nikos Kazantzakis is a perennially popular classic.

Greek Art (1985) by John Boardman will enhance your appreciation of the art of Ancient Greece.

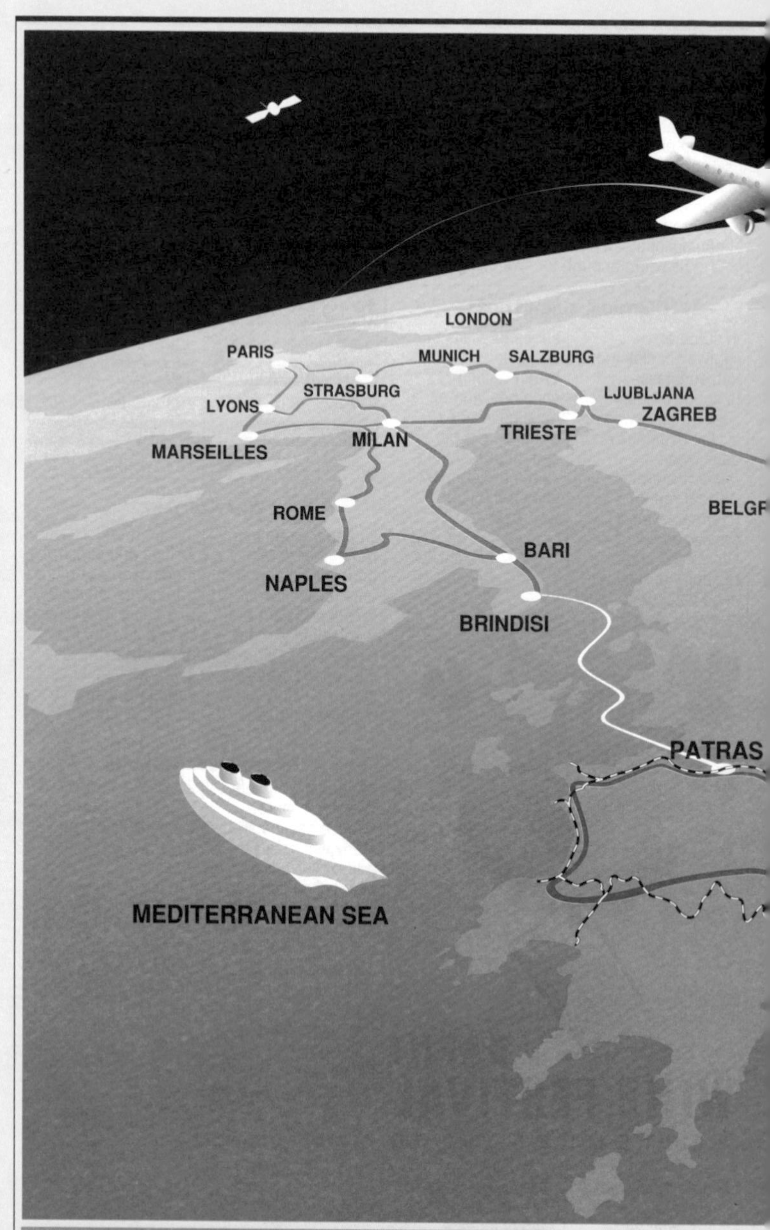

Traveling costs

	Time	Average Cost
From the U.S.		
Direct flight from New York	9 hours	\$756–\$2138 return
From the U.K.		
Direct flight from London	3½ hours	£178–£491 return
By coach (summer only)	3 days	£218 return

Distances between Athens and major European cities

Paris	1,825 miles
London	1,900 miles
Berlin	1,825 miles
Rome	775 miles
Madrid	2,350 miles
Amsterdam	1,800 miles

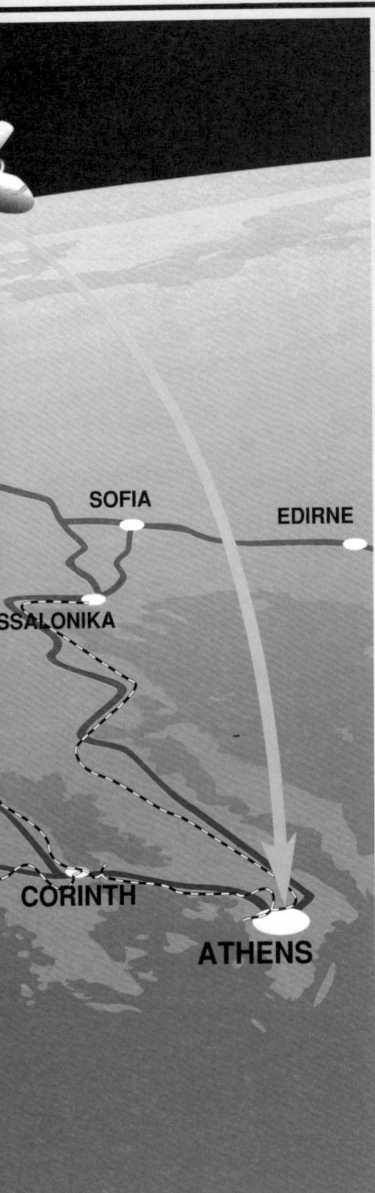

By air

From the U.S.

American Airlines
New York to Athens with stopover in either London or Brussels $698–$2080 (coach class).
Chicago to Athens with stopover in either Frankfurt, Munich or Zurich $768–$2798 (coach class).
Los Angeles to Athens with stopovers in New York or Chicago and a European city $918–$3398 (coach class)

TWA
New York to Athens direct $756–2138.
Chicago to New York then direct to Athens $832–$2398.
Los Angeles to New York then direct to Athens $1032.

From the U.K.

British Airways
Direct daily flights from London Heathrow to Athens depart at noon and 11pm, and from London Gatwick at 9.45am. Full fare £491 return.

Charter flights
Apart from the special deals offered by major airline companies, travel agents have many charter flights on offer.

Getting from the airport to the town center
Hellenikon Airport, near Athens, has two terminals: West (Tel. 981 12 01 or 969 94 66) for Olympic Airways, and East (Tel. 969 69 91) for other airlines. Buses and shuttles provided by Olympic Airways run a service between the airport and the town center: between 5.30am and 12.30pm (every 30 minutes), 160 drachmas; between 12.30am and 5.30am (every hour), 200 drachmas.

By rail

Regular departures from London's Victoria station, via Paris.
Tel. 071 834 2345.

By car

From the U.K. you should allow five to six days by road, driving through France, Germany, Austria and Hungary.

By car and ferry

You can catch a ferry in Venice, Ancona, Bari, Brindisi or Otranto. It is advisable to book at least two months in advance.

Cheap fares

- British Airways offer cheap fares to Athens from Monday to Thursday of £178 return and on weekends £189 return. Flights are generally cheaper off season.
- Young people can use an InterRail Card for cheap train fares all over Europe.

◆ MAP OF ATHENS

Kerameikos Cemetery ▲ 200.

The Olympieion ▲ 216.

The Propylaea ▲ 136, on the Acropolis.

The Hephaisteion ▲ 191, in the Agora.

Bus tickets

THE MOUNT LYCABETTUS FUNICULAR

You will see signs for the entrance to the funicular as soon as you reach Vasilissis Sophias Avenue. This will take you to the top of the highest hill in Athens. It operates from 9am to 12.45pm (10am to 12.45pm on Tuesdays).

THE METRO SYSTEM

Athens has only one metro line, which you can take when sightseeing. It links Piraeus and Kifissia, and runs through the city's liveliest areas: Thissio, Monastiraki, Syntagma, Omonia and Victoria. The ticket for one zone costs 75 drachmas. The metro is open daily from 5.30am to midnight.

BUSES

The city has an extensive network of buses. This is a convenient and inexpensive form of transport (75 drachmas, whatever the length of journey). Tickets can be bought from the kiosks. The bus routes are indicated on the map of Athens provided by the Tourist Police. Ordinary bus stops are blue, trolley-bus stops yellow.

ΠΛΑΤΕΙΑ
ΑΓ. ΑΙΚΑΤΕΡΙΝΗΣ
ΙΣΤΟΡΙΚΗ ΜΟΝΗ ΤΟΥ ΣΙΝΑ

ΛΕΩΦΟΡΟΣ
ΝΙΚ. ΠΛΑΣΤΗΡΑ
ΗΡΩΪΚΟΣ ΣΤΡΑΤΗΓΟΣ κ ΠΟΛΙΤΙΚΟΣ

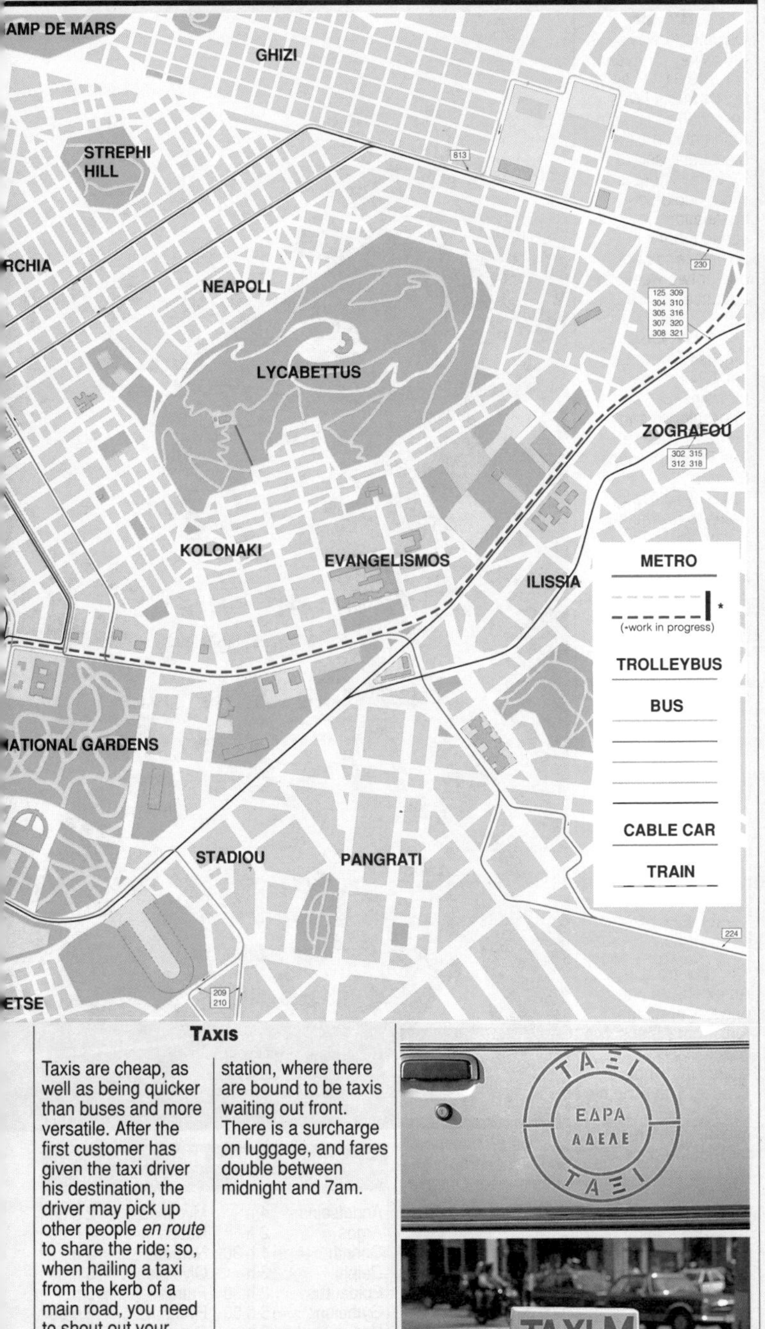

Taxis

Taxis are cheap, as well as being quicker than buses and more versatile. After the first customer has given the taxi driver his destination, the driver may pick up other people *en route* to share the ride; so, when hailing a taxi from the kerb of a main road, you need to shout out your destination clearly in Greek. You may find it simpler to head for large hotels and restaurants or the station, where there are bound to be taxis waiting out front. There is a surcharge on luggage, and fares double between midnight and 7am.

BY AIR
Olympic Airways (96, Syngrou Avenue, Tel. 926 91 11) fly from Athens (West Terminal) to Kalamata, in Messenia, and to Kythera. There is a wider choice of destinations in season, but it is advisable to book one or two weeks in advance.

BY RAIL
LARISSA STATION, Tel. 524 06 46: for trains to Thessaloniki and northern Greece.
THE PELOPONNISSOS STATION, Tel. 513 16 01: for trains to Patras and Kalamata.

INFORMATION (IN ATHENS): 6, Sina Street, Tel. 362 44 02; 17 Filelinon Street, Tel. 323 67 47 and 323 62 73; 1 Karolou Street, Tel. 522 24 91

GENERAL BUS AND TRAIN INFORMATION:
Railway Company of Greece (OSE), 1, Karolou Street, Tel. 522 24 91.

BY COACH
An extensive public network of routes runs from Athens' two coach stations and covers the whole of Greece. Traveling by coach is more expensive than by rail, but the price is still reasonable and coaches are extremely punctual. Timetables and reservations at the coach stations and from the Tourist Police.
COACH STATION TERMINAL A
100, Kifissiou Street Tel. 512 49 10. Catch the 051 bus from the junction of Zinonos and Menandrou streets (near Omonia Square) to get there. Coaches for the Peloponnese.
COACH STATION TERMINAL B
260, Liossion Street. The 024 bus goes there from Amalias Avenue. Coaches for Attica and Boeotia.

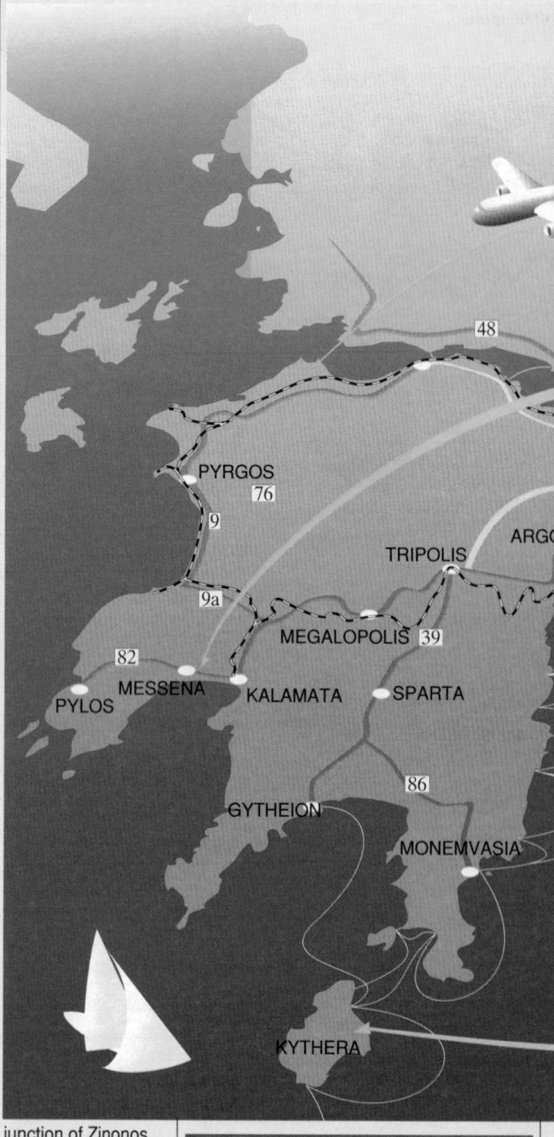

COACH ROUTES FROM ATHENS

Destination	Journey time	Destination	Journey time
Andritsaina	4 h	Mycenae	2 h 30
Argos	2 h	Nauplion	2 h 30
Corinth	1 h 30	Nemea	3 h
Delphi	3 h	Olympia	5 h 30
Epidaurus	2 h 30	Patras	3 h
Gytheion	5 h 30	Pylos	5 h 30
Hosios Loukas	3 h	Pyrgos	5 h
Kalamata	4 h 30	Sparta	4 h 30
Karitaina	4 h	Marathon	0 h 40
Megalopolis	3 h 15	Sounion	2 h
Monemvasia	7 h	Thebes	1 h 30

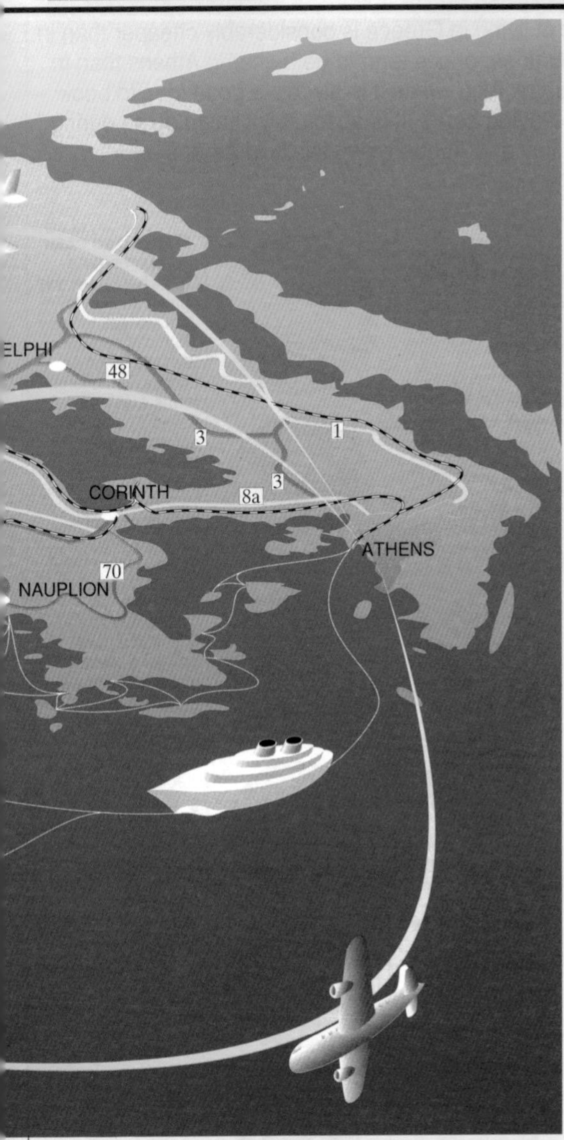

Boats and ferries from Piraeus

Destinations:
- Southern Peloponnese: Paralia, Geraki, Monemvasia, Neapolis, Elafonissos, Gytheion, and Kythera (Haghia Pelagia, Kapsali).
- The Saronic Gulf: Salamis, Aegina, Poros, Hydra, Spetses and Nauplion.
- To Patras, via Corinth and Aigion.

Information:
GNTO, Tel. 322 31 11 Piraeus Port Police; Tel. 451 13 11 or the Piraeus-Zea Marina, Tel. 452 71 07

Chartering a yacht
Contact the Athens Association of Yacht Charterers, Tel. 982 71 07

Car hire

It is extremely easy to hire a car or motorcycle. Be warned, however, that although the main roads have been resurfaced, most of the minor roads in the Peloponnese have not yet been asphalted.

Hertz
12, Syngrou Avenue, Tel. 922 01 02; East Terminal, Tel. 961 36 25; West Terminal, Tel. 981 37 01

Avis
46-48, Amalias Avenue, Tel. 322 49 51

Autorent
94, Syngrou Avenue, Tel. 923 25 14; – 66 14; – 65 29; – 84 38.

Budget Rent-A-Car
8, Syngrou Avenue, Tel. 921 47 71

Kosmos Rent-A-Car
9, Syngrou Avenue, Tel. 923 46 97

Distance between Athens and major Greek cities

City	Distance	City	Distance
Andritsaina	174 miles	Mycenae	56 miles
Argos	114 miles	Nauplion	92 miles
Corinth	54 miles	Nemea	81 miles
Delphi	106 miles	Olympia	203 miles
Epidaurus	100 miles	Patras	133 miles
Gytheion	175 miles	Pylos	194 miles
Hosios Loukas	94 miles	Pyrgos	215 miles
Kalamata	160 miles	Sparta	159 miles
Karitaina	138 miles	Marathon	24 miles
Megalopolis	122 miles	Sounion	43 miles
Monemvasia	234 miles	Thebes	52 miles

Although the cost of living in Greece is considerably cheaper than in most other EC countries, prices tend to be higher in Athens than in the rest of the country. Also, while it is always a good idea to book your hotel before leaving home, it is absolutely vital to do so during the high season (July and August), especially in Athens.

IN CASE OF LOSS OR THEFT

TOURIST POLICE ATHENS:
923 92 24
969 95 23
981 40 93
AEGINA: (297)
223 91
233 33
DELPHI: (285)
829 20
HYDRA: (298)
522 05

MONEY MATTERS

The Greek unit of currency is the drachma. This is subdivided into 100 lepta, which are now hardly ever used. You will come across 1 drachma, 2 drachma, 5 drachma, 10 drachma, 20 drachma and 50 drachma coins – but coins of the same value can be different sizes, which often leads to mistakes. The notes currently in circulation are worth 50 drachmas, 100 drachmas, 1,000 drachmas and 5,000 drachmas.

EXCHANGE RATE

The exchange rate for drachmas is 360 drachmas to £1, 240 drachmas to $1. Traveler's checks as well as U.S. dollars and sterling are accepted by all banks, as well as many hotels, travel agents and shops. However, banks still offer the best exchange rate. You can also change Eurocheques at post offices and the yellow post-office vans ▲*384*.

BANKS AND CASH DISPENSERS

Greek banks are only open from 8am to 2pm Monday to Thursday, and from 8am to 1.30pm on Fridays. In the larger towns it isn't difficult to find a bank or an automatic cash machine, but it is not a good idea to head for the mountain regions without sufficient cash. In remote places there are few banks and even fewer cashpoints, so you will need to take traveler's checks, plus enough money to survive on until you reach the next big town. However, nowadays the use of credit cards is gradually becoming more widespread. On the islands, you will find that some bureaux de change and banks are usually open near the harbor at weekends.

CREDIT AND DEBIT CARDS

Credit and debit cards, such as Mastercard and Visa, are accepted in most hotels and quality restaurants, as well as in shops. They can also be used to make withdrawals from the cashpoints of the Commercial Bank of Greece and the Ionian Bank. Eurocheques can be changed in banks as well as in post offices.

ACCOMMODATION

The prices within each category tend to vary according to the facilities they offer – so a Category C hotel can be more expensive than a Category B hotel.

LUXURY HOTELS
Spacious air-conditioned rooms or suites, with bathroom. Sumptuous facilities such as swimming pools, private beaches, saunas, tennis courts, bars, restaurants, tavernas and shopping arcades.

CATEGORY A HOTELS
Comfortable air-conditioned rooms, with bathroom. More often than not they have a swimming pool, restaurant and bar.

CATEGORY B HOTELS
Rooms may or may not be air-conditioned, with bathroom or shower room. Often have a taverna or a restaurant.

CATEGORY C HOTELS
Fairly comfortable, unexceptional rooms, with shower room and private WC.

CAMPING
There are around one hundred campsites in the Peloponnese, and about fifty between Mount Parnassus and Cape Sounion. Although some stay open all year round, most are only open from April or May to October. They are not graded.

RENTING A ROOM
There are often rooms to rent in private houses in small towns and villages, both in the mountains and by the sea. Ask at local branches of the Tourist Police.

OTHER ACCOMMODATION
You can also rent apartments and other kinds of furnished accommodation, such as bungalows in holiday villages.

AVERAGE PRICES, AND NUMBER OF HOTELS IN EACH CATEGORY

Average price	Athens	Attica	Peloponnese
LUXURY £110–180 $160–270	14	7	1
CAT. A £45–60 $70–90	17	45	32
CAT. B £25–40 $40–60	69	76	103
CAT. C £12–25 $20–35	114	110	186

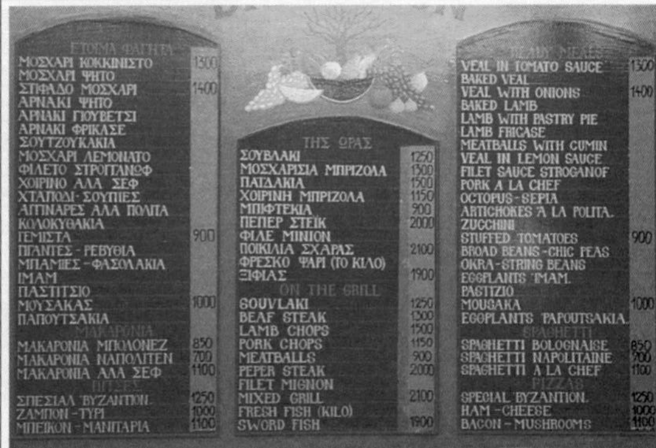

EATING OUT

STARTERS (PIKILIA)
Dolmádhes: rice in vine leaves
Fasolakia: green beans
Khoriatiki: Greek salad (tomatoes, cucumber, olives, onions, feta cheese)
Kreatopitta: meat pasty
Piperies gemistes: stuffed sweet peppers
Piperies salata: pepper salad
Melitsano gemistes: stuffed eggplants
Melitsáno salata: cold puréed eggplant
Spanachopita: spinach pasty
Tárama: taramasalata
Tiropitta: cheese pasty
Tzaziki: yoghurt, cucumber, garlic dip.

FISH (PSARI)
Astakos: lobster
Bakaliaros: salt cod
Gharídes: prawns
Glossa: sole
Gopes: fried fish
Kalamarákia: squid
Ksifias: swordfish
Óctapodi: octopus
Pestrofa: trout

MEAT (KREAS)
Arnáki: lamb
Brizóla: cutlet
Kefthèdes: meatballs
Khirino: pork
Kokorètsi: stuffed offal roasted on a spit
Kotópoulo: chicken
Moschari: veal
Mousakás: Moussaka
Psitó: roasted meat
Souvlákia: meat kebabs on a skewer
Vrastó: boiled meat

DESSERTS (GHLIKO)
Baklavás: filo pastry with almonds and honey
Bougatsa: sweet custard pie
Froúta: fruit
Ghiaoúti: yoghurt
Koulourakia: biscuits sprinkled with sesame seeds
Loukouma: Turkish Delight
Tirí: cheese

DRINKS
Bíra: beer
Kafé: coffee
Krasí: wine
Neró: water

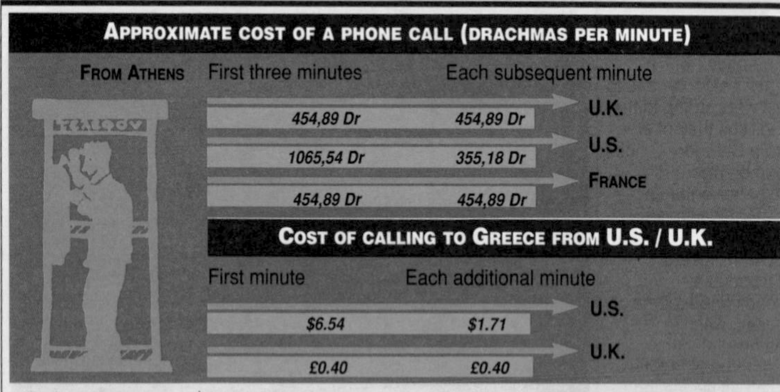

APPROXIMATE COST OF A PHONE CALL (DRACHMAS PER MINUTE)

FROM ATHENS	First three minutes	Each subsequent minute
U.K.	454,89 Dr	454,89 Dr
U.S.	1065,54 Dr	355,18 Dr
FRANCE	454,89 Dr	454,89 Dr

COST OF CALLING TO GREECE FROM U.S. / U.K.

	First minute	Each additional minute
U.S.	$6.54	$1.71
U.K.	£0.40	£0.40

TELEPHONE AND TELEGRAMS

In large towns centers run by the OTE (Telecommunications Company of Greece) are open from 7am to 11pm. You can also make phone calls from phone boxes and kiosks, as well as from hotels and restaurants.

PHONING THE U.S. OR U.K. FROM GREECE: Dial 00 1 for the U.S., 00 44 for the U.K., then the area code and number you require.

PHONING GREECE FROM THE U.K. OR U.S: From the U.S. dial 011 30, from the U.K. dial

010 30 (00 30 from April 16,1995), then the area code (1 for Athens) and the number you require.

INFORMATION
For international calls: 161/162.

SOME USEFUL AREA CODES

Include the 0 at the start of the code if you are phoning within Greece.

Aigion: (0691)
Aegina: (0297)
Athens: (01)
Corinth: (0741)
Delphi: (0265)
Epidaurus: (0753)
Ermioni: (0754)
Gytheion: (0733)
Glyfada: (01)
Hosios Loukas: (0267)
Hydra: (0298)
Itea: (0265)
Kalamaki: (01)
Kalamata: (0721)
Karpenissi: (0237)
Kifissia: (01)
Kiparissia: (0761)
Lamia: (0231)
Piraeus: (01)
Loutra Ipatis: (0231)
Loutra Killinis: (0623)
Loutraki: (0744)
Methoni: (0723)
Mistra: (0731)
Mycenae: (0751)
Monemvasia: (0732)
Nauplion (Tolo): (0752)
Nemea: (0746)
Olympia: (0624)
Patras: (061)
Poros: (0298)
Porto Heli: (0754)
Pylos: (0624)
Pyrgos: (0621)
Sicyon: (0742)
Sounion: (0292)
Sparta: (0731)
Spetses: (0298)
Thebes: (0262)
Tiryns: (0752)
Tripolis: (071)
Xilokastron: (0743)

POSTAL SERVICES

Most post offices are open Monday to Friday from 7.30am to 3.30pm, and closed on Saturdays. They only handle the distribution of mail (telecommunications are the responsibility of the OTE). You can receive mail sent *poste restante* (general delivery) to the central post office in each town. At the height of the tourist season yellow mail vans, providing the same services as post offices, travel the city streets.

IN ATHENS
The main post offices are on Eolou Street and Syntagma Square; they are open Monday to Friday from 7.30am to 8pm, and Saturday from 7.30am to 2pm. (The other post offices in Athens are open at the times given above.) For information Tel. 323 75 73.

SOME USEFUL NUMBERS

EMERGENCY ASSISTANCE
Police: 100
Hospitals: 106
Pharmacies: 107
Ambulance: 166
Fire brigade: 199

PRACTICAL INFORMATION
Roadside assistance: 104
Tourism: 171
Coaches: 142
Trains: 145

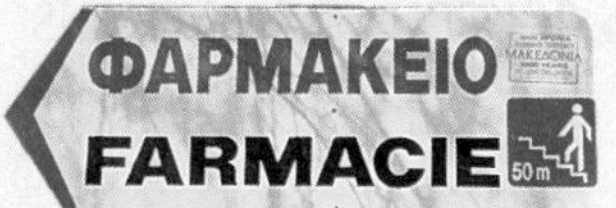

Tourist information

Greek National Tourist Offices (GNTO) in Athens
- Head office
2, Amerikis Street,
Tel. 322 31 11-9
- Information desk,
East Terminal,
Tel. 969 95 00
- Information desk,
National Bank,
2, Kar. Servias Street,
Tel. 322 25 45
- Information desk,
National Bank,
1, Ermou Street,
Tel. 323 41 30
- Athens Festival office,
4, Stadiou Street,
Tel. 322 14 59 and
322 31 11-9

Greek National Tourist Offices (GNTO) outside Athens
Piraeus
Marina Zea, 185 04
Piraeus,
Tel. 413 57 16, 413 47 09, 413 57 30
Patras
Iroön Politekhniou Street,
Tel. (61) 65 33 58/61

Newspapers

Foreign daily newspapers and magazines are available in Athens and the major towns (albeit at elevated prices). There are also several English-language newspapers and magazines published in Athens, such as *The Athenian* and *Athenian News*.

SOME SAMPLE PRICES

Coffee or tea: 80 to 200 drachmas

1 breakfast: 600 to 1,000 drachmas

1 litre of petrol: 200 to 240 drachmas

A meal in a taverna: 2,400 to 5,200 drachmas

1 glass of wine or beer: 200 to 400 drachmas

1 postcard with stamp: 90 drachmas

1 museum admission: 400 drachmas

1 double room: 8,000 to 12,000 drachmas

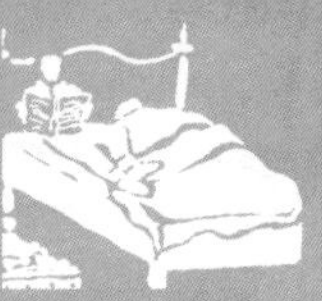

Greek time

GMT + 2 hours, so 7 hours ahead of U.S. East Coast time.

Shopping hours
Shops are generally open from 8.30am to 1.30pm, and from 5pm to 8pm.

Siesta
Most shops and services close down during the hottest part of the day. Siesta time is generally from 2pm to 4pm, but may start around 1.30pm and last to 5pm.

1. Erechtheion, Porch of the Caryatids.

2. Goulandris Museum: Cycladic figurine, 3rd Century BC.

3. Acropolis Museum: hound, c. 530 BC.

4. The Small Metropolis, in Plaka.

. Benaki Museum: 18th-century breastplate in the shape of a caravel.

7. Byzantine Museum: iconostasis.

6. National Historical Museum: Ephebos, 340 BC.

8. Theseion (or Hephaisteion), in the Agora.

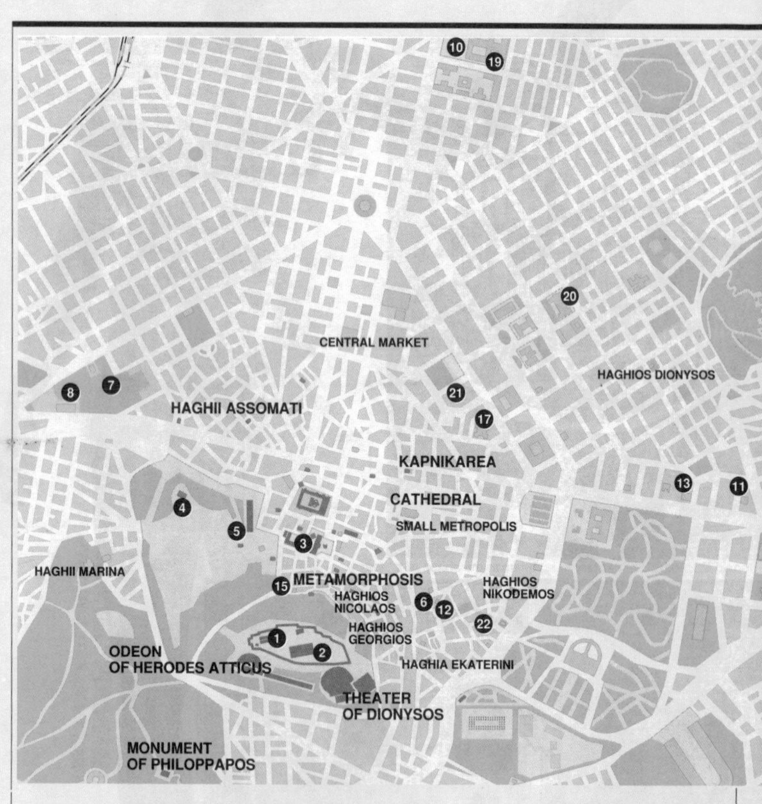

1• Acropolis, archeological site	Tel. 321 02 19	Open Mon. to Fri. 8am-5pm; Sat., Sun. and holidays 8.30am-3pm.
2• Acropolis, museum	Tel. 323 66 65	Open Tues. to Fri. 8am-5pm; Sat., Sun. and holidays 8.30am-3pm; Mon. 11am-5pm.
3• Roman Agora, archeological site	Corner Pelopida and Eolou Sts Tel. 324 52 20	Open 8.30am-3pm; closed Mon.
4• Ancient Agora, Hephaisteion and museum 5•	Tel. 321 01 85	Open 8.30am-3pm; closed Mon.
6• Museum of Greek Popular Art	6, Hatsim Ihali Street, Tel. 324 39 87	Open Tues. and Thurs. 9am-9pm; Wed., Fri., Sat. and holidays 9am-1pm, 5pm-9pm; closed Mon.
7• Kerameikos Cemetery and Museum 8•	148, Ermou Street Tel. 346 35 52	Open Mon. 11am-5pm; Tues. to Fri. 8am-5pm; Sat., Sun. and holidays 8.30am-3pm.
9• National Picture Gallery	50, Vassilisis Konstantinou Ave. Tel. 721 10 10	Open Tues. to Sat. 9am-3pm; Sun. and holidays 10am-2pm; closed Mon.
10• National Archeological Museum	44, Patission Street Tel. 821 77 17	Open Mon. 11am-5pm; Tues. to Fri. 8am-5pm; Sat., Sun. and holidays 8.30am-3pm.
11• Museum of Cycladic and Ancient Art (Nicolas P. Goulandris Foundation)	4, Neofitou Douka Street Tel. 724 97 06	Open Mon. to Fri. 10am-3.30pm; Sat. 10am-2.30pm; closed Tues. and Sun.
12• Museum of Greek Folk Art	17, Kidathineon Street Tel. 321 30 18	Open Tues. to Sun. 10am-2pm; closed Mondays.
13• Benaki Museum	1, Koumbari Avenue and Vassilisis Sophias Avenue Tel. 361 16 17	Open 8.30am-2pm; closed Tues.

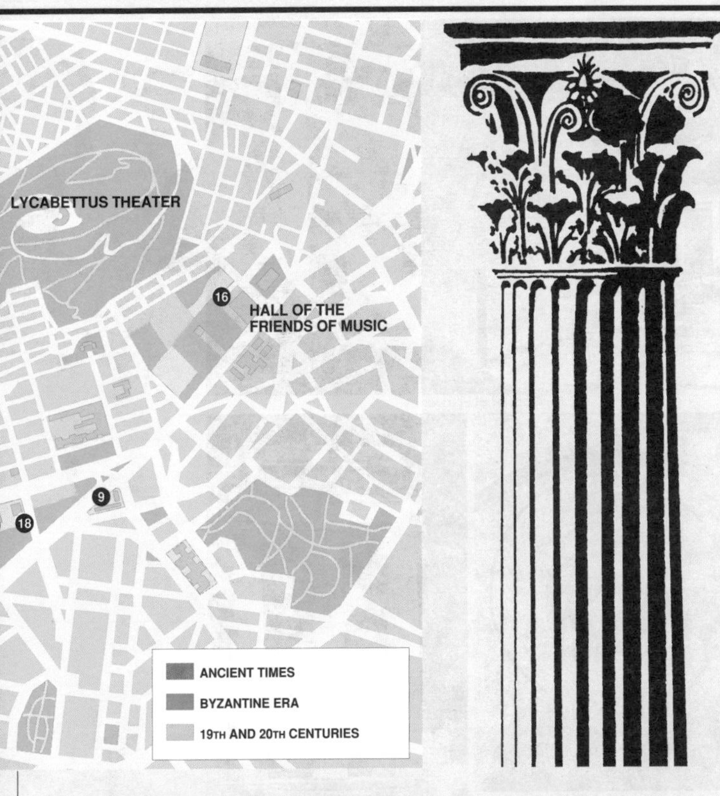

14• Byzantine Museum	22, Vassilisis Sophias Avenue Tel. 723 15 70	Open 8.30am-3pm; closed Mon.
15• Canellopoulos Museum	Corner Theorias - Panoss sts Tel. 321 23 13	Open Tues. to Sat. 8.30am-3pm; closed Mon.
16• Eleftherios Venizelos Museum	Eleftherias Park Tel. 722 42 38	Open Tues. to Sun. 10am-3pm; closed Mon.
17• National Historical Museum	13, Stadiou Street (Syntagma Square) Tel. 323 76 17	Open Tues. to Fri. 9am-1.30pm; Sat., Sun. and holidays 9am-12.30pm; closed Mon.
18• Military Museum	Vassilisis Sophias Avenue Tel. 729 95 43	Open Tues. to Sun. 9am-2pm; closed Mon.
19• Numismatic Museum	1, Tossitas Street Tel. 821 77 69	Open Tues.to Sat. 8.30am-1.30pm; Sun. and holidays 9am-2pm.
20• Museum and Center of Greek Theater	50, Acadimias Street Tel. 362 94 30	Open Mon. to Fri. 9am-3pm; Sun. and holidays 10am-1pm; closed Sat.
21• Museum of the City of Athens	7, Paparigopoulou Street (Klafthmonos Square) Tel. 323 01 68	Open Mon., Wed., Fri., Sat. and holidays 9am-1.30pm; closed Tues., Thurs. and Sun.
22• Jewish Museum	36, Amalias Avenue Tel. 323 15 77	Open every day 9am-1pm; closed Sat.
23• Daphni Monastery	Road to Corinth (near the car park) Tel. 15 81 15 58	Open 8.30am-3pm; closed Mon.
24• Kaisariani Monastery	4 miles from Athens Tel. 723 66 19	Open 8.30am-3pm; closed Mon.

◆ Museums and sites in Attica, Boeotia and the Peloponnese

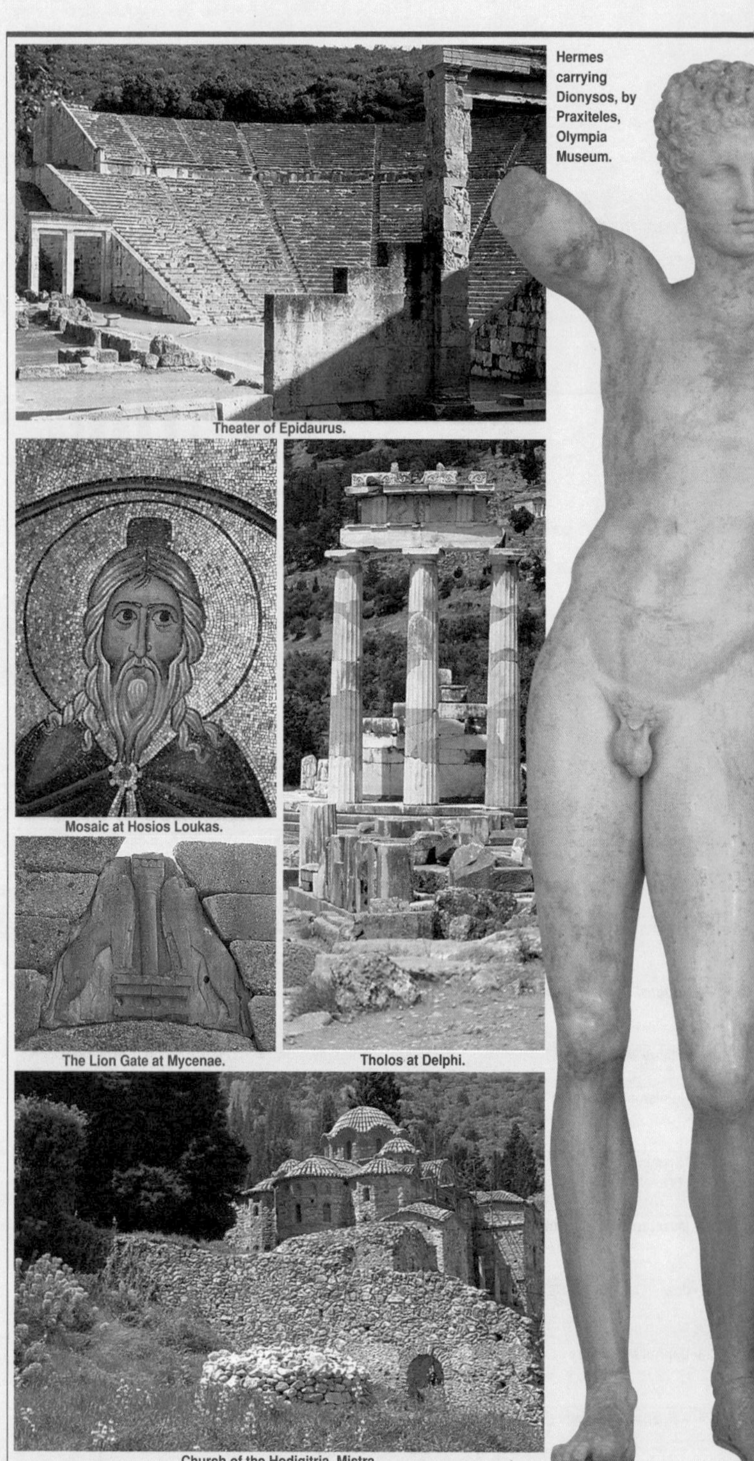

Theater of Epidaurus.

Hermes carrying Dionysos, by Praxiteles, Olympia Museum.

Mosaic at Hosios Loukas.

The Lion Gate at Mycenae.

Tholos at Delphi.

Church of the Hodigitria, Mistra.

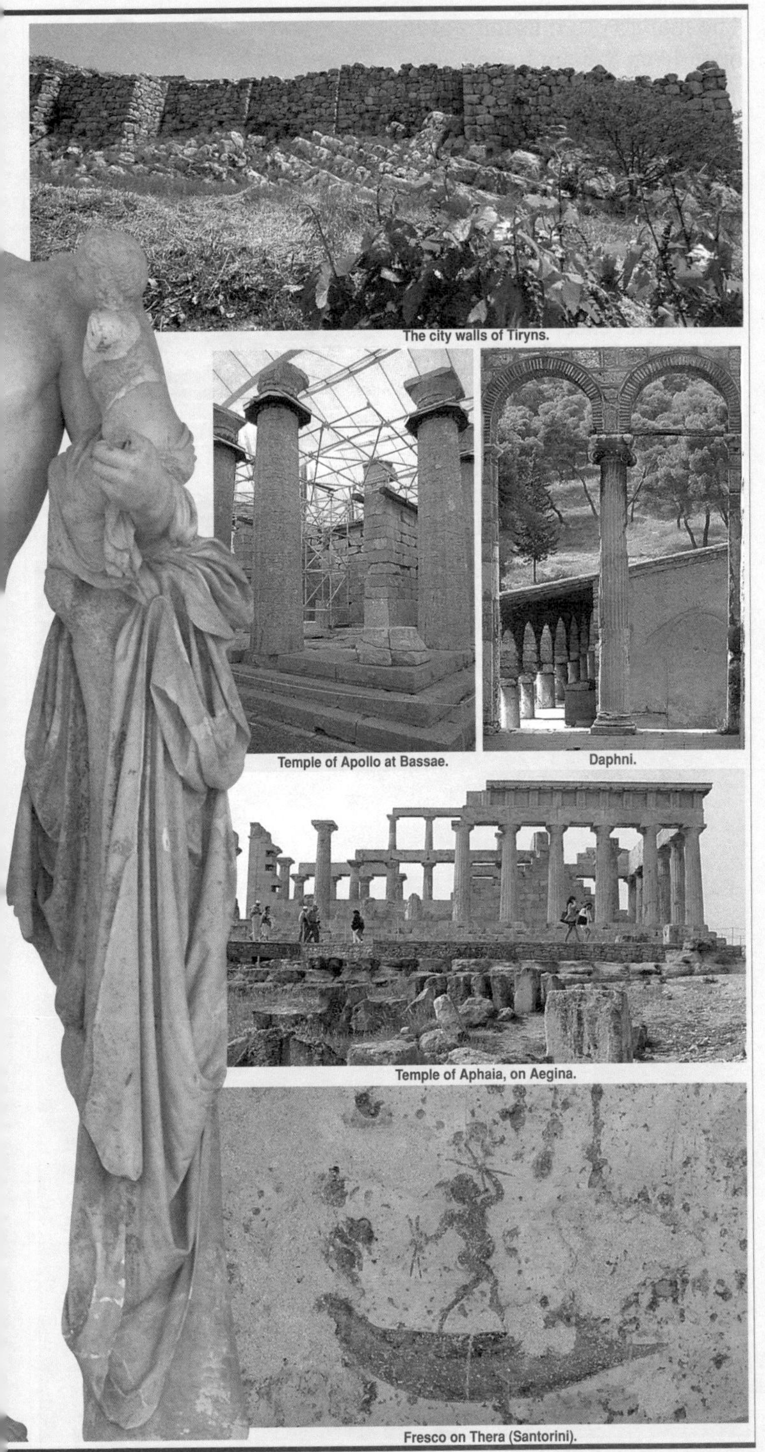

The city walls of Tiryns.

Temple of Apollo at Bassae.

Daphni.

Temple of Aphaia, on Aegina.

Fresco on Thera (Santorini).

◆ MUSEUMS AND SITES IN ATTICA, BOEOTIA AND THE PELOPONNESE

The majority of museums are open from 8.30am to 3pm and are closed on Mondays. However, some open at different times on different days of the week, so it is best to check with the local branch of the Tourist Police. The cost of admission is usually very reasonable, except for the well-known archeological sites and major museums. Admission to some sites and museums is free or half price for EC students. Photography is permitted on payment of a supplementary charge. It is advisable to visit the archeological sites early in the morning, to avoid the heat.

The monastery at Hosios Loukas.

The sanctuary at Eleusis.

The odeon at Patras.

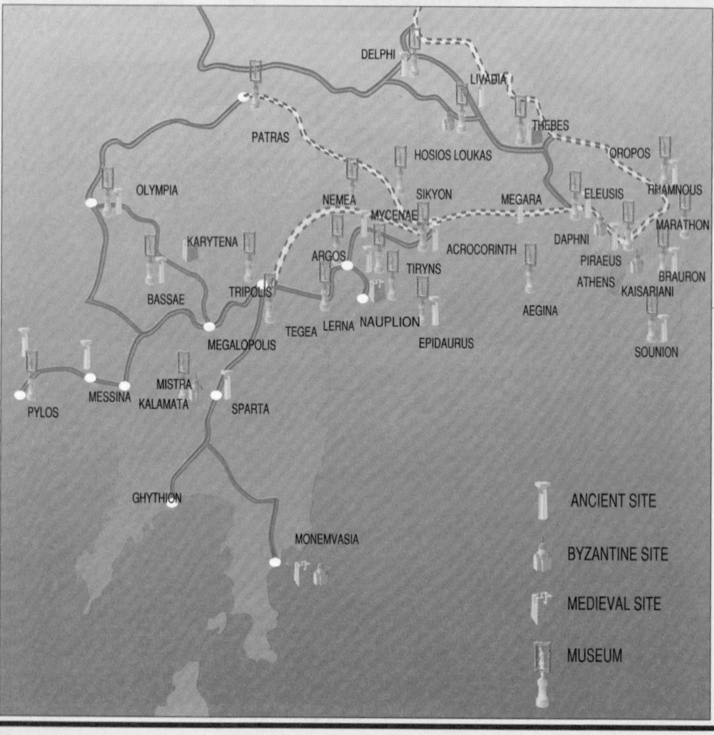

• ARGOS	7 miles from Nauplion	
Argos Museum	Tel. (751) 288 19	Open 8.30am-3pm.
Sanctuary of Hera	6 miles from Argos	Open 8.30am-3pm; closed Mon.
• BASSAE (Bassai)	9 miles from Andritsaina	Undergoing restoration,
Temple		but open 8.30am-3pm.
• BRAURON (Vravrona/Vraona)	5 miles from Marcopoulo	
Archeological site and museum	Tel. (294) 270 20	Open 8.30am-3pm; museum closed Mon., Thurs. and Fri., site closed Mon.
• CORINTH (Korinthos)		
Museum and site of Ancient Corinth	4 miles from Corinth Tel. 741 312 07	Open Mon. 11am-5pm; Tues. Fri. 8am-5pm; Sat.-Sun. 8.30am-3pm.
Archeological site of Acrocorinth	7 miles from Corinth Tel. (741) 314 43	Open Mon. to Fri. 8am-5pm; Sat., Sun. and holidays 8.30am-3pm.
Isthmia Museum	5 miles from Corinth Tel. (741) 372 44	Open 8.30am-3pm; closed Mon.
• DELPHI (Delfi)		
Archeological site	Tel. (265) 823 13	Open Mon. to Fri. 8am-5pm; Sat. and Sun. 8.30am-3pm.
Delphi Museum	Tel. (265) 823 13	Open Mon. 11am-5pm; Tues. -Fri. 8am-5pm; Sat.-Sun. 8.30am-3pm.
• AEGINA (Egina)		
Aegina Museum	Tel. (297) 222 48	Open 8.30am-3pm; closed Mon.
Temple of Aphaia	6 miles from Aegina town Tel. (297) 323 98	Open Mon. to Fri. 8am-5pm; Sat. and Sun. 8.30am-3pm.
• ELEUSIS (Elevsina/Elefsis)		
Museum and archeological site	Corner of Iera and Gioka Sts Tel. 554 60 19	Open 8.30am-3pm; closed Mon.
• EPIDAURUS (Epidavros)	11 miles from Palea Epidavros	
Museum and site	and 7 miles from Ligourio Tel. (753) 220 09	Open Mon. 11am-5pm; Tues.-Fri 8am-5pm; Sat. and Sun. 8.30am.
• HOSIOS LOUKAS	23 miles from Delphi	
Byzantine monastery	Tel. (267) 222 28, 227 97, 225 62	Open 8.30am-3pm.
• MARATHON (Marathonas)	4 miles from the city	
Museum and tumulus	Tel. (294) 551 55	Open 8.30am-3pm; closed Mon.
• MYCENAE (Mykine)	8 miles from Argos	
Archeological site	Tel. (751) 665 85	Open Mon. to Fri. 8am-5pm; Sat. and Sun. 8.30am-3pm.
• MISTRA (Mystras)	3 miles from Sparta	
Site and museum	Tel. (731) 253 63	Open 8.30am-3pm.
• NAUPLION (Navplion)		
Museum	Syntagma Square Tel. (752) 275 02 and 246 90	Open 8.30am-3pm; closed Mon.
Fortress of Palamidi	Up steps from Nikitara Square Tel. (752) 280 36	Open Mon. to Fri. 8.30am-5pm; Sat. and Sun. 8.30am-3pm.
• NEMEA	15 miles from Argos	
Archeological site and museum	Tel. (746) 227 39	Open 8.30am-3pm; closed Mon.
• OLYMPIA	12 miles from Pyrgos	
Archeological site	Tel. (624) 225 17 and 225 79	Open Mon. to Fri. 8am-5pm; Sat. and Sun. 8.30am-3pm.
Archeological museum	Tel. (624) 225 29 and 227 42	Open Mon. 11am-5pm; Tues.-Fri. 8am-5pm; Sat.-Sun. 8.30am-3pm.
Olympic Games Museum	Tel. (624) 225 44	Open Mon. 12-6pm; Tues.-Fri. 8am-7pm; Sat.-Sun. 8.30am-3pm.
• OROPOS	6 miles from Skala Oropos	
Amphiareion, archeological site	Tel. (295) 621 44	Open 8.30am-3pm; closed Mon.
• PATRAS (Patra)		
Archeological museum	Tel. (61) 275 408 and 276 207	Open 8.30am-3pm; closed Mon.
• PYLOS		
Archeological museum	Tel. (624) 224 48	Open 8.30am-3pm; closed Mon.
• PIRAEUS (Piraias)		
Archeological museum	31, Har. Trikoupi Street Tel. 452 15 98	Open 8.30am-3pm; closed Mon.
Naval Museum	Themistokleous Quay Tel. 451 68 22	Open 8.30am-1pm; closed Mon and Sun.
• RHAMNOUS (Ramnus)	12 miles from Marathon	
Archeological site	Tel. (294) 694 77	Open 8.30am-3pm; closed Mon.
• SOUNION	6 miles from Laurion	
Temple of Poseidon	Tel. (292) 393 63	Open 10am to nightfall.
• THEBES (Thiva)		
Archeological museum	Tel. (262) 279 13	Open 8.30am-3pm; closed Mon.
• TIRYNS	4 miles from Argos	
Archeological site	Tel. (752) 226 57	Open Mon. to Fri. 8am-5pm; Sat., Sun. and holidays 8.30am-3pm.
• TRIPOLIS		
Archeological museum	Tel. (71) 232 397	Open 8.30am-3pm; closed Mon.

Greece, the birthplace of the Olympic Games, is a paradise for sports enthusiasts: sailing, water skiing, golf, tennis, horse riding, mountain climbing and skiing are all available.

WATERSPORTS

You are spoilt for choice when it comes to watersports: sailing, jet-skiing, surfing, water skiing etc. Not to mention the simple joy of swimming. Information is available from watersports centers on the beaches or from the local branch of the Tourist Police: wherever you are, they will be able to direct you to the nearest beaches and tell you which have sports facilities. Options include learning to windsurf or chartering a sail ship, either for the day or for a mini-cruise. Prices are set by the Tourist Police and are comparable to prices elsewhere in Europe.

BEACHES

Attica, Boeotia and the Peloponnese boast a vast number of beaches, some fifty of which have full amenities. Most do not provide any shelter from the sun; so be very careful in midsummer and avoid the hottest part of the day, which is the perfect time for a siesta in the shade or indoors. The best time to go to the beach is between 4pm and sunset.

NEAR ATHENS

You can get to the beaches and seaside resorts on the Apollo Coast by bus: **GLYFADA** (bus 205), **VOULA** (bus 122), **KAVOURI**, **VOULIAGMENI** (buses 188 and 153), Varkiza (buses 115 and 116), **LOUTSA** (buses 304, 305, 306 and 316), near Rafina, **LAGONISSI** (bus for Sounion: 14, Mavromateon Street).

UNDERWATER FISHING

The Greek sea bed is strictly protected, and underwater fishing is expressly forbidden except in certain restricted areas, a list of which can be obtained from the Greek National Tourist Organization. Antiquities and amphoras form part of a preserve and cannot be exported.

WALKING

The European hiker's trail E4 crosses the Peloponnese from Aigion in the north, to Gytheion in the south, passing through Kalavrita, Arcadia, Tripolis and Sparta. Due to the area's mild climate, it is possible to do this walk at any time of year; however, the best times for walking are May-June and September-October. Sweaters for the evenings and waterproofs are a must, even in summer. The entire distance of the trail (155 miles) can be covered in about two weeks at the rate of five to seven hours a day. But you can also use the E4 for a stroll or a short walk.

WHERE TO OBTAIN INFORMATION

From the Greek Federation of Excursion Clubs (4, Dragatsaniou Street, Athens, Tel. 323 41 07) or from the Greek Federation of Skiing Clubs, which is responsible for this stretch of the E4.

GOLF

The only major golf club is at Glyfada, 10 miles from Athens, on the Apollo Coast. It has an eighteen-hole golf course, with two lengths (about 6,750 yards and 5,600 yards). There are changing rooms, restaurants and a bar. Tel. 894 68 20

TENNIS

There are tennis courts near most beaches that have full amenities, provided by the Greek National Tourist Organization, as well as in sports clubs and centers. Large hotels, self-catering accommodation and holiday villages often have their own tennis courts and equipment.

Snow-capped Mount Taygetos.

Cavern at Diros.

SKIING

The skiing season in the Greek mountains lasts from December to April.

BOEOTIA:
MOUNT PARNASSUS
KELARIA-FTEROLAKKAS
Tel. (0234) 226 89, 226 94 and 226 95
GERONTOVRAHOS
Tel. (0267) 313 91

THE PELOPONNESE:
MOUNT AROANIA (HELMOS)
VATHIA LAKKA
Tel. (0692) 226 61 and 221 74
MOUNT MENALO
OROPEDIO OSTRAKINAS
Altitude 5,250 feet
Tel. (071) 232 243 and (796) 222 27

MOUNTAIN REFUGES

BOEOTIA:
MOUNT GIONA
LAKA KARVOUNI
Altitude 6,000 feet
Tel. 363 45 49
MOUNT PARNASSUS
Starting out from Arakhova, you can climb the main peak, which rises to an altitude of 8,350 feet.
SARANTARI REFUGE
Altitude 6,250 feet
Tel. (234) 226 40
ATTICA:
MOUNT PARNES
The Fortress of Phyle is at an altitude of 2,000 feet.
BAFI REFUGE
Altitude 3,800 feet
Tel. 321 24 29, 321 23 55 and 246 90 50
FLABOURI REFUGE
Altitude 3,800 feet
Tel. 246 15 28
VARIBORIS REFUGE
Altitude 2,000 feet
Tel. 321 24 29

THE PELOPONNESE:
MOUNT TAIYETOS
VARIVARA-DEREKI REFUGE
Altitude 5,250 feet
Tel. (1731) 225 74 and 241 35
MOUNT KILNI (ZIRIA)
OROPEDIO REFUGE
Altitude 5,000 feet
Tel. (0691) 252 85
PORTES REFUGE
Altitude 5,500 feet
Tel. (0741) 243 35 and 299 70
MOUNT AROANIA (HELMOS)
DIASSELO AVGOU REFUGE
Altitude 6,900 feet
Tel. (0692) 226 11
MOUNT PARNONAS
ARNOMOUSGA REFUGE
Altitude 4,600 feet
Tel. (0731) 225 74 and 241 35
MOUNT PANAHAIKO
PSARTHI REFUGE
Altitude 4,650 feet
Tel. (061) 273 912

INFORMATION

GREEK FEDERATION OF MOUNTAINEERING CLUBS,
5, Milioni Street,
106 73 Athens,
Tel. 364 59 04

GREEK SKIING AND ALPINE FEDERATION,
7, Karageorgi Street, Servias,
105 63 Athens,
Tel. 323 01 82

CAVES

Early in its history, the Greek Speliological Society discovered and explored some 7,500 caverns, chasms and other geological formations (*karstiks*). Some of these natural phenomena have been opened to the public.

ATTICA
KOUTOUKI CAVE
VILLAGE OF PEANIA
Tel. 664 21 08
Discovered accidentally in 1926, this cave is nearly 1,700 feet above sea level. It is situated on the east slope of Mount Hymettus, two miles from the village of Peania (Liopessi) in the district of Messogia. It covers about 4,500 square yards and comprises a main cavern, with several compartments walled off by groups of stalactites, stalagmites and columns in various colors. The artificial lighting is artistically concealed.

ADMISSION
400 drachmas
STUDENTS
200 drachmas
CHILDREN
100 drachmas

THE PELOPONNESE:
DIROS CAVERN
BAY OF DIROS
Tel. (733) 522 223
This cavern was discovered at the end of the 19th century. It is situated on the west coast of the Laconian peninsula in a downcast fault in the Bay of Diros, about 25 miles from Gytheion and 3 miles from Pyrgos Diros. The cavern is formed by an underground river flowing along two parallel passages and various secondary channels. Nearly 3 miles of the underground river have been explored, as well as about half a mile of dry cave. In one of the sections the fossilized skeleton of a panther was discovered, the only one ever found in the Peloponnese. A visit to the cave involves a walk (about a third of a mile) and a boat trip (three quarters of a mile) through lakes and galleries. You will see variegated limestone stalactites as well as huge stalagmites and white columns rising from the water. Long waits are to be expected for entrance.

CAVE AND LAKE TRIP:
1,200 drachmas
CAVE ONLY:
600 drachmas

Actors from the National Theater.

Hall of the Friends of Music.

Athens offers a great deal in the way of evening entertainment, including music clubs that cater for all tastes: *rembetika, bouzouki*, folk music and jazz. Summer is the prime time for festivals, the most famous of which are the ones held in Athens, Epidaurus and Patras. Summer is also the most pleasant time for going to the cinema, as there are open-air film shows.

SUMMER ENTERTAINMENT

ENTERTAINMENT IN ATHENS

SON ET LUMIERE AT THE ACROPOLIS
Tel. 922 62 10
Daily shows in English.
Price 500 drachmas (reduced price tickets offered for students on production of a valid ID card).
You can buy your tickets at the entrance to the show, or at the Athens Festival office, Tel. 322 14 59

FOLK DANCING
From May to September the Dora Stratou Theater on the Hill of Philopappos (Hill of the Muses) organizes displays of folk dancing every evening at 10.15pm, with additional performances on Wednesdays and Sundays at 8.15pm. Tickets cost from 1,000 to 1,400 drachmas. Information and bookings: Tel. 324 43 95 (9am-2pm) and 921 46 50 (7-11pm).

FESTIVAL OF ATHENS

From June to September. Includes shows, concerts and ballets at the Lycabettus Theater, and classical music, modern music and folk dancing at the Odeon of Herodes Atticus. Information and tickets (Mon. to Sat. 8.30am-2pm and 5-7pm; Sun. 10am-1pm): Festival Office, 4, Stadiou Street, Tel. 322 14 59, or 322 31 11-9.

ODEON OF HERODES ATTICUS
From mid June to late September. Performances start at 9pm in June-August, 8.30pm in September. Tickets can be bought two weeks in advance. Information and tickets (5-9pm on days when there are performances): Odeon of Herodes Atticus (blue bus 230 from Syntagma Square, opposite Parliament), Tel. 323 27 71.

EPIDAURUS

FESTIVAL OF CLASSICAL DRAMA
Late June to late August.
Performances start at 8pm. Tickets can be bought ten days in advance. Information and tickets (Thurs., Fri. and Sat., 9am-1pm and 6pm-9pm): from the ancient theater in Epidaurus, Tel. (752) 226 91. Also available from the Athens Festival office.

PATRAS

FESTIVAL OF DRAMA, MUSIC, DANCE AND OTHER ARTS
June to September.
Information:
Tel. (61) 272 911 and 279 866.

BOOK FAIRS

Organized in Athens by the Greek publishers' associations. One is held in the Zappeion (Tel. 363 00 29) in May, and another in Pedion Areos (Tel. 362 19 61) in September.

LYCABETTUS THEATER
Open-air theater seating 4,000 people. Tickets can be bought ten days in advance. Information and tickets (7-9pm on days when there are performances): Lycabettus Theater, Tel. 722 72 09.

Carnival poster.

Carnival workshop.

Horses and clown at the Patras carnival.

CINEMA

Most cinemas that operate during the summer are open-air (some of them are even in the middle of the countryside, as on Aegina). Films are always shown in the original language, and American and European productions are widely distributed.

SOME CINEMAS IN ATHENS

ATHINEA: 50, Haritos Street, Tel. 721 57 17
VOX: 82, Themistokleou Street, Tel. 330 10 20
RIVIERA: 46, Valltetsiou Street, Tel. 363 77 16
CINÉ PARIS: Plaka, Tel. 322 20 71
DEXAMENI REFRESH: Dexameni Square, Tel. 362 39 42

WHAT'S ON IN ATHENS

For up-to-date information about shows, films, concerts and night clubs in Athens, buy the English-language publication *Athenscope.*

REMBETIKA SONGS AND MUSIC CLUBS

The first *rembetika* songs date from 1800 and were sung by the underprivileged classes. This working-class genre of music was banned in 1936, but made a comeback several years ago. You can now hear *rembetika* – which is often compared to the *blues* – performed in several clubs that have an authentic ambience. Although some clubs may open as early as 10pm, they do not really get going before midnight, and "evenings" can run into the small hours of the morning. Most of the clubs serve drinks and snacks throughout the night.

REMBETIKA CLUBS

In Athens:
FRANGOSYRIANI
57, Arahovis Street, Exarchia
Tel. 360 06 93
Closed Thurs.
REMBETIKI ISTORIA
181, Ippokrastous Street, Exarchia
Tel. 642, 49 37
Closed Mon. to Wed.
REMBETIKI NICHTA
102, Formionos Street, Pangrati
Tel. 766 99 03
Closed Wed.
MINORE
34, Notora Street, Exarchia
Tel. 823 86 39
Closed Mon. and Tues.
TAKSIMI
29, Isavron Street, Exarchia
Tel. 363 99 19
Closed Wed.
In Piraeus:
AMIFORI
47, Vassilis Yorgiou Street
Tel. 411 58 19.

HALL OF THE FRIENDS OF MUSIC

The singer, Alexandra Triandi, had the idea of founding a cultural center. In 1956 the government donated the land necessary for its construction; in 1981 the Organization of the Hall of the Friends of Music was founded; and ten years later the Megaron was inaugurated, remedying the capital's lack of cultural facilities. The hall boasts a huge auditorium, which can seat two thousand people, and a smaller one seating five hundred. The two auditoria are used for various types of event: orchestral concerts, chamber music recitals, operas, plays and ballets. The larger-scale events form the subject of original publications. There is a program of activities specifically aimed at a younger audience, and a record club for music lovers.
Information and tickets:
Megaron, Vasilissis Sophias and Kokali Streets,
Tel. 728 23 33.

ROCK, JAZZ AND TRADITIONAL MUSIC

There are many jazz, *bouzouki* and folk music clubs in Greece.

SOME VENUES

In Athens:
AGATHI
100, Kifissias Avenue
Tel. 514 65 66
Jazz and rock.
AMBELOFYLLO
3, Samothrakis Street, Karayanni, Kapseli
Tel. 867 88 62
Greek music.
ESMERALDA
50, Kefallinias Street, Kapseli
Tel. 867 12 90
Bouzouki club.
Closed Tuesdays.
HALF NOTE
Corner of Nikiforou Duranou and Patriarhou Fotiou streets, Kolonaki
Tel. 364 18 41
Excellent jazz club.
Closed Tuesdays.
RAVANASTRON
60, Dimitsanas Street, Ambelopiki
Tel. 644 95 34
Traditional Greek and Turkish music.
RODON
24, Marni Street
Tel. 524 74 27
Jazz and rock.
WEST CLUB
268, Vouliagmenis Avenue
Tel. 971 61 45, 925 38 47
Jazz and rock.

In Monemvasia:
ANGELO
In the main street
Great jazz in the evenings, classical music during the day.

In Aegina:
LA BELLE EPOQUE
Pileos Street (at right angles to the quay)
Sixties music.

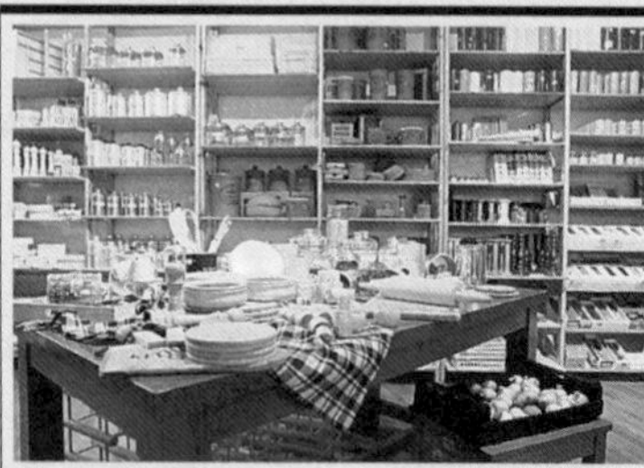
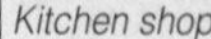
Kitchen shop.

Typical Greek wine shop.

Athens boasts a vast array of shops, as well as markets. There are temptations everywhere you turn: arts and crafts, clothing, leather, rare books, antiques, flowers, spices, wine etc. You never know what you may find as you wander through the streets of Athens.

LUXURY GOODS

Athens' most stylish shopping center is in the Kolonaki quarter ▲ 228. This is the home of the big names in Italian and French designer clothing (Versace, Montana, Valentino and Gianfranco Ferré at the *Galeries Jade*, Chanel exclusively at *Morel*) as well as in Greek *haute couture* (the great classicists Filimon, Aslanis and Parthenis, and the avant-garde designer Dafni Valente). *Sotris* stocks international *haute couture* clothing and Greek ready-to-wear. Despite its name, *Artisti Italiani* (36, Abatzoglou Street, Nea Ionia) is devoted to Greek designers. The collections by Christian Dior, which are harder to find, are shown on the first floor of 10, Likavitou Street.

CRAFTS

You will certainly be tempted by Greek crafts, including multicolored woollen rugs (made near Delphi), wooden objects, leather goods, embroidery and, naturally, the leather sandals and woven bags which were all the rage in the seventies and are now back in fashion.
Useful addresses:
National Organization of Greek Crafts
9, Mitropoleos Street, for woodcarvings and a range of woollen rugs and bedspreads.
Tanagrea
15, Mitropoleos Street, for pottery.
Greek Women's Institution
13, Voukourestiou Street, for embroidery.

FLEA MARKET

Every weekday morning there is a flea market, from 8am to midday, on Avicinas Square and around the Church of Haghios Philippos. In an atmosphere reminiscent of Oriental bazaars, bric-a-brac dealers from all over Greece unpack their odd assortment of wares – old furniture, rugs, icons, carved chests, oil cans, churns, wooden seals etc. – among which you may stumble across a bargain. Haggling is mandatory, but preferably in Greek.

JEWELRY

The two leading Athenian jewelry stores, *Lalaounis* and *Kessaris*, face each other on Panepistimiou Street. They are renowned for their original pieces inspired by classical or Byzantine motifs. In Leventi Street the small eccentric store of the designer *Armandos Moustakis* specializes in costume jewelry.

BARGAIN HUNTING

Athinas Street, the home of the second-hand-clothes dealers, is a good place for bargains.

MONASTIRAKI ▲ 186

The main shopping areas in Monastiraki are Ermou Street, Pireos Street and Andrian Street. Here you will find leather articles at give-away prices, as well as many other inexpensive goods: rucksacks, tapestries, spices, jewelry etc.

FURNITURE AND DECORATIVE OBJECTS

Traditional Greek furniture and ornaments, and also original modern designs.
Useful addresses:
Deloudis
3-5, Spefsipou Street. A designer of ultra-modern furniture.
Meli Interiors
24, Skoufa Street. In the Greek tradition of uncluttered lines.
I gata pou tin lene Ucello
19, Al. Soutsou Street. A designer's fresh look at traditional style.
John Stefanidis
6, Patrarhou Ioakim Street. The acme of classicism.

OPENING HOURS

Shops catering for tourists stay open from 8am to 8pm during the week; some open from 8.30am to 3pm on Sunday. Most other shops open from 8.30am to 3pm on Monday, Wednesday and Saturday; from 8.30am to 1.30pm and 5pm to 8pm on Tuesday, Thursday and Friday; and are closed on Sunday.

Athenian market.

Street seller.

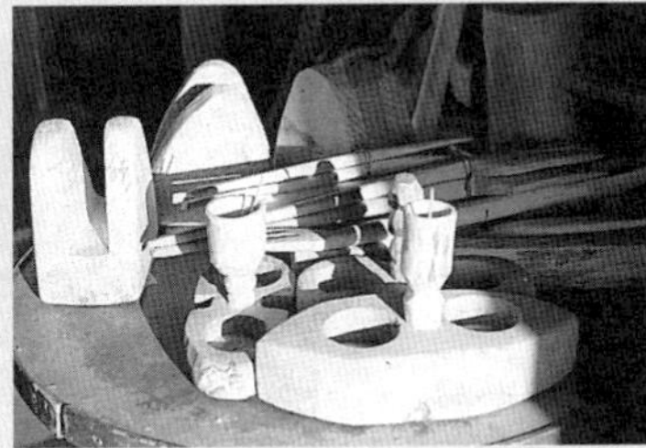
Greek crafts.

The capital of Greece offers a number of activities that are free – such as visits to churches and, on Sundays, to museums. The parks cry out for you to take a stroll.

GIFTS

You will find old or second-hand books, antiques and plenty of objets d'art in the Monastiraki quarter and in Plaka.

USEFUL ADDRESSES

The Art Group
13, Thisseos Avenue
Objets d'art.
O Perris
104, Kifissias Avenue
Objets d'art.
Kourdisti Maimou
17, Iperidou Street, Plaka
Unusual or rare objects, antique mechanical toys.
Calypso
40-42, Voulis Street, Plaka
Crafts, woven goods, jewelry.
Alexandros Kostas
3, Avicinas Square, Monastiraki
Second-hand goods and knick-knacks.
Niki Eleftheriadis
18, Filikis Eterias Street
Second-hand goods, rare objects and jewelry.
Te panda ri
35, Haritos Street, Kolonaki
Perfumes and pot-pourri.
Onirokosmos
6, Proklou Street, Pagrati
Traditional toys, perfumes and a small coffee lounge.
Zografies
44, Amfitritis, Palio Faliro
Painted glass.
Outopia, antiques
3-5, Skoufa Street, Kolonaki
Restored 19th-century furniture.

FOOD MARKETS

The central food market (a large building on Athinas Avenue) is a hive of activity. The fish and meat stalls and the shouts of stallholders and customers all contribute to its atmosphere. The fruit market, next to the central food market, is the cheapest in Athens.

MUSEUMS

Athens boasts more than a dozen museums that are free on Sunday. Free guided tours are also organized every weekend by the local authorities.
Call 424 30 33 for information on the program, which changes weekly.

PARKS AND WALKS

The National Gardens ● *34* (open from 7am until nightfall) are a haven of peace and coolness. They provide a setting for the neoclassical Zappeion exhibition hall, as well as the Botanical Museum (1, Amalias Street) founded in 1980. Strolling along its serpentine paths, you will encounter a number of ancient remains, including fragments of mosaics and vestiges of Roman baths, Hadrian's city wall and Pisistratus' aqueduct. A building shaped like a pagoda, next to the Zappeion, serves as a cafeteria; behind it there is an open-air cinema (the daily program starts at 8.30pm). The most attractive walks in Athens are those to high-up spots – such as Mount Lycabettus (900 feet), dominated by the white chapel of Haghios Georgios, and the Hill of the Muses – which afford splendid views of the city and the Acropolis.

CHURCHES

Athens has some fine churches. The 11th-century Church of the Holy Apostles, to the south of the Stoa of Attalos, contains a number of magnificent Byzantine paintings. Panaghia Grigoroussa, in Taxiarkhon Street, is a recently built church renowned for its gold *ex voto* offerings. Athens Cathedral ▲ *183*, in Mitropoleos Square, was built in the 19th century with stones from seventy-two demolished churches. The 11th-century Kapnikarea ▲ *186*, in Ermou Street, is a tiny gem of Byzantine architecture. The Small Metropolis ▲*183* (behind the cathedral), which dates from the 12th century, is richly decorated with marble blocks, friezes and bas-reliefs. Here you can attend a music-filled Greek Orthodox service. The major festivals, particularly Easter, are celebrated with great gusto.

SITES

Entrance to the major sites is free for students from EC countries.

A zakharoplasteion serves pastries and non-alcoholic drinks.

An open-air café in one of the narrow streets of Plaka.

A traditional Athenian street scene: street vendors walk up and down offering different kinds of pastries and snacks.

Greek hospitality adds to the enjoyment of Greek food. Even modest meals are eaten in a sociable, convivial atmosphere, continuing the tradition of banqueting from ancient times.

BREAKFAST

Breakfast is not really part of the Greek tradition. In the morning Athenians tend to make do with black or white coffee and buy *koulouri*, rounds of breads sprinkled with sesame seeds, on the way to work.

LUNCH

Athenians rarely take a lunch break: most arrive at work at 8am and return home around 3pm. Main meals are eaten at home with the family. It is, however, common practice to drink coffee at the office and to offer visitors something to drink: all office blocks or ministries have a *kafetzis*, which in response to a simple phone call will provide coffee, mineral water or orange juice, and even sandwiches and pastries.

IN THE STREET

If you are peckish or want to have lunch on the move there are street vendors on virtually every corner, displaying a tempting array of pastries filled with cheese (*tiropitta*), spinach (*spanakopitta*) or meat (*kreatopitta*) and, for dessert, yoghurts and sugared pastries filled with fruit or cream (*bougatsa*). At lunchtime young Athenians head for the fast-food restaurants which are springing up all around the city center; older people with more money go to the bistros where Italian coffee and pastries are served.

THE "KAFENION"

Greek cafés used to be very much a masculine domain: a meeting place for the *parea* (groups of friends belonging to the same profession or political faction), a place where you could play cards or *tavli* (a type of backgammon), linger over coffee, read the newspapers, recite your *komboloi* (rosary), or simply relax and pass the time of day. These traditional bastions of Greek masculine society began to disappear in the 1970's, to be replaced by more conventional cafés.

THE "OUZERI"

At lunchtime the *ouzeri* take over. Here, with your *ouzo*, beer or wine (usually white), you can enjoy an array of little snacks or appetizers called *meze*. Journalists, artists, politicians, university lecturers and writers meet here between 1pm and 4pm. The most popular *ouzeri*, situated between Syntagma and Kolonaki, are *Apotsos* (on Stadiou Street) and *Steki* and *Yali Kafene* (near Kolonaki Square).

TAVERNAS AND RESTAURANTS

Single people tend to be regular customers at the restaurants that open at midday. The Plaka district offers the best choice. The restaurants on Filomoussou Eterias Square and Adrianou Street serve excellent traditional cuisine, as do those around the Aerides. You should try to arrive by 2pm if you want to take your pick of everything on the menu. Restaurants (*estiatoria*) are more sophisticated than traditional tavernas, and this is reflected in their prices. After lunch, from around 3.30pm onward, Athenians usually return home to take a siesta until around 5.30pm.

ATHENS À LA CARTE

The Acropolis.

Kifissia Station, in Athens.

ATHENS IN A DAY

8.30AM. Spend the morning visiting the Acropolis ▲*130*, Athens' most impressive cultural legacy from the classical era, which should not be missed during a visit to the city.
11AM. Take the Peripatos, a circular road winding down the north slope of the Acropolis, toward Plaka. You will find yourself in Anafiotika, one of the capital's oldest working-class areas. As its name implies, its first inhabitants originally came from Anafi, an island in the Aegean Sea. Visit the 17th-century Church of Haghios Symeon, then Haghii Anargyroi, a little further down on Pritaniou Street. Take Mnisikleous Street on the right, and then turn left onto Lisiou Street to reach the Aerides, a 19th-century bourgeois neighborhood. Visit the Museum of Musical Instruments ▲*181* at the very end of Markou Avriliou Street, then the ruins of the nearby Ottoman Medrese as well as the Fethiye Cami'i (Victory Mosque), on Pelopida Street.
1PM. Have lunch in one of the many friendly and traditional tavernas you passed on your way, such as the *Palia Plakiotiki Taverna* (26, Lisiou Street). Grills, vegetables cooked in tomato sauce and braised meats are the connoisseurs' favorite dishes.
2.30PM. From nearby Monastiraki Square, take the metro (which crosses the city of Athens from north to south) to the suburb of Kifissia.
3.30PM. When you arrive at Kifissia Station, head for Platanos Square and walk along Kasseveti Street. Stop to have coffee and cake at *Varsos*, which is also famous for its crystallized fruit, which you can buy to take away. Levidou Street, lined with countless interesting shops, will take you to the Natural History Museum, which has many interesting exhibits of Greek flora and fauna.
5PM. Take time to stroll through the shady streets of Kifissia ▲ *262*, which was the Athenians' favorite summer resort in the 19th century. Many of the villas built by wealthy families have survived here and there among the modern structures. It is worth making a short detour to look at the Cecile Hotel on Kefalari Square, which has now been converted into luxury offices.

6.30PM. Take the train (in the opposite direction to that in which you have just come) to the port of Piraeus ▲ *243*.
7.30PM. On arrival at Piraeus, walk across the beautiful Kastella Hill to reach Turkolimano harbor.
8PM. Have dinner in one of the many restaurants which line the quay of this attractive little harbor. Sample some of the many traditional Greek specialties such as grilled or fried fish with zucchini and *khorta* (steamed wild greens).
10PM. Before heading back to Athens (catch bus 40 or 49), take a gentle stroll along the quays and round off the day with a nightcap in one of the many harbor cafés.

Restaurant terrace in Plaka.

Street vendor in Monastiraki.

Byzantine fabric.

Haghios Georgios, on Mount Lycabettus.

ATHENS IN TWO DAYS

FIRST DAY

9AM. Spend your first morning visiting the Acropolis, the supreme architectural achievement of the classical era. Don't miss the museum on the site which contains many interesting artefacts.

12AM. Descending from the Acropolis via the Peripatos, stroll around the Plaka district until lunchtime. There are several Byzantine churches at the foot of the Acropolis, including the Metamorphosis tou Soteira and Haghios Nicolaos. There are a great many stalls lining the pedestrianized streets, selling plaster models, souvenirs and reproductions of classical or Byzantine jewelry. Have lunch in one of the many welcoming tavernas to be found in this district, such as *Xinos* in Angelou Geronta Street.

2PM. Visit the National Archeological Museum, which has an outstanding collection of pottery, sculpture, bronzes and silverware from the Mycenean, Archaic, classical and Hellenist eras, as well as Minoan frescos.

5PM. Take the metro (45 minutes) to Kifissia, an extremely attractive suburb of Athens. Stop for a breather in one of the cafés on Kefalari Square. Before you move on, go window-shopping in Athens' most stylish shopping center, near Kifissia Station.

8PM. Back in the city center, have dinner at the *Sigalas* taverna, in Monastiraki Square, or (on the other side of the Acropolis) at *Dionysos*, in Dionysiou Areopagitou Street, at the foot of the Hill of the Muses. Between June and September, you can complete your evening by going to one of the shows put on at the Odeon of Herodes Atticus as part of the Festival of Athens.

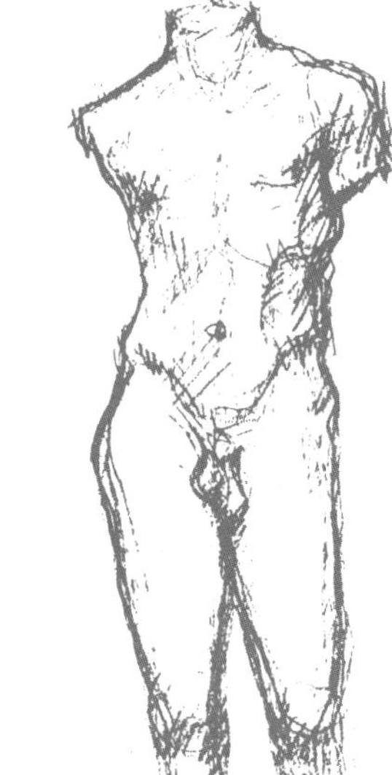

SECOND DAY

9AM. Begin your second day with a visit to the Goulandris Museum and/or the Byzantine Museum, situated fairly close to each other on Vassilisis Sophias Avenue. Afterward, cross the elegant quarter of Kolonaki to Dexameni Square, from where you can begin your ascent of Mount Lycabettus (the "hill of wolves") either by climbing the stairs or by taking the funicular ▲ *378*.

12AM. At the top, 900 feet up, you will enjoy a splendid view of the entire city, crowned by the Acropolis and lapped by the sea. You can have lunch either here, or lower down at *Vladimiros* on Aristodimou Street.

3PM. Take a taxi or bus (118 or 122, from Olgas Street) to one of the beaches on the Apollo Coast at Voula or Vouliagmeni where you can spend the afternoon.

8PM. Return via Glyfada, where you can have dinner in one of the restaurants on the seafront or in the central square.

12 MIDNIGHT. After a stroll along the beach, head for a *rembetika* music club (the show may go on until 5am). You will need to take a taxi back to Athens.

Delphi.

Acronauplia.

ATHENS AND THE PELOPONNESE IN A WEEK

1ST DAY
Athens
2ND DAY
Athens
3RD DAY
Argolis (120 miles)
4TH DAY
From Mycenae to Monemvasia (140 miles)
5TH DAY
Mistra, Laconia and the Mani (147 miles)
6TH DAY
Olympia and Arcadia (217 miles)
7TH DAY
Delphi, Hosios Loukas, Daphni (186 miles)

FIRST DAY

MORNING. Start with a visit to the Agora (open from 8.30am), which is dominated by the fine Doric building of the Hephaisteion (Theseion) ▲ *191*. Then head for Plaka ▲ *178*, which is liberally scattered with Byzantine churches and ancient monuments including the Roman Agora, the Tower of the Winds, the Churches of the Metamorphosis tou Soteira, Haghios Nicolaos and Haghia Ekaterini, the Monument of Lysikrates, and, further north, the Small Metropolis. It is easy to find a pleasant taverna in this area for lunch.
AFTERNOON. Spend the afternoon at the National Historical Museum (open until 5pm). Behind the museum stretches the elegant district of Kolonaki, where you can stop for a drink and, later, have dinner in one of its many restaurants.
EVENING. Between June and September you can go to one of the shows put on as part of the Festival of Athens ▲ *396*; or you may prefer to stroll through Kolonaki and then ascend to the top of Mount Lycabettus ▲ *378*, where you can feast your eyes on the lights of the city, crowned by the Acropolis.

SECOND DAY

MORNING. You can easily spend an entire morning visiting the Acropolis ▲ *130* (open from 8.30am) – a vast and world-renowned ancient site whose most famous monuments include the Temple of Athena Nike, the Parthenon, the Erechtheion and the Propylaea, as well as a museum.
AFTERNOON. After lunch, if it is too hot, go back to the hotel for a short siesta, or take refuge from the heat and bustle of the city in a museum such as the Byzantine Museum ▲ *227* (open until 3pm) or the Benaki Museum ▲ *226* (open until 2pm). Around 4pm head for the Apollo Coast, where you will find several good beaches in Voula and Vouliagmeni. As the afternoon draws to a close, you can continue on to Cape Sounion ▲ *258*, where the superb ancient site is open in summer until sunset.
EVENING. On your return to Athens, stop at Piraeus ▲ *243* to sample the traditional Greek seafood specialties in one of the many restaurants in Microlimano, the "little harbor" packed with gaily colored yachts.

THIRD DAY

MORNING. Hire a vehicle and take the E94 expressway, which goes to the Peloponnese via Eleusis (Elevsina) and Megara. You will drive over the dizzy heights of the bridge crossing the Corinth Canal (50 miles from Athens). Visit the site of the ancient city of Corinth (4 miles further on) ▲ *296*, the ruins of its Temple of Apollo and its small museum with its fine collection of ceramics. Finally, take the coast road south to Epidaurus ▲ *316* (43 miles away). Here, in the midst of woodland, you will find one of the best preserved ancient theaters. Stop at the harbor of Palea Epidavros for lunch.
AFTERNOON. Tiryns ▲ *306* lies 19 miles to the west, via Nauplion. Stop to admire its splendid city walls, before heading for Nauplion ▲ *308* (4 miles away), where you can relax on the terrace of one of the seafront cafés.
EVENING. Finish off the day with a walk in the old town, which will take you to the foot of the Byzantine citadel, the Fortress of Palamidi, before dining in one of the harbor tavernas.

Patras.

Mistra.

FOURTH DAY

MORNING. Before leaving Nauplion, visit the Archeological Museum on the second floor of a Venetian house. Take the road to Mycenae ▲ *300* (14 miles to the north), a famous site well worth a visit, where you can admire the Lion Gate and the tombs reputed to be those of Homer's legendary king of Mycenae, Agamemnon, and his wife Clytemnestra. Retrace your steps to Argos ▲ *320* (6 miles away), where you can pick up the coast road to Leonidion (about 50 miles), a small city at the center of a cultivated plain dominated by the foothills of Mount Parnon.
AFTERNOON. Climb the road to Kosmas (19 miles), with its houses huddled together on the mountainside. Have lunch here, then continue to Geraki (10 miles further on). Perched on a promontory, it towers above the countryside which is studded with little chapels. Rejoin the coast road at Monemvasia (40 miles), and spend the rest of the afternoon relaxing on the beach at Pori (2 miles away).
EVENING. After dinner take a stroll through the narrow streets of Monemvasia; walk along the city walls and, if there is still enough light, climb up to the Church of Haghia Sophia.

FIFTH DAY

MORNING. Retrace your steps to Geraki, where you can pick up the road to Mistra ▲ *333* (59 miles to the northwest). Spend the morning visiting this fascinating Byzantine city, built in terraced rows up the hillside. Its restored churches boast some superb frescos. Have lunch in Sparta ▲ *323* (3 miles away).
AFTERNOON. Explore the extraordinary lunar landscapes and distinctive architecture of the villages in the Mani ▲ *341*.
EVENING. Stop for the night in the attractive little seaside village of Aeropolis ▲ *348* (85 miles in total), near the caves of Diros ▲ *395*.

SIXTH DAY

MORNING. Make your way back to Arcadia ▲ *321*, via Kalamata and Megalopolis (87 miles). From the picturesque village of Karitaina (10 miles away), take the road running alongside the gorge of the Alpheios River; this leads to Andritsaina (18 miles further on), a small village full of

old-world charm which is a pleasant place to stop for lunch. As the Temple of Bassae is presently being restored, continue on as far as Olympia ▲ *352* (34 miles).
AFTERNOON. The famous site and museum at Olympia are so beautiful and fascinating that you will find it well worth your while spending the entire afternoon here. Afterward pick up the E55 at Pyrgos (11 miles away). This is a fast route to Patras ▲ *360* (60 miles), where you can catch a ferry that will drop you off near Naupaktos.

SEVENTH DAY

MORNING. Take the E65 to Delphi ▲ *263* (70 miles), where you can easily spend the entire morning visiting the site and its museum ▲ *274*, with its superb collection of ancient Greek art. Drive back to Itea (8 miles), on the coast, for lunch.
AFTERNOON. Visit Hosios Loukas ▲ *254* (24 miles away) – one of the finest monasteries in Greece along with the one at Daphni, which you will find in the suburbs of Athens (84 miles by the E962a). Both boast some outstanding examples of Byzantine mosaics.

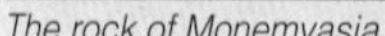

The rock of Monemvasia.

Streets in Monemvasia.

EXCURSION TO MONEMVASIA

You can catch a hydrofoil direct to Monemvasia from Piraeus: the journey takes three and a half hours. Alternatively, there is a bus early in the morning to Monemvasia from Athens. You can also make the trip by car from Sparta or Gytheion.

Monemvasia

Kythera

THE BYZANTINE AND VENETIAN LEGACIES
Monemvasia stands picturesquely on a rocky island, inaccessible by sea and linked to the mainland by a long bridge, the only means of entry, from which it derives its name (Monemvasia means "single entrance").
Conquered by the French in 1249, the city passed into the hands of the Byzantines in 1262. There then ensued a period of relative prosperity. Several churches, houses and palaces, most of which are now in ruins, were built within the new walls. After the fall of the Byzantine Empire in 1453, Monemvasia was occupied by the Venetians from 1464 to 1540, then again from 1690 to 1715. The Venetian influence is the more obvious, as the original buildings and restorations dating from that era have survived better than the Byzantine ones.

A SPELLBINDING TOWN
Monemvasia is beyond compare: its isolation is more or less complete, its serenity belongs to another age. For more than a century the city gate has stood open day and night; and once you have passed through it, you will find yourself in a totally different world. Here there are no cars and no shops (apart from several that sell souvenirs). There are, however, a number of restaurants and cafés, discreetly nestling in the clefts of the imposing rock crowned by the old fort.

STONE DREAMS
In Monemvasia time seems to have stood still. Arcades, staircases, sea walls, churches adorned with Byzantine paintings, narrow cobbled streets, imposing and humble dwellings, all combine to create a fascinating backdrop. Inaccessible on all sides, the rock is surrounded by the sea, which gives visitors the feeling that this enchanting ancient town is floating and unreal.

THE LOWER TOWN
This backs onto the rock and is surrounded on three sides by the city walls built by the Venetians in the 16th century, which in places sport the Lion of Saint Mark. The lower town has only four churches that still hold services. The cathedral (Christos Elkomenos) is a Byzantine basilica with a 13th-century dome restored by the Venetians. It still has two marble Imperial thrones and a templum. Haghios Nicolaos and Panaghia Kritikia are both 17th-century churches; the latter contains a famous icon. The lower town's fourth church, dating from the 14th century, is consecrated to Panaghia Myrtidiotissa.

Mylopotamos, on Kythera.

Bas-relief on a church on Kythera.

The harbor of Kapsali, Kythera.

Side by side on the central square, Plateia Dzamioui, stand the ancient 12th-century cathedral, Christos Elkomenos, extensively restored and modified, and the Paleo Djami, a mosque which dates from the short Turkish occupation (between the end of the 16th and the beginning of the 17th century).

THE UPPER TOWN
This is reached through the arched corridor of a monumental gate. Scattered ruins lie where the Byzantine upper town once sprawled. Only the 12th-century Church of Haghia Sophia remains proudly standing. Its dome, which resembles that of the katholikon at Hosios Loukas ▲ *254*, rests on squinches and has sixteen windows. Inside, there are fragments of 13th-century frescos and marble motifs. The portico, with its three arches, was added by the Venetians.

STAYING IN MONEMVASIA
The people who live here are warm and extremely welcoming, and take great pride in their ancient town. The cuisine is simple but tasty: primarily freshly caught fish and seafood. Several old buildings, including a convent, have been converted into pensions.

PENSIONS
CASTRO (CAT A)
Tel. 0732 61 413
KELIA (CAT A)
Tel. 0732 61 520
MALVASIA II (CAT A)
Tel. 0732 61 323
VYZANTIO (CAT A)
Tel. 0732 61 351
ANO MALVASIA (CAT B)
Tel. 0732 61 323

MALMSEY WINE
Called Malvoisie by the Franks, Monemvasia gave its name to one of the most famous wines of the Middle Ages: Malmsey, a sweet, syrupy white wine. It was exported as far as France and England and served at royal tables. Unfortunately, the vineyards have long since disappeared.

THE ISLAND OF KYTHERA

Situated south of the Peloponnese, Kythera is the stuff that dreams are made of. By painting his masterpiece *Embarkation for Cythera*, in 1717, Watteau contributed greatly to the legend of this island which, in poetry, is the allegorical home of the gods of Love. In classical times the island was called Porphyris, "the purple island", because of the abundance of murex shells, which were used to make purple dye. Herodotus states that a temple dedicated to Aphrodite was another reason for its fame during the classical era, and Homer called the goddess "the Kytherian with the beautiful crown". But there is no trace of that temple now. After the disappearance of the Minoans, the island was occupied by the Achaeans, the Dorians, the Argives and then the Spartans. The Athenians captured it in 424 BC, during the Peloponnese War ● *46*. For a very long time the property of the Venetians, the island is now administered by Attica.

VISITING THE ISLAND
Take the main road south toward the capital, which is also called Kythera. You will first pass the ruins (walls, chapels, houses) of Paleopolis, a Byzantine city founded in the 12th century, then those of the Byzantine and Venetian city of Mylopotamos, close by the charming village of the same name. If you follow a footpath for 40 minutes, you will come to the grotto of Haghias Sophias, which contains some frescos and a mosaic floor. The main town in the south of the island, Khytira or Chora, still has narrow cobbled streets and a ruined fort, dating from the Middle Ages, perched on one of the two hills that encircle the town. There are also some Byzantine churches, remodeled by the Venetians or the Franks; and the collections of the Archeological Museum include several Byzantine and post-Byzantine icons, as well as some Minoan and Mycenean pottery. A stone's throw away, on the coast, is a wonderful little harbor, Kapsali, with a pension and two tavernas.

GETTING TO KYTHERA
By ferry: from Neapolis (37 miles south of Monemvasia) alight at Haghia Pelaghia, which is linked to Kythera by the road that crosses the island from north to south. There are also ferry services, three times a week, from and to Piraeus (twelve hours) and Gytheion. From the ferry, you can catch a bus to the town of Kythera or to Kapsali.
By air: in summer there is a daily flight (one hour) from and to Athens. The airport is in the northwest part of the island.
Accommodation:
KALOKERINES KATIKIES*, Kapsali*
Tel. (801) 312 265.

The small harbor of Poros.

Floating market, Aegina.

Chartering a yacht

You can charter a boat from many of the ports and coastal resorts in Greece. You can arrange a sailing holiday through a specialist agent. They will provide all the information you need and can take care of all the necessary formalities.
In the U.K:
Greek Island Sailing Club
66 High Street
Walton-On-Thames
Tel. 0932 220416

Boarding

Most chartered boats are moored in the marinas of Kalamaki and Glyfada, situated conveniently near Athens' Hellenikon Airport. So, flight times and other factors permitting, you can get off the plane and jump straight onto your boat. You should allow half a day for stocking up on provisions and departure formalities with the port police. An abundant supply of drinking water is essential, as water points on the islands and the Peloponnese coast are few and far between – and they are not always open when you need them. As for food, it is quite possible to avoid cooking at all during your trip, as there are almost as many tavernas as there are coves in this area.

Nightlife

As a rule, people who regularly sail in Greek waters often like to anchor in a harbor during the day in order to take advantage of the markets and tavernas. They also know that during the summer the harbors and seaside resorts are bustling with life at all hours. In the evenings the night clubs open just before midnight and close at daybreak, when the first ferry or hydrofoil is due. If you want to spend a quiet night, it is therefore best to avoid the busier ports and find a more deserted, sheltered bay.

Choice of routes

For a week's charter it is preferable to opt for a short trip. That way you can enjoy your voyage without worrying about encountering the *meltemi* on your way back. This north wind, which reaches force four or five in July and August, can occasionally gust as high as seven or eight.

The Saronic Gulf

Besides being close to Athens, the Saronic Gulf has a great deal to offer those who love sailing. There are plenty of places to anchor in the islands, and with a small boat you can draw into isolated and peaceful coves and beaches. Moreover, the sailing is relatively safe and easy, as these waters are free of sandbanks, dangerous currents or reefs. The only drawback is the wind that blows in the summer, the dreaded *meltemi*, which can make your return journey last twice as long as your outward one. Leaving from Athens, you can plan an enjoyable, yet sensible trip: sail out as far as Spetsai or Porto Heli, in the south, and allow two whole days for your return.

The island of Aegina.

AEGINA ▲ *364*
Set out from Kalamaki and head for the island of Aegina. You can stop at Haghia Marina, near the hill topped by the Temple of Aphaia. Spend the night in the main port, Aegina, in the western part of the island, and take the opportunity to visit the city, which on summer evenings tends to be bustling with crowds of Athenians on vacation. Hydrofoils (which run between the island and Marina Zea in Piraeus all year round) make the island very accessible for people living in the capital, and many have a second home here. The island remains, however, a haven of tranquility and its atmosphere is provincial. If peace and quiet is what you are looking for, head for Perdhika, a little fishing port in the south of the island. There are plenty of restaurants both in the town of Aegina and in Perdhika that serve a wide variety of excellent fish. In fine weather you can anchor in the cove of Haghia Marina in the northeast of the island, to the south of the cape of the same name. At the westernmost tip of the bay you can cast anchor in front of a sandy beach, and a landing stage enables you to stock up on supplies at the little village. On the west coast the port of Aegina, which is sheltered from southerly and westerly winds, is easily accessible and suitable for mooring; you can draw alongside the entire length of the quay in the eastern dock of the old harbor to fill up with water and fuel.

ANGISTRI
Much less widely known than its big sisters, the tiny island of Angistri, off Aegina, is also much quieter. This is the perfect place to relax. The island has a little harbor, Milo, sheltered from the north, which affords extremely attractive mooring. Yachts anchor in the quay between the breakwaters and the jetty. Further south, you will find good mooring anywhere in the Bay of Marathon, as well as in the attractive harbor of Perdhika. Akra Perdhika in the Moni channel, between Perdhika and the islet opposite, is dangerous to approach, so exercise extreme caution.

METHANA
The next stop, in the south, is a little seaside resort in the Peloponnese, which is also a thermal spa with sulphur springs and a pleasant spot for lunch. The entrance to the cove is blocked by an islet and a sandbank, indicated by a beacon. Enter the harbor with a draught of about six feet along the west quay. You can refuel and replenish your water supply here.

POROS ▲ *368*
The charming little coastal town of Poros faces Galatas on the mainland of the Peloponnese. You will have no problem replenishing fuel and water supplies here. You can also do your shopping in the supermarkets, which will deliver to your boat on request; you can even buy bags of ice cubes here, a must in summer. The harbor is used regularly by warships, hydrofoils and fishing smacks, so it is often difficult to find a berth. There are a great many tavernas and restaurants along the main quay, renowned for their excellent food and particularly for their fish specialties. This area is the hub of the town's nightlife. The island's two main tourist attractions are the Monastery of Zoodochos Pighi (make sure your clothing is suitable for visiting it) – which has a fine gilded iconostasis – and, a little higher up, the ruins of a sanctuary dedicated to Poseidon. The harbor of Poros is well sheltered, and there are several places to moor. The northwestern approach is easily accessible, even at night (the channel poses more difficulties and you have to sail along the coast). You can also come alongside the jetty situated to the north of the clock tower, or along the quay toward the harbor's south entrance. The maritime traffic is very heavy: many boats ply the waters of Poros throughout the day. To the southeast, the Bay of Poros provides good moorings that are quieter, though less sheltered.

HYDRA ▲ *367*
From Poros head southwest, passing the cove of Rigani between the coast and the island of Hydra. When deciding where to spend the night, you

The island of Poros.

The island of Hydra.

have a choice between the tranquillity of the island of Dhokos, the provincial charm of the small town of Ermioni (on the mainland) or, finally, the exciting nightlife of the beautiful port of Hydra, the loveliest of all the Greek islands – which will give you an opportunity to explore the town's attractive neighborhoods, built in terraces up the hillsides. As early as the 18th century wealthy shipbuilders were building their homes here: the house belonging to the Boudouris family, with its private chapel, or those of Bougaris, Koundouriotis and Tombazis, are worth a look, although unfortunately they cannot be visited. Take the time to stroll along the quays, and to sit on a café terrace and watch the world go by. Do not miss a visit to the beautiful shops here, as well as the art galleries and jewelry stores. In the evening treat yourself to a meal in one of the fashionable tavernas, the haunt of artists, painters and writers. The harbor is easily accessible and popular with yachts, which are often moored in several rows during the tourist season. Water and fuel is available on the quay, and food can be bought in the town. There is a fruit market every morning in a little street near the harbor. If you want to moor in the harbor for the night, you should arrive early, well before evening. Failing that, head eastward to the small port of Madraki, twenty-five minutes walk from the town. This is well sheltered, except when the wind is blowing from the northwest, and has a good firm sea bed of sand and seaweed, making it a secure place to anchor. It is also much quieter than the harbor of Hydra, which can be very lively at night.

Ermioni

This fishing port opposite the island of Hydra is also a pleasant place to stop. Although nowadays it looks more like a seaside resort, it has lost none of its charm. Ermioni is easily accessible by rounding Cape Kastri and continuing westwards toward the far end of the bay. Anchor inside the main mole on the east side, or by the small mole. There is a water point on the quay, and fuel can be obtained from the service station in town.

Dhokos

There are several places to moor in the large bay of this small deserted island opposite Hydra. The sea bed is good holding-ground. On your approach, watch out for the numerous rocks to the east of the mouth of the bay, below the only house on the island.

Spetsai ▲ *368*

Spetsai is the greenest island in the Saronic Gulf. The town is only ten minutes on foot from the harbor of Balitza, where you can fill up with fuel and water. This is the place to go for good open-air tavernas and stores. It is a pleasant shopping area: there are no cars in the shady streets, and the stores are well-stocked. Strolling through the residential area, you will see some fine 19th-century villas, surrounded by gardens that are a blaze of color whatever the season. The church of Haghia Triada, built in 1793, with its carved wooden iconostasis is also worth a visit. If you want to swim, leave the harbor and head for the beaches on the south side of the island, which is dotted with idyllic little coves. On the opposite coast, the bays of Porto Heli and Tolo provide good mooring. At the easternmost tip of the town of Spetsai, Balitza is one of the safest harbors in the area and in the summer is frequented by a great many yachts. The western approach is a little tricky because of the numerous reefs. To fill up with water and fuel, head for the west quay at the far end of the harbor. You can spend the night here, generally anchored astern, or otherwise head for the harbor to the south of the lighthouse at the east mouth of the bay.

The island of Spetsai.

Useful addresses

- View
- Central location
- Isolated
- Luxury restaurant
- Typical restaurant
- Budget restaurant
- Luxury hotel
- Typical hotel
- Budget hotel
- Car park
- Supervised car park
- Television
- Quiet
- Swimming pool
- Credit cards accepted
- Reductions for children
- Pets not allowed
- Music
- Live music
- Room with telephone

♦ Under £35 / $50
♦♦ £35–£120 / $50–$180
♦♦♦ Over £120 / $180

	Page	Price	View	Quiet	Garden, Terrace	Bar	Car Park	Restaurant	Air Cond.
ATHENS									
Acropolis House	418	♦	●	●					●
Adonis	418	♦		●	●	●			
Adrian	418	♦♦	●	●	●	●			●
Amalia	420	♦	●			●		●	●
Andromeda	423	♦♦♦		●		●	●	●	●
Aphrodite	418	♦		●	●	●			●
Astir Palace Athens	420	♦♦♦	●	●	●	●	●	●	●
Athenian Inn	420	♦				●			
Athens Hilton	420	♦♦♦			●	●	●	●	●
Ava	418	♦		●	●				
Divani Palace	423	♦♦		●	●	●		●	●
Capsis-Esperia	420	♦♦				●		●	●
Electra	418	♦♦				●		●	●
Hera	423	♦	●	●	●	●			●
Herodion	424	♦♦			●	●			●
Le Grande Bretagne	420	♦♦♦				●		●	●
Lycabettus	420	♦				●		●	
N.J.V. Meridien Athens	420	♦♦♦				●	●	●	●
Omiros	418	♦	●	●	●	●		●	●
Pan	418	♦				●			
Parthenon	424	♦				●			●
Phoebus	418	♦	●	●					
Royal Olympic	424	♦♦	●		●	●		●	●
St-George Lycabettus	420	♦♦	●	●	●	●	●	●	●
AEROPOLIS									
The Tower	425	♦		●					
ANDRITSAINA									
The Pan	424	♦		●					
ARACHOVA									
Parnassos	424	♦	●						
CORINTH									
Le Belle Vue	425	♦	●						
ANCIENT CORINTH									
O Tassos Pension	424	♦		●	●			●	
DELPHI									
Amalia	425	♦	●	●		●		●	●
Kouros	425	♦	●	●					
AEGINA									
Brown Hotel	426	♦		●	●	●	●		
GYTHION									
The Aktaeon	426	♦	●	●					
HOSIOS LOUKAS									
The Koutriaris	429	♦		●					

	Page	Price	View	Quiet	Garden, Terrace	Bar	Car Park	Restaurant	Air Cond.
HYDRA									
El Greco	426	◆		●	●	●	●	●	●
KALAMATA									
Élite Hotel	426	◆◆	●				●		●
KIFISSIA									
The Pentelikon	426	◆◆◆		●	●	●	●	●	
KIPARISSIA									
Kiparissia Beach	427	◆	●	●		●	●		●
LOUTRAKI									
Agelidis Palace	427	◆◆	●	●		●		●	
Beau Rivage	427	◆	●	●					
MARATHON									
The Marathon	427	◆		●			●		
MEGALOPOLIS									
The Leto	427	◆		●					
METHONI									
The Castello	427	◆	●	●	●				
NAUPLION									
King Othon	428	◆		●	●				
Xenia Palace	428	◆◆	●	●	●	●	●	●	
OLYMPIA									
Altis	428	◆	●	●	●	●		●	●
Europi	428	◆	●	●		●	●	●	
PATRAS									
Astir	429	◆			●	●	●		
Porto Rio	429	◆	●	●	●	●	●	●	
PILOS									
Karalis Beach	430	◆	●	●		●	●	●	
PIRAEUS									
The Park	430	◆		●	●	●		●	●
POROS									
The Saron	430	◆	●						
CAPE SOUNION									
The Belvedere Park	430	◆◆	●	●	●	●	●	●	
SPARTA									
The Menelaion	431	◆		●		●		●	
SPETSAI									
Possidonion Hotel	431	◆	●	●	●		●		
TIRYNS									
Amalia	431	◆◆	●	●	●	●	●	●	
TRIPOLIS									
The Galaxy	431	◆				●			
XYLOKASTRON									
The Hermes	431	◆		●	●		●		

◆ Choosing a Restaurant

◆ Under £12 / $18
◆◆ £12–£18 / $18–$25
◆◆◆ Over £18 / $25

	Page	Price	View	Eating outside	Setting	Greek specialties	Fish specialties	Live music	Air cond.
ATHENS									
Athinaikon restaurant	419	◆				●	●		
Bretania	421	◆			●	●			
Byzantine restaurant	419	◆◆◆				●			●
Café Biz	421	◆◆		●					●
Delfi restaurant	416	◆				●	●		●
Democritos taverna	419	◆				●	●		
Dionysos restaurant	423	◆◆◆	●	●		●	●		
Eden restaurant	416	◆							
G.B. Corner restaurant	419	◆◆◆				●			●
Gerofinikas restaurant	419	◆◆			●	●	●		●
Ideal restaurant	419	◆◆◆			●	●	●		
Il Posto Café	422	◆		●	●				
Kidathineon restaurant	416	◆	●	●		●			
Kostoyanis taverna	419	◆◆				●	●		
Le Grand Balcon restaurant	419	◆◆◆	●	●		●	●	●	●
Metropol Café	418	◆	●		●				
Nefeli restaurant	416	◆	●	●		●			
Neon Café	419	◆						●	●
O Platanos taverna	416	◆		●		●			
Ouzeri Scolarheion	417	◆		●		●		●	
Palia Plakiotiki Taverna	417	◆		●	●	●		●	
Palia Taverna	423	◆◆		●	●	●			
Petrino taverna	419	◆◆			●	●	●		
Sigalas taverna	417	◆				●			
Strophilia Café	418	◆			●	●			
Ta Nissia restaurant	419	◆◆◆		●	●		●		●
Telis taverna	420	◆				●			
Tristrato Café	418	◆			●	●			
Xinos taverna	417	◆◆	●	●	●	●		●	
Zonar's Café	420	◆			●	●			
Zorba's taverna	417	◆		●		●	●		
ANCIENT CORINTH									
Dionysos taverna	424	◆		●					
ARACHOVA									
Laka taverna	424	◆				●			
BRAURON (VRAVRONA)									
Xanolia taverna	425	◆		●			●		
DELPHI									
O Baxos taverna	425	◆	●	●		●			
Topiki Gevsi	425	◆	●		●	●		●	

	PAGE	PRICE	VIEW	EATING OUTSIDE	SETTING	GREEK SPECIALTIES	FISH SPECIALTIES	LIVE MUSIC	AIR COND.
AEGINA									
DIONYSOS TAVERNA	426	◆		●			●		
GLYFADA									
OUI 2 DISCOTHEQUE	424	◆◆	●	●				●	
GYTHION									
APHOI LAMBROU TAVERNA	426	◆	●	●		●	●		
HYDRA									
KONTILENIAS TAVERNA	426	◆◆	●	●			●		
KIFISSIA									
BOKARIS TAVERNA	426	◆◆		●	●	●			
KIPARISSIA									
ST NECTANOS	427	◆	●	●					
LOUTRAKI									
REMEZO TAVERNA	427	◆		●		●	●	●	
MARATHON									
TO LIMANAKI	427	◆	●			●	●		
METHONI									
KLIMATARIA TAVERNA	427	◆	●				●		
MISTRA									
TO CASTRO	427	◆				●			
NAUPLION									
KALAMARAKIA TAVERNA	428	◆		●			●		
SAVOURAS TAVERNA	428	◆	●				●		
OLYMPIA									
PRAXITELIS TAVERNA	428	◆							
ROMANTIKA TAVERNA	428	◆				●			
PATRAS									
EVANGHELATOS	429	◆				●			
PYLOS									
4 EPOXE TAVERNA	429	◆	●	●	●		●		
POROS									
TOU SOTIRI TAVERNA	430	◆	●	●	●	●			
SALAMIS									
FARO TAVERNA O CHRISTOS	430	◆	●	●			●		
SPARTA									
DIONYSOS RESTAURANT	431	◆			●	●			
SPETSAI									
MOURAYO RESTAURANT	431	◆◆◆	●	●			●	●	
THEBES									
TAVERNA	431	◆			●	●			

◆ General Information

ATHENS

Useful information

Tourist office
2, Karageorgi Servias
Tel. 13 22 27 30

Post office
100, Eolou Street
Tel. 13 2160 23

Cash dispensers
National bank
2, Karageorgi Servias
Tel. 13 22 27 30
City Bank
8, Othonos Street
Tel. 13 22 74 71
Credit Bank
40, Stadiou Street
Tel. 13 26 00 00

Events

Festival of Athens
Athens Festival Office
4, Stadiou Street
Tel. 13 22 14 59
June 12–Sept. 23. Drama, music and dance at the Odeon of Herodes Atticus. Advance bookings at the Festival Office and on the evening of the performance from 5pm at the theater.

Lycabettus drama festival
Athens Festival Office
4, Stadiou Street
Tel. 13 22 14 59
Open-air theater seating 4,000. Involved in the Festival of Athens. Advance bookings ten days before at the Festival Office, and at the theater from 7–9pm on the evening of the performance.

Son et lumière at the Acropolis
Athens Festival Office, or at the entrance to the show on the Pnyx
Tel. 13 22 14 59
Apr.–Oct., daily, in all languages (depending on program times). Length of display: 40 minutes. Book your seats at the Festival Office, or buy tickets at the entrance.

◆

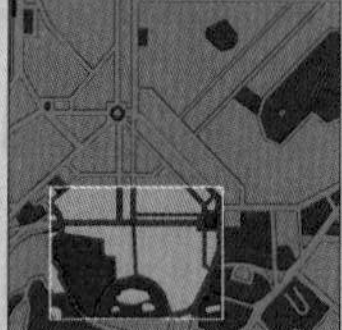

MONASTIRAKI
PLAKA

Culture

Acropolis archeological site
Tel. 13 21 02 19
Open Mon.–Fri. 8.30am–7pm; Sat., Sun. and hols. 8.30am–2.45pm Free admission on Sun.

Acropolis Museum
Acropolis
Tel. 13 23 66 65
Museum and site open Mon.–Fri. 10.30am–4.30pm, Sat., Sun. and hols. 8.30am–2pm.

Ancient Agora, Hephaisteion and Agora Museum
Site of the ancient Agora
Tel. 13 21 01 85
Open 8.30am–2.30pm. Closed Mon. Free admission on Sun.

Archeological site of the Roman Agora
Tel. 13 24 52 20
Open 8.30am–3pm. Closed Mon.

Canellopoulos museum
Junction of Theorias Street and Panos Street
Tel. 13 21 23 13
Open 8.30am–3pm. Closed Mon.

Jewish Museum
36, Amalias Avenue
Tel. 13 23 15 77
Open 9am–1pm. Closed Sat. Free admission.

Kerameikos Cemetery Museum and Site
148, Ermou Street
Tel. 13 46 35 52
Open Mon.–Fri. 8am–3pm; Sat., Sun. and hols. 8.30am–3pm. Closed Mon. Free admission on Sun.

Restaurants

Delfi Restaurant
13, Nikis Street
Tel. 13 23 48 69
Open 11.30am–1.30pm. Closed Sun. and hols.
Typical taverna décor and friendly atmosphere. Very popular with local people. Specialties: grills, fish.

Eden Restaurant
12, Lissiou Street and Mnissikleous, Plaka
Tel. 13 24 88 58
Open 11am–midnight.
Vegetarian restaurant with cheerful décor. Specialties: vegetables, moussaka, mushroom flan.

Kidathineon Restaurant
Filomouson Square, and 1, Farmaki Street, Plaka
Tel. 13 23 42 81
Open 10am–midnight.
The terrace is extremely pleasant. Specialties: veal with eggplant, veal with onions, lobster.

Nefeli Restaurant
24, Panos Street
Tel. 13 21 24 75
Open 11am–midnight. Closed out of season.
Reasonably priced restaurant with very good food and a panoramic view of the city. Ideal for lunch.

O Platanos taverna
4, Dioginous Street, Plaka
Tel. 13 22 06 66
Open noon–4.30pm, 8pm–midnight. Closed Sun.
Quiet, in a neoclassical building on a delightful square. Excellent traditional cuisine.

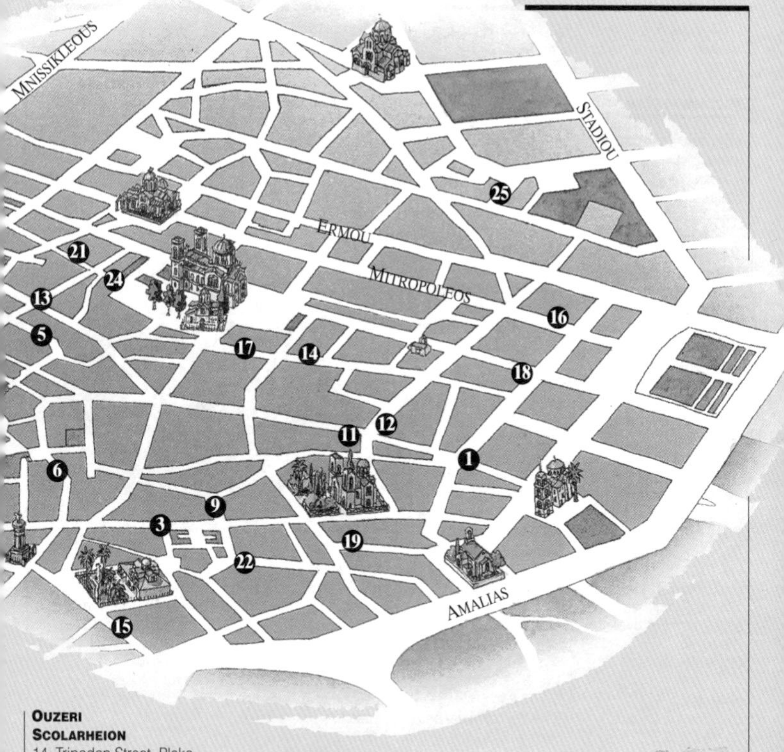

MNISSIKLEOUS
STADIOU
ERMOU
MITROPOLEOS
AMALIAS

OUZERI SCOLARHEION
14, Tripodon Street, Plaka
Tel. 13 24 76 05
Open 11am–4pm, 7pm–11pm.
At the foot of the Acropolis, but slightly off the beaten track, this café is a student haunt. Garden upstairs and fin-de-siècle décor.
⌂

PALIA PLAKIOTIKI TAVERNA
26, Lissiou Street, Plaka
Tel. 13 22 87 22
Open 11am–4pm, 7pm–midnight.
Dine alfresco to the strains of a quartet in one of Plaka's best eating places, which was built in 1882. Specialties include veal in wine sauce, braised veal.
⌂

SIGALAS TAVERNA
2, Monastiraki Square
Tel. 13 21 30 36
Open 7am–2am.
One of the oldest tavernas in Athens in a lively neighborhood near the flea market. Specialty: excellent "giros pita".
⌂

XINOS TAVERNA
4, Angelou Geronta Street, Plaka
Tel. 13 22 10 65
Open 8pm–midnight. Closed Sat., Sun. and out of season.
One of the most tucked-away tavernas in Plaka and perhaps the most delightful. Lovely gardenia-filled garden. Inside, works by naive painters adorn the walls. Excellent music and cuisine.
⌂

ZORBA'S TAVERNA-RESTAURANT
15, Lissiou Street, Plaka
Tel. 13 22 61 88
Open 7pm–midnight.
Small, attractively decorated restaurant

MONASTIRAKI PLAKA

RESTAURANTS
1. DELFI
2. EDEN
3. KIDATHINEON
4. NEFELI
5. O PLATANOS TAVERNA
6. OUZERI SCOLAREION
7. PALIA PLAKIOTIKI TAVERNA
8. SIGALAS TAVERNA
9. XINOS TAVERNA
10. ZORBA'S

HOTELS
11. ACROPOLIS HOUSE
12. ADONIS
13. ADRIAN
14. APHRODITE
15. AVA
16. ELECTRA
17. OMIROS
18. PAN
19. PHOEBUS

NIGHTLIFE
20. DISCOTHEQUE BOOZE
21. TRADITIONAL HELLENIC-STYLE CAFÉ
22. CAFÉ-PATISSERIE TRISTRATO
23. THE COFFEE SHOP
24. METROPOL
25. STROPHILIA

serving traditional Greek cuisine.

ACCOMMODATION

ACROPOLIS HOUSE (PENSION)
6, Kodrou & Voulis Street, Plaka
Tel. 13 22 23 44
Fax 13 22 62 41
In a side street, this former 19th-century mansion with old frescos has been converted into a pension. Family atmosphere. One of the best hotels in the neighborhood, and popular with artists and intellectuals. Some rooms have air conditioning. Breakfast.

ADONIS (PENSION)
3, Voulis & Kodrou Street, Plaka
Tel. 13 24 97 37
Fax 13 24 97 41
Good location, friendly service. Sliding scale of prices, terraced garden. Breakfast.

ADRIAN
74, Adrianou Street
Tel. 13 22 15 53
Fax 13 25 04 54
Closed Nov.–Feb.
Small modern hotel in the heart of Plaka, with a breathtaking view from the shady terrace. Friendly service, bar, air conditioning.

APHRODITE
21, Apollonos Street
Tel. 13 23 43 57
Fax 13 22 60 47
In a quiet street near the center of Plaka. Friendly, helpful service. Bar and air conditioning: excellent buffet breakfast (for a surcharge). One of the best in its category.

AVA (FURNISHED STUDIO APARTMENTS)
9, Lissikratous, Plaka
Tel. 13 23 66 18
Fax 13 23 74 78
Family hotel, extremely good location between the Acropolis and the National Gardens. Friendly service.

ELECTRA
5, Ermou Street, Syntagma
Tel. 13 22 32 22
Fax 13 22 03 10
Central and very comfortable. Friendly service. Restaurant, bar, air conditioning. Breakfast.

OMIROS
15, Apollonos Street, Plaka
Tel. 13 23 54 86
Near Plaka's tourist center, but a little off the beaten track. Rather charmless, but in an excellent location. View of the Acropolis from the terrace. Bar, restaurant, air conditioning. Breakfast.

PAN
11, Mitropoléos Street, Syntagma
Tel. 13 23 78 16
Fax 13 23 78 10
Near the cathedral and Syntagma Square, in a neighborhood that hums with activity day and night. Rather anonymous modern hotel.

PHOEBUS (PENSION)
12, Petra Street, Plaka
Tel. 13 22 01 42
Good location, a short distance from the center of Plaka. Quiet, family pension with view of the Acropolis. Bar, friendly service and sliding scale of prices.

BARS AND NIGHTLIFE

BOOZE DISCOTHEQUE
Junction of Ermou Street and Asomaton Street
Tel. 13 25 28 89
Open 1.30pm–8am.
In the trendy neighborhood of Thissio, at the foot of the Acropolis. Twenty-seven DJs take turns to play a varied and original choice of music. Young clientele.

METROPOL CAFÉ
Mitropoleos Square and 1, Pandrossou Street
Tel. 13 22 01 97
Open 7am–2am.
Closed Sun.
Extremely friendly service, delicious pastries and attractive surroundings. Tasty breakfasts and snacks (salads, sandwiches).

STROPHILIA
7, Karytsi Street
Tel. 13 23 48 03
Open 8pm–2am.
Closed Aug.
Wine bar popular with artists and students. Convivial, friendly atmosphere. Serves over sixty Greek wines and various dishes of the day.

THE COFFEE SHOP
13, Dioskoupon Street
Tel. 13 21 96 07
Open 10am–1am.
Closed Nov.– end Feb.
Café and snack bar at the foot of the Acropolis, shady square, student haunt.

TRADITIONAL HELLENIC-STYLE CAFÉ
36, Pandrossou Street
59, Mitropoléos Street
Tel. 13 21 30 23
Open 9.30am–7pm.
Closed Sun.
Frequented by lecturers and students. "Rembetika" music, very friendly welcome, traditional "meze". Peaceful and cool, crafts on sale.

TRISTRATO CAFÉ-PÂTISSERIE
Geronta & Daidalou Street
Tel. 13 24 44 72
Open noon–midnight.
Attractive café, ideal for romantic trysts. Sample their range of delicious Viennese pastries in quiet, comfortable surroundings.

CRAFTS

NATIONAL ORGANIZATION OF GREEK CRAFTS
9, Mitropoleos Street
Tel. 13 22 10 17
Woven fabrics from Macedonia, embroidery from Mykonos, carvings, silverware.

TANAGREA
15, Mitropoleos Street
Tel. 13 22 33 66
Ceramics.

TRIKALA
31, Voulis Street
Tel. 13 22 49 32
Fax 13 24 91 04
"Flokati" carpets and bedspreads.

BOOKSTORES

ELEFTHEROUDAKIS
4, Nikis Street
Tel. 13 22 93 88
Fax. 13 23 98 21
Some works, especially art books, in English.

ANTIQUES

ANTIKA
4, Leoforou Amalias Street
Range of antiques, and less expensive objects suitable as souvenirs.

◆

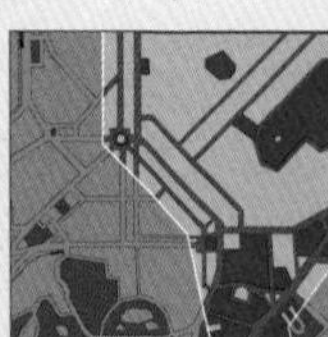

OMONIA
EXARCHIA
SYNTAGMA
KOLONAKI

CULTURE

BENAKI MUSEUM
1, Koumbari Street
(corner of Vas. Sophias Avenue)
Tel. 13 61 16 17
Open 8.30am–2pm. Closed Tues.

BYZANTINE MUSEUM
22, Vas. Sophias Avenue
Tel. 17 23 21 78,
Open 8.30am–3pm. Closed Mon.

CENTER FOR FOLK ART AND TRADITIONS
6, Hadzimihali Street
Tel. 13 24 39 87
Open 9am–1pm, 5pm–9pm. Closed Mon. Free admission.

MUSEUM OF CYCLADIC AND ANCIENT ART
4, Néofitou Douka Street
Tel. 17 22 83 21
Open 10am–2pm. Closed Tues., Sun. Free admission on Sat.

MUSEUM OF THE CITY OF ATHENS
7, Paparigopoulou Street
Tel. 13 24 61 64
Open 9am–1.30pm. Closed Tues., Thurs. and Sun.

NATIONAL ARCHEOLOGICAL MUSEUM
44, Patission Street
Tel. 18 21 77 17
Open Tues.–Fri. 8am–7pm; Mon. 12.30–7pm; Sat. Sun. and hols. 8.30am–3pm.

NATIONAL GALLERY AND A. SOUTSOS MUSEUM
50, Vas. Konstantinou Avenue
Tel. 17 23 59 38
Open 9am–3pm. Closed Mon.

NATIONAL HISTORICAL MUSEUM
13, Stadiou Street
Tel. 13 23 76 17
Open Tues.Fri. 9am–1.30pm; Sat. Sun. and hols. 9am–12.30pm. Closed Mon. Free admission on Thurs.

THEATER MUSEUM
50, Akadimias Street
Tel. 13 62 94 30
Open Mon.–Fri. 9am–3pm; Sat. and hols. 10am–1pm.

RESTAURANTS

ATHINAIKON RESTAURANT AND OUZERI
2, Themistekleous Street
Tel. 13 63 84 85
Open 11am–4pm, 7pm-11pm. Closed Sun.
A good, quiet restaurant with air conditioning behind Omonia Square. Décor in the style of a Paris bistro. Mainly frequented by students. Specialty: seafood.

BYZANTINE RESTAURANT
Hilton Hotel
46, Vas. Sophias Avenue
Tel. 17 25 02 01
Open 8.30am–2am.
Attentive service and air conditioning. Delightful restaurant with weekly Spanish nights and Italian nights. Specialties: buffet, salmon.
P

DEMOCRITOS TAVERNA
23, Democritou Street, Kolonaki
Tel. 13 61 92 93
Open 11.30am–4pm, 8pm–1am. Closed Sun. and Aug.
Understated but attractive surroundings. Tasty cuisine. Well-trained staff serve a prestigious clientele from the world of politics and the arts. Specialties: chicken souvlaki and kalamari in wine sauce.

G.B. CORNER RESTAURANT
Grande Bretagne Hotel
Syntagma Square
Tel. 13 23 83 61
Open 7am–1am.

This plush restaurant (piano bar) lives up to expectations. Traditional Greek dishes and French cuisine. Top-quality service.

GEROFINIKAS RESTAURANT
10, Pindarou Street, Kolonaki
Tel. 13 62 27 19
Open noon–11.30pm. Closed public hols.
This intimate restaurant is one of the best meeting places in Athens, and very peaceful as it is separated from the street by a long corridor. Air conditioning. Excellent cuisine (the seafood is worth a special mention). Specialties: lamb fricassée, veal in lemon sauce, lobster thermidor.

IDEAL RESTAURANT
46, Panepistimiou Avenue
Tel. 13 30 22 00
Open 11am–4.30pm, 8pm–2am. Closed Sun.
A quiet restaurant in a shady main road. Good service; pink 1900's décor. Specialties: toasted pancakes, prawns with feta cheese, vine leaves.

KOSTOYANIS TAVERNA
37, Zaimi Street
Tel. 18 21 24 96
Open 7pm–midnight. Closed Sun. and Aug.
Near the National Archeological Museum. Has a shady patio and an extremely varied menu. Specialties: fish kebabs, prawns, cheese flan.

LE GRAND BALCON RESTAURANT
St George Lycabettus Hotel
2, Kleomenous Street
Tel. 17 29 07 11
Open 10am–11pm. Closed Mon, Tues.
The restaurant overlooks the city. Piano music and singers. Air conditioning. Exquisite Greek and European cuisine.

NEON CAFÉ
8, Omonia Square
Tel. 15 23 64 09
Open 8am–2am.
The Neon Café has been here since 1924. It is now a very popular snack bar serving Greek and European dishes.

PETRINO TAVERNA
32, Themistokleous Street
Tel. 13 60 41 00
Open noon–4pm, 8pm–midnight.
A quiet restaurant in the lively neighborhood of Omonia. Air conditioning and attractive décor. Specialty: eggplant with cheese.

TA NISSIA RESTAURANT
Hilton Hotel
46, Vas. Sophias Avenue
Tel. 17 25 02 01
Open 11am–4pm,

7pm–midnight.
Closed out of season.
One of the most stylish restaurants in Athens, overlooking the city. Air conditioning. Excellent authentic cuisine. Specialties: seafood.

TELIS TAVERNA
86, Evripidou Street
Tel. 13 24 27 75
Open 10am–11pm.
In a working-class area near Omonia Square. Very typical. Specialty: grills.

ZONAR'S CAFÉ
9, Panepistimiou Avenue
Omonia
Tel. 13 23 05 72
Open 9am–12.30am.
One of Athens' great meeting places, perfect for a coffee or a quick bite to eat. Frequented by elderly Athenians. Large 1930's dining room. Not to be missed. Specialties: cheese flans, petits fours.

ACCOMMODATION

AMALIA
10, Amalias Avenue
Tel. 13 23 73 01
Fax 13 23 87 92
Near Parliament and the National Gardens. Modern hotel, restaurant, bar, air conditioning.

ASTIR PALACE ATHENS
Panepistimiou Avenue and Vas. Sophias Avenue, Vouliagmeni
Tel. 13 64 31 12
Fax 13 64 28 25
Extremely comfortable, recently built hotel, rather anonymous. Two private beaches on the Bay of Vouliagmeni. Restaurants, swimming pools, tennis, bars, shops, air conditioning. Breakfast.

ATHENIAN INN (PENSION)
22, Haritos, Kolonaki
Tel. 17 23 80 97
Fax 17 23 95 52
In the heart of Kolonaki near the neighborhood's stylish cafés. Cosy, well-kept family hotel. Decorated with works by local artists. Friendly, helpful service. Breakfast.

ATHENS HILTON
46, Vas. Sophias Avenue
Tel. 17 22 02 01
Fax 17 21 31 10
The extremely luxurious Hilton does not stint on marble and provides a wide range of facilities. There are restaurants, bars, swimming pool, air conditioning. All rooms have a balcony. Breakfast.

CAPSIS
22, Stadiou Street
Tel. 13 23 80 01
Fax 16 44 48 30
In a main road near the Ethnological Museum and Parliament. It has all the period charm of an old-fashioned hotel. Restaurant, bar, air conditioning.

LE GRANDE BRETAGNE
Syntagma Square
Tel. 13 23 02 51
Fax 13 23 83 61
The most captivating of Athens' palaces in an elegant late 19th-century structure, meticulously decorated. Extremely friendly service. Bar, restaurant. Breakfast.

LYCABETTUS
6, Valaoritou Street, Kolonaki
Tel. 13 63 55 14
Reasonable hotel. Bar, restaurant.

N.J.V. MERIDIEN ATHENS
1, Voukouresstiou-Stadiou, Vassileos Georgiou.
Tel. 13 25 53 01
Fax 13 23 58 56
No surprises. Its central location is an advantage. Two restaurants, a shopping arcade, bar. Luxury facilities and well-trained staff.

ST-GEORGE LYCABETTUS
2, Kleomenous Street
Tel. 17 29 07 10
Fax 17 29 04 39
In a residential area of Kolonaki, this peaceful luxury hotel affords a superb view of the city . Restaurant, bar, outdoor swimming pool and top-notch amenities with staff to match.

BARS AND NIGHTLIFE

APOTSOS
10, Panepistimiou Avenue
Open 10am–5pm. Closed Sun. and Aug.
Wide range of ouzo and meze, attractive décor. Near Syntagma Square, at the far end of a shopping arcade away from the traffic.

BAR DADA
57, Arachovis Street, Exarchia
Tel. 13 60 77 51
Open 1pm–3am.
In a trendy area.

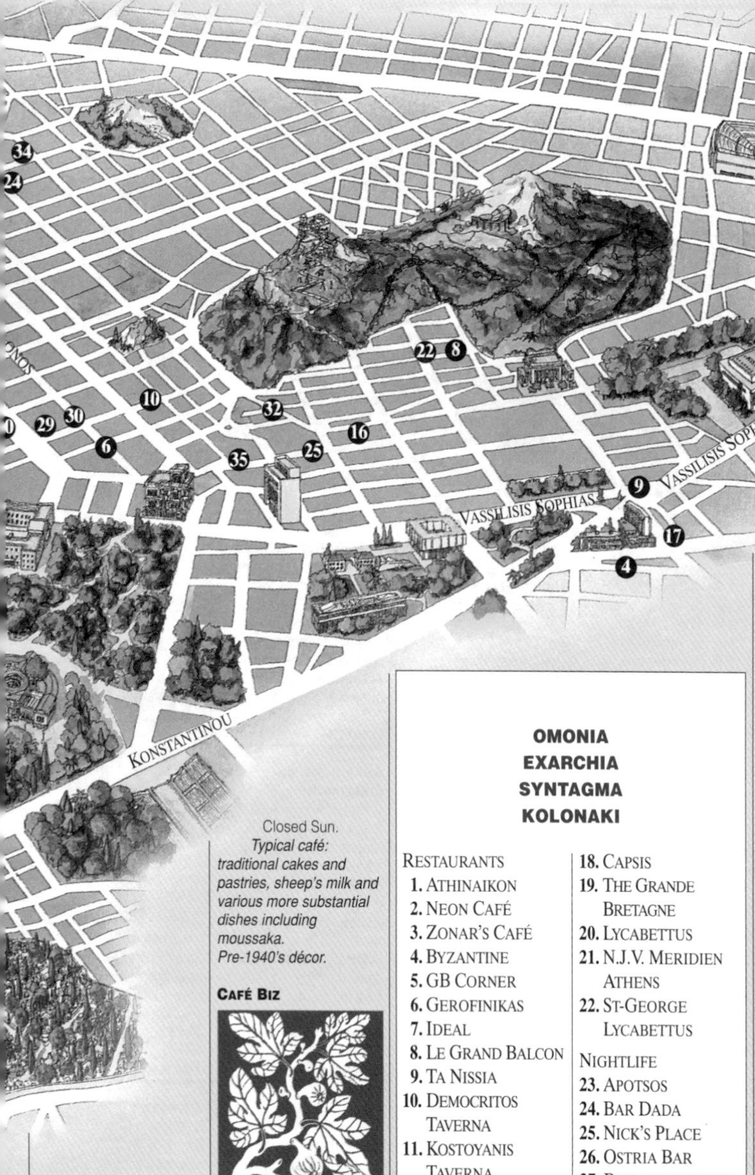

BAR OSTRIA
6, Oikononou Street,
Exarchia
Tel. 13 30 09 07
Open 3pm–2am.
Musical ambience, rock and jazz.

BRETANIA
Omonia Square
Tel. 15 22 26 44
Open 7am–2am.
Closed Sun.
Typical café: traditional cakes and pastries, sheep's milk and various more substantial dishes including moussaka. Pre-1940's décor.

CAFÉ BIZ
21, Voukourestiou Street
Open 10am–11pm.
Closed Sun.
Near Syntagma and Voulis, stylish café-restaurant. Shady terrace in a pleasant pedestrianized street. Tables inside, air conditioning.

DEXAMENI SQUARE
At the end of Xanthipou

OMONIA
EXARCHIA
SYNTAGMA
KOLONAKI

RESTAURANTS
1. ATHINAIKON
2. NEON CAFÉ
3. ZONAR'S CAFÉ
4. BYZANTINE
5. GB CORNER
6. GEROFINIKAS
7. IDEAL
8. LE GRAND BALCON
9. TA NISSIA
10. DEMOCRITOS TAVERNA
11. KOSTOYANIS TAVERNA
12. PETRINO TAVERNA
13. TELIS TAVERNA

HOTELS
14. AMALIA
15. ASTIR PALACE ATHENS
16. ATHENIAN INN
17. ATHENS HILTON
18. CAPSIS
19. THE GRANDE BRETAGNE
20. LYCABETTUS
21. N.J.V. MERIDIEN ATHENS
22. ST-GEORGE LYCABETTUS

NIGHTLIFE
23. APOTSOS
24. BAR DADA
25. NICK'S PLACE
26. OSTRIA BAR
27. RUE DE LA PRESSE
28. BRETANIA
29. CAFÉ BIZ
30. IL POSTO CAFÉ
31. ZONAR'S CAFÉ
32. DEXAMENI SQUARE
33. EXARCHIA SQUARE
34. KAVOURAS
35. LE QUARTIER

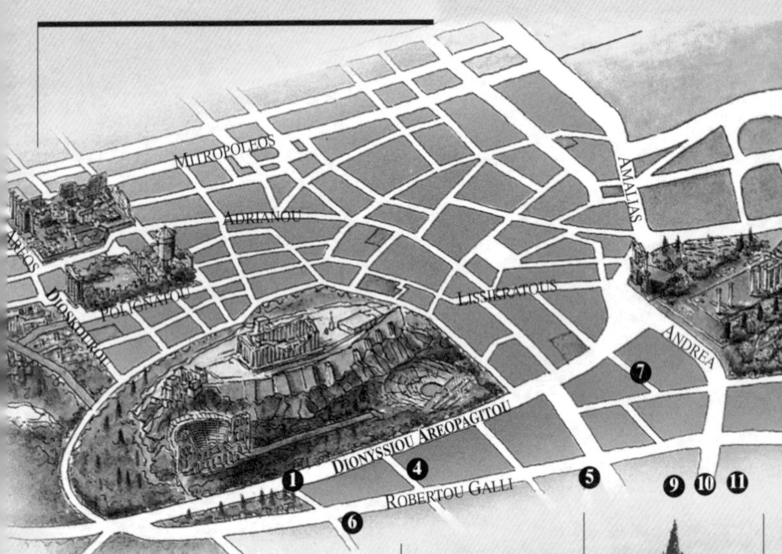

Street, Kolonaki
Open 10am–midnight.
There are a number of traditional cafés on this large irregular square. Family atmosphere, cool.

EXARCHIA SQUARE
An assortment of cafés, restaurants and tavernas offering all sorts of music (mainly rock). Eclectic clientele, with the emphasis on students.

IL POSTO CAFÉ
19, Voukourestiou Street
Tel. 132 62 85 50
Open 5.30–11pm.
Closed Sun.
Recently opened trendy café with modernist décor. Terrace in a pedestrianized street, small dining room inside. Quick lunches and cocktails. Near Syntagma.

KAVOURAS
64, Themistokleous Street
Tel. 13 61 02 02
Open 7pm–2am.
Closed Sun.
Good traditional music, attractive décor, friendly, Greek clientele.

LE QUARTIER
Patriarchou Ioakeim Street, Kolonaki
Open 9am–midnight.
A student haunt on the liveliest square in Kolonaki. Near the neighborhood's trendy stores and chic boutiques.

NICK'S PLACE
26, Spesippou Street, Kolonaki
Tel. 17 24 12 35
Open noon–2am .
In an elegant neighborhood. Musical ambience, rock.

RUE DE LA PRESSE BAR
44, Valtetsiou Street, Exarchia
Tel. 13 30 13 69
Open 5pm–2am.
In a trendy neighborhood,

has a very pleasant garden. Musical ambience, rock.

ZONAR'S CAFÉ
9, Panepistimiou Street
Tel. 13 23 03 36
Open 9.30am–midnight.
Huge café-patisserie with 1930's décor – wood paneling, ceiling fan, mirror etc. A veritable institution, frequented by business people and elderly ladies. A bit pricey, but worth a visit.

CRAFTS

ANNA ANGELOU SIKELIANOU
1, Panou Aravantinou Street (behind the Hilton)
Embroidery and woven fabrics.

PANIJIRI
23, Kleomenous Street
Tel. 13 45 13 78
Original crafts, model boats carved out of wood from old ships.

BOOKSTORES

KAUFFMAN
28, Stadiou Street
Tel. 13 22 21 60
One of the capital's best bookstores, extremely well stocked with travel guides, literature and general works, as well as international newspapers and magazines.

PANDELIDES
9, Amérikis Street
Tel. 13 62 97 63
Some English-language books, especially on art.

REYMONDOS
18, Voukourestiou Street, Syntagma

Tel. 13 64 81 89
Stocks some English-language books as well as a selection of international newspapers and magazines.

JEWELRY

ANDREADIS
7, Amerikis Street
Tel. 19 34 64 17
Reproductions of antique jewelry.

GRECO GOLD
4, Stadiou Street, Syntagma
Tel. 13 22 14 72
Craft designs.

MATI
20, Voukourestiou Street
Tel. 13 62 62 38
Traditional Greek jewelry.

ZOLOTAS CHRYSSOTHEQUE
10, Panepistimiou-Venizelou Street
Tel. 13 61 37 82
Jewelry in ancient and Byzantine styles.

ANTIQUES

LES BEAUX-ARTS
18, Voukourestiou Street
Tel. 13 61 98 88
Statuettes and bronzes, items from the 17th, 18th and 19th centuries.

MINTZAS
22, Pindarou Street
Icons, "ex voto" figures etc.

ART GALLERIES

ATHENS
4, Glykonos Street
Tel 17 25 17 17
Artists shown include Alexiou, Baskalakis, Makroulakis, Nanolides, Prekas, Tsarouchis, and Zamboura.

KREONIDIS

24, Kanari Street, Kolonaki
Tel. 13 60 65 52
and 13 61 86 09
Artists shown include Anrithakis, Droungas, Karas, Mytaras, Philolaos and Xenakis.

NEES MORPHES
9, Valaoritou Street
Tel. 13 61 61 65
Artists shown include Adamacos, Houliaras, Moraïti and Tetsis.

ZOUMBOULAKIS
7, Kriezotou Street
Tel. 13 63 19 51
2, Kolonaki Square
Tel. 13 60 82 72
Artists shown include Fassianos, Ghika, Karella, Moralis, Samios and Tsarouchis.

◆

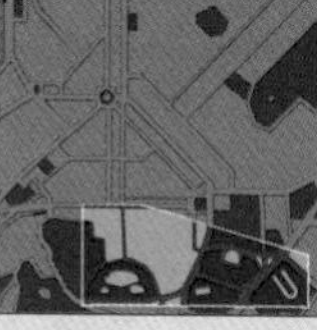

MAKRIGIANI

CULTURE

TEMPLE OF OLYMPIAN ZEUS (OLYMPIEION)
Junction of Vas. Olgas and Amalias avenues
Tel. 19 22 63 30
Open 8.30am–3pm. Closed Mon.

THEATER OF DIONYSOS
Dionysou Areopagitou Street
Tel. 13 22 46 25.

RESTAURANTS

DIONYSOS RESTAURANT
Dionysou Areopagitou (opposite the Acropolis)
Tel. 19 23 31 82
Open 11am–4pm, 7pm–11pm.
At the foot of the Hill of the Muses, with a view of the Acropolis. Well-trained staff, muted atmosphere and high-class cuisine. Specialties: Dionysos pastry, fish.

PALIA TAVERNA
35, Markou Mousourou Street
Tel. 19 02 44 93
Open 7pm–2am. Closed July 20– mid Aug.
One of the oldest tavernas in Athens (1896), behind the stadium. Pleasant garden, large dining room (former barn), period photos and furniture; guitar music and singers; friendly, helpful service. First-class Greek specialties; Peloponnesian cuisine, good selection of wine.

MAKRIGIANI

RESTAURANTS
1. DIONYSOS
2. PALIA TAVERNA

HOTELS
3. ANDROMEDA
4. DIVANI PALACE ACROPOLIS
5. HERA
6. HERODION
7. PARTHENON
8. ROYAL OLYMPIC

NIGHTLIFE
9. BARBARELLA DISCOTHEQUE
10. BOUZOUKI IPHIGENIA
11. BOUZOUKI REGINA

ACCOMMODATION

ANDROMEDA
22, Timoleontos Vassou Street
Tel. 16 43 73 02
Fax 16 46 63 61
Small, recently built luxury hotel (17 rooms, 13 studio apartments and suites) in a residential area 15 minutes walk from the center. Bar, restaurant. Very comfortable.

DIVANI PALACE ACROPOLIS
19, Parthenonos, Makrigiani
Tel. 19 22 29 45
Fax 19 22 96 50
Modern hotel near the Acropolis. Luxurious and very comfortable.

HERA
9, Falirou Street, Makrigiani
Tel. 19 23 66 82
Fax 19 23 56 18
New hotel with good service but unremarkable décor. Terrace with view of the Acropolis. Bar, air conditioning.

HERODION
4, Robertou Galli,
Makrigiani
Tel. 19 23 68 32
Fax 19 23 58 51
Extremely comfortable modern hotel situated near the ramparts of the Acropolis. Garden, bar, shops, air conditioning. Breakfast.
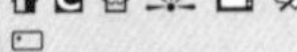

PARTHENON
6, Makri Street
Tel. 19 23 45 94
Fax 19 23 57 97
Very clean, well-run hotel with friendly service. Situated a short distance from the tourist center near the Arch of Hadrian. Air conditioning. Breakfast.

ROYAL OLYMPIC
28–32, Diakou Street
Tel. 19 22 64 11
The atmosphere of this hotel conjures up the peacefulness and bygone luxury of the 1970's. The hotel also boasts perhaps the finest view of Athens from its terrace, taking in the Temple of Olympian Zeus (Olympieion), the Acropolis and the National Gardens. Two top-notch restaurants.

BARS AND NIGHTLIFE

BARBARELLA DISCOTHEQUE
253, Singrou Avenue
Tel. 19 42 56 01
Open 10am–6am.
A varied range of trendy modern music including funk, rap, techno and, later in the evening, traditional Greek music. Air conditioning.

BOUZOUKI IPHIGENIA
201, Singrou Avenue
Tel. 19 34 94 44
Open 10pm–3am.
Closed Weds.
Traditional Greek music.

BOUZOUKI REGINA
140, Singrou Avenue
Tel. 19 22 89 02
Open 10pm–3am.
Closed Weds., Sun.
Traditional Greek music, air conditioning.

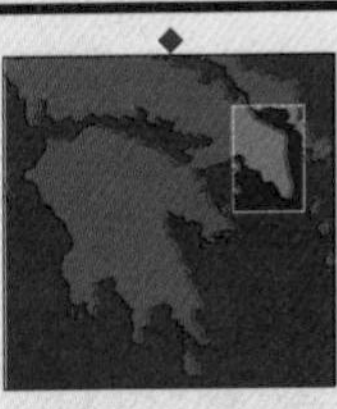

GLYFADA

BARS AND NIGHTLIFE

OUI DISCOTHEQUE
33, Vas. Georgiou Street,
Glyfada
Tel. 18 94 14 56
Open 10am–6am.
Closed out of season.
On the beach. 1960's music, air conditioning.

OUI 2 DISCOTHEQUE
81, Vas. Georgiou Street,
Glyfada
Tel. 18 94 95 85
Open 10am–6am.
Closed out of season.
On the beach. Music from the 1950's, 1960's and 1970's. Restaurant.

SUMMER LOFT DISCOTHEQUE
2, Pavlou Street, Glyfada
Tel. 18 94 30 72
Open 10am–6am. Closed out of season.

ILIOUPOLIS

CULTURE

MUSEUM OF GREEK POPULAR ART
17, Kidathineon Street
Tel. 13 22 90 31
Open 10am–2pm. Closed Mon.

OUTSKIRTS OF ATHENS

CULTURE

DAPHNI MONASTERY
Road to Corinth
(near the campsite)
Tel. 15 81 15 58
Open 8.30am–3pm.

KAISARIANI MONASTERY
Four miles from Athens
Tel. 17 23 66 19
Open 8.30am–3pm. Closed Mon.

ANCIENT CORINTH

USEFUL INFORMATION

Postcode 20007

ANDRITSAINA

USEFUL INFORMATION

Postcode 27061
Town Hall Tel: 626 06 26

CULTURE

TEMPLE OF BASSAE
Six miles from Andritsaina
Undergoing restoration, but open to the public. Free entry. Open all day.

CULTURE

ARCHEOLOGICAL SITE OF ACROCORINTH
Tel. 74 13 14 43
Open 8.30am–3pm. Closed Mon. Free admission.

CORINTH MUSUEM
Four miles from Corinth, near the archeological site.
Tel. 70 13 12 07
Open 8.30am–3pm.

RESTAURANTS

DIONYSOS TAVERNA
On the square.
Tel. 74 13 10 15
Open noon–3pm, 6pm–1am.
Extremely pleasant terrace and delightful service. Convivial atmosphere in the evenings. Specialties: fried cheese, spit-roasted meat.

ACCOMMODATION

O TASSOS PENSION
As you enter the village
Tel. 74 13 12 25.
A traditional pension situated just over a quarter of a mile from the archeological site. Friendly service, terrace with view of the village square or of New Corinth. There is also a taverna of the same name.

ACCOMMODATION

THE PAN
As you enter the town.
Tel. 62 62 22 13
Open all year
Best value for money in town. This small, friendly family hotel is less than a quarter of a mile from the center and cafés.

ARACHOVA

USEFUL INFORMATION

Postcode 32004
Town Hall Tel: 267 312 50

RESTAURANTS

LAKA TAVERNA
On the main square.
Tel. 26 73 16 28
Open 8am–midnight.
Traditional taverna-café-grocery, friendly service, regional cuisine. Specialties: meat soup, "fromella" toasted cheese, grilled lamb and mutton.

ACCOMMODATION

PARNASSOS
As you enter the village coming from Delphi
Tel. 26 73 13 07
Fax 26 73 11 89
Open all year.

Traditional family pension, a stone's throw from the center, cafés and restaurants. View of Itea and the Gulf of Corinth. Bathroom on the upper floor only.

AREOPOLIS

USEFUL INFORMATION

Postcode 23062
Town Hall Tel: 733 512 39

ACCOMMODATION

THE TOWER
Pyrgos Kapetanakou
Tel. 53 35 12 33
A beautifully converted tower, in the old town, housing a family hotel. Breakfast.

ARGOS

USEFUL INFORMATION

Postcode 21200
Town Hall Tel: 751 224 25

CULTURE

ARCHEOLOGICAL SITE OF LERNA
Tel. 75 14 75 97
Open 8am–3pm. Closed Mon.

ARGOS MUSEUM
Tel. 75 12 88 19
Open 8.30am–3pm.

BRAURON (VRAVRONA)

USEFUL INFORMATION

Postcode 19003

CULTURE

BRAURON MUSEUM AND ARCHEOLOGICAL SITE
Tel. 29 47 10 20
Open 8.30am–2pm. Closed Mon.

RESTAURANTS

XANOLIA TAVERNA
Tel. 294 710 20
Open 9am–1am.
The terrace of this charming taverna is quiet and pleasant. Specialty: fish.

CORINTH

USEFUL INFORMATION

Postcode 20100

TOURIST OFFICE
33, Koliatsou Street
Tel. 741 232 83

ACCOMMODATION

LE BELLE VUE
40, Damaskinou Street
Tel. 74 12 20 88
Only five minutes from the station, facing the sea and on the busiest square (cafés and patisseries). Rooms are practical but rather characterless.

DAPHNI

USEFUL INFORMATION

Postcode 25004

EVENTS

WINE FESTIVAL
Daphni Park, just as you enter the monastery.
The festival is held from early August to early September. It features displays of traditional dancing and tasting of all the Greek wines.

CULTURE

DAPHNI MONASTERY
Open Tues.–Thurs. 8am–3pm, Sat. and Sun. 8.30am–3pm. Closed Mon.

DELPHI

USEFUL INFORMATION

Postcode 33054

TOURIST OFFICE
45, Apollonos Street
Tel. 265 822 20

CULTURE

DELPHI ARCHEOLOGICAL MUSEUM
At the entrance to the archeological site.
Tel. 265 823 12
Open Wed.–Fri. 8am–7pm; Mon. 8.30am–7pm; Sat. and Sun. 8.30am–3pm. Free admission for students.

DELPHI ARCHEOLOGICAL SITE
Tel. 265 823 12
Open Mon.–Fri. 8am–7pm. Sat. and Sun. 8.30am–3pm. Free admission for students.

RESTAURANTS

O BAXOS TAVERNA
82, Apollonos Street
Tel. 265 824 48
Open 8am–1am.
View of the gulf from the terrace. Faultless service, very friendly owner. Three menus. Specialty: Greek cuisine.

TOPIKI GEVSI
19, B. Pavlou Street
Tel. 265 820 71
Open 7.30am–midnight.
Superb view, varied menu and wide selection of Greek wines. Piano bar in the evenings. Tasty Greek specialties.

ACCOMMODATION

AMALIA
Apollonos Street
Tel. 265 821 01
Fax 265 822 90
Large hotel dating from the 1970's. Old-fashioned but charming, roomy and peaceful. Bars, restaurant, air conditioning. View of the gulf. Breakfast.

KOUROS (PENSION)
23, Vassileos Paviou (opposite Zorba's Taverna).
Tel. 265 824 73
Fax 265 826 29
Open all year
Well-kept family hotel. Excellent service. Delightful and very comfortable.

AEGINA

USEFUL INFORMATION

Postcode 18010

TOURIST OFFICE
Paraliaki Street
Tel. 297 223 91

CULTURE

AEGINA MUSEUM
Tel. 297 226 37
Open 8.30am–3pm. Closed Mon.

TEMPLE OF APHAIA
Tel. 297 323 98
Open Mon.–Fri. 8am–5pm, Sat. and Sun. 8.30am–3pm.

RESTAURANTS

DIONYSOS TAVERNA
40, Pan. Irioti Street
Tel. 2972 45 21
Open 11am–midnight.
Small restaurant, part of the fish market. A shady spot where you can sample excellent seafood, fish and octopus.

ACCOMMODATION

BROWN HOTEL
3, Toti Hatzi Street, Peralia
Tel. 297 222 71
Fax 297 258 38
Closed Dec.–Mar.
South of the harbor and facing the beach, bar, view of garden, charming traditional house. Breakfast.

ELEUSIS

USEFUL INFORMATION

Postcode 19200

CULTURE

ELEUSIS ARCHEOLOGICAL SITE AND MUSEUM
1, Lera Street
Tel. 155 460 19
Open 8.30am–3pm. Closed Mon.

EPIDAURUS

USEFUL INFORMATION

Postcode 21054
Town Hall Tel: 753 412 50

CULTURE

EPIDAURUS ARCHEOLOGICAL SITE
Tel. 753 412 49
Open 8am–7pm
Closed Mon.

EVENTS

FESTIVAL OF EPIDAURUS
Ancient theater of Epidaurus.
Tel. 75 22 26 91
End June to end Aug. Information from Athens Festival Office. Seats can be booked ten days in advance in Athens or Epidaurus.

GYTHEION

USEFUL INFORMATION

Postcode 23200
Town Hall Tel: 733 222 10

RESTAURANTS

APHOI LAMBROU TAVERNA
On the harbor, opposite the landing stage.
Tel. 733 221 22
Open 11am–11.30pm
Terrace on the jetty, traditional Greek cuisine. Specialties: swordfish and shellfish.

ACCOMMODATION

THE AKTAEON
On the jetty.
Tel. 733 222 94
Open all year.
This hotel is in an old traditional house with basic comforts but full of charm. View of the harbor, sunny rooms.

HYDRA

USEFUL INFORMATION

Postcode 18040

TOURIST OFFICE
Navarchou N. Votsi Street
Tel. 298 522 05

RESTAURANTS

KONTILENIAS TAVERNA
To the right of Hydra harbor (ten minutes walk)
Open 11am–3pm, 6pm–midnight.
Closed out of season.
Overlooks a little harbor. Perfect after a swim. Specialties: large prawns with cheese, lobster.

ACCOMMODATION

EL GRECO
Greco Gold Office, on the harbor. Tel. 298 532 00
Fax 298 535 11
Closed Nov.–Mar.
Modern hotel a short walk from the bustle of the harbor. Garden, café, bar and restaurant. Friendly service. Air conditioning.

KALAMATA

USEFUL INFORMATION

Postcode 24100

TOURIST OFFICE
46, Aristomenous Street
Tel. 721 231 87

ACCOMMODATION

ÉLITE HOTEL
2, Navarinou Avenue (on the beach at Kalamata)
Tel. 721 250 15
Fax 7218 43 69
Open all year.
Modern hotel with 50 rooms, in the town's tourist center. Private beach, swimming pool, tennis. Air conditioning.

KIFISSIA

USEFUL INFORMATION

Postcode 14562

CULTURE

NATURAL HISTORY MUSEUM
13, Levidou Street
Tel. 180 864 05
Open 9am–2.30pm. Closed Fri.

RESTAURANTS

BOKARIS TAVERNA
Socratous Street
Tel. 180 125 89
Open 7.30pm–3am.
A very pleasant taverna in a delightful garden. Excellent food, including a variety of Greek specialties and wines.

ACCOMMODATION

THE PENTELIKON
66, Deligiani Street, Kefalari
Tel. 180 128 37
Fax 180 106 52
Closed Oct.–May
Neoclassical-style palace with bars and restaurant (international cuisine and Greek specialties). Tree-lined grounds,

terraces, tennis courts. Near the town center, restaurants and cafés. Breakfast.

KIPARISSIA

USEFUL INFORMATION

Postcode 24500
Town Hall Tel: 761 222 80

RESTAURANTS

ST NECTANOS
Kiparissia Beach
Tel. 761 248 81
Open noon–11pm.
This is one of the town's few restaurants. Situated very close to the Kiparissia Beach Hotel. Shady terrace near the sea. Friendly, helpful service.

ACCOMMODATION

KIPARISSIA BEACH HOTEL
By the beach
Tel. 761 44 92
Fax 761 2 44 95
Open all year.
Recently built hotel with all mod cons, overlooking the beach. Bar, nearby taverna, friendly service, air conditioning. Breakfast.

LOUTRAKI

USEFUL ADDRESSES

Postcode 20300

TOURIST OFFICE
7, El. Venizelou Street
Tel. 741 422 58

RESTAURANTS

REMEZO TAVERNA
8, Korinthou Street
Tel. 741 215 00
Open noon–midnight.
Alfresco family taverna near the seafront, in the town center. Variety of Greek specialties including seafood pancakes, shellfish and fish.

ACCOMMODATION

AGELIDIS PALACE
19, G. Lekka Street
Tel. 741 422 51
Fax 741 262 86
Open all year
Small palace at the water's edge. In the style of a 1900's seaside resort with modern comforts, neoclassical architecture and décor. Bar and restaurant.

BEAU RIVAGE
1, Possidonos Street
Tel. 741 423 23
Fax 741 411 28
Closed Nov.–Mar.
Recently renovated turn-of-the-century hotel on the seafront. Charming, comfortable and welcoming. Breakfast.

MARATHON

USEFUL INFORMATION

Postcode 19007
Town Hall Tel: 294 662 82

CULTURE

MARATHON MUSEUM AND TUMULUS
Tel. 294 554 62
Open 8.30am–3pm. Closed Mon.

RESTAURANTS

TO LIMANAKI
Timvos Beach
Tel. 294 553 06
Open noon–3pm, 6pm–midnight.
This is one of many tavernas and ouzeris bordering a popular beach, just a few minutes from Marathon's site and hotel. Very typical. Specialties: seafood.

ACCOMMODATION

THE MARATHON
Timvos Beach
Tel. 294 551 22
Fax 294 552 22
Only 25 miles from Athens and a few hundred yards from Marathon's tumulus and beach, this 1950's hotel retains its old-fashioned charm. Attentive service.

MEGALOPOLIS

USEFUL INFORMATION

Postcode 22200
Town Hall Tel: 791 222 65

ACCOMMODATION

THE LETO
14, P. Kefala Street
Tel. 791 223 02
Fax 791 224 60

The best hotel in town. Has a convivial, family atmosphere.

METHONI

USEFUL INFORMATION

Postcode 24006
Town Hall Tel: 723 312 55

RESTAURANTS

KLIMATARIA TAVERNA
Methoni Beach
Tel. 723 315 44
Open 9.30am–midnight. Closed evenings during the winter.
Delightful taverna by the beach and near the archeological site. Good quality cuisine. Specialties: fish, Methoni rosé wines, onion flans.

ACCOMMODATION

THE CASTELLO
In the town center
Tel. 723 313 00
Closed Nov.–Apr.
Less than a quarter of a mile from the beach and the site. This is a very comfortable family hotel, smartly kept, totally renovated, friendly service. Pleasant garden, several rooms with view of the site.

MYCENAE

USEFUL INFORMATION

Postcode 21200
Town Hall Tel: 751 662 31

CULTURE

MYCENAE ARCHEOLOGICAL SITE
Tel. 751 665 85
Open Mon.–Fri. 8am–7pm, Sat. and Sun. 8.30am–3pm.

MISTRA

USEFUL INFORMATION

Postcode 23100
Town Hall Tel: 731 933 68

CULTURE

MISTRA ARCHEOLOGICAL SITE AND MUSEUM
Tel. 731 933 77
Open 8.30am–3pm.

RESTAURANTS

TO CASTRO
At lower end of village.
Tel. 731 935 26
Open 11.30am–3.30pm, 6.30pm–midnight.
Restaurant serving traditional Greek cuisine, conveniently close to the archeological site.

NAUPLION

USEFUL INFORMATION

Postcode 21100

TOURIST OFFICE
Ethnosinelefseos Square
Tel. 752 277 76

CULTURE

FORTRESS OF PALAMIDI
Can be reached by steps from Nikitara Square ▲ *311*
Tel. 752 280 36
Open 8.30am–5pm. Closed after 3pm on Sat. and Sun.

NAUPLION MUSEUM
Syntagma Square
Tel. 752 275 02
Open 8.30am–3pm. Closed Tues.

RESTAURANTS

KALAMARAKIA TAVERNA
42, Papanikolaou
Tel. 752 285 62
Open 7pm–midnight.
In a quiet side street in the old town. A restaurant with terrace and interior garden that is an absolute must. Friendly, helpful service. Specialties: grilled fish, stuffed noodles, kebabs.

SAVOURAS TAVERNA
5, Bouboulinas Street
Open 7pm–1am.
Friendly taverna serving excellent cuisine. Specialties: squid, grilled fish.

ACCOMMODATION

KING OTHON
3, Farmakopoulo Street
Tel. 752 275 85
Peaceful hotel situated in the heart of the old town in a turn-of-the-century building. You can have breakfast in the garden. Shady terrace, full of charm.

XENIA PALACE
Hill of Acronauplia
Tel. 752 289 81
Fax 752 289 87
Large luxury hotel at the foot of the hill of Acronauplia on the outskirts of Nauplion. Superb view of the harbor and the old town. Bars, restaurants, chalets, private beach, garden, night club. Breakfast.

NEMEA

USEFUL INFORMATION

Postcode 20500
Town Hall Tel: 746 222 35

CULTURE

NEMEA SITE AND MUSEUM
Tel. 746 227 39
Open 8.30am–3pm. Closed Mon.

NAUPLION

RESTAURANTS
1. KALAMARAKIA TAVERNA
2. SAVOURAS TAVERNA

HOTELS
3. KING OTHON
4. XENIA'S PALACE

OLYMPIA

USEFUL INFORMATION

Postcode 27065

TOURIST OFFICE
13, Douma Street
Tel. 624 231 00

CULTURE

ARCHEOLOGICAL MUSEUM
Tel. 624 225 29
Open Tues.–Fri. 8am–7pm, Mon. noon–6pm, Sat., Sun. 8.30am–3pm.

OLYMPIA ARCHEOLOGICAL SITE
Tel. 624 225 17
Open 8am–7pm.

RESTAURANTS

PRAXITELIS TAVERNA
Spiliopoulou Street
Tel. 624 235 70
Open 11am–3pm, 5pm–midnight.
Situated in a quiet street, this taverna serves inexpensive traditional dishes. Varied menu. Specialty: grilled rabbit.

ROMANTIKA TAVERNA
Town center
Tel. 62 42 22 10
Open 9am–midnight
Closed Nov.–end Jan.
Traditional Greek cuisine and several house specialties.

ACCOMMODATION

ALTIS
On the road out of town heading toward the site, on a small modern square.
Tel. 624 231 01
Fax 624 224 59
Situated a little over a quarter of a mile from the ancient site, this hotel offers comfortable, modern rooms, terrace, balcony, garden, bar, restaurant, shops, air conditioning. Has a gallery that shows contemporary Greek art.

EUROPI
1, Drouva Street
Tel. 624 226 50
Fax 624 227 00
This roomy, extremely comfortable little hotel offers all mod cons and a view of the site. Bar, restaurant. Breakfast.

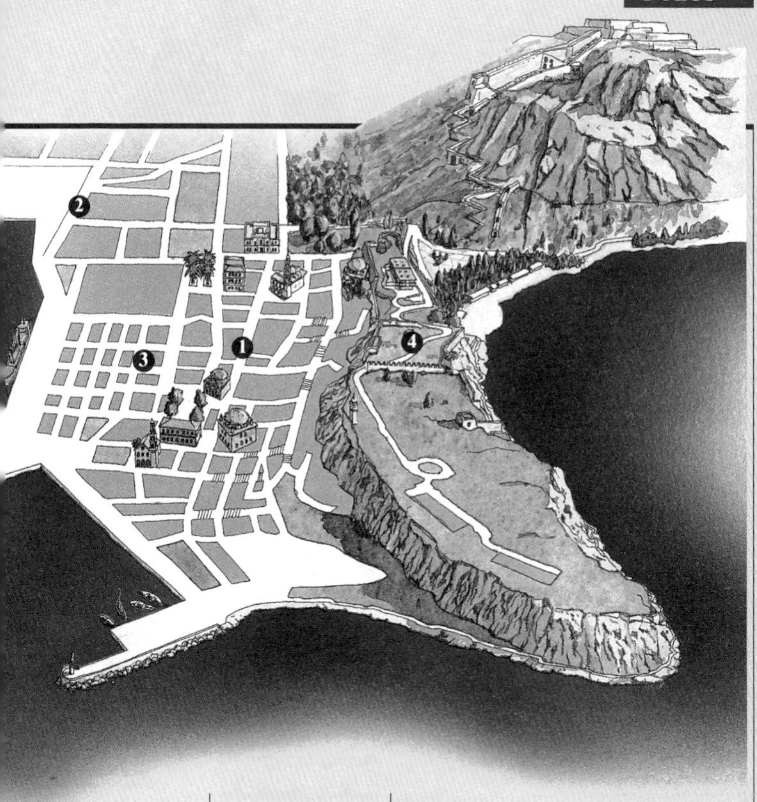

HOSIOS LOUKAS

CULTURE

MONASTERY OF HOSIOS LOUKAS
Between Delphi and Thebes.
Tel. 267 222 28
Open 8.30am–2pm, In summer 4–6pm.

ACCOMMODATION

THE KOUTRIARIS
6, Ethnikis Antistassis Square, Distomo
Tel. 267 222 68
Fax 267 225 11
About 6 miles from the Monastery and 9 miles from the beach, this friendly hotel is situated on the village's pleasant, shady square.

PATRAS

USEFUL INFORMATION

Postcode 26500

TOURIST OFFICE
40, Othonos & Amalias
Tel. 612 209 02

CULTURE

ARCHEOLOGICAL MUSEUM
Tel. 612 750 70
Open 8.30am–3pm. Closed Mon.

RESTAURANTS

EVANGHELATOS
Haghiou Nikolaou Street
Tel. 612 777 72
Open 6pm–midnight.
Traditional restaurant, one of the oldest in Patras, which serves excellent food.

ACCOMMODATION

ASTIR
19, Hagiou Andreou Street
Tel. 6127 75 02
Fax 612 775 24
This 1970's hotel is the major hotel in Patras, near the harbor, shops, cafés, banks and travel agencies. Bar, terrace. Breakfast.

PORTO RIO (HOTEL AND CHALETS)
Rhion Beach
Tel. 619 921 02
Fax 619 922 12
Closed Nov.–Mar.
Just 5 miles from Patras, this modern tourist complex is near the archeological site. It offers a wide range of sports activities, bars and restaurants, terraces and gardens. Breakfast.

PYLOS

USEFUL INFORMATION

Postcode 24001
Town Hall Tel: 723 222 21

CULTURE

CITADEL OF NAVARINO
Tel. 731 253 63
Open 8.30am–3pm.

NESTOR'S PALACE
About 10 miles from Pylos.
Tel. 763 314 37
Open 9.30am–2.30pm.

RESTAURANTS

4 EPOXE TAVERNA (FOUR SEASONS)
On the seafront, at the far end of the village.
Open 6pm–midnight.
Situated near the archeological site and the Karalys Hotel, this typical Greek taverna serves a wide variety of fish. Terrace and large dining room. Specialties: fish, shellfish.

Accommodation

Karalis Beach (pension)
Paralia Street (on the seafront)
Tel. 723 230 21
Fax 723 229 70
At the foot of the citadel, surrounded by pine trees. Friendly service, beach and mooring, restaurant, bar, mod cons, peaceful.

PIRAEUS

Useful information

Postcodes 18531–18539

Tourist office
43, Akti Miaouli
Tel. 145 236 70

Culture

Naval Museum
Akti Themistokleous
Tel. 14 51 68 22
Open 8.30am–1pm. Closed Mon. and Sun.

Piraeus Archeological Museum
31, Har. Trikoupi Street
Tel. 145 162 64
Open 8.30am–3pm. Closed Mon.

Accommodation

The Park
103, Kolokotroni & Gladstonos Street
Tel. 14 52 46 11
Although situated on a square in the town center, close to the harbor, this modern hotel is pleasant and peaceful. Friendly service. Bar, restaurant, attractive terrace, air conditioning. Breakfast.

POROS

Useful information

Postcode 18020

Tourist office
Haghiou Nicolaou (summer only)
Tel. 298 224 62

Restaurants

Tou Sotiri taverna
On the harbor, to the right.
Tel. 298 224 07
Open noon–midnight.
Original nautical décor, shady terrace. Extremely good food. Specialties: snails, pork with onions, braised lamb.

Accommodation

The Saron
On the jetty
Tel. 298 222 79
Fax 298 236 70
Closed Nov.–Mar.
Right in the center of the village, this hotel is full of old-world charm. Attractive rooms with views of the sea and the harbor (rather noisy in high season). Friendly service and good value for money. Breakfast.

RHAMNOUS

Culture

Rhamnous Archeological Site
Rhamnous, Kato Souli
Tel. 294 262 70
Open 8.30am–3pm. Closed Mon.

SALAMIS

Useful information

Tourist office
Junction of Salaminos Avenue and Thermoplion
Tel. 1 465 11 00

Restaurants

Faro Taverna O Christos
Adriresti Beach, just in front of Haghios Nikolaos.
Open 11am–11pm.
Near the beach. Extremely friendly service, pleasant shady garden overlooking the sea. Specialty: fish.

SKALA OROPOS

Useful information

Postcode 19015

Culture

Archeological Site of the Amphiareion
Tel. 29 56 21 44
Open 8.30am–3pm.

CAPE SOUNION

Useful information

Postcode 19500

Culture

Temple of Poseidon
Cape Sounion
Tel. 292 93 63
Open 10am–nightfall.

Accommodation

The Belvedere Park
Cape Sounion
Tel. 292 391 02
Hilltop hotel and chalets in magnificent grounds. ten minutes' walk from the beach. Tennis, golf, disco, bar. Friendly service in breathtaking surroundings.

SPARTA

Useful information

Postcode 23100

Tourist office
8, Hilonos Street
Tel. 731 267 72

Culture

Archeological Museum
True Dionisiou Daphni
Tel. 731 285 75

SPETSAI

VIDA PRÁCTICA

Código postal 18050

OFICINA DE TURISMO
Dapias (sólo en verano)
Tfno. 731 287 01

RESTAURANTES

RESTAURANTE MOURAYO
Palio Limani
Tfno. 298 737 00
Abierto 19 h-4 h.
Cerrado fuera de temporada.

Tranquilo, aislado, terraza frente al mar, piano-bar y música griega a partir de las 2 h. Muy apreciado, buena recepción. Especialidades: cocina francesa, pescado. 4.200-5.800 PTA.

ALOJAMIENTO

HOTEL POSSIDONION
En el muelle, a la derecha del puerto.
Tfno. 298 722 08
Cerrado de nov. a marzo.
Magnífico hotel de estilo neoclásico con jardín, terraza, sala de música, decoración exquisita, acogida muy atenta, jardín-terraza frente al mar. 4.000-7.000 PTA. Desayuno 800 PTA.

SUNIÓN (CABO)

VIDA PRÁCTICA

Código postal 19500

VIDA CULTURAL

TEMPLO DE POSEIDÓN
Cabo Sunión.
Tfno. 292 93 63
Abierto 10 h-24 h. 360 PTA.

ALOJAMIENTO

BELVEDERE PARK
Cabo Sunión.
Tfno. 292 391 02
Hotel y bungalows situados en un magnífico jardín. Tenis, golf, restaurante, discoteca, bar. A 10 min a pie de la playa. Buen recibimiento en un hermoso marco. 6.700-9.600 PTA.

TEBAS

VIDA PRÁCTICA

Código postal 32200

RESTAURANTES

TABERNA
Epaminonda, 64
(junto al hotel Meletiou).
Abierto 10 h-15 h 30, 17 h-24 h.
En el centro-ciudad, en la calle más comercial, cerca del mercado y de los cafés más populares. Taberna reciente pero tradicional bien atendida. Especialidades griegas tradicionales (sólo plato del día). 700-1.700 PTA.

TIRINTO

VIDA PRÁCTICA

Tfno. Ayuntamiento:
752 362 80

VIDA CULTURAL

RECINTO ARQUEOLÓGICO
Tfno. 752 226 57
Cerrado temporalmente (no hay información de la fecha de apertura ni del horario).

ALOJAMIENTO

AMALIA
Carretera de Nauplia-Argos.
Tfno. 752 244 01
Hotel neoclásico de reciente construcción. Próximo al mar, apartado de la ciudad. Restaurante, bar, jardín. 8.500 PTA. Desayuno 900 PTA.

TRÍPOLI

VIDA PRÁCTICA

Código postal 22100

OFICINA DE TURISMO
Georgiou, 7
Tfno. 71 22 30 39

VIDA CULTURAL

MUSEO ARQUEOLÓGICO
Evangelistrias, 6
Tfno. 71 269 06.
Abierto 8 h 30-14 h 30.
Lunes cerrado.

ALOJAMIENTO

GALAXY
B. Georgiou
Tfno. 71 22 51 95
Hotel sin especial encanto situado en la plaza de la catedral y próximo al bazar de Trípoli, justo antes de la animada plaza Makariou. Bar. 3.000 PTA. Desayuno 400 PTA.

XYLOKASTRON

VIDA PRÁCTICA

Código postal 20400

OFICINA DE TURISMO
Frantzi, 1
Tfno. 74 32 23 31

ALOJAMIENTO

HERMES
J. Ioannou, 95
Tfno. 74 32 22 50
Pequeño hotel familiar a la entrada de la ciudad, cerca de la playa y del centro, de los cafés y los restaurantes situados en el bosque de pinos de al lado. Muy buena recepción. Terraza. 1.700-2.000 PTA.

APPENDICES

ESSENTIAL ◆ READING ◆

◆ BOARDMAN (J.): *Greek Art.* London and New York, 1989.
◆ FINLEY (M.I.): *The Ancient Greeks.* Harmondsworth and New York, 1987.
◆ WOODHOUSE (C.M.): *Modern Greece: A Short History.* 5th rev. ed. London, 1991.

◆ MYTHOLOGY ◆

◆ GRIMAL (P.): *A Concise Dictionary of Classical Mythology.* Oxford, 1990.
◆ KERENYI (C.): *The Gods of the Greeks.* London, 1974. *The Heroes of the Greeks.* London, 1974.

◆ PHILOSOPHY ◆

◆ ARISTOTLE: *Poetics* (many editions). *Rhetoric* (many editions).
◆ GUTHRIE (W.K.C.): *A History of Greek Philosophy.* Cambridge, 1962–82.
◆ PLATO: Clarendon Plato Series, Oxford.
◆ VERNANT (J.-P.): *The Origins of Greek Thought.* Cornell UP, 1982.

◆ RELIGION ◆

◆ BURKERT (W.): *Greek Religion of the Archaic and Classical Epochs.* Oxford, 1985.
◆ TIMIADIS (E.): *Le Monachisme orthodoxe.* Buchet-Chastel, 1981.
◆ VERNANT (J.-P.): *Myth and Thought Among the Greeks.* London, 1983.

◆ TRADITIONS ◆

◆ LOSFELD (G.): *Essai sur le costume grec.* De Boccard, 1977.
◆ PAPAMANOLI-GUEST (A.): *Grèce: fêtes et rites.* Denoël, 1991.
◆ PARADISSIS (C.): *Greek Cookery.* 5th ed. IBD Ltd., 1985.

ANCIENT ◆ HISTORY ◆

◆ BOARDMAN (J.), GRIFFIN (J.) and MURRAY (O.): *The Oxford History of the Classical World.* Oxford, 1986.
◆ BRANIGAN (K.), VICKERS (M.): *La Grèce antique.* Armand Colin, 1981.
◆ CAMP (J.): *The Athenian Agora.* London and New York, 1987.
◆ DELCOURT-CUVERS (M.): *Périclès.* Gallimard, 1940.
◆ DUCREY (P.): *Guerres et guerriers dans la Grèce antique.* Payot, 1985.
◆ EFFENTERRE (H. van): *La Cité grecque : des origines à la défaite de Marathon.* Hachette, 1985.
◆ FAURE (P.): *La Vie quotidienne en Grèce au temps de la guerre de Troie.* Hachette, 1975.
◆ FINLEY (M.I.): *The World of Odysseus,* rev. ed. Harmondsworth and New York, 1979. *Early Greece: The Bronze and Archaic Ages.* 2nd ed. London, 1981.
◆ FLACELIERE (R.): *La Vie quotidienne en Grèce au siècle de Périclès.* Hachette, 1959.
◆ FINLEY (M.I.): *The Ancient Greeks.* Harmondsworth and New York, 1987. *The World of Odysseus,* rev. ed. Harmondsworth and New York, 1979. *Early Greece: The Bronze and Archaic Ages.* 2nd ed. London, 1981.
◆ FITZHARDINGE (L.F.): *The Spartans.* London and New York, 1980.
◆ FUSTEL DE COULANGES (D.): *La Cité antique.* Flammarion, 1984.
◆ GREEN (P.): *Alexander the Great.* Berkeley, 1992. *Alexander to Actium: The Hellenistic Age.* Berkeley and London, 1990.
◆ HATZFELD (J.): *History in Ancient Greece.* New York, 1968.
◆ HERODOTUS: *The Histories* (many editions).
◆ LÉVÊQUE (P.): *The Greek Adventure: A Cultural and Historical Study of the Ancient Greeks.* London, 1968.
◆ LANE FOX (R.): *Alexander the Great.* London, 1973.
◆ MOSSÉ (C.): *La Grèce ancienne.* Seuil, 1986. *La Grèce archaïque d'Homère à Eschyle: 8e-6e siècles av. J.-C.* Seuil, 1984. *Histoire d'une démocratie: Athènes.* Seuil, Points Histoire, 1980.
◆ PAUSANIAS (P.): *Guide to Greece.* Vol. 1: *Central Greece.* Harmondsworth, 1971.
◆ POLIGNAC (F. de): *La Naissance de la cité grecque.* La Découverte, 1984.
◆ ROUSSEL (P.): *Sparte.* De Boccard, 1960.
◆ SNODGRASS (A.M.): *An Archeology of Greece.* 1987.
◆ THUCYDIDES: *History of the Peloponnesian War* (many editions).
◆ VANNIER (F.): *Le Quatrième Siècle grec.* Armand Colin, 1983.
◆ VIDAL-NAQUET (P.): *La Démocratie grecque vue d'ailleurs.* Flammarion, 1990.

MODERN ◆ HISTORY ◆

◆ CLOGG (R.): *Parties and Elections in Greece.* London, 1987.
◆ DAKIN (D.): *The Unification of Greece 1770–1923.* London, 1972.
◆ RAYMOND (J.-F. de): *La Grèce de Gobineau, ministre de l'empereur à Athènes (1864-1868).* Belles Lettres, 1985.
◆ WOODHOUSE (C.M.): *The Struggle for Greece, 1941–1949.* London, 1976.

◆ CIVILIZATION ◆

◆ BOULANGER (N.) and SANDRIN (P.): *L'Antiquité dévoilée par ses usages.* Belles Lettres, 1979.
◆ BROWN (P.): *Society and the Holy in Late Antiquity.* San Francisco, 1982.
◆ CARTLEDGE (P.): *The Greeks: A Portrait of Self and Others.* Oxford and New York, 1993.
◆ CHAMOUX (F.): *La Civilisation grecque à l'époque archaïque et classique.* Arthaud, 1963.
◆ COGNE (C.): *Grèce.* Éditions Autrement, série Monde n°39, 1989.
◆ DELVOYE (C.), ROUX (G.): *La Civilisation grecque de l'Antiquité à nos jours.* Renaissance du livre, 1969.
◆ MYLONAS (G.E.): *Mycenae, Rich in Gold.* Athens.
◆ RACHET (G. and M.-F.): *Dictionnaire de la civilisation grecque.* Larousse, 1968.
◆ ROSTOVTSEFF (M. I.): *Histoire économique et sociale du monde hellénistique.* Laffont, 1989.
◆ SLESIN (S.), CLIFF (S.), ROZENSZTROCH (D.): *Greek Style.* London and New York, 1988. ◆ TREUIL (R.), DARCQUE (P.), POURSAT (J.-C.), TOUCHAIS (G.): *Les Civilisations égéennes du néolithique à l'âge du bronze.* PUF, 1990.
◆ VASSILIS (A.): *Les Grecs d'aujourd'hui.* Balland, 1979.
◆ VERNANT (J.-P.): *Myth and Society in Ancient Greece.* Zone Books, 1988.
◆ WALBANK (F.W.): *The Hellenistic World.* London, 1981.

◆ GUIDES ◆

◆ ANDRONICOS (M.): *National Museum.* Athens, 1975.
◆ *The Blue Guide to Greece* (many editions).
◆ CAMP (J.): *The Athenian Agora.* 4th rev. ed. Athens, 1990.
◆ PAPAHATZIS (N.): *Ancient Corinth.* Athens, 1985.
◆ ROLIN (O.): *Athènes.* Autrement, «Les villes rêvées», 1986.
◆ STOURNARAS (N.) AND CORBETIS (N.) (Eds.): *Delphi.* Athens.
◆ TATAKI (A. B.): *Sounion : le temple de Poséidon.* Athenon, Errance, 1989.
◆ YALOURIS (A. and N.): *Olympie : le musée et le sanctuaire.* Athenon, Errance, 1989.

◆ ARTS ◆

◆ BOARDMAN (J.): *Greek Sculpture: The Archaic Period.* London and New York, 1978. *Greek Sculpture: The Classical Period.* London and New York, 1987.
◆ BRUNEAU (P.): *La Mosaïque antique.* Presse universitaire Paris-Sorbonne, 1987.
◆ CHARBONNEAUX (J.), MARTIN (R.), VILLARD (F.): *Grèce archaïque.* Gallimard, «L'Univers des formes», 1984.
◆ COOK (B.F.): *The Elgin Marbles.* London, 1984.
◆ COURBIN (P.): *Céramique géométrique de l'Argolide.* De Boccard, 1966.
◆ DEMARGNE (P.): *Naissance de l'Art grec.* Gallimard, «L'Univers des formes», 1985.
◆ GINOUVES (R.): *L'Art grec.* PUF, 1989.
◆ MAFFRE (J.-J.): *L'Art grec.* Flammarion, «La Grammaire des styles», 1984
◆ METZGER (A. and H.),

SICRE (J.-P.): *La Beauté nue : quinze siècles de peinture grecque.* Phébus, 1984.
◆ PAPAOIANNOU (K.): *L'Art grec: les sites archéologiques de la Grèce et de la Grande Grèce.* Citadelles, 1972.
◆ POURSAT (J.-Cl.): *Les Ivoires mycéniens.* École française d'Athènes, 1977.
◆ RACHET (G.): *Delphes: le sanctuaire d'Apollon.* Laffont, 1985.
◆ RAVAISSON (F.): *L'Art et les mystères grecs : entretien avec Alain Pasquier.* L'Herne, 1985.
◆ ROLLEY (C.): *Les Bronzes grecs.* Office du Livre, 1983.
◆ TOUCHEFEU-MEYNIER (O.): *Thèmes odysséens dans l'art antique.* De Boccard, 1968.

◆ MUSEUMS ◆

◆ ANDRONICOS (M.): *The Greek Museums.* Athens, 1981.
◆ COLIGNON (M.): *Catalogue des vases peints du Musée national d'Athènes.* De Boccard.
◆ Poursat (J.-C.): *Catalogue des ivoires mycéniens du Musée national d'Athènes.* École française d'Athènes, 1978.
◆ ROLLEY (C.): *Musée de Delphes : bronzes.* École française d'Athènes, 1980.

ANCIENT ◆ LITERATURE ◆

◆ AESCHYLUS: The Plays (many editions).
◆ ARISTOPHANES: The Comedies (many editions).
◆ EASTERLING (P.E.) AND KNOX (B.M.W.) (Eds): *The Cambridge History of Classical Literature.* Vol. 1: *Greek Literature.* Cambridge, 1985.
◆ EURIPIDES: The Plays (many editions).
◆ HOMER: *The Iliad* and *The Odyssey* (many editions).
◆ SAPPHO: *Poetarum Lesbiorum Fragmenta.* (Lobel, E., and Page, D. L., Eds.) London, 1955.
◆ SOPHOCLES: The Tragedies (many editions).
◆ VERNANT (J.-P.), VIDAL-NAQUET (P.): *Myth and Tragedy in Ancient Greece.* Zone Books, 1988
.◆ XENOPHON: *History of My Time.* Harmondsworth. *The Persian Expedition.* Harmondsworth, 1981.

MODERN ◆ LITERATURE ◆

◆ CAVAFY (C.): *Collected Poems.* Rev. ed. Princeton, 1992.
◆ ELYTIS (O.): *Axion Esti.* Anvil Poetry, 1980. *Selected Poems.* Anvil Poetry, 1991.
◆ KAZANTZAKIS (N.): *Zorba the Greek.* London.
◆ MILLER (H.): *The Colossus of Maroussi.* New York.
◆ RITSOS (Y.): *Exile and Return: Selected Poems 1967–74.* Anvil Poetry, 1988.
◆ SEFERIS (G.): *Complete Poems.* Anvil Poetry, 1990.

TRAVEL, ◆ ESSAYS ◆

◆ BARRES (M.): *Voyage de Sparte.* Trident, 1987.
◆ BOARDMAN (J.) and LA ROCCA (E.): *Eros in Greece.* London, 1978.
◆ BUFFIERE (F.): *Les mythes d'Homère et la pensée grecque.* Belles Lettres, 1957.
◆ DURRELL (L. G.): *The Greek Islands.* London and Boston, 1978.
◆ GREEN (P.): *Classical Bearings: Interpreting Ancient History and Culture.* London and New York, 1989.
◆ PITTON DE TOURNEFORT (J.): *Voyage d'un botaniste: 1. L'Archipel grec.* La Découverte, 1985.
◆ TSIGAKOU (F.-M.): *The Rediscovery of Greece: Travellers and Painters of the Romantic Era.* London, 1981.

ACKNOWLEDGEMENTS

We would like to thank the following for permission to reproduce the extracts on pages 106 to 120.

◆ THE BODLEY HEAD: Excerpt from *Old and New Athens* by Demetrios Sicilianos, translated by Robert Liddell, published by Putnam in 1960. Reprinted by permission of the Bodley Head, a division of Random House (UK) Ltd.
◆ GERALD DUCKWORTH AND COMPANY LTD: Excerpts from *The Station* by Robert Byron (1931). Reprinted by permission.
◆ FARRAR, STRAUS & GIROUX, INC: Excerpts from "Greek Diary: Notes on Liberated Athens", from *Europe Without Baedeker* by Edmund Wilson. Copyright © 1947, 1966 by Edmund Wilson, copyright renewed 1974 by Elena Wilson. Reprinted by permission.
◆ HARCOURT BRACE & COMPANY and CHATTO & WINDUS LTD: Excerpts from Diary entries April, 1932, and May, 1932, from *The Diary of Virginia Woolf, Volume IV: 1931–1935*, edited by Anne Olivier Bell, copyright © 1982 by Quentin Bell and Angelica Garnett. Rights in Canada administered by Chatto and Windus Ltd., London. Reprinted by permission.
◆ HARVARD UNIVERSITY PRESS: Excerpt from Dec. 19, 1850, letter from Gustave Flaubert to Louis Bouilhet from *The Letters of Gustave Flaubert, Vol. 1, 1830-1857*, selected, edited, and translated by Francis Steegmuller, Cambridge, Massachusetts: The Belknap Press of Harvard University Press, copyright © 1979, 1980 by Francis Steegmuller. Reprinted by permission.
◆ HARVILL: Excerpt from *On the Shores of the Mediterranean* by Eric Newby (1984). Reprinted by permission of Harvill, an imprint of Harper Collins Publishers Limited, London.
◆ A.M. HEATH & CO. LTD: Excerpt from *The Private Sea*, by Peter Mayne, published by John Murray in 1958. Reprinted by permission.
◆ DAVID HIGHAM ASSOCIATES: Excerpt from *A Three-Legged Tour of Greece*, by Dame Ethel Smyth, published by William Heinemann in 1927. Reprinted by permission.
◆ JOHN MURRAY (PUBLISHERS) LTD: Excerpt from *Mani – Travels in the Southern Peloponnese* by Patrick Leigh-Fermor, published by John Murray in 1958. Reprinted by permission.
◆ NEW DIRECTIONS PUBLISHING CORPORATION: "Self-Indulgence" and "The Greek Chronicles" from *The Colossus of Maroussi* by Henry Miller, copyright © 1941 by Henry Miller. Reprinted by permission. (In the UK: Excerpts from *The Colossus of Maroussi* by Henry Miller, published by William Heinemann Ltd, reprinted by permission of Reed Consumer Books)
◆ PETERS FRASER & DUNLOP GROUP LTD: Excerpts from *Labels – A Mediterranean Journey*, by Evelyn Waugh, published by Duckworth in 1930. Reprinted by permission.
◆ UNIVERSITY OF OKLAHOMA PRESS: Excerpt from *Traveling with the Innocents Abroad: Mark Twain's Original Reports from Europe and the Holy Land*, edited by Daniel Morley McKeithan. Copyright © 1958 by the University of Oklahoma Press. Reprinted by permission.
◆ WATSON, LITTLE, LTD: Excerpt from *The Selected Letters of Edward Lear*, edited by Vivien Noakes, published by Clarendon Press, Oxford in 1988. Reprinted by permission.
◆ WEIDENFELD AND NICOLSON: Excerpt from *The Diaries of Evelyn Waugh*, edited by Michael Davie (1976). Reprinted by permission.

◆ A ◆

◆ ACANTHUS: Stylized representation of the leaves of a Mediterranean plant, used as a decorative motif on Corinthian capitals.
◆ ACROPOLIS: High place, such as a hill or rock, serving as a fortified site for the most important public buildings of a Greek city.
◆ ACROTERS: Plinths designed to take a statue or ornament, on top of a pediment. Also, ornaments adorning the ridge of a roof.
◆ ADYTON: The inner sanctum of a temple, which only priests were allowed to enter.
◆ AGORA: Marketplace, which also served as a meeting place for citizens.
◆ AISLE: Lateral division running parallel to the central nave of a church.
◆ AMBULATORY: Gallery enclosing the choir.
◆ AMPHIPROSTYLE TEMPLE: Temple with columnar porticos at the front and rear, but not at the sides.
◆ AMPHITHEATER: Round or oval building with tiered seating where gladiators or animals engaged in combat.
◆ AMPHORA: Two-handled vessels used for storing and transporting liquids.
◆ ANCIENT ALTARS (THREE TYPES): *Bomos*, a raised aedicule on a stepped base; *bothros*, an altar hollowed out in the ground, forming a sort of trough; *eschara*, a hollow altar in the shape of a hearth.
◆ ANTAE: Pilasters or corner columns at the end of the *cella* of a temple.
◆ APSE: Polygonal or semicircular space opening into an aisle, generally at the east end of a church.
◆ APTERAL TEMPLE: Rectangular (literally "wingless") temple without porticos at the sides.
◆ ARCHITRAVE: The bottom section of the entablature, resting on the columns.
◆ ARCHIVOLT:: Molding along the curve of an arch or portal.
◆ ATLAS OR TELEMON: Male statue acting as a column, to support an architectural element.
◆ ATRIUM: Courtyard at the entrance of an ancient building or paleo-Christian church.

◆ B ◆

◆ BARREL VAULT: Semicircular vault.
◆ BASILICA: Original model for Christian churches, with either one or several aisles.
◆ BOND: The cut and shape of the constituent elements of a wall. From the 11th and 12th centuries onward, the brickwork of Greek churches alternated bricks and ashlar for decoration.
◆ BOULEUTERION: Council chamber in ancient Greece.

◆ C ◆

◆ CAPITAL: The uppermost part of a column, which sits on top of the shaft.
◆ CARYATID: Female statue acting as a column, to support an architectural element.
◆ CAVEA: The tiered seating for spectators in an ancient theater or amphitheater.
◆ CELLA OR NAOS: The main chamber of an ancient temple, which contained the cult statue.
◆ CHOIR: The part of a church, often partitioned off by a screen, reserved for the officiating priests. It generally includes the altar.
◆ CHURCH PLANS:
BASILICAL PLAN: By analogy with paleo-Christian basilicas, an oblong plan with several aisles. The central aisle is illuminated by high windows.
INSCRIBED GREEK CROSS WITH CUPOLA: A development of the cruciform paleo-Christian plan. The pilasters supporting the dome were replaced at the beginning of the 11th century by columns.
OCTAGONAL PLAN: Octagon inscribed in a square and crowned by a cupola resting on eight columns linked by arches.
TRICONCH PLAN: Often combined with the inscribed-cross plan in Greece.
◆ CIRCUS: Edifice, with tiered seating, used for chariot races. Basically rectangular in shape, it was rounded at either one or both ends.
◆ CORBEL: Cantilevered section of a building.
◆ CORINTHIAN ORDER: The base of the column is made up of a plinth, a torus, two scotias between fillets separated by twin baguettes, and another torus. The shaft is fluted. The capital consists of a bell (generally decorated with acanthus leaves), an abacus and volutes (scrolls); at the center of the abacus, between the stems ending in the volutes, rises a stalk holding a flower.
◆ CORNER SQUINCHES: Small arches supporting the tambour of a cupola, formed across a reflex angle and below a cant-wall. Sometimes used instead of pendentives.
◆ CUNEUS: Wedge-shaped section (between two stairways) of the *cavea* in an ancient theater.
◆ CUPOLA: Dome, supported by pendentives or corner squinches resting on columns or pilasters, used to crown a square space.

◆ D ◆

◆ DEME: Administrative division, borough.
◆ DESPOT: Governor of a province in the Byzantine Empire.
◆ DIAZOMA: Promenade halfway up or at the top of the tiered seating in an ancient theater.
◆ DIPTERAL TEMPLE: Rectangular temple with a peristyle that has two rows of columns on either side.
◆ DOG-TOOTH CORDONS: Carved serrated moldings, commonly used to decorate the window surrounds in Byzantine churches.
◆ DORIC ORDER: The column is baseless. The shaft, which is fluted, is separated from the capital by one or more annulets (rings). The capital consists of a gorgerin (necking), an echinus (with ovolos or decorations shaped like a horse's nose) and an abacus. The gorgerin is separated from the echinus by a single fillet or baguette or by three fillets.

◆ E ◆

◆ ENTABLATURE: Section between the columns and the pediment, consisting of the architrave and the frieze.
◆ EXEDRA: Semicircular recess containing benches.
◆ EXTRADOS: The outer curve of an arch or dome.

◆ F ◆

◆ FRIEZE: The horizontal band between the pediment and the architrave. On a Doric temple, the frieze is composed of alternating triglyphs and metopes.

◆ H ◆

◆ HEROÖN: Shrine dedicated to a hero, often in the form of an altar or funerary monument.
◆ HIGOUMENOS: Head of a Greek Orthodox monastery.
◆ HYPETHRAL TEMPLE: A temple whose *cella* is open to the sky.

◆ I ◆

◆ ICONOSTASIS: In Orthodox churches, the screen separating the nave from the sanctuary, generally decorated with mural paintings and/or icons.
◆ IN ANTIS: A pair of columns placed between the projecting side walls of the *naos* are said to be *in antis*. In a temple *in antis* the *pronaos* and *opisthodomos* have no portico.
◆ IONIC ORDER: The base of the column consists of a plinth, two scotias separated by two baguettes, and a torus. The shaft is fluted. The capital is composed of an echinus, volutes and an abacus. The echinus is generally decorated with ovolos. The space between the volutes may be adorned with festoons; the abacus then often has a flower at the center.

◆ K ◆

◆ KATHOLIKON: Principal church of a monastery or parish.

◆ KERKIDES (MAENIANUM): Section of the *cavea* between two stairheads in an ancient theater.
◆ KORE/KOUROS: Archaic statue representing a maiden (*kore*) or a youth (*kouros*).

◆ M ◆

◆ MEGARON: The main hall of a Mycenean palace. Rectangular in shape, it comprises a porch (supported by two columns), a vestibule and a square room, in the center of which is a hearth surrounded by four columns.
◆ METOPES: The square spaces in a Doric frieze, often plain but sometimes decorated with motifs.
◆ MONOPTERAL TEMPLE: Circular temple, with no *cella*, whose roof is supported by columns.
◆ MOSAICS: A more costly form of ornamentation than mural paintings, between the 10th and 13th centuries mosaics were generally reserved for Imperial institutions.
◆ MURAL PAINTINGS (PROTOCOL): Christ Pantocrator (Almighty) is depicted in the cupola; a series of great feast days, from seven to twelve, generally decorates the lunettes and vaults; apostles, patriarchs and prophets appear on the upper sections of walls and pillars. This basic protocol was vastly enriched from the 10th and 11th centuries onward.
◆ MYSTERIES: Initiatory religious rites.

◆ N ◆

◆ NARTHEX: The vestibule of a church, often topped by a tribune and sharing the same roof as the nave.
◆ NAVE: The central aisle of a church.
◆ NOME: Greek administrative division (roughly corresponding to a county).

◆ O ◆

◆ ODEON: Semicircular or semi-oval roofed theater, with tiered seating, for concerts.
◆ OPISTHODOMOS: Chamber (at the opposite end of a temple from the *pronaos*) at the rear of the *cella*, which may or may not lead into it.
◆ ORACLE: Message from the gods relayed by a priestess. By extension, the shrine where the oracle could be consulted.
◆ ORCHESTRA: Lower than the *cavea* in an ancient theater, the circular area (between the first row of spectators and the *pulpitum*) across which the actors and chorus moved.
◆ ORDER: Denotes both the constituent parts of the column (base, shaft, capital) and its entablature (architrave, frieze and cornice). See Doric, Ionic and Corinthian orders.
◆ ORTHOSTAT: The side walls of the structure formed by the *pronaos*, *cella* and *opisthodomos*.

◆ P ◆

◆ PALESTRA: Training ground for athletes.
◆ PARASKENIA: Supporting walls, at right angles to the *skene*, on either side of the stage in an ancient theater.
◆ PARODOS: Side entrance to the *cavea* in an ancient theater.
◆ PEDIMENT: Triangular gable consisting of a tympanum enclosed by a cornice.
◆ PENDENTIVES: Squinches, characterized by the concave triangular shape of their intrados, achieving a transition between the square space defined by the walls and the cupola.
◆ PEPLOS: Women's garment.
◆ PERIBOLOS: Monumental boundary wall or fence enclosing a sanctuary or *cella*.
◆ PERIPTERAL TEMPLE: Rectangular temple that has a peristyle consisting of a single row of columns, around all four sides.
◆ PERISTYLE: Colonnade surrounding a temple or other building. When calculating the number of columns, those at the corners are counted twice.
◆ PITHOS: Large jar.
◆ PODIUM (KREPIDOMA): Masonry platform supporting the *pronaos*, *cella* and *opisthodomos*. Can either be stepped or completely surrounded by long steps; has three levels, the *euthynterion* (lower section), the *krepis* (middle section) and the stylobate (upper section, on which the columns stand).
◆ POLIS: Independent, autonomous city or city-state.
◆ PORCH: Vestibule or portico forming an avant-corps at the entrance to a church.
◆ PORTICO: Open gallery with a colonnade or colonnades. Also, a colonnade leading to the entrance of a building.
◆ PRONAOS: Portico or antechamber with or without portico leading to the *cella*. A *pronaos* formed by extending the walls of the *cella* is said to be *in antis*.
◆ PROPYLAEA: Columnar porch at the entrance to a sacred precinct, *agora* or palace.
◆ PROSKENION (PROSCENIUM): Stage, in front of the *skene*, on which the actors performed in an ancient theater.
◆ PROSTYLE TEMPLE: Temple with a columnar portico at the front, but not at the rear or sides.
◆ PRYTANEUM: Public building, seat of the *prytaneis* who were responsible for the city's administrative and political stability.

◆ R ◆

◆ RHYTON: Drinking vessel for libations.

◆ S ◆

◆ SEKOS: Inner room of a temple.
◆ SKENE: Structure in front of which the actors performed in an ancient theater, with a wall facing the *cavea*.
◆ STADIUM: Edifice designed for foot-races, with tiered seating for the spectators.
◆ STOA: A roofed portico or gallery with an open colonnade on one side and a wall, providing shade and shelter, on the other.
◆ STUCCO: A mixture of plaster and marble dust used for decorating surfaces. By extension, the decorative motif itself.
◆ STYLOBATE: The top step of the masonry platform supporting the walls and/or colonnades of a temple.

◆ T ◆

◆ TAMBOUR: Cylindrical substructure of a cupola, generally with an octagonal exterior.
◆ TEMENOS OR HIERON: Sacred precinct, often surrounded by an enclosing wall (*peribolos*); may not have a temple, merely one or several altars.
◆ TEMPLE: Sanctuary and abode of a god or goddess. The temple contained the divine image – but not the altar, which was outside.
◆ THEATER: Semicircular building, with tiered seating, for performances of drama.
◆ THOLOS: A round building. Temple with a round *cella*, in some cases surrounded by a peristyle.
◆ TRANSEPT CROSSING: Junction of the transept and nave of a church.
◆ TRANSEPT: Transverse aisle at right angles to the central nave of a church.
◆ TRIBUNES: High open galleries over the central aisle, a characteristic feature of Greek churches and the early basilicas in Constantinople.
◆ TYMPANUM: On the façade of a temple, the surface enclosed by the cornice and the sloping sides of the pediment. In church architecture, the space between the lintel and the archivolt of a portal.

◆ V ◆

◆ VOLUTE: Ornamental scroll or spiral motif.
◆ VOMITARIUM: Entrance to the *cavea* in an ancient theater.
◆ VOUSSOIR: The curve or part of the curve of a vault.

◆ BASICS ◆

Yes: *ne*
No: *okhi*
With: *me*
Without: *khoris*
What: *ti*
Why: *ghati*
Where: *pou*
When: *pote*
How: *pos*
And: *ke*

◆ COURTESIES ◆

Please: *parakalo*
Thank you: *efkharisto*
Thank you very much: *efkharisto para poli*
Sorry / Excuse me: *signomi, me sinkhorite*
Don't mention it / Please / Be my guest: *tipota*
Goodbye: *kherete, adio*
Hello: *kalimera*
How are you?: *ti kanete ?*
Very well: *poli kala*
OK: *entaxi*
Good evening: *kalispera*
Good night: *kalinikhta*
Hi / Goodbye: *ghiasou*

◆ TIME & DATES ◆

Now: *tora*
Later: *meta*
What time is it?: *ti ora ine ?*
Morning: *proï*
Midday: *mesimeri*
Afternoon: *apoghema*
Evening: *vradhi*
Night: *nikhta*
Today: *simera*
Tomorrow: *avrio*
Yesterday: *khtes*
Day: *imera*
Week: *evdhomadha*
Monday: *dheftera*
Tuesday: *triti*
Wednesday: *tetarti*
Thursday: *pempti*
Friday: *paraskevi*
Saturday: *savato*
Sunday: *kiriaki*
Month: *minas*
January: *ianouarios*
February: *fevrouarios*
March: *martios*
April: *aprilios*
May: *maïos*
June: *iounios*
July: *ioulios*
August: *avghoustos*
September: *septemvrios*
October: *oktovrios*
November: *noemvrios*
December: *dhekemvrios*
Year: *khronos*

◆ NUMBERS ◆

One: *ena*
Two: *dhio*
Three: *tria*
Four: *tesera*
Five: *pende*
Six: *eksi*
Seven: *efta*
Eight: *okto*
Nine: *enia*
Ten: *dheka*
Twenty: *ikosi*
Thirty: *triada*
Forty: *sarada*
Fifty: *penida*
Sixty: *exida*
Seventy: *evdhomida*
Eighty: *oghdhoda*
Ninety: *enenida*
Hundred: *ekato*
Thousand: *khili*

◆ TRAVEL ◆

Airport: *aerodhromio*
Plane: *aeroplano*
Boat: *karavi*
Port / Harbor: *limani*
Station: *stathmos*
Train : *treno*
Luggage: *aposkeves, pramata*
Porter: *akhthoforos*
Car: *aftokinito*
Driving license: *adhia odhighiseos*
How much does it cost per day?: *poso kostizi tin imera ?*
Taxi : *taxi*

◆ ON THE ROAD ◆

Road: *dhromos*
Garage: *garaz*
My car has broken down: *to aftokinito ekhi vlavi*
Fill it up, please: *to ghemizete me venzini, parakalo*
Petrol: *venzini*
Normal, Super, Unleaded: *apli, souper, amolivdhi*
Can you check...: *parakalo eleghkhete...*
The oil: *to ladhi*
The tyres: *ta lastikha*

◆ DIRECTIONS ◆

Are we on the right road for...?: *imaste sto sosto dhromo ghia ... ?*
Sea: *thalasa*
Mountain: *vouno*
Village: *chorio*
Beach: *paralia*
North: *voria*
South: *notia*
East : *anatolika*
West : *dhitika*

◆ IN TOWN ◆

Bus: *leoforio*
Which bus is for...?: *pou ine to leoforio ghia...?*
Bus stop: *stasi*
Where is...?: *pou ine...?*
How far?: *poso makria ine ?*
Near: *konda*
Far: *makria*
Right: *dheksia*
Left: *aristera*
Center: *kentro*
Street: *dhromos, odos*
Avenue: *leoforos*
Square: *platia*

◆ MONEY ◆

Bank: *trapeza*
Money: *khrimata*
I would like to change some money: *thelo na alaxo merika khrimata*
Do you take credit cards?: *pernete pistotiki karta ?*
Traveler's checks: *traveler's cheques*

◆ SIGHTSEEING ◆

Open: *anikto*
Closed: *klisto*
Ticket: *isitirio*
Church: *eklisia*
Castle: *kastro*
Palace: *palati*
Ruins: *archea*
Museum: *mousio*
Temple: *naos*
Theater: *theatro*
May I take a photo?: *boro na paro mia fotografia ?*
Entrance: *isodhos*
Exit: *exodhos*

◆ FOOD & DRINKS ◆

Restaurant: *estia torio*
Taverna: *taverna*
Lunch: *mesimeriano*
Dinner: *vradhino*
Menu: *kataloghos*
May we have a table, please?: *boroume na ekhoume ena trapezi ?*
Black coffee: *enan kafe*
White coffee: *enan kafe me ghala*
A tea: *ena tsaï*
A dessert: *ena ghliko :*
Hot: *zesto*
Cold: *krio*
A glass: *ena potiri*
The plate, the dish: *piato*
Water: *nero*
Mineral water: *metaliko nero*
Wine: *krasi*
Bottle: *boukali*
Beer: *bira*
Meat: *kreas*
Fish: *psari*
Vegetables: *khortarika, lakhanika*
Potatoes: *patates*
Bread: *psomi*
Sugar: *zakhari*
Rice: *rizi*
Salad: *salata*
Soup: *soupa*
Cheese: *tiri*
Fruit: *frouta*
The bill: *loghariasmos*

◆ ACCOMMODATION ◆

I would like a room: *tha ithela ena dhomatio*
A single, double room: *tha ithela ena mono, ena diplo domatio*
With twin beds: *me dhio krevatia*
With bath: *me banio*
With shower: *me dous*
How much does it cost per night: *pia ine i timi gia mia nikhta ?*
Breakfast: *proïno*

◆ AT THE POST OFFICE ◆

Where is the nearest post office?: *pou ine to kontinotero takhidhromio ?*
The post office: *to takhidhromio*
Stamp: *ghramatosimo*
Letter: *ghrama*
Postcard: *karta*
Telegram: *tileghrafima*
Can you put me through to the following number?: *borite na mou parete afton ton arithmo... ?*

◆ EMERGENCIES ◆

Pharmacy: *farmakio*
I need a doctor: *khriazome ena ghiatro*
Dentist: *odhontogiatro*
Ambulance: *asthenoforo*
Hospital: *nosokomio*
Policeman: *astinomikos*
Police station: *astinomia*

◆ SHOPPING ◆

Kiosk: *periptero*
Shop: *maghazi, katastima*
Cheap: *ftino*
Expensive: *akrivo*
Market: *agora*
Bakery: *fournos*

◆ USEFUL PHRASES ◆

I don't understand: *dhen katalaveno*
I'd like...: *theo...*
Where can I phone from?: *pou iparkhi tilefono ?*
How much is it?: *poso kostizi... ?, poso kanei ?*
It's too expensive: *ine poli akrivo*
What is it?: *ti ine afto ?*
When does ... open?: *ti ora anighi ?*
When does ... close?: *ti ora klini ?*
A packet of cigarettes, please: *ena paketo tsigara, parakalo.*
Can you help me?: *borite na me voïthisete?*

List of illustrations

Maps: Pierre-Xavier Grézaud, Jean-François Binet and Jean-François Péneau.
Illustrators : Jean-François Binet: 84-89, 94-95, 170-171, 180, 190-193, 210-211, 215, 289, 290, 291, 325, 334, 393. Pierre-Xavier Grézaud: 12-13, 80-81, 128-129, 178-179, 184-185, 194-195, 200-201, 205, 206, 220, 244-245, 258-259, 264, 296, 300, 309, 317, 322-323, 328, 374-375, 380-381, 389, 392-393, 406. Sophie Lavaux: 19, 20, 22-23, 28-29, 30-31, 32-33, 34. Stéphane Marcie: 78-79, 83, 84-85, 86-87, 196, 197. Jean-François Péneau: 62-63, 64, 77, 78-79, 82-83, 84-85, 86-87, 90-91, 96, 231, 323, 364, 368, 369, 409, 410. Maurice Pommier: 375, 384, 385. Philippe Marchand: 26-27, 290.

Abbreviations used:
Coll.: collection
Ph.: photo
ENBA: École nationale des Beaux-Arts
EFA: École française d'Athènes.

INDEX

◆ B ◆

◆ C ◆

◆ CORINTH ◆

◆ D ◆

◆ DELPHI ◆

◆ **E** ◆

◆ **EPIDAURUS** ◆

◆ **F** ◆

◆ **G** ◆

◆ **H** ◆

◆ **I** ◆

◆ **J** ◆

◆ **K** ◆

Post
O.T.E.
Isminis
Haghia Sophias
Aristomenous
Peoniou
Drosopoulou
Alsos
Domokou
Samou
Patission (28. Oktovriou)
Ioulianou
Metaxa N.
Filadelfias
Michail Voda
Larissa Station
(Stathmos Larissa)
Ipirou
Argous
Ioanninon
Polytekhneion
Attiki
Liossion
Aristoteleous
Marni
National Archeologica
Museum
Peloponnisos Station
(Stathmos Peloponnisou)
Tritis Septemvriou
Pl. Anexartisias
Kapodistriou
Chalkokondili
Palamidiou
Favierou
Deligiani
Karolou
National Theater
Leof. Konstandinopoleos
Lenorman
Benaki Virg.
Hag. Konstandinou
Achileos
Deligiorgi
Sokratous
Pl. K. Kotzias
El. Venizelou
Meg. Alexandrou
Leonidou
Keramikou
Kolokinthous
Pireos
Menandrou
Sofokleous
Stadiou
Pl. Odiou
Central market
Thermopilon
Salaminos
Evridipou
Pl. Eleftherias
Praxitelous
Dipilou
Hag. Assomaton
Eolou
Athinas
Evangelistria
Iera Odos
(Sacred Way)
Haghia Triada
Kerameikos
(ancient cemetery)
Haghii Asomati
Pl. Avikinas
Pl. Thistou
Eptachalkou
Adrianou
Monastiraki
Tzisdarakis
Mosque
Pl. Agoras
Agora
Tower of
the Winds
Large and Small
Metropolis
Hephaisteion
Stoa of Attalos
Iraklidon
Dioskouron
Mnissikleous
Nileos
Apostolou Pavlou
Plaka
Akamantos
D. Eginitou
Theorias
Acropolis
Acropolis
Museum
Propylaea
Akteou
Pnyx
Odeon of
Herodes Atticus
Theater of
Dionysos
Dimofontos
Dionysiou
Areopagitou
Kidandion
Perikleous
Rovertou Galli
Lofos Nymfon
(Hill of the Nymphs)
Monument
of Philopappos
Garivaldi
Erechthiou
Makrigiani
Troon
Eoleon
Kallisthenous
Dimitrakopoulou
Drakou
Mouson
Doras-Stratou
Theater
Anteou
Gen. Kolokotroni
Panetoliou
Veikou
Markou Botsari